Internet Commerce and Software Agents: Cases, Technologies and Opportunities

Syed Mahbubur Rahman
Minnesota State University, Mankato, USA

Robert J. Bignall
Monash University, Malaysia Campus

IDEA GROUP PUBLISHING
Hershey • London • Melbourne • Singapore

Aquisitions Editor:	Mehdi Khosrowpour
Managing Editor:	Jan Travers
Development Editor:	Michele Rossi
Copy Editor:	Maria Boyer
Typesetter:	Tamara Gillis
Cover Design:	Deb Andree
Printed at:	Sheridan Books

Published in the United States of America by
Idea Group Publishing
1331 E. Chocolate Avenue
Hershey PA 17033-1117
Tel: 717-533-8845
Fax: 717-533-8661
E-mail: cust@idea-group.com
Web site: http://www.idea-group.com

and in the United Kingdom by
Idea Group Publishing
3 Henrietta Street
Covent Garden
London WC2E 8LU
Tel: 44 20 7240 0856
Fax: 44 20 7379 3313
Web site: http://www.eurospan.co.uk

Library of Congress Cataloging-in-Publication Data

Rahman, Syed Mahbubur, 1952-
Internet commerce and software agents / Syed Mahbubur Rahman, Robert J. Bignall.
p. cm.
Includes bibliographical references and index.
ISBN 1-930708-01-7 (paper)
1. Electronic commerce. 2. Business--Data processing. I. Bignall, Robert J. II. Title.

HF5548.32 .R34 2000
658.8'4--dc21 00-050545

British Cataloguing in Publication Data
A Cataloguing in Publication record for this book is available from the British Library.

Internet Commerce and Software Agents: Cases, Technologies and Opportunities

Table of Contents

Preface

The Internet has created tremendous business opportunities and is revolutionizing the whole structure of retail merchandising and shopping. Internet usage around the world is said to be doubling every 10 days. The number of people on the Internet is expected to increase tenfold from around 100 million in 1999 to one billion by 2005. The biggest transformation resulting from this is in the area of Internet commerce, which is enabling participating businesses to simultaneously serve both domestic and foreign customers, even from the first day of their operation. There are many examples demonstrating that organizations can reap benefits if they can innovate successfully using Internet commerce. Consequently, marketers may spend large sums to create and promote online brands. According to an April 2000 Forrester research report, the rush for customer acquisition will swell the online promotions market to $14 billion by 2005. So there is no doubt that it will be imperative for businesses to be part of the global Internet commerce community. With the development of Internet trading, the amount of business information available on the Internet is growing at an extraordinary speed. Management, security, legal and other issues are arising accordingly. Existing businesses are seeking answers to the question of if and how they may adapt their business processes to meet the new demands and new startups are arising to take advantage of the shifting strategic horizons of Internet commerce.

As the Internet grows, it is becoming infeasible for customers and merchants to manually visit each Web site, analyze the information there, and thus to make sound business decisions regarding the trading of goods or services. Under such circumstances it is inevitable that buyers may miss finding the best deal in the vast ocean of information. In this scenario the use of software agent technologies, both mobile and stationary, offers a new paradigm for trading on the Internet and presents a revolutionary approach to conducting analysis and market research. Software agents may be designed to be capable of automating the more routine, tedious and time-consuming tasks involved in today's trading processes. They may be able to negotiate and make autonomous decisions and commitments on behalf of their owners. With knowledge about the habits and shopping trends of the e-consumers, accurate and personalized user profiles may be created. Agent technologies may use this knowledge to establish a much higher degree of sales confidence and create loyal and sustained relationships with customers. However, software agents for Internet commerce still have some way to go before they can fully demonstrate all of their potential advantages and ensure participant trust with regard to their privacy and the security of the transactions they undertake.

This book addresses, in 20 chapters, many of these major Internet commerce issues and the challenges to be met in achieving automated and secure Internet trading using software agents. Topics covered include the development of intelligent tools, business models to maximize the benefits of agent technologies, agent-based payments, recommender systems, web based smart card agents, Internet lottery systems and wireless virtual communities. The chapters are grouped into the following interrelated sections.

- Internet commerce and applications
- Agents in e-commerce: introduction and impact
- Agents in e-commerce: frameworks, applications and cases
- A human interface to software agents
- Payment systems, recommender systems and the future

The chapters in the first section provide some background and an overview of some problems and concerns, in an effort to rationalize the building of web-enabled enterprise information systems for conducting business transactions over the Internet. An improved understanding of Internet commerce is provided through this overview plus some requirements, benchmarks, development and implementation methodologies and approaches to successfully achieving the ultimate goal of producing robust, effective, and viable Web-enabled enterprise information systems. The second chapter considers the impact of Internet commerce on export marketing strategies The main determinants of an electronic export marketing strategy are examined and the chapter discusses how firms can best capitalize on Internet commerce for their particular types of products and services. This chapter also represents a first attempt to incorporate new technologies into existing theory on export entry strategy, as well as providing a basis to conduct future research to measure the effects of Internet commerce on export performance. The next chapter of this section deals with the issue of consumer trust and confidence in Internet commerce, which is fundamental to its eventual success. If consumers cannot be confident that personal information is safe and secure, the Internet will never reach its economic potential. There is thus a very strong incentive for the Internet business community to provide a safe and acceptable business environment for consumers. The next chapter addresses the policymakers who need to recognize the inherent complexity and unique dynamics of the global Internet mass market in the 21st century. The final chapter in this section considers a specific Internet commerce application domain, namely Internet Lottery Commerce. This chapter provides a structured guide for senior executives and strategic planners who are planning on or interested in Internet lottery deployment and operation. The chapter demonstrates the case for applying the guidelines it proposes for the lottery business.

Section two provides an overview of agent technologies, with the definitions, properties, security issues and future research and challenges for software agents in electronic commerce. The second chapter in this section provides a socio-technical perspective on intelligent agents. It argues that the new business environment requires a re-conceptualization of knowledge management. Therefore, the infrastructure and technological functionality needed to support knowledge management will be an important topic of future research. A framework is proposed that is based on the data lifecycle and on knowledge discovery using intelligent agents. One of the key ideas of this chapter is that in this period of profound social and economic changes, managers should focus on the meaning of information, not on the technology that collects it. The next chapter considers how agents can facilitate the various activities necessary for successful e-commerce. It also identifies the different types of intelligent agents that are currently being utilized in different e-commerce models and markets. A generic architecture for designing and implementing such agents is presented.

Section Three provides different frameworks for specific applications and demonstrates these with cases. The concepts covered in Section Two are elaborated upon and extended with examples. The first chapter in this section includes an overview of different reasoning and negotiation strategies among agents, followed by a discussion of the issues relevant to the architecture, design and implementation of multi-agent systems based on constraint technology and software patterns. The focus is on the implications of the theoretical work on design. The next chapter presents a conceptual framework for designing and developing software agents that will enable customized electronic commerce, and highlights several effective techniques for building specific constructs within this framework. Some of the key characteristics of customized electronic commerce are demonstrated by experimentally prototyped software agents. Examples are Electronic Tour Agents, Electronic Property Agents and Electronic Auction Agents. Technical feasibility is demonstrated based on available market products and existing research findings. In the following chapter some of the key challenges in turning agent research into commercial applications are presented with an overview of electronic commerce business models and a discussion of how they can benefit from the new developments in agent technologies. The discussion is illustrated with examples of the work that is being undertaken in projects from the IST Research Programme of the European Union. Following this, a Secure Agent Fabrication, Evolution & Roaming (SAFER) architecture for agent-based e-commerce is presented. SAFER provides services for agents in e-commerce and establishes a rich set of mechanisms to manage and secure them. The definitions and functions of the various components in the SAFER architecture are explained. This chapter also illustrates three main aspects of the SAFER architecture, namely agent fabrication, agent evolution and agent roaming.

The issues of usability, security, and mobility are major concerns for e-commerce implementations that aim to gain widespread public acceptance. To address these issues the next chapter in Section Three proposes a combination of software agents and smart cards to build a smart card agent environment. A functional overview of the proposed environment and a design is presented to illustrate how these two technologies can be integrated to offer e-commerce services with high usability, security, and mobility. A prototype implementation of the concept has demonstrated how the various agents can work with a smart card agent in a secured way. In the subsequent chapter in this section the tendering process is analysed with framework solutions proposed highlighting the benefits of the online tendering system. In the next chapter a component framework is introduced for a multi-agent-based architecture to support inter-company integration implemented with Java, and in the final chapter of the section wireless virtual communities are discussed.

It may be argued that high quality, personalized customer service will be one of the more significant drivers of e-commerce success. Thus, a more human visual interface to the Web will be an important step towards making agent technology more accessible and user-friendly to online consumers. The chapter in section four discusses the development and underlying components of a prototype 3-D audio-visual virtual salesperson talking head. Such an interface has the potential to automatically generate a voice response to many of the routine natural language queries received from customers by organisations.

Internet-based payment mechanisms are an integral part of Internet commerce. Payment systems have evolved from metal coins, paper notes, and bank checks to savings cards, credit cards, and now electronic forms through an abstract representation of commodity values. Development of secure payment systems over an open network is a basic prerequisite to the success of online commerce. The first chapter in Section Five discusses these issues. It presents a brief survey of some existing types of payment systems and focuses on mobile agent-based computing trends in e-commerce. An e-payment scheme designed for agent-based SAFER e-commerce is also proposed and explained in detail. Incorporating cryptographic techniques with software agent technology the scheme aims to provide a flexible and secure financial infrastructure for Internet commerce. In the next chapter a new payment mechanism is proposed for the use of software tools on demand, which charges users according to how much they have used a given tool. This amounts to pay-per-use rental. The chapter discusses the benefits of pay-per-use for users and producers with evidence for the critical issues in designing a system to support pay-per-use. The third chapter in this section focuses on the application of software agents together with cryptographic technology in automating and securing the processes of negotiation and payment, which are the principal and most time-consuming steps during Internet trading. A software-agent-mediated Internet trading framework integrating negotiation and payment procedures is proposed.

The final chapter introduces the concept of recommender systems as a successful Internet commerce tool. It demonstrates their similarities to and differences from traditional data analysis and knowledge discovery methods. Also included is a detailed analysis of recommender system interfaces for some Internet commerce applications. The chapter describes how they are being used to make profits by generating and maintaining customer loyalty. A taxonomy of the application space for distributed recommender systems is then presented. Some frameworks for implementing distributed recommender systems are discussed and several implementation models are described.

The nature and range of the topics covered means that this book can be used by business professionals, technologists, academics, students and policymakers. Professionals from the business community may use it to improve their understanding of the technical concepts involved in present and future Internet commerce, something that is necessary if they are to participate in the emerging global marketplace. The book will also enable technologists to achieve a better understanding of the trading applications to which Internet technology and software agents may be applied. We are confident that the discussions of some of the key business and technical issues of this growing technology, supported by the cases demonstrated, will help the book's varied audience to expand their knowledge and motivate further contributions to their fields.

Credit for the successful publishing of this book is due to many people, including the chapter authors who contributed their ideas and expertise and many colleagues who have contributed invaluable suggestions in their thorough reviews of each chapter. We would like to take this opportunity to thank the editorial staff at IGP who patiently supported us at all times. Finally, thanks are due to our family members who have given us their constant support even when missing our company for extended periods of time.

Syed Mahbubur Rahman
Robert J. Bignall

Section One: Introducing Internet Commerce and Software Agents

Chapter I

Engineering Issues in Internet Commerce

Xue Li
University of New South Wales, Australia

ABSTRACT

Engineering Internet Commerce is about building Web-enabled enterprise information systems to carry out business transactions over the Internet. This engineering task is related to three aspects: the requirement specification, the Internet technology, and the development methodology. In the requirement specification, the business analysis and design is conducted to create a semantic business model that will reflect both the business and the system requirement. With the Internet technology, the modern information technology infrastructure is investigated in order to transform a business model into an implementation model. The system analysis and design will be performed and the architecture issues should be discussed. With respect to the development methodology, an efficient way to build enterprise information systems is addressed. This chapter is to provide an overview of the problems, concerns, and the background in an effort to rationalize the Internet Commerce Engineering.

INTRODUCTION

From an engineering viewpoint, we are dealing with three worlds, the **real world**, the **perceptual world,** and the computerized **virtual world**. The real world is every thing existing in the physical world. The perceptual world exists in human brains. And the virtual world is existing in the Internet. The engineering activity is to transform ideas in the perceptual world into the real world (e.g., electronic engineering) or into the virtual world (e.g., information engineering).

The real world is objective. It changes and evolves. The perceptual world is subjective. It is individual and cognitive. It is configured in the best interests of human desire and survival. The perceptual world is intangible and reflects human understanding of and interactions with the real world. To an enterprise, the perceptual world is an asset that will control and guide business planing and strategic decisions. On the other hand the virtual world is reflective. It is an implementation of our perceptual world. In the virtual world, the digital signals are interchanged as an efficient way of information exchange.

The concept of the three-world is to help the understanding of the relationships between the objects that are considered in the Internet Commerce (IC) Engineering. The success of business is becoming more dependent on the successful applications of information technology. An unrealistic perception of the business world may result in unfruitful business systems on the Internet, and consequently cause business failure. In general, the perceptual world should be proactive, that is to interpret the real world in the best way to satisfy business goals.

This chapter is to address the high level issues of IC Engineering for building IC systems. IC Engineering is considered in three aspects: the requirement specification, the Internet technology, and the development methodology. We will discuss the problems, concerns, and background related to these three aspects in an effort to rationalize IC Engineering. Figure 1 illustrates this idea.

The **requirement specification** is a process that generates business requirement specifications and other necessary documents such as the explanatory files. The outcome is regarded as a business model. The process is for the business analysis and design that maps business information needs to the Internet technology.

The **Internet technology** is characterized by the object-oriented technology, Internet working, and the Client-server architecture (Umar, 1997). The system analysis and design techniques are used to derive an implementation model that is a mapping between the business model and the technological details with regard to the system components and the architecture.

The **development methodology** is applied to give a map that shows the path of the system development. It provides answers on how to apply what technology on which business applications. There is a phenomenon that both business and the Internet may experience rapid changes. This requires growth management to be built into the system development. Currently many development methodologies rely on the underlying software tools supplied by the major software market players.

An **IC system** is an information system that provides Web-enabled services including:

- the operational business transactions carried out over the Web;
- the ability to maintain system security and data integrity in a Web environment; and
- the strategic business planning and decision support in advanced Web-applications such as data warehousing, on-line analytical processing, data mining, and enterprise knowledge management.

The growth of the Internet has been exponential in every aspect, including its size and the capacity. Many businesses are now engineering their information systems onto the Internet. Despite the Y2K problem in the legacy systems, the information system evolution towards the Internet is not a trivial problem. **IC Engineering**

Figure 1. The Engineering Process of Internet Commerce Systems

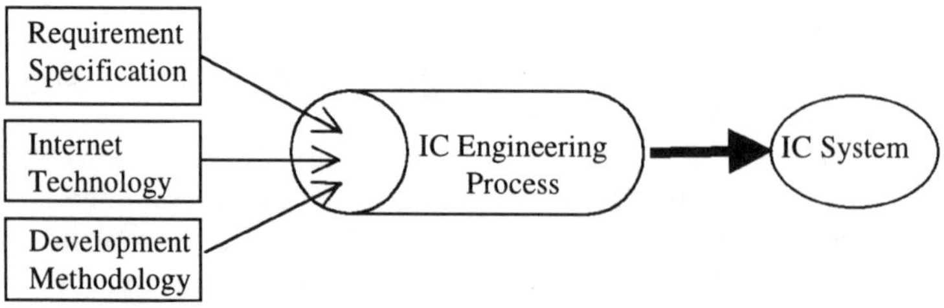

is about how to build a Web-enabled enterprise information system for businesses. The engineering may also need to deal with the legacy systems that were developed without regards to the Internet. The trend has already begun that many businesses are now starting using Web sites for their information needs. More and more software engineers are now employed to bring legacy systems onto the Internet.

The understanding of business is fundamental. However, it sometimes is not simple because the understanding of the applicability of the technology is a progressive process. It is like a marriage. It requires the mutual understanding between the business requirement and the technology applicability. It may require a recursive refinement process during the system development. It is evident that the new innovative technology may impact on the business and change the business process. Therefore, the requirement specification in IC Engineering can be affected by the Internet technology. If the requirement specification is subject to a recursive refinement process, the development methodology should also play a role in the requirement specification. In fact, these three aspects of IC Engineering are overlapped. For example, a prototyping methodology may be applicable to the system development to accommodate the recursive refinement of the system requirement specification. In this case, the prototyping is a reflective process that incorporates the system requirement dynamically.

The IC Engineering should integrate the requirement specification, the Internet technology, and the development methodology into a progressive and reflective process. This is mainly because we are now in an unprecedented fast-changing world. The consistency between the real world and the virtual world means a successful engineering that is very much dependent on the reflectiveness of our perceptual world. Hence in building the IC systems, we need a tight connection between the fast-changing world and the system built. Comparing to the classical software engineering approaches, the IC Engineering is a process incorporated with the ability of dealing with the fast-changing environment.

The requirement specifications will be discussed in the next section. Then benchmarking will be discussed as business-critical specifications. We will emphasize the current IC technologies. During the discussion, we will compare and contrast some different IC system architectures. The methodology issues are then discussed. We will give an overview of the implementation techniques towards the end of this chapter. The conclusions are presented at the end of this chapter.

IC REQUIREMENT SPECIFICATION

One of the challenges in the Information Age is that consumers are now accessing same information via the web. This gives consumers a larger variety of options and thus businesses are facing a bigger and more competitive market.

The IC requirement specification is a process of the business analysis and design that is to create logistic models, process models, or semantic business models for the business-trading environment. This section will not be discussing how to create those models (see Davis, 1993; and Kotonya, 1998) but rather explaining the problems and concerns in doing so.

In terms of business transactions, there may be mainly two types of IC systems on the Internet, **business-to-business** and **business-to-customer**. In a business-to-business system, most transactions are automated by using EDI (Electronic Data Interchange) or EDI/XML (Plaplante, 1998). The network traffic is predictable and stable. The transactions are mostly in batch mode. In a business-to-customer system, most transactions are manual. The network traffic is unpredictable and dynamic. Also the most transactions are in on-line mode.

We identify three major concerns in the IC requirement specification: the **business vision**, the **assessment criteria**, and the **system viability**. A successful business must have a vision. We will analyze two cases to demonstrate the importance of the business vision. The perceptions that developers may have in their minds may be business-centric or customer-centric. Then, we discuss the assessment criteria for benchmarking the Web-enabled enterprise information systems. We identify four factors for the business-critical applications, which are availability, reliability, security, and performance of the systems. Finally, we discuss the system viability of a business application in terms of the growth management as the ability of coping with changes.

Having a Vision: Business-Centric Versus Customer-Centric Applications

A business vision is about the perception that we posses towards the success of a business. To have a vision is to identify the success factors and foresee the changes. It will fundamentally affect the design and the implementation of a system. We may view a system in many different ways. For example, it can be viewed on what and how a system does, or on changes a system can bring. In this subsection, we compare and contrast two opposite views on a business information system, from within the business and from its outside. The concepts are the business-centric systems and the customer-centric systems. They are treated as a case study for establishing a business vision in the IC Engineering.

Business-centric systems are those systems specialized in business activities. They may require prerequisite knowledge and training of users. Traditionally, non-Web business information systems are almost all business-centric because consumers do not need to directly interact with the computer systems. Operators of business systems are trained and designated. There is no need to create interfaces especially for the targeted consumers who want to visit the business via computer systems. Business is conducted normally through facsimile, telephone, mail, or face to face. In business-to-business type systems, business-centric application still has its *raison d'être* because there are mostly still machine-to-machine batch transactions and the specialized interfaces. However when the Internet comes into play, the business-centric style increasingly becomes a problem to the general users. **Customer-centric** systems are applications that are designed in a way that is to put the customer's needs first. The system will try to satisfy customers in all possible ways. Therefore a customer can use the system without much knowledge of computing. And a customer can get as much information as he/she can.

Let us discuss an example. We may have retail businesses to be put on-line for Web users. We discuss this example in two different viewpoints: one is from a customer-shopping viewpoint, the other is from a product-sale viewpoint. From this example we try to show that the customer-centric development is important to the IC requirement analysis.

Case One

In a customer-shopping-oriented design, a business is shown to the customers to view, to search, and to buy their products. General shoppers will be able to log onto the Internet shopping service to do the Web shopping with a minimum knowledge of computer. We call it as Shopping World.

Much like the real shopping activities, the Shopping World may be a Web service that provides users with a walk-through experience on gaining information or doing on-line transactions for geographically locatable objects of the businesses. For example, the system may represent a large shopping center for general shopping lovers with the pictures and the floor plans. It provides information for the shoppers in a way that they would see in the real-world shops. All shops are presented in a cross-referenced structure. The customers are able to *walk* into the shop and browse the items, order and pay for the products. Of course there will be many questions or helps that may be asked from customers to a shop. The Shopping World may also use a search engine to answer questions such as, Where do I find a dry cleaner for my suit? Which shops sell the screws sized 1.5 mm in diameter and 5 cm in length? In a way, the Shopping World can help people find where to buy things.

Case Two

In a product-sale oriented design, individual shops may have their own Web sites. A shopping center may then have a general Web page to link them together. The whole service is then presented as a list of categorized businesses. This requires a customer to understand the words and the categorization system used by that Web site. In addition to a bombardment of advertisements, a customer may have to rely on a search engine interface to find what he/she needs. This search process may have to go from general to specific in terms of the categorization of the goods. In other words, the business is conducted as a catalogue-based on-line ordering system. Whenever a customer finishes a business with a shop, she/he then has to restart a Web journey again for the next item to buy.

The main problem for Case Two is that it is business-centric. It puts the **shops' sales** information ahead of the **customers' shopping** information. The information is presented by the system in a way that may be suitable for the individual shops to maintain their own Web sites but difficult for a customer, who may have little knowledge of the sales business, to do shopping. A shopper may need to buy things from many shops in a way she/he wants but not in a way the shops organize their businesses. For example, a business-centric Web site can restrict to a top-down presentation of their business information using a rationalized general-to-specific fashion in either search or presentation services. While a customer-centric Web site may disregard the rationale of the categorization of goods but use a specific-only way to search and use the services. It is common that one may buy some items without knowing what categories they are. Currently we can see both kinds of Web sites on the Internet. For example, *shopping carts* as a Web-shopping concept for shopping lovers has been used in many Web sites as a similar case to the above-mentioned Case One. Unfortunately, we can still see many businesses' Web sites that are in situations of Case Two. They are still very much relying on the search engines to discover them. It is revealing that the customer-centric business systems are taking advantage of the re-visitors or the visitors who receive the message passed by the satisfied pre-visitors. Many successful Web-enabled businesses have shown that their success is mainly because of the satisfaction provided to the customers. The trend shows that the business-centric Web applications are phasing out.

On the other hand, the abuse of Web technology in many systems does not provide customers with a simple method one normally uses in everyday shopping. For example, many search engines provide a multi-threaded search result (represented as a tree) instead of a simple linear search (represented as a list). Yet the simple search method may imply a powerful back-end help that can be dynamic and context-sensitive on various problems during the shopping, such as the locations, prices, or on-sale information.

We can view the retail business as a two-sided story that is about the customers' shopping activities and the shops' sale effort. So a multi-threaded search may help to maximize the opportunities of the sale but be less pleasant for a shopper. Instead, providing shoppers with a linear and pleasure-driven search may give a better imitated shopping experience that is much more enjoyable than real-life shopping.

There are still many questions yet to be answered to distinguish a business-centric and a customer-centric system. We discuss some of these aspects in the next section such as Web databases and data mining. The investigations on general *pull* technology in the shopping activities or *push* technology in business sales may also improve the satisfaction of Web-shopping lovers.

Benchmarking: Business-Critical Applications

Successful IC Engineering requires an assessment benchmark that brings the confidence and better understanding to the IC. The building of business-critical applications requires quality assurance. Under these assumptions, we identify availability, reliability, security, and the performance of a system as the critical factors for business applications. One needs to start from the analysis of business functions and specify the requirements for the system. A top-down design methodology can then be applied to bring a perfect marriage between business functions and Internet technology.

Availability

That a system is available may imply that it is accessible, scalable, and attractive. Hence the availability of a system is a measurement of its accessibility, scaleability, and attractiveness. The accessibility of a system harnesses the Internet technology for its business solutions. On the one hand, a system should be accessible for supplying a range of business services. On the other hand, a system should be accessible for providing a variety of business transactions. There should be no limit on supporting the businesses whether they are selling tangible or intangible goods, whether businesses are located in a shopping mall or as a warehouse-based distributor, whether they are the business partners in a suppliers chain or in a virtual enterprise. Moreover, different types of users of a system may have different purposes, such as for front-end business operations, for executive information needs, for decision supports, or for enterprise knowledge management. The accessibility can be achieved by a unified "on-the-web" standard user interface. It may provide users a great help on accessing information but may introduce security problems and other concerns. The Intranet and Extranet technologies can be applied as a leverage of business functions on the Web.

The **scalability** of a system means that it is capable of being tailored to suit a different environment or is flexible to satisfy different business needs. When considering the environment, the system may be scalable for deployment on mainframe machines, on personal computers, or on portable devices such as mobile phones. In this case the software should be platform independent, capable of dealing with different types of network traffics, and capable of processing a different volume of data. When considering the business needs, the system may be scalable for different customized software configurations so that the system is installed to suit particular business needs.

Availability may also refer to the **attractiveness** of the Web site. The metrics of attractiveness consist of two factors: the publicity and the satisfaction. Both of these two factors are important for system viability. Without the publicity, the system will have no users. Without the satisfaction, the system will be useless. The analysis of the Web site attractiveness may start with the statistics of the user numbers. It may give the numbers of first-time visitors, second-time visitors, or the number of customers who have done business with the Web site (and come back again). On the other hand, there may be many attributes that affect the attractiveness of the Web site. The Web data mining technique may be used to discover the significance of those attributes (see next section).

Reliability

Reliability is about the robustness and soundness of a system. It can be operationally related, so the system can be recovered from either software or the hardware crashes. It may also require backups in order to recover from environmental disasters. On the other hand, it can be application related. It is very hard to have a system bug-free. In many cases the error is not easy to classify as a logical error or a system error. A logical error could be a design error or a data error. In many cases, it may give no error message. A system error could be an operating system run-time error, network traffic problem, or a software-interfacing problem. A system error message may not indicate the real problem, but just report on the failure of a system operation. When an error is discerned, it is sometimes necessary to repeat an error in order to fix it. Theoretically, any error should be repeatable. However, the ability of repeating an error is very much dependent on the understanding of the error.

There are generally two ways to provide application reliability, the **verification** and the **software test**. These two ways may compensate each other. The verification is a process that uses the theorem proof technique to check the system specification against the system requirement, while the software test is a process that checks the system implementation against the system specification.

In system verification, a reasoning machine is used to reason the artifacts in the specifications for achieving the goals of the requirement. The verification process is based on a formal specification language that can provide the formal syntax and semantics. A specification language can be either executable or non-executable. A non-executable specification language may provide a non-ambiguous semantic specification and an implementation-independent document. It requires a translation process to perform the verification in an executable programming language. While an executable specification language may have a built-in verification process and can provide an executable program file for a system in a target computer language, an executable specification language may also reduce the software test work because the built-in verification process can be executed automatically whenever the target system program is to be generated.

In a software test, the system is tested in many ways, such as the static and dynamic tests. **Static tests** are performed in a bottom-up fashion. Step-by-step, all components are tested before they are put together. Each component is tested against the specifications and their pre-post conditions. A *window-technique* can be used to exhaustively test all functions of a system for all possible input. The static tests are *ideal and deterministic* in a sense that the test environment is known and the output is predefined. An error can be regarded as a kind of system side effect. The complexity in static tests is that the system side effects are inherent in the system implementation. A metaphor of proving a side-effect-free system is "to know what you do not know." Another problem is that it may be difficult to feed a system with all possible input permutations. Although it is sometimes infeasible or unnecessary, the decision on a non-exhaustive test can be subjective and problematic, particularly to the reused system software components.

Dynamic tests target the system's overall functions and the performance. Therefore, the process should be top-down. The system is to be tested in a dynamic and changing environment in order to find system problems from general to specific. Referring to a system's architecture, the system dynamics are considered in two dimensions: (1) the major business data flows between major system components (e.g., between clients and servers), and (2) the main business transactions in each stream of the data flow (e.g., the transition from product browsing to on-line ordering). By using this two-dimensional approach, the *bottleneck problems* can be isolated in terms of when, where, and what the problem manifested. For example, a crash (or stress) test can be used to find out the most vulnerable part of a system. In this case, the system is engaged in an extreme situation in either maximum system load (of resource usage including the network traffic) or the maximum system charge (of log-on users or on-line services). The complexity of the dynamic tests is that the tests are mostly conducted in a test environment and the simulation of the system dynamics may be incomplete or incomprehensible.

Other issues may also affect the system availability, such as the virus protection, the network security, and the system administration, including recovery, security control, performance tuning, etc. In dealing with a changing world, the availability can also be affected by the system viability in coping with the changes. Overall, the availability is the ability that keeps the system constantly alive on the Internet.

Performance

The performance is a dynamic factor of the system. It is related to three aspects of a system. First, there is a **cost-effective** decision made in the system design phase that is to bring a best integration of the software and the hardware at a cost within the system development budget. This decision is meant to give the system performance a base line. Second, there is a system architecture problem. In a client-server paradigm, the network traffic and the network dynamics are both considered in providing a balance in the principles of distributed computing. In considering the network traffic, the performance is a problem of the **distributed database management** in order to minimize the network traffic by using techniques such as RPCs (remote procedure calls), or data fragmentation and data replica cache techniques. In considering the network dynamics, the performance is problem of the **network management** that is associated to the network topology and the configuration to maintain the network reachability and the high-level interoperability. Third, the performance is a system administration matter in the performance tuning process that is to find a balance of the trade-offs between the system storage space and the system responding time in a dynamic business environment. Within a changing environment, the performance problem may involve the above three aspects recursively.

Security

The security problem of an IC system is about the authenticity, confidentiality, and data integrity for the Web-enabled business transactions. It is very important and crucial to an IC system. This problem is inherent in the Internet security and deserves a detailed discussion elsewhere.

A Viability Study: Growth Management

Growth management is the strategy on how to deal with changes. The *business reconceptualization* is discussed in many research papers on how to rebuild business in facing the opportunities and challenges in the Information Age. Here is a to-do list:

- Anticipate and monitor changes in the business environment.
- Assess the changes and find out what the impact could be in both aspects of losses or

gains in business.

- Understand the reason for changes and analyze the triggers or conditions of changes.
- Build the business model that is able to incorporate changes.

If the business model cannot reflect and represent the changes, the business model then needs to be changed. There are two ways to do so: (1) Change or redesign the business model. This involves the *reverse engineering* process. (2) Use a trial-and-error approach. This is to modify the system in order to adopt a change. The second way has been used by many systems to cope with the Y2K problem.

Growth management reflects the viability of a system. The strategies used to deal with changes can either be exploitative or defensive.

IC TECHNOLOGY

IC technology is the application of Internet technology on the building of IC systems. In this section we discuss three prominent issues: Web architecture, Web databases and data mining, and Web intelligence.

Web Architecture

Web architecture concerns how the information flows among the system components and how the system components are organized. We will firstly give an overview on a progressive and reflective procedure of building Web business applications. This idea shows how Web architecture is established. Then, we introduce the basic concepts of front-end and back-end system components. Based on those concepts, the client-server paradigm will be discussed in the context of the information flow and the system software deployment. Finally we consider the system architecture in contrast with the business structure that can be *vertical* or *horizontal* in terms of business connections.

Progressive and Reflective IC Engineering

Globalization and deregulation are two main drives to the changes of the business environment. The impact from the growth of the Internet has also accelerated these changes. IC Engineering is challenging these changes by using a progressive and reflective process to build the IC systems.

Figure 2 is used to illustrate the idea that an IC system can be developed progressively with reflection of changes. The initial IC system may be a few primitive information pages. Then the interactive features may be added on to establish a basic trading environment to allow customers to search for or purchase the goods and services. The operational business transactions are supported at this layer. Web-enabled database applications are deployed at this layer. When a trust has been built on the system, a full-fledged business information system can be built on the Web using **Corporate Portals** (Finkelstein, 2000). Corporate Portals are the Web applications that provide a unified information gateway for distributing, analyzing, consolidating, and managing information across and outside an enterprise. Corporate Portals are also called Enterprise Information Portals (EIP). The trend has already started that the Corporate Portals are used to unify the effort of the enterprises to integrate their information access methods. For example, Corporate Portals can be configured with data warehouses to enable different users to access information for their needs, such as Executive Information Systems (EIS), Decision Support Systems (DSS), On-line Analytical Processing (OLAP), and Knowledge Management Systems (KMS). Above the Corporate

Portals layer, the **Intelligent Agents** (Wooldridge, 1995) can be built to retrieve, discover, reason, or deliver the knowledge for various needs. They can be used for business purposes such as buying and selling products, or be used for strategic purposes. For example, Intelligent Agents can be proactive to mine data in data warehouses in order to discover the trends or changes in a business environment, or be reflective in order to solicit expert advice to review business policies. Although enterprise knowledge is available at the Corporate Portals layer, it is about its accessibility and maintenance. At the Intelligent Agents layer, enterprise knowledge is available with the interests of its manipulation and application.

Figure 2. Progressive and Reflective IC Engineering

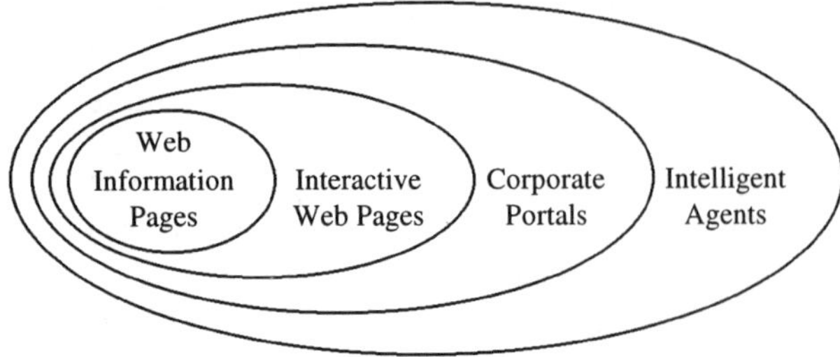

Front-End and Back-End Concepts

All Web-enabled applications have two ends, front-end for the user support and the back-end for the system support. The front-end has the responsibility to:

- provide user interfaces,
- implement the representation logic,
- implement the application logic, and
- specify the interfaces with back-end components.

The back-end includes all those invisible system components that must be used to support the functions of front-end. The back-end may include functions of:

- database management,
- data communication,
- multimedia management, and/or
- security control (e.g., firewall).

It is important to distinguish the system front-end and back-end components. Front-end is application oriented and business specific. It should be user friendly, flexible, and competent for business functions. The tools used to develop front-end should be easy to learn, easy to use, yet functionally sufficient. Meanwhile, the back-end is implementation oriented and business independent. It should be highly efficient, standard, and versatile for supporting different requirements. For example, the front-end of an IC system can be built based on XML, VRML, or SMIL (Synchronised Multimedia Integration Language, from W3C, www.w3c.org) tools, and the back-end can be built based on CORBA (from ODMG) or ADO (ActiveX Data Objects, from Microsoft®), for relational or object-oriented databases. By the distinction between the front-end and back-end components, we can develop an IC system separately and we have a better chance to organise the system for different business environments. As a result of the distinction between front-end and back-end components, the programming tasks are also discussed as **client-side** and **server-side** programming tasks (Morrison, 2000).

Client and Server Paradigm

In a client-server application, a client can initiate the information request and expect the server to reply. Here are two concerns: (1) the information flow between client and server, and (2) the software deployment between client and server. The Web applications are often decomposed into **two-tiers** or **three-tiers** (Umar, 1997b). In two-tiered architecture, when a Web application is to be deployed on the Internet, there are at least three ways to deploy the software components: a *thin client*, a *medium client*, or a *fat client*. This is decided based on the principle to minimize the information flow between client and server and to maximize the system performance. Figure 3 is used to illustrate this idea.

As a thin client, the software is deployed in a minimum. A simplest case is that the client only needs a Web browser to access the service. The representation logic is presented in the Web pages specified by a URL. Other kinds of thin clients may have to install light client-control software where the Web-browsing facility is embedded. In this case, the user may not see a standard Web browser but a customized business-specific application. The problem with a thin client is that it does not support application logic and database logic. So, the transactions are all performed on the server side. This may cause frequent accesses to the server for fetching or processing data. Then the responding time may fluctuate according to the status of the server that may be heavy loaded. The advantage of the thin client is that the light client software deployment may reduce the cost to the user and increase the accessibility from general Web users.

As a medium client, the software is deployed based on a balanced tuning of two factors: the network performance and the distributed database management. The network performance concerns the dynamics of the network traffic. From a network management viewpoint, the software deployment should have the least possibility of bursting data transmissions and should request the least number of data communication channels. This requires the client software to be able to buffer the data in advance to reduce the possible data bursting; or to cache the data whenever they are buffered to reduce the chances of further requests of data communications. From a distributed database viewpoint, the data processing should be as local as possible. This requires the client software to locally support the representation logic, or the application logic, or even the database logic. It also requires the database fragmentation or the database replication in a way that can reduce the chances of moving data around. The medium client implies a complexity in the design of a balance between the front-end and the back-end software deployment for both client and server. It also introduces the complexity of the database management. However the advantage is obvious that the client software is deployed in the best way to maximize the system performance.

As a fat client, the system functions are mostly housed on the client side (e.g., automatically downloaded as .JAR files in an HTML page). This is sometimes a good idea for the semi-off-line clients or mobile desktop clients. In this case, the client is responsible

Figure 3. Software Deployment of Client-Server Components

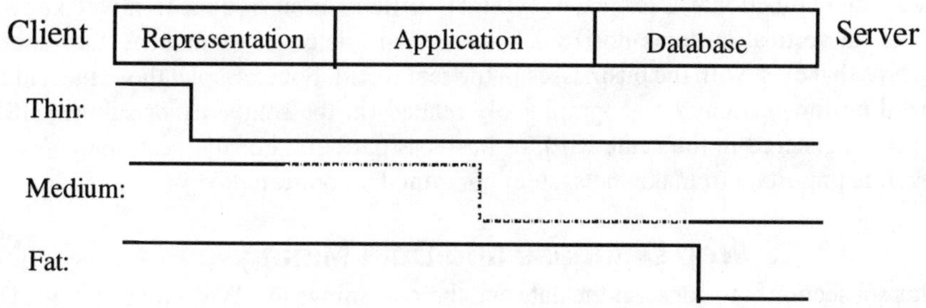

for virtually all application processing. The request to the server side is limited to a minimum, such as the replica consistency maintenance, data dictionary, or the data validation services. A fat client may make IC Engineering more complicated and expensive.

In three-tiered architecture, an application is decomposed into three levels of control: client, Web server, and back-end database management system. The middle-tier application is mostly referred as a Web listener plus the firewall control. The three-tiered-client server architecture provides a better balance between the application control and the system performances. More detailed discussions can be found in Dickman (1995) and Umar (1997b).

The client-server paradigm can be incorporated into two kinds of IC frameworks, the **site-based** or the **agent-based** frameworks. In a site-based framework, the information flow is basically in a request-reply pattern: the client asks for information, then the server replies. This request-reply pattern executes as either RPC (Remote Procedure Call) or RDA (Remote Data Access). In this pattern, the essence is the data and data processing. It is called site-based because the value of information is decided at the site: the one who is asking for information. In an agent-based framework, the information flow is basically in a goal-satisfying pattern: the agent travels to the server and interacts with the server for the goal to be achieved. The agent carries the goal and the knowledge. The server provides the inference mechanism and information for agent to reason out the goal. In this pattern, the essence is the knowledge and goal achieving. It is called agent-based because the agent, who has the autonomy to make decisions on behalf of its creator, decides the value of information. An agent is characterized by its mobility, intelligence, and autonomy.

Vertical Structure Versus Horizontal Structure

There are two forms of IC systems in terms of business connections, the vertical or the horizontal. IC system architecture is said to be **vertical** if it is an individual business and built as an isolated Web application totally relying on the advertisement of its URL or on the search engines to publicize it. This is particularly the case for small and specialized businesses. IC system is said to be **horizontal** if it is a Web application system that is cross-linked with other Web application systems in a way of its business nature. Many IC systems building a network of trading partners as a *virtual enterprise* can be regarded as horizontal structured systems because there are multidimensional connections with other different businesses.

To gain information from vertical structured Web sites, a Web surfer may use a search engine that often returns a formidable list of results in a non-preferable order. Some very skillful Web surfers may find their expected Web sites. The horizontal structured web sites, on the other hand, are more accessible in a sense that businesses are linked together in cross-references. Unfortunately, many of the current IC systems are still vertically structured and struggling for their survival. Although there are many ways to make IC systems appear more attractive or more functional, a vertical IC system is difficult to survive until it is well known.

To make vertical systems horizontal, we need to discover or identify the natural relationships that exist with the businesses in the real world. For example, those individual specialized businesses may be geographically related (in the same city or suburb), ISP-related (i.e., registered in the same ISP), or business partners. For the best interests of a business, it is important to make the system horizontally connected.

Web Database and Data Mining

This subsection is to consider the data and their meanings in a Web environment. The

Web database is discussed in terms of the interconnectivity and interoperability. The Web data mining is considered in terms of the knowledge discovering of **rule-based** patterns and **topology-based** patterns for the publicity problems and the attractiveness problems of Web sites.

Web Database

The database management system (DBMS) provides functions for storing and accessing data. The DBMS is characterized by its platform independence and application independence. The platform independence allows the DBMS to be implemented on different operating environments, so that the database can be scalable and portable. The application independence allows the DBMS to be shared by different applications at different abstraction levels. The DBMS can be measured in terms of data integrity, security, accessibility, and reliability. The distributed DBMS (DDBMS) is a system that can handle the data fragmentation and replication over data communication networks.

IC systems need database support at the back-end. This challenges the DBMS to have its data Web-accessible. A Web database is a database that has its data accessible for Web applications (Morrison, 2000), so the data can be inserted, retrieved, or updated from within a Web-addressable unit (e.g., an HTML document). A Web-addressable (i.e., hypertext-linked) unit is given as a URL (Uniform Resource Locator) that can be a document, a program of a business transaction, or an interactive user action (e.g., sending e-mail or downloading software). There are generally two different ways to make a database Web-enabled: a **connection-based** approach or a **content-based** approach. In the connection-based approach, a standard protocol is proposed to specify an interface between data and programs. Examples can be the CORBA architecture using a Java-based programming environment to manipulate data over the Internet, or the ADO architecture (Gutierrez, 2000) using Microsoft® proprietary ActiveX technique for the data interfacing in the network environment. In the content-based approach, a standard protocol is proposed to specify the meaning (content) of the data for different applications. Examples are the ICE (Information and Content Exchange, www.w3c.org) and XML/EDI (www.xmledi.com). In this approach, the data need to be extracted from the database according to the content-based protocols before they are exchanged. So the interaction is performed in terms of the document exchange instead of the interfacing.

The main difference between the connection-based and content-based approaches is that the former is computing-centric, while the latter is business-centric. The connection-based approaches are considered in terms of the independence between platforms and applications, so those application programs can share and exchange data over different database architectures. The essential point here is the interconnectivity of the databases. The content-based approaches are considered in terms of the independence between business data and business applications, so those different business applications can share and exchange enterprise information for the suppliers chain, purchasing, manufacturing, shipping, auditing, and other business transactions. The central point here is the interoperability that makes the data understandable to each other applications.

In a top-down design viewpoint, the content-based approaches should be considered and evaluated before we consider the Web database implementations. However the engineering concerns can always be constrained by the availability of the web database techniques for their ability to support the content-based approaches.

Web Data Mining

The Web data mining (WDM) activity is to automatically discover rules, patterns, or associations from the Web-collected data. The WDM can be applied on two categories of data recorded: the business transactions and the Web-user patterns. The purpose of the WDM can be either for the improvement of the business functions or for the enhancement of the Web site attractiveness. The data mining on the business transaction data is the traditional data mining, while the data mining on the user-Web patterns is an emerging research topic, for which further discussion is given as follows.

For the understanding of Web user patterns, current research follows two directions: computing *rule-based* patterns (Mobasher, 1997), or computing *topology-based* patterns (Chen, 1998; Lin, 1999). In a rule-based approach, the input of the data-mining algorithm is a relational database, and the output is a set of association rules that report the intrinsic relationships between data items. In a topology-based approach, the input of the data-mining algorithm is a set of directed graphs that represent the user accesses to the Web business components, and the output is a pattern of a specific topology, which represents the frequent user traversal in a Web environment. Business components are the Web-addressable units. By using the topology pattern, we can find out the causal relationships between the frequently visited Web-addressable units and the scenario of the Web-visiting activities.

For the approach of rule-based patterns, we discuss the **popularity problem** of Web sites (Li, 2000). We identify four kinds of visitors regarding a Web site: the first-time visitors (FV), the second-time visitors (SV), the visitors who have elected to do business with the Web site (FB), and the visitors who come back to do the business again (SB). The number of FVs may reflect the successfulness of the Web publicity. The number of SVs may reflect the successfulness of the Web site construction. The number of FBs may show the usefulness of the Web site. And the number of SBs may demonstrate the overall attractiveness of the Web site, including the successfulness of the business functions.

There are many questions to be answered in order to understand the user behavior. We need to identify the factors that would affect the determination of the numbers of FVs, SVs, FBs, and SBs. Thus, a database is needed to record the data about the visitor's profile as well as the data that attribute Web sites. Hopefully then we may able to tell what kind of Web sites may attract large numbers of the four categories of visitors. By using a system log, Web site visitors can be classified into one of the above four categories. For example if such a database is available, we may be able to use data mining algorithms to find out if a "free e-mail account" is a good way to attract the FV to a Web site. Or we may be able to verify that "the most effective way to publicize a web site in retail business is the local newspaper advertisements," etc. So the rule-base data mining in this case can be used to find a cost-effective way to attract a large number of first-time web site visitors.

It may be useful to understand not only how but also why a user visits the Web site. We now discuss the **satisfaction problem** of Web sites as an example of the topology-based Web data mining approach. We may consider the satisfaction problem in two phases: how and why. If we can understand how users behave in visiting Web sites, we may have a better idea to organise the Web site. If we know why user is attracted to visit a Web site, we may be able to make Web sites more satisfactory to the user needs. We assume that the metric of the satisfaction is the frequency of Web visits. A larger number of the frequency implies a higher level of the user satisfaction. By viewing the frequently visited topology pattern of the hypertext-linked Web business components, we may find out what business components are visited frequently and how they are visited.

We assume that a system log is used to record the detailed information about Web accesses in a local system. The system log should provide the information on the following items: the user identification, the current focused Web business component, the duration of the visit, and the previously visited business component. The system log then can give the history of the Web access activities of users. By using the user identification, we are able to group the Web activities in terms of users. By using the duration of transitions, we may know the average time spent by a user in that function. By recording the focus and the previously visited business components, we can draw a direct graph of the Web visit. The nodes in the graph represent the Web-addressable units, and the edges represent the transitions of the visits. The edges are weighted by the frequency of the user's visits. Then we can collect a set of graphs from different users. The task now is to compute a topology pattern that is the most common to all graphs in the set. This topology pattern would show how users have visited the Web site.

After the topology pattern of the Web access is discovered, the further study is to find out why this pattern is. This triggers the further investigation on the properties of the topology pattern. It should reveal the scenario of the user visit, the causal connections between the Web-addressable units, and orientations of the user visits towards the attributes of those business components. This further study may require a new phase of the Web data mining that needs to collect the topology patterns from all different Web sites that use different Web-addressable units for different business components. When this kind of database becomes available, we would be able to run the data mining algorithm again to find an interpretation for a frequently visited Web site.

The research on web data mining has just started and needs much more attention.

Web Intelligence

Web intelligence is to apply artificial intelligence in the WWW (World Wide Web) environment. To this end, the intelligence refers to the knowledge and the application of knowledge in problem solving. Knowledge can bring change and knowledge itself may change. If we view the Internet as a network of servers and clients, we can then see that the collection of servers and clients is representational of the virtual world that reflects the image of our perceptual world. In the virtual world, knowledge can be discovered, stored, transported, and applied.

Intelligent Search Engine

In information search, the problem is to search an information base thoroughly. The fundamental question is to understand, first, what is to be searched. So, the key issue is to decide the search criteria in terms of both denotations and connotations provided by user explicitly and implicitly. We may view the Internet as a huge distributed information base; the searched result can then be said complete if the search goal is decidable. A search goal is decidable if all implicated meaning can be explicitly expressed by the search syntax. Figure 4 shows a complete search paradigm on the Internet. There have been three generations of Internet search engines.

The **first-generation search engines** use a simple keyword search methodology. It has two stages. Stage One is to use a software agent program (called *spider* or *robot*) to fetch information from the Internet. Then a database is used to store the categorized information. Stage Two is to search the database to provide the resource (URL) addresses according to user request. The first-generation search engines are characterized by a fetch-store database approach. It is sometimes difficult for a user to digest a vast amount of returned search result. Depending on the quality of a search engine, a user may have to use different search engines to get the information.

The **second-generation search engines** use a *meta-search* technique that uses software agents to simultaneously search multiple first-generation search engine databases and bring back the data and then compile them dynamically to satisfy users' requests. The second-generation search engines are characterized by a fetch-processing analytical approach. The advantage of the second-generation search engines is that they pay attention to the content of search result and present the content in a way that is best suitable to users. For example, some search engines can provide a multidimensional URL graph as a user interface to allow a user to pursue the further search. A *fish-eye* technique can be used to *zoom in* or *zoom out* in a URL graph. The second-generation search engine can be content-based in a sense that the *search pattern* can be recognized in the search process. The meta-search for the universal resource discovery is a research paradigm that is aimed to provide the structural information for the Web data.

The **third-generation search engines** are characterized by a semantic-driven approach. The main advantage is that "it knows what it is trying to find." Or in other words, it is a goal-driven search. It has the ability to learn from search behaviors of the user. During the search a user profile may be used or updated. Compared to the second-generation search engine, the third-generation search engine is the content-based search plus the interpretation. It is an **incremental search** on all previously searched results. By using the context-sensitive analysis, the search pattern is recognized from its context. For example, ontologically a word "menu" in a software user guide must be different from that in a restaurant blurb. One of the advantages of the third-generation search engines is that it has greater search power than traditional database-oriented search engines. In addition to the ability to query structured data, it can also *filter* or *digest* unstructured data.

There is no reason the third-generation search engines should replace the first two generations of search engines. Actually, they will all coexist for their own applications. In implementation, the intelligent mobile agents can play a role in third-generation search engines.

In Internet Commerce, the availability of business information is crucial. According to the types of business (i.e., business-to-business or business-to-customer), the information flow can be categorized based on the business work flow. Either about product advertisement or about the current status of service delivery, business transactions may generate an infinite number of pieces of information and need to be organized in a way suitable for search agents.

Reflective Reasoning

Agent server on the Internet provides an environment for intelligent agents. Intelligent agents work with the server in an *open system* environment. Thereby the inference engine in the server should be able to deal with the dynamics in the knowledge management and manipulation. The server should be reflective to the changes of the domain knowledge. This requires a *causal connection* between its modeling mechanism and domain knowledge. The causal connection works like a mirror: it reflects changes in the real world into an image-recording system. If the mirror is not functioning well, the recorded image can be distorted. The causal connection modeling is a meta level activity that the server can incorporate changes into the knowledge base. The knowledge representation approach also needs to be reflective: the representation on both domain and meta knowledge.

Figure 4. The Internet Information Search Space

	Searched	Non-Searched
Wanted	Expected	Minimized
Unwanted	Minimized	Expected

To allow an inference engine

Figure 5. Web-Enabled Legacy Systems

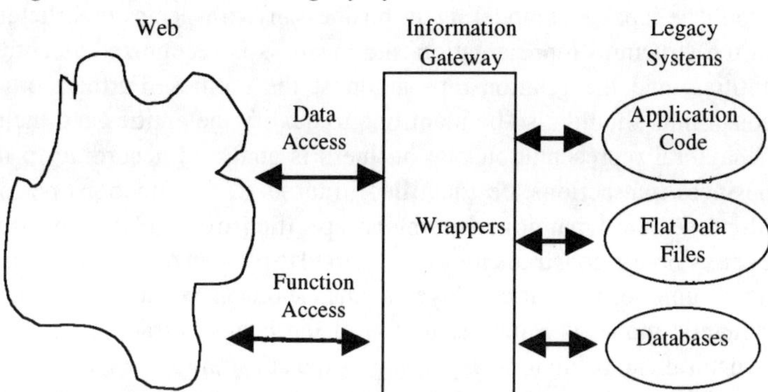

capable of reflective reasoning, it requires the reasoning of *meta knowledge* triggered by exceptions in a reasoning process. It is context sensitive and retrospective in order to provide agents the answers that are normally not derivable from a first-order inference engine. The reflective reasoning is treated as an interrupt in the first-order reasoning process and will derive the goals that can handle abnormal situations of normal reasoning process. A kernel high-order reasoning mechanism will need to be built in an agent server. Although the research work on reflective reasoning has been started early (Maes, 1988), its reflection to the Internet intelligent agents is yet to be seen.

Counter Inference

Agents are often dealing with conflict interests. When an agent is working in a closed system environment, the outcome is predictable in a sense that the inference engine is a search machine working on the knowledge base plus the calculation of confidence factors. However, in an open system environment, the goals are dynamic (i.e., changing and conflict), the knowledge bases are inconsistent, the reasoning strategies vary. The interaction between agents may yield win-lose situations (e.g., game playing) or win-win situations (e.g., negotiation). The kernel inference engine in an agent server should take the counter goals from different agents and progresses with the goal-refinement and reflective control on the inference process. The counter inference engine in this sense should be objective, and meta knowledge used in the control should be domain-knowledge independent.

In practice, an agent server should integrate the inference engine with both the reflective reasoning and the counter inference.

IC DEVELOPMENT METHODOLOGY

IC development methodology is a procedural work that can be followed step-by-step to create the IC systems. In this section, we are not going to give the detailed procedures but instead discuss some issues that can affect the application of proper procedures. Firstly we discuss the modelling methodologies that provide the formal method for catching semantics of IC systems. Then we discuss the methodologies that are used to make *legacy systems* Web accessible. Finally, we give an overview of the system development methodologies that are applicable to different engineering environments.

Modelling of IC Systems

The modeling of an IC system is to create a semantic model for the representation of the business in a trading environment. It is a conceptualization process. In this process, we need to use a syntactical tool to represent the concepts in the business environment. This tool should be capable of modeling the business in two aspects: the structural and the behavioral. In the structural representation, the business is recognized as entities, properties of the entities, and the relationships amongst the entities. Furthermore, the domain (static) constraints should also be identified to qualify the entities and their relationships. In the behavioral representation, the business is analyzed according to its work flow. So the business transactions are identified in terms of the functions performed by the entities. Moreover, the dynamic constraints are specified to control the transitions of the data updates. For example, a constraint may be specified to prevent the update on the employee data under the assumption that "an employee's salary should never be decreased." To sum up, a business semantic model is a representation of the business-trading environment in terms of its structural and behavioral aspects, plus the constraints.

The modeling process has two general questions to be answered: the **semantic completeness** and the **representation uniqueness**. By the semantic completeness, two aspects are considered: (1) everything in the business-trading environment will be described; (2) anything expressed within the resulting model is true in the business-trading environment. By this two-way checking we can be sure that the business semantic model derived from the modeling process is a true representation.

By the representation uniqueness, two aspects are concerned: (1) the *semantic non-ambiguity* is maintained; (2) the *minimum representation* is achieved. The semantic non-ambiguity requires that the typing system enforce both the unique naming convention and the elementary domain values. Therefore complex values can be constructed from elementary values without semantic ambiguity. The minimum representation requires that all derivable artifacts cannot be directly stored but represented as formulas or the derivation rules, so that there is no redundancy in the system representation. The minimum representation will guarantee that the smallest number of syntactic units is used to produce the model. So this ensures a way of standardization for the modeling process. By checking on the representation uniqueness, we can be sure that the business semantic model derived from the modeling process is a *good* representation.

There have been many modeling methodologies proposed in recent years. The current consensus is the UML (Unified Modeling Language) promoted by the OMG (www.omg.org). The UML can be used to visualize, specify, construct, and document artifacts of the systems ranging from enterprise information systems to distributed Web-based applications (Booch, 1999).

From a Legacy System to a Web-Enabled System

Many methodologies available currently are:

- the traditional software design and implementation methodologies which have little support for the system evolution towards the Internet information systems, or
- the software tool-based design and implementation methodologies that are applicable only on that tool. This leaves little room for a software engineer to minimize his/her effort in transforming a legacy system into a Web-enabled system.

The legacy systems are defined and viewed in many different ways (Alderson, 1999; Umar, 1997). In our discussion we regard the legacy systems as the systems that are disadvantaged by not having their data and functions Web accessible. So, the question now is to consider how we can convert the legacy systems into the Web-enabled systems. There are two fundamental issues: (1) How do we make legacy data Web accessible? (2) How do we make legacy systems run in the Web environment? The former is a **data conversion** problem; the latter is a **system integration** problem.

For both problems *middleware programming* can provide the solutions. In middleware programming, the legacy systems are *wrapped* with Web-accessible interface-protocol specifications, called *wrappers*. One example of the interface-protocol specifications is the IDL (Interface Definition Language) in the CORBA architecture (www.odmg.org). The IDL-specified CORBA wrappers are Web accessible (Umar, 1997). The wrappers form a software layer that allows the legacy systems to exchange data or to interact with the Web. We call this layer the information gateway that solves the data conversion and the system integration problems for the legacy systems. Figure 5 (p. 22) illustrates this idea.

Methodologies in System Development

Many different approaches to IC system development currently exist. These approaches are applicable to different situations in the system development. We identify four different system development methodologies according to the focus of the developers: user-driven, data-driven, process-driven, and system-driven.

The user-driven methodology is to let the user play the important role in the system development. It is an iterative process that is to build a prototype first and then the user will be working with the developer to improve the system functions. This approach is usually focused on small applications, and the system can be quickly built and refined.

The data-driven methodology is used as a formal top-down refinement methodology. Following down a few successive stages, the system is developed. This approach starts with the formal specifications of the system requirement. Then the data model is derived. Based on the data model, the system transactions are defined and implemented. This methodology provides a chance to perform the verification for checking the system specification against the requirement. The data-driven methodology follows a formal software-engineering path and is good for the large systems that have clearly specified system requirements.

The process-driven methodology is used for the systems that consider the understanding of the system functions more important than that of the data structure. In this kind of system, the fundamental processes are identified before the specification of a data model. This methodology is suitable for systems that have complicated functions but have relatively simple data structure.

The system-driven methodology is applied on the existing system to reverse engineer it to a new one. By reverse engineering, the new system interfaces and added functionality will be integrated with the old system. This will minimize the effort of creating a new system from the beginning. The new requirements can be compared with the old requirements to improve the system quality.

In IC Engineering, all four methodologies may be applicable. For example, a prototyping approach may be a good way to quickly develop a system for the demonstration of ideals. But it may be difficult for further development regarding the change of the underlying system architecture. A reverse engineering approach may be helpful on redeveloping a new system similar to an old one. But it is difficult to formally verify the new system because the reverse engineering may not be able to guarantee that the reversed system will be a true recovery of the old one. Sometimes, the reverse engineering may have to "reinvent the wheel," in which the problems were overcome before.

IC IMPLEMENTATION

In this section we consider how we can implement an IC system properly. The implementation is an issue of the **applicability** of the Internet technology. The availability does not equal the applicability. The issue of the implementation is to understand the needs of the system and select the most suitable technology to implement the system. Instead of comparing and contrasting different technologies in detail, we discuss the background of the implementation. Firstly, we discuss the independent relationships existing in the implementation environment. The understanding of this may help us in selecting tools and back-end systems for the implementation. Secondly, we discuss the component technology that is used to construct a system. Finally, we give a brief list of the critical factors in IC Engineering.

Implementation Independence

When system development comes to an implementation phase, it faces an intricate task: the decisions on building tools, on adherence of protocol standards, and on system construction. The complexity consists in the diversity of the current available technological products and the proprietary protocols that are all tangled. In this subsection, we identify the independent relationships that may help us to consolidate the decisions in an effort to unify the implementation process. The following independent relationships are identified:

- front-end and back-end system independence,
- platform independence, and
- proprietary protocol independence.

The front-end is independent from the back-end so that the implementation work can have different focuses, as mentioned in the previous discussions of Web architecture. However, this implies that we have to design a standard interface for the data flow between front-end and back-end systems. For example, XML can be used to specify Corporate Portals (Finkelstein, 2000) as front-end and access the back-end of standard relational or standard (ODMG) object-oriented databases. Another example is to use some scripting programs embedded in an HTML document (e.g., CGI, Java applets, or ActiveX components) in the front-end system and use CORBA (www.odmg.org) or ADO (Gutierrez, 2000) for the back-end support for accessing databases. It may be worthwhile to mention that some front-end supporting functions may have minor compatibility problems, such as that between the Netscape Internet Explorer. In this case, the front-end development should limit the functions to use only those compatible features.

Platform independence is implemented by choosing a development tool that is supported by all operating systems. It is not difficult to implement the platform independence as long as we use OMG/ODMG Standard and Java, XML, tools. Many *off-shelf* tools are now providing developers a freedom to implement systems on different platforms.

Proprietary protocol independence is an effort to improve the interconnectivity or the interoperability of the system for the potential incremental development. Many software companies provide the tools that are not designed for an open system environment. Although they may provide some API (Application Program Interfaces) for standard protocols, the integration of these tools may require an extra effort on leaning and programming of the API, and an extra layer of the system software for the bugs. The *middleware* programmers are now still in high demand. It is expected that with the development of the convergence of the universal protocols on the Internet, the proprietary protocol should have less interest for its existence.

Component Technology

The component technology (Szyperski, 1998) is developed based on the assumption of the open system environment. This technology is characterized by the reusability, portability, and the interoperability within an open system environment. A component is an independent and portable program that has its functions defined within the component interface. A component interface consists of *interface elements* that are the ontological descriptive notions of the interface including the syntax, semantics, and the functions of the component. A component has the ability to respond to the events that trigger the execution of the component or the interaction with other components. Components can cooperate together in a pre-designed architecture to perform the tasks of data processing or the process control.

The component-based systems are constructed based on a framework of the *component packaging*. When a system is designed, the system functions are refined from top-down to generate framework of components. The component packaging is the grouping of the functions to composite a system. On the other hand, the *system assembly* is considered to respond to the events that may happen to the system. The system assembly is regarded as a process that organizes the components in terms of the event control.

In building the IC systems, the component-based system development may start with the transformation from a business model into a component-based architecture. Then the system is assembled based on the transactions in the business trading. Currently the available tools are the EJB (Enterprise JavaBeans) from Sun Microsystems® and the ETS (Enterprise Transaction Server) from Microsoft®. Both of them are used for the component-based and transaction-oriented applications. In EJB, transactions are packaged as the JavaBean objects. In ETS, transactions are packaged as the COM (Component Object Model) objects.

The future, however, is still considering using the component technology in a higher level of the component packaging, that is to group the components in terms of the business types instead of the transactions. Furthermore the packaged components should be Web addressable so a business (e.g., a virtual enterprise) can be established based on the systems that are already functioning. We may call this business-oriented component technology Web Addressable Business Objects (WABO). Since the WABO is Web addressable, it inherits all properties from the component technology, plus it is interconnected and interoperable. In designing a WABO-based system, we need to concentrate on the business requirements and the business functions. After that, the WABO-based system should be generated automatically for the implementation of the business model.

Critical Factors for IC System Development

To bring a project to success, there are three important aspects: the **business management**, the **project management**, and the **technology management**. For simplicity of our discussion, we itemize the important points as follows:

Business Management

- From a business point of view, ensure the success of the idea.
- Keep the business idea alive.
- Manage the financial support.
- Direct and steer the process and the new ideas of the project.
- Make contact with the business partners.
- Supervise and monitor the project progress.

Project Management

- Prom a management point of view, ensure the success of the project.
- Plan and schedule the project.
- Discover the problems and predict the possible impasse of the project development.
- Provide the information and the assessment for the business strategies.
- Organise the execution of the project (provide resources and personnel).
- House keeping (documentation, financing, marketing, etc.).

Technology Management

- From a technology point of view, ensure the success of the project.
- Make sure the best technology and the effective and efficient methodologies are applied to the implementation of the project.
- Provide the expertise and knowhow to solve the problems in the process of implementation.
- Implement the project.
- Help the project manager with the planning and the scheduling.

The critical factors of the success in IC Engineering are that:

- The constant communication must be maintained to ensure the consensus of the project.
- Timing is important—a sense of entrepreneur.
- Be informative—monitor the Web for new ideas and new developments in Web technology.
- Necessary resources must be guaranteed.
- Provide a simple yet functional and attractive model for the illustration of the idea.

CONCLUSIONS

The ultimate goal of IC Engineering is to produce robust, competent, and viable Web-enabled enterprise information systems. In this chapter, we have tried to reason out some important factors in building such systems. A scenario of IC Engineering may start with the creating of a business model in the process of business analysis and design, then transform it into a system model that has its main interests in the system architecture and components. Finally the system implementation will be carried out. Within this scenario, three aspects are considered: requirement specification, Internet technology, and development methodology.

To achieve success in IC Engineering, this chapter has given an overview of some current important issues. It aimed to provide a better understanding on the questions such as:

- What is IC Engineering about?
- What is an IC system?
- What are the general requirements for an IC system?
- How do we benchmark an IC system?
- How do we develop such a system?
- How do we implement such a system?
- How do we make an IC Engineering project successful?

We consider IC Engineering as a progressive and reflective process. Within this process, we should not only understand what we are doing, but also manage what we are doing. This chapter has given some rationale on the issues of this process. Many IC tools provided by major software competitors are still weak in interoperability and interconnectivity mainly because of their proprietary protocols. It is expected that in the near future. We may be able to build IC systems faster and easier by assembling systems with the plug-and-play WABO.

REFERENCES

Alderson A., & Shah H. (1999). Viewpoints on legacy systems. *Communications of ACM*, 42(3), 115-116.

Booch G., Rumbaugh J., & Jacobson I. (1999). *The Unified Modelling Language User Guide*. Addison Wesley.

Chen M.S., Park J.S., & Yu P.S., (1998). "Efficient Data Mining for Path Traversal Patterns". *IEEE Transactions on Knowledge and Data Engineering*, 10(2), 209-221.

Davis A.M. (1993). *Software Requirements Objects, Functions, and States*. Prentice Hall.

Dickman A. (1995). "Two-Tier versus Three-Tier Applications". *Information Week*, Nov., 13, 74-80.

Finkelstein C., & Aiken P. (2000). *Building Corporate Portals with XML*. McGraw-Hill.

Glushko R.J., Tenenbaum J.M., & Meltzer B. (1999). "An XML Framework for Agent-Based E-Commerce". 42(3), March, *Communications of ACM*, 106-114.

Gutierrez D.D. (2000). "*Web Database Development for Windows Platforms*". Prentice Hall.

Kotonya G., & Sommerville I. (1998). "*Requirements Engineering–Processes and Techniques*". Wiley.

Laplante M. (1998). "Making EDI Accessible with XML". *E.COM Magazine*, 4(2), March, 23-26.

Li X., & Low G. (2000). "Fuzzy Logic in Web Data Mining", Session on Fuzzy Systems, *Proceedings of the 4th World Multiconference on Systemics, Cybernetics, and Informatics* (SCI' 2000), Orlando, USA, July.

Lin X. (1999). "Efficiently Computing Frequent Tree-Like Topology Patterns in a Web Environment" *Proceedings of the 31 IEEE International Conference on Technology of Object-Oriented Languages and Systems* (TOOLS 31), 440-447.

Maes P. (1988). "Computational Reflection", *Knowledge Engineering Review*, 3(1), 1-19.

Mobasher B., Jain N., Han E.H., & Srivastava (1997). "Web Mining, Pattern Discovery from World Wide Web Transactions". *Proceedings of the 9th IEEE International Conference on Tools with Artificial Intelligence* (ICTAI'97).

Morrison M., & Morrison J. (2000). "*Database-Driven Web Sites*". Web Warrior Series, Thomson Learning.

Szyperski C. (1998). "Component Software—Beyond Object-Oriented Programming". Addison-Wesley / ACM Press.

Wooldridge & Jennings N.R. (1995). "Intelligent Agents: Theory and Practice." *The Knowledge Engineering Review,* 19(2), 115-152.

Umar A. (1997). "*Object Oriented Client/server Internet Environments.*" Prentice Hall.

Umar A. (1997b). Chapter 6: Web-Based Application Software Architectures. "*Application (Re)Engineering—Building Web-Based Applications and Dealing with Legacies*". Prentice Hall.

Chapter II

Internet Commerce and Exporting: Strategies for Electronic Market Entry

Munib Karavdic
Macquarie Bank, Australia

Gary D. Gregory
University of Wollongong, Australia

INTRODUCTION

A host of new products and services are now available to more than a half-billion consumers. Firms now have greater opportunities to customize their product/service offerings as well as rely on standardized offerings as a preference. Global firms have the opportunity to customize their advertising and sales promotion messages to specific customer segments without the significant cost once involved in developing numerous messages for numerous markets. This communication segmentation strategy allows firms to achieve real dissemination strategies because of the elimination of wasted audience coverage and better-targeted messages aimed at the core benefits sought by various consumer segments. This is the new business world created by the Internet.

As a result of recent technological advances in market entry, many firms are now beginning to increase their marketing and export functions. An emerging part of new technologies development involves electronic transactions over the open network, the Internet. An important Internet characteristic is its global coverage. Using the Internet as an access to the international market, firms generate significant revenues. For example, the music CD distributor CDNow, as a pure on-line company generated 21 percent of its total revenue from international markets in the first quarter of 1998; Dell, a computer manufacturer, generated 20 percent; and FastParts, an electronic components distributor, generated 30 percent. With other numerous examples of generating international revenue on-line, the Internet has already been proven a strategic tool in the exporting process.

In this chapter we examine Internet marketing strategy for exporting and possible implications for firms using electronic technologies. The first part of this chapter presents Internet commerce as a specific entry mode to global markets using advanced technologies, represented by the Internet. Part Two introduces a model for Internet exporting strategies utilizing key components in the marketing mix (i.e., product, promotion, place, and price). The focus of this model is on the interaction between Internet commerce activities and software agents, and the potential impact on the exporting process. Applying the model of Internet-based exporting strategy to businesses, Part Three develops a strategic matrix that classifies firms based on the degree of product transferability and their capitalization on Internet technologies in exporting. Particular emphasis is given to the role of software agents in the electronic exporting process at different stages in strategy development. Finally, we summarize the impact of Internet commerce on exporting activities and highlight the benefits of incorporating new technologies into an exporting strategy.

EXPORTING USING INTERNET COMMERCE

The information technology revolution, manifested through the Internet, has intensified the dynamics of the global market, both stimulating consumer demand and reducing domestic and international entry barriers. Businesses are now beginning to increase their international marketing and export functions by using the Internet to receive customer orders and handle inquiries (Hamill, 1997; Bennett, 1997; Samiee, 1998). There are three possible directions in Internet commerce, business to business (B2B), business to customer (B2C), and customer to customer (C2C). The biggest volume of trade has been generated by B2B relationships, typically suppliers to large companies such as General Electric, Mercedes Benz, etc. Also, Cisco and Oracle, technology companies, have transferred almost all their products to domestic and international companies using the Internet. B2C includes normal retail activities using the Internet commerce, such as book selling by Amazon.com or computer selling by Dell. Firms also use their retail operations to sell products into the global market.

C2C is a new model of the Internet-based relationship where consumers can trade using auction-designed Web sites such as ebay.com in the U.S., qxl.com in Europe, or sold.com.au in Australia. At present, for global operations the first two models are more appropriate. Going global is not just about getting first mover advantage and being ahead of the pack, it is increasingly becoming imperative for their success for all firms to invest in Internet commerce activities (Knight & Cavusgil, 1996). There are no geographic boundaries to using the Internet infrastructure—it is open, scaleable, and allows an instantaneous global presence. It is becoming the gateway through which manufacturers and service providers gain access to world markets without relinquishing control, and where physical distance is no longer an issue (Hoffman & Novak, 1995). There are numerous implications for firms if they use the Internet in exporting activities. The size of the company is not as crucially important for exporting through the Internet as it was for the traditional ways of exporting. On the other hand, cost reduction in finding new buyers and an improvement in the speed of information dissemination are the key benefits for exporters. These benefits increase companies' price competitiveness, provision of product/service information, and observation of buyer behavior. To gain the full benefits of the Internet in the exporting process, buyers need to have Internet access, a basic level of understanding of on-line trading, and a significant amount of trust in the companies they deal with. In developed countries there is a 'critical mass' with very fast growth of on-line trading. According to the latest International Data Corporation (IDC) survey, there are significant numbers of on-line consumers in developing countries, despite the conventional opinion that these are not e-commerce markets. As many as one-third of survey respondents in nations such as Chile, China, and India said they had made on-line purchases in the past three months (IDC, 1999). The Internet establishes an absolutely different environment for exporting activities and determines different exporting strategies (Hamill & Gregory, 1997).

Despite the fact that Internet commerce is a new research paradigm, the mainstream academic literature has ignored its increasing importance (Hamill, 1997; Samiee, 1998). Current exporting models focus on export strategy into a single market (or country). Because the Internet is able to provide instantaneous access to numerous global markets, recent technological advances force us to rethink whether existing theoretical frameworks are sufficient to explain today's export entry strategies. While past research suggests that new technologies may affect the export entry mode decision, there is little evidence to support the actual incorporation of technology into exporting theory. However, recent research suggests that electronic marketing using the Internet may actually serve as an entry mode into international markets (Gregory & Karavdic, 1998). According to these authors, Internet commerce is a potential entry mode for businesses that involve a high usage of standardized interactive technologies, and in which most international activities may be finalized electronically. Although the Internet is best known among these interactive technologies, others include intranets, extranets, electronic data interchange (EDI), and mobile commerce. Capitalizing on the high usage of standardized interactive technologies, Internet commerce differs from 'traditional' modes of entry by (1) providing higher levels of transnational interactions among global firms and their partners, (2) improving the access and selection of products and services, (3) simplifying administrative and distribution procedures, and for improving communications with foreign partners and customers (Gregory & Karavdic, 1998). Furthermore, electronic market entry into countries has the potential to help in establishing alliances and the sharing of ideas with firms in the global marketplace, enabling 'customer-driven' relationships and long-term interactive relationships with overseas clients/customers.

MODEL OF INTERNET EXPORTING STRATEGY

Past research has identified a number of impediments to export market entry and export volume growth, such as information acquisition and transport (Kedia & Chokar, 1986), market access and physical distance (Dicht, Koeglmayr, & Mueller, 1990; Johanson & Vahlne, 1990), export promotion, and the costs associated with these activities (Czinkota and Johnston, 1983; Johanson & Vahlne, 1990; Rabino, 1980; Samiee & Walters, 1991). Using Internet commerce in exporting activities, it is possible to overcome many of these impediments, resulting in more cost-effective exporting. The model presented in Figure 1 is an extension and modification of existing theoretical exporting models. While previous research explains export marketing strategy with product and promotion adaptation, support of foreign distributor/subsidiary, and price competitiveness (Cavusgil & Zou, 1994), our model conceptualizes Internet marketing strategy as a function of product transferability, marketing communication, number of foreign distributors/subsidiaries, price competitiveness, and Internet commerce activities.

The purpose of the model is to explore Internet export marketing strategy in terms of the capitalization on Internet activities during the export process. There is a perception that the success of Internet commerce applications mainly depends of the Internet marketing strategy employed. To explore this framework we first review mainstream exporting literature and research related to the Internet and e-commerce. Next, we provide case studies of present companies' activities on the Internet to support important linkages within our model.

Figure 1. Model of Internet Exporting Strategy

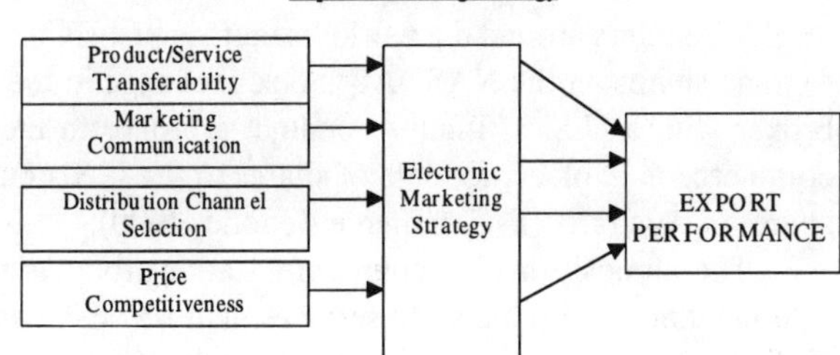

Export Marketing Strategy Development

Product/ service transferability

Product/service characteristics are very important in both ways of exporting, traditional or using Internet marketing. Although there is some evidence that for traditional exporting activities product adaptation leads to an increase in demand from local buyers, exporting using Internet commerce allows the possibility of changing the product or service into digital form, leading to a greater impact on export performance. However, product and service transferability depends on the degree of 'intangibility' of the product or service. As Figure 2 indicates, the more intangible the products/services, the greater the opportunities for exporting. For example, home furnishings are tangible, and because of that, opportunities for their Internet transfer are very low. A different situation occurs with financial services and computer software, which can be intangible and gain benefits from direct exporting using Internet transfer.

Products/services with a high level of intangibility are able to be transferred electronically in digital form. Examples of such commodities include telecommunications, computer software, music, video entertainment, financial services/insurance, mathematical and biological algorithms, semiconductors, database content, and so on. These differ, obviously, from home furnishings, agricultural products, electronic appliances, or any other products from traditional manufacturing. There are certain things that obviously can be transferable,

Figure 2. Degree of Intangibility and Internet Export Opportunities

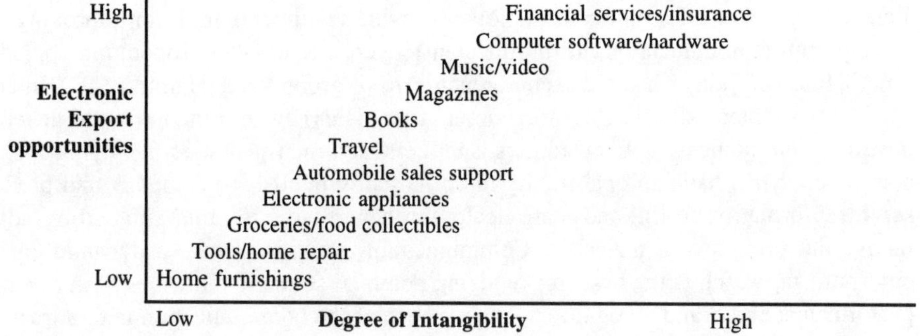

for example financial services. Financial service providers are pure information businesses. The times when investments physically changed hands are long gone. With the Internet, money transfers around the world instantaneously. Currently, if a trader in Australia wants to trade shares on the NASDAQ stock exchange in the U.S., all he/she has to do is find a broker with a U.S. affiliate or contact a broker in the U.S.. Very soon, when Internet commerce is in place, the sale of shares in the U.S. could be used to fund the purchase of shares in Australia (E-Commerce Beyond, 2000).

The supposition is that pure information products are even easier to exchange over the Internet than the products and services in those other cases that still have a physical nature. Unlike intangible products and services, books cannot be sold solely using the Internet. Books can be ordered on the Internet, paid for, and after sales service can be received, but for now they cannot be distributed using the Internet. So intangibility is not merely the shift from manufacturing towards a service-based economy. There are new products that have no physical manifestation or weight, and they are characterized by infinite expandability. Intangible objects cannot be transferred, but merely replicated: the originating agent in a transaction cannot physically and credibly relinquish ownership of the object. Product categories with inefficient transaction processes and sophisticated customers, including automobiles, PCs, electronics, and consumable products, will move quickly to the electronic marketplace and also have opportunities to supplement physical exporting using electronic channels. For example, in 1999 in the U.S. only 2.7 percent of new cars were sold on the Internet, but as many as 40 percent of buyers involved the Internet during the purchase process, to compare prices or to look at the latest models (*Economist*, 2000).

Internet export opportunities depend on the degree of intangibility. As mentioned earlier, a low degree of intangibility results in fewer Internet export opportunities (Figure 2). There is empirical evidence that exporting through the Internet (especially for products with a high degree of intangibility) has a significant influence in reducing the physical distance, transport, documentation and payment, resource constraints, import controls, and foreign market risk (Bennett, 1997). In other words, Internet export opportunities lie in each of these factors and depend on the degree of intangibility. It is very important to emphasize that firms with low intangibility of products/services can still have successful international operations replacing the other transferable functions such as sales, communication, after sales service and customer support.

Marketing communication

Maintaining efficient communications with foreign customers (current and prospective), suppliers, agents, and distributors is critically important to successful entry into international markets (Axelsson & Easton, 1991; Blankenburg, 1992; Christopher et al., 1991; Cowles, 1996; Grönroos, 1996; Gummerson, 1996; Mattson, 1996; Johanson & Vahle, 1992). New information technologies provide a number of tools for improving and/or supporting communication with the different players in international operations including e-mail, Internet Relay Chat, video conferencing, news groups, etc. (Hamill, 1997). Internet use for sales is increasing, but the most common use of this new information media generally is still to communicate with customers, suppliers, and intermediaries. Applying Internet commerce, firms have an opportunity to cut costs by publishing company and product/service information on-line and using electronic channels to disseminate marketing, advertising, and promotional materials. Communication activities create a dynamic content environment, which is the basis for realizing potential strategic outcomes such as export performance and brand recognition. The purpose of the communication is to attract and inform potential buyers and position the company in the global market (Simeon, 1999).

It is very difficult to attract buyers in domestic markets, and in the global market it is even harder. However, using powerful search engines, portal Web sites, or infomediaries, attracting customers becomes simplified. If an Australian company, for example, advertises via a banner on the Yahoo or Excite portal Web site, there is a real chance that millions of Internet users around the world will see it. How much effort companies need to put into Internet marketing depends on numerous determinants such as current global brand recognition, product/service attractiveness, marketing budget for export promotion, and so on. In traditional methods of attracting customers, cultural differences are obvious, especially language. But with the Internet, companies like CNN can broadcast news around the world in nine or more languages.

Once people are attracted to a Web site, the next step is to provide relevant information. The most critical Internet capability is the presentation of information about products, services, people, events, or ideas. Companies with a strategic orientation to Internet commerce can achieve both feedback and the dissemination of information. To achieve this a company should have a pure customer-oriented strategy. If customers can find information relevant to them, it is very likely that they will establish a relationship with a manufacturer/exporter.

The final outcome of a proper communication strategy should be the company position in domestic and international markets. Positioning relates to the ways in which the products and services help create a company image or market position. To value add, to have something unique to offer, is a key factor in positioning when companies use Internet commerce. Value adding can result in attracting or informing clients, or in new forms of distribution, communication, and customization or personalization of product offerings. The best example of a very successful positioning strategy is bookseller Amazon.com. Customer perception is that Amazon brings a bookstore to their home computer. They can search through several million titles, and through that search they are able to read opinions from other readers about buying books.

Distribution Channel Selection

The effect of Internet commerce on marketing channels has been quite dramatic. The channel structure dissolved to some extent. Existing intermediaries were driven out of business and new types of intermediaries emerged.

The speed with which an electronic market develops for any product will depend on the inefficiencies in current transactions and the level of sophistication of buyers. Transaction inefficiencies can arise from poor information flow, complex or multitiered distribution channels, and fragmented supplier and customer bases, among other factors (Weiber & Kollmann, 1998; Palmer & Griffith, 1998). Customer sophistication is measured by their ability to define clear product specifications, their understanding of the difference between vendors, and how comfortable they are about buying products without actually seeing them.

Using Internet commerce, exporters can shorten or eliminate supply chains and respond rapidly to customer needs (Klein & Quelch, 1997; Sarkar, Butler, & Steinfield, 1996). There are many established examples where products are shipped directly from the manufacturer to the end consumer, bypassing the traditional staging posts of the wholesaler's/exporter's warehouse, foreign representative or distributor, retailer's warehouse, and retail outlet. The extreme example arises in the case of products and services that can be delivered electronically, when the supply chain can be eliminated entirely. This has massive implications for financial services, the airline industry, the entertainment industry (film, video, music, magazines, newspapers, etc.), information industry (including all forms of publishing), and for companies concerned with the development and distribution of computer software. The corresponding customer benefit is the ability to rapidly obtain the precise product that is required, without being limited to those currently in stock at local suppliers.

With the emergence of Internet commerce, two opposing views on market mediation have emerged: the issue of disintermediation versus reintermediation.

The Internet gives consumers increased access to a huge selection of products and services, but at the same time causes a restructuring and redistribution of profits among the stakeholders in the marketing channel. It makes a shift from traditional marketing channels to electronic markets that lower coordination costs, with the possibility of eliminating foreign retailers, representatives, and wholesalers entirely as customers deal directly with overseas manufacturers or service providers. This reduction or elimination of intermediaries is referred to as the disintermediation process (Hamill, 1997; Benjamin & Wigland, 1995; Samiee, 1998).

There are obvious benefits in replacing traditional intermediaries in the supply chain of products and services. Direct manufacturer/customer contacts are not always successful since suppliers and consumers do not always perceive value in the same way. Though the need for the traditional middleman in the export distribution channel is diminishing because products can be distributed directly, the collection and dissemination of information is overwhelming (Quelch & Klein, 1996). The argument for the disintermediation process is that Internet commerce will facilitate the removal of many of the processes that now exist between buyers and sellers in the traditional marketplace. The basic assumption is that intermediaries make the transfer of goods and services inefficient. This may be particularly true for small and medium-sized firms (SME) where the Internet provides low-cost access to global markets (Bennett, 1997). Using a disintermediation process (Figure 3) through Internet commerce is seen as a way to make the transaction structure more efficient by automating and centralizing business processes, and eliminating intermediaries.

According to Palvia and Vemuri (1998), the implications of the increased role of electronic markets on intermediaries will most likely be that:

- the number of intermediaries will decrease across all industries and marketing channels;
- the reduction of intermediaries will take place more efficiently in service rather than in manufacturing industries;
- reputable brand name products and services will have a greater advantage in direct sales and will minimize the role of middlemen;
- new forms of intermediaries will emerge to fill the demands in Internet commerce transactions;
- Internet channels and distribution will become an important part of the core functions of a business.

The role of the middleman, however, will not entirely disappear. Middlemen provide some crucial services for international markets, which an individual company can provide only with difficulty or at great cost. Rather, some intermediaries will take on new roles to provide value in different ways from traditional intermediaries. Since acquiring information takes time and is a costly activity, some firms will have a relative advantage in (1) their knowledge of international transactions or techniques of production, (2) international market requirements, or (3) the types of administrative activity necessary to adapt to particular kinds of fluctuations or uncertainties in demand or supply in the international market. With the process of reintermediation, intermediaries will redesign their roles in international markets (Figure 3). The roles can be of two kinds: (1) collaborate in product/service information gathering and sharing with other intermediaries (foreign representative and portal Web site); or (2) become an infomediary or portal intermediary who finds and compares offers made worldwide and sells the best solution to buyers. Software agent technologies will have a very significant impact on the automation of business processes in new intermediary roles.

With the rise of the Internet marketplace new opportunities for intermediaries in marketing channels are:

- to deliver the information the customer needs at a specific moment anywhere in the world;
- to build a lasting relationship with the consumer and to learn more about him or her in the process;
- to invent roles for intermediaries as value-adding players.

Marshall Industries, once a typical middleman distributing electrical components, has put all its business on the Internet and redesigned its old role to become an information based intermediary. Marshall's Web sites provide its 40,000 customers with a range of Internet-based services from technical characteristics to interactive training sessions and new product introductions (*The Economist*, 1999).

The challenge ahead is to constantly enhance the value proposition that is presented to the customer. This includes building a permanent relationship, preparing for continuous change, and managing the relationships of both internal and external additional international intermediaries and partners in a marketing channel.

Price Competitiveness

The Internet will lead to the increasing unification of prices in international markets and to the narrowing of price differentials as consumers become more informed about prices in different countries (Hamill, 1997). When using the Internet in the exporting process, companies may reduce their cost structure significantly. There is some evidence that the Internet markets are much more efficient than traditional markets in respect to a price policy (Smith, Bailey, & Brynjolfsson, 1999). Because the Internet allows low search, entry, and operational costs, it will lead to low relative price levels. Reduction of market entry costs can limit the price premiums by current players on the international markets by increasing actual or potential competition (Milgrom & Roberts, 1982). Furthermore, price dispersion on the Internet should be lower because of the high level of customer price awareness. Also, because of the nature the Internet and the involvement of unknown parties in the process, important sources of price dispersion are brand and trust.

As mentioned in the previous section, technologies enable usage of different applications, such as software agents or intelligence brokers, that can help in the electronic exchange process. Involving them in the relationship process, customers will be able to negotiate the price electronically in an auction module. The auction module is an automatic system where customers place bids for a particular product or service. Before the auction stage, customers are able to set up product category requirements based on their demographics, relevant life-style, and/or psychographic information (Elofson & Robinson, 1998). To avoid potential losses in the auction module, suppliers provide sealed-price bids within a limited time frame. For example, eBay created a new market with efficient person-to-person trading in an auction format on the Internet. Buyers are encouraged to trade on eBay due to the large number of items available. Similarly, sellers are attracted to eBay since they can conduct business where there are the most buyers. eBay provides over four million new auctions and

Figure 3. Rebuilding the Export Value Chain

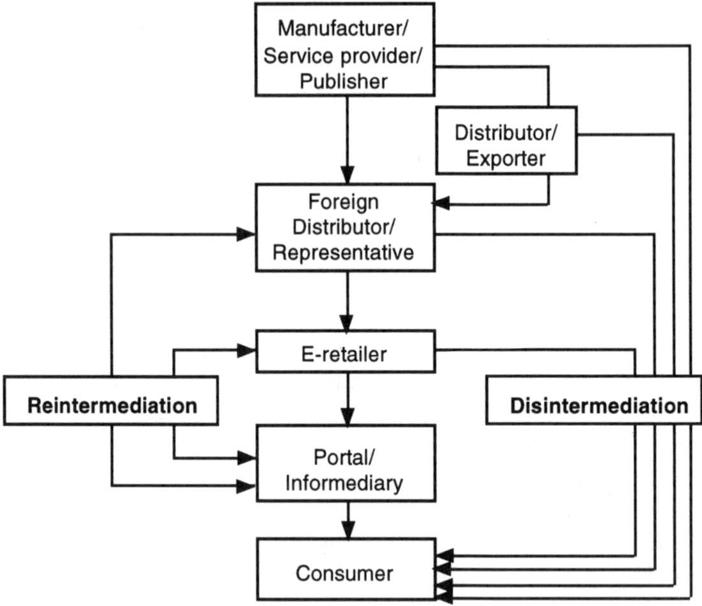

450,000 new items every day from which users may choose (www.ebay.com). In Australia, a similar type of Web service, but on a smaller scale, is provided by sold.com.au.

The benefit of dynamically negotiating a price for a product via an auction is that the seller is relieved from having to determine the value of the good. This decision is pushed into the marketplace (Maes et al., 1999).

A good example of the new price policy is in firms with products/services based on information transfer. Publishers, broadcasters, marketers, bankers, brokers, teachers, and lawyers all make money by transferring information. However, the Internet has caused the price of information to plummet and upstarts are undermining long-established price structures. Prices are tumbling because the Internet creates a market in which the scarcity, quality, and relevance of information fall.

We expect a new equilibrium to emerge, with prices perhaps lower than they once were, but more stable. Also, supply will meet demand on the international markets and the quality or relevance of products/services based on information will be restored.

Internet Commerce Strategy

Internet commerce enables firms to export products and services directly to customers (B2C) or through on-line foreign representatives, wholesalers, and retailers (B2B). For new entrants and firms that traditionally export directly to customers, such as mail order and catalog firms, international Internet trading is a natural progression, with numerous direct-channel advantages.

Internet commerce in international trading not only offers opportunities to suppliers, but also offers several benefits to final customers. Firstly, Internet commerce provides a global presence for companies and global choice for customers. The boundaries of the Internet are not defined by geography or national borders, but rather by the coverage of computer networks (Hamill, 1997). Internet commerce enables the smallest suppliers to achieve a global presence and to conduct business worldwide (Bennett, 1997). A customer can select from all potential global and domestic suppliers of a required product or service, regardless of their geographical location. Secondly, Internet commerce has a big influence on communication with clients enabling interaction, mass customization, and personalized products and services. With Internet interaction, companies are able to gather detailed information on the needs of each individual customer and automatically tailor products and services to those individual needs. This results in customized products comparable to those offered by specialized suppliers but at mass market prices (Elofson & Robinson, 1998).

Thirdly, Internet commerce enables substantial cost savings and substantial price reductions. Having in mind that export companies face a very high level of costs and price competitiveness, these benefits are very important. While the cost of a business transaction that entails human interaction might be measured in dollars, the cost of conducting a similar transaction electronically might be measured in cents. While these various opportunities and benefits are all distinct, they are to some extent interrelated. Fourthly, improvements in competitiveness and quality of service may in part be derived from mass customization, while the shortening of supply chains may contribute to cost savings and price reductions. With a reduction in the number of intermediaries or a redefinition of existing distribution channels, searching for products and services will be dramatically simplified for international buyers. Hence, any business process involving electronic trading with suppliers and final customers offers the potential for substantial cost savings, which can in turn be translated into substantial price reductions.

Fifthly, Internet commerce has improved potential competitiveness and quality of service. Suppliers are able to improve competitiveness by becoming "closer to the customer." Many companies are employing Internet technology to offer improved levels of pre- and post-sales support, with increased levels of product information, guidance on product use, and rapid response to customer inquiries. The corresponding customer benefit is improved quality of service. Answering questions and solving customer problems is a typical on-line activity. Taking problem solving a step further, service providers aggressively target Web customer self-service systems. Also, from their Web sites, they distribute software fixes and updates for customers to download and install on their own computers.

Dell Computer is a good example of international electronic trading (B2C). Dell launched its e-commerce capability in 1996 and in 1999 generated revenues of more than $14 million per day in Internet sales, up from an average of $5 million per day in June of 1998. At present, on-line sales account for 25 percent of Dell's total revenue. The company expects this percentage to increase to 50 percent by the end of 2000. The company has a history of sidestepping traditional retail channels, so it was easy to move to electronic trading without conflicting with any existing sales channels. In order to maximize its on-line business, Dell is currently engaged in a project to develop Web pages for its top 30 suppliers. The idea is that the computer company's top customers will be able to access Dell's manufacturing lines directly to determine when they need to place their next order. Dell currently runs a six-day inventory, dramatically reduced from its previous inventory of 30 days due to the introduction of new technology. Worldwide, Dell now holds the number two position in the computer company rankings (Nua Internet Surveys, 1999).

Internet commerce is still largely non-automated. This fact has a big impact on direct buyers. With the huge amount of information available, buyers are sometimes confused by numerous offers for the same product. If they buy a product or service directly, they are responsible for collecting and interpreting information about that product or service. It is even more complex for international buyers. To simplify the purchasing process, software agent technologies have been introduced. This enables the automation of several very important stages in the purchasing process, such as need identification, product and merchant brokering, negotiation, purchase and delivery, product services, and evaluation (Maes et al., 1999). For example, Amazon.com offers its customers a service called zBubbles, an exciting new shopping tool. With zBubbles, customers learn about products and where to buy them, share their experiences with other shoppers, and buy anything Amazon.com sells instantly. Another example is PersonaLogic (www.personalogic.com) which enables customers to make a short-list of products that meet their needs by helping them define a number of product features. These examples present possible ways of automating the trading processes using software agents to transform the way companies conduct business (Maes et al., 1999). Today, there are several products that turn customer service calls into Web-based forums— putting discussions between customer service representatives and customers, and among customers, on-line. These discussions become knowledge repositories that help the company develop stronger customer relationships and improve and maintain quality control (Hagel & Armstrong, 1997).

STRATEGIC MATRIX FOR ELECTRONIC MARKETING ACTIVITIES

As discussed earlier, there are numerous implications of Internet commerce for export activities and it is almost impossible to present all of them because of the very fast rate of Internet development. To explain the possible implications of Internet commerce, we have developed a framework based on two major components: capitalization on Internet commerce and product/service transferability. Product/service transferability is chosen because the physical nature of the product itself impacts on a firm's ability to transfer its products/ services electronically. Previous research has identified that the most significant hurdle in electronically based exporting is the physical nature of product transfer, whereas other factors in the marketing mix such as price and communication can be overcome using electronic means. Using a three-by-three matrix, nine scenarios are developed for using Internet commerce (Figure 4). Basically, the more easily products/services are transferable, the greater are the opportunities for capitalizing on Internet commerce. However, there are sufficient opportunities for companies with a limited level of product/service transferability to use electronic technologies. The objectives in developing this matrix are to investigate market entry using electronic means, to classify Internet exporting strategies, to serve as a map for firms using the Internet for marketing, and to describe the role of software agents in the Internet-based exporting process.

A description of how companies may define their placement in this framework follows, together with a rationale for each of the suggested scenarios in the cells of the model.

Limited Product and Service Transferability

On-line and off-line models are being combined to sell every product or service, including those once considered ill-suited to on-line sales, such as airline products, laundry products, groceries, perishable goods, cars, apparel, appliances, and other goods.

Firms with limited product and service transferability and low capitalization on Internet commerce sometimes use the Internet to provide a presence. By **maintaining an**

Figure 4. Internet Commerce and Exporting Through the Electronic Trade

Capitalization of Internet Commerce				
	High	Value-chain integration	Direct and electronic export to customers	Mass customization
	Medium	Intra-firm electronic export transactions	Dual export activities	Process-based electronic exporting
	Low	Maintaining an Internet presence	Combining the Internet presence with others traditional means	Failing to capitalize
		Limited	Mixed	Complete
			Product/Service Transferability	

Internet presence, these firms utilize the Internet as an opportunity to replace existing communication materials such as brochures, catalogs, product description, or firm information. These are companies that have not generated a substantial number of orders, and may in fact not be receiving any orders, but still maintain their Internet presence (O'Keefe et al., 1998). They use the Internet as an entry mode only to maintain electronic marketing communications.

As we mentioned earlier, despite the limitation of product or service transferability, there is a possibility that firms can organize their international electronic trading and start to generate substantial exports. The main function of **intra-firm electronic export transactions** is to support the existing channel structure by simplifying order transactions and administrative procedures. Firms might sell their products on-line through retail and wholesale on-line channels. Also, improved efficiency, after-sales activities, and customer support can result in significant cost reductions. In the airline industry, for example, the Boeing Company's decision to put its repair manuals on the Internet has resulted in big payoffs for its customers. United Airlines estimates that electronic access to aircraft repair documentation will trim its repair process (approval and distribution) by almost 80 percent [www.boeing.com].

With **value-chain integration,** exporters do not need to decide on which overseas market to address, as customers throughout the entire Internet world are able to place orders (Bennett, 1997). Value chain integration is defined as "a process of collaboration that optimizes all internal and external activities involved in delivering greater perceived value to the ultimate customer" (*The Economist*, 1999). Exporters have a link with end users and have their own distribution network. The distribution function is reduced to physical distribution only. The main contribution of high capitalization on Internet commerce for a limited level of transferability is developing long-term relationships with clients and establishing a high level of communication, international trade activities, some distribution functions, and after-sales service and customer support. Answering questions and solving customer problems is a typical on-line activity that supports the client relationship. For example, Procter & Gamble's Tide laundry detergent Web site uses automated problem solving to recommend treatments for a range of laundry problems. Also, value-chain integration is occurring in other industries, such as auto retailing (General Motors and Auto-By-Tel) and trade publishing (Cahners and VerticalNet). Unlike transferable products, cars cannot be sold solely using the Internet. Automotive companies have set up a dense network of dealers tightly controlled by their often complex domestic and international sales organizations. The sales process, especially for export, involves substantial information costs and transaction costs in order to establish some market transparency and allow customers to make an informed buying decision. Cars require a physical infrastructure for storage and distribution. However, the Internet is used to make the sales process more efficient, to provide convenience and total care concepts (from comparative vehicle information to financing and insurance), and to enable different types of interaction between dealer and buyer.

Software agents are able to built extensive Internet-based information platforms—often linking the offerings of multiple dealers—to facilitate product comparison, to establish communication links between buyers and manufacturers, and to enable transactions (or at least their preparation) without the necessity to physically move either people or vehicles. It is possible to identify two broad categories of on-line dealerships: service and information brokers (Selz and Klein, 1997). Service brokers are companies such as DealerNet and Auto-By-Tel that offer on-line information, pricing and on-line quoting, additional services like finance, insurance, etc., and a direct link to a car dealer in a country or region of the client's choice. Information brokers are companies such as AutoVantage and Look4Cars that offer on-line information, pricing, and a broker service to bring together potential buyers and sellers. However, they do not offer the possibility of on-line quotes or additional services.

Mixed Product and Service Transferability

Mixed product and service transferability embodies the possibility of becoming transferable if exposed to a product which can be transformed into digital form. This means that products in this category can participate in the export process in both ways, tangible and intangible. Good examples are book publishing and the traveling industry. There are two main groups of companies that belong this category. The first group consists of companies that are already in the exporting business and who try to apply the advantages offered by the Internet to their business. This group of companies, which **combine an Internet presence with other traditional means**, includes industries that are now increasingly experimenting with on-line offerings. The dominant issue for these firms, however, has been channel conflict with their traditional intermediaries. *Encyclopedia Britannica*, for example, decided to market its wares on the Internet using a subscriber-based model. At the same time traditional channels were in operation, but because of the huge success of Britannica On-line, management announced they would no longer produce a printed version. Companies like this are being challenged to find ways to build stronger product offerings so as to deflect the potential for intense pressure on price structures.

Companies that capitalize on electronic access to markets are often start-ups that develop completely new tools for sales, administration, distribution, and after-sales-service for clients. For example, Software.net, an on-line software retailer, allows customers to purchase and download software directly from its Web site. These types of companies establish **dual export activities**, which means that they will create good relationships with their foreign partners by supporting existing business in a much more efficient way or by establishing a new channel that could bypass their partners and create a competing channel. They are better able to utilize Internet commerce to penetrate new markets where channel structures have not been developed. CDNow, as an example, is able to offer worldwide customers recordings that, even after shipping and handling costs, are priced lower than at foreign retail outlets. Companies in this group are generating potential exports through Internet commerce, but still performing exporting functions using traditional modes of distribution.

Companies that are able to fully capitalize on Internet commerce in the international market are those providing both **direct and electronic exports to customers**. They develop electronic information about a company and its business, replace existing physical brochures and product/service descriptions, develop interaction with existing channel members, develop electronic advertising and promotion functions, develop electronic channels, and establish supporting/servicing functions. Along with direct sales, channel intermediaries also exist in the virtual marketplace as on-line retailers and wholesalers. At the service level, selling takes place at a wide range of service-specific Web sites—from sites that sell computers and electronic equipment, to those that sell hard-to-find and out-of-print books. For example, Amazon.com is one of the first service companies using electronic trading and is definitely the best-known bookseller on the Internet. Its well-publicized success as an on-line intermediary is a result of a database of more than two million titles in its virtual inventory and its use of Internet technology to provide services that a traditional book retailer cannot. Through effective use of software agents, Amazon.com is able to provide inventory, delivery, and a personalized and community buying experience that is unequaled in the physical market place. When an Amazon customer buys several books, a software agent is able to update a customer profile based on the book contents and automatically offer available products that have a match with the identified profile. This strategy can be applied to any buyer in the world.

As a result, these companies convert all their activities to a purely electronic business operation and use Internet commerce as the main tool in their export activities. This enables them to achieve a high level of capitalization on Internet commerce and improve their export performance.

Complete Product and Service Transferability

Firms with the ability to completely transfer products and services electronically are in a position to fully utilize the capabilities of Internet commerce. Naturally, not all companies with complete product/service transferability capitalize on Internet commerce using the benefits of the Internet as a tool for accessing the international marketplace. While Internet commerce enables these companies to achieve higher export performance, some companies **fail to capitalize** on the benefits of Internet commerce. In this group companies use the Internet to maintain their presence despite the fact that their products are highly transferable. Similar to companies with limited product transferability, companies in this group also utilize the Internet to replace existing brochures, product descriptions or firm information, or to support their existing distribution channel structure. For businesses that have limited product transferability, these activities may be considered as full utilization, yet for firms with complete transferability these same activities represent a failure to capitalize.

Internet commerce is growing most rapidly in those sectors with intangible products or services, where it offers the greatest benefit to suppliers and consumers. This includes software, journals, music samplers, images, etc. A second group of firms with a high level of transferability of products and services are capitalizing on Internet commerce by reducing their exporting costs. **Process-based electronic exporting** enables the development of electronic channels on the Internet, through the distribution of products, promotion, and communication with customers and clients, and through after-sales support and servicing. Usually these companies belong to the group of 'start-ups' that have developed the necessary strategies and tools for accessing the international marketplace. For this group of companies, we can say that they achieve a medium level of capitalization on Internet commerce. For example, brokerage firms such as E*Trade are rapidly establishing electronic channels over the Internet. Brokers, dealers, and traders sell securities, clearinghouse services, and related financial services on-line. In fact, more than half the services offered by brokerage houses are now delivered electronically, from order entry to electronic quote reporting. On-line trading firms offer significant advantages to investors. For example, on-line investors can view their portfolios any time. Most Internet brokers also provide up-to-the-minute news headlines and stories about companies held, and free quotes on domestic and international stocks, bonds, and mutual funds. Some even send e-mail at the end of the day with closing quotes for an entire investment portfolio. Trading confirmations are also generally sent via e-mail.

The key advantage of using the Internet and Internet commerce as a method to access international markets is the ability to give end users the option to create their own products or services and receive them electronically. This phenomenon is referred to as **mass customization**. Internet commerce enables companies to bypass intermediaries, putting them in direct contact with their end users. Companies that fully utilize the benefits of the Internet can expect significant export revenue generation. For this group of companies with a high level of product transferability and high capitalization on Internet commerce, communication is a vital aspect for the successful marketing of products and services. The utilization of Internet commerce for communication purposes can enable companies to achieve a competitive advantage in the international marketplace. They use communication for product support but also to develop active interaction with end users trying to identify and satisfy their needs. In this case end users have an active approach in creating company offerings incorporating their cultural, social, and other characteristics. To achieve mass customization exporters have to use different types of software agents. Software agents will reduce transaction and search costs for both buyers and sellers with a particular common interest by aggregating both parties through content, community building, and export commerce. Having in mind these opportunities, companies are able to design a product for a particular niche in the global marketplace and distribute it with a very low level of risk. Companies with highly transferable products are further capitalizing on the low cost of the Internet as a mode of communication, distribution, and product/service support. Low costs in finding new clients, administrative procedures, distribution, and after sales service enable companies to improve their export performance.

Finally, software agents have an important role in the electronic exporting process. Firstly, they can fulfill the classic intermediary role, aggregating and matching demand and supply. Secondly, agents add value by performing additional roles such as the role of an infomediary (Hagel and Rayport, 1997)—mediating consumer and supplier information, or as an assembler of formerly discrete products and services—offering a new value proposition.

CONCLUSION

The primary purpose of this chapter is to examine the main determinants of an electronic export marketing strategy and describe how firms can capitalize on Internet commerce for varying types of products and services. A strategic matrix was presented that would allow firms to develop strategies capitalizing on Internet commerce to meet specific exporting needs. This chapter also represents a first attempt to incorporate new technologies into existing theory on export entry strategy, as well as providing a basis to conduct future research to measure the effects of Internet commerce on export performance.

Firms characterized by relatively high levels of product intangibility will most likely be the first to embrace Internet commerce as a strategic mode to propel their globalization efforts. Internet commerce will encourage such global manufacturers to switch their strategic emphasis from a traditional production orientation to product design because these firms will benefit from faster and cheaper sources of information regarding foreign customer preferences. Likewise, Internet commerce will change the face of international service businesses across a broad array of diverse fields including education, management, advertising, sales promotion, engineering, and medical consulting and delivery systems.

Internet commerce for many industries will lead to a process of disintermediation, namely a reduction in the number and types of distribution channel members now linking manufacturers and global consumers. Instead of first promoting a firm's products/services to a domestic market and then eventually seeking global customers, Internet commerce will force many new firms to simultaneously serve both domestic and foreign customers from the first day that they open their business doors. The new electronic technology will create a seamless global consumer market for many high technology/high knowledge industries, thus accelerating the current spread of high technology knowledge worldwide. In this new age, geographical barriers will no longer allow many domestic retailers to remain complacent under the old business assumptions that they are the only "game in town" available to local consumers. Rather, electronic "net-shopping" will enhance various forms of interfirm competition within an industry, thus increasing the quality and diversity of products and services available to increasing numbers of affluent global consumers, often at significant price discounts compared to conventional brick and mortar retail distribution outlets. In this era of global electronic shopping, a firm will define different levels of global standards for their products and services depending upon that firm's specific cultural and geographical perspectives.

Utilization of Internet commerce will further increase global trade. The Internet in its broadest sense has already had a major impact on large trading corporations. The real question is: will the Internet enable international trade to be dominated by relatively few multinational companies? Although cross-border cooperation is increasing, generally this is involving less direct control (via equity holdings) than in the past, and is more oriented to joint ventures in R&D and market development. This is true of the traditional manufacturing and distribution industries, including IT. It would appear to be less true for industries dealing in products with a high level of intangibility, where it would not seem necessary to be a true multinational in order to dominate the global market. Software agents will dominate more and more in electronic marketing. They will create sustained and loyal relations with customers, and they will grow, organize, and sustain relationships within export operations.

Can the majority of existing businesses adapt their working processes to meet the new demands, or will the real advantage go to vigorous new start-ups willing to deal with the shifting strategic horizons of electronic commerce? There is little doubt that organizations that can innovate successfully using electronic commerce will reap benefits. The most innovative of the multinational companies have already benefited. Equally, there are many small companies that have been able to develop a global presence through higher export performance, without the necessary capital investment once required by traditional entry strategies.

The impact of the Internet on the exporting process will grow rapidly in years to come. To determine this, there are a numerous areas of international business that should be tested empirically. Some of these are new ways of product design, client relationships, role of intermediaries, price structures, and the whole process of doing business internationally that occurs as a result of the implementation of electronic technologies.

REFERENCES

Axelsson, B., and Easton, G. (Eds.) (1991). *Industrial Networks: A New View of Reality.* Rouletge, London.

Benjamin, R., and Wigand, R. (1995). Electronic market and virtual value chains on the information superhighway. *Sloan Management Review,* Winter 36(2), 67-72.

Bennett, R. (1997). "Export marketing and the Internet; Experiences of Web site use and perceptions of export barriers among UK businesses." *International Marketing Review,* 14(5), 324-344.

Blankenburg, D. (1992). " The foreign market entry process: A network perspective." In Moller and Wilson (Eds.), *Business Marketing: Relationships and Networks.* PWS Kent, Belmont, CA.

Cavusgil, S. T. and Zou, Sh. (1994). Marketing strategy–Performance relationship: An investigation of the empirical link in export market ventures. *Journal of Marketing,* 58. (January), 1-21.

Christopher, M., Payne, A., and Ballantyne, D. (1991). *Relationship marketing: Bringing Quality Customer Service and Marketing Together.* Butterworth, London.

Cowles D.L. (1996). "To trust or not to trust." *MCB Electronic Conference on Relationship Marketing,* http://www.mcb.co.uk/confhome.htm.

Czinkota, M.R., and Johnston, W.J. (1983). "Exporting: Does sales volume make a difference?" *Journal of International Business Studies,* 14(1), 147-53.

Dicht, E., Koeglmayr, H., and Mueller, S. (1990). "International orientation as a precondition for export success." *Journal of International Business Studies,* 21(1), 23-40.

EITO (European IT and Telecommunication Organization). (1997), 219-221.

Elofson G., and Robinson, W. N. (1998). "Creating a custom mass-production channel on the Internet." *Communication of the ACM,* 41(3), 56-62.

Gregory, G., and Karavdic, M. (1998). "New technologies and foreign market entry: Assessing electronic exchange entry modes (EEEM) and the impact on the internationalization process." *Academy of International Business Annual Meeting in Vienna.*

Grönroos, C. (1996). "From marketing mix to relationship marketing: Towards a paradigm shift in marketing." *MCB Electronic Conference on Relationship Marketing,* http://www.mcb.co.uk/confhome.htm.

Gummerson, E. 1996, "Why relationship marketing is a paradigm shift: Some conclusions from the 30Rs approach," MCB Electronic Conference on Relationship Marketing, http://www.mcb.co.uk/confhome.htm.

Hamill, J. (1997). "The Internet and international marketing," *International marketing review,* 14(5), 300-323.

Hamill, J., and Gregory, K. (1997). "Internet marketing in the internationalization of UK SMEs." *Journal of Marketing Management,* in Hamill, J. (Ed.), Special edition of internalization, 13(1-3).

Hagel, J., and Armstrong, A. (1997). *"Net Gain: Expanding Markets Through Virtual Communities."* Harvard Business School Press, Boston, Massachusetts.

Hagel J., and Rayport J.F. (1997). "The new Infomediaries". *McKinsey Quarterly,* 4, pp. 54-70.

Hoffman, D.L., and Novak, T.P. (1996). "Marketing and hypermedia computer-mediated environments: conceptual foundations." *Journal of Marketing,* Vol. 60, July, pp.50-68.

International Data Corp. (IDC) (1999), Project Atlas: On-line survey responses from about 29,000 Internet users in more than 100 countries, http://www.idc.com.

Johanson J., and Vahle, J.E. (1992), "Management and foreign market entry" *Scandinavian International Business Review,* 1(3).

Johanson J., and Vahle, J.E. (1990), "The mechanism of internationalization" *International Marketing Review,* 7(4), 11-24.

Kedia, B.L., and Chokar, J. (1986), "Factor inhibiting export performance of firms: An empirical investigation." *Management International Review,* 26(4), 33-43.

Klein, L.R., and Quelch, J.A. (1997), "Business-to-business market making on the Internet." *International Marketing Review,* 14(5), 345-361.

Knight, Gary, A., and Tamer, S., Cavusgil (1996). The born global firm: A challenge to traditional internationalization theory. *Advance of International Marketing,* Volume 8: 11-26.

Maes, P., Guttman, R.H., and Moukas, A.G. (1999), "Agents that buy and sell." *Communication of the ACM,* 42(3), 81-91.

Mattson, J. (1996), "Beyond service quality in search of relationship values." *MCB Electronic Conference on Relationship Marketing,* http://www.mcb.co.uk/confhome.htm.

Milgrom, P., and Roberts, J. (1982), "Limit pricing and entry under incomplete information, Econometrica." Volume 50, pp. 443-460.

O'Keefe, M.R., O'Connor, G., and Kung, H-J. (1998), "Early adopters of the Web as a retail medium: Small company winners and losers." *European Journal of Marketing,* 32(7,8), 629-643.

Palmer, J.W., and Griffith, D.A. (1998), "An emerging model of web site design for marketing." *Communication of the ACM,* 41(3), 45-51.

Palvia S.C., and Vemuri V.K. (1998) "The impact of electronic commerce on traditional marketing channels". *Proceedings of the 1998 AIS Conference,* Baltimore, pp. 447-449.

Quelch, J.A., and Klein, L.R. (1996), "The Internet and international marketing." *Sloan Management Review,* Spring, pp. 60-75.

Rabino, S. (1980), "An examination of barriers to exporting encountered by small manufacturing companies." *Management International Review,* 20(1), 67-73.

Samiee, S. (1998), "Exporting and the Internet: A conceptual perspective." *International Marketing Review,* 15(5), 413-426.

Samiee, S. and Walters, P.G.P. (1991), "Segmenting corporate export activities: Sporadic versus regular exporters" Journal of the Academy of Marketing Science, 9(2), 93-104.

Sarkar, M.B., Butler, B., and Steinfield, C. (1996), "Intermediaries and cybermediaries: A continuing role for mediating players in the electronic marketplace." *http:www.usc.edu/dept/annenberg/vol11/issue3/sarkar.html.*

Selz, D., and Klein, S.(1997), "Emerging electronic intermediaries—The Case of the automotive industry". *Proceedings of 10th Bled EC Conference,* Bled, Slovenia, pp. 316-336.

Simeon, R. (1999), "Evaluating domestic and international web site strategies." *Internet Research: Electronic Networking Applications and Policy,* Vol. 9, No. 4., pp. 297-308.

Smith, D.M., Bailey, J., and Brynjolfsson (1999), "Understanding digital markets: Review and assessment." *MIT Sloan School, Working paper,* http://www.e-commerce.mit.edu/papers/ude/ude99.html

The Economist (1996), "Taming the Beast; Living with the Car". June 22, survey section.

The Economist (1999), "A survey of business and the Internet: The net imperative." June 26.

The Economist (2000). A survey of e-commerce: Shopping around the web. February 26.

Weiber, R., and Kollmann, T. (1998), "Competitive advantages in virtual markets—perspectives of information-based marketing in cyberspace." *European Journal of Marketing,* 32(7,8), 603-615.

Chapter III

Consumer Trust and Confidence in Internet Commerce

Shahul Hameed
Kolej Tafe Seremban, Malaysia

INTRODUCTION

The Internet network is rapidly becoming more and more popular among companies as an avenue to do business. It has made it easy for them to advertise, market their products and services, and communicate with their customers. Advertising and marketing on the Internet offers the promise of huge profits. Sellers, though, are not the only ones to reap benefits from the Internet. Purchasing products over the Net has also become extremely beneficial. It is faster than the traditional process of mail ordering, and various on-line support forums provide advice that is not found in manuals, catalogs, or brochures.

Over the last few years, retail and computer experts have called the Internet the hottest marketing trend and the new consumer market. There are a number of benefits which Internet commerce could potentially deliver to consumers—convenience, wide choice of products, better product information, new types of products and services, and even lower prices. Nevertheless, the actual volume of consumer buying on the Internet is still small, a tiny fraction of worldwide consumer purchases. At the heart of this phenomenon of Internet commerce are the most essential concerns of the consumer—trust, confidence, and protection.

Trust, itself, represents an evaluation of information, an analysis that requires decisions about the value of specific information in terms of several factors. Methodologies are being constructed to evaluate information more systematically, to generate decisions about increasingly complex and sophisticated relationships. In turn these methodologies about information and trust will strongly influence the growth of the Internet as a medium for commerce.

In this new business environment, consumers find themselves increasingly in the driver's seat, holding a tremendous amount of purchasing power over providers and sellers. They are empowered because they now have access to a worldwide assortment of suppliers—the Web gives them the power to buy from anyone, anywhere, anytime. The consumers, therefore, want to have control over the collection and use of their personal data and to have appropriate redress mechanisms available in the event of a problem.

The explosive growth of the Internet has promised a new shift of power to consumers. This chapter takes a look at the changing environment of the Internet and its opportunities for consumers, and examines the issues that Internet commerce throws into sharp focus—trust, confidence, and protection of consumers.

The Consumer Is the Major Player

The Internet has offered a breakthrough in marketing efficiency. Where traditional marketing often treats customers as an undifferentiated mass, the Internet allows the seller to discover and exploit the buyers' individual interests. Traditional marketing relies on disparate media for advertising, research, sales, promotional activities, coupon distribution, and customer support. The Internet, by contrast, permits the sellers to put these separate channels of customer communication into a single, focused, coherent response mechanism. Sellers or merchants can create awareness, educate, generate trials, reward loyalty, provide customer support, and generally simplify the customer's life. As Godin (1999) says, the Internet is surely "the greatest direct marketing medium of all time." Indeed, the Internet gives customers an unprecedented degree of control over the entire marketing process.

As consumers become proficient at using the Internet, they'll take the lead in satisfying their own needs. This is particularly true of the devoted customers of particular companies, but mainstream consumers will eventually jump in, too. (Hill and Rifkin, 1999). The Internet gives consumers the ability to access a great deal of information about the benefits and prices of various products and services. For instance, in the publishing business, when a particular topic interests them, consumers will use the powerful search engines available to contact whoever has the content they need—whether it's a bookseller, a book publisher, a magazine, or even an author. Not only will customers grant these providers permission to send additional information; they'll actively solicit information. They will engage in dialogue very much as equals with marketers—and they will be eager to buy when they have found the right match.

Thus, in this global, hyper-competitive environment, those who can survive are the ones who understand the shift away from today's pushing of products and services, to a more pull-oriented model. Because consumers are faced with an ever-increasing choice of products and services to buy from an ever-increasing choice of products and services to buy from an ever-increasing number of vendors, their expectations shift from selecting what they want to buy to defining it. The economy will, thus, become increasingly demand-driven with the customer dictating the rules of trade.

Internet commerce has been revolutionary for business as it potentially shifts greater power from the business to the consumer. Nevertheless, many problems impede its growth. Central to these problems are consumer's trust and confidence. Some of the greatest areas of concern are security and privacy of personal information, the safety of international trade, and the lack of a uniform payment system.

Though there are many obvious advantages for consumers and organizations to do business on-line, consumers have learned to be wary of Internet commerce. "Many businesses are reporting that the level of sales over the Internet has been disappointing" (Survey Net).

Currently, marketers can only segment their audiences, conduct onetime targeted campaigns, or make crude attempts at personalization, where consumers open a piece of mail that addresses them by name in the cover letter. A few companies such as Amazon.com have begun to grasp the importance of learning about and catering to their customers. Amazon.com "remembers" its customers' reading preferences and alerts each with an individualized e-mail when a new book by a favorite author is about to ship. Some companies with vast amounts of consumer spending data have not had such experiences. For instance, American Express announced that it was forming partnership with KnowledgeBase Marketing, a database marketer that manages customer data on 175 million Americans, and launched an avalanche of negative press and customer outcry. Two months later, American Express quietly ended plans to work with KnowledgeBase and issued a statement assuring customers that it had no intention of sharing its American Express card member data.

Marketers can, therefore, consider the effectiveness of a two-way active dialogue that builds understanding and trust.

Two-Way Trust-Based Relationships

Marketers are learning that the best way to reassure customers is to establish trust-based relationships with them. There are three critical components to building an effective, trust-based relationship:

- *Voluntary participation*: On-line consumers are free to go wherever they want—and leave whenever they choose. To attract and retain on-line customers, marketers must empower and delight rather than pressure and persuade—which is a dynamic shift in marketing. Consumers must feel as though their interaction with the marketer is within their own control. In absence of that control, consumers will exit the relationship.
- *Fair exchange of value*: In the new medium, marketers need to realize that every contact they have with their customers is not necessarily calculated to prompt a sale. Rather, cultivating a relationship with customers means that if marketers ask consumers for something—a piece of personal information—they need to be prepared to offer something of value in return. This practice emphasizes the culture of trust, a critical element too often absent in today's on-line marketplace and which will be dealt with later in the chapter.
- *Privacy*: Because consumers place trust in the marketer when they impart personal information, it is incumbent that the marketer treat that information with respect and demonstrate a commitment to privacy. Privacy is the bedrock of trust, and if consumers feel vulnerable to invasion of that privacy, they will not only be unwilling to form a relationship, but may defame that marketer to other potential customers.

Key Issues Affecting Users' Trust and Confidence

The concept of consumer confidence and trust is clearly multifaceted. It can be addressed from a number of different, sometimes overlapping perspectives encompassing a potentially enormous array of concerns. The issues range from privacy and fraud to taxation and protection of children on the Internet.

Fraud, Law Enforcement, and Security on the Internet

Though the Internet provides a wealth of opportunities and resources for consumers and businesses like any communications medium, it is inherently neutral, and can also be accessed by criminals. Because criminal acts can be performed with unusual speed on-line, and without any face-to-face or even telephone contact, it may seem that Internet criminality is unique. Instead, most acts of fraud and other crimes are Internet versions of crimes with long histories in the world of bricks and mortar. Examples are credit card fraud, theft of proprietary data, get-rich-quick schemes, libel, unlawful solicitation, conspiracy, and more.

A main issue that concerns today's on-line consumers is the ease of cross-border transactions. A cross-border transaction takes place when a consumer purchases a product from a different country. The numerous laws dealing with international trade that are enforced in conventional commerce simply cannot be effectively enforced in the Internet marketplace. Sales tax laws are among those that will be extremely difficult to maintain over the World Wide Web. The international commerce laws that will heavily affect consumers are those that deal with the prevention of fraudulent business operations. Fraud on the Internet is an increasingly difficult problem for enforcement agencies because it is so easy to start a business.

The cost of opening a business on the Internet is extremely low compared even to mail order types of fraudulent businesses. Confidence artists and thieves welcome the new market that the World Wide Web has created. They prey upon the weakly protected and uninformed consumers who dare to do business on the Internet. Such con men can move easily from one Web address to another and change the properties of their deceitful shadow companies. For example, they frequently give information about a product that does not exist. When a consumer orders one of the nonexistent products, the con man promises delivery and accepts payment. When the product does not arrive as promised, the consumer often attempts to return to the home page from which he or she has made the transaction only to find that the home page is no longer there. The problem of fraud is much more prevalent in Internet commerce because the laws that prevent consumer deception are not being enforced. Policymakers, therefore, must remember that the problem is not the Internet as a medium, but rather the criminals who have imported an old crime to a new venue.

Internet and its Influence on Children

Some of the content and activities on the Internet are appropriate for adults but unsuitable for children. It would be worth the challenge to identify and use strategies directing children's access whilst at the same time preserving for society at large, the functionality and freedom of the Internet medium.

The Internet, in the future, will be the means by which today's youth carry out job assignments, find others who share their interests, publish their thoughts and creative works to the world, and experience other cultures and viewpoints in ways never before possible. Children are tomorrow's electronic consumers and merchants, parents and educators. Imbuing them with a fear or dislike of the Internet as a medium would handicap them economically and culturally. Developing safeguards, nevertheless, is important against some of the excesses of those that abuse the Internet. Finding ways to empower parents allowing them to customize their children's experiences according to their own individual values and priorities.

Privacy

There is little doubt that the ability to control the collection and flow of their personal data is a key concern of Internet users and prospective users. The public debate over privacy must not be one-sided. The differences between aggregate data and personally identifiable information must be recognized. It must accommodate differences in privacy expectations among individuals. It must take into account that the more information available to Web site operators, search engines, and marketers, the more they can help tailor the user's on-line experiences in ways the user finds worthwhile.

A balance, then, in the collection and use of data would be desirable. As elsewhere, an absolute approach is neither desirable nor workable. Industry has recognized this, and has undertaken several initiatives aimed at inducing Internet sites to post privacy policies and to disclose the types of information gathered, if any, and the uses to which such information may be put.

According to the Tenth Edition of *Merriam Webster's Collegiate Dictionary*, privacy and security mean:

the quality or state of being apart from company or observation; freedom from unauthorized intrusion.

Security is the quality or state of being secure... measures taken to guard against espionage or sabotage, crime, attack, or escape.

The Internet has not changed the kind of commercial collection and use of consumer data that has been taking place for years, but it is making possible significant changes to the scope, scale, and effectiveness of these data practices. The Internet is also changing the public perception of what data-driven businesses are doing. This is not surprising. As consumers have begun to appreciate the Internet's power to deliver to them information about people, products, and events around the world, they increasingly wonder what information about them is being collected and used by others.

Collection of data by on-line businesses is comparable in kind to the off-line practices. Some collection is explicit, such as when a consumer purchases a product on-line that must be shipped to him, he must supply his shipping address. Some companies require registration—including name and address—before allowing free or sample software to be downloaded, though there are no mechanisms in place to prevent the consumer from submitting an alias and fake address. Some companies ask users to register just so that they know who is visiting. Companies can track visitors who come to their Web site, and they can discern where they came from. This capability is built into most Internet browsing software. For example, when a consumer visits a Web site, that site can, in the background, send a "**cookie**" to the consumer's computer. A cookie allows the Web site to track what the consumer does while visiting, and it can allow the Web site to know when that consumer revisits the site.

Cookies are not designed to identify someone by name—in other words, the cookie tells a Web site that user S3528766 is back. However, if the consumer registers at the site, then the cookie allows the site to recognize the consumer by name—which can be convenient for the consumer, obviating the need, for example, to sign in each time and enter a Web site password. Many sites that charge for access, as well as those that simply require registration, make use of this functionality.

Another consumer privacy concern is not just about the use of personal data. It is also about invasion of consumers' peace and quiet. The issue is Internet junk mail, which is a major problem on two counts. First, it clogs the "mail server" facilities of companies providing e-mail service to consumers, thereby slowing consumers' access to the e-mail specifically addressed to them and that they want to receive. Second, the fear of ending up on mailing lists, resulting in new waves of unwanted electronic junk mail, discourages people from registering at Web sites, encourages those who do register to submit false information, and impinges on people's desire to participate in political discourse taking place in on-line communities. So-called "filtering" software can reduce the annoyance factor by helping consumers separate out the unwanted e-mail and send it directly to the trash bin. However, filtering is not entirely effective, especially as marketers have started to disguise their junk e-mail in order to slip through along with the legitimate e-mail; also, filtering does not solve the problem of clogged mail servers.

Some consumer groups have been promoting federal legislation that would ban junk e-mail, just as so-called "junk faxes" were banned by federal law in 1991. However, any law which limits speech—and a law banning junk e-mail would necessarily fall within that category—must embody the least intrusive means of achieving a legitimate goal of government. Otherwise, it will be struck down by the courts for violating the constitutional guarantee of free speech provided by the First Amendment. In the case of junk faxes, no means other than a ban was seen as providing consumers a chance to prevent substantial cost shifting from the seller to the buyer. On the other hand, requiring that junk e-mail be labeled as such could be reasonably effective in protecting consumers' interests while meeting the substantial First Amendment concerns.

Beyond cookies, tracking, database proliferation, and junk e-mail, another major privacy issue is security—the possibility that on-line communications will be overheard. Whether a consumer is sending e-mail to a friend, financial records to an accountant, or a credit card number to an on-line auction, people are concerned that someone might intercept the communication and use it to invade the sender's privacy or commit fraud.

While the consumers' level of concern about security of credit card information is understandable in light of both news stories and myths about the exploits of computer hackers, technology actually makes it less likely that credit card information will end up in the wrong hands when it is used on-line than when it is used in a local store. First, most on-line transactions involving a credit card are automatically encrypted, unless a consumer has an older Internet browser that lacks that capability, in which case merchants generally suggest that the consumer fax or call-in the credit card number. Second, in light of the profit potential of Internet commerce for merchants and credit card issuers, as well as for companies that design, build, and sell the software, hardware, and services that make Internet commerce possible, all parties are continually looking for ways to improve security. Third, while credit card information is processed automatically during a typical Internet commerce transaction—that is, with no human intervention—such is not the case at a store or restaurant. Also, in the virtual world, there are no carbon-copy receipts to be fished out of a trash can. Finally, under federal law, credit card companies may hold a consumer responsible for no more than $50 if her credit card is used fraudulently, and in instances in which the card holder has not been negligent, the bank that issued the card often waives any such charge. This long-standing consumer protection law applies equally to the new world of Internet commerce.

Many individuals discuss privacy and security as if they are the same. Actually, they are different and distinct, sometimes at odds with each another. When individuals conduct private transactions, there is an assumption that personal information is not being divulged to others. When a transaction is secure, it is thought to be protected from assault or corruption. In this context, privacy is the ability of an individual to keep his identity confidential in the course of a transaction. An anonymous transaction, using cash as the means of payment, maintains privacy; the transaction, however, is not secure. Credit cards, on the other hand, offer security, but not privacy.

Internet Taxation

The tax status of electronic transactions has become an increasingly pressing issue as the potential scale of the consumer Internet has become clear. A wise solution would be a uniform, fair, certain, and administratively simple one. It is clear that a disastrous scenario would be the development of different state-by-state Internet taxation schemes, creating an unpredictable consumer market on the Internet. If businesses are burdened with unpredictable tax regimes governing the Internet, the medium's potential economic benefits to consumers could be seriously thwarted. For their part, some state and local officials claim loss of sales tax revenues will devastate their budgets. In fact, many estimates of potential tax revenue lost due to electronic commerce are seriously overstated. It is also important to balance any potential loss in sales tax revenue with the significantly increased benefits to the economy brought about by Internet commerce.

With the rapid transformation of commerce on the Internet, it must be understood that the issues surrounding it should not and, in fact, cannot be viewed as discrete and insular. There is an inherent interconnectedness of all the issues and the certainty in the knowledge that the most important factor in the success of the Internet is the degree of confidence that consumers have in this new medium.

What Is Trust?

Trust, according to Giddens (1990), is defined as "confidence in the reliability of a person or a system, regarding a given set of outcomes or events, where that confidence expresses faith in the probity or love of another, or in the correctness of abstract principles (technical knowledge)." The primary condition that creates a need for trust is lack of full information, generally associated with a person who is separated in time and space or a system whose workings are not fully known. A user, when lacking complete information about a system, has to develop a trust-related attitude towards it. Even dealing with any commercial organization necessarily requires a trust-related attitude. When transactions with such complex systems are mediated by a technological system such as an electronic commerce platform, the importance of trust is heightened. Therefore, trust has to be dynamically generated and worked on. In interpersonal relationships, one party's actions, particularly self-disclosure or lack thereof, can reinforce, diminish, or destroy the other party's trust.

Trust is central to any commercial transaction. Typically, it is generated through relationships between transacting parties, familiarity with procedures, or redress mechanisms. Developing new kinds of commercial activities in a computer-mediated environment largely hinges on assuring consumers and businesses that their use of network services is secure and reliable, that their transactions are safe, and that they will be able to verify important information about transactions and transacting parties, such as origin, receipt and integrity of information, and identification of parties dealt with.

Consumers are seriously concerned about a number of dimensions of trust:

- Trust in the **security of value** passed during the transaction with 'vendors' who are 'virtual' in a disconcertingly ineffable way.

The forms of value that are involved include:

- Money paid and received,
- goods and services offered and acquired, and
- assurances that a refund is available for unsatisfactory goods and services.
- Trust in the **security of personal data** while it is in transit during the electronic transaction.
- Trust in the **privacy of personal data** arising from electronic transactions.
- Trust in the **subsequent behavior of the other party to the electronic transaction**. In particular, there is a fear among consumers, based on prior experiences with marketers in other contexts, that they are likely to make unwarranted assumptions about the nature of any relationship that may arise from the transaction.

Trust is also defined as "the assured reliance on the character, ability, strength, or truth of someone or something, or one in which confidence is placed." When conducting a transaction in the 'real' world, as opposed to the virtual world, there is a level of trust at work gained through experience. Any system using currency has deep-seated trust. When someone purchases any merchandise and pays for it by cash, the merchant trusts that these bills are legal tender, not counterfeit, and will be accepted when he tenders them for deposit or purchase. For some, the currency of the United States is considered the safest in the world because a majority trusts that the United States government will always fully back it.

This level of trust has not yet reached Internet commerce. For Internet commerce to flourish and reach its full potential, the same level of trust as in the real world must be developed, so that the consumers, merchants, and banks will have faith in the new system.

Merchants, consumers, and financial institutions all need to be confident of the identity with which they conduct business. Only when all of the above parties are truly able to trust who they are dealing with on-line will this business model really take off. These concerns are in the areas of:

- *Identification*: the method that provides the means to recognize a user to a computer system.
- *Authentication*: the act of positive identification, coupled with a level of certainty before granting specific rights or privileges to the individual or station that has been positively identified.
- *Authorization*: the act of granting a user or program the requested access.

Trust encompasses issues wider than security and consumer protection. It would be useful to distinguish between *hard trust* and *soft trust.* Issues of hard trust involve authenticity, encryption, and security in transactions. Issues of soft trust deal more with control, comfort, and caring, which involve human psychology, brand loyalty, and user-friendliness. It is important to see that the problem of engendering trust is not simply technical in nature, as trust also involves making psychological, sociological, and institutional adjustments.

The key aspect of control is the consumer wanting to be in control of the information about himself or herself and the transaction. The consumer wants to be able to determine the level of privacy and be able to authenticate the provider of goods and services and the person receiving the payment.

Comfort is directly linked to previous use, familiarity, and reputation; security measures, warranting structures that vouch for quality and reliability; minimizing risk and capped liability. In many spheres such as health, consumers want to be also assured they are cared for, with the provider showing benevolence, intimacy, and a desire to communicate.

Such soft trust factors derive strongly from diverse cultural contexts, such as that of the Asia Pacific region, and if consumers in such regions are to trust in Internet commerce, it must go with a cultural understanding of the way they perceive money and commerce, and how these fit with their ideas of marriage and family.

The level of trust and confidence, the acceptance, and the subsequent use of the Internet for a wide variety of purposes, including business commerce, depends on the attitude that the user has toward computers and technology. The user could be a consumer, merchant, or expert. What clearly emerges is that people have varying comfort levels. Some are ready to fully embrace technological change and the Internet with its seemingly unlimited potential, while others are very reluctant to move quickly into the realm of cyberspace. There are also other individuals whose attitudes toward the Internet fall somewhere in between.

A lot of effort is being invested in developing trust through 'authentication.' A first approach is '**value authentication.**' This is similar to the biting of a coin to see if it feels like its really 'coin of the realm,' and holding up a bank note to the light to see if it looks like the real thing. On the Internet, forgery of digital money is feasible, but not if the people minting it use the electronic equivalents of complex visual designs, watermarks, and hidden metallic strips.

A second approach is called '**eligibility authentication,**' which calls for checking that the person being dealt with actually has a particular capability that they claim to have. For example, does the person have a license to sell those kinds of goods; are they a member of the relevant industry or professional association; do they have their company's authority to sign a contract of this nature; and do they qualify for a special tariff or price-list (e.g., because they're a tradesman who buys at wholesale price) or a discount (e.g., because they are an old-age or invalid pensioner)? There is a need for electronic equivalents of membership cards, concession cards, letterheads, and calls back to the company's premises, in order to establish confidence.

A further approach is '**person authentication,**' which involves ensuring that the other person is who they claim themselves to be. There are some kinds of transactions that only the person in question should be permitted to perform (such as access to personal data). Other interactions necessarily involve an ongoing relationship between the parties (such as health care and the advancing of credit).

These authentication techniques are based on particular mathematical techniques commonly referred to as **cryptography**. The particular application of cryptography that most assists in authentication is the technology called '**digital signatures.**' These are long numbers that are able to demonstrate conclusively that a particular message must have come from a particular person or organization, and, moreover, that the message has arrived without being modified along the way. This achieves a standard of evidence for a court of law that is much higher than has ever been possible with conventional signed documents. Thus, with cryptography, one gets access to control, which means data is controlled and access is granted according to a predetermined policy. Cryptography also creates privacy so that unauthorized people on the Web cannot see the contents of messages being sent. It brings integrity, which means that when the data is received, some mechanism tells the user whether it has been altered or destroyed.

Encryption

From time immemorial, people have used cryptography to scramble messages to maintain their confidentiality. At the origin, the message is scrambled and at the destination it is unscrambled as per a prearranged logic.

To understand encryption, let us look at an example. If you want to send the message: 'Hello world' on the Internet you may encrypt it by replacing each letter by the next letter so 'h' becomes 'i', 'e' becomes 'f', and so on. As per this scheme, the encrypted message is 'Ifmmp Xpsme.' At the receiving end, replacing the letter by the previous letter to obtain the original message decrypts this message.

There are four elements to the encryption system:

- The plain text—the message to be encrypted. In our example, it is 'Hello world'.
- The key—that is the string or digits. In our example, it is "1"
- The ciphertext is the encrypted message. In our example, it is 'Ifmmp Xpsme'.
- Cryptographic algorithm—this is the logic to combine the plain text with the key to generate the 'ciphertext'. It is also used to convert the ciphertext to plain text using the key. In our example, the cryptographic algorithm for encryption is 'replace each letter by the letter that succeeds it by the number represented by the key'. The logic for decryption is reverse of this. As per this scheme if the key was '2', the ciphertext would have been 'Jgnnq Yqtnf'.

Encryption technology is going to play a critical part in protecting confidentiality, authenticity, and security. Trust on-line is going to be created when security issues have developed along these lines. The customers, merchants, and financial institutions must trust that it is safe to conduct business on-line. The industry must reassure all parties by actually developing technologies that essentially substantiate trust.

Security Tools and Technologies

Secure Socket Layer (SSL) and **Secure Electronic Transaction (SET)** are two key protocols that exist to ensure secure on-line transactions today. SSL was designed to provide privacy between two communicating applications. It authenticates the server and can also be applied to the client. It requires a reliable transport protocol for data transmission and reception and is used widely to provide authentication and privacy on the Internet.

SET, which is from Visa and MasterCard and widely endorsed by financial and technology companies, was designed for conducting secure credit card transactions on the Internet. It has an advantage of ensuring that only the card holder and the acquiring bank are able to see the actual credit card when a transaction is paid for using the credit card. The merchant never sees the number, ensuring a high degree of security for the transactions. Future versions of the SET protocol are expected to support other payment types including cash.

Elliptic Curve Cryptography (ECC) is a new cryptography system that uses the algebraic system defined on the points of an elliptic curve to provide public-key algorithms. These algorithms can be used to create digital signatures, provide secure distribution of secret keys, and provide a secure means for the transmission of confidential data.

Smart cards offer another important approach. These contain tiny embedded computer chips with logic and nonvolatile memory. The cards can contain software that monitor network intrusions or tampering and watch out for abnormal network usage in the same way a bank puts a temporary hold on a credit card after a flurry of purchases.

Security in smart cards is typically insured by a combination of digital signature and public-key technology. There are many different algorithms in use for smart cards, but all act to verify the authenticity of cards and to prevent misuse or fraud. Smart cards incorporate write-once memory that cannot be modified once it has been programmed. This allows each card to contain a unique identification number. Limits are typically placed on the number of erroneous attempts, preventing brute force access.

Digital Signatures

Digital signatures enable the encoding and authentication of transactions, purchase orders, and the like. The way that digital signatures work is that the sender of a message 'signs' it using a '**private key**' that only they should have. The key that unlocks the signature is different from the private key, and is widely available (and hence called the sender's '**public key**'). Anyone who receives a message can check that it decodes using the public key, and feel confident that only the person who possesses that private key could possibly have sent the message.

For digital signatures to assist in establishing trust in virtual commerce, a public key will have to be reliably associated with a person. That person will need to present evidence of their identity to a 'certification authority' (CA). The CA will then post in a public place (an electronic public place) certification that the particular public key is associated with an identified person.

However, strong encryption raises concerns about concealed criminal activities and the ability of governments to carry out legitimate law enforcement activities, including taxation. Some governments have approached this issue by limiting the strength of encryption products for export and calling for mechanisms to ensure access to private cryptographic keys. Others have taken the position that the cryptography market should not be limited and that access to private cryptographic keys held by third parties would compromise security and erode trust in the system. Since no clear solution is in view, the best course may be to agree to disagree and accept that multiple solutions may have to coexist.

Possible Solutions

Given these obstacles to Internet commerce, companies hoping to broaden their market by utilizing the Internet have begun to create solutions to some of the problems that cause consumer mistrust and dissatisfaction.

Development of Industry Self-Regulatory Mechanisms

The concept of industry self-regulation for Internet business has some attractions – the Internet business community has a strong incentive to provide consumers with an acceptable environment in which to do business in order to promote on-line commerce; industry codes are well adapted to providing detailed, flexible guidance on matters related to a particular area of business, such as Internet commerce; and the borderless nature of the Internet may not pose the same problems for self-regulatory mechanisms as it does for regulation based on national law.

A Code of Conduct

A code of conduct for Internet selling which was widely accepting and adhered to by Internet vendors and recognized by consumers could provide a solution to many of the problems of consumer protection in an on-line marketplace. However, there are a number of obstacles to achieving a code of conduct for Internet selling.

In practice, industry codes tend to operate within national boundaries and be administered by industry associations at a national level; gaining wide adherence to a code dealing with Internet commerce poses problems where Internet selling involves participants in a very broad range of business sectors making internal industry organization difficult; and to be effective, a code would need a strong basis for achieving compliance, especially if it sought to provide a mechanism for resolving disputes between vendors and consumers.

Role of Major Industry Players

Various businesses such as payment system operators and mall operators that have a key role in Internet commerce are well positioned to reduce the risks to consumers who purchase on-line. Business such as these could reduce risks by limiting access to facilities to businesses that they regard as reliable. For example, credit card networks or other payment system operators may only grant merchant status to businesses that can demonstrate their soundness or meet certain standards in their dealings with consumers. A mall operator could take similar responsibility for vetting the businesses using its services, and accepting responsibility for assisting in the resolution of consumer disputes and protecting consumers from unfair trading practices. The basis for adopting this role could be the contractual relationship with client businesses or the potential sanction of refusing them further service.

Adopting this sort of role provides an additional service to consumers who use the relevant payment system or mall, and provides a business benefit by encouraging consumer use.

A number of major credit and charge card networks already have "charge-back" systems for re-crediting consumer payments in the case of fraud, nondelivery, delivery of products not meeting description, and a range of other circumstances. The effect of these arrangements is that consumers who pay for goods using credit and charge cards can generally seek redress through the card issuer in these situations.

Role of Consumer Affairs Agencies

State, territory and federal fair trading bodies may need to consider cooperative arrangements to deal with issues in Internet commerce. One fundamental aim of fair trading agency arrangements should be to identify the appropriate agency to consider a complaint arising from Internet commerce and the referral of the complainant to the appropriate body.

The charge-back system considerably predates Internet commerce, but is well adapted to an on-line environment given the global reach of the major credit card networks. This has prompted a program of work by the OECD Committee on Consumer Policy to explore the potential of charge-back as a means of redress in a global marketplace (OECD, 1996).

The effect of major industry players adopting a role of providing protection for consumers with whom they have an involvement may not be a cohesive system of consumer protection for on-line commerce as a whole. Consumers need to have clear accessible information about the role of major players in vetting their business clients, the facilities they offer for dispute resolution, and the areas in which liability is accepted for consumer losses. It will also be beneficial for consumer protection mechanisms offered by major business to be aligned to the greatest extent possible.

Consumer Education

There are a number of areas where consumer education and information strategies could assist consumers in making decisions about their involvement in on-line commerce.

Consumer education is widely advocated as a means of tackling some problems with on-line commerce, such as exposure to malpractice and weaknesses in consumer protection mechanisms. However, it has acknowledged limitations. There is a great variety of information which may be relevant to the on-line consumer, and the task of making sure that it is not only available to, but is actually accessed by those who might benefit from it is a daunting one. Consumer education may, however, supplement other measures to protect on-line commerce.

Some of the areas that could be the subject of consumer education are:

- How to recognize fraudulent offers and information about particular scams. A consumer alert system of this sort is operating in the USA.
- Advising on specific considerations in purchasing goods and services over the Internet. Issues such as delivery time and cost, costs of importing goods, and the vendor's policies on return of goods and privacy may have special significance in the context of on-line commerce. Consumers need to know what they should be asking vendors to avoid later complications.
- Advising people about consumer protection risks inherent in cross-border transactions.
- Advising people about what they can do if they have difficulties with an Internet vendor. Advice on this subject could include information about both industry-based and government avenues.

Building Trust – A Simple and Successful Case Study from India

Bababazaar.com

Baba Bazaar has been one of the first Indian commercial sites on the Internet offering the convenience to order fresh vegetables and other related food products of various companies, including Nestles and Dabur, over the Net. Currently, Baba Bazaar caters only to select areas in Chandigarh, Delhi, New Delhi, Noida, and parts of Gurgaon. They have plans to extend operations to other major cities for nationwide operations.

Baba Bazaar launched its Web site storefront in early 1998. The initial response was mixed. However, their promotional strategy has facilitated building an extensive customer base. At present, Baba Bazaar has a customer base of more than 2,000. This base is growing steadily. They are adding to their base, 8 to 10 new customers every day.

Baba Bazaar started with the sale of vegetables, as they felt that being a very basic commodity, the market potential was unlimited. From vegetables, they moved on to other food products to become a one-stop shop for foodstuffs. As the volume of business grows, they plan to go in for backward integration and start sourcing the vegetables from the farmers. This will ensure that consumers get better and fresher vegetables and food products.

Baba Bazaar had devised an inexpensive but engaging procedure of securing the transactions and building 'relationship.' To become a preferred Baba Bazaar shopper, the customer has to fill out a simple registration form on-line. The details furnished in this form are verified telephonically by the staff of Baba Bazaar. On verification, the shopper (customer) is issued a shopper access password, which is required to be used at the time of ordering goods on the site. This password is sent to the shopper by courier to ensure security along with the 'User's manual.' This manual introduces Baba Bazaar to the shoppers and guides them through it. This has enabled them to initiate a 'relationship' building process before the shopper places the first order. It has also allowed them 'to build trust' and give the shopper a positive impression of the business-essential ingredients for the development and growth of their 'on-line' business.

The shoppers are required to make payment on delivery and have been given the following options:

- Cash on delivery
- Postdated checks for up to one week from the time of the delivery
- At the time of the next delivery

This procedure has been designed for the following reasons:

- In India customers do not entertain payment before receiving the goods and/or services.
- High processing cost of credit cards transactions, which according to them is about 4-5% of the total transaction cost. This would increase the cost of the goods.
- Low penetration of credit cards.
- Absence of secure payment gateways.

The procedure has enabled them to ensure the prices of goods are competitive, build an extensive database of their shoppers' specific needs and requirements, and provide their shoppers personalized service.

The owners of Baba Bazaar developed the Web storefront in-house because available software was unable to provide a seamless integration of their operations. This has also enabled them to incorporate shoppers' suggestions and update the Web site on an ongoing basis. The Web site is simple, and the product display assists shoppers in making their shopping decisions and is easy to navigate. The order form is simple to complete and an order can be placed with a few clicks of the mouse. What started off as a basic commercial Web site quickly grew to be a consumer centered Web site. This was primarily due to the overwhelming response to the site, and the felt-need to grow by ensuring fulfillment of the customers' expectations. This strategy has also ensured steady growth in business.

CONCLUSION

Internet commerce has been evolutionary in its development and has the potential to be revolutionary in the way it shifts great power from businesses to consumers.

From the customers' perspective, Internet commerce means using the Internet to identify suppliers, select products or services, make purchase commitments, complete final transactions, and obtain services.

At present many problems impede the growth of Internet commerce. The technologies that make the World Wide Web and I-commerce possible have some potentially negative aspects. Privacy issues are a major concern for many since there are means to collect consumer information easily with digital tools. Transaction security is equally important.

The issue of consumers' trust and confidence in Internet commerce is fundamental to its eventual success. If consumers cannot trust that personal information is safe and secure, the Internet will never reach its economic potential. More particularly, the Asian consumer is wary of conducting an on-line transaction for fear of the Internet eroding the Asian culture, values, and business systems.

In order to address increased consumer access and engender greater trust in Internet commerce, it is wise to distinguish between hard and soft trust issues. 'Hard trust' issues involve authentication, encryption, and security in transactions. 'Soft trust' issues involve helping improve user interface with Internet commerce systems.

Whilst hard trust issues need timely resolutions, with government and business working together to ensure the privacy of consumers and the fidelity of transactions, emphasis must be placed on the consumer being at the center of policy and business strategy and recognition made on the interrelationships between the economy, social relations, and cultural values.

Given these obstacles to Internet commerce, businesses hoping to broaden their market by utilizing the Internet have begun to create solutions to some of the problems that cause consumer mistrust and dissatisfaction. These include self-regulation by the industry, a widely accepted code of conduct, and consumer education.

The Internet business community has a very strong incentive to provide a safe and acceptable business environment for consumers. The vendors' primary incentive is the growth in the on-line market that presumably will occur from their improvements to the on-line marketplace. Even though it may cost the suppliers more to make changes to ensure security, they will attempt to do it anyway in order to ease the concerns of potential consumers. One method to promote the creation of a code of conduct for vendors is for the government to mandate such a code, although it will be difficult to enforce government power over an industry that virtually lacks regulation.

Consumer education is perhaps the most plausible option to combat safety problems on the Internet. As these fears of Internet consumers dissipate, as they will in time, more and more consumers will begin to purchase goods and services over the Internet. The progress that has already been made and the continued efforts of the industry and individual vendors alike to erase consumer-trust and confidence issues will, no doubt, induce many more buyers to take advantage of the consumer opportunities provided by Internet commerce.

In order for the Internet to live up to its potential as the global mass market medium of the 21st century, policymakers must recognize this complexity and the unique dynamics at work in the Internet marketplace as they perform their valuable role of public oversight. Industry must respond to consumer expectations with improving products and services, and with business practices that improve the on-line consumer experience.

REFERENCES

Business and the Internet. (1999). *The Economist*, June 26, 3-34.

Dennis, E.E., and Pease, E.C. (1994). Preface. *Media Studies Journal*, 8 (1), xi-xxiii.

Erickson, J. (1999). Middlemen beware: The Net is matching global buyers and sellers. *Asiaweek*, March 19, 46.

Giddens, A. (1990). *The Consequences of Modernity*. Stanford University Press, Stanford, CA.

Godin, S. (1999). *Permission Marketing: Turning Strangers into Friends, and Friends into Customers*. Simon & Schuster.

Hill, Sam, and Rifkin, Glenn. (1999). *Radical Marketing: From Harvard to Harley, Lessons from Ten that Broke the Rules and Made it Big*. Harper Business.

Hoffman, D., Novak, T., and Chatterjee, P. Commercial Scenarios for the Web: Opportunities and Challenges. http://cwis.usc.edu/dept/annenberg/vol1/issue3/hoffman.html.

Hughes, L. (1995). *Internet Security Techniques*, pp.11-12.

Privacy Commissioner. (1996). Information Sheet 3. *The European Data Protection Directive*, December, 1.

Rivest, R. L., Shamir, A., and Adleman, L. M. (1978). A method for obtaining digital signatures and public key cryptosystems. *Communications of the ACM*, 21(2), 120-126.

Survey-Net at http://www.survey.net/.

The Internet Age. (1999). *Business Week*, October 4.

United States Federal Trade Commission (FTC). (1996). *Anticipating the 21st Century: Consumer Protection in the New High-Tech Global Marketplace*. May, p.23.

Waters, N. (1996). Privacy in Cyberspace—Is it an Illusion? Paper delivered to *On-line Services Regulation Forum 23-24,* April, Sydney, p.2.

http://www.anu.edu.au/people/Roger.Clarke/DV/RogersDVBibl.html.

http://www.anu.edu.au/people/Roger.Clarke/DV/.

Chapter IV

Deploying Internet Commerce in Lottery Businesses: An Executive Guideline

Nansi Shi
Singapore Pools (Pte) Ltd., Singapore

David Bennett
Aston University, UK
University of South Australia, Australia

INTRODUCTION

Commerce is essentially the exchange of goods and services in various forms between sellers and buyers, together with associated financial transactions. Electronic Commerce (EC) is the process of conducing commerce through electronic means, including any electronic commercial activity supported by IT (information technology) (Adam and Yesha, 1996; Kambil, 1997; Yen, 1998). In this sense, EC is not totally new. Industries have used various EC platforms such as advertising on TV and ordering by telephone or fax. Internet Commerce (IC), or Web Commerce, is a specific type of EC (Maddox, 1998; Minoli D. and Minoli E., 1997). While some traditional EC platforms such as TV and telephone have been used to build "TV-gambling" and "telephone-betting" systems for conducting lottery business, Internet Lottery Commerce (ILC) has been assessed as the most promising type of EC in the foreseeable future. There are many social and moral issues relating to the conduct of lottery business on-line. However, this chapter does not debate these but deals only with business and technology issues.

The purpose of this chapter is to provide a structured guide to senior executives and strategic planners who are planning on, or interested in, ILC deployment and operation. The guide consists of several stages: (1) an explanation of the industry segment's traits, value chain, and current status; (2) an analysis of the competition and business issues in the Internet era and an evaluation of the strategic resources; (3) a planning framework that addresses major infrastructure issues; and (4) recommendations comprising the construction of an ILC model, suggested principles, and an approach to strategic deployment.

The chapter demonstrates the case for applying the proposed guideline within the lottery business. Faced with a quickly changing technological context, it pays special attention to constructing a conceptual framework that addresses the key components of an ILC model. ILC fulfils the major activities in a lottery commerce value chain—advertising, selling and delivering products, collecting payments for tickets, and paying prizes. Although the guideline has been devised for lottery businesses, it can be applied to many other industry sectors.

BACKGROUND – LOTTERY BUSINESS

To introduce new IT into a company effectively, it is first necessary to understand the company's business in terms of inherent traits, the value chain, IT heritage and current status.

Inherent Traits of the Lottery Business

The lottery business has obtained significant commercial benefits from using EC, mainly due to its inherent traits that have positive and negative influences on deploying and operating ILC applications. These traits are as follows:

Digitized Goods

A *lottery product* is a combination of digits, which entitles people to participate in a particular game within a certain period of time and under certain rules. A typical lottery product consists of a ticket number associated with particular game data such as the drawn number and date, security code, etc. While various forms of ticket numbers represent different products, the associated data are essential for identifying the availability and uniqueness of a lottery product.

While lottery products may be generated using diverse media, they are traditionally printed as paper tickets. Classified by their selling mode, there are two main lottery tickets, namely **static** and **dynamic** tickets. Static lottery tickets are preprinted on paper, so are also called **preprinted tickets**. When consumers want to buy preprinted tickets at an agent, they can only select the numbers from among those on the tickets available for sale. Dynamic lottery tickets, on the other hand, will be printed according to consumers' preferences. That is, when a consumer selects a preferred number the seller can produce a ticket to fit the individual's order. Fundamentally, a dynamic ticket is a customized product. While static or preprinted tickets usually are sold manually, dynamic tickets are generally sold via electronic means. The term **on-line tickets** refer to tickets sold at on-line terminals that are connected to, and controlled by, back-end computer systems.

In short, lottery products are "digitized goods." Examples of digitized goods include software, reports, CD-ROMs, and so on (Treese and Stewart, 1998). Distributing digitized goods is a "bit-moving operation" which transfers data from one place to another (Cash et al., 1992).

Value and Consumption

The difference that distinguishes most digitized goods from lottery products are prospective value and the manner of consumption. After a predefined time a lottery game's numbers are drawn, then a lottery product will be either (1) entirely consumed and worthless, or (2) used as a claim against a prize. In the first case, the customer's investment will have entirely disappeared, otherwise the return on the investment could be huge. The top prize in a lottery can often be several million times the cost of a ticket. For example, in 1998 in the United States, one jackpot reached 195 million U.S. dollars. The total amount used as a single prize can be between 50% and 90% of the total betting amount. Such a huge prize is attractive to lottery players since the investment leverage is possibly much bigger than for other investments in the short term. This suggests that the payment of prizes is a key factor to consumers and is more critical than in many other businesses' post-sale services.

National Assets and Laws

The "manufacture" of lottery products basically involves the generation of combinations of digits, which is much easier than producing other digitized goods such as software or reports. It does not rely on other raw materials, so even a small firm is able to operate a lottery business. Thus it is sometimes called "easy money," so a large proportion of lottery proceeds will often be used for good causes and public benefits such as national projects, education, charities, social welfare, and other public programs, rather than for the profits of private organizations. Lottery operations are able to collect huge amounts of money from millions of individuals who usually place bets involving small amounts of money. The benefit of a national lottery operation is that the government can collect large sums of money from large numbers of people and use part of the collected money for the public good. Thus in most countries the operation of a lottery is a national monopoly, and there are laws and regulations to control lottery operators and banning foreign lottery businesses within their borders. In addition, such laws and regulations give consumers more confidence in playing lotteries or other games.

Being conscious of the social and ethical issues related to gaming, many governments have set up laws to limit its scope. To operate a lottery business, the most important condition is to follow local laws and usually it is necessary to obtain a license from the government. A lottery firm should also be aware of the local culture, ethical basis, or regulations of the country in which it is operating. Although there has been a lot of argument against gaming by those who want to restrict, or even prohibit, the activity, there has been little serious debate of the affects of a lottery—most people regarding it as rather harmless.

Lottery Commerce Value Chain

The trait analysis suggests that the commercial processes of a lottery are information driven and network based. While several models such as the "value chain," "supply chain," and "generalized exchange processes" can be used to model the lottery process, we have adopted the value chain approach in this chapter.

Popularized by Porter (1985), the value chain concept has been widely adopted as an analytical framework to examine value-adding activities (Cash et al., 1992; Yen, 1998). It is useful for conceptualizing the role of information systems (IS) in a firm, especially regarding its interaction with different activities that can be carried out within the firm in bringing a product or service to customers (Andreu et al., 1992; Porter and Millar, 1985). When a customer buys a product, it is merely one step in a complex process, at each step of

Figure 1. Lottery Commerce Value Chain

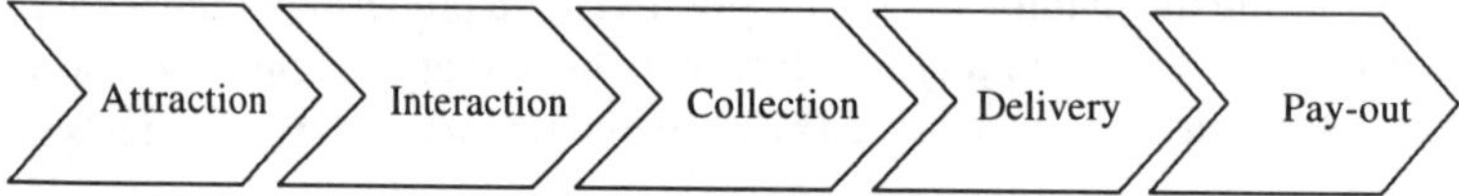

which something of value would be added along the way. Generally, different industry sectors have different models of value chain. Even in businesses that may appear outwardly to be very similar, differences in emphasis can have major effects. Looking at a value chain for a business helps to define areas of focus—what the business is best at, or where the greatest emphasis should be placed.

Figure 1 shows the five primary activities in a lottery commerce value chain.

Attraction of players includes such diverse marketing activities as advertising, promotion, announcing drawn results, and relevant information. **Interaction** with players occurs when they want to know more details or need help to play the lottery. After the business system records the numbers chosen by a consumer, it checks and validates whether the numbers are valid. If they are not, the business system rejects the purchase and informs the consumer. Otherwise, the business will manufacture a product (generate the combination of digits or data). Then the business will **Collect** the payment from the player, and **Deliver** the product (the "ticket") to the player. **Payout** of prizes is the most expensive activity in a lottery business, but is the most exciting and attractive one for players. In many other businesses, the last activities are post-sales services or reaction to customer requests, which may not have much effect on the margin compared with the total cost incurred in the value chain. Within the value chain, the money spent on prize pay-outs may amount to 55% to 90% of total ticket sales. In the other words, the post-sales services will consume the greatest part of the margin, but add big value for some consumers. These activities are linked together in the value chain, so if any of them breakdown, the whole business is affected.

History and Current Status of IT Use

IT is the preparation, collection, transport, retrieval, storage, access, presentation, and transformation of information in all its forms via voice, graphics, text, video, and images (Boar, 1994). IT can profoundly affect business activities, sometimes simply by improving effectiveness, or sometimes by fundamentally changing the activity (Cash et al., 1992). While IT and communication are able to process and transfer digitized goods, today's lottery firms are operating computerised on-line systems to sell lottery products at special on-line terminals located within agents. That is, lottery industries have used various EC platforms to exchange goods between firms and agents. This is a typical "Business-Agent-Consumer" (BAC) model.

ISSUES IN THE INTERNET ERA

The Vision – Shifting the Commerce Model

There are some problems with the BAC model. A business cannot reach all consumers anywhere and anytime, so many potential consumers may not have the chance to purchase tickets in time for a lottery draw. Moreover, the business has to pay money or commission to the agents. The vision is therefore to reach individual consumers directly. The commerce model, therefore, shall be shifted from predominantly BAC to predominantly the direct "Business-Consumer" (BC) model.

Although there are several ways to realize the vision, the Internet permits direct access from creators of value to consumers, and greatly reduces the cost associated with distribution. Internet Commerce (IC) or Web commerce is one type of the more general EC (Maddox, 1998; Minoli D. and Minoli E., 1997). EC in general and IC in particular differ from traditional commerce in the way information is exchanged. EC encompasses several methods of connecting buyers and sellers, while IC is one of a battery of on-line services that consumers may ultimately be interested in. The most obvious changes are those of geography, time, and cost structure. It is not necessary for an individual company to create an expensive distribution channel to enter a new marketplace.

Internet Lottery Commerce (ILC), a particular IC application in the gaming industry, involves the use of the Internet for advertising, selling and delivery of lottery products, collecting payments for tickets, paying-out prizes, and providing other services in the lottery commerce value chain.

Competitive Analysis of the Lottery Business in the Internet Era

IC has dictated the forces of change within the business environment and could well lead to the worst nightmare for traditional lottery businesses. Any decision to sideline an IC strategy is likely to result in a weakened market position that leaves businesses with no choice but to rethink their strategy. When considering the impact of IC on their traditional businesses, firms may view it as a threat or opportunity. The economic and competitive forces in an industry segment were the result of a broader range of factors than the strengths and weaknesses of established combatants in a particular industry.

To provide direction for strategic planners and senior executives, an Industry and Competitive Analysis framework (Porter, 1980) is based on the premise that an industry segment's competition depends on five basic forces: intra-industry rivals; new entrants; substitute products or services; buyers; and suppliers. It is a useful framework to analyze the competitive advantages using IT (Cash et al., 1992). Here, we adopt the method to undertake a competitive analysis of the lottery business in the IC era.

Traditional Intra-Industry Rivals can compete using price, product, distribution, and service to attract consumers. Using the global Internet connection, some bigger lottery corporations are able to occupy the world market based on their expertise and technology. These corporations can easily provide the same products as others provide now. There may be only a few winners combining attractive prices, good service, and a worldwide distribution network, while others will become smaller survivors, or even losers.

New Entrants into the Industry Segment traditionally bring additional capacity, substantial resources, and often this brings reduced prices or an increase in existing firms' costs. In the Internet era, more interesting things start to happen when competition crosses between various industry segments. The Internet can bring formerly unrelated enterprises into direct competition. Whilst the traditional lines between some industries are becoming blurred or may disappear, who owns the customer relationship will be a winner. Some areas are becoming open markets, like delivery or selling digitized goods or money transfer services on-line. For example, in on-line music sales, music recording companies and IT companies are fighting for what each company hopes will be its domination of the industry (Yih and Anderson, 1999). Similarly, the on-line lottery business is now becoming another open market with some sectors of industry, like banks armed with money transfer mechanisms and global distribution networks, having the knowledge and technology to go into the lottery business.

Substitute Products or Services attract traditional consumers. Since producing different lottery products is basically to generate different variations on the generation of combinations of digits, even small firms are able to provide various products and services over the Internet. These substitute products and services may emerge every day and can be disseminated very quickly. Therefore, although a firm has the opportunity to sell its products to the whole world, the threat is ever-present that other more attractive products and better services may attract away its traditional consumers.

Bargaining Power of Buyers will raise the cost of many activities and reduce margins. If more Web sites become available that provide lottery products, consumers will have more bargaining power. In such cases, consumers will demand that businesses payout greater prize monies or provide more services. A firm may have to force ticket prices down, increase quality, and provide more services in responding to greater competition.

Suppliers' Bargaining Power has implications such as lower prices for supplies or increased operating cost through more expensive bought-in services. When the firm operates with ILC, it may no longer need traditional vendors to supply raw materials, such as paper, but will need infrastructure services such as networks and payment systems, which will be supplied by IC system developers and maintainers. The bargaining power of suppliers may increase when the firm becomes more reliant on their services, particularly if there are no alternative sources of supply. In the Internet era, no firm can do everything itself, so it will have to face this problem. This is particularly so for small firms because of their lack of resources (Poon and Swatman, 1997).

Strategic Resource Evaluation

Business issues for ILC cross the entire range of business activities in a value chain, from attracting consumers to fulfilling their orders, and from collecting wagers to prize payment. Every firm has many questions to ask in evaluating new activities. Adopting the method suggested by Cash et al. (1992), this section assesses the ultimate impact of a planned ILC by addressing the following critical questions: Can ILC build barriers to entry? Can ILC retain current consumers and attract new consumers? Can ILC generate new products and services? Can ILC change the basis of competition?

If the answer to one or more of the above questions is "Yes," ILC is a strategic resource that requires attention at the highest level.

In the five forces analyzed above, the threats from traditional rivals and new entrants are the most crucial ones. Existing national laws are the strongest barriers to combat such threats. However, it is difficult for any government to prevent people from betting over the Internet. Laws may be changed so that legal barriers could eventually disappear. For existing firms the response to the threat may be to build its own ILC system in order to take advantage of cost-effectiveness and differentiation in product and service. In the open battleground that will be created, ILC is a weapon for success or survival, and the best defensive strategy is to take the offensive. If a firm's ILC applications are cost effective and attractive, it can effectively bar new entrants and may dominate the market.

As always, it is very important to keep a very clear view of the value provided to consumers.

The prime objective of rivals is to attract away another company's consumers. ILC enables various means, such as switching cost, differentiation, and entry barriers to retain loyalty among customers and attract new ones within both the local and global domains. Even when customers are outside the country, they can play the lottery via a firm's Web site; otherwise if the firm does not deploy an ILC application, it may lose the battle when its customers shift to others that do use the technology.

The Internet short circuits traditional distribution chains in a way that can change the nature of competition. Since ILC reaches individual consumers with multimedia interfaces and global connections, it enables the delivery of many new services and products electronically, such as informing winners and paying-out prizes through via the Internet. In this way ILC can soon become an effective means of barring new entrants, retaining current consumers, attracting new ones, and generating new services, thereby changing the basis of competition. Therefore, ILC can be viewed as one of critical strategic resources that not only reduces the threat but also enables firms to extend their business into broader domains.

FRAMEWORK OF PLANNING

The variety of potential competitive and strategic uses of IT are as broad and complex as the industries within which the uses have evolved. To plan for these IT uses, top management needs a comprehensive framework that should provide a strategic rather than a tactical perspective (Cash et al., 1992). Figure 2 demonstrates our conceptual framework for addressing high level issues and essential components in planning ILC.

Social Environment

Although many organizations can provide infrastructure services, lottery businesses can only apply such services within certain social environments.

Standards

Internet interconnection agreements are as heterogeneous as their users and the traffic along the networks connected by the Internet. Changes in interconnection agreements and pricing strategies are evident as new services (Bailey et al., 1998). No single model of interconnection will dominate the Internet. In establishing connections users can potentially increase the congestion costs of other users, so a scalable interconnection framework to support end-to-end delivery of integrated services will be required. Infrastructure service providers need a set of open standards in the areas of network, security, encryption, information sources, and exchange. While there are many organizations working on such standards, the Internet Engineering Task Force (IETF) and World Wide Web Consortium (W3C) play very important roles in establishing Internet standardization. The IETF is a large open international community concerned with the evolution of the Internet architecture and smooth operation of the Internet. It makes recommendations to the Internet Engineering Steering Group (IESG) and facilitates technology transfer from the Internet Research Task Force (IRTF) to the wider Internet community. The W3C is an international association to lead the World Wide Web to its full potential by developing common protocols that promote its evolution and ensure its interoperability. Generally, the IETF addresses specific issues of Internet protocols while W3C addresses the architecture of the Web.

Figure 2. Schematic Diagram of a Conceptual Framework

<table>
<tr><td colspan="5">Internet Lottery Commerce Applications</td></tr>
<tr><td colspan="5">Infrastructure Services</td></tr>
<tr><td>Network service</td><td>Directory service</td><td>Security service</td><td>User access service</td><td>Payment services</td></tr>
<tr><td colspan="5">Social Environment</td></tr>
<tr><td>Standards</td><td>National Laws</td><td colspan="2">Industry Regulation</td><td>Participants</td></tr>
</table>

National Laws

While the Internet technologies enable global lottery operations, national or local laws may restrict the opportunities created. Morality and taxation issues are two reasons for governments legislating for Internet gaming activities. People also need to know that when they undertake commercial transactions on-line, they enjoy the same legal protection as they do with traditional businesses. Lottery firms have to follow laws and should explicitly address legal issues involved to avoid problems later.

The legal situation for Internet gaming around the world is concentrated on three main geographical areas—The USA, Australia and New Zealand, and Europe, where regulators are actively thinking about the development of a legal framework. While Australia and New Zealand are trying to regulate this newly evolving form of gaming, the USA has so far strongly opposed gaming via the Internet. Europe is examining the issues, but has not decided yet whether a regulation for Internet gaming is wanted or needed.

Firms must pay attention to legal issues no matter where and to whom they would like to offer Internet lottery services. This will make sure that such services are acceptable to the targeted consumers so they feel comfortable when purchasing tickets on-line.

Industry Self-Regulation

There is no formal body that regulates the Internet gaming industry (Martin, 1999). As such, industry participants have initiated their own efforts toward creating an independent regulatory body that would involve both the Internet gaming developers and operators. These regulations aim to increase confidence that an Internet lottery is a responsible activity. One of the proposed regulations is to limit Internet gaming within national borders, so an operator only allows residents within the same country to be Internet lottery players. However, only certain countries have accepted this regulation.

Participants

Participants consist of businesses and individual customers. One of the most essential issues for any business is "Who is the customer?" (Treese and Stewart, 1998). Very different strategies should be adopted in order to sell effectively to different customers. Firms often do not have a clear understanding of the answer, and sometimes the answer is subtler than it at first appears. As advances in communication and transportation make "globalization" possible for businesses to operate worldwide, businesses and customers may be located anywhere.

Infrastructure Services

Network Services and Directory Services

Network services allow businesses to link over the Internet, while directory services allow people to search for web sites based on search criteria using common search engines like "Yahoo" and "Excite." Generally, a local Internet Service Provider (ISP) or Internet Access Service Provider (IASP) provides such services.

Security Services

Customers' concerns relate to the integrity and security of electronic transactions. Security services provide secure identification and communication, and data integration over the Internet, involving various technologies like "Smart Card," "Public Key," "Digital Identification," and "Digital Signatures." Identifying the authenticity of buyers and sellers on the Internet is one of the most important issues of Internet commerce. Some organizations provide digital identification or certification authority services, which enable both buyers and sellers to identify each other when they process transactions over the Internet.

Table 1. Payment System

Style \ Implementation	Closed	Opened
Credit	***Account***	*Credit Card, Credit Links/Account*
Debit	*Deposit Account, Customer Card*	*ATM Card, Debit Card, E-Purse, E-Cheque*

Payment Services

Payment services enable secure payments over the Internet. One of the reasons consumers prefer not use the Internet for financial transactions is because of the perceived lack of security, especially when traditional ways of making transactions are regarded as robust and sound. Today on the Internet, more than two dozen commercially ready payment systems/protocols of various types are available for business (Austin, 1997; Yen, 1998). But there is the lack of a widely adopted transaction mechanism (Poon and Swatman, 1997). Some reasons for having various payment systems developed are due to special considerations regarding levels of security, speed, and customers' requirements. Table 1 shows some available payment systems for ILC applications.

A closed implementation means that a payment mechanism is only available within a closed environment, such as an enterprise or community. An opened implementation refers to a national or international money transfer mechanism by which all organizations or individuals can transfer money between them. Credit is an easy and reliable form of payment, and has been adopted and practised by some lottery firms. In lottery commerce, the daily receivable amount is usually much more than the amount payable so credit payment is technically appropriate. However, the opportunity of using credit may encourage people to bet beyond their means so some governments do not allow its use in lotteries. Debiting is an alternative method, which uses stored amounts of money on a cash card or electronic purse (e-purse), which is useful when the betting amount is small. While a debit card or Automatic Teller Machine (ATM) card can be used for the transfer of up to a few thousand dollars, an electronic check (e-check) can transfer larger amounts. Both open and closed debit accounts can be used to transfer from small to large amounts of money.

In a lottery business, the money transferred includes both payments for tickets and prize pay-outs. While winning prizes can range from small to huge amounts (e.g., from $10 to more than $100 million), generally they are small. Thus firms need different payment mechanisms. Using a closed system a firm can closely control and monitor cash flows, but it needs more resources to do so. Using an open system, a firm can focus its energy on its core business, although it needs to pay for the money transfer services. Some companies, therefore, have started to provide money transfer services for gaming businesses (IGI, 1999).

RECOMMENDATIONS

Internet Lottery Commerce Model

Based on the infrastructure services, firms can deploy their ILC. Figure 3 shows an integrated model of the lottery commerce process and provides a wider picture for studying and planning ILC.

This model generalizes the exchange processes between businesses and consumers in the lottery commerce value chain. In each step of the value chain, the behavior of businesses and consumers are different when exchanging goods or services. Communications and computing serve as the glue between businesses and consumers in these exchange processes. The assumptions of the value chain are that competitive advantage arises from value created for customers that exceeds the cost of creating that value. By understanding more about its own value chain and the value chain of customers, a company has a greater ability to create value for those customers.

Electronic-Consumers (E-Consumers)

An **e-consumer** refers to a person who is able and willing to use the required electronic tools (e.g., computer and software) to search for and buy products. Typical lottery e-consumers are people who have confidence in Internet transactions and believe ILC can provide them with more convenience and privacy.

Electronic-Business (E-Business)

An **e-business** refers to an organization that has reliable, scaleable, and secure systems for use by its customers and the internal organization for managing major business processes. An e-business comprises two functions—that of the **electronic-firm** (e-firm) and the **electronic-agent** (e-agent). The e-firm function refers to the internal organization processes while the e-agent function refers the interface for dealing with on-line processes that exchange goods and services between the firm and its customers. An e-agent, supported by back-end systems, uses a set of IT applications or in-front systems that simulates the commercial behavior of human agents. The face of an e-agent is the Web site. Almost all today's lottery firms are e-firms since they have back-end systems used by internal departments for processing business transactions. The outstanding issue for these firms to deploy ILC, therefore, is to deploy an e-agent that can fulfill the traditional functions of agents. Customers interact with an e-agent through its Web site to search for information and buy goods. In considering and using the IT heritage, focusing on e-agent is a more effective and faster way for a lottery firm to establish its ILC.

Figure 3. Business-Consumer Internet Lottery Commerce Model

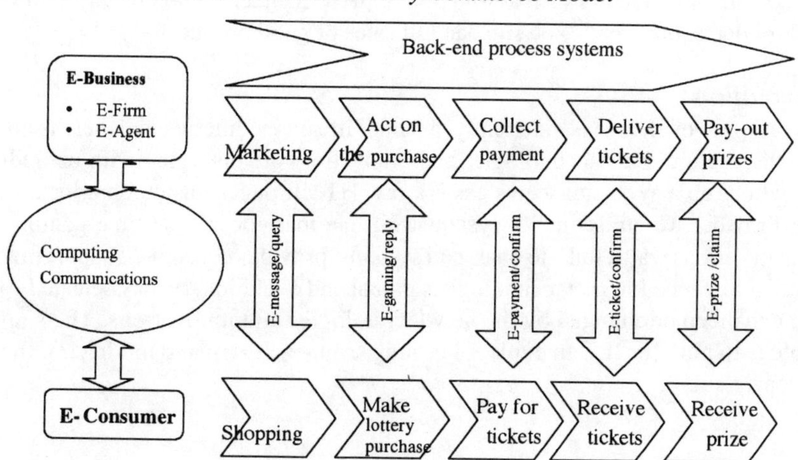

Electronically Exchanged Goods and Services

While the Internet brings new capabilities to businesses, an ILC system does not change the lottery business processes in the value chain but changes the ways of exchanging goods and services. The fundamental change is that the exchange is through the Internet. Following the value chain, the goods and services exchanged between the e-agent and e-consumer are modelled as electronic messages or data. Thus a data-oriented analysis can reflect the critical issues.

Principles

To be a winner in the Internet era, the generic strategy of a firm is the achievement of global cost and differentiation leadership. To a lottery business, the generic competitive advantage is to provide a different gaming service with a new commerce style, and the generic competitive scope is to attract more consumers. Putting various technologies and business requirements together to form a secure, high-performance, and integrated ILC can be challenging, but the principles presented here should provide some useful guidance. It should be noted that these principles are not isolated but related each other.

Start Early and Keep It Simple

The Internet creates thousands of opportunities for business. The challenge for a company now is to select and act on one or a few opportunities. The time is crucial for occupying the marketplace. Starting early gives a firm enough time to obtain customers' trust and gain experience. The Internet short-circuits traditional distribution chains in a way that can change the nature of competition. Although the legal context is not entirely clear, early participants are driving the market's growth and preparing to occupy the potential marketplace at the earliest opportunity when the legal obstacles have been removed. A simple solution is recommended at the early stage. Deploying a complex system at once will take a long time, and whatever is done will need to change as context and technologies change, as they inevitably will.

Security

At the early stage, building a simple but secure prototype is the best practice. A simple solution lets a firm focus on security, while it is critical to building consumers' trust (Ratnasingham, 1998). Security is the most critical factor in building consumers' trust compared with other factors such as function or performance. A good ILC system will not sell bad products, but a bad Web site can kill sales of good products.

Evolution

A fast pace of change is, inherently, a fact of life on the Internet and there is no end in sight to this feature. New technologies and innovations are emerging with unpredictable speed. Setting up a Web site seems easy: a few HTML pages hosted on a local Internet Service Provider. Contrast such a system with one that allows real-time gaming, takes payment in various ways, links to back-end systems, provides consumer support functions, and is reliable. Since Internet technology is global and evolutionary, any selected solution may be enhanced or changed by the new technologies and innovations. The suggested principle is to plan for ILC to evolve, learning from each step and modifying the plans as appropriate.

Build Customer Trust

Who owns the customer relationship and trust is the winner in the Internet era. For the ultimate long-term success of an on-line lottery business, it is essential to develop a credible reputation bolstered by a vigorous regulatory system. As consumers interact with a Web site, they determine whether or not they trust it. A recent study (Cheskin and Studio Archetype, 1999) identifies six items in which trust is established: seals of approval, brand, navigation, fulfillment, presentation, technology. The trust life-cycle consists of "untrust," "build trust," "confirm trust," and "maintain trust." Hence, starting early is necessary to build customers' trust.

Customer Retention

The most important thing is not what attracts customers' attention but what retains that attention. In other words, the more important consideration is not why customers navigate a Web site, but what may cause them or seek out or, once found, spend time with a Web site. The way to retain customers is to provide them with confidence and benefit. About one-third of Internet users consider that if they feel they may experience a loss by shopping on-line, they will avoid completely buying on the Internet. The long-term survival of a retail operation depends on one thing: excellent customer service. With more choices than ever available to today's discerning consumers, and their coveted loyalty increasingly difficult to earn, it is every seller's goal to keep the customer coming back for more.

Business-Driven but not Fashion-Driven

While growing the market value of business is the primary objective, the suggested ILC shall shift focus from cost-cutting to market-share growth. Building ILC applications is to enhance a lottery firm's primary commerce activities in its value chain rather than catching up with a new fashion. It allows a firm to focus on what it is doing and what it is getting for its investment. The planned ILC shall enable exchange of e-messaging, e-ordering, e-purchasing, e-ticketing, and e-pay-outs between players and the company via the Internet.

Long-Term Benefit and Competitive Advantage

While global Internet commerce will fundamentally change the way of conducting lottery business, commercial benefits may not be yielded in a short term. This is mainly due to the need to build consumers' trust over time, and there are many uncertain things in the legislative, business, and technology areas. Table 2 shows how various benefits may be yielded using ILC.

Direct benefits are readily quantifiable by means of such techniques as numbers of new consumers or other quantitative evidence. Indirect benefits are not so easily quantifiable but they have a significant effect on the business. Short-term benefits should be realized within a few months, while long-term ones may take much longer and can be unpredictable. As the Internet provides a cheaper distribution channel, an implemented ILC application will reduce the cost in interaction, collection, and delivery actions, which will generate direct benefit within a short period. Moreover, a new way of planning will attract some new consumers who would like to participate in a lottery via the Internet, which will increase sales. A well-implemented ILC system will secure consumer loyalty and provide a better communications channel between them and the business which will build and maintain their trust. Such consumer trust is essential and provides direct benefit for companies, thereby contributing to success in a long term. Firms are able to use their deployed ILC infrastructure

Table 2. Four Categories of Benefits of ILC

	Short term	Long term
Direct	*Save in communication cost* *Generate short -term revenues*	*Secure returning consumers* *Long-term customer relationship*
Indirect	*Potential business opportunities* *Advertising and marketing*	*Ongoing business transformation* *New business initiatives* *Market share occupation*

as survival weapons to reduce threats from the five forces mentioned earlier and to capture potential business opportunities in the Internet era. These are indirect or intangible benefits for firms, especially with a long-term view. Looking forward to long-term benefits is the key motivation for ensuring effective ongoing ILC activities.

Quick Response

The World Wide Web has changed rapidly with both rapid growth in use and dramatic evolution in protocol, systems, and applications. The waiting time for accessing Web sites, however, is becoming an important event in the Internet search, especially with the popularity of multimedia technology and the exponential increase in the number of Web users (Nah et al., 1998). Visitors evaluate technology largely in terms of speed and function (Cheskin et al., 1999). When the access time greatly exceeds the perceived and tolerable waiting time, the consumers' trust will be affected. Zona Research (1999) reports that an Internet on-line buyer's maximum waiting time for downloading is eight seconds, and if the waiting time is too long, the number of EC transactions in the USA could reduce by 4.35 billion each year. Reducing download time is therefore essential if an on-line merchant wants to retain customers. Some service providers, including America On-line, clearly recognize the importance of access time to users.

Sufficient Capacity

The significant and basic aspect of undertaking commerce via the global Internet is that the customers come from anywhere and anytime throughout the world. The number of a firm's on-line customers may be many more than expected, so its Web site and back-end systems may not handle such huge customer requirements. For example, popular good Web sites have needed to shut down when the number of visitors became too many to handle. This not only reduces business, but also impacts negatively on a firm's image and its customer trust.

Smart Sourcing

While complete "Insourcing" is extremely expensive to create and maintain, total "Outsourcing" may tie a firm to the fortunes of one vendor. "Smart-sourcing" uses a mix of off-the-shelf products and vendors, but may be one main integrator.

Strategic Deployment Approach

In the ILC model, the interactive transactions between e-consumers and e-agents are modelled as five categories of exchanged data. Each of the exchanged data categories are associated with several business processes. Focusing on the exchanged data will identify the critical issues and corresponding solutions. However, it is not necessary for a firm to deploy

Table 3. Data-Oriented Solution Selection Guide

Solutions \ Data	E-message	E-order	E-purchase	E-ticket	E-prize
Security	1	2	2	2	2
Response Speed	1	2	2	2	3
Capacity	1	2	2	2	3
Convenience	1	2	2	2	3
Privacy	1	2	2	2	3
Effectiveness	1	2	2	2	3
Efficiency	1	2	2	2	3
Integration	1	3	3	3	3

its ILC applications to handle all processes at one time. Table 3 proposes an evolving deployment approach. As a guide, this approach suggests three main deployment stages—(1) Web site for Basic Presence and Prospecting, (2) ILC Prototype of business integration, and (3) Full ILC application for business transformation. The numbers "1," "2," and "3" indicate stage 1, 2, and 3, as well as related data issues and solutions. For example, in Column 2 (e-message), all rows have the same number "1." This suggests that all solutions for transferring e-messages must be implemented in Stage 1. At Stage 1, a firm sets up its Web site to present corporate information, draw results and press releases, e-mail support, and provide simple search facilities. At Stage 2, the firm deploys its initial Web site to an ILC prototype that is incorporated into the business model, and the integration of business processes takes place. At Stage 3, the firm extends its prototype to a full ILC system, and the firm must align and transform its business strategy with the EC initiatives throughout the organization. The strategic values are increased from low to high when the firm moves from Stage 1 to 3.

FUTURE TRENDS AND RESEARCH ISSUES

Global Winners

The commercial processes of a lottery are typically information-driven and network-based processes. This feature determines that on-line lottery businesses would yield significant commercial benefits using Internet commerce. Technically, it seems anybody can undertake on-line lottery business anywhere over the Internet, so the on-line lottery market is becoming an open battleground. With affordable access to the global Internet, the traditional barriers of time, distance, and geography will no longer be issues. While the Internet enables small companies to compete in the global market, they will face stronger rivals from around the world. A lottery firm in different situations may be a winner, survivor, or even a victim. In the future, there may only be about less than 10 global winners and many victims. Another possible trend is that some firms form joint ventures to become groups of companies.

Management Talent

To be a success, a firm should fully use its competitive advantages that consist of four layers—technology infrastructure, business model, strategy, and talent management. While firms are able to obtain the same technology and adopt the same model and strategy, management talent may become the most critical success factor in the knowledge economy.

Organization Model

Who owns ICL in an organization is a critical factor for success. In reality, a successful ILC is almost always a combined effort, drawing on the strength of many different groups within a firm. Success of any innovation will be affected by organizational conditions, such as the marketing strategy, availability of marketing and IT resources, senior management factors, interdepartmental dynamics, and organizational systems (Milley and Marcolin, 1998). Deploying a successful and profitable ILC involves cross-enterprise involvement with the focus on building relationships and developing knowledge to create new business opportunities.

Change Management

The fast pace of technological change is inherently a fact of life in the Internet era, and there is no end in sight. The new technology, however, will open up new opportunities (Cash et al., 1992). To be a success, any ILC design should be based on a coherent architecture in order to accommodate any new technology as it becomes available. Setting up a Web site seems easy: a few HTML pages, hosting on a local ISP. Contrast such a system with one that allows real-time catalogue updates, keeps and uses consumer profiles, takes payment in various ways, links to inventory and fulfillment systems, and provides consumer support functions.

Emerging Technologies

Mobile computing technology and IP telephony enable firms to offer their customers mobile lottery playing services. With Wireless Application Protocol (WAP), people may use a mobile phone to play lotteries in the future. Internet-based interactive TV is another channel by which lottery firms can distribute their products and services. Internet2, the most exciting evolution in the Internet, will be available within the next few years and solve the performance issues.

SUMMARY

The Internet era forces all industry sectors to reconsider their business model based on emerging technologies. The lottery business is one industry sector which will be strongly impacted by the new era. To be a winner in undertaking business on the Internet, executives should have right vision and strategies. This chapter has aimed to provide current and potential executives in the lottery industry a feasible guideline to deploy Internet Lottery Commerce (ILC) applications. Since ILC is one type of Internet commerce, this executive guideline may be partially applicable to other industry sectors, particularly the model, principles, and strategies.

ACKNOWLEDGMENT

The authors would like to offer thanks to the editors and reviewers for their efforts and valuable comments on this chapter.

REFERENCES

Adam, N. R., and Yesha, Y. (Eds.) (1996). *Electronic Commerce – Current Research Issues and Application*. Springer.

Andreu, R., Ricart, J. E., and Valor, J. (1992). *Information Systems Strategic Planning – A Source of Competitive Advantage*. NCC Blackwell.

Austin, T. W. (1997). Betting on digital money. *EC.COM*, May, 8-10.

Bailey, J. P., McKnight, L. W., and Sharifi, H. S. (1998). Critical business decision for Internet services. Khosrowpour, M., (Ed.). In the *Effective Utilization and Management of Emerging Information Technologies*, IDEA Group Publishing, pp. 555-564.

Boar, B.H. (1994) Practical steps for aligning information technology with business strategies. AT&T bell Laboratories, John Wiley & Sons, Inc.

Cash, J.I., McFarlan F.W., and McKenney, J.L. (1992), Corporate Information Systems Management—The Issues Facing Senior Executives. Third edition, Irwin, Homewood, IL.

Cheskin and Studio Archetype (1999). eCommerce trust study. A joint research project by Cheskin Research and Studio Archetype/Sapient, January, www.studioarchetype.com/cheskin.

IGI (1999). *Internet Gaming International*, 2(3).

Kambil, A. (1997) Doing business in the wired world. *Computer*, 30(5), 56-61.

Maddox, K. (1998) Web Commerce – Building a Digital Business. John Wiley & Sons, Inc.

Martin, J. (Ed.) (1999). Internet & E-Commerce – Effects on the Gambling Industry, report of the Intertoto Working Group - Games of Chance Via New Media.

Milley, R., and Marcolin, B. (1998). "Under what conditions does the World Wide Web add value to marketing?" Khosrowpour, M., (Ed.), *In the Effective Utilization and Management of Emerging Information Technologies*, IDEA Group Publishing, pp. 541-548.

Minoli, D., and Minoli, E. (1997). Web Commerce Technology Handbook. McGraw-Hill.

Nah, F. H., Siau, K., Kim I., and Zhang W. (1998). "WWW: World-Wide Wait." Khosrowpour, M. (Ed.), In the *Effective Utilization and Management of Emerging Information Technologies*, IDEA Group Publishing, pp. 174-179.

Poon, S., and Swatman, P.M.C. (1999). "An exploratory study of small business Internet commerce issues." *Information & Management,* 35, pp. 9-18.

Porter, M. E. (1980). Competitive Strategy: Technique for Analyzing Industries and Competitors. The Free Press.

Porter, M. E. (1985). Competitive Advantage: Creating and Sustaining Superior Performance. The Free Press.

Porter, M. E., and Millar, V. E. (1985). "How information gives competitive advantage." *Harvard Business Review*, July-August, 149-160.

Ratnasingham, P. (1998). "Trust in Web-based electronic commerce security." *Information Management & Computer Security*, 6(4), 162-166.

Treese, G. W., and Stewart, L. C. (1998). Designing Systems for Internet Commerce. Addison Wesley Longman, Inc.

Yen, V. C. (1998) "An integrated planning model for electronic commerce." Khosrowpour, M. (Ed.), In the *Effective Utilization and Management of Emerging Information Technologies*, IDEA Group Publishing, pp. 174-179.

Yih, T. F., and Anderson, L. (1999) "Music giants fight a corporate war on-line." *ICommerce*, IDG Communications, May/June, 18-21.

Zona Research. (1999) "The Need for Speed." www.zonareasearch.com/promotions/needforspeed.

Section Two: Agents in E-Commerce: Introduction and Impact

Chapter V

Software Agents in Electronic Commerce: An Overview

Maria Indrawan
Monash University, Australia

ABSTRACT

The explosive growth of Internet-based electronic commerce has increased the consumer's choices of goods and merchants. To find a suitable good and merchant with acceptable sales terms is a very tedious task. Agent technologies promise to simplify these tasks for consumers. This chapter presents an overview of electronic commerce systems based on software agent technology. A survey of current existing and prototype systems are presented. One of essential requirements of a successful e-commerce system is security measurement. This paper also discusses security issues related to implementing agent-based e-commerce.

INTRODUCTION

Electronic commerce stems from the demand within business and government to make better use of computer technology to improve customer interaction, business processes and information exchange both within an enterprise and across enterprises. In the early days of electronic commerce, the emphasis was placed more on information exchanges within and across enterprises or business-to-business electronic commerce through the use of EDI. There have been some reservations expressed by the business community, especially small businesses, regarding EDI solutions in electronic commerce. The main reservations result from the high costs associated with developing EDI and limited interaction with customers. The latter point shows that there is little support for customer-to-business electronic commerce. In order to support the customer-to-business model, a different technology is required. Such an alternative technology is provided by the Internet technology.

The maturity of Internet technology has opened opportunities for businesses to develop customer-to-business electronic commerce. Indeed, this type of commerce has grown rapidly in the last few years. Forrester Research estimates that Internet-generated transactions will grow exponentially from a combined worth of about US $14 billion in 1997 to US $327 billion within five years (Ma, 1999). This figure shows that there is still around

US $313 billion worth of unrealized potential transactions to date. Electronic purchases are still largely non-automated. While information about different products and vendors are readily available, and orders and payments can be dealt with electronically, human involvement is still required in all stages of the buying process. A human buyer is still responsible for collecting and evaluating information on products and merchants before making decisions on buying a product from a particular merchant and entering the purchase and payment stage. To exploit the full potential of electronic commerce, some of the tasks need to be automated. This automation is made possible by the introduction of software agents to electronic commerce.

The software agent is a new computing paradigm that allows a piece of program to act as an agent to perform a task on behalf of a human. The field is far from mature but it has great potential in automating customer-to-business electronic commerce. Indeed, there are some research organizations which have launched their prototypes of software agents for electronic commerce in the Internet in the last few years. In this paper, we present and discuss the current trend and challenges in developing electronic commerce based on the software agent paradigm. We have organized this paper as follows: Section Two introduces the reader to the definition and properties of software agents. Specifically, the properties that benefit electronic commerce will be highlighted. Section Three discusses how software agents can be used in different stages of buying activities according to the Mercantile model (Kalakota & Whinston, 1996). Examples of existing systems or prototypes to this model will be presented. Section Four discusses the existing technologies that can support the development of agent-based systems. These technologies include programming languages, and human computer interaction. Security is an important issue in implementing agent-based e-commerce systems. Section Five discusses the security requirements of such systems and the possible mechanism and/or technologies to meet these requirements. As a new technology, agent based e-commerce has not reached its full potential due to limited support of the existing technologies. Section Six discusses research challenges to deliver the full potential of agent-based e-commerce. Finally, in Section Seven, we provide a conclusion.

SOFTWARE AGENTS

Definition and Properties

Before we can discuss the properties of software agents, we first have to define what we mean by the term 'software agent.' In doing this, we immediately run into difficulties, as some key definitions in this field lack universal acceptance. Some of these definitions are as follows:

> "An agent is a computer system, *situated* in some environment, that is capable of *flexible autonomous* action in order to *meet its design objective* ... by flexible we mean the system is *responsive, proactive, and social*" (Jennings, Sycara, & Wooldrige, 1998).

> "Software agents are programs to which one can *delegate* (aspect of) a task. They differ from "traditional" software in that they are *personalized, continuously running,* and *semiautonomous*" (Maes, 1994).

> "...we define an agent as referring to a component of software and/or hardware which is *capable of acting* exactly in order *to accomplish tasks on behalf* of its user" (Nwana, 1993).

Although software agents are defined differently by these people, there is some agreement between them regarding the key concepts of software agents. For example, they all agree that an agent should act on behalf of its user (which is the design objective in Jenning's definition). Other key concepts of agents such as whether agents should be fully autonomous or semiautonomous, or whether agents should have personalized capability, or whether agents should have social ability to interact with other agents, will depend greatly on the intended application domain of the software agents. For example, for the purpose filtering e-mail or newsgroup articles, an agent does not need to interact with other agents, hence social capability is not required. However, in an automatic purchasing system, a buying agent may need to be able to negotiate with the selling agents.

An attempt to find a universally accepted definition of software agent may in fact be futile or counterproductive. It will be more beneficial to identify ideal properties of agents and then determine which of these properties are required by a software agent to serve the requirement of the application domain where the agent is situated. In the next section, we will identify properties of software agents which are useful in the electronic commerce domain.

Properties of Software Agents that are Useful to Electronic Commerce

From the definitions supplied in the previous section, we can conclude that software agents may exhibit one or more of the following properties:

- the capacity to accomplish tasks on behalf of users
- autonomy
- the capacity to be personalized
- social capability
- intelligence
- purposeful/goal oriented behavior
- mobility

Different properties are required to automate different stages of buying-selling activities. It is important to realize that ordering products on the World Wide Web by clicking a "BUY" button on a Web page is inherently complex and the processes involved may differ for different products or services. To understand the role of software agents and the important properties of agents in electronic commerce, it is useful to have a general consumer behavior model. A generalized consumer interaction model, divided into steps, is depicted in Figure 1.

Figure 1. Consumer Interaction Model

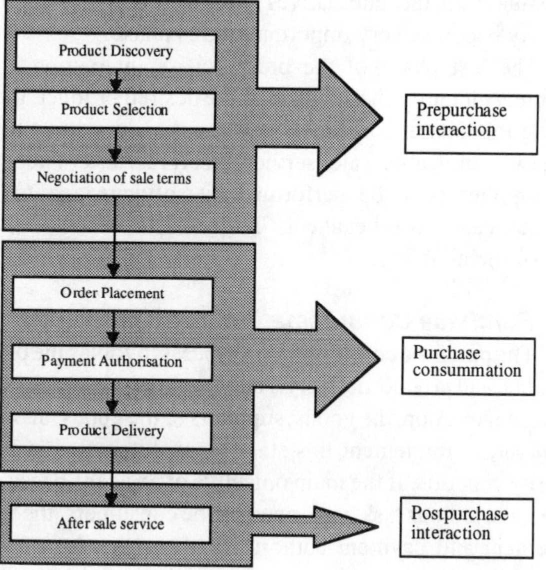

Using this model, a software developer can easily

modularize e-commerce systems into different subsystems. The challenge in building software agents for e-commerce lies in creating agents which are appropriate for each subsystem and providing interfaces and communication between agents on different subsystems so that these agents work as a team to complete a whole commerce process.

Pre-purchase Interaction

The pre-purchase interaction phase includes discovery, search, and selection of products and negotiation phases. The discovery process characterizes the consumer becoming aware of some unmet need. Within this stage, the consumer can be stimulated through product information. On-line suppliers may exploit the benefits of software agents by collecting customer profiles and deliver personalized product information to the customer. For example, according to the purchase records, a customer may always buy a book written by particular author, and a message can be sent to this customer each time a new book is published by this author.

The search stage involves finding a set of products in a large information space that meet requirements specified by the consumer. Each of the products found may have different attributes and in the selection phase, the attributes of these products are compared. The consumer then chooses a product that has attributes which meet the specifications. In electronic commerce, this means that a consumer needs to search the Internet using a search engine like Yahoo (http://yahoo.com) or Excite (http://excite.com) for different on-line stores for a specific product. In this situation, software agents can help automate the search process. The users can specify in the agent's interface the product's attributes they desire and deploy the agent in the Internet. The agents then should autonomously 'travel' on different sites in the Internet to collect information regarding the attributes of the product and its supplier. To be able to fulfill the task in this phase, the properties of agents important for this phase are autonomy, mobility, and the capacity to be personalized.

Once a set of supplier or alternative products (in the case of the desired product not being available) is identified, a consumer then decides on an appropriate supplier or alternative product. To automate the tasks in this phase, the software agent needs to be able to evaluate all the alternatives presented and make a decision. Thus, the intelligence property becomes very important in this phase.

The last phase of the pre-purchase interaction is the negotiation process. Once consumers identify the supplier of the desired product, they enter into a negotiation phase. During this phase, consumers and suppliers negotiate the sale terms such as the product price, warranty, after-sales service, etc. If this task of negotiation on behalf of the consumer and supplier is to be performed by software agents, the agents need to be able to communicate with other agents. To do this, the software agents involved in this process need to have social ability.

Purchase Consummation

The purchase consummation process involves the placement of order, authorization of payment, and product delivery. At the surface, these tasks seem very straightforward because during negotiation, the goods, suppliers of the goods, and the sales terms have been decided. However, to implement this stage as an automated system requires a very high level of security supports. If the main objective of an agent-based electronic commerce is to simply reduce the tedious task performed by the consumers, the implementation of automatic order placement and payment authorization may not be desirable. The relative advantage of automating these activities would not make up for the high level of security risks. In section

5.0, we will discuss current issues and techniques to enable the implementation of this stage.

Post-purchase Interaction

The role of the software agent in post-purchase interaction is more interesting from the point of view of supplier than consumer. From the supplier point of view, software agents can be used to collect consumer profiles and provide personalized after-sale service.

From this Mercantile model perspective, we can identify the roles of agents as mediators in electronic commerce. The personalized, continuously running, autonomous, mobile, and sociable nature of agents make them well-suited for mediating those consumer behaviors involving information filtering and retrieval, personalized evaluation, complex coordinations, and time-based interactions. Specifically, these roles correspond to the pre-purchase interactions.

MEDIATING ELECTRONIC COMMERCE USING SOFTWARE AGENTS

Purchase consummation and post-purchase interaction are parts of customer-to-business electronic commerce. However, their applicability to agent-based electronic commerce are less interesting than the pre-purchase interaction stage, as we discussed earlier. For this reason, we limit our discussion in this section to the pre-purchase interaction.

Product Discovery

Agent technology is useful to some extent in automating or assisting the consumer in the product discovery stage. It can play an important role for repetitive purchases such as buying of supplies or predictable purchases such as habitual buying. The agent can monitor continuously a set of sensor or data stream and take actions when certain pre-specified condition occurs. Examples of such monitoring agents are abundant in the stock market domain. Amazon.com (http://amazon.com) is one on-line business that provides its customer with a "notification agent" called "Eyes." It monitors the catalog of books for sale and notifies the customer when certain events occur that may be of interest to the customer.

Product Search

The product search phase of themercantile model is where consumers determine what to buy and where to buy the product based on the need identified in the product discovery stage. There are two different stages in this phase from the point of view of software agent designs. These serve as mediators, namely, in product brokering and merchant brokering.

Product Brokering

Bakos (1997) shows that software agents can reduce the product search cost. The reduced cost is achieved through automatic critical evaluation of retrieved product information. Examples of software agents that support product brokering are Firefly (http://www.firefly.com, Shardanand & Maes, 1995), PersonaLogic (http://personalogic.com), and Tete-a-Tete (http://ecommerce.media.mit.edu/Tete-a-Tete; Guttman and Maes, 1998).

Firefly helps consumers find products using automated collaborative filtering (ACF). ACF works by comparing consumer profiles. The profiles are built from product ratings that are given to particular products. In the case of a product that is highly recommended by one shopper but has not been included for another shopper with a similar profile, this product will be recommended to the other shopper. For example, from the profiles of two shoppers, it may be deduced that they like books written by Dr. Seuss. Suppose one of the shoppers recently bought a new release of Dr. Seuss's autobiography and highly recommends this book. On the hand, the other shopper may not be aware of this new release. Firefly will suggest this new book to the second shopper. Essentially, Firefly uses the opinions of like-minded people to offer recommendations. Currently it is used to recommend products such as books and music.

PersonaLogic, unlike Firefly, can be considered as a traditional product brokering agent. The system filters out unwanted products within a given domain by allowing shoppers to specify constraints on a product's features. The system returns a list of products that satisfy all the constraints in order of relevance.

Merchant Brokering

The merchant brokering stage compares merchant alternatives for a given product. Andersen Consulting's BargainFinder (http://bf.cstar.ac.com/bf) was the first merchant brokering service. Given a specific product, BargainFinder requests its price from different merchant sites and compares the price of the item. One major disadvantage of this system is that a request for price has to come from the 'central site' (e.g., BargainFinder). On-line merchants can easily block requests from the centralized site, thus reducing the exposure of the request. However, BargainFinder has been useful because it offers a valuable insight into the issues involved in price comparisons.

The problem of centralized requests is solved by Jango (http://www.jango.com, Doorenbos, Etzioni, & Weld, 1997). This system allows the request to originate from each consumer's Web browser. This request is then simultaneously sent to merchant sites selected from a list maintained by Excite Inc. for the price.

A more sophisticated agent system for merchant brokering is Kasbah (Chavez, Dreilinger, Guttman, & Maes, 1997) from MIT Media Lab. It is a multi-agent classified ad system. A user who wants to sell or buy an item creates an agent. The agent is given strategic directions such as acceptable deals, acceptable price range, and a date by which to complete transaction. Using these strategic directions, the agent is deployed to a centralized agent marketplace. In this virtual marketplace, these buying and selling agents interact and perform tasks on behalf of its owner. The latest version of Kasbah incorporates a distributed trust and reputation mechanism called Better Business Bureau. Upon completion of a transaction, both parties may rate how well the other party managed their half of the deal. Agents can then use these ratings to determine if they should negotiate with agents whose owners fall below the user-specified reputation threshold.

Negotiation

Negotiation is an important part of any commerce. The benefit of dynamically negotiating a price instead of fixing it is that it relieves the merchant from the need to determine the value of the good *a priori*. Rather, this burden is pushed to the marketplace itself. However, there are impediments to using negotiation. Negotiation may involve a very complex procedure and can frustrate consumers. A negotiation may also occur for an extended period of time, which does not cater to impatient or time-constrained consumers. Today, support from software agents as mediators to e-commerce can be considered the most challenging task. Most of the existing agent systems support only product discovery and selection. Examples of agent systems that support negotiation are AuctionBot (http://auction.eecs.umich.edu; Wuman, Wellman, & Walsh, 1998), Kasbah, and Tete-a-Tete.

In Kasbah, once a buying agent finds a matching selling agent, the only valid action for the agents in the negotiation protocol is that performed by the buying agents to offer the bid without restrictions on time and price. The selling agent will respond with either "yes" or "no." It will provide buyers with one of three negotiation strategies, namely, anxious, cool-headed, and frugal. These strategies correspond to linear, quadratic, and exponential functions respectively for increasing the bid for a product over time. The simplicity of the negotiation protocol may be considered as a weakness of this system because it does not concern itself with optimal strategies or convergence properties as suggested in Sierra, Faratin,and Jennings (1997). However, it can be argued that the simplicity of the negotiation heuristic makes it intuitive for users to understand what their agents are doing in the marketplace.

AuctionBot is a general purpose Internet auction server. It is different from most of auction sites, in that it provides an application programmable interface (API) for users to create their own software agents, which may autonomously compete in the AuctionBot marketplace. The encoding of the bidding strategies is left to the users. A user who wants to sell a number of items creates a new auction. This is done by choosing an auction type and associated parameters such as clearing times, methods of resolving bidding ties, the number of sellers permitted, etc. Buyers and sellers can then bid according to the multilateral distributive negotiation protocols of the created auction. The seller bids the reserve price and lets AuctionBot manage and enforce buyer bidding according to the auction protocol and parameters.

The Fishmarket (http://www.iiia.csic.es/Projects/fishmarket/newindex.html; Rodriquez, Noriega, Sierra, & Padget, 1997) project is not currently used in a real-world system, but is worth looking at. It has hosted tournaments whereby opponents' handcrafted bidding strategies (Rodriquez, Noriega, Sierra, & Garcia, 1998) are compared along the lines of Alexrod's prisoner's dilemma tournaments (Axelrod, 1984).

Tete-a-Tete provides a more sophisticated negotiation model. It allows negotiation based on multiple terms such as warranty, delivery times, service contracts, and other merchant value-added services, not merely on price as in other agent systems. Like Kasbah, the negotiation takes the form of multi-agent, bilateral bargaining. However, it does not use a simple raise and decay function as in Kasbah. Instead, Tete-a-Tete shopping agents follow an argumentative style of negotiation with sales agents and use the evaluation constraint captured in product brokering and merchant brokering stages as dimensions of a multi-attribute utility. This utility is used by a consumer's shopping agent to rank merchant offerings based on how well they satisfy the consumer's preference.

SOFTWARE AGENT TECHNOLOGY FOR ELECTRONIC COMMERCE

Most of the technologies supporting today's agent-mediated electronic commerce systems stem from AI research, including the extraction of meaning from ambiguous Web pages (Allen, 1987), planning trips (Linden, Hanks, & Lesh, 1997; Weld, 1996), learning users' music preferences (http://www.firefly.com, Shardanand & Maes, 1995), negotiating delivery contracts (Sandholm, 1993), and deciding on which car to buy (Gmytrasiewicz, Durfee, & Wehe, 1991). AI's contribution has been mainly in the development of the software agent model.

Content-Based filtering

One of the AI application domains which influences and contributes to the development of software agents is that of content-based filtering systems (Lewis & Sparck-Jones, 1996; Indrawan, Ghazfan, & Srinivasan, 1996). These systems process information from various sources and try to extract useful features and elements concerning its content. This technology is useful for product and merchant brokering.

Human Computer Interaction

Most of the current e-commerce sites provide on-line catalogues. However,they are merely enhanced price lists with search capabilities. Shoppers may still find it difficult to search the intended product. This difficulty may be reduced by a number of techniques taken from Human Computer Interaction research.

One of the approaches under consideration is the introduction of interfaces that are similar to 'real-world' interactions. This can be achieved through the use of 3D VRML technologies. The shoppers will find that they are browsing a virtual shop similar to their experience of browsing shop windows. Although promising (Richmond, 1996), these shopping environments have not yet lived up to expectations due to the awkwardness of navigating 3D worlds with 2D interfaces. The consideration of bandwidth requirement also limits the support of this interface.

Another useful approach is the introduction of virtual sales agents using animated graphical characters that interact in natural language with the consumer (http://www.extempo.com, Elliott & Brzezinski, 1998). This virtual sales agent can be used to personalize Web stores according to the particular personality of consumer.

Protocols and Programming Language

Currently, information in Web pages is delivered in format-oriented, handcrafted hypertext markup language (HTML), making it understandable only through human eyes. Software agents and search engines have difficulty using the information because it is not semantically coded. This problem can be partly overcome by using appropriate tags or software that 'scrapes' Web pages to extract contents. However, these ad-hoc approaches do not scale. Property tags require browser plug-ins and scraping approaches require a customized script for each Web site. XML, a simplified meta-language derived from SGML, is emerging as the standard for self-describing data exchange in the Internet application. XML has the ability to encode information and services with meaningful structure and semantics that computers can readily understand. However, it is still far from a complete solution. XML does not have any standards for representing high-level concepts, such as standard business process (Glushko, Tenenbaum, & Meltzer, 1999). CommerceNet and member organizations are working towards such common ontologies (Tenenbaum, Chowdhry, & Hughes, 1997).

The research in the software agents has introduced several agent-based languages and protocols such as Knowledge Query and Manipulation Language (KQML) (Finin, Fritzson, McKay, & McEntire, 1994; Mayfield, Labrou, & Finin, 1996), Knowledge Interchange Format (KIF) (http://www.logic.stanford.edu/kif), and Ontolingua (Gruber, 1992). These protocols and languages were designed to enable heterogeneous agents to communicate at the knowledge level. In electronic commerce this knowledge would include the definition and semantics of consumer profiles, merchants, goods, services, and negotiation protocols.

SECURITY ISSUES IN AN AGENT-BASED ELECTRONIC COMMERCE SYSTEM

Konrad, Fuchs, and Barthel (1999) suggest that security issues in electronic commerce depend *only partly* on technical security and the knowledge of security gaps and ways of closing them. To build a secured agent-based e-commerce system requires 'trust' on socio-technical systems, which include users, business practise and related institutions, not just 'trust' on the technical systems. With this in mind, human interaction during transaction is still desirable. Indeed, most of the current agent-based e-commerce still requires human interaction when dealing with order placement, payment authorization, and product delivery activities due to the lack of socio-technical security mechanisms that meet the level of maximum acceptable risk.

Security in electronic commerce can be seen as a multilevel security system. For example, a higher-level security is required for an agent dealing with payment authorization compared with an agent dealing with product selections. The level of security required for the application influence the degree of mobility of an agent (Jansen & Karygiannis, 1999), as depicted in Figure 2. A highly mobile agent will have a greater probability of being 'attacked' and require more difficult mechanisms in keeping track of its activities and fitness. This highly mobile agent will be appropriate to be used in the product selection stage. On the other hand, an agent that performs highly secured activity, such as payment authorization, needs to be restricted in its mobility to reduce the chances of being maliciously altered by irresponsible agents or hosts.

The vertical bar in Figure 2 represents a cutoff point for the designer to decide which agents will be static and which agents will be mobile. The decision will be made based on the available security mechanisms, performance requirements, sensitivity of the agent's code and data, maximum acceptable risk, and the level of functionality required.

Mobile Agent Security

In a mobile agent environment, both the agents and the hosts face the security threats. The degree of the threats increases with the openness of the network. In a closed Local Area Network, contained within one organization, it is possible to trust all the hosts, whereas in open network like the Internet, it is not possible to trust all the hosts. The introduction of mobile code in an open network raises several security issues:

- Protecting sensitive data in the servers/hosts from malicious agents.
- Protecting sensitive data in the agents from malicious hosts or agents.
- Protecting agent's code, control flow, and results from agents or hosts.
- Protecting the hosts from malicious agents that used up the hosts' resources and prevent other agents in the hosts from progressing.

The mobile agents systems need to be equipped with several types of security mechanisms for detecting and foiling such attacks. These include *privacy* mechanism to sensitive data and code, *authentication* mechanism to establish the identity and trust between communicating parties, and *authorization* mechanism to provide agents with controlled access to server resources. In a relatively closed market, it is possible to include a *social control* mechanism. The mechanism involves the introduction of an Electronic Institution or trusted third-party which provides necessary trust on the electronic commerce transactions between agents, supervise the agents' commitments, and provide backup/support to those users whose agents are damaged by others. The Better Business Bureau, previously mentioned, is an example of an attempt to build such a mechanism, although it is still far from ideal.

Ametas (Zapf, Helge & Kurt, 1998) is a mobile agents prototype that is aimed to support security in the electronic marketplace. It provides not only the mechanisms for encryption and integrity, but also authorization of users and agents. All these mechanisms are controlled by several policies, such as domain access policy and delegation policy.

Figure 2. Security Requirement vs. Mobility

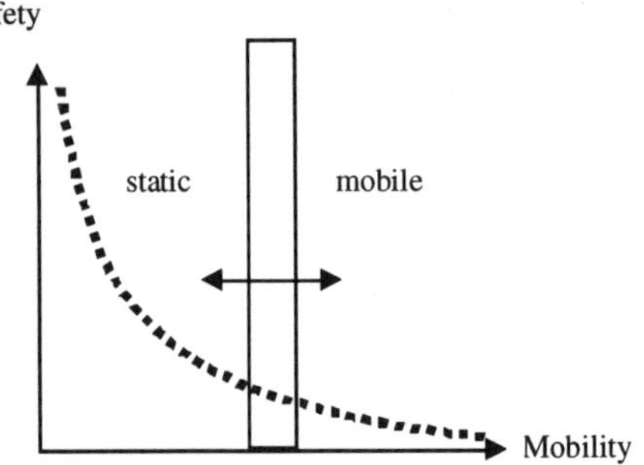

Mole (http://www.informatik.uni-stuttgart.de/ipvr/vs/projekte/mole) provides a different approach to security. It is based on the idea that an agent can only be executed "exactly once," that is, once an agent is launched, it should never be lost until its task is completed. To support this idea, Mole uses the monitor nodes to observe and monitor the activities of the agents. Similar to this approach, Kotzanikalaou, Katsirelos, and Mastorakis (1999) proposed the use of a static agent as a master agent, which controlled several slave agents, that can roam across the network.

FUTURE RESEARCH AND CHALLENGES

The challenges put forward by businesses to exploit a new way of doing business online have been partly answered by the inclusion of software agents into electronic commerce. The first generation software agent systems currently found in the Internet have provided good support to the first two stages of the buying process, namely product discovery and product/merchant search. There is some work to be done in order to support the next stage of the buying process—negotiation. The main challenge will be to find a common ontology for heterogeneous agents to communicate or exchange information during negotiation.

Providing a trusted environment in which agents may work is also a challenge for software agent researchers. Security and privacy issues will be paramount for software agent systems to be successful. The security issue should be handled at both a low level (network security) as well as a high level (ethics, game rules). Only by providing a good level of support of both low-level and high-level security, can the purchase consummation stage be implemented using agent technologies.

The next generation of software agents for electronic commerce needs to be able to facilitate commerce within complex multimedia information systems. Research areas such as speech recognition, image recognition, and natural language will play a major role in making this requirement a reality. Providing more natural human-computer interaction is also required of next generation software agent systems. The fulfillment of these requirements will transform on-line commerce activities in such a way that they are made closer to commercial activities in the physical world.

CONCLUSION

Agent technologies provide a new approach to conduct electronic commerce. Early electronic commerce applications based on EDI are concentrated on providing business-to-business interaction. Agent technologies have enabled support for both business-to-business and customer-to-business interactions. Another advantage of agent-based e-commerce is the relatively low setup cost compared with the EDI. Agent systems can use the existing network infrastructure such as the Internet to support their operations, which in turn can reduce the setup cost. In addition, the fact that the Internet is globally available, benefits suppliers/merchants by providing a larger market.

Agents can also help merchants in automating their market research activities by monitoring consumer's buying behavior in the Internet. This can be achieved by exchanging information with the buyer's agent or other merchant's agent.

From the point of view of consumers, agent-based e-commerce provides advantage by reducing, if not eliminating, the tedious task of product selection and negotiation. Agent systems will also enable consumers to perform near-exhaustive searches of suitable products and suppliers.

The major disadvantage of an agent-based system would be the level of security risk involved. The risk would increase as the mobility of the agent increases. Mobile agents have a high risk of getting their information/program changed by malicious agents or hosts. There are some security measures that can be applied to reduce this risk, however, it is still far from ideal. The security requirements of an agent-based e-commerce system are multifaceted because they encompass technical and social consideration. Until the security risk involved is reduced to the level accepted by the users, we will see that fully automated purchasing using agents will not be popular because the consumers would not trust the systems. For this reason, existing agent-based electronic commerce systems limit their implementation to product discovery, selection, and negotiation. They still require a human to manually place the order and conduct the payment. Of course, it does not mean that electronic transaction cannot be used. Electronic transactions using digital cash still can be used. However, the actual authorization of the order placement and payment will be performed by a human, instead of automatically performed by agents.

The development of agent-based electronic commerce is still in the infancy stage. It promises to deliver efficient customer-to-business and business-to-business support. The realization of its full potential will depend on the improvement in the agent technologies, especially in the area of security and negotiation model.

REFERENCES

Allen, J. (1987). *Natural Language Understanding*. Benjamin Cummings.

Axelrod, R. (1984). *The Evolution of Cooperation*. Harper Collins.

Bakos, Y. (1997). Reducing buyer search costs : Implications for electronic marketplaces. *Management Science, 43*(12).

Chavez, A., Dreilinger, D., Guttman, R., & Maes, P. (1997). A Real Life Experiment in Creating and Agent Marketplace. *Proceedings of the Second International Conference on Practical Application of Intelligent Agents and Multi-Agent Technology (PAAM'97)*, London, UK.

Doorenbos, R., Etzioni, O., & Weld, D. A Scalable Comparison –Shopping Agent for World Wide Web. *Proceedings of the First International Conference on Autonomous Agents (Agents'97)*, Marina del Rey, CA.

Elliott, C., & Brzezinski, J.(1998). Autonomous Agents as Synthetic Characters. *AI Magazine 19(2)*, 13-30.

Finin, T., Fritzson, R., McKay, D., & McEntire, R. (1994). KQML as an Agent Communication Language. *Proceedings of the Third International Conference on Information and*

Knowledge Management, 456-463.

Glushko, R.J., Tenebaum, J.M., & Meltzer, B. (1999). An XML Framework for Agent-based E-commerce. *ACM Communication, 42(3)*, 106-114.

Gmytrasiewicz, P., Durfee, E., & Wehe, D. (1991). A Decision Theoretic Approach to Coordinating Multi-agent Interactions. *Proceedings of the Eleventh International Joint Conference on Artificial Intelligence.*

Gruber, T. (1992). *Ontolingua: A Mechanism to Support Portable Ontologies,* Technical Report KSL 91-66), Stanford University Knowledge Systems Laboratory.

Guttman, R., & Maes, P. (1998). Agent-mediated Integrative Negotiation for Retail Electronic Commerce. *Proceedings of the Workshop on Agent Mediated Electronic Trading (AMET'98)*, Minneapolis, Minnesota.

Indrawan, M., Ghazfan, D., & Srinivasan, B. (1996). Bayesian Network as a Retrieval Engine. *Proceedings of the Fifth Text Retrieval Conference*, 437-444.

Jansen, W., & Karygiannis, T. (1999). *Mobile Agent Security* (NIST Special Publication 800-19), National Institute of Standards and Technology, Gaithersburg, MD, USA.

Jennings, N. R., Sycara, K., & Wooldridge, M. (1998). A Roadmap of Agent Research and Development. *Autonomous Agents and Multi-Agent Systems, 1.* Kluwer Academic Publisher, Boston, 275-306.

Kalakota, R., & Whinston, A. B. (1996) . *Electronic Commerce—A Manager's Guide.* Addison Wesley.

Konrad, K., Fuchs, G., & Barthel, J. (1999). Trust and Electronic Commerce—More than a Technical Problem. *Proceedings of the Eighteenth Symposium on Reliable Distributed Systems*, Lausanne, Switzerland, IEEE Computer Society, 360-365.

Kotzanikolaou, P., Katsirelos, G., & Chrissikopoulos, V. (1999). Mobile Agents for Secure Electronic Transactions. Mastorakis, N.E. (Ed.), *Recent Advances in Signal Processing and Communications*, World Scientific Engineering Society, 363-368.

Lewis, D.D., & Sparck-Jones, K. (1996). Natural Language Processing for Information Retrieval. *ACM Communication, 39(1)*, 92-101.

Linden, G., Hanks, S., & Lesh, N. (1997). Interactive Assessment of User Preference Models: The Automated Travel Assistant. *Proceedings of the Sixth International Conference on User Modeling.*

Ma, M. (1999). Agents in E-commerce. *ACM Communications, 42(3)*, 79-80.

Maes, P. (1994). Agents that Reduce Work and Information Overload. *ACM Communication, 37(7)*, 31-40.

Mayfield, J., Labrou, Y., & Finin, T. (1996). Evaluating KQML as an agent communication language. In Wooldrige, M., Muller, J.P., and Tambe, M. (Eds.), *Intelligent Agents II (LNAI Vol. 1037)*, 347-360.

Nwana, H.S. (1993). Software Agents: An Overview. *Knowledge Engineering Review, 11(3)*, 1-40.

Richmond, A. (1996). Enticing On-line Shoppers to Buy – A Human Behavior Study. *Proceedings of the Fifth International World Wide Web Conference*, France.

Rodriquez, J., Noriega, P., Sierra, C., & Garcia, P. (1998). Competitive Scenarios for Heterogeneous Trading Agents. *Proceedings of the Second International Conference in Autonomous Agents (Agents'98).*

Rodriquez, J., Noriega, P., Sierra, C., & Padget, J. (1997). FM96.5: A Java-based Electronic Auction House. *Proceedings of the Second International Conference on the Practical Application of Intelligent Agents and Multi-Agent Technology (PAAM'97)*, London, UK.

Sandholm, T. (1993). An Implementation of the Contract Net Protocol Based on Marginal Cost Calculations. *Proceedings of the Eleventh National Conference on Artificial Intelligence (AAAI'93)*, Wahington DC.

Shardanand, U., & Maes, P. (1995). Social Information Filtering: Algorithm for Automating 'Word of Mouth'. *Proceedings of the Computer-Human Interaction Conference (CHI'95)*, Denver, CO, May 1995.

Sierra, C., Faratin, P., & Jennings, N. (1997). A Service-Oriented Negotiation Model Between Autonomous Agents. *Proceedings of the Eighth European Workshop on Modeling Autonomous Agents in a Multi-Agent World (MAAMAW'97)*, Ronneby, Sweden.

Tenenbaum, J., Chowdhry, T., & Hughes, K. (1997). eCo System: An Internet Commerce Architecture. *Computer* 30(5), 48-55.

Weld, D. (1996). Planning-Based Control on Software Agents. *The Third International Conference on Artificial Intelligence Planning Systems (AIPS'96)*, Edinburgh, Scotland.

Wuman, P., Wellman, M., & Walsh, W. (1998). The Michigan Internet AuctionBot: A Configurable Auction Server for Human and Software Agents. *Proceedings of the Second International Conference on Autonomous Agents* (Agents'98), May.

Zapf, M., Helge, M., & Kurt, G. (1998). Security Requirements for Mobile Agents in Electronic Markets. *Proceedings of the International IFIP/GI Working Conference, TREC'98, Lecture Notes on Computer Science Vol. 1402*, Springer-Verlag, 205-217.

Chapter VI

Software Agents in Today's Digital Economy: Transition to the Knowledge Society

Mahesh S. Raisinghani
University of Dallas, USA

"The future business culture will be one in which innovation is necessary, learning is constant, organizations need to act collaboratively, and work is its own reward...It will not be business. It will not be government. It is the social sector that may yet save the society." ——Peter F. Drucker

EXECUTIVE SUMMARY

One of the most discussed topics in the information systems literature today is software agent/intelligent agent technology. Software agents are high-level software abstractions with inherent capabilities for communication, decision making, control, and autonomy. They are programs that perform functions such as information gathering, information filtering, or mediation (running in the background) on behalf of a person or entity. They have several aliases such as agents, bots, chatterbots, databots, intellibots, and intelligent software agents/robots. They provide a powerful mechanism to address complex software engineering problems such as abstraction, encapsulation, modularity, reusability, concurrency, and distributed operations. Much research has been devoted to this topic, and more and more new software products billed as having intelligent agent functionality are being introduced on the market every day. The research that is being done, however, does not wholeheartedly endorse this trend.

The current research into intelligent agent software technology can be divided into two main areas: technological and social. The latter area is particularly important since, in the excitement of new and emergent technology, people often forget to examine what impact the new technology will have on people's lives. In fact, the social dimension of all technology is the driving force and most important consideration of technology itself. This chapter presents a socio-technical perspective on intelligent agents and proposes a framework based on the data lifecycle and knowledge discovery using intelligent agents. One of the key ideas of this chapter is best stated by Peter F. Drucker in Management Challenges for the 21st Century *when he suggests that in this period of profound social and economic changes, managers should focus on the meaning of information, not the technology that collects it.*

INTRODUCTION

Although there is no firm consensus on what constitutes an intelligent agent, there are certain characteristics that intelligent agents (also referred to as software agents in this chapter) display. When a new task is delegated by the user, an intelligent agent determines precisely what its goal is, evaluates how the goal can be reached in an effective manner, and performs the necessary actions. It learns from its past experience in order to respond to unforeseen situations with adaptive, self-starting, and temporal continuous reasoning strategies. It needs to be not only cooperative and mobile in order to perform its tasks by interacting with other agents, but also reactive and autonomous to sense the status quo and act independently to make progress towards its goal (Baek et al., 1999; Wang, 1999). Software agents are goal-directed and possess abilities such as autonomy, collaborative behavior, and inferential capability. Intelligent agents can take different forms, but an intelligent agent can initiate and make decisions without human intervention and has the capability to infer appropriate high-level goals from user actions and requests and take actions to achieve these goals (Huang, 1999; Nardi et al., 1998; Wang, 1999). The intelligent software agent is a computational entity that can adapt to the environment, making it capable of interacting with other agents and transporting itself across different systems in a network. "The state of the running program is saved, transported to the new host, and restored, allowing the program to continue where it left off" (Kotz and Gray, 1999).

The following is a roadmap of this chapter. This chapter takes a closer look at the current state of research on intelligent agents by first examining the technological issues. This is followed by discussion of the transition to the knowledge society and the data lifecycle and knowledge discovery using intelligent agents, and then a proposal for an integrated framework in the form of a sense-making model of knowledge management for new business environments. Next, the social and ethical implications of intelligent agent software technology are discussed, followed by a summary and conclusion.

THE CURRENT STATE OF RESEARCH ON SOFTWARE AGENTS

Software agents were first used several years ago to automate repetitive behavior in simple tasks such as filtering and sorting information and making basic price comparisons (Maes et al., 1999; Kirsner, 1999). This first phase of software agents has been superceded by sophisticated software agents that keep a detailed profile of demographics and psychographics and can track interests and preferences in order to offer customized services in business-to-business, business-to-consumer, and consumer-to-consumer e-commerce based on some embedded mobility meta-data (Maes, 1999; Wong et al., 1999). In automated negotiation in retail e-commerce, electricity markets, manufacturing planning and scheduling, distributed vehicle routing among independent dispatch centers, and electronic trading of financial instruments, computational agents find and prepare contracts on behalf of the real-world parties they represent (Sandholm, 1999). Examples of intelligent software agents in e-commerce include Andersen Consulting's BargainFinder (http://bf.cstar.ac.com/bf/) and Lifestyle Finder (www.lifestyle.cstar.ac.com/lifestyle) in the virtual retailing domain; Agents Inc.'s Firefly (www.firefly.com) and Open Sesame (www.opensesame.com) using collaborative filtering and behavior-based user profiling respectively; and Monster Board's (www.monster.com) use of intelligent search engines to help job seekers find jobs on the Internet (Turban et al., 1999). Gloshko et al. (1999) believe that over time, most merchant Web sites will provide agent-searchable catalogs that supply product descriptions and information about price and availability. The stage is set for several applications that can benefit from the mobile agent paradigm: personal assistance by monitoring and notifying/information dissemination (sometimes manifested in intelligence tools to combat or predict criminal activity by aiding in case investigation, such as the Coplink Concept Space application, which uncovers relationships between different types of information in Tucson Police Department's records management system), secure brokering, distributed information retrieval, telecommunication networks services, work flow applications, and parallel processing (Lange & Oshima, 1999; Hauk & Chen, 1999).

Agent technology, particularly intelligent agent technology, is one of the most discussed topics in information systems literature today. Much research and many articles have been devoted to this topic, and more and more new software products billed as having intelligent agent functionality are being introduced on the market every day. The articles and research that are being done on this topic, though, do not wholeheartedly endorse this trend. A growing number of computer information professionals recognize that there are certain problems and issues surrounding intelligent agent terminology and technology that must be resolved if agent technology is to continue to develop and mature. The current research into intelligent agent software technology can be divided into two main areas: technological and social. The latter area is particularly important since, in the excitement of new and emergent technology, people often forget to examine what impact the new technology will have on people's lives. In fact, the social dimension of technology is the driving force and most important consideration of technology itself. The technology is not created and produced for its own sake, but to improve people's lives. Technology and computers and software are not created simply to see what the human mind can achieve; they are created for the sake of human beings.

TECHNOLOGICAL ISSUES

The first and most fundamental technological aspect that must be considered is what constitutes an intelligent software agent. What is the definition of an intelligent software agent? It is here that the first major problem for intelligent agent technology emerges. "In order for this term [intelligent agent] to have any effectiveness, there must first be a universal definition that can be agreed upon and used consistently" (Vinaja and Sircar, 1999). Unfortunately, though, there is in fact no commonly agreed upon definition of an intelligent agent or even an (software) agent. Many proposals for a formal definition of "intelligent agent" have been made, but none has been widely accepted (Franklin and Graesser, 1996). The following are a few of the more promising definitions:

> "An agent is anything that can be viewed as perceiving its environment through sensors and acting upon that environment through effectors." (Russell and Norvig, 1995)

"Let us define an agent as a persistent software entity dedicated to a specific purpose. 'Persistent' distinguishes agents from subroutines; agents have their own ideas about how to accomplish tasks, their own agendas. 'Special purpose' distinguishes them from other entire multifunction applications; agents are typically much smaller." (Smith, Cypher, and Spohrer, 1994)

"Intelligent agents are software entities that carry out some set of operations on behalf of a user or another program with some degree of independence or autonomy, and in so doing, employ some knowledge or representation of the user's goals or desires." ("The IBM Agent")

"An **autonomous agent** is a system situated within and a part of an environment that senses that environment and acts on it, over time, in pursuit of its own agenda and so as to effect what it senses in the future." (Franklin and Graesser, 1996)

"Autonomous agents are computational systems that inhabit some complex dynamic environment, sense and act autonomously in this environment and by doing so realize a set of goals or tasks for which they are designed." (Maes, 1994).

Some of the key terms found in the preceding definitions are: sensing, environment, persistent, 'own agendas,' autonomy, goals, and knowledge. Ma (1999) defines intelligent/mobile/multi-system/profiling agents as working through actions and characterizes agents as "atomic, software entities that operate through autonomous actions on behalf of the user-machines and humans—without human intervention." Each of these terms seems to appropriately describe characteristics of an intelligent agent, yet none of them has gained wide recognition as *the* definition of a software (intelligent) agent. Woolridge and Jennings (1996) give a compelling reason why a definition consensus has not yet been reached. They point out that agent technology is so popular partly because the idea of an agent is extremely intuitive. The intuitive aspect of the term "intelligent agent" has resulted in many different ideas of what an agent is. As Franklin and Graesser (1996) point out, most of the definitions proposed thus far seem to have originated from particular examples that the people who have proposed the definitions already had in mind. It is important to note here that the same intuitive aspect of the term "intelligent agent," while making it difficult to establish a broadly accepted formal definition, actually makes marketing a product billed as incorporating intelligent agent software technology much easier.

Another reason that a consensus has not been reached is that much of the agent research is proprietary. Companies that sponsor the research do not want to give away their work for free, since they have made significant monetary contributions to that research. The problem is analogous to that experienced with object technology. Standardization of new technology is difficult because no one wants to give away their work, especially to would-be competitors. Intelligent agent technology will continue to suffer from this difficulty either until the companies and individuals with the proprietary information recognize that sharing it will benefit everyone, including themselves, or until they recoup enough of their expenditures to feel justified in making their research available. Moreover, it is not possible to discuss standardization of intelligent agents because they should be unique and customized for each business application separately.

A third reason for the difficulty in reaching a generally approved definition of what comprises an intelligent software agent, which is probably the most important reason of the three outlined in this chapter, is that so-called intelligent agent software does not seem to be qualitatively different from any other software. "Is it an agent, or just a program?" (Franklin and Graesser, 1996). In their article of the same title as the previous question, Franklin and Graesser note, correctly, that all software agents are programs. They go on to state that not all programs are agents, the implication being that some programs, then, are in fact agents.

This third reason for the difficulty in reaching a generally approved definition of "intelligent agent software" revolves around a key term, "quality." The term "intelligent agent" does not simply mean a more complicated program. If it did, not much controversy would have been generated about what an intelligent software agent actually is. If "intelligent agent" only signified a more complicated program, the term "intelligent agent" would mean that a so-called intelligent agent software program was simply more complex and possibly more useful than other typical computer programs. This sense of "intelligent agent" is a *quantitative* sense.

However, those who are doing research into so-called intelligent agent software technology do not mean that an intelligent agent is only more complicated than other computer programs. A so-called intelligent agent is two *qualitative* steps removed from a mere computer program. First it is an agent. An agent is, broadly speaking, someone or something that acts. Examples of more widely known agent systems include AuctionBot, BargainFinder, Firefly and Kasbah. Agents such as DealTime already comb the catalogs of on-line sellers to keep an eye on what prices are right for interested shoppers, then relay the opportunity back to the shopper to pursue. Some other agents are also able to channel the accumulation of user preferences into personalization services like those that recommend books or movies, based on user ratings of a given set of titles. To understand the potential for intermediaries, imagine adding a bidding agent to the mix. It is just a matter of time before the agents are sophisticated enough to act by making less risky purchases themselves, as on-line bill payment systems do for routine or small bills. Smart refrigerators will be able to order provisions when they run low, and cars will be able to automatically call up maps of any given area. Day traders may replace themselves with automated day traders that buy certain stocks under a specific price and sell once they reach higher prices. However, in order to act, the thing that acts must have a purpose or a goal. This is included in the third and fourth proposed definitions set forth earlier. Do any computer programs have their own goals or purposes? Not really. All a computer program does is perform a set of instructions that were programmed into it. An intelligent software agent is no different from any other computer program in this respect. It simply has more possibilities than less complicated computer programs.

Even if we do grant that a computer program may act, it certainly does not act autonomously as the fourth definition asserts. For something to act autonomously, it must have independence and freedom. Philosophically, for something to be autonomous, it must have knowledge of what it is doing and it must *will* to do what it is doing. Computer programs do not *will* to do anything. Whatever they do is programmed into them. Again, we reiterate that the program may be quite complex and be able to react to many different events, but the key is that the computer simply reacts, it does not act on its own.

The word "react" further clarifies the inherent limitations of computer programs and why they cannot truly be called intelligent or autonomous agents. An agent, in the true sense of the word, initiates action. True agents are proactive as well as reactive. They have beliefs, intentions, and desires. It is absurd to speak of computer programs of any sort as having desires. This, then, sums up the problems with calling computer programs "intelligent agents." Due to the various difficulties that have been raised concerning calling specific computer programs intelligent agents, it is rather unlikely that a formal definition of an intelligent software agent will ever be satisfactorily formulated.

This leaves us with a question. What are we to make of the all of the software currently on the market or in production that is billed as having intelligent agent functionality? Certainly we do not wish to demean all of the research that has gone into these products. Products such as e-mail filters, help engines (e.g., the Microsoft Chapterclip), data warehousing tools, news filters, etc. all have the potential to be highly useful to human beings. But look at how they work. They are all based on the detection of patterns in conjunction with explicit user commands and preferences. At their core, all of these computer programs are based on pure mathematics and logic. The e-mail filters reject messages which do not comply to the user's defined preferences. The news filters may be more complex than the e-mail filters in that they search the Internet for news in user-defined subject areas. The help engines and data warehousing tools search for patterns, but the programs do not generate the patterns on their own. They have the patterns built into them.

The news and searching tools (often marketed as intelligent agents), while having great potential given the explosion of information accessible on the Internet, pose an interesting problem. The problem is this: if many users have news searching "intelligent agent" tools constantly searching for information on the Internet, isn't it likely that the Internet may be clogged up by too many of these searching tools? It is likely that each person would have quite a number of these programs running in order to get a wide variety of information. To further complicate this picture, there is also the possibility that these "intelligent agents" will be programmed with the capability to spawn other agents. Imagine if one of these agents had an error (bug) built in which caused the program to continuously spawn agents to search the Internet. What if each one of these spawned programs also spawned other programs to search the Internet?

Furthermore, it is conceivable that a certain number of the agents searching the Internet for information would get lost, that is, they would not return with the requested information to the entity which spawned them. Thus, one can begin see the technical dangers in having such "intelligent agents." They might create severe bottlenecks on the already crowded Internet.

BENEFITS OF INTELLIGENT AGENTS: APPLICATIONS IN E-COMMERCE

There are potentially many reasons for using intelligent agents. Three reasons will be discussed. First, intelligent agents can assist an organization tremendously by reducing support costs. A study done by Jupiter Communications (Kirley et al., 1999) suggests that there is solid rationale to justify on-line systems to handle pre-sale product inquiries, post-sales first-level support, and general Web site service requests. It is recommended for sites generating more than 15,000 service incidents per month to consider implementing chatter bots and systems for auto-response e-mail. This could have a positive ROI for the organization if implemented properly. The first area we should look at automating is the first-level Customer Service Representative (CSR) position.

Jupiter Communications (Kirley et al., 1999) made the following assumptions in their study:

- The automated system would cost about $250,000.
- This system would reduce 25% of service requests with remaining service requests being escalated to the CSR.

- A first-level CSR has a base salary of approximately $28,000 per year. This model does not account for any other savings realized by a reduction in the number of staff or physical plant.

Most of the inquiries to first-level CSRs are very basic and simple and could be addressed by a chatter bot, knowledge base, or e-mail auto-response. For example, if you hired 10 first-level CSRs, which amounts to $280,000 per year vs. $250,000 per year, you will have generated an extra $30,000 in operating expenses that could have been saved. As you can see, over the long run you will have substantial savings in implementing this system to address first-level CSR requests instead of hiring more CSRs. In turn, this will lead to increased customer satisfaction, because the customer will get immediate answers to simple requests, and complex requests that do not map to the intelligent agent's technologies algorithm will be routed to a live CSR.

Second, intelligent agents can assist in addressing the issue of "information overload." They can filter out unnecessary information through powerful search engine technology that enables users to retrieve information that is relevant and specific to them. This is an incredible benefit that any user can benefit from immensely. It not only saves the user hours of time in doing a search, but also can be used as a mechanism for researching and shopping by allowing the user to negotiate through the use of intelligent agent technology once he/she filters down to the exact items he/she is interested in purchasing. A great example of this technology is the product BullsEye 2, a search engine with customizable intelligent agents (Dow Jones Interactive Newsstand, 2000a).

Third, intelligent agents can assist tremendously in system management by automating many tasks and providing useful alert mechanisms to request human involvement when necessary. Ultimately, the goal would be to have a self-healing system that would correct itself when it encounters potential system problems. Some excellent examples of this are *Social Intelligence Server* from NetSage and Unicenter Neugents from Computer Associates. The recent announcement of this technology for Windows NT is but a first step on a long road that may well bring us to the world of truly self-managing systems (Mason, 1998; Muller, 1998). This technology uses a predictive model that will warn of an impending problem before it actually occurs. Additional applications of intelligent agents include operating systems agents, spreadsheet agents, user interface agents, workflow and task management agents, software development agents, and negotiation agents. Intelligent agents will become more critical as networks continue to grow on an international basis. More importantly, in today's global economy, having the capability to effectively monitor local and remote systems will be essential for organizations that are under pressure to minimize staff and reduce operating costs.

TRANSITIONING TO THE KNOWLEDGE SOCIETY

The transition from the industrial age to the information age to the knowledge age is a continuum that is evolutionary. A final destination will never be reached, since new knowledge and experiences are continually added and refined and outside forces can create a change in corporate strategy. Although there have been several definitions of knowledge management published, the one which conveys the concept best in the context of this chapter is by Malhotra (1999):

> "Knowledge Management caters to the critical issues of organizational adoption, survival, and competence in the face of increasingly discontinuous environmental change. Essentially it embodies organizational process that seeks synergistic

combination of data and information processing capacity of information technologies, and the creative and innovative capacity of human beings."

This definition not only recognizes the discontinuous environment but also the importance of both techno-centric and sociocentric approaches. Jacobs (1996) refers to four phases in the development of the knowledge-based economy, which overlap to some extent. In the first phase, there is an increasing importance of information by virtue of information and communication technologies being applied. In the second phase, there is a shorter product/technology lifecycle. In the third phase, there is an evolution from the supply-side economy to the demand-side economy, with the growing importance of consumers and their individual wishes. This is one area where intelligent software agents can help with knowledge mining of customer profiles by collecting and analyzing the customer's demographic, psychographic and geographic information. The fourth phase is the rising of the network economy, in which human networks are crucial for dealing with specialization and the combination of different forms of knowledge. The traditional view of knowledge management mostly relies on the prepackaged or taken for granted interpretation of the knowledge. Such knowledge is generally static and does not encourage the generation of multiple and contradictory viewpoints in a highly dynamic and ever-changing environment. The concepts of "best practices" and "efficiency optimization" cannot provide the competitive advantage that companies may be striving for. This is where the concept of intelligent agents acting as catalysts of knowledge management is not only effective but also essential for the organization's survival.

According to Churchman (1971): "To conceive of knowledge as a collection of information seems to rob the concept of all its life...Knowledge resides in the user and not in the collection. It is how the user reacts to a collection of information that matters." Intelligent agents can facilitate the process of filtering and reacting to information. Since they are heterogeneous, robust, fault-tolerant, and able to encapsulate protocols, adapt dynamically and execute asynchronously and autonomously, they can reduce the network load, and overcome network latency (Lange and Oshima, 1999). Kotz and Gray (1999) state that the rise in the use of mobile agent technology on the Internet will be due to several factors such as availability of increased bandwidth, need of technology to ease information overload, increasing need for individual customization to meet user expectations, increasing use of mobile devices, dependence of Internet technology by mobile users, and proxy sites which will provide for the specific needs of individual users.

A case in point is the footwear manufacturer Nike, which does not own any factories and whose physical assets are a much smaller part of its total worth than its knowledge assets. Thus it is more appropriate to label Nike as a knowledge company instead of a manufacturer of footwear, since the real value of their company is their knowledge and expertise in designing and marketing products, not manufacturing them. The next section takes a closer look at the transformation of data into knowledge and proposes a sense-making model of knowledge management for new business environments.

DATA LIFECYCLE AND KNOWLEDGE DISCOVERY USING INTELLIGENT AGENTS: A PROPOSED FRAMEWORK

To better understand how to manage data and knowledge, it is necessary to trace how and where data flows in organizations. Businesses do not run on data. They run on information and their knowledge of how to put that information to use successfully. Knowledge fuels results. Everything from innovative product designs to brilliant competitive moves relies on knowledge. Therefore, knowledge has already been an underlying component of business. However, tacit and/or explicit knowledge is not readily available, especially in today's rapidly changing world. In many cases, knowledge is continuously derived from data. However, such a derivation may not be simple or easy (Turban, Mclean, and Wetherbe, 1999).

The transformation of data into knowledge may be accomplished in several ways. In general, it is a process that starts with data collection from various sources. These data are stored in a database. Then the data can be preprocessed and stored in a data warehouse. To discover knowledge, the processed data may go through a transformation that makes it ready for analysis. The analysis is done with data mining tools, which look for patterns, and intelligent systems, which support data interpretation. The result of all these activities is generated knowledge. Both the data, at various times during the process, and the knowledge, derived at the end of the process, may need to be presented to users. Such a presentation can be accomplished by using presentation tools, and the created knowledge may be stored in a knowledge base (Turban, Mclean, and Wetherbe, 1999).

It is essential to develop a system architecture for implementation of a knowledge management system. Brook Manville, Director of Knowledge Management at the consulting firm McKinsey & Co. in Boston, proposes three architectures needed for implementing a shift from traditional emphasis on transaction processing, integrated logistics, and work flows to systems that support competencies for communication building. This conceptualization is proposed in the form of a sense-making model of knowledge management for new business environments. The framework proposed is:

- A new information architecture that includes new languages, categories, and metaphors for identifying and accounting for skills and competencies.
- A new technical architecture that is more social, transparent, open, flexible, and respectful of the individual user.
- A new application architecture oriented towards problem solving and representation, rather than output and transactions.

The application of this framework will facilitate business model innovation necessary for sustainable competitive advantage in the new business environment characterized by dynamic, discontinuous, and radically paced change. This proposed architecture helps integrate the key ideas of this chapter, i.e., a socio-technical perspective of intelligent agents facilitating the transition to the knowledge society. The social and ethical implications are discussed in the next section.

SOCIAL AND ETHICAL IMPLICATIONS

In *Management Challenges for the 21st Century*, Peter F. Drucker suggests that in this period of profound social and economic changes, managers should focus on the meaning of information, not the technology that collects it. The social implications, as might be expected with a relatively new and partially developed technology, include both positive and negative issues. The author recognizes that the current discussion and research into intelligent agent software technology deals quite sparingly on the topic of the social and ethical implications of this new technology. This lack of serious consideration of the impact of intelligent agent software technology on people's lives is a problem that this chapter hopes to begin to address.

The first area that must be addressed is the philosophical nature of technology itself. Technology is created by human beings for human beings. According to Quinn (1992), technology has created major new opportunities for improved productivity and value added in many areas. All new technology must be tested in order to see if it meets the requirements of the person(s) who have invented it, and one of the tests must be: does the new technology provide significantly more benefit to mankind, or a portion of mankind, than it causes harm? This is the most general test of any new technology, and it is also the most important, since if the new technology fails this test, it should not be implemented at all. So let us apply this test to the new intelligent agent software technology.

To begin with, let us consider the positive aspects of intelligent agents. One of the benefits of intelligent agents is that they have the potential to assist humans in the tedious work of searching for information on the Internet/World Wide Web. The amount of information and data both on the Internet and in corporate databases is already enormous, and it is continuing to grow exponentially. For any given search by a human being, however, much of the information available on the Internet and in databases is of little value. The intelligent agent is supposed to aid in the search by filtering out information and data which is of little or no value, with little human intervention. If the intelligent agents are successful in this task, they certainly can provide a significant benefit to human beings.

Unfortunately, intelligent agents also have the potential to harm human beings. First, if human beings rely too much on intelligent agents, they (human beings) may possibly lose too much freedom. This is a problem with technology and computers in general. A very good article by Jaron Lanier describes in detail the potentially harmful effects of technology on humans. Lanier objects to the use of the words "intelligent agent" to describe any type of computer program. His argument centers around the concept that computers contribute substantially to the dulling of the human mind and human creativity. Confining oneself to an artificial world created by some human programmer(s) does limit human potential. This argument, though, lends itself more to the development of children's minds rather than human beings in general.

Another objection Lanier raises is that human beings end up degrading and lowering themselves when they accept computer programs as "intelligent agents." This argument is more applicable than the first to human beings in general. While information technology professionals and others who know what intelligent agents actually are and how they function realize the limitations and scope of so-called intelligent agents, the general public who are the intended audience and users of intelligent agents are less aware of those inner-workings and limitations. These are the people whom Lanier suggests will be psychologically harmed by "intelligent agent" terminology. When individuals begin to think of computers as actually possessing intelligence and autonomy, they will begin to treat the computers like people rather than the (helpful) tools which they are intended to be. The result of treating computers like people will actually be that people begin to view themselves and others around them as computers. "As a consequence of unavoidable psychological algebra, the person starts to think of himself as being like the computer" (Lanier). This is a serious problem that must be avoided at all costs.

Another more technical problem that Lanier raises is this:

> "If info-consumers see the world through agent's eyes, then advertising will transform into the art of controlling agents, through bribing, hacking, whatever. You can imagine an 'arms race' between armor-plated agents and hacker-laden ad agencies."

The point here is that if intelligent agents are used to find useful information, what will end up happening is that the agents themselves will be manipulated by producers of goods and services. Imagine an agent that is searching for airline flight information being manipulated by the various advertising agents sent out by the more clever airline companies. This problem is not insurmountable for those creating intelligent agents, but it is a significant problem that needs to be addressed.

SUMMARY AND CONCLUSION

The technological, social, and ethical issues notwithstanding, the new business environment is characterized not only by a rapid pace of change but also the dynamically discontinuous nature of such change. This new business environment requires a re-conceptualization of knowledge management as it has been understood in information systems practice and research. In conclusion, knowledge management is a process, not a technology. However, technology's importance as an enabler of the process should not be ignored. The infrastructure and technological functionality needed to support knowledge management will be the topic of future research.

Perhaps the toughest part about knowledge management—besides defining it—is finding what you need when you need it. While intelligent agent technology has potential to be useful to mankind, many fundamental problems remain to be solved. These problems are both technical and social or ethical in origin, and require careful thought and consideration by those who are developing intelligent agent technology. This chapter has been critical of the current state of intelligent agent software technology in the hope of making these developers aware of problems they do not seem to have taken into account. The issues such as lack of standardization in mobile agents may cause lack of identity traceability due to multiple transfers among networks. The security concerns relate to machine protection without artificially limiting agent access rights. Finally, there are issues surrounding performance and scalability, such as the performance effects that high levels of security would have on the network, as well as the effects of having multiple mobile agents in the same system. These issues are fundamental to the well-being of those for whom intelligent agent technology is ultimately intended, and need to be carefully considered. Intelligent agent software technology has made some progress but has much, further to go before it can and should be accepted as a tool to improve the quality of people's lives. The emergence of intelligent mobile/software agents not only will change the way that we communicate across networks, but also have a profound impact on the way that we accomplish many tasks.

REFERENCES

Baek, S., Liebowitz, J., Srinivas P., and Granger, M. (1999). Intelligent agents for knowledge management—toward intelligent Web-based collaboration within virtual teams. In J. Liebowitz (Ed.), *Knowledge Management Handbook* (pp. 11-1–11-23). Boca Raton: CRC Press LLC.

IntelliSeek BullsEye 2, the ultimate Web search application, becomes a desktop portal and it's free! (2000a). *Dow Jones Interactive Newsstand*, January 18, 1–2.

HP E-Service innovation uses intelligent-agent technology to provide a personalized shopping experience. (2000b). *Dow Jones Interactive Newsstand*, January 28, 1–2.

Franklin, S., and Graesser, A. (1996). Is it an agent, or just a program?: A taxonomy for autonomous agents. *Proceedings of the Third International Workshop on Agent Theo-*

ries, Architectures, and Languages. New York: Springer-Verlag.

Glushko, R. J., Tenenbaum, J. M., and Meltzer, B. (1999). An XML framework for agent-based e-commerce. *Communications of the ACM*, 42(3), 106–109. Available: ABI/ Inform Abstracts, http://rupert.alc.org/library/web2/pex frame.htm [October 19, 1999].

Hauk, R.V., and Chen, H. (1999). Coplink: A case of intelligent analysis and knowledge management. *Proceedings of the Twentieth Annual International Conference on Information Systems*, Charlotte: ICIS.

Huang, M. J. (1999). Intelligent diagnosing and learning agents for intelligent tutoring systems. *Journal of Computer Information Systems*, Fall, 45–50.

Kerley, D., Seamus, M., and Graves, L. (1999). Automating service: Reducing support costs through bots and agents—Outlook: Marketplace ripe for intelligent service solutions. *Jupiter Communications*, March, 1–2.

Kirsner, S. (1999). The bots are back. *CIO, 12:14*, Section 2, 26–28.

Kotz, D., and Gray, R. (1999). Mobile agents and the future of the Internet. *ACM Operating Systems Review, August.*

Jacobs, D. (1996). Het kennisoffensief. Slim concurren in de kenniseconomie. *Alphen aan den Rijn/Diegem.*

Lange, D. B., and Oshima, M. (1999). Dispatch your agents, shut off your machine. *Communications of the ACM, 42(3)*, 88–89.

Lanier, J. Agents of Alienation. Available: http://www.well.com/user/jaron/agentalien.html.

Ma, M. (1999). Agents in e-commerce. *Communications of the ACM, 42(3)*, 78–80.

Maes, P. (1994). Agents that reduce work and information overload. *Communications of the ACM*, July, 108.

Maes, P. (1999). Smart commerce: The future of intelligent agents in cyberspace. *Journal of Interactive Marketing, 13(3)*, 66–76.

Maes, P., Guttman, R. H., and Moukas, A. G. (1999). Agents that buy and sell. *Communications of the ACM, 42(3)*, 81–87.

Malhotra, Y. (1999). Deciphering the knowledge management hype. Available: www.brint.com.

Mason, P. R. (1998). Secret agents: CA announces the first release of Unicenter Neugents. *International Data Corporation*, December, 1–3.

Muller, N. J. (1998). Intelligent agents for network operations. *Datapro*, July, 17–18.

Nardi, B.A., Miller, J.R., and Wright, D. J. (1998). Programmable intelligent agents. *Communications of the ACM, 41(3)*, 96–104.

Quinn, J. B. (1992). *Intelligent Enterprise: A Knowledge and Service Based Paradigm for Industry*. New York: The Free Press.

Russell, S. J., and Norvig P. (1995). *Artificial Intelligence: A Modern Approach*. Englewood Cliffs: NJ: Prentice Hall.

Sandholm, T. (1999). Automated negotiation. *Communications of the ACM, 42(3)*, 84–85.

Smith, D. C., Cypher, A., and Spohrer, J. (1994). KidSim: Programming agents without a programming language. *Communications of the ACM, 37(7)*, 55–67.

Turban, Mclean, and Wetherbe (1999). *Information technology for management: Making connections for strategic advantages*. New York: John Wiley & Sons, Inc., pp. 255–258 and 498–503.

The IBM agent. Available: http://activist.gpl.ibm.com:81/WhiteChapter/ptc2.htm.

Vinaja, R., and Sircar S. (1999). Agents delivering business intelligence. *Handbook of IS Management*. Boca Raton: Auerbach Publications, pp. 477–490.

Wang, S. (1999). Analyzing agents for electronic commerce. *Information Systems Manage-*

ment, Winter, 40–46.

Wong, D., Paciorek, N. and Moore, D. (1999). Java-based mobile agents. *Communications of the ACM, 42(3)*, 92–95.

Woolridge, M., and Jennings, N. R. (1996). Pitfalls of agent-oriented development. *Intelligent Agents*, Section 4.2. Berlin: Springer-Verlag.

THINKING OUT OF THE BOX

Q.1. How can the scope of an intelligent software agent be identified?
(Hint: The following three different functionalities need to be evaluated:
(a) Implied Constraint Identification
(b) Explicit Constraint Requirements Analysis, and
(c) Product Class and Feature Identification)

Q.2. How can managers best model, simulate, and integrate proposed intelligent software solutions into the existing information systems infrastructure?

Q.3. In an era of increasing organizational complexity and heightened international competition, what kinds of organizational practices can successfully enhance the transition to the knowledge era?

Q.4. What theoretical foundation/s and design methodology can be used to measure the quality of the decisions made by intelligent software agents or presented as alternative choices to the decision-maker?
(Hint: Expected-Utility Theory)

Q.5. How can we structure the specifications of agent behaviors as well as the agent designs so that it is easy to identify, replace, and reuse parts of an agent's behavior in a knowledge management system?
(Hint: Build families of agents after paying attention to the commonalities and variabilities that the members of an agent family represent.)

Chapter VII

Intelligent Agents for Electronic Commerce: Trends and Future Impact on Business Models and Markets

Merrill Warkentin
Northeastern University, USA

Vijayan Sugumaran
Oakland University, USA

Ravi Bapna
Northeastern University, USA

ABSTRACT

A characteristic feature of the explosive growth in electronic commerce is the rapid innovation and adoption of new technologies, which results in the creation of new business relationships between consumers, firms, and markets. One such technology that is profoundly changing the dynamics of the electronic marketplace is 'intelligent agent' technology. Agents have the ability to autonomously carry out various activities on behalf of their principals. At a micro-economic level, agents can help buyers and sellers achieve greater efficiencies of information exchange in the electronic business-to-consumer and business-to-business domains. Additionally, they facilitate the creation of vertically integrated portals that have a significant impact on the macroeconomic landscape. Using many real-world examples, we characterize the different roles that software agents play in the various e-commerce business models and also touch upon their impact on creation of new market structures. We address price-matching versus price-comparison agents. We highlight the various purchase decision criteria evident in various vertical markets and suggest the need for a cross-industry product (and service) attribute data representation model, based on the expanded capabilities of XML. We contrast the autonomous price comparisons enabled by agents with the expanded criteria comparisons facilitated by the e-commerce rating sites. We discuss the public policy implications of these second-

generation e-commerce agents with regard to data representation standardization and consumer information privacy. We present future directions for intelligent agent functions that encompass standard representation of decision criteria such as delivery and payment options, return policies, service, quality, trust, and reputation.

ELECTRONIC COMMERCE BUSINESS MODELS

Electronic commerce is the electronic exchange (delivery or transaction) of information, goods, services, and payments over telecommunications networks, primarily the World Wide Web. E-commerce activities include the establishment and maintenance of *on-line relationships* between an organization and its suppliers, dealers, customers, strategic partners, regulators, and other agents related to (or in support of) traditional delivery channels. These activities may be business-to-consumer ("B2C" such as direct book sales to the general public by www.amazon.com), business-to-business ("B2B" such as corporate procurement or supply chain management using a secure extranet), consumer-to-consumer ("C2C" such as a public auction at www.ebay.com), or within a business (such as an employee intranet or an enterprise resource planning (ERP) system). This environment enables organizations to re-engineer their internal and external functions and activities, increasing both efficiency and effectiveness. Firms can automate existing processes and dramatically reduce cycle times throughout the supply chain. They can enhance communication, collaboration, and cooperation between knowledge teams (including virtual teams) using *intranet* technologies as well as between the organization and members of its external constituent organizations using *extranet* technologies.

As in traditional markets ("brick and mortar"), e-buyers need to find sellers of products and services; they may need expert advice prior to purchase and for service and support afterwards. There is often a tremendous amount of information that the buyer must evaluate before s/he can make any final purchase decisions. Similarly, e-sellers need to find buyers and they need to provide expert advice about their product or service. Both buyers and sellers need to automate handling of their transaction processing and "electronic financial affairs."

Ideally, in an on-line shopping environment, buyers should be able to find the products that meet their requirements from different sources, compare the products (and the sources) using multiple selection criteria, determine the product that best meets their needs, and purchase it through a secure transaction. Sellers on the other hand, should be able to not only attract new customers by making available up-to-date information about their products and services, but also maintain their customer base by providing exciting opportunities and incentives.

Several categories of new types of businesses have evolved to take advantage of the unique opportunities within this new environment. There are a number of ways these new business models can be viewed. The following sections categorize these emerging business models.

Content, Community, and Commerce Strategies

Business models that have emerged in this era of e-commerce activity have been categorized a number of ways. Most models explicitly leverage the ubiquitous and universal availability of the World Wide Web as a platform for communication between and among organizations and individuals. Web-based e-commerce models were traditionally oriented toward one of three basic purposes—*Content*, *Community*, and *Commerce* (transactions). (See Figure 1a.) The first includes sites offering news, reports, publications ("e-zines"), music, or other soft goods. (A classic example is www.nytimes.com.) "Community" is the second category, which includes sites that provide focused niche discussions, fora, or chatrooms and sites that offer free e-mail and/or free Web-hosting space. (A classic example is www.tripod.com.) The final type includes all sites that directly sell either "soft goods" (documents, reports, music, software) or "hard goods" (requiring common carriers or shippers) by implementing order-entry, order-fulfillment, and payment processing on-line. (A classic example is www.amazon.com.) However, in today's environment, most e-commerce site managers feel compelled to satisfy all three objectives. For example, visit www.garden.com (see Figure 1b) and find *content* (articles about gardening, advice from the "garden doctor," etc.), *community* (24 live chats about gardening with people around the world, celebrity chats, and a forum to get advice from other gardeners or to showcase your gardening photographs), and *commerce* (with help for buying the right plants for your soil, sun, and other conditions).

Sell-Side Versus Buy-Side Strategies

Another perspective on e-commerce business models is the focus on either the "sell side" or the "buy side." Traditional inter-organizational networks, which used technologies such as electronic data interchange (EDI) or electronic funds transfer (EFT), were developed for use *between* businesses. The purpose was to facilitate the exchange of inventory data or transactional data, and these systems benefited both buyers and sellers. Modern e-commerce systems, usually built on the Web platform, support activity between businesses, and also facilitate various business activities between consumers and businesses. Web sites with the greatest initial success were those which were focused on direct selling to individual consumers (the "sell side"), such as www.dell.com. However, mature e-businesses have developed strategies to leverage this platform to improve their purchasing functions (the "buy side"). E-procurement and electronic supply chain management are two examples of this focus.

Figure 1. Web-Based E-Commerce Model Purposes

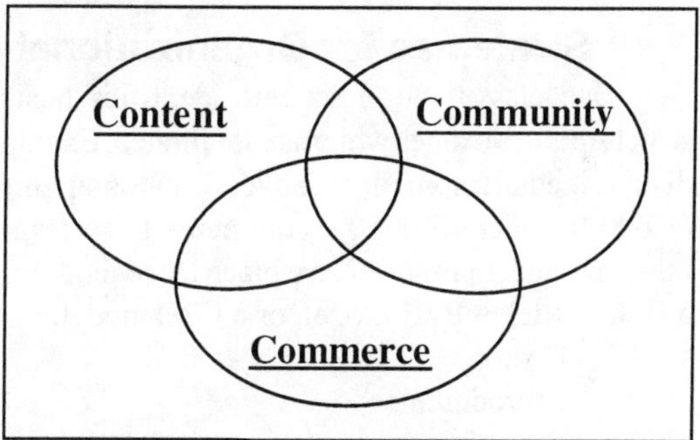

Figure 1b. Strategic Combination of E-Commerce Purposes

System Orientation Categories

Another potential taxonomy is one which identifies e-business strategies by whether they focus on (1) internal or "back-office" functions and activities (such as order fulfillment or inventory management), (2) external inter-organizational activities (such as procurement and supply chain management), or (3) external "customer-facing" activities (such as sales and service). E-business strategies aimed at the first domain are implemented with enterprise resource planning

(ERP) software from companies such as SAP or PeopleSoft. These internal exchanges of information are also facilitated by the adoption of *intranet*, groupware, and knowledge management technologies. The second category of e-strategy initiatives traditionally utilized electronic data interchange (EDI) technologies to facilitate the seamless and automatic exchange of various information between companies and their strategic partners. These activities are now also being supported by the use of *extranets*, which utilize a secure IP platform to enable firms to safely exchange orders and other information over the Web. The final category is the most obvious function within e-commerce. Direct selling models, along with various newer models, use *public internet* sites to reach global audiences with a standard presentation media and display format.

E-Commerce Models Categorized by Penetration Level

Another way of categorizing the role of e-commerce in a firm's overall strategy is to identify the level of "penetration" that e-commerce technology has had on the firm's managerial perspective and on its internal and external processes. The first level is "awareness," followed by the "brochureware" stage in which the Web content is static and simply descriptive of the company. The next step is often loading catalogs onto a Web site (either static or dynamic), followed by actually taking orders on-line. Some firms will employ sophisticated secure on-line payment systems. The next level includes back-office functionality, such as order processing and order fulfillment. Some firms incorporate electronic customer relationship management (CRM) features to enhance the customer intimacy. Firms may use e-mail order confirmations, allow customers to check on the order status on-line, recall the shipping and billing options for the user (to prevent unnecessary keystroking), recognize the user's interests by recording them in a cookie file, or suggest related products and services based on the results of data mining and profiling. Finally, firms may link their electronic systems to those of their suppliers, distributors, and dealers in a powerful inter-organizational network to support effective supply chain management objectives, including integrated production lifecycle planning.

Strategies for Organizational Structure and Linkages

One classification scheme identifies business models by the inter-organizational structure and linkages which are facilitated. Examples include intermediaries, infomediaries, disintermediaries, auctions, buyers' unions, aggregators, consolidators, and others. Timmers (1998) has identified 10 e-commerce business models, extended here to include several other models. In Figure 2, we place these models into a framework which identifies each as a B2C model, a B2B model, or a C2C model.

1. E-shop
2. E-procurement
3. E-auction
4. E-mall
5. 3rd-party marketplace
6. E-communities
7. Value chain service provider
8. E-integrators
9. Collaboration Platforms
10. Information brokers, trust, and other services
11. E-exchanges or industry spot markets for commoditized products

Figure 2. E-Commerce Business Models

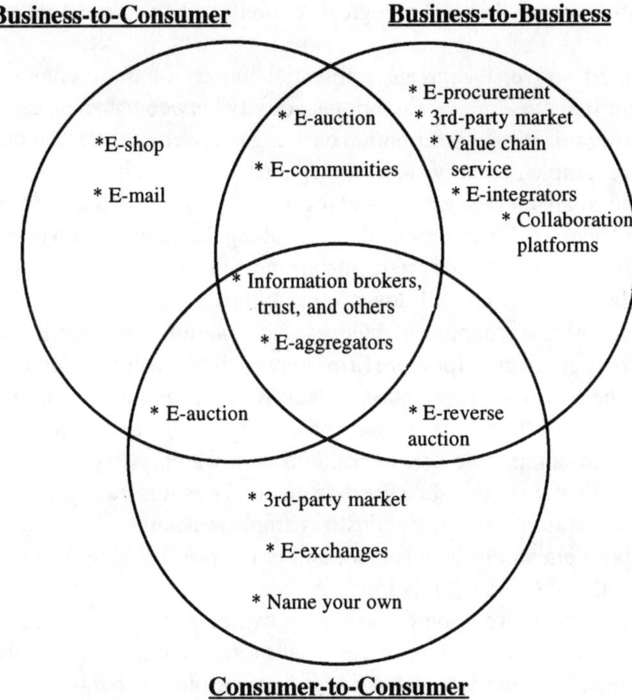

12. E-reverse auctions that allow buyers to request competitive pricing offers from multiple sellers
13. Name your own price
14. E-aggregators that consolidate demand
15. Quantity discounters

Given this background, it seems clear that technologies that assist in the information exchange process in electronic markets will have a positive impact on the economic players as well as overall market efficiency. We discuss the role of information exchange in electronic markets and present an overview of intelligent agent technology before discussing the role of agents in electronic markets.

THE ROLE OF INFORMATION EXCHANGE IN E-COMMERCE

The fundamental characteristic of the World Wide Web which has contributed the most to its widespread impact on commerce is its *standard representation* for information display embodied in HTML and its *standard representation* for the transmission of such data embodied in the HTTP and IP protocols. Any individual wishing to participate in this ubiquitous network of networks, whether they use a Wintel client, a Mac, a UNIX workstation, or other computer, and whether they use Netscape, Internet Explorer, or other browser, need only to connect and view the material served by the millions of computers in this IP landscape. However, the HTML markup language (along with GIF and JPG standards and extended by Javascript and other technologies) is useful only for creating a common definition for visual display of information. The Web is meant to be seen. Further opportunities to leverage this technological revolution require more data representation standards.

As discussed above, the greatest potential impact of the e-commerce revolution probably lies not in the realm of transactional activity between businesses and consumers, but in the inter-organizational information exchange between sellers and other businesses. One prominent example is supply chain strategic partnerships. In this situation, businesses link their production planning systems and inventory systems with those of their suppliers, distributors, and dealers. By doing so, all parties along the supply chain benefit from faster, more accurate information, thereby reducing the inefficiencies, time lags, and overreactions in production levels (both up and down!) that typified the pre-e-commerce era of wild business cycles. Other exchanges of business information can benefit the firm in other significant ways. Yet, in order for more firms to participate in this revolution, there must be an evolution in the on-line representation of data. When firms currently pursue supply chain management activities, they must expend considerable resources to either restructure their data to make them compatible (*data scrubbing* and warehousing) or they must employ complicated *middleware* to translate the data on the fly as it is transmitted from one site to the other. Neither option is ideal. If industries employed standardized data representation schemes, this problem would be resolved, and in the process, intelligent agents could be used in beneficial ways discussed below.

Prices represent information cues relating overall supply and demand levels; better information leads to more accurate prices (that more accurately reflect the relative total supply and demand). To the extent that prices become more accurate, vertical market can achieve greater overall efficiency (fewer "mistakes" in over-purchasing, under-purchasing, and purchasing at excessive prices). Pockets of waste or excessive inventories are exposed and quickly cleared in the efficient market. As markets improve, the overall economy also achieves greater efficiencies, thereby benefiting all who participate. As a social policy, it can be argued that efforts to promote technologies and standards that improve information exchange in electronic markets will improve the ability of the world economy to allocate resources. Worldwide standards of living would increase, jobs would be created, and wealth would accumulate. We present an overview of intelligent agent technology in the following section before discussing the role of agents in electronic markets.

INTELLIGENT AGENT TECHNOLOGY: CATEGORIES AND CAPABILITIES

Nwana et al. (1998) define agents as "software entities that have been given sufficient autonomy and intelligence to enable them to carry out specified tasks with little or no human supervision." There is no standard definition for intelligent agents, but they are generally described (Decker et al., 1997; Specter, 1997; Hendler, 1996) as programs that act on behalf of their human users to perform laborious and routine tasks such as locating and accessing necessary information, resolving inconsistencies in the retrieved information, filtering away irrelevant and unwanted information, and integrating information from heterogeneous information sources. In order to execute tasks on behalf of a business process, computer application, or an individual, agents are designed to be goal driven, i.e., they are capable of creating an agenda of goals to be satisfied. Agents can be thought of as intelligent computerized assistants.

Several types of intelligent agents have been proposed and implemented (Collis & Lee, 1999; Dasgupta et al., 1999; Eriksson et al., 1999; Guttman et al., 1999; Klemm, 1999; Maes et al., 1999; Rachlevsky-Reich et al., 1999; Powley et al., 1997; King & O'Leary, 1996; Rich & Sidner, 1997). While there is no consensus on what the architecture of an agent should be, there is agreement on what are some of the properties of agents. Sycara et al. (1996) list the following as desirable characteristics of intelligent agents:

(a) taskable—take directions from human agents or other agents,
(b) net-centric—distributed and self-organizing,
(c) semiautonomous—perform tasks on its own,
(d) persistent—doesn't require frequent attention,
(e) active—able to initiate problem solving activities,
(f) collaborative—delegate tasks to other agents and work cooperatively with other agents,
(g) flexible—deal with heterogeneity of other agents and information sources, and
(h) adaptive—accommodate changing user needs and task environments.

Cooperative intelligent agent systems contain agents (intelligent computerized assistants) that are capable of acting autonomously, cooperatively, and collaboratively to achieve a collective goal. An agent by itself may not have sufficient information or expertise to solve an entire problem; hence mutual sharing of information and expertise is necessary to allow a group of agents to produce a solution to a problem. Cooperating agents can communicate (exchange information) and collaborate (work together on a common task or sub-task).

Grosof et al. (1995) lays out the desirable technological characteristics for intelligent agent technologies. They stress embedability, which includes the ability to have inferencing capability in conjunction with procedural invocations. It also includes the ability to symmetrically inter-operate with other software and the attribute of light-weightedness. This also implies the ability to reuse code, reuse knowledge bases and the necessity of standards of communication such as XML. If these agents are to add value to businesses, then they should have a user-friendly interface for the authoring of rules. Various multifunctional agent architectures have been implemented that support some or all of these above technological characteristics (Nissen and Mehra, 1998; Grosof et al., 1995; Maes et al., 1999). All of these utilize the object-oriented approach, which facilitates code reuse and embedability. In light of these desirable characteristics, a combination of Java, C++, and XML will be utilized in creating autonomous and mobile intelligent agents.

AGENT ARCHITECTURE IN ELECTRONIC COMMERCE

Based on the desired properties listed above, we propose the following generic architecture (shown in Figure 3) for intelligent agents in an electronic commerce environment. The agent primarily consists of the following components: (a) agent interface, (b) domain- independent component, (c) domain-dependent component, (d) control/procedural knowledge component, and (e) local data component. The responsibilities of each of the components as well as their internal modules are discussed below.

Agent Interface: The agent interface component is primarily responsible for facilitating agent communication. Agents communicate with each other by sending messages and the agent interface facilitates this process. Also, the agent interface provides mechanisms for the human agent to interact with the software agent, as well as deal with the heterogeneity of the agents within the environment. It also provides mechanisms for data/knowledge exchange during problem solving. The agent interface can also be customized based on the user tastes and needs, as well as the current problem characteristics.

Domain-Independent Component: Regardless of the application domain in which the agent operates, there are certain fundamental activities that the agent has to carry out. For example, the agent must be able to gather data from a variety of sources, cleanse it, and transform that data for further processing. This domain-independent component consists of the following modules: (a) Data Access—responsible for relevant data collection from a number of sources; (b) Data Summarization—responsible for cleansing and summarizing the data for processing both by the agents as well as humans; (c) Conflict Resolution—responsible for dealing with inconsistent and imprecise information, since the agent can acquire data from heterogeneous data sources; and (d) Agent Communication— this module contains knowledge about the basic communication primitives and protocols applicable to a specific domain.

Domain-Dependent Component: The domain-dependent component contains domain-specific knowledge that enables the agent to work on a problem in that domain. Based on the objectives of the problem, the agent identifies specific goals to be achieved and for each goal a task hierarchy is created. Each task may consist of one or more actions to be executed. The agent also operates with a set of beliefs appropriate to that domain as well as internal and external functions. Specifically, the domain-dependent component contains the following modules: (a) Goal—contains the goal hierarchy corresponding to the problem at hand; (b) Belief—contains the set of beliefs about the environment, and the agent federation; (c) Task—contains task hierarchies corresponding to each goal node in the goal hierarchy; (d) Action—actions corresponding to each task in the task hierarchy; (e) Transaction—the transactions that have to be carried out during task execution; (f) Functions—external functions that the agent needs to utilize during problem solving; (g) Capabilities—set of operations that the agent can perform; and (h) Role—the various roles the agent will take on during cooperative problem solving.

Control-Knowledge Component: This component contains the control and procedural knowledge needed to actually execute the various tasks corresponding to a particular goal and generate outputs. If the agent is working cooperatively with other agents, then it also synthesizes the outputs from those agents and generates the final result. This component also processes messages from other agents and responds to service requests. This component consists of the following modules: (a) Planning—generate the goal hierarchy as well as the corresponding task and action hierarchies; (b) Reasoning—work with precise and imprecise information; (c) Transaction Processing—processing the necessary transactions and updating data stores; and (d) Message Processing—processing the incoming messages and responding to service requests, and sending the outgoing messages.

Local Data Component: The local data component is the memory space that the agent uses where it stores facts, intermediate results, the status of various tasks that are in progress, etc. This component reflects the "state" of the agent and is tightly coupled with the other components.

The following section discusses the functions performed by agents within the electronic marketspace.

Figure 3. Intelligent Agent Architecture

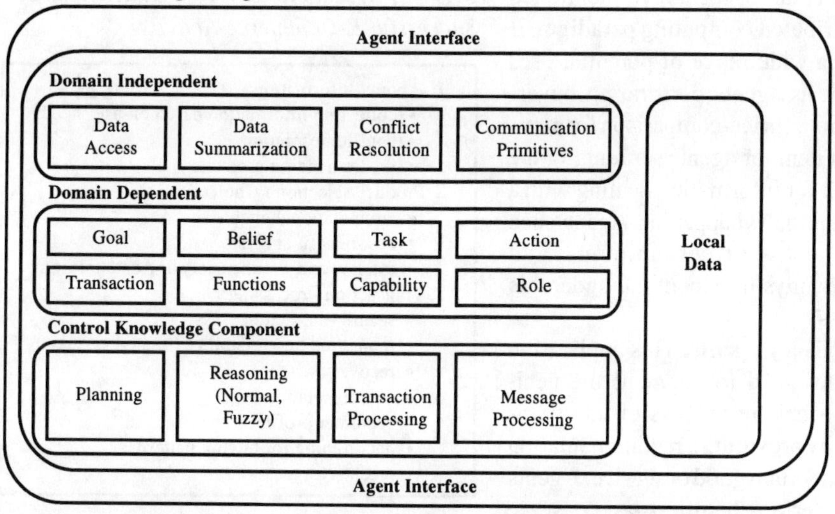

AGENT FUNCTIONALITY IN ELECTRONIC COMMERCE

Intelligent agents can assist in electronic commerce in a number of ways. Agents, also known as robots or simply "bots," can assist buyers in the shopping process by recommending purchases that meet the buyer specifications. The agent or bot might rank potential e-tail Web sites based on the buyer's profile of purchase decision criteria (price, service, return policy, shipping options, etc.). Agents can also assist sellers by providing product or service advice to prospective buyers. This alleviates the problem of information overload and the time it takes to sort through it. Further, with standard data representation schemes for prices and other product characteristics, agents could be easily employed to perform sophisticated inter-organizational queries, which would dramatically improve the overall efficiency and effectiveness of cooperative efforts.

There are four key dimensions of successful electronic commerce activity: a) product information, b) product selection/choice, c) transaction processing, and d) customer relationship. Figure 4 shows some of the activities within each of these dimensions that can be implemented using intelligent agents.

Traditionally, intelligent agent technology has drawn upon the varied fields of distributed computing, artificial intelligence, software engineering, and consumer buying behavior research. With advances in e-commerce technology, additional fields such as supply-chain management, logistics, and decision support systems now influence agent technology. To begin understanding the roles these agents play in the various e-commerce models, we first examine the various kinds of tasks performed by these agents. Nissen and Mehra (1998) group agent applications into four classes:

1. **Information filtering.** This application of agent technology is typically utilized for screening incoming information channels like e-mail or Webcast multimedia. Potential applications include dealing with information overload by having the agent detect a certain class of e-mails that could be either discarded as spam or automatically answered using a knowledge base.
2. **Information retrieval.** This application utilizes the mobility of the agent that arises

as a result of the above-mentioned distributed computing paradigm. It has a wide range of potential uses such as agents performing buyer-initiated price-comparison for a certain item, or agents scrounging the Web for information dealing with a certain news happening. Agents such as www.pricescan.com and www.mysimon.com fall under this class.

3. **Advisory agents.** This application is designed to augment the decision-making process of its principal by providing a recommendation for a certain good or service. Agents that perform help desk tasks or serve as electronic concierges like www.askjeeves.com fall under this category.
4. **Performative agents.** These agents go beyond the advisory function described above and typically undertake transaction processing on behalf of their principals. In the process they effect state changes in the overall system. For instance, the on-line auctioneer www.onsale.com allows consumers to utilize an agent called *Bid Watch®* to automatically place bids on their behalf, freeing up the consumers from the tedium of monitoring the auction. Consumers specify the maximum dollar amount they are willing to pay for the item under consideration, and the agent keeps placing incremental bids on the consumer's behalf until the current minimum required bid to get into the winners list becomes greater than the consumer's maximum willingness to pay.

Figure 4. Agents Role in Key Dimensions of Successful E-Commerce Activity

1. Product Information:
   - collecting information based on user needs
   - conflict resolution
   - recommending products
2. Product Selection / Choice:
   - computational agents
   - cost/benefit analysis
   - off-line and & time analysis / data mining
3. Transaction Processing:
   - secure transactions
   - reputation and reliability (trusted systems)
   - recovery
4. Customer Relationship:
   - customer profile
   - data mining for buying patterns
   - incentives

AGENT IMPACT ON BUSINESS-TO-CONSUMER MARKETS

The objective of this section is to illustrate the various ways in which intelligent agents impact *consumer*-related e-commerce business models. This is accomplished in both the business-to-consumer and in the consumer-to-consumer domain. The majority of agent applications under these categories assist e-shopping in some form or the other, and are often referred to as 'shopping bots.' We begin with a discussion of some agent categories in this space and show that bots can go beyond e-shopping for consumers.

Consumer-Oriented Agent Categories

Bots can perform many kinds of tasks for consumers, some very simple and others quite complex. For example, www.MySimon.com pinpoints the lowest price on hundreds of products, www.CareerSite.com can notify one when a job opening matches one's career goals, and www.MovieCritic.com builds a knowledge base about one's tastes and suggests movies that one might like. We present and extend Wolff and Rutten's (1999) taxonomy of Web-based agents or bots. We include examples wherever available and, in some cases, offer a detailed discussion.

1. Intelligent Shoppers
   - Auction bots
   - Recommendation bots
   - Shopping bots
2. Automated Agents (that do your work for you)
   - Off-line browsers
   - Surf help bots—NetSumm
   - Scrubbers
   - Form fillers—FormAgent
3. Search Bots and Metacrawlers
4. Digital Secretaries
   - E-mail bots—SmartBot, SmartOne, Snoop
   - Travel bots—Automated Travel Agent
   - Translation bots
   - Reference bots
   - Reminder and alert bots
5. Intelligent Money Managers—Business and financial bots
   - Stock bots—NavigateOne, JustQuotes
6. Daily Life Agents
   - News bots—AdHound, Backweb
   - Job bots—CareerAgent, CareerSite
   - Real estate bots
   - Dating bots
   - Entertainment—eGenie, Interactive Characters
   - Reading Recommendations—Alexandria Digital Literature

In the next section we focus on the first of the above-mentioned six categories and explore the role of intelligent agents in business-to-consumer e-commerce.

Intelligent Agents for Price Comparison

An undisputed fact that has emerged from the increased utilization of Web-based shopping technologies by consumers is the increased power that is available for those who seek it. By power we mean the ability to make better-informed decisions that are not constrained by the tyranny of geography, time, or information scarcity. In fact, the phrase *caveat emptor* (meaning "buyer beware") might now be replaced by *caveat mercator*, implying that a fundamental power shift has occurred in the favor of consumers. Information-retrieving intelligent agents have a big part to play in the shift in balance of power and are now ubiquitous in B2C e-commerce models such as e-shops, e-malls, and e-auctions. They offer consumers order-of-magnitude better ways to shop.

However, the success of an intermediary such as intelligent agents is dependent on providing value to all its constituencies. Thus, from a seller's perspective, the agents provide a technology that significantly increases the volume of interested buyers to their site, and the click-throughs from agents' sites represent consumers that have done their homework and are ready to purchase.

Books and CDs: Compare the pre-e-commerce process for purchasing commodities like books and CDs with the current solutions provided by Web sites like www.amazon.com, www.barnesandnoble.com, and www.books.com (now owned by barnesandnoble.com). It is well known that Amazon pioneered the creation of this now vast channel, and traditional brick-and-mortar Barnes and Noble played the role of the counter-puncher, even spinning off its Web business as a separate entity with its own initial public offering. What was interesting about www.books.com was that it offered consumers the service of an intelligent agent, which at their behest would detect the current price for the book under consideration at Amazon and Barnes and Noble, and subsequently lower its own price if it was higher than either competitor. To conduct such a search in the pure brick-and-mortar environment is obviously far too costly.

Similar price comparison agents now exist for a wide variety of merchandise. www.shopper.com (a C/NET property) offers price-comparison for a vast variety of computer hardware and software. Mysimon.com and www.pricescan.com extend the range of this service to include a variety of merchandise. At this point it is useful to categorize two different kinds of comparison-shopping services provided by these bots.

- *Price Comparison*—The consumer specifies an item of interest and the bot scours the partnering merchants for prices and availability. Examples are www.pricescan.com, www.mysimon.com, www.shopper.com.
- *Price Matching*—The consumer specifies an item of interest and a maximum willingness to pay. The bot scours the partnering sellers who are willing to accept that price. Examples are www.dealtime.com and www.nesttag.com.

Table 1 categorizes a few of the currently popular shopping bots and the product categories for which they offer their services. The list, while not exhaustive, shows the kinds of goods and services that are offered by the different agent categories. Not surprisingly, commodities such as books and music appear widely, whereas only one shopping bot offers comparison-shopping for specialty items such as jewelry.

Inside Shopping Bots: Mechanics and Policy Issues

All of the above-mentioned price-comparison bots either maintain their own product catalog databases that are frequently updated by their agents, or connect in real-time to the partnering merchant databases. Thus, when a consumer searches for the lowest price for a Palm V, the personal digital assistant, a database lookup is performed. The resulting screen displays several rows, each containing a hyperlink to the merchant that typically (but not always) takes the consumer directly to the product page on the merchant Web site, price, availability, and in some cases actual shipping costs.

In some cases the lowest posted price hyperlink takes one to a brochure Web site with an 800 number of a brick-and-mortar merchant rather than to the product page on an e-merchant's catalog. This implies that the above-mentioned comparison-shopping services do not limit themselves to pure e-merchants. While this offers consumers greater choice, it also opens up questions regarding how and by whom is the price-comparison database updated. Thus, one of the key determinants of the success of these intelligent agents will lie in the open and public declaration of their 'ownership of update' policy. For instance, www.bottomdollar.com declares, "In addition, the real-time nature of the Bottom Dollar technology allows merchants to seamlessly manage their inventory with confidence that the pricing changes are automatically picked up in real time with the next product search."

It is important to note that while many of the above-mentioned Web sites claim that they "scour the Internet" giving the false impression of an ubiquitous search, in reality they are only connecting to their respective trading partners who have agreed to be included. In a later section, we will examine issues relating to the adoption of an ubiquitous data representation format such as XML, which would make a true global comparison feasible. We examined the Web sites mentioned in Table 1 for an explicit policy statement regarding the kind of

Table 1. Types of Shopping Bots and the Product Categories They Address

Product Category	Price Comparison Agents					Price Matching Agents	
	Pricescan.com	Mysimon.com	Shopper.com	DealPilot.com	Bottomdollar.com	Dealtime.com	Nextag.com
Books	X	X		X			X
Computer Hardware	X	X	X		X	X	X
Computer Software	X	X	X		X		X
Electronics	X	X			X	X	
Movies	X	X		X			X
Music	X	X		X			X
Office	X	X	X		X		
Sporting Goods	X						
Video Games	X				X	X	
Watches	X						
Appliances						X	
Holiday Decorations						X	
Food and Beverage		X			X	X	
Hardware						X	
Health and Beauty		X			X	X	
Home and Garden						X	
Jewelry & Accessories						X	
Kids and Toys		X			X	X	
Pet Supplies						X	
Sports and Leisure		X				X	
Apparel		X					
Flower and Gift		X					
Personal Finance		X					

relationships that were created between the comparison sites and the participating merchants. Among other things, we were interested in determining whether merchants had to pay to be listed and the frequency of updates. Such a policy statement, or lack thereof, would influence consumer confidence in the bot. The results are presented in Table 2.

It is clear from Table 2 that a wide variety of inter-organizational relationships are being adopted by the comparison-shopping sites. Many sites have arrangements with merchants to display the retailers' goods in a search. The results given by a shopping bot may be skewed toward merchants that have agreements with a specific site. Nevertheless, by providing large amounts of information quickly and easily, they put shoppers in a position of power.

Intelligent Agents and e-Auctions

An interesting result of the remarkable strides taken in e-commerce is the fact that the time-tested posted-price mechanism is no longer the only choice available for the exchange of assets. On-line auctions, brought about by the synergetic combination of Internet technology and traditional auction mechanisms, represent a significant new dimension to e-markets. The efficiencies of bringing together the three Cs of e-commerce, namely content, commerce, and community, are nowhere more evident than in the consumer-to-consumer domain. www.ebay.com pioneered the growth in this area by creating an easy-to-use, community-centric auction platform that allows millions of consumers to buy and sell merchandise. Accordingly, they have created a vast secondary market, which hitherto was constrained by geography, time, and space. Secondary markets such as these have a positive impact on the macroeconomic health of participating markets by providing greater information exchange between buyers and sellers, quickly identifying shortages and excess inventory, and increasing the volume of economic activity. This near-perfect exchange reduces vast amounts of waste and spoilage, while bringing small pockets of demand into the marketplace as well. That same Barbie doll that is currently out of vogue in a certain segment of the global economic landscape could well have significant demand elsewhere. Ebay plays the role of the market that bridges the information gap that existed in facilitating the reallocation of such assets.

Interestingly, these e-auctions are not readily understood if one's perspective is constrained by the physical limitations of traditional auctions. One has to consider nuances of the emerging e-marketplace, such as the presence of automated intelligent agents that allow individuals to monitor and participate in multiple auctions simultaneously. Bapna, Goes, and Gupta (1999) discuss the presence of simultaneous substitutable on-line auctions, which allow an individual shopping for a computer, for example, to simultaneously bid at Onsale.com or Yahoo.com. This economic

Figure 5. Intelligent Agent Example (Screen Capture)

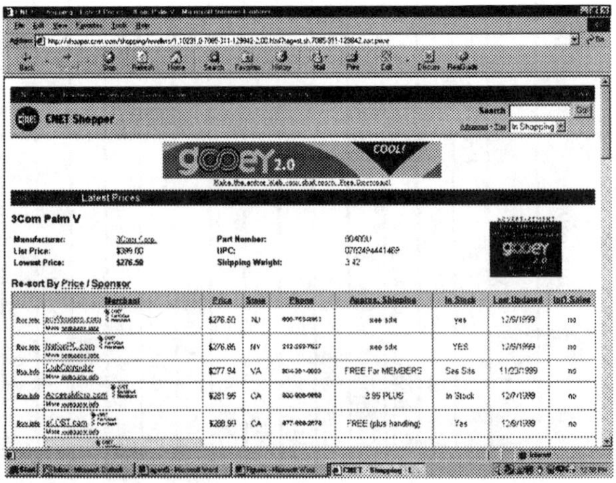

process impacts the efficiency of not just the isolated auction under consideration but also the external market in which it takes place. Intelligent agents like www.auctionrover.com, www.auctionwatch.com, and www.biddersedge.com are specifically designed to make tracking such simultaneous substitutable on-line auctions easy for the consumer. Users can go into the above-mentioned Web sites and key in their desired item. The agent then gives a list of all current auctions that meet the search criteria.

Auction Bots: Incentives and Branding

It is, of course, well known that Ebay and AuctionWatch are currently engaged in a long and protracted battle against this very technology. In November 1999, Ebay blocked AuctionWatch's ability to search through its auctions and post a current list on the AuctionWatch Web site. "This is anticonsumer and threatens the very basis of the Internet, which is freedom of information," said Dan Neary, vice president for marketing and sales at AuctionWatch.com. "Our search engine is no different than other search engines, such as Yahoo."

Ebay disputes the analogy, suggesting that its site is not defined by the mere listing of items up for bid, but by the surrounding experience, which includes chat rooms and an item's bidding history, for example. In addition, a spokesman for Ebay said the company objects to having its auction listings "commingled" with listings from other auction houses, a practice he said could dilute the Ebay brand name.

While neither AuctionWatch nor BiddersEdge currently include auction listings from Ebay, AuctionRover is the only company that currently does so. However, Ebay listings are displayed on a separate tab, that utilizes the Ebay logo, on their Web site from the listings of all the other auction sites that fall under the 'Global Auction' category. This is the part of the branding that Ebay, the clear current front-runner, wishes to preserve.

Table 2. Shopping Bots and Policy Disclosure

Shopping Bot	Policy on Web site	Merchant Relationship	Frequency of updates (as per Web site's policy)
www.Bottomdollar.com	Comprehensive	Sellers do not pay to be listed. Revenue through referral programs.	Real time
www.DealPilot.com	Comprehensive	Merchants pay commission on actual sales.	Real time
www.Dealtime.com	Comprehensive	Chooses merchants based on III-party ratings.	Very frequently
www.Mysimon.com	Not directly available on Web site. Partially available through press releases.	Sellers do not pay to be listed. Revenue through referral programs.	
www.Nextag.com	Not directly available on Web site. Partially available through related links on Web site.	Not clear	Sellers send electronic updates frequently.
www.Pricescan.com	Comprehensive and upfront	Sellers do not pay to be listed. Revenue from advertising and sale of pricing information.	Daily updates
www.Shopper.com	Absent		

Another concern that Ebay raised relates to the frequency of updates issue we touched upon earlier. Ebay claimed that the AuctionWatch search results did not accurately reflect the current state of its auctions and that the information was outdated, a claim that AuctionWatch rejects.

Ultimately, it will be the market forces that decide whether or not such information aggregation is desirable for e-auctions. It is conceivable that Ebay will rethink its position and determine how it can form strategic alliances with such agents, as it has done with AuctionRover, for the benefit of both buyers and sellers.

AGENT IMPACT ON BUSINESS-TO-BUSINESS MARKETS

It should be noted that while the above examples have human consumers as the principals, intelligent agent technology is by no means limited to this. In fact the principals themselves could be other agents, or firms or even markets. In electronic vertical markets (between businesses within a specific industry), agents have been developed to support the information exchange function (see Figure 6). For instance, Application Service Providers (ASPs) like www.CommerceOne.com, that builds and hosts vertically integrated trading communities on the Internet, utilize intelligent agents to aggregate horizontal information such as shipping patterns. Subsequently, the agent can use this information to negotiate competitive advertising rates with adserver companies such as www.DoubleClick.com and www.adforce.com. Ultimately, the B2B e-commerce space will far exceed the volume of transactions in the B2C space, given the volume of corporate procurement (about half of all Fortune 1000 spending) and given its mission critical status. No one who shops at a brick-and-mortar bookstore instead of buying books on-line is jeopardizing his or her financial future. But for a corporate procurement officer, to lag behind while competitors move toward e-procurement and tightly integrated supply chain management practices could threaten the company's very existence! And because a high percentage of corporate procurement is regular, routine, repeated business, agents can play a particularly valuable role to improve the information exchange between the many buyers and sellers in these markets.

DISCUSSION AND EMERGING TRENDS

This paper describes how agents can facilitate various activities necessary for successful e-commerce. It provides a discussion of various e-commerce business models from differing perspectives and presents a taxonomy based on criteria such as sell side versus buy side, system orientation, penetration level, and organizational structure. The multitude of e-commerce models that exist have been placed in a framework, extending Timmers' (1998) classification. The paper also addresses the importance of information exchange in e-commerce and how intelligent agents can be employed in these environments to enhance commerce activities, particularly focusing on acquisition and analysis of data. The paper identifies different types of intelligent agents that are currently being utilized in e-commerce and presents a generic architecture for designing and implementing such agents. Specific roles and functions that intelligent agents can perform in different e-commerce models and markets have been discussed in detail.

Various trends in technology and business will impact the ability of intelligent agents to provide greater functionality to firms that employ them. One ongoing research focus that will impact the utility of e-commerce agents is the development of systems that exhibit *emergent behavior*. Emergent behavior is a term applied to system behaviors that are not programmed—actions that are demonstrated as a result of machine learning algorithms and heuristics. Systems that are programmed to recognize patterns in their environment and develop strategies for success, especially if their behavior can continuously adapt to changing environmental conditions (such as pricing patterns, delivery responsiveness, etc.) will have a significant effect on the overall efficiency of electronic markets. As agents become more intelligent, firms using them will become more profitable as their supply chain management processes become more responsive to changes in availability, price, and other market conditions.

A second important trend is the issue of protecting the privacy of individuals in these new electronic markets. The potential for e-commerce to facilitate the unwanted exchange of personal information via cookie files and shared profiles (third-party adserver networks such as DoubleClick) has been extensively documented and debated at the national and international level. Privacy experts recently called on the United States Federal Trade Commission (FTC) to investigate the practices of adserver networks. In 1999, the U.S. Congress passed the far-reaching "Financial Services Modernization Act" which poses a significant challenge to the ability of e-commerce sites to collect data on individuals. The European Union, with its clear articulation of personal information privacy rights, has also expressed concern over the recent developments in sophisticated targeting and profiling through shared data mining processes. Clearly, independent cooperative agents may provide an even greater threat to the privacy rights of individuals and organizations. This debate should proceed to ensure a balance between the benefits of this technology and its potential for abuse.

E-commerce environments are complex and contain a multitude of tasks that are non-deterministic and fuzzy. In the traditional commerce world, human experts make tough decisions and judgment calls based on their expertise and in cooperation with other experts, while in an e-commerce environment, the same task knowledge has to be codified into software components that can replicate the behavior of the human counterparts. One can envision an e-commerce environment as a community of cooperative problem-solving agents, where each agent has its own roles and responsibilities. Such multi-agent systems are essential to open digital marketplaces, particularly considering the different roles an organization may have to play such as a buyer, seller, broker, etc. This type of intelligent agent-based e-commerce system is similar to the

Figure 6. Vertical Markets and Seller-Buyer Information Exchange

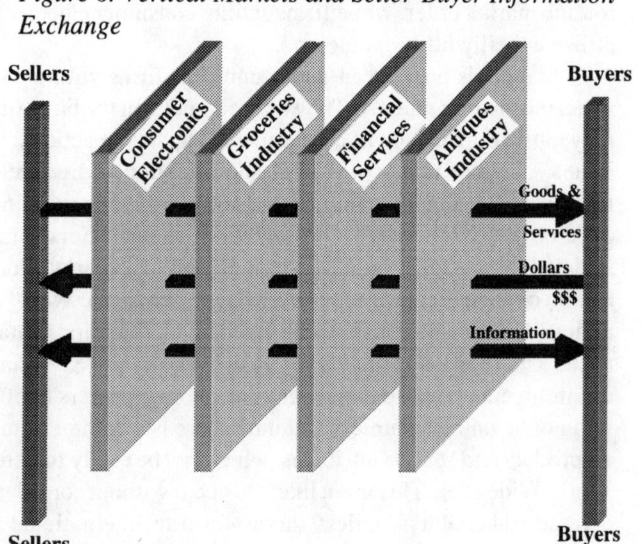

systems proposed in the distributed artificial intelligence arena which support coordination, communication, and collaboration between multiple agents. These systems consist of a network of autonomous agents that asynchronously solve smaller pieces (subproblems) of a large problem; the results of the individual agents are synthesized to generate the solution to the overall problem. The agents in these systems use either task sharing or data sharing to cooperate with other agents. Hence, proper care must be taken in designing the coordination mechanisms.

The purchase lifecycle starts with shopping comparisons, progresses to the actual sales transaction, and continues through order fulfillment and after-sales service. The initial shopping comparisons include criteria beyond price. Consumers also evaluate delivery options, payment options, return policies, service, quality, trust, and reputation. Future shopping agents will assist consumers in comparing these other decision criteria. To do so, they must be able to collect this data from electronic sellers in a standard format, which must be established. This data must be collected and updated in order to maintain its value to consumers in a meaningful way as they evaluate Web sites in their shopping decision process. Sellers will be motivated to participate in this standardization effort when they observe that shopping agents are driving customers to Web sites that adopt the emerging standards.

One fundamental requirement for all inter-organizational systems is the existence of a standard data representation scheme. Firms or other organizations which exchange information about any product or service must recognize and utilize a common method for representing the attributes (and attribute values) for those products and services. At the most basic level, language barriers have kept companies from cooperating throughout business history. Yet even with a common spoken and written language, most firms developed their own representation scheme for inventory information, order processing information, and information about every activity and function of the firm. When two firms wished to engage in electronic data interchange (EDI), they had to adopt the same "EDI standard." (We might speak of global and local standards. It's been said that the great thing about standards in computing is that there are so many of them to choose from!) In other words, two automobile parts manufacturing firms engaged in EDI might use one method of representing a specific routine market order, while firms selling consumer electronics to Wal*Mart for resale may utilize a totally different method.

Standards provide an opportunity for firms within an industry to share information when it is in their interest. They may compete on the basis of product features and price, yet they must cooperate on issues related to legislative action, employment planning and union issues, or other matters. This is another area where intelligent agents may be used to facilitate data gathering and comparison activity. Various industries are already working to develop new XML-based representation schemes. For example, the Chemistry community is developing CML, an XML-based chemical markup language, to become the *lingua franca* of chemical information exchange across the Web. "There are also XML initiatives underway that will transform the exchange of graphics data. It would not be surprising … to see a markup language emerging in every field" (Spedding, 1999). But the true potential of intelligent agents to empower all economic players to efficiently exchange information will not be unlocked unless and until there is a common standard for the representation of all product and service attributes, which can be easily transferred and interpreted across the World Wide Web. This is not likely to occur without considerable efforts on the part of many diverse stakeholders, unless there is a true international effort or major governmental involvement. International cooperation between governments (the World Trade Organization) and between nongovernmental organizations (IEEE and ISO) has already established standards in other technical and trade areas. As a policy issue, it can be argued that an international standardized data representation scheme for product and service attributes is an issue for consideration as well. It certainly would establish a platform for improving the efficiency of world trade.

The phenomenal growth in e-commerce is fueled by rapid adoption of new technologies, including 'intelligent agent' technology. E-commerce agents can help buyers and sellers achieve greater efficiencies of information exchange in the electronic business-to-consumer and business-to-business domains. They also facilitate the creation of vertically integrated portals (vortals) that represent significant new marketspaces. Current shopping agents or "shopbots" may be price-matching or price-comparison agents, but they are evolving to encompass decision criteria besides price, such as delivery and payment options, return policies, service, quality, trust, and reputation. To succeed in this endeavor, developers must employ a cross-industry product (and service) attribute data representation model, based on the expanded capabilities of XML. If these trends come together, the future growth of electronic commerce will be enhanced for business-to-consumer and for business-to-business buyers and sellers.

REFERENCES

Andreoli, J., Pacull, F., & Pareschi, R. (1997). XPECT: A framework for electronic commerce. *IEEE Internet Computing*, 1(4), 40-48.

Bapna, R., Goes, P., & Gupta A. (1999). "A Theoretical and Empirical Investigation of Multi-item On-line Auctions." *Information Technology and Management*, Vol. 1, No. 1, pp. 1-23.

Collis, J., & Lee, L.C. (1999). "Building Electronic Marketplaces with the ZEUS Agent Tool-kit. " *Lecture Notes in Computer Science*, Issue 1571, Springer-Verlag, pp. 1-24.

Corradi, A., Cremonini, M., Montanari, R., & Stefanelli, C. (1999). "Mobile Agents Integrity for Electronic Commerce Applications" *Information Systems*, Vol. 24, No. 6, pp. 519-533.

Dasgupta, P., Narasimhan, N., Moser, L.E., & Melliar-Smith, P.M. (1999). "MAgNET: Mobile Agents for Networked Electronic Trading," *IEEE Transcript.on Knowledge and Data Engineering*, Vol. 11, No. 4, pp. 509-525.

Decker, K., Pannu, A., Sycara, K., & Williamson, M. (1997). "Designing Behaviors for Information Agents." *Proceedings of Autonomous Agents '97*, Marina del Rey, CA, Feb. 5-8, pp. 404-412.

Eriksson, J., Finne, N., & Janson, S. (1999). "SICS MarketSpace – An Agent-Based Market Infrastructure." *Lecture Notes in Computer Science*, Issue 1571, Springer-Verlag, pp. 42-53.

Garcia, P., Gimenez, E., Godo, L., & Rodriguez-Aguilar, J.A. (1999). "Bidding Strategies for Trading Agents in Auction-Based Tournaments." *Lecture Notes in Computer Science*, Issue 1571, Springer-Verlag, pp. 151-165.

Grosof B. N., Levine D. W., Chan H. Y., Parris C. J., and Auerbach J. S. (1995) Reusable Architecture for Embedding Rule-based Intelligence in Information Agents., *Proceedings of the Workshop on Intelligent Information Agents*, Tim Finin and James Mayfield (Eds.), ACM Conference on Information and Knowledge Management (CIKM-95), Baltimore, MD, Dec. 1-2.

Glushko, R.J., Tenenbaum, J.M., & Meltzer, B. (1999). "An XML framework for Agent-Based E-commerce." *Communications of the ACM*, 42(3), 106-114.

Guttman, R.H., & Maes, P. (1999). "Agent-Mediated Integrative Negotiation for Retail Electronic Commerce." *Lecture Notes in Computer Science*, Issue 1571, Springer-Verlag, pp. 70-90.

Guttman, R.H., Moukas, A., & Maes, P. (1998). "Agent-Mediated Electronic Commerce: A Survey." *Knowledge Engineering Review*, June, pp. **.

Hendler, J. (1996). "Intelligent Agents: Where AI Meets Information Technology," *IEEE Expert*, Vol. 11, No. 6, pp. 20-23.

Huhns, M.N., & Vidal, J.M. (1999). "Online Auctions." *IEEE Internet Computing*, Vol. 3, No. 3, pp. 103-105.

King, D., & O'Leary, D. (1996). "Intelligent Executive Information Systems." *IEEE Expert*, 11(6), 30-35.

Klemm, R. P. (1999). "WebCompanion: A Friendly Client-Side Web Prefetching Agent," *IEEE Trans. On Knowledge and Data Engineering*, 11(4), 577-594.

Maes, P., Guttman, R.H., & Moukas, A.G. (1999). "Agents that Buy and Sell." *Communications of the ACM*, 42(3), 81-87, 90-91.

Nissen, M.E., & Mehra, A. (1998). "Redesigning Software Procurement through Intelligent Agents." *Proceedings of the AAAI Workshop on AI in Reengineering and Knowledge Management*, pp. **

Nwana, H., Rosenschein, J., Sandholm, t., Sierra, C., Maes, P., & Guttmann, R. (1998). "Agent-Mediated Electronic Commerce: Issues, Challenges and Some Viewpoints." *Proceedings of 2nd International Conference on Autonomous Agents*, Minneapolis, MN, May 9-13, 189-196.

Park, S, Durfee, E. H., Birmingham, W. P. (1999). "An Adaptive Agent Bidding Strategy Based on Stochastic Modeling." *Proceedings of 3rd Annual Conference On Autonomous Agents*, Seattle, WA, May 1-5, 147-153.

Powley, C., Benjamin, D., Grossman, D., Neches, R., Postel, P., Brodersohn, E., Fadia, R., Zhu, Q., & Will, P. (1997). "Dasher: A Prototype for Federated E-commerce Services," *IEEE Internet Computing*, 1(6), Nov/Dec, 62-71.

Preist, C. (1999). "Commodity Trading Using An Agent-Based Iterated Double Auction." *Proceedimgs of 3rd Annual Conference On Autonomous Agents*, Seattle, WA, May 1-5, pp. 131-138.

Rachlevsky-Reich, B., Ben-Shaul, I., Chan, N.T., Lo, A.W., & Poggio, T. (1999). "GEM: A Global Electronic Market System." *Information Systems*, 24(6), 495-518.

Rich, C., & Sidner, C. (1997). "COLLAGEN: When Agents Collaborate with People." *Proceedings of Autonomous Agents '97*, Marina del Rey, CA, Feb. 5-8, pp. 284-291.

Schlueter, C., & Shaw, M. (1997). "A Strategic Framework for Developing Electronic Commerce." *IEEE Internet Computing*, 1(6), Nov/Dec, 20-28.

Shaw, M. J. (1999). "Electronic Commerce: Review of Critical Issues." *Information Systems Frontiers: A Journal of Research and Innovation*, 1(1), July, 95-106.

Smith, H., & Poulter, K. (1999). "Share the Ontology in XML-based Trading Architectures." *Communications of ACM*, 42(3), 110-111.

Spector, L. (1997). "Automatic Generation of Intelligent Agent Programs." *IEEE Expert*, 12(1), 3-4.

Spedding, V. (1999). "Scientists reopen the XML Files." *Scientific Computing World* 49, October/November 1999, p. 3.

Steinmetz, E., Collins, J., Jamison, S., & Sundareswara, R. (1999). "Bid Evaluation and Selection in the MAGNET Automated Contracting System." *Lecture Notes in Computer Science*, Issue 1571, Springer-Verlag, pp. 105-125.

Sycara, K., Pannu, A., Williamson, M., and Zeng, D. (1996). "Distributed Intelligent Agents." *IEEE Expert*, 11(6), 36-45.

Timmers, P. (1998). "Business Models for Electronic Markets." *Electronic Markets*, 8(2), 1998, 3-8.

Warkentin, M., Bapna,R., Sugumaran,V. (2000). "The Role of Mass Customization in Enhancing Supply Chain Relationships in B2C E--Commmerce Markets." *Journal of Electronic Commerce Research*, 1(2), 1-17

Wolff, M., & Rutten, P. (1999). *BotGuide: The Internet's Hottest Tools that Work the Web For You.* New York: HarperCollins Publishers.

Section Three: Agents in E-Commerce: Frameworks, Applications, and Cases

Chapter VIII

Design Agents with Negotiation Capabilities

Jana Dospisil and Liz Kendall
Monash University, Australia

INTRODUCTION

Agents are viewed as the next significant software abstraction, and it is expected they will become as ubiquitous as graphical user interfaces are today. Multi-agent systems have a key capability to reallocate tasks among their members, and this may result in significant savings and improvements in many domains, such as resource allocation, scheduling, e-commerce, etc. In the near future, agents will roam the Internet, selling and buying information and services. These agents will evolve from their present-day form—simple carriers of transactions—to efficient decision makers. It is envisaged that the decision-making processes and interactions between agents will be very fast (Kephart, 1998).

The importance of automated negotiation systems is increasing with the emergence of new technologies supporting faster reasoning engines and mobile code. A central part of agent systems is a sophisticated *reasoning engine* that enables the agents to reallocate their tasks, optimize outcomes, and negotiate with other agents. The *negotiation strategy* used by the reasoning engine also requires high-level interagent communication protocols and suitable collaboration strategies. Both of these subsystems—a *reasoning engine* and a *collaboration strategy*—typically result in complicated agent designs and implementations that are difficult to maintain.

Diversity in reasoning and strategies has led to "homegrown" agent development done independently from scratch. This has led to the following problems (Bradshaw, 1997):

- **Lack of an agreed definition:** Agents built by different teams have different capabilities.
- **Duplication of effort:** There has been little reuse of agent architectures, designs, or components.
- **Inability to satisfy industrial strength requirements:** Agents must integrate with existing software and computer infrastructure. They must also address security and scaling concerns.

This chapter explores current concepts and directions in negotiation and collaboration strategies in Multi-agent systems. The focus is on coupling the theoretical underpinning of negotiation processes with trends and directions in software engineering and design. In particular, the implications of the theoretical work on design are discussed.

In this chapter we provide an overview of different reasoning and negotiation strategies among agents and then we move to issues relevant to the architecture, design, and implementation of Multi-agent systems based on constraint technology and software patterns. In the second section we discuss the fundamentals of negotiation strategies and protocols based on the following theories:

- Game theoretical models of bargaining and negotiation (analytical strategies),
- Evolutionary (machine learning) computational approaches,
- Constraint technology.

Particular attention is paid to constraint technology, scheduling, and resource-allocation strategies. Finally, we present two software engineering approaches for building agent systems:

1) Plug-in components for agents, and
2) Software patterns.

BACKGROUND

Selected Negotiation and Reasoning Techniques

It is necessary to coordinate the activities of a set of autonomous agents, and some of them could be mobile agents, while others are static intelligent agents. We usually aim at decentralized coordination which produces the desired outcomes with minimal communication. Many different types of *contract protocols* (cluster, swaps, and Multi-agent, as examples) and *negotiation strategies* are used. The evaluation of outcomes is often based on marginal cost (Sandholm, 1993) or game theory payoffs (Mass-Colell, 1995). Agents based on constraint technology use complex search algorithms to solve optimization problems arising from the agents' interactions. In particular, coordination and negotiation strategies in the presence of incomplete knowledge are good candidates for constraint-based implementations.

The focus of any negotiation strategy is to maximize outcomes within the rational boundaries of the environment. The classification of negotiation strategies is not an easy task since a negotiation strategy can be realized by any algorithm which evaluates outcomes, computes appropriate actions, and follows the information exchange protocol.

Negotiation is a search process. The participants jointly search a multidimensional space (e.g., quantity, price, and delivery) in an attempt to find a single point in the space at which they reach mutual agreement and meet their objectives. For many-to-many coupling or interaction between participants, the market mechanism is used, and for one-to-many negotiation, auctions are more appropriate. The market mechanism often suffers from an inability to scale down efficiently (Osborne, 1990) to smaller numbers of participants. On the other hand, one-to-many interactions are influenced by strategic considerations and involve interactive bargaining where agents search for *Pareto efficient* agreement.

Three distinct techniques are reviewed in the following subsections:

i) Analytical (game theory-based approach),
ii) Evolutionary approaches (genetic algorithms approach), and
iii) Constraint technology and constraint agents.

Analytical Approach (Game Theory)

The principles of bargaining and negotiation strategies in Multi-agent systems have attracted economists. Early foundations and mathematical models were investigated by Nash (1950), and the field is still very active. *Game theory* is a collection of analytical tools designed to understand and describe bargaining and interaction between decision makers. Game theory uses mathematical models to formally express real-life strategies (Osborne, 1994; Fudenberg, 1991). The following is a model of interactive negotiation in which each negotiator chooses his or her finite plan of actions. The model consists of a finite set of players (N), a set of actions (A_i), and a preference relation on a set of action profiles or outcome:

$$a = \left(a_j\right)_{j \in N}$$

We denote the preference relation as

$\underset{\approx i}{\text{£}}\ on A = \times_{j \in N} A_j$ for each player. In another words, there is the requirement that the preferences of each player i, be defined over A. The preference relation of a player i can be represented by a payoff function (or utility function) u_i in the sense that we can specify the strategic game as

$$\langle N, (A_i), (u_i) \rangle$$

We also may define a function that associates a set of consequences with action profiles. Sometimes we need to model a situation in which the consequence of an action is affected by a random variable whose values are not known to the players before they take their actions. We can model such a situation as a strategic game with a set of consequences C, a probability space Ω, and a function

$$g : A \times \Omega \rightarrow C$$

This means that $g(\alpha,\omega)$ is the consequence when the action a is taken and the random variable value is ω. In this case, the profile of actions induces a lottery on C.

The high level of this abstraction allows the model to be applied to a variety of situations. The model places no restrictions on the set of actions available to the player. With regard to mathematical models, there already exist many sophisticated and elaborate strategies for specific negotiation problems. The Contract Net Protocol (CNP) (Smith, 1980; Sandholm, 1993) represents the model of decentralized task allocation where agents locally calculate their marginal costs for performing sets of tasks. The pricing mechanism in Sandholm (1993) generalizes the CNP to work for both cooperative and competitive agents. In Zeng (1996) bilateral negotiation based on the Bayesian method is presented. It demonstrates the static nature of the model. The learning effect is achieved by using dynamic updates of a knowledge base, which is consulted during the negotiation process.

Most of the studies assume perfect rationality (flawless deduction, marginal costs are computed exactly, immediately and without computational cost), and the infinite horizon of strategic bargaining. These are not realistic assumptions. More advanced studies deal with coalition formation and negotiation strategies in the environment of multiple self-interested or cooperative agents with bounded rationality (Sandholm, 1993) and bargaining with deadlines.

Analytical strategies have the advantage of stable and reliable behavior. The main disadvantage is the static nature of the model resulting in potential predictability of the outcomes. The other problems are associated with the notion of perfect rationality. It cannot be assumed that an agent can resolve many NP-hard problems instantly.

Contracts in automated negotiations consisting of self-interested agents are typically designed as binding (impossible to breach). In cooperative distributed problem solving, commitments are often allowed to be broken based on some local reasoning. Frequently, the protocols use continuous levels of commitment based on a monetary penalty method (Sandholm, 1993). Unfortunately, the inflexible nature of these protocols restricts an agent's actions when the situation becomes unfavorable. The models which incorporate the possibility of decommitting from a contract with or without reprisals (Sen, 1994; Smith, 1980) can accommodate some changes in the environment and improve an agent's status. However, all of these protocols are somewhat restricting with respect to evolving, dynamic situations.

Evolutionary Strategies

With *evolutionary strategies*, the data used as the basis for negotiation, as well as the algorithm operating on the data, evolve. This approach provides more efficient learning, supports the dynamics of the environment, and is adaptable. However, only a few implementations have been attempted, and these have been of only simple negotiation strategies (Oliver, 1996). *Genetic algorithms* are probably the most common technique inspired by evolution, in particular by the concepts of natural selection and variation. The basic genetic algorithm is derived from the hypothesis that the candidate solutions to the problem are encoded into "chromosomes." Chromosomes represent a solution or instance of the problem at hand encoded into a binary string. The algorithm then operates on this binary string. It begins with a randomly generated set of candidate solutions. The set of candidate solutions is generated as a random string of ones and zeroes. Each chromosome is evaluated and the fitness of the chromosome is the value of the objective function (or the utility if we want to maximize the outcome). A new population is created by selecting individuals to become parents. A thorough description of the genetic algorithm approach can be found in Goldberg (1989).

A very large amount of research has been carried out in the application of evolutionary algorithms to situations that require decisions to be made. Examples include coalition games, exchange economies, and double auctions. This technique is inspired by the concept of variation and natural selection. The intelligent agents are modeled using classifier systems to select decisions. Although the resent research shows that multi-agent systems of classifiers are capable of learning how to play Nash-Markov equilibria, the current limitations of computational resources and the instability of "homegrown" implementations significantly constrain the nature of the strategies. The important question is what design and implementation techniques should be used to ease this conflict and to provide the resources required for genetic learning to operate in an unrestricted way. It is believed that the ability of agents to learn simple games would be beneficial to electronic commerce.

Constraint Agents

The potential of constraint-based agents is still to be fully realized and appreciated. One of the possible frameworks for constraint-based agents is outlined in Nareyek (1998). This framework considers agents as a means for simplifying distributed problem solving. An agent's behavior and the quality of solutions depend on the underlying action-task planning system. The recent results with some constraint planners and Constraint Satisfaction Problems (CSP,) indicate the potential advantages of this approach.

Constraint satisfaction and constraint scheduling problems

In order to understand the concepts of constraint solving technology and constraint solvers, we provide a brief overview of CSP and constraint solver technologies. A constraint satisfaction problem (CSP) is defined by a set of variables (Mackworth, 1977):

$$V = \{v_1, v_2, \ldots v_m\}$$

Each variable can assume a value from the domain

$$D = \{d_1, d_2, \ldots\ldots, d_m\}$$

There is also a set of constraints

$$C = \{c_1, c_2, \ldots\ldots, c_n\}$$

Finding a solution to a CSP means finding a value assignment for each variable such that all constraints are satisfied. The basic process is iterative. First select a variable for instantiation, then select a value and assign it to the variable and determine whether the assignment is consistent with all of the constraints. If an inconsistency is detected, backtrack; otherwise iterate for the next variable.

The complexity of this process can be reduced by heuristics which are applied to order the variables or values. Complexity reduction can also be achieved by using the arc consistency method. Arc consistency is based on selecting a single variable from a constraint network and checking the consistency of each value in the domain. All inconsistent values are then removed.

The classic formulation of a resource constrained scheduling process used in manufacturing applications aims at reducing a search space by making a number of strict assumptions about operations, resources, and processing times. We have investigated the assumptions presented in the literature (Bellman, 1982; Coffman, 1976). In general, the assumption is that all required information is available at the beginning of processing, and it remains constant over the entire presentation schedule.

A significant difficulty is added to the problem if a dynamic environment is considered. The constraints in fact produce the additional bounds that can change during the real-time processing. Both the search space and the solution space are modified during the scheduling process, as well as during the actual real-time processing, as new constraints are added and existing constraints are relaxed. The assignment of pairs of activity-resource values must be an adaptable process that allows the resource to adjust performance according to available capacity. It must also be able to adjust the activity processing time. Alternatively, providing we have previously captured statistical data about a resource fluctuation, we may be able to adjust parameters prior to the start of the scheduling process.

It has been recognized that CSP techniques and tools are useful in the implementation of flexible and extensible scheduling systems in manufacturing, transportation, and planning. Scheduling is a decision-making process that assigns activities to resources in time. Activities and resources can be constrained in a number of aspects, and the scheduling process has to resolve them. Activity constraints include duration, start times, end times, and precedence constraints. Resource constraints include capacity, availability, and resource setup time constraints. The constraints, together with the search algorithm, define the space of admissible solutions.

Le Pape (1994) classifies scheduling problems into three categories according to the degrees of freedom in positioning resource supply and resource demand intervals in time:

- Pure scheduling problems (e.g., job-shop machine scheduling),
- Resource allocation problems (e.g., allocation of people to tasks), and

• Joint scheduling and resource allocation problems.

These three categories in fact represent a large variety of scheduling problems. The existence of such a variety of scheduling problems prompted the development of a number of constraint solvers and scheduling procedures which are designed to deliver optimal or near optimal schedules for a particular range of problems.

Desired Properties of Constraint Agents

Agents operating with only partial knowledge of the surrounding environment are prime candidates for the implementation of reasoning using constraint solvers. Agents can share and exchange knowledge in a distributed fashion. The suggestion-correction process used in negotiation strategies corresponds to mapping constraint satisfaction problems to search algorithms and heuristics (Tsang, 1993). The planning and scheduling systems can be treated as CSPs that allow the use of constraint solvers to support the planning activity of an agent. However, similar to analytical tools, constraint solvers represent static models of CSP. In order to achieve flexibility in the decision-making process, the solver has to be able to incorporate an agent's essential characteristics:

i) reactive behavior,
ii) rational behavior with bounded resources,
iii) social abilities,
iv) mobility (lightweight core).

Reactive behavior is characterized by the agent's ability to absorb new information and restrict or relax its actions. When constraint solvers face the relaxation of constraints, they recompute the entire problem. Relaxation in constraint planners and schedulers nearly always results in reduced stability and possibly reduced quality of solutions. Despite the recent implementation of constraint solvers in graphical applications (Sadeh, 1995; Borning, 1995) with real-time computation and stability, constraint relaxation and adaptive behavior still represent some difficulties for practical applications.

An agent's *rational behavior* and fast reaction to the changes in its environment are difficult to support with constraint solvers. Some scheduling systems incorporate this idea and extend or replace deliberative planning with behavior rules (ILOG, 1996). The majority of existing constraint solvers compute the search for solutions off-line. An approach to eliminate this problem is the development of an anytime algorithm (Zilberstein, 1995) and constraint hierarchies (Zanden, 1996). Some CSPs are suitable for iterative local search techniques, such as annealing, tabu search, or genetic algorithms (Kautz, 1996). Additional information on suitability can be found in Tsang (1993).

Representation of time in traditional planning systems is based on Allen's model of temporal relations (Allen, 1985) and usually implemented with STRIPS like programs. This representation does not seem suitable for multi-agent interaction with complex temporal relationships and commitment protocols. Problems arise with respect to concurrency and events that last over a period of time.

Social abilities mean interaction, negotiation, coordination, and/or cooperation among agents. A language, or interaction protocol, typically supports these social skills. The ultimate goal of cooperation and coordination is to reach a globally optimal solution independent of the language or protocol used. If we map the cooperation goals into distributed problem-solving strategies and let each agent play the role of a cooperating computational unit instead of an autonomous negotiator, it is then possible to deploy distributed constraint satisfaction problem-solving strategies.

Multi-agent solutions to the distributed constraint problems require new types of design frameworks based on replaceable components which can accommodate the local autonomy of agents, several negotiation strategies, cooperative problem solving, on-line search for solution, and support agent rational behavior.

DESIGN TECHNIQUES FOR NEGOTIATING AGENTS

Overview

In this section, we summarize the requirements for negotiating agents and derive the essential architectural requirements. We have identified the following four fundamental *agent building blocks* which have to be present in the system:

Problem solving engine: Many aspects of negotiation can be modeled as distributed problem solving. There is a large body of work on algorithms, optimization, and heuristics for problem solving.

Representation: Agents reason or solve problems about things, concepts, and objects. These have to be represented in a form that can be processed by the agents.

Interaction and collaboration: In order to facilitate meaningful collaboration among agents, we need to specify different protocols and protocol primitives, such as contract proposal, commitment, penalty enforcement to support composite actions (i.e., auction), contract net, and bargaining.

User interface and support for interaction with humans: Negotiation has to be carried out in the context of existing human authorization and modification rights. Automated negotiation processes are always coupled with existing organizations in order to maximize the outcome.

Agent design must accommodate static agents as well as trends in mobile agents. The lightweight architecture required for mobile agents, and an efficient and flexible negotiation strategy, are not mutually exclusive. The main issue is to provide a framework which guarantees that the negotiating agent is not overloaded with the complex intelligence which may not be used. We see an agent as a lightweight core with the ability to 'borrow' the intelligence it requires from the hosting environment.

In order to explain the architectural elements of the framework, we briefly review *agent properties* and *behavioral features*. An agent (Wooldridge, 1994) is:

i) autonomous—acts without human intervention,
ii) social—collaborates with other agents via structured messages,
iii) reactive—responds to environmental changes, and
iv) proactive—acts to achieve goals.

It is the combination of these behaviors that distinguishes an agent from objects, actors (Agha, 1986), and robots. Agent behavior is summarized in Figure 1. Agents

Figure 1. Model of Agent Behavior (Kendall, 1995)

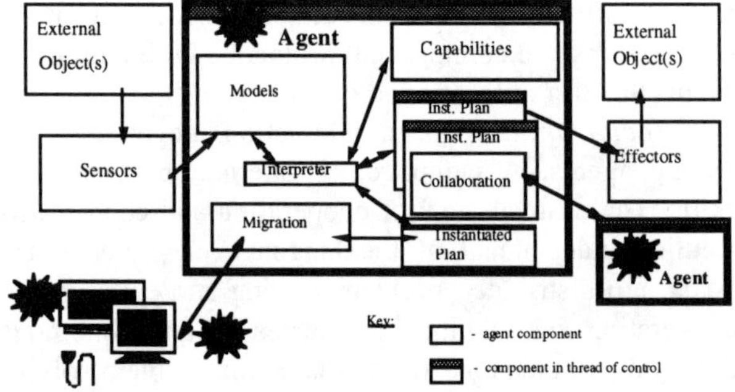

review models of the world and themselves to select a capability or plan to address the present situation. Once invoked, each plan executes in its own thread, and several of these may execute concurrently. Agents negotiate with each other; agent collaboration across disciplines may require that semantics can be exchanged. Three sample capabilities are shown in Figure 1. One involves an effector; the other two feature collaboration with other agents, either within the original society or external to it. If the agents are in different societies, they must migrate, either virtually or in reality, in order to collaborate.

In the following subsections, we present two design techniques:

i) Plug-in components, and
ii) Design patterns.

Both satisfy the *decomposition requirements, agent properties,* and *behavior features* and can accommodate analytical and evolutionary approaches, as well as constraint-based reasoning.

Components for Agent Design

Overview

In component-based design of negotiating agents, we need to support two entities: *negotiation protocol* and *negotiation strategy*. *Negotiation strategy* can be seen as a private formalized strategy responsible for computation of appropriate actions and outcomes. The generated actions and outcomes depend on the role the agent assumes, the negotiation protocol used, and the agent's relationship with other parties (e.g., cooperating self-interested agent).

Negotiation protocols, together with other constraints, restrict interaction between participating agents. There exists theoretical basis to understand the formal concepts of *negotiation protocols* (e.g., Sandholm, 1993; 1998; Decker, 1995; Smith, 1980). Each protocol follows the rules outlined below:

i) A goal which is associated with a set of parameters (attributes);
ii) Relationships among participants,
iii) Time-out and termination conditions, and
iv) Binding rules with regard to penalty, commitment, and decommitment.

From the design perspective, we need to map the above rules into a set of request and response messages, and a set of interfaces which each agent has to implement. The format of the messages (ontology) and the interfaces to support the protocols must be specified and disclosed.

The motivations for developing negotiating agents are to simplify electronic commerce, reduce the complexity of routine transactions, filter the enormous amount of information collected at a given time, and support mobile device users by asynchronous communication (Chess, 1995). The important criteria of the design are the achievement of *decision autonomy*. Each agent prefers to follow its own *negotiation strategy* which is internal (private) to the agent and not disclosed to the participating parties.

The outcome evaluation strategy is typically based on the utility function. However, the subsequent computed action depends on the reasoning module (negotiation strategy used). If the selected strategy is not producing the desired results, the agent should be able to move to a different strategy while still conforming to the given negotiation protocol. Alternatively, the negotiation can be terminated and restarted with a new protocol and strategy, providing the involved participants reach mutual agreement in this matter. Therefore, we need to build negotiation protocols and strategies as

Component-based software development is one of the most common approaches found today. In this approach, a component is a module equipped with a rich interface that can be plugged in and out of an application, as needed. The richness of the interface plays an important role, since each interchangeable component follows or subscribes to the same interface. This means that it has the same format for messaging or interaction with other components, or with a user. A restricted interface would reduce interchangeability of the component.

Two examples of plug-in, component-based agent architectures are discussed in the following subsections: DYNAMICS (Tu, 1998) Architecture and Constraint Agents.

Example 1: Dynamics Architecture

The architecture of DYNAMICS is based on three main components (see Figure 2):

1. *Communication module* which is responsible for interagent messaging. It delivers and processes any kind of messages exchanged among negotiating agents. The interoperability among different agents is provided through KQML (Finin, 1994).
2. *Protocol module* is responsible for the correctness of all incoming and outgoing messages, and the examination of proper treatment of activities by the participating agents. The role of this module is to inspect the content of each incoming or outgoing message. Implementation flexibility is achieved by the central protocol engine which is capable of intercepting protocols with complex semantics.
3. *Strategy module* which implements a negotiation strategy by producing proper actions with regard to the negotiation state, knowledge base, environment situation, and incoming messages. This module is the interface between the strategy module and the protocol for dynamically typed parameters.

Figure 2 shows a negotiation-enabled agent in the DYNAMICS architecture. The modular structure has obvious advantages: each module has clearly defined interfaces and functionality and can be developed independently. This enables different implementations or algorithms to be used with the strategy module. In addition, the protocol module can be developed and certified by a third-party instance. In this way, clear separation of 'private' strategy and 'public' communication is achieved.

Most of the application semantics are components which can be added or removed at run-time. The agents are plug-in container objects with minimal orthogonal functionality: mobility and persistence. The plug-in components are classified into the following types:

- *Roles* represent the semantics of a business entity, such as seller or buyer. By adding a role to a plug-in container, we extend the object's interface and corresponding implementation (to support dynamic binding).
- *Substitutes* provide means for replacement of an existing interface.
- *Configuration* supports dynamic reconfiguration of an application. It allows reconfiguration of the rule-based negotiation strategy.

The implementation of DYNAMICS is based on the Voyager system which provides the basic functionality for building mobile agents from well-defined components. *IPluggable* is the interface which all the objects acting as plug-in containers must implement. The interface provides *plug* and *unPlug* methods to add or remove the component from the container. This architecture is flexible, and it would be suitable for most types of reasoning engines. It permits the replacement or substitution of negotiation strategies as well as coordination protocols.

Example 2: Constraint Agents

Figure 2. Main Components of Negotiation Enabled Agents (from Tu, 1998)

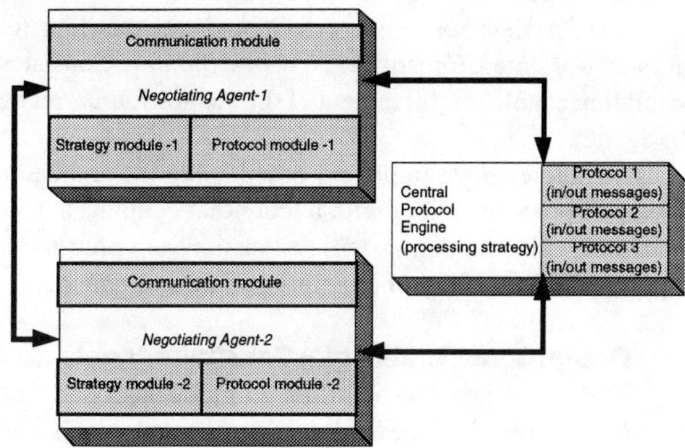

Constraint agents deal with incomplete knowledge. The typical problem-solving process consists of four steps:

- Problem decomposition into mutually interrelated subproblems,
- Finding solution subproblems,
- Detecting conflicts, and
- Refining the search space, applying constraint relaxation.

The quality of the solution and the time complexity are directly related to the type of problem. Some work has already focused on identifying the best performing algorithms and heuristics. For example, in Tsang (1993), the important point has been made: "Studying the relative performance of algorithms and heuristics is of limited value unless we identify certain characteristics for the problem set." This issue is very true for agents. We need to pinpoint the characteristics of the problem in terms of the environment, the outcome evaluation, and the type of processing (or width of the problem space) in order to claim that a particular combination of heuristics and algorithm is the best for this problem space. The design framework must be capable of using solvers and heuristics as plug-in components.

In Figure 3, we present the basic model of a component-based agent with a constraint solver (Dospisil, 1999) used as the evaluation and reasoning component. The model is composed of the following building blocks:

- *User Interface* component offers an interface between a user and an agent. The user gives a high-level request for a task to be performed, and this is translated into a collaboration request.
- *Communication Interface* is the module which supports agreed interfaces between different agents. It is composed of a set of protocols which facilitate interaction with the environment and support sending and receiving messages over the network.
- *Decision and Problem Description* module is a central module for these agents. It evaluates incoming information and invokes the appropriate processes, e.g., it calls the *Problem Solver* to evaluate the current status, or it calls the *Collaboration Module* to acquire further information from the user or peer agents. It also implements the negotiations strategy and agent-binding rules (penalty, commitment, and decommitment protocols).
- *Problem Solver*, after accepting a problem description from the *Collaboration Module*, invokes a goal-driven search to obtain one or more solutions.
- *Collaboration Module* keeps listening to the *User Interface* as well as the *Communication Interface*. Any incoming message is analyzed and relevant collaboration processes are invoked. The results are mapped into high-level problem descriptions (variables, domains, and constraints; requests for relaxation; or restriction of possible actions) and communicated to the *Decision and Problem Description* module. In

addition, the *Collaboration Module* also accepts the actions generated by the *Decision and Problem Description* module and translates them into corresponding outgoing messages to the user or to peer agents.

The *Problem Solver's* internal composition is depicted in Figure 4. The central part is an object-oriented *Constraint Network Builder.* Consistency checking and search space rebuilding enable reinforcement of the suggestion-correction process between the user and the agent.

An interesting component-based 'plug-in' architecture is also suggested in Bartak (1997). It proposes a tool with a core that contains a general hierarchy solver and meta-interpreter. The domain-specific extensions are plug-in modules. The tool is flexible and supports the reusability of domain-specific components.

Design Considerations for Constraint Agents

The major problem with this component-based framework in which one or more constraint solvers are used as plug-in components arises from the difficulties associated with the description of the constraint satisfaction problem (CSP) itself. The representation of the problem can be either under-constrained or over-constrained. In either case, the agent is dealing with incomplete knowledge and it cannot determine which of the generated solutions is optimal and suitable to use in further negotiation.

Present approaches to integrating constraint solvers into an agent's core use object-oriented techniques. Application activities and resources are modeled as the application objects. Two private variables within these objects are declared as constrained variables, and the constrained relationship between these variables defines dependency between these two objects together. The unclear issue here is the information hiding (encapsulation) as supported by object-oriented languages. In order to create a constraint on the variable outside of the application object, e.g., within the solver, so it can be maintained by the solver, the variable has to be exported from the object using a programmer's interface. However, the constraint solver may have difficulties in maintaining the constraints on the external object variables. There is no way for the constraint solver to know whether there is a mechanism within the object that relates their values or if another solver is accessing these variables. In addition, such implementations do not allow matching of algorithms with the problem and easy replacement of the solver or heuristics.

One of the most important criteria used to judge constraint solvers is their performance. In order to provide reactive and proactive behavior, it is important for the solver to generate the solution quickly enough to maintain responsiveness. This becomes more difficult to achieve as the number of constraints and variables becomes larger.

Figure 3. Component Based Agent Model with Constraint Solver (from Dospisil, 1999)

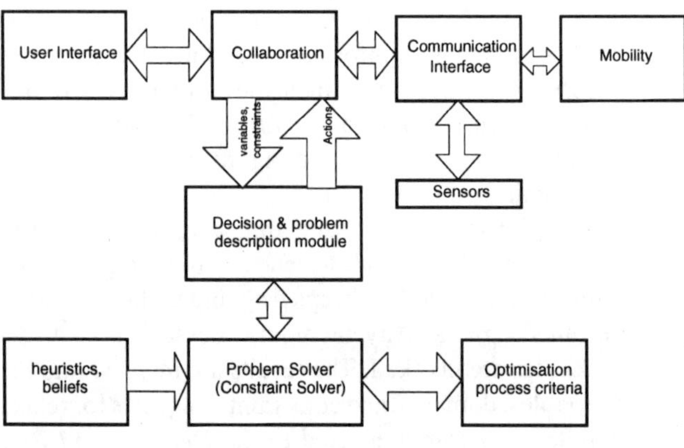

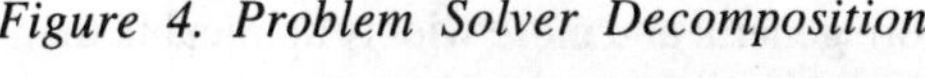

Figure 4. Problem Solver Decomposition

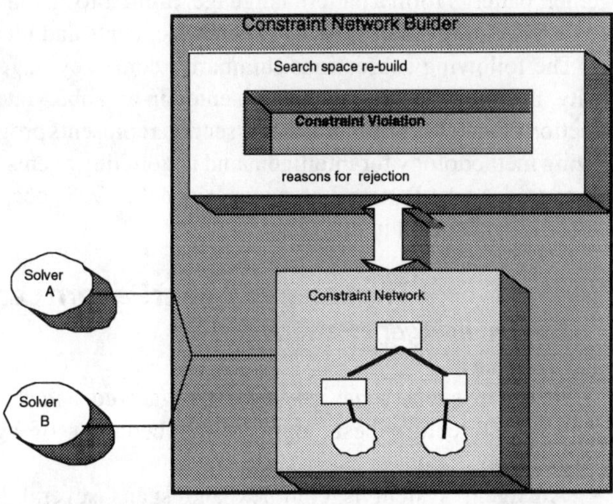

A pre-built constraint solver may be able to maintain constraints efficiently. However, declarative definitions of constraints are difficult to use in high-level agent building tools. The programmer has to understand the details of the consistency mechanism to prevent undesirable interactions when data structures are accessed from multiple procedures, since changing a data structure to maintain one relationship may invalidate another relationship. A constraint solver can process a set of constraints, taking into account any interaction between them. The need to understand the details of the algorithm within the solver undermines a major advantage of constraint solvers, namely that they provide a declarative way to define relationships which are to be maintained.

There has been very little work in incorporating constraint solvers into the reasoning and negotiation strategies of agent systems. The slow acceptance of constraint solvers seems to have been caused by three reasons:

1. Many constraint solvers only support a limited range of constraints.
2. It is difficult to understand and control constraint solvers. When the programmer defines a set of constraints, it may not be obvious how the constraint solver will maintain them.
3. If the search space is large, then on-line performance of constraint solvers may not be satisfactory for some application domains, e.g., in Eaton (1997).

The solver must allow for various types of search strategies, backtracking, and revision algorithms. The new category of *flexible schedulers* appeared in ISIS (Fox, 1984), OPIS (Smith, 1987), and FlyPast (Mott, 1988). Their architecture allows dynamic adaptation to the problem at hand.

Patterns of Negotiating Agents

A software pattern is a recurring problem and its solution; it may address conceptual, architectural, or design problems. A pattern is described in a set format to ease its dissemination. The format states the problem addressed by the pattern and the forces acting on it. There is also a context that must be present for the pattern to be valid, a statement of the solution, and any known uses. Optional sections include variations, a sample use, and a discussion of consequences.

Patterns and components are closely related concepts, and both are indicative of high-quality approaches to software design. However, component-based approaches are totally *prescriptive*; a developer directly uses the given interfaces and components. Alternatively, pattern-based approaches are *generative;* a developer employs a pattern to generate their own particular solution. While an example may be used to illustrate a pattern, the pattern is more general and more widely applicable than any one given example. Taken together, patterns form a pattern language. Similar to any language, a pattern language is a way for developers to express or *generate* concepts and ideas.

The following subsections summarize some key patterns of negotiating agents; for brevity, many of the patterns are presented in an abbreviated "patlet" form. The selected collection of patterns presented in this section represents progress toward a pattern language or living methodology for intelligent and negotiating agents. We have termed the language the Layered Agent Pattern Language (Kendall, 1998) because it is based on the layered architecture presented in this chapter.

The Layered Agent Pattern Language

The Layer Agent Pattern

Problem:

How can agent behavior be best organized and structured into software? What software architecture best supports the behavior of agents?

Forces:

- An agent system is complex and spans several levels of abstraction.
- There are dependencies between neighboring levels, with two-way information flow.
- The software architecture must encompass all aspects of agency.
- The architecture must be able to address simple and sophisticated agent behavior.

Solution:

Agents should be decomposed into layers (Buschmann, 1996) because:

i) higher level or more sophisticated behavior depends on lower level capabilities,
ii) layers only depend on their neighbors, and
iii) there is two-way information flow between neighboring layers. The layers can be identified from the model of the agent's real world; Figure 5 structures the basic model in Figure 1 into seven layers.

In Figure 5, the left side of the figure depicts top-down information flow, while the right side depicts bottom-up flow. Reading the right side, an agent's beliefs are based on sensory input. When presented with a problem, an agent then reasons to determine what to do. When the agent decides what to do, it can carry it out alone, or it can collaborate with other agents. Once the approach to collaboration is determined, messages are formulated or translated; the messages may then be delivered to distant societies by mobility.

Top-down, distant messages arrive at mobility. An incoming message may be translated into the agent's semantics. The collaboration layer determines if the agent should process a message. If the message should be processed, it is passed on to the next layer (actions). When an action is selected for processing, it is passed to the reasoning layer, if necessary. Once a plan is placed in the actions layer, it does not require the services of any lower layers, but it can call on the services of higher ones.

Variations:

The Layered Agent Architectural Pattern shown in Figure 5 is a general architecture that addresses simple and sophisticated agents. All agents do not have the seven layers. A translation layer is only needed for multidisciplinary agent societies, and many agent societies have one collaboration layer that agents share. If an agent's beliefs do not change, sensors are not needed; mobility layers may also be combined. Further, aspects of the Layered Agent pattern may only be conceptual; direct connections between nonadjacent

Figure 5. The Layered Agent Architectural Pattern

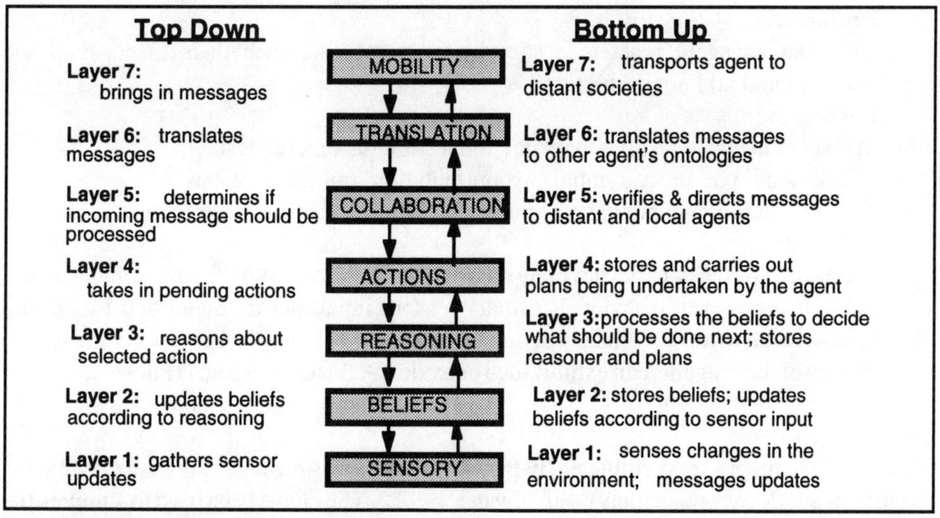

Top Down		Bottom Up
Layer 7: brings in messages	MOBILITY	**Layer 7:** transports agent to distant societies
Layer 6: translates messages	TRANSLATION	**Layer 6:** translates messages to other agent's ontologies
Layer 5: determines if incoming message should be processed	COLLABORATION	**Layer 5:** verifies & directs messages to distant and local agents
Layer 4: takes in pending actions	ACTIONS	**Layer 4:** stores and carries out plans being undertaken by the agent
Layer 3: reasons about selected action	REASONING	**Layer 3:**processes the beliefs to decide what should be done next; stores reasoner and plans
Layer 2: updates beliefs according to reasoning	BELIEFS	**Layer 2:** stores beliefs; updates beliefs according to sensor input
Layer 1: gathers sensor updates	SENSORY	**Layer 1:** senses changes in the environment; messages updates

layers can be used to address performance issues.

Known Uses:

There are many layered agent architectures. GRATE (Wooldridge, 1994) features domain, cooperation, and control layers, equivalent to sensory, beliefs, reasoning, action, and collaboration. Touring Machines (Ferguson, 1991) consist of perception, action, and control. InterRRaP (Muller, 1994) has four layers: cooperation, plan-based, behavior-based, and world interface.

Sample Usage:

A sample use of the Layered Agent is in Figure 6. In this, the individual agents each have senses, beliefs, reasoning, and actions. Because the societies are centralized, the agents share a collaboration layer and a translation layer. Three agent societies also share a common mobility layer.

The Sensory, Beliefs, and Reasoning Layers

The Sensory and Beliefs layers maintain the agent's models of its environment and itself. There are four conceptual patterns that are relevant. These patterns are distinct from one another according to the presence or absence of three factors: a symbolic model; a knowledge based, prescriptive solution; and interaction with a human user. The following table summarizes these four patterns:

Sensory, Beliefs, & Reasoning Problem	Symbolic Model	Prescribed Solution	Human Interaction	Solution	Pattern
How can an agent simply react to a stimulus or a request?	-	-	-	Utilize a stimulus/response type of behavior.	Reactive Agent
How can an agent select a plan to achieve a goal?	X	X	-	The agent reasons about a symbolic model to select a capability.	Deliberative Agent
How can an agent address problems when no solution is known?	X	-	-	Represent the problem's constraints, and let the agent find a solution.	Opportunistic Agent
How can an agent adapt to the needs of a human user ?	-	-	X	Provide the agent with parametric user models & sensors to monitor the user's actions.	Interface Agent

The Reactive Agent:

Problem:

How can an agent react to a stimulus or a request when there is no symbolic representation and no known solution?

Forces:

- An agent needs to be able to respond to a stimulus or a request.
- There may not be a symbolic representation for an application.
- An application may not have a knowledge-based, prescriptive solution.

Solution:

A Reactive Agent does not have any internal symbolic models of its environment; it acts using stimulus/response behavior. It gathers sensory input, but its Belief and Reasoning layers are reduced to a set of situated action rules. A single Reactive Agent is not proactive, but a society of these agents can exhibit such behavior. A Reactive Agent is known as a weak agent.

Known Uses:

Reactive theory was originated by Brooks (1986) and Agre and Chapman (1987), and reactive agents have been widely used (Nwana, 1997a). They have been used to simulate the behavior of ant societies and to utilize such societies for search and optimization (Ferber, 1994).

The Deliberative Agent:

Problem:

How can an agent select a capability to proactively achieve a goal within a given problem context?

Forces:

- An agent should be capable of intelligent behavior, selecting a plan to achieve a goal.
- For some applications, a symbolic representation or model of the environment can be specified.
- Some problems have a knowledge-based solution that can be identified by experts.

Solution:

A Deliberative Agent possesses symbolic reasoning models of its environment and its own capabilities within its Beliefs and Reasoning layers. It selects a plan or a capability that can achieve a goal in the context of the present situation. A Deliberative Agent is known as a strong agent.

Known Uses:

Deliberative Agents were originated by Cohen (1990) and Georgeff (1993), and they have been widely used by Jennings (1996) and others (Nwana, 1997a).

The Opportunistic Agent:

Problem:

How can an agent opportunistically address problems, identifying an approach that is not known *a priori*?

Forces:

- A problem can have a symbolic representation but not have a knowledge-based, prescriptive solution.
- For these applications, only constraints may be known; these indicate what can not be done.

Figure 6. Centralized Collaboration and Translation and Shared Mobility Layers

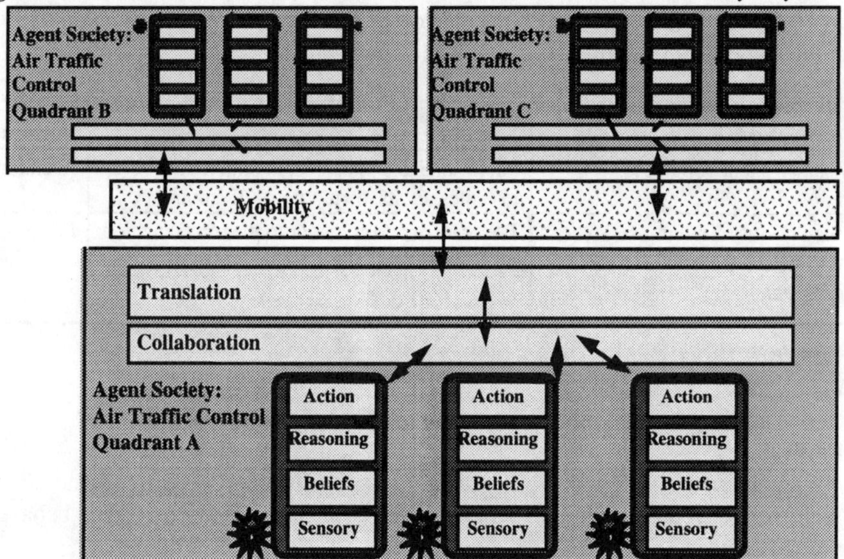

- An agent needs to be able to avoid known constraints but still move toward a solution.

Solution:

An Opportunistic Agent does not attempt to have prescriptive plans to address a problem. Rather, its Beliefs consist of constraints found in the problem, and its Reasoning or capabilities accomplish constraint propagation and satisfaction. Problems with a symbolic representation but with no known *a priori*, prescriptive solution can be solved this way. Opportunistic agents are also known as constraint agents.

Known Uses:

Fox (1984), Sadeh (1995), and Sathi (1989) have pioneered this approach and used it successfully in distributed scheduling and resource allocation.

The Interface Agent:

Problem:

How can an agent adapt to the needs of a human user?

Forces:

- Some agents work directly with a human user.
- The needs of human users are variable, but there may be certain types of recognizable behavior.

Solution:

An Interface Agent collaborates with a user. Typically, only one agent is utilized. This kind of agent observes the user and adapts to his or her needs by identifying what kind of user they are and their types of computer usage. An Interface Agent's beliefs are parametric user models, and their sensors monitor the user's actions.

Known Uses:

Maes (1994) has led the development of Interface Agents, also called Personal Assistants (Nwana, 1997b).

The Action Layer

The Action layer carries out the plan selected by the Reasoning layer. There is a need for the layer to be able to schedule and prioritize actions. Many conceptual and design patterns can be found in this layer, and detailed descriptions can be found in Kendall (1998). Two of the patterns are summarized in the following:

Action Problem:	**Solution:**	**Pattern:**
How can an agent commit to behavior ?	An instantiated plan is an Intention that executes in its own thread of control.	Intention
How can priority handling and other forms of behavior be added to an intention dynamically?	Decorate or add behavior to the run () method of the intention thread, where a plan executes.	Prioritizer

The Intention:

Problem:

How can an agent commit to performing reactive and proactive behavior?

Forces:

- An agent needs to be able to commit to proactive and reactive behavior.
- Behavior executes with the beliefs that the agent had when it (the behavior) was initiated.
- An agent may have many actions executing concurrently.
- An agent impacts the environment through effectors; it collaborates as needed.

Solution:

An Intention represents *the commitment of an agent to being in a state where it believes it is about to actually perform a set of actions* (Cohen, 1990). An instantiated plan is an Intention that executes in its own thread of control; it executes until completion, unless it is suspended. A plan's goals are stated in invocation conditions; additional criteria may be in context conditions. Conditions and plans reside in the Reasoning layer (Figure 5). If the conditions are satisfied, the plan is instantiated and executed by an Intention in the Actions layer. All variables and expressions in the plan are evaluated, based on the agent's beliefs, at the time of instantiation, when the agent commits to performing the plan. An Intention can be specialized to a Collaboration Intention and a Reaction Intention (Figure 7). Once an Intention is created, it does not require the services of any of the lower layers; collaboration can involve higher layers.

Known Uses:

Intentions were first introduced by Georgeff and Lansky (1993), as part of their Belief-Desires-Intentions (BDI) agent architecture. Intentions provide the proactive and reactive behavior of many strong and weak agent systems, (including, Cohen, 1990; Jennings, 1996).

The Prioritizer:

Problem:

How can priority handling and other forms of behavior be added to an intention dynamically?

Forces:

- Intentions need to be assigned priorities.
- Priority handling should be attached to an object, and not a class, because the type of Intention (Reactive or Collaborative) is not known before run time.

Solution:

Additional responsibilities can be attached to an Intention dynamically following the Decorator pattern (Gamma, 1994). The Prioritizer pattern can be used to decorate the run() method of the Intention Thread, where action plans are executed. The run() method is declared in Runnable interface and is called whenever a thread is started. Additional priority handling can be added dynamically to it by using the decorator object..

The Collaboration Layer

In the Collaboration layer, the agent determines its approach to cooperating or working with other agents. Conceptual, architectural, and design patterns are utilized for messaging (Conversation), centralization (Facilitator), decentralization (Agent Proxy), and social policies (Protocol, Emergent Society); they are summarized below:

Collaboration Problem:	**Solution:**	**Pattern:**
How can messaging between agents occur in sequences ?	Agent messaging can occur within a context established by previous messages.	Conversation
How can agents collaborate without direct knowledge of each other ?	Encapsulate agent interaction in a Facilitator that coordinates agents within a given society.	Facilitator
How can agents collaborate directly with one another ?	Provide a Proxy to control access to the agent and to provide distinct interfaces. Store and retrieve conversations.	Agent Proxy
How can agent collaboration be prescribed ?	Establish conversation policies that explicitly characterize communication sequences.	Protocol
How can agents cooperate to achieve goals when there is no established protocol ?	Though stimulus/response behavior, each agent can stimulate its neighbors. Complex patterns of behavior emerge when viewed globally.	Emergent Society

The Conversation:

Problem:

How can structured messaging between agents occur in sequences rather than in isolated acts ?

Forces:

- Successive messages between agents are often related.
- Endless loops of messages between agents need to be avoided.

Solution:

A Conversation (Bradshaw, 1997) is a sequence of messages between two agents, taking place over a period of time. There are termination conditions for any given occurrence, and Conversations may give rise to other Conversations. In some agent societies, messages between agents may occur only within the context of conversations; isolated messages are not supported.

Known Uses:

COOL (Barbucaenu, 1995) and AgenTalk (Nwana, 1997a) supports Conversations between agents, as does KAoS (Bradshaw, 1997).

Figure 7. Intentions in the Action Layer, Plans and Conditions in the Reasoning Layer

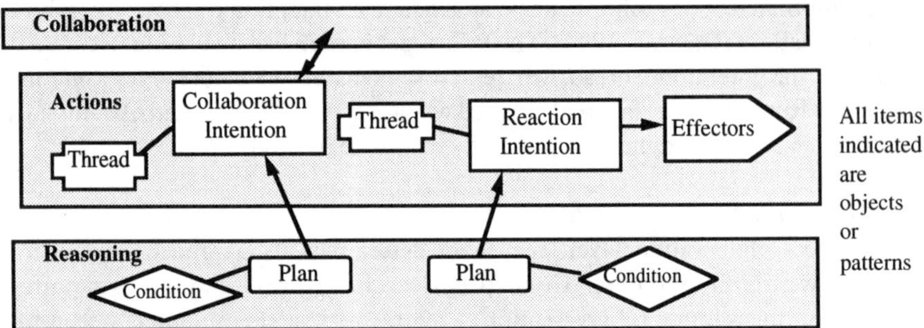

Centralized Collaboration: The Facilitator

Problem:

How is an agent able to freely collaborate with other agents without direct knowledge of their existence?

Forces:

- Each agent may not have knowledge of every other agent.
- Proliferating interconnections and dependencies increase complexity, complicate maintenance, and reduce reusability.

Solution:

Each Mediator (Gamma, 1994) is associated with a multitude of Colleagues, objects that rely on it for all communication. The Facilitator is based on the Mediator, and it provides a gateway or clearinghouse for agent collaboration (Bradshaw, 1997). With a Facilitator, agents do not have to have direct knowledge of one another for collaboration, and agents within the same society share a single Collaboration layer.

Known Uses:

ARCHON (Jennings, 1996), PACT (Tenenbaum, 1992), and other agent applications have utilized Facilitators, referring to this approach as a federated agent architecture (Nwana, 1997a)

Decentralized Collaboration: The Agent Proxy

Problem:

How can agents collaborate directly with one another?

Forces:

- An agent may not have a Facilitator to represent it. Then, each agent must communicate directly with other agents, support different interfaces, and maintain collaboration knowledge.
- Agents collaborate with each other via structured messages; there are many agent dialects.
- Bottlenecks encountered in a centralized architecture need to be avoided.
- An agent must be able to recover Conversations that it is involved in.

Solution:

A Proxy (Gamma, 1994) controls access to the Real Subject; it can also provide a distinct interface. Each Agent Proxy class (Figure 8) would subscribe to a certain interface. An agent must be able to determine its behavior based upon the state of the conversation it is involved in. One agent may be engaged in several conversations simultaneously, requiring context switching. The Memento pattern (Gamma, 1994) externalizes an object's state so that the state can be restored later. Agent Proxies that support conversations must store and recover their state, delegating this to a Memento.

Protocol:

Problem:

How can agent collaborative behavior be prescribed to follow certain policies?

Forces:

- Agents need to be able to follow certain conventions or policies for collaboration.

Solution:

Conversation policies (Bradshaw, 1997) or Protocols prescriptively encode regularities that characterize communication sequences between users of a language. Agent Protocols explicitly define what sequences of which messages are permissible between a given set of participating agents.

Known Uses:

COOL (Barbuceanu, 1995) prescribes a particular form of agent negotiation. KAoS (Bradshaw, 1997) and AgenTalk (Nwana, 1997a) stipulate several protocols or conversation policies, including contract net, inform, offer, and request (Bradshaw, 1997). In the contract net protocol, one agent asks for bids for tasks it needs performed, and other agents respond, if they are available to do the work. If a bid meets the originating agent's criteria, it can award the work to the successful bidder.

The Emergent Society:

Problem:

How can agents collaborate without known protocols? How can Reactive Agents collaborate?

Forces

- There may not be known agent protocols for a given application.
- Reactive Agents need to be able to collaborate and carry out proactive behavior together.
- Reactive Agents simply react to stimuli and are not capable of any knowledge- based behavior.

Solution:

Each individual agent, even a Reactive Agent, can provide a stimulus to a neighboring agent. As each individual agent reacts to stimuli provided by their neighbors, the net result is the Emergent Society. Complex patterns of behavior can emerge from these interactions when the society is viewed globally (Nwana, 1997a). No model exists for this behavior, although economic and game theory have been applied successfully. Reactive Agents and agents from Emergent Societies have reduced Collaboration layers; they merely provide stimuli to neighboring agents.

Known Uses:

All Reactive Agent systems (Ferber, 1994) rely on the Emergent Society for collaboration (Nwana, 1997a).

Other Collaboration Patterns

Many more collaboration patterns can be found in Deugo (2000). Some of these are briefly summarized in this subsection.

Blackboard Pattern:

Problem:

How can you ensure the cohesion of a group of specialized agents?

Forces:

- It is difficult to hard-wire agent collaboration if the locations of the collaborating agents are not fixed.
- Agents may have been independently designed, making it difficult to enforce a common way of collaborating.
- Collaboration can be expressed using the data access mechanisms of the coordination medium. This means that the coordination logic is embedded into the agents.

Figure 8. The Agent Proxy Pattern for Decentralized Collaboration

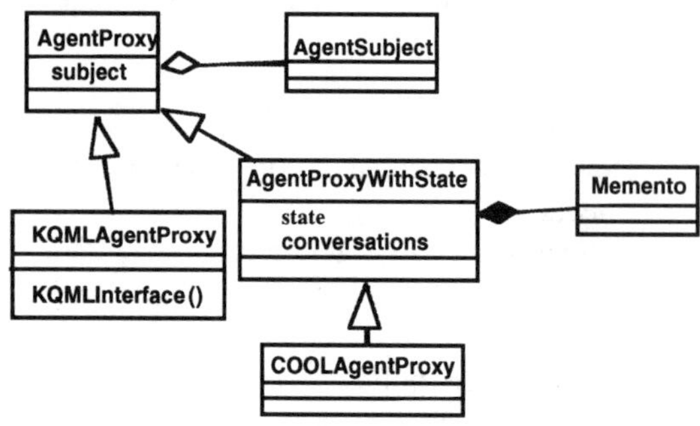

Solution:

The solution to the problem involves a blackboard where agents can add data and subscribe for data updates. Agents can also modify data and erase it from the blackboard. The agents continually monitor the blackboard for changes and signal when they want to add, erase, or update data.

When multiple agents want to respond to a change, a supervisor decides who may make a modification. The supervisor also decides when the blackboard has sufficiently progressed and a solution to the task has been found. The supervisor acts as a scheduler for the other agents, deciding when and whether to let them modify the blackboard. It does not facilitate their interaction with each other. The structure and main interactions of this pattern are shown in Figure 9.

Known Uses:

The blackboard concept first appeared in Hayes-Roth's BB1 system (Hayes-Roth, 1985). Many agent-based systems have employed the blackboard pattern (Talukdar, 1986; Weiss, 1992).

Meeting Pattern:

Problem:

How can agents agree to coordinate their tasks and mediate their activities?

Forces:

- Messaging between agents located within the same environment is fast, secure, and simple.
- Remote agents require several messages and interactions with other agents across the network.
- Direct interaction is a simple technique that is easy to implement.

Solution:

Create a place for agents to meet. Let an agent call for a meeting at that meeting place. Permit interactions to occur in the context of the meeting. These will enable agents to communicate and synchronize with one another, coordinating their activities.

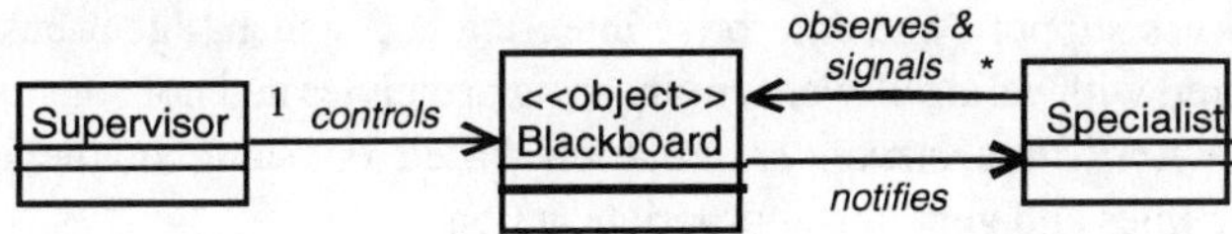

Figure 9. Role Diagram of the Blackboard Pattern (Deugo, 2000)

The first part of the solution involves the construction of a named meeting place in the context of an existing environment. A meeting is an event, and the Meeting Manager is responsible for notifying agents when one is proposed. The Meeting Manager accepts messages from agents that want to register for notification of specific meetings. The Meeting Manager also accepts messages from remote or local agents interested in calling a meeting and informs registered agents of when the meeting will occur. The Meeting Manager also has the responsibilities of controlling the meeting, registering agents as they arrive, and deregistering them as they depart.

Known Uses:

IBM's Aglet's framework makes use of a meeting (Aridor, 1998). Concordia (Wong, 1997) also uses the pattern. Place-oriented communication (Kitamura, 1999) is another example.

Negotiating Agents Pattern:

Problem:

How can you detect and resolve conflicting intentions between agents?

Forces:

- Agents need to align their actions and resolve conflicts.

Solution:

In this solution, agents make their intentions explicit, exchanging constraints on what the other agents are allowed to do. In response to the disclosures, the agents may replan their actions to avoid detected interactions with their own intentions. The solution involves an initiator who starts a negotiation by declaring its intention to its peers, which are all the other agents who must be consulted. The peers take on the role of critics in the negotiation. They test if there is a conflict. If there is none, a critic accepts the proposed action; otherwise it makes a counterproposal or rejects the action. Counterproposals contain alternative actions that are acceptable to the critic. Rejections indicate that there is an impasse that can only be handled outside the negotiation framework. Figure 10 shows the structure of this pattern.

An agent can be an initiator and a critic in different negotiations at the same time. Therefore we create another role, that of a participant, which contains the initiator and critic roles. Participants often act on behalf of other agents for whom they are negotiating. For instance, an initiator may negotiate on behalf of a buyer agent about the terms of a transaction. Once the terms have been determined, the buyer pays the negotiated amount to the seller and receives the good.

Known Uses:

This pattern is popular in the telecommunications (Griffeth, 1993) and the supply-chain domains (Barbuceanu, 1998). The concept of market sessions in MAGNET (Steinmetz, 1999) also exemplifies this pattern. The supply chain role model in the ZEUS agent building toolkit introduces similar roles: negotiation initiator and partner (Collis, 1999).

CONCLUSION AND FUTURE TRENDS

Agents are fairly complex and ambitious software systems. They will be entrusted with advanced and critical applications, such as network administration, workflow/business process support, and enterprise integration. As such, agent-based systems must be engineered with valid software engineering principles and not constructed in an ad hoc fashion.

Analytical strategies are tools based on static mathematical model to evaluate outcomes and generate appropriate action. With *evolutionary* or *genetic approaches*, the learning process is more effective and models are adaptable. The advances in *constraint technology* enable the design and implementation of planning and scheduling tasks to be treated as constraint satisfaction problems. The agent concept then can be used to support dynamic adaptation and collaboration of local or distributed problem-solving modules.

Figure 10. Role Diagram of the Negotiating Agents Pattern (Deugo, 2000)

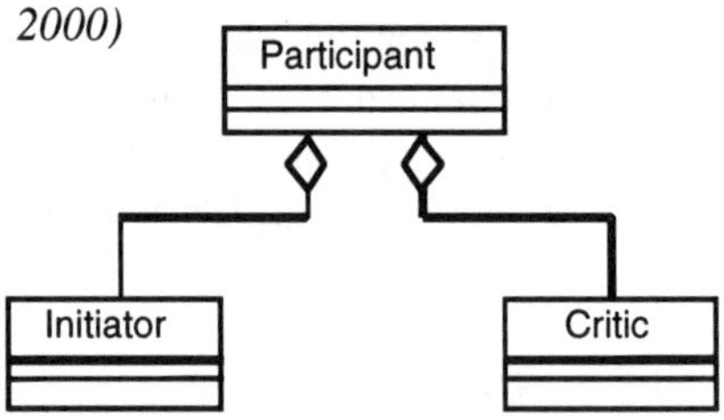

Design and implementation of any reasoning strategies and collaboration protocols can lead to complex systems, and these issues can also lead to code that is difficult to maintain. The protocols of interaction are complicated and they typically have many levels or states. If a reasoning engine is very large and complex, it restricts and slows an agent's mobility, rationality, and real-time responsiveness. In recent years, patterns of agent collaboration and negotiation, and some useful components and architectures have emerged. Reusable components and generative patterns can greatly improve the quality of agent designs and implementations.

Any agent, and mobile agents in particular, should have the capability to adapt their negotiation strategy and protocol according to the tasks at hand. In order to match tasks with the appropriate negotiation and collaboration strategies, the agent should have the ability and the means to select a negotiation strategy as a component and then "plug" it in for use. This is addressed by the components described earlier. It is also provided by the layered architecture and the collaboration patterns covered subsequently in the chapter..

These approaches to designing and implementing an agent must address the following considerations:

- An agent's specific role or roles may not be known at the compilation time. New roles and new capabilities need to be added at runtime.
- Simple and special-purpose agents have limited negotiation processes and therefore have limited capabilities. On the other hand, more sophisticated capabilities require more processing time.
- With mobility, the required functionality may need to be loaded on demand. New negotiation mechanisms can be supported by the agent's ability to 'search' for a given component, and satisfy a particular interface in a plug-and-play or plug-and-work fashion.

The coordination of a set of largely autonomous agents focuses on three particular issues:

- *Resource allocation.* The outcome of an agent's strategies is to use knowledge to allocate resources and distribute products while maximizing their utility.
- *Rationality aspect.* Most of the theoretical models assume that an agent's behavior is

rational in terms of knowledge and goals. The problems with incomplete knowledge are difficult to model.

- *Decentralized decision making*. Individual agent decisions impact the behavior of the overall society.

H. Nwana in (Nwana, 1998) discusses the contradiction between the research in agent coordination and reasoning, and the reality of implementing real applications. He suggests that we should continue with "borrowing and consolidation" using already established AI work. This evolutionary path requires adaptable design techniques to support the trends in AI. With regard to the two design techniques (patterns and components) presented in this chapter, we are experiencing a paradigm shift in agent technology. Instead of building specific negotiation strategies and protocol cores for each problem domain, we build agents with robust, adaptable core capabilities. The agent's negotiation strategy and protocols are then components or pattern-based building blocks which are "borrowed" and matched with the task at hand.

Future trends in the design of negotiating agents will undoubtedly track those in software engineering in general. Interesting and valuable future developments are expected to appear in the areas of separation of concerns and aspect-oriented programming (AOP). Object-oriented techniques, components and patterns have revolutionized software engineering. However, as software applications get more ambitious and complicated, object technology reaches its limits, especially due to its inability to address behavior and functionality that crosscuts an object hierarchy. Research completed by E. A. Kendall and described in (Kendall, 1999b) has considered how the separation of concerns and AOP can be used to improve the quality of agent designs. Role modelling is another key area for future research, and this area is also detailed in (Kendall, 1999b).

REFERENCES

Agha, G. (1986). *A Model of Concurrent Computation in Distributed Systems*. Cambridge: MIT Press.

Agre, P. E., and Chapman, D. (1987). Pengi: An implementation of a theory of activity. *Proceedings of the 6th National Conference of Artificial Intelligence*.

Allen, J.F., and Hayes, P.J. (1985). A common-sense theory of time. *Proceedings International Joint Conference on Artificial Intelligence*, 528-531.

Aridor, Y. and Lange, D. (1998). Agent design patterns: Elements of agent application design, *The Second International Conference of Autonomous Agents, IEEE.*

Barbuceanu, M. and Fox, M. S. (1995). COOL: A language for describing coordination in multi-agent systems", *First International Conference on Multi-Agent Systems*.

Barbuceanu, M. (1998). Coordination with obligations. *Second International Conference on Autonomous Agents*. IEEE. 62-69.

Bartak, R. (1997). A plug-in architecture of constraint hierarchy solvers. *Proceedings of the Conference Practical Applications of Constraint Technology*. 359-369.

Bellman, R., Esogbue, A., and Nabeshima, I. (1982). *Mathematical Aspects of Scheduling and Applications*. Oxford: Pergamon Press.

Borning, A., (1995). The OTI constraint solver: A constraint library for constructing interactive graphical user interfaces. *Proceedings of the 1st International Conference on Principles and Practice of Constraint Programming*, 624-628.

Bradshaw, J. M., S. Dutfield, P. Benoit, and Woolley, J.D. (1997). KAoS: Toward an industrial-strength open distributed agent architecture. Bradshaw, J.M. (Ed.), *Software Agents*, AAAI/

MIT Press.

Brooks, R. A. (1986). A Robust Layered Control System for Mobile Robot. *IEEE Journal of Robotics and Automation.* RA-2(1).

Buschmann, F., Meunier, R., Rohnert, H., Sommerlad, P., and Stal, M. (1996). *Pattern-Oriented Software Architecture: A System of Patterns.* Wiley.

Chess, D., Grosof, B., Harrison, C., Levine, D., Parris, C., and Tsudik, G.. (1995). Itinerant agents for mobile computing. *Technical Report RC 20010*, IBM Research Division, T.J. Watson Research Center.

Coffman, J. (Ed.) (1976). *Computer and Job-Shop Scheduling Theory.* New York: Wiley.

Cohen, P. R., and Levesque, H. J. (1990). Intention is Choice with Commitment. *Artificial Intelligence,* 42(3).

Collis, J., and Ndumu, D. (1999). The Role Modelling Guide. *In: ZEUS Methodology Documentation.* British Telecom Laboratories.

Decker, K., and Lesser, V. (1995). Analyzing the Need for Meta-Level Communication. Computer Science Department, University of Massachusetts, *Technical Report* 93-22.

Deugo, D., Weiss, M., and Kendall, E. (2000). *Reusable Patterns for Agent Coordination,* Tolksdorf, R (Ed.), *in Coordination of Internet Agents: Models, Technologies, and Applications.*

Dospisil, J. (1999). Design Framework for Constraint-Based Agents. *Technical Report.* SoNC, Monash University.

Eaton, P.S., Freuder, E.C., and Wallace, R.J. (1997). Constraint-Based Agents: Assistance, Cooperation, Compromise. *Report.* Computer Science Department, University of New Hampshire.

Ferber, J. (1994). Simulating with Reactive Agents. E. Hillebrand and J. Stender (Eds.), *in Many Agent Simulation and Artificial Life*, Amsterdam, IOS Press, 8–28.

Ferguson, I.A. (1991). Towards an Architecture for Adaptive, Rational, Mobile Agents. *Proceedings of the Third European Workshop on Modelling Autonomous Agents and Multi-Agent Worlds* (MAAMAW-91).

Finnin, T., Fritzson, R., McKay, D., and McEntire, R. (1994). KQML as an Agent Communication Language. *In Proceedings of the Third International Conference on Information and Knowledge Management* (CIKM''4), ACM Press.

Fox, M.S., and Smith, S.F. (1984). *ISIS: A Knowledge-Based System for Factory Scheduling.* Expert Systems, 1(1), 25-49.

Fudenberg, D., and Tirole, J. (1983) Sequential bargaining with incomplete information. *Review of Economic Studies,* 50, 221-247.

Fudenberg, D., and Tirole, J. (1991). *Game Theory. Cambridge*: MIT Press.

Gamma, E.R., Helm, R., Johnson, R., and Vlissides, J. (1994). *Design Patterns: Elements of Reusable Object-Oriented Software.* Addison-Wesley.

Georgeff, M.P., and Lansky, A.L. (1993). "Reactive Reasoning and Planning." *Proceedings of the Sixth National Conference on Artificial Intelligence,* Seattle, WA.

Goldberg, D.E. (1989). *Genetic Algorithms in Search, Optimisation and Machine Learning.* Reading, MA: Addison-Wesley.

Griffeth, N., and Velthuijsen, H. (1993). Reasoning about goals to resolve conflicts. *International Conference on Intelligent Cooperating Information Systems*, 197–204, IEEE.

Hayes-Roth, B. (1985). A Blackboard Architecture for Control. *Artificial Intelligence*, 251-321.

ILOG. (1996). *ILOG SCHEDULER User's Manual.*

Jennings, N.R., P. Faratin, M. Johnson, P. O'Brien, and M. Wiegand. (1996). "Using Intelligent Agents to Manage Business Processes." *First International Conference on the Practical*

Application of Intelligent Agents and Multiagent Technology, London.

Kautz, H., and Selman, B. (1996). Pushing the Envelope: Planning, Propositional Logic, and Stochastic Search. *Proceedings of the Thirteenth National Conference on Artificial Intelligence* (AAAI-96), 1194-1201.

Kendall, E.A., Malkoun, M.T., and Jiang, C.H. (1995). A Methodology for Developing Agent-Based Systems for Enterprise Integration, Enterprise Integration '95. IFIP TC5 *SIG Working Conference on Models and Methodologies for Enterprise Integration*, Heron Island, Australia.

Kendall, E.A., Murali Krishna, P.V., Pathak, C.V., and Suresh, C.B. (1998). Patterns of Intelligent and Mobile Agents. *Proceedings of Autonomous Agents '98.*

Kendall, E., Murali Krishna, P.V., Pathak, C.V., and Suresh, C.B. (1999a). A Framework for Agent Systems. *Implementing Applications Frameworks: Object-Oriented Frameworks at Work*, Fayad, M., Schmidt, D.C., Johnson, R. (Eds.) Wiley & Sons.

Kendall, E. (1999b). Role Model Designs and Implementations with Aspect-Oriented Programming. *Proceedings of the 1999 Conference on Object-Oriented Programming Systems, Languages, and Applications* (OOPSLA'99), ACM Press, November.

Kephart, J. O., Hanson, J.E., Levine, D.W., Grosof, B.N., Sairamesh, J., Segal, R.B., and White, S.R. (1998). Dynamics of an Information-Filtering Economy. *Proceedings of Second International Workshop on Cooperative Information Agents* (CIA-98), Paris, July 4-7.

Kitamura, Y, Mawarimichi, Y., and Tatsumi, T. (1999). Mobile-Agent Mediated Place-Oriented Communication, *Proceedings of the Third International Workshop on Cooperative Information Agents,* LNAI 1652, Springer, 232-242.

LePape, C. (1994). Using a Constraint-Based Scheduling Library to Solve a Specific Scheduling Problems. *Proceedings of the AAAI-SIGMAN Workshop on AI Approaches to Modelling and Scheduling Manufacturing Processes*, TAI, New Orleans, Louisiana.

Mackworth, A.K. (1977) Consistency in Network Relations. *Artificial Intelligence*, 8(1), 99-118.

Maes, P. (1994). Agents that Reduce Work and Information Overload. *Communications of the ACM*, 37(7), 31–40.

Marriott, K., Sargeant, T., and Armstrong, T. A (1996). C++ constraint solver. *Proceedings of Summer USENIX Conference*, Nashville, June.

Mass-Colell, A., Whinston, R., and Green, J.R. (1995). *Microeconomic Theory.* Oxford University Press.

Mott, D.H., Cunningham, J., Kelleher, G., and Gadsden, J.A. (1988). Constraint-Based Reasoning for Generating Naval Flying Programmes. *Expert Systems*, 5(3), 226-246.

Muller, J.P., M. Pischel, and M. Thiel, (1994). Modelling interacting agents in dynamic environments, *Proceedings of the Eleventh European Conference on Artificial Intelligence* (ECAI-94), Amsterdam.

Nareyek, A. (1998). Constraint-Based Agents. *Technical Report*, German National Research Center for Information Technology, Berlin.

Nash, J. (1950). The Bargaining Problem. *Econometrica*, 18, 155-162.

Nwana, H. S., Lee, L., and Jennings, N.R. (1997a). Coordination in Multi- Agent Systems. *in Software Agents and Soft Computing, Towards Enhancing Machine Intelligence,* Nwana H.S., and Azarmi, N. (Eds.), Springer.

Nwana, H. S., and Ndumu, D.T. (1997b). An Introduction to Agent Technology. *in Software Agents and Soft Computing, Towards Enhancing Machine Intelligence*, Nwana, H.S., and Azarmi, N. (Eds.), Springer.

Nwana, H.S., and Ndumu, D.T. (1998). A Perspective on Software Agents Research. *In ZEUS Methodology Documentation*, British Telecom Laboratories.

Oliver, J.R. (1996). On Artificial Agents for Negotiation in Electronic Commerce. PhD Thesis, Wharton.

Osborne, M.J., and Rubinstein, A. (1990) *Bargaining and Markets*. Academic Press.

Osborne, M.J., and Rubinstein, A. (1994). *A Course in Game Theory*. Cambridge: The MIT Press.

Sadeh, N.M., and Fox, M.S. (1995). Variable and Value Ordering Heuristics for the Job Shop Scheduling Constraint Satisfaction Problem. *Technical Report* CMU-RI-TR-95-39. Carnegie Melon University.

Sandholm, T. (1993). An implementation of the contract net protocol based on marginal cost calculations. *American Association for Artificial Intelligence,* 256-262.

Sandholm, T.W., and Lesser, V.R. (1998). Issues in Automated Negotiation and Electronic Commerce: Extending the Contract Net Protocol. *Readings in AGENTS,* Huhns, M.N., & Singh, M.P. (Eds.), Morgan Kaufmann, pp. 66-73

Sathi, A., and Fox., M. (1989). Constraint- Directed Negotiation of Resource Allocations," *In: Distributed Artificial Intelligence* 2, Gasser, L., and Huhns, M. (Eds.), Morgan Kaufmann.

Sen, S., and Durfee, E., (1994). The role of commitment in cooperative negotiation. *International Journal of Intelligent Cooperative Information Systems*, 3(1), 67-81.

Smith, R.G. (1980). The Contract Net Protocol: High-Level Communication and Control in a Distributed Problem Solver. *IEEE Trans. on Computers,* C-29(12), 1104-1113.

Smith, S.F. (1987). A Constraint-Based Framework for Reactive Management of Factory Schedules. *Proceedings of the First International Conference on Expert Systems and the Leading Edge in Production Planning and Control,* Charleston, South Carolina, 204-213.

Steinmetz, E., Collins, J., and Jamison, S., et al. (1999). Bid Evaluation and Selection in the MAGNET Automated Contracting System. In: Noriega, P. and Sierra, C. (Eds.), *Agent-Mediated Electronic Commerce*, 105-125, LNAI 1571, Springer.

Talukdar, S., Cordozo, E., and Leao, L. (1986) Toast: The Power System Operator's Assistant. *IEEE Expert*, 53-60, July.

Tenenbaum, J.M., J.C. Weber, and T.R. Gruber. (1992) Enterprise Integration: Lessons from SHADE and PACT, in Enterprise Integration Modeling," Petrie, C.J. (Ed.), *Proceedings of the First International Conference*, MIT Press.

Tsang, E., and Borrett, P.K. (1993). *Foundation of Constraint Satisfaction*. Academic Press.

Tsang, E., Borrett, J., and Kwan, A. (1994). An Attempt to Map the Performance of a Range of Algorithm and Heuristic Combinations. *Technical Report*, University of Essex, September CSM-210.

Tu, M.T., Griffel, F., Merz, M., and Lamersdorf, W. (1998). A Plug-in Architecture Providing Dynamic Negotiation Capabilities for Mobile Agents. *Distributed Systems Group*, Computer Science Department, University of Hamburg

Weiss, G. (1999). *Multiagent Systems*. MIT Press.

Weiss, M., and Stetter, F. (1992). A Hierarchical Blackboard Architecture for Distributed AI Systems. *Fourth International Conference on Software Engineering and Knowledge Engineering,* 349-355, IEEE.

Wong, D., Paciorek, N., Walsh, T., DiCelie, J., Young, M., and Peet, B. (1997). Concordia: An Infrastructure for Collaborating Mobile Agents. *Proceedings of the First International Workshop on Mobile Agents.*

Wooldridge, M.J., and Jennings, N.R. (1994). Agent Theories, Architectures, and Languages. *European Conference on Artificial Intelligence '94 Workshop on Agent Theories, Architectures, and Languages,* Amsterdam, Carbonell, J.G., and Siekmann, J. (Eds.), Springer–Verlag.

Zanden, B. (1996). An incremental algorithm for satisfying hierarchies of multi-way dataflow constraints. *ACM Transactions on Programming Languages and Systems*, 18(1), 30-72.

Zeng, D., and Sycara, K. (1996). How Can an Agent Learn to Negotiate?. Muller, J.P., Wooldgridge, M.J., and Jennings, N.R. (Eds.), *Intelligent Agents III: Agent Theories, Architectures, and Languages (Proceedings of European Conference on Artifical Intelligence'96)*, LNCS. Springer, August.

Zilberstein, S., and Russell, S. (1995). Approximate Reasoning Using Anytime Algorithms. In Natarajan, S. (ed.), *Imprecise and Approximate Computation*, Kluwer Academic Publishers.

Chapter IX

Customised Electronic Commerce with Intelligent Software Agents

William K. Cheung, C.H. Li, Ernest C.M. Lam, and Jiming Liu
Hong Kong Baptist University, Hong Kong

This chapter describes a conceptual framework for designing and developing software agents that will enable customized electronic commerce (CEC) and highlights several important constructs as well as their interrelationships within the framework. In particular, it examines the enabling technologies under two categories, namely, on-line cataloging and recommendation. In order to demonstrate some of the key characteristics of customized electronic commerce, this chapter also presents three prototyped software agents, namely, ETA (Electronic Tour Agent), EPA (Electronic Property Agent), and EAA (Electronic Auction Agent).

INTRODUCTION

Electronic commerce on the Internet is about on-line exchange of information, services, and products. Customers look for products that meet their needs and dealers try to identify potential customers of their products. Matching products with potential customers is a nontrivial process.

The Web provides an affordable and convenient way for information exchange between customers and dealers. Keyword search engines have been available nowadays in many company Web sites for helping visitors (and potential customers) to identify products that they are interested in. However, as the size of the virtual marketplace (i.e., the Web) is tremendously large and is growing at a tremendously fast pace, matching customers and dealers in Internet commerce remains a costly process—customers often experience a hard time in digging up and comparing product information available in the Web, whereas dealers spend a great effort in advertising their products.

With the advent of the software agent technology, the goal of agent-based customized electronic commerce is to alleviate the aforementioned problems by empowering customers in accessing and using electronic commerce services and enabling dealers to gain competitive advantages in finding customers for their products and in providing services without frictional costs. A naive definition of a software agent is a program that can act on behalf of its owner, which is originated from the field of intelligent agents (Russel & Norvig, 1995; Nwana, 1996). A generic model of an intelligent agent is typically defined with at least a goal (e.g., locating products relevant to customer interests), an input interface (e.g., a Web page crawler), a performance element (e.g., identifying matches between the interests and Web pages), an actor (e.g., sending customized messages to the customers automatically), and a learning element (e.g., improving the matching relevancy based on the customer feedback).

Needs for Customized Electronic Commerce

Advances in Internet technology are overwhelming such that connectivity on demand and media on demand have now become a reality. Making the best use of Internet technology is fast emerging to become the norm of daily business and life. Such a norm will present at least four immediate implications for customizing electronic commerce systems with intelligent software agents:

1. **Trading Opportunities.** What we know as steady, constant supply and demand in a traditional marketplace may soon be replaced by electronic selling and buying in a boundary-less Internet marketplace.

   The Web provides a new means of trading commodities. The interests of customers as well as the availability of products from dealers can change dynamically from time to time. These changes may be short-termed or long-termed, making the analysis of the overall market complicated. What usually happens in present day electronic commerce is: (1) a dealer sells his or her items simply because these are the *only* items that he or she has at the moment, or (2) a customer buys a certain item simply because it is the *last* item that he or she can find that partially fits his or her need. In some cases, customers may not even know exactly what they are looking for. Software agent-based customized electronic commerce attempts to change the existing on-line buying and selling into the following new scenarios: (1) a dealer identifies and offers what exactly customers are interested in, and (2) a customer finds and purchases what he or she really loves by comparing the captured customer interest with product information in a just-in-time manner.
2. **Customer Relationship.** What used to be a face-to-face customer-business relationship will soon be replaced by a virtual customer-business relationship. The needs of the customers can be very specific. Simpleminded one-to-one marketing will be too costly to be justified unless there are some (semi-) autonomous ways of achieving that.

   Many existing Web sites are at present constructed based on a set of static projections and fixed assumptions. It would be helpful to develop and deploy on-line intermediaries in the electronic marketplace that can provide or pawn auxiliary services, evaluate the quality of products, and provide recommendations on related or similar products. From the dealers' point of view, each customer is unique in both demographic (e.g., age, gender, occupation, and location) and psychographic (e.g., friendship, trust, like-mindedness, gossip, and opinion) senses. Software agents will be able to detect what customers' buying patterns are forming and how they are structured, and hence effectively manage the on-line commerce. Collaborative recommendation agents can help individual customers aggregate into groups, which can in turn form a dynamic marketplace.

3. **Proliferation of Information.** What is supposed to make us better informed for business and leisure may soon be found to be hard to digest, simply because of information overload in diversity, source, scope, and exchange/updating rate. For instance, there can be a large number of similar products available from numerous dealers on the Web. The results returned by keyword search engines will obviously be too much to examine and choose from.

   It would be necessary that there exist intermediaries that identify efficient information channels, remove noises, and create new shortcuts. Software agents as information content mediators can play an important role in dynamically creating pull-and-push advertising. Here, by pull-and-push advertising we mean that a customer expresses his or her favorites during the interaction with the agents (pull advertising) and in return the agents search and deliver the information about the favorite items dynamically to the customer (push advertising), Such agents can also increase the positive externality of products, that is, the better people are informed about certain products, the more likely the products will be sold.
4. **Ease of Use.** What is supposed to be a means for improving people's quality of life may soon be proven to be a real burden of frequent adaptations and long learning curves. Electronic commerce on the Internet is a chaotic, less mature marketplace. The descriptions about the same products in the catalogs of different company Web sites can be very different. Customers often have to spend extra time and effort in browsing and understanding them for quality and price comparisons. Software agent-based customized electronic commerce is aimed to help Internet customers cope with this situation by providing more intelligent interfaces and hence benefit from even-increasingly sophisticated Internet technology.

In view of the aforementioned challenges, recently we started a project on customized electronic commerce (CEC) using intelligent software agents. We refer to software agents as Web programs that can mediate among various heterogeneous Web sites, monitor contents and notify customers, perform precision information filtering, and provide tailored delivery according to the specialized needs of customers, proactively.

Emerging Personalized Internet Services

The trend of incorporating *personalized* (or customized) services into company Web sites has been observed in recent years. For example, being a registered member of Amazon.com (one of the biggest on-line bookstores in the world), their system greets you when you visit their home-page, and if you have bought something from them before, customized product recommendations will be provided automatically without answering questions. Another good example is the product of an Internet toolbar from Entrypoint.com, where users can specify their interests in different aspects of information by filling in a form, and personalized latest news will be pushed to them accordingly. In addition, there have been an increasing number of commercially available products that contain certain ingredients of personalization. Their goals are to add values to company Web sites by enabling a better understanding of customers based on demographic information, past purchase behaviors, and real-time click streams, and providing personalized services (i.e., personalized experience, personalized contents, and personalized sales suggestions and offers).

Current State of the Industry

Several companies have started to adapt to the new demand of personalizing

Web sites by developing server technologies that can filter customer browsing and purchasing behaviors in visiting Web sites and make customer-specific product recommendations in somewhat one-to-one marketing or customer management.

For instance, Microsoft Site Server 3.0 supports Personalized Web Pages, E-mails, and Channels (i.e., push technology). It contains tools for setting up Site Vocabulary and Rule Builder. This server technology has already been adopted by business giants such as Dell. Dell's system configurator allows for identifying and specifying desired configurations for desktop applications.

Andromeda's Personalization Server 3.0 (or LikeMinds) provides content-based Preference Engine for filtering and analyzing soft constraints/preferences of customers, Product Matching based on product similarity measurements, collaborative Purchase Engine based on identified customer purchasing patterns, and collaborative Clickstream Engine based on customer navigation patterns. Andromeda's technology has been adopted by Levi's in its Style Finder.

Net Perception's Recommendation Engine Suite is yet another real-time recommendation agent technology, with the capability of collaborative filtering, as has been incorporated in Amazon.com, CDNow.com, and Ticketmaster On-line. Other vendors of personalization tools include BroadVision.com, Inference.com, Personify.com, etc. A related repository can be found at the Web site of Personalization.com.

Other examples of personalized Web sites include Autobytel for assisting customers in narrowing down their choices of cars, and Lands' End for creating, editing, and viewing customized virtual models prior to buying.

Technical Issues

Technical issues in building a personalized Web store vary with respect to the complexity of personalization to be supported. Smart personalization will require active tailoring, rich profiles, and granularly tagged contents. Some of the common issues will include:

- User Profiling
  - how to plan when to observe users' interaction behaviors in order to acquire user profiles;
  - how to extract user profiles, by means of explicitly filling in forms or implicitly extracting related information such as the number of visits, the types of ad clicked, etc.; and
  - what models are to be employed in profiling, predefined stereotypes, or dynamically overlaid user-model structures.
- On-Line Cataloging
  - how to effectively retrieve information in a just-in-time manner to support specific customer needs; and
  - how to interpret and integrate different information sources for precision filtering.
- Matchmaking
  - how to store, manipulate, and mine user information efficiently and securely; and
  - how to plan and execute the adaptation to what users need.

In the literature, there have been different prototypes reported by academic and research institutions for studying and addressing the aforementioned issues.

Ardissono et al. (Ardissono, Barkero, Goy, & Petrone, 1999) have proposed a knowledge-based multi-agent architecture for personalized Web stores that can support cooperative dialog with users by suggesting and exploring different views of product descriptions through dynamically formed hypertextual pages. During interaction, the system builds user profiles by classifying users into stereotypical user classes, with respect to a set of socio-demographic parameters.

Billsus and Pazzani have implemented several agents. News Dude is a personal news agent that is motivated by a desire for ubiquitous information access and will be used as an intelligent, IP-enabled car radio that retrieves Web news based on user interests and voice feedback (Rucker & Polanco, 1999). They also developed an adaptive Web site agent for recommending scholarly publications according to the interest of the individual user in an implicit manner (Pazzani & Billsus, 1999).

Segal & Kephart (1999) developed an intelligent assistant for organizing e-mail called MailCat which can provide shortcuts to users for filing e-mails by recommending the most relevant folders that exist.

Gossip is a personal assistant that can gather information on the Internet catering to user interests by interacting with a group of distributed mobile agents for potential contributions on certain related topics (Tryllian, 1999).

The Characteristics of Customized Electronic Commerce (CEC)

A survey on some earlier agent-mediated electronic commerce systems, including those prototyped at MIT Media Lab, has been provided by Guttman et al. (Guttman, Moukas, & Maes, 1998; Maes & Moukas, 1999). These earlier systems emphasize a role of software agents that stems directly from traditional marketing Consumer Buying Behavior research. This role encompasses supports in six stages of consumer-buying activities; they are need identification, product brokering, merchant brokering, negotiation, purchase and delivery, and service and evaluation.

In our work, we take one step further beyond the present notion of agent-mediated electronic commerce and define software agent-based customized electronic commerce (CEC) in a broader sense. In the contexts of different electronic commerce applications, customers may demand different values, and hence software agents may have different objectives in customer empowerment. Their complexity will also depend on the complexity of electronic commerce systems.

Generally speaking, the objectives of CEC software agents are to enable electronic commerce systems to exhibit some or all of the following five characteristics:

1. **Content Support.** To provide customers with immediate access to the most relevant information. This support encompasses a wide spectrum of information filtering and delivery activities, such as dynamically locating, integrating, and comparing various heterogeneous Web sources, including databases, data warehouses, news wire, financial reports, newsletters, newsgroups, outbound e-mails, electronic bulletin boards, and hypermedia documents, and based on customers' profiles, tailoring and delivering the retrieved information to the customers. The provided summary information must be just-in-time (i.e., delivered whenever is needed), relevant (i.e., focused on whichever topics the customers are concerned with), and up-to-minute (i.e., refreshed whenever a new piece of information arrives). An example of applications with this type of agent support is comparison shopping that utilizes software agents with mobile and filtering capabilities.

2. **Interface Support.** To provide customers with a user-friendly style of presentation that personalizes both the interaction with customers and the content presentation. This activity involves the creation of various cognitive aids, including tables, charts, executive summaries, indices, and personalized visual assistants (e.g., graphically animated personas and virtual-reality avatars). Software agents as interfaces must offer the ease of using electronic commerce systems. The provided cognitive aids must be concise (i.e., accessible with as few manipulations as possible and as less memorization as possible) and consistent (i.e., understandable based on customers' previously customized cognitive styles).
3. **Motivational Support.** To motivate customers to enter and reenter a certain electronic commerce service. While an ever-greater proliferation of content continues to consume individuals' attention, e.g., through push technology to sell something or to support customers, software agents can play a crucial role in creating a captive audience, in educating it constantly, and even in kicking away customers' old purchase habits. To be motivational is to add value. The motivational rewards or incentives can be created by offering free access to certain information and utility resources (e.g., free software download), opportunities to participate in multi-user information/commodity exchange activities (e.g., collaborative recommendation, chat, bidding, and auction), and scheduled plans for promotional deals.
4. **Decision Support.** To assist customers in making decisions. Such decision support may be in the forms of evaluations or recommendations on the various features of certain specific items, cost-benefit analysis, inference support for optimizing utility and resources with respect to functional, time, and cost requirements, and model-based trend analysis and projections concerning new patterns of demand.
5. **Delegation Support.** To act on behalf of customers in electronic commerce activities. The tasks that software agents may delegate to achieve include matchmaking, server monitoring, negotiation, bidding, auction, transaction, transfer of goods, and follow-up support. This mode will empower a new paradigm shift from customer-centric to customer-delegated electronic commerce. The delegations of these tasks may be carried out in either semiautonomous (with customers' intervention on decisions) or fully autonomous manners.

With the above-mentioned software agent supports, not only will the richness and depth of electronic commerce services increase and new value be created, but also new forms of products and services will emerge and hence exploit the new business opportunities, as offered by the shared accessibility and availability of the Internet.

On the other hand software agent applications in electronic commerce have been, and will continue to be, the best seeds for the growth of intelligent agent technology field. As software agent technologies become more mature and standardized (e.g., through XML ontology and/or AML—Agent Markup Language), we may envision a realm that is not in the physical business world at all, where the rules of traditional business and economics are discarded and the only limitations are those of the imagination. We may expect that one day, market shares in the current physical space we live in may soon become irrelevant and outdated.

This chapter is *not* an explicit account for computational algorithms in modeling customers' interests or preferences and customizing electronic commerce systems. Yet, its primary objective is to provide a conceptual framework for designing and developing software agents that will enable customized electronic commerce, and highlight several effective techniques for building specific constructs within this framework. To evaluate the technical feasibility of the frameworks, this chapter reviews related enabling technologies based on products found in the market and research works reported in the literature. In order to demonstrate some of the key characteristics of customized electronic commerce, this chapter also describes three experimentally prototyped software agents.

The Outline of this Chapter

The remainder of this chapter is organized as follows. Section 2 provides the overview of a proposed CEC framework. Sections 3 and 4 take an in-depth look at some of the enabling technologies for building CEC modules. These technologies are grouped into two categories, namely, On-Line Cataloging and Recommendation. Section 5 describes three implemented software agents, namely, ETA (Electronic Tour Agent), EPA (Electronic Property Agent), and EAA (Electronic Auction Agent), in order to illustrate how value-added CEC systems can be effectively developed and readily deployed. Section 6 discusses several insights gained from our CEC project. Finally, Section 7 concludes the chapter.

THE CEC FRAMEWORK

The CEC framework to be described in sequel is aimed at providing a conceptual architecture with the necessary components for building an agent-based customized electronic commerce system, which can support *autonomous, customized,* and *just-in-time* services for electronic customer-to-business commerce. The proposed framework can be deployed to empower company Web sites with improved customer interaction or to support some intermediary on-line companies for providing customized product and merchant brokering services.

Framework Overview

In order to support the characteristics of CEC described in an earlier section, it is necessary for the corresponding system to be able to:

- understand the preference of individual users who are the identified potential customers (*user profiling*);
- monitor, retrieve, understand, manage, and present on-line product information (*on-line cataloging*); and
- customize the content and the presentation style of the retrieved information based on the individual user preferences (*matchmaking*).

Figure 1 illustrates an overview of the CEC framework composed of three main functional modules, namely, *generic user profiling module, generic on-line cataloging module*, and *generic matchmaking module*.

Generic User Profiling Module consists of components for identifying users and capturing their *personal preference profiles*. The profiles can be captured either explicitly by filling in forms or implicitly via some autonomous agents, and the captured profiles form the basis for customizing other components in the framework.

Generic On-Line Cataloging Module consists of components for monitoring, retrieving, and converting on-line information of merely syntactical type to one with semantic order for storage. The introduction of the semantic structure can facilitate both personalized presentation within this module and support tailor-made product recommendation in the matchmaking module.

Figure 1. An Overview of the CEC Framework (Components marked with smileys require user profile information.)

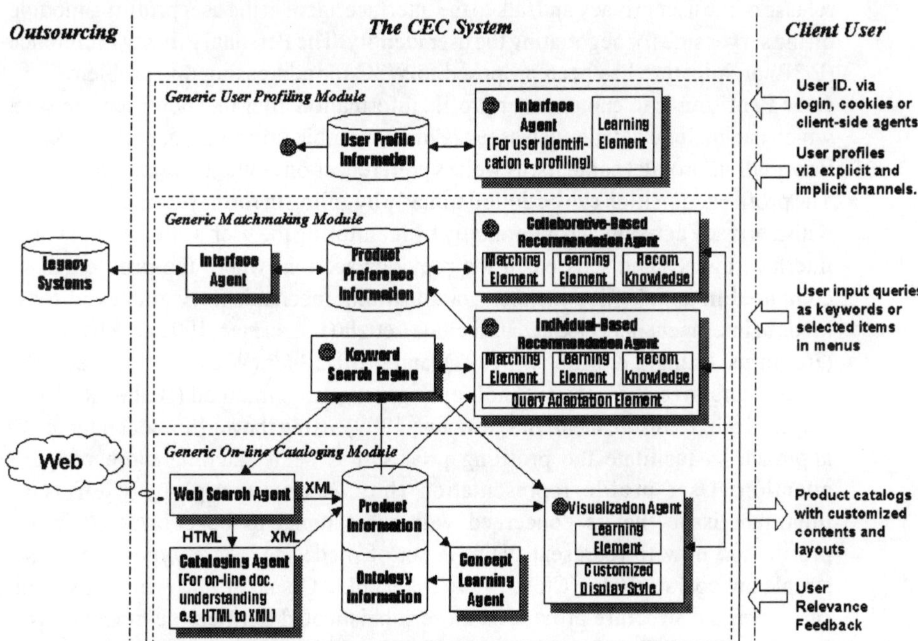

Generic Matchmaking Module consists of components for matching the retrieved product information with (1) individual user profile information, (2) product preference information of other customers, and sometimes together with (3) user input queries as well, to provide customized product recommendations.

Various intelligent software agents together with several related databases form the crucial components of the framework where the importance of the software agents lies in their characteristics of autonomy, mobility, rationality, and interactivity that are proved to be essential features for CEC. More detailed descriptions on the functionality and on the operation of the three functional modules are provided in the following sections.

Generic User Profiling Module

The two main functions of this module are user identification and profiling, which can be achieved by incorporating an agent interfaced with a database for storing the acquired user information.

- **Interface Agent for User Identification and Profiling**
  - **User Identification** is currently found in most of the company Web sites via membership registration. The identity of a visitor is identified by checking his or her user name and password. An authenticated session can then be established with the session state either encoded in the URL, stored on the server side, or stored on the client side (using cookies). To achieve automatic identification of a registered user, his or her identity information can be stored in the cookie of his or her machine. However, one has to understand that a cookie is weak in privacy protection since its content is open to the host(s) of the Web page visited as long as it is enabled. A complete clickstream can be

automatically captured by the hosts without one's knowing. An alternative is to install a proactive interface agent on the client (user) side which can safeguard the release of the user privacy and talk to the interface agent in the user profiling module on the server side for negotiating the user identity. The Personal Privacy Preference (P 3P) architecture has been proposed to W3C for addressing this problem.

User Profiling is to capture user profile information after the identification step, which can include details such as users' demographic information, preferences on information/product contents, as well as preferences on content presentation styles. The profile acquisition can be done explicitly by filling in forms (normally together with a privacy agreement) or implicitly by monitoring the user's clickstream via an interface agent, as discussed in the previous section, where the profile can be computed in an adaptive manner via a learning mechanism. Examples of these kinds of intelligent interface agents include Letizia (Lieberman, 1995), WebWatcher (Joachims, Freitag, & Mitchell, 1997), and ProfBuilder (Wasfi, 1999). Recently, as the interactive character technology is getting more matured (Ball et al., 1996; Hayes-Roth, Johnson, Gent, & Wescount, 1999), using the multimodal interactive approach to facilitate the profiling process has been catching more people's attention. User profile representation (http://www.um.org) by itself is an important issue that is concerned with what items to be considered in the profile and how to represent them. A set of predefined stereotypes provides a simple but coarse model (Chin, 1989; Takeuchi & Otsuki, 1988) while a dynamically overlaid structure provides a more sophisticated but flexible model (Rosis, Pizzutilo, Russo, Berry, & Molina, 1992). The choice of the modeling approaches greatly affects the efficiency and the effectiveness of the customized system and should be carefully picked according to what is really needed.

- **User Information Database** maintains user identity and profile information and forms the basis for all the related customization processes. The security aspect is important due to the data privacy expectations of customers on the Web. Under a secure platform (such as P3P), automatic information exchange is desirable for achieving productive electronic commerce. Such a need implies that using conventional database systems may not be a good choice for the user information database, as efficient information exchange among heterogeneous sources is not supported. XML is going to play an important role in addressing this problem. Related issues are discussed later..

Generic On-Line Cataloging Module

The goal of this module is to support just-in-time messaging by (1) monitoring, retrieving on-line information from distributed data sources, (2) analyzing it on the fly, and (3) generating a product catalog dynamically. To support a small company Web site with relatively static product information, the cataloging module probably degenerates to a simple database system. For large enterprises or intermediary on-line companies, searching information from distributed heterogeneous data sources becomes a need and the generic on-line cataloging module to be described is required in its full form. Before proceeding, it is worth noting that most of the data sources contain documents in HTML format with only layout information and that is the reason why on-line document understanding is here required. In the future, as more and more Web sites becomes XML-compliant, the heterogeneous situation will be reduced to merely the problem of semantic heterogeneity.

In order to provide on-line cataloging services, our on-line cataloging module consists of the following components:

- **Web Search Agent** acts as an interface between a CEC system and the Internet for obtaining up-to-minute on-line information from the Web. It can be implemented as a standard document retrieval system downloading related information from the Web (also called a spider or a crawler) or can be implemented as a mobile crawler which can be dispatched from a host and hop from one server to another, obtaining and carrying the required information before going back to the original host. The shopbot proposed by Doorenbos et al. (Doorenbos, Etzioni, & Weld, 1997) is an good example of stationary Web spider for comparison shopping. The mobile agent technology so far is still in an immature stage. Sim & Chi (1999) discussed the stationary and mobile Web search agents and proposed a new mobile agent framework in which the logical parts (corresponding to the standard services required the agents) are left in the servers, instead of carrying around. Other than mobility, the intelligence of the crawling process is another issue. Breath-first search is one of the feasible choices. McCallum *et al.* (McCallum, Nigam, Rennie, & Seymore, 1999) have successfully applied reinforcement learning to develop an adaptive Web crawler.
- **Cataloging Agent** is responsible for analyzing the layouts and the content of the on-line documents retrieved by the Web Search Agent to reconstruct the semantic order and store them preferably as XML documents in the product information database. In the literature, these kind of wrappers have been proposed (Hsu, 1998; Cohen, 1998). Cohen (1999) proposed how machine learning techniques can be used to combine different wrappers and derive page-independent heuristics for extracting data from Web pages. So far, the HTML standard has no restriction on Web page design and thus a generic on-line document understanding algorithm for heterogeneous Web sites may be difficult. Also, heterogeneous ontologies are commonly adopted by different data sources which make the derivation of a generic algorithm even harder. A partial solution is to develop a set of cataloging agents, each being delegated to analyze a particular Web page based on some predefined rules. However, the locations and layouts of Web pages are still subject to unexpected changes of any kind; the use of XML with a shared ontology should be the ultimate solution in the future (Glushko, Tenenbaum, & Meltzer, 1999).
- **Product Information and Ontology Information Database** maintains the retrieved product and ontology information. As mentioned in the previous sections, using XML-based database management systems should be a good choice. Recently, different database system vendors have extended their database systems to support searching on XML data and documents. The latest version of Oracle database system Oracle8i is an XML-enabled database system which contains an XML Development Kit (XDK) so that XML content management can be readily achieved. Besides, IBM has included an XML Extender in its DB2 Universal Database. Informix got its Web DataBlade module, which is included in its Informix Internet Foundation.2000, to bridge the gap between the traditional relational data and XML documents.
- **Concept Learning Agent** is responsible for automatically generating ontology information by analyzing information from heterogeneous data sources. Various techniques, in particular natural learning processing and machine learning, for knowledge acquisition from text can be used (Assadi, 1998; Williams & Tsatsoulis, 1999). Autonomy.com developed products with the concept learning capability for sorting documents into predefined categories.

- **Visualization Agent** presents customized product information in a customized fashion based on the user preferences indicated in his or her profile. Due to the great variety in information nature, different predefined visualization models can be adopted, ranging from simple table-like organizations to sophisticated graphical constructs. The presentation style customization is then achieved by modifying the settings of a chosen visualization model. The visualization agent may also contain a learning element to automatically adapt the settings for reflecting the user's latest preferences (Desmarais, Maluf, & Liu, 1996; Andre, Rist, & Muller, 1998; Bauer, 1996).

Generic Matchmaking Module

The generic matchmaking module is used to match up registered customers, and possibly together with their input queries, with the on-line product information collected via the on-line cataloging module to achieve product recommendation and precision information filtering. Related components include:

- **Individual-Based Recommendation Agent** provides product/information recommendation (c.f. filtering) services merely based on individual user profiles. The customization can be achieved by a query adaptation element and a product-profile matching element.
  - **Query Adaptation Element** is to adapt an input query based on user profile information (e.g., context-sensitive meanings of keywords), user relevance feedback information (e.g., ratings on items in previous search results), as well as product ontology information (e.g., words with similar meanings). An on-line learning element is mostly required for supporting the adaptation, especially for incorporating the relevance feedback information.
  - **Matching Element** achieves precision filtering by matching the adapted query with the product information using information retrieval (Frakes & Baeza-Yates, 1992) and machine learning techniques (Russel & Novig, 1995). The matching results retrieved from the product database can be further ranked (thus customized) by computing their similarities from the user profile, where the similarity measures can also be obtained via learning.
- **Collaborative Recommendation Agent** adopts a word-of-mouth approach and provides recommendations based on the opinions of customers with similar preference patterns. Similar to the individual-based recommendation agent, it contains a matching element and a learning element, but the formulation and the underlying algorithms are different.
  - **Matching Element** functions similarly as that of the individual-based recommendation agent and provides recommendations by computing the correlation between the user preference pattern with other customers'. The preferences of the similar customers form the collaborative recommendations. Such a paradigm is commonly called *collaborative filtering* (Goldberg, Nichols, Oki, & Terry, 1992; Resnick, Iacovou, Suchak, Bergstorm, & Riedl, 1994).
- **Product Preference Information Database** maintains the product preference information from users and can be conceptually interpreted as a product-customer matrix, where each entry indicates the preference rating of a customer on a particular product.

- **Interface Agent for Legacy System Interaction.** The product preference information based on individual user-explicit input, which is known to be costly to obtain, the information can also be induced from the information (e.g., individual's purchase history) stored in the legacy information systems of the corporation and their partners. Corresponding interface agents are responsible for communicating with the legacy systems for accessing the information.

Agent Communication

An important feature of our CEC framework is that it is agent-based where tasks are accomplished in a cooperative manner. Therefore, effective communication among the agents via a standardized protocol is necessary. This echoes our previous discussion on the use of XML and is especially true for tasks where the agents have to communicate intensively to accomplish a common goal. A good example is the negotiation process between customers and dealers in an electronic marketplace. Other than the communication concern, the need for achieving secure communication should also be stressed. For more details, interested readers are referred to Maes and Moukas (1999), and Wong, Paciorek, and Moore (1999).

ON-LINE CATALOGING

Personalized On-Line Catalog

As electronic commerce continues to develop, various product and service information is available through Web pages and the Web has become a global database for both consumers and dealers. The integration and access to such information as a heterogeneous database has become an increasingly important issue. Once integrated, the product information in Web pages would become a homogeneous on-line catalog where users can search for product information without browsing different Web sites. However, users would still face the problem of information overload. Personalized on-line catalogs differ from traditional catalogs in that they are generated on demand, covering relevant product information from different sources and tailored for the preference and personal profile of the user. As personalized on-line catalogs contain different product information from different dealers, it also forms the basis for agent-based product brokering and merchant brokering.

XML

Extensible Markup Language (XML) is used as the core structure for implementing the on-line catalogue (W3C-XML, 1998). The XML is a subset of Standard Generalized Markup Language (SGML). The XML has several features that bring compelling benefits to various Web-based applications. Firstly, XML can flexibly integrate data from various sources. Secondly, the syntax of XML is freely extensible. Thirdly, XML has universal and inter-operable support from all major venders, including IBM, Microsoft, and SUN. Since its proposal, most of the main software developers have been incorporating and developing software and applications to take advantage of this unique and powerful language. To name a few of the numerous applications currently being developed around the XML: on-line auction, Web commerce, supply chain integration, natural language translation, agent discovery, and content management (Goldfarb & Prescod, 1998).

Heterogeneous Source Integration

As the Web is quickly becoming the largest information source in various disciplines including commerce, Web pages contain a large amount of timely product information. To integrate the information in different Web pages as a homogeneous on-line catalog, we have to:

- acquire an understanding of the layout and design of specific Web pages according to a standardized model, and
- derive a shared ontology so as to support precision content integration in a highly autonomous and flexible way.

XML—A Common Syntactic Representation of Knowledge

The design of HTML as a formatting language for visual communication poses difficulty to the automated understanding of HTML pages. Data in HTML pages are often marked up by their formatting tags from which the semantic about the data is not available. Although the employment of XML in future Web pages would alleviate the problem of document understanding, HTML would still be a significant channel for information dispersion, especially for the consumer market.

To facilitate document understanding, the HTML document is modeled by an object-oriented approach. The W3C has recommended a specification on document object model (DOM) for both HTML and XML. The DOM is specified initially for accessing and manipulating HTML pages for dynamic effects and off-loading processing on the client browser. However, the object hierarchy structure of the DOM facilitates HTML document understanding. The current specification for DOM level 1 defines a language- and platform-neutral API for accessing and manipulating HTML and XML documents. Understanding and translation of content is achieved via analyzing and specifying object structure in the DOM. The DOM interface is specified using the Object Management Group Interface Definition Language (OMG IDL) and has been implemented on various platforms using COBRA, COM, and Java Virtual Machine.

To summarize, the transition from HTML to XML bears the advantages of:

1. allowing agents to mediate between two or more heterogeneous sources,
2. distributing processing load from servers to clients,
3. supporting different views of the same data to different users (under different appliances), and
4. ease of integration with intelligent agents.

A Shared Ontology

The use of an ontology has long been used to supplement and enhance the conventional search engine. Among the commercial search companies, Yahoo.com is famous for its broad and deep organizations of knowledge for assisting users to identify information in the Web. In the academic community, FindUR, developed by McGuinness (1998), is another example of a knowledge-enhanced search engine.

Recently a lot of efforts have been spent by different on-line companies, like Yahoo.com shopping and Amazon.com, to develop a broad and deep ontology to support their e-commerce business (McGuinness, 1999). Having a shared ontology for e-commerce is important, especially if a large-scale electronic market is to be established, which normally involves a large party of customers and dealers. Ontology.org is an independent industry and research forum focussed upon the application of ontologies in Internet commerce. In general, it is easy to mix up the meaning of vocabulary and taxonomy with that of ontology. According to the definition of Ontology.org, an ontology is more than just an agreed vocabulary and a taxonomy of terms. An ontology provides a set of well-founded constructs that can be leveraged to build meaningful higher level knowledge. Also, it includes richer relationships between terms than simply contributing to the semantics and taxonomy of the term.

Bauer et al.'s paper (Bauer & Dengler, 1999) provides a good example about how a domain-specific ontology is used in developing an Internet Travel Arrangement Assistant (ITA). In their work, a variant of frame logic is used for the concept representation. For example, to represent the concept of Flight with a set of attributes like carrier, departure city, destination city, etc., the following expression is used:

```
Flight [  carrier Æ Airline;
       departure Æ CityCode;
       destination Æ CityCode;
       travel_date Æ Date;
       departure_time Æ Time;
       arrival_time Æ Time;
       number Æ Flight_Number;
       .... ]
```

It is noted that the concepts about Airline, CityCode, Time, etc. are in turn represented using similar constructs. This construct is based on the Flight concept together with the contents of the ITN Web site and is described by the following schema:

```
itnflight (    Flight.carrier: Airline,
       Flight.departure: CityCode,
       Flight.destination: CityCode;
       Flight.travel_date: date_us_2;
       Flight.departure_time: time_12_3;
       Flight.arrival_time: time_12_3 )
```

Referring back to our framework, it is the responsibility of the Cataloging Agent to convert the format of the Web site (HTML) to a data format described by the schema (derived from the shared ontology) using XML as the syntactic representation.

One of the main obstacles for developing a shared ontology to support open-interoperable e-commerce systems lies in the semantic heterogeneity—the semantics of a term varies from one content to another. So far, using a domain-specific ontology in a fixed context seems to be a more common practice. For the Bauer et al. work we just discussed, the ontology is derived specifically for travel arrangement. Amazon.com's ontology is specific to books. Chemdex.com has established a shared ontology of life science products. In view of the situation, Cui and O'Brien (2000) argue that ontology engineering will be a major effort of future application development; they developed a software tool called Domain Ontology Management Environment (DOME) which can facilitate the users to convert traditional meta-data like database schemas to an ontology as well as directly manipulate the ontology.

Personalized Content via XML

The implementation of personalized on-line catalog also depends on standards of personal privacy. The growing needs in the provision of personalized services through the Web, along with the issues of standardization and regulations, have resulted in various proposals being submitted to the World Wide Web Consortium (W3C). The Information and

Content Exchange (ICE) protocol has been proposed by various corporations including Adobe Systems and Sun Microsystems (W3C-ICE, 1998). The ICE protocol defines the roles and responsibilities of content syndicators and subscribers; defines the format and method of content exchange; and provides supports, management, and control of syndication relationships. The Platform for Privacy Preference (P3P) Specification is proposed by W3C for expression of privacy practices and enables users to exercise preferences over those practices (W3C-P3P, 1999). The Personalized Information Description Language (W3C-PIDL, 1999) is proposed by NEC Corporation. The PIDL is a language with syntax developed using Extensible Markup Language (XML) for facilitating personalization of on-line information by providing enhanced interoperability between personalized applications. The above proposals address different areas in Web-based personalized content delivery for the public in general Internet services, such as portals and Net communities, and will also be important for the development of on-line cataloging.

RECOMMENDATION

Since the advent of the Web, people have been enjoying the ease of accessing information, which however leads to the struggle of the well-known information overload problem. Keyword search engines are often used to filter out information based on some input keywords, but very often the results returned by the search engines are still too much for the users. Similar difficulties are also encountered for product and merchant brokering. Recommendation is a technology that is aimed at filtering information using the user-oriented approach. It takes into consideration (1) the similarity between the information content and the user profile as well as (2) the similarity among the user preference patterns, and recommends information content in a customized manner. Related algorithms can be cataloged into *individual-based* and *collaborative-based.*

Individual-Based Approach

This approach provides customized recommendations by computing the similarity between the content of the information acquired and the profile of a single user (matching). Particular algorithms to be used for the underlying matching process are determined by the profiling model adopted. Roughly speaking, a user profile can be represented by either a set of constraints, a vector of preference ratings, or some more sophisticated models where model training is typically involved.

- **Constraint-Based Recommendation** casts the recommendation problem as a constraint satisfaction problem (CSP), where the user profile is typically represented by a set of hard or soft constraints on some predefined product attributes (c.f. domain variables). The hard constraints can sort out a set of feasible recommendations, and the soft constraints can be used to rank those recommendations accordingly. Very often, "real" user profile may not coincide with the one captured the first time (due to the noise in user input), and relevancy feedback for iterative constraint fine-tuning is typically required. KRAFT is one of the famous knowledge-based systems based on CSP (Gray et al., 1997), which has been in the context of an e-commerce environment (Preece, Hui, & Gray, 1999). Tete-a-Tete (http://ecommerce.media.mit.edu/Tete-a-Tete) is yet another one under this category. This kind of algorithm is particularly suitable for applications such as air-ticket booking, where user preference is actually a mix of hard and soft constraints (ranges of dates for departure and arrival, preferred airlines, budget on airfare, etc.). Other examples include the Autobytel Web site that requests a user to input preference ranges for different domain variables as constraints to narrow down his or her choice of cars.

- **Content-Based Recommendation** typically represents a user profile as a vector of preference ratings on some predefined product attributes to indicate user preferences. Other models are also possible, including rule-based systems (Basu, Hirsh, & Cohen, 1998), Bayes classifier (Mooney & Roy, 1999), artificial neural networks, etc. Model training is typically involved in building the profile model. Recommendations can then be induced using the corresponding reasoning techniques. In particular, for profiles represented as vectors of preference ratings, a product is only recommended if its attribute vector is close enough to the user profile based on a certain distance metric. Other than simple vector representation, associated rules are also commonly used. Agrawal et al. (Agrawal, Mannila, Srikant, Toivonen, & Verkamo, 1996) used associated rules for representing user profile and proposed a fast algorithm for automatically deriving them. The rules derived from the customer database, which are something like (`Product = AppleJuice Æ CouponUsed = Yes`), are then used in a rule-based system for matchmaking. Adomavicius and Tuzhilin (1999) discussed the possibility of having spurious or obvious rules being derived and proposed a computer-aided tool for rule validation. This kind of algorithm is particularly suitable for applications with products embedding a rich set of discriminative attributes that are hard to be specified by the user but can be effectively extracted by computers. A good example is Web page recommendation (Joachims et al., 1997; Lieberman, 1995). A weighted keyword vector can readily be extracted according to user navigation history. Web pages with their keyword vectors similar to the extracted user profile are recommended. Generally speaking, similar techniques can be applied to products with detailed description information available on-line (Mooney & Roy, 1999).
- **Integration with Keyword Search.** Before jumping to another approach, it is important to note that keyword search, though not perfect in filtering information, is still a very useful tool to be kept in company portals. Recommendation techniques, in fact, can be integrated into keyword search engines. The possible ways of integration include customizing input queries as well as customizing search results based on the user profile. Taking the search engine of an on-line bookstore as an example, the word "communication" may mean personal interaction to a psychologist but telecommunication to an engineer. A customized keyword search engine should be able to sort out the characteristics of the user and provide customized book recommendations accordingly. Together with ontology information integration, McGuinness (1998) has demonstrated how more robust and customized search engines can be achieved by adopting the knowledge-based approach. Also, Inquirus 2 is a meta-search engine which adopts a similar idea of combining query and information into need categories to support personalized ordering of search results (Glover, Lawrence, Gordan, Birmingham, & Giles, 1999).

Collaborative-Based Approach

This approach provides customized recommendations to a user by matching his or her preference patterns with those of the other customers, with the assumption that there exists a large amount of preference ratings from a reasonably large group of customers. Possible algorithms include simple pattern correlation based on some similarity measures and statistical model-based techniques (Breese, Heckerman, & Kadie, 1998). As this approach does not require the content information about the user and the products, it is one of the earliest approaches used for product recommendation. The GroupLens Research Project (http://www.grouplens.org) at the University of Minnesota has been studying the problem since 1992, and the developed techniques have been turned into commercial products by the company Net Perception (http://www.netperception.com). As it is highly likely that there can be a large number of missing values for each preference pattern, especially when the total number of products is large (also known as the sparsity problem); different model-based algorithms have been proposed for improving its overall performance, where matching learning techniques are typically required (Ungar & Foster, 1998; Hofmann & Puzicha, 1999).

This kind of algorithm is particularly suitable for companies that used to keep the records of customer purchase history and feedback information in their corporate information systems. Also, companies that sell a large variety of products will find collaborative-based recommendation useful. Working examples include the Web sites of Amazon.com, CDNow.com, Ticketmaster On-line, etc.

Integration of Content-Based and Collaborative-Based Approaches

Recently there have been substantial research and development works on integrating the content-based and collaborative-based approaches for building hybrid recommendation systems. Such an integration assumes that both the customer purchase and preference information, as well as detailed product description information, are available for analysis and the objective is to further improve the overall recommendation accuracy. Some positive preliminary results have been reported (Balabanovic & Shoham, 1997; Condliff & Lewis, 1999; Good et al., 1999; Aggarval, Wolf, Wu, & Yu, 1999) and further investigation is still required for any affirmative conclusion.

THREE CASE STUDIES

In order to illustrate how the enabling technologies discussed in the previous two sections can be deployed in CEC systems, we have prototyped three different agent-based systems: Electronic Tour Agent (ETA), Electronic Property Agent (EPA), and Electronic Auction Agent (EAA). As tabulated in Table 1, it is noted that the three systems are implemented in order to highlight some important components of the proposed CEC framework, which is supposed to be relatively more general and complete.

Electronic Tour Agent (ETA)

Travel planning used to be a nontrivial task where various types of considerations have to be taken care of, including which airlines to take, in which hotels to stay, what budget to meet, etc. As most of the information is available on the Web nowadays, software agents can be developed for retrieving and comparing related information for assisting the planning process. Electronic Tour Agent (ETA) is under this category.

ETA is a constraint-based recommendation agent that provides customized traveling tour recommendations by searching related tours in the product database that satisfy the user input constraints. The domain variables of the tours include budget, destination, dates of departure, transportation, hotel, etc. The user profile is the set of constraints on each of the variables that can be either hard (with expressions such as "before," "after," "below,"

Table 1. An Architectural Overview of the Three Implemented Software Agents—ETA, EPA and EAA

Modules	Components	ETA	EPA	EAA
Generic User Profiling	Interface Agent for User Identification & Profiling	✓	✓	
	User Profile Database		✓	
Generic Matchmaking	Individual-Based Recommendation Agent			
	⇒Constraint-Based	✓		
	⇒Content-Based		✓	
	Collaborative-Based Recommendation Agent			
	Product Preference Database		✓	
	Keyword-Based Search Engine			✓
Generic On-Line Cataloging	Web Search Agent			✓
	Cataloging Agent			✓
	Product Database	✓	✓	
	Ontology Database			
	Concept Learning Agent			
	Simple Visualization Agent	✓	✓	✓

"must," etc.) or soft (with expressions such as "around," "preferred," "don't care," etc.) to be set by the user. The domain variables are then quantified and the weights of the variables are set accordingly. The agent returns tour information that satisfies the hard constraints and at the same time is close to the satisfaction of the soft constraints. A score, a normalized weighted sum of the domain variables, is given to each of the retrieved records to indicate the level of satisfaction. Figure 2 includes two snapshots of the ETA agent.

Electronic Property Agent (EPA)

Property buying and selling is a very common activity in cities like Hong Kong. Related transactions happen on a daily basis and properties' market prices are dynamically changing from time to time. This dynamic nature of the content indicates the potential of using software agents that can be delegated to keep track of the latest properties available and provide tailor-made recommendations to users.

Electronic Property Agent (EPA) is a content-based recommendation agent that provides customized property recommendations by matching user profile with property information stored in the product database. Instead of extracting features, domain variables of the properties like price per square foot, floor, number of bedrooms, view, and orientation, are used in their original forms, where each can only take a finite set of values. The probability distribution on all the possible values of the domain variables forms the profile representation. Navíe Bayesian classification algorithm is adopted in its learning and matching elements for learning the profile and performing the inference respectively. The Bayes factor is computed for each property as the score of relevancy. The technique adopted in the implementation is similar to Mooney et al.'s work on book recommendation (Mooney & Roy, 1999).

For the operation, at the very beginning when a registered user has not rated any properties at all, no recommendation is provided. Instead, a basic search function is provided to assist users in looking for properties that they are interested in. After the user provides his or her rating on a certain property, his or her profile will be generated accordingly and will adapt itself along with the user's further ratings. Based on the

Figure 2. Snapshots of ETA: (a) Capturing user preferences in terms of hard and/or soft contraints. (b) Recommendation results returned by the agent.

(a)

(b)

Travel Agent

The Results

Agency	Package#	Price	Distination	Type	Hotel	Days	Trans.	Stops	Duration	Score
Red	PKB05	4095	Beijing	Tour	5 star	5	Plane	10	1/1/99-31/12/2000	100%
Red	PKB05X	4498	Beijing	Tour	6 star	5	Plane	10	1/1/99-31/12/2000	100%
Yellow	TCA	4898	Beijing	Tour	5 star	5	Plane	10	28/9/99-2/12/99	100%
Red	PKB06	4498	Beijing	Tour	5 star	6	Plane	12	1/1/99-31/12/2000	89%
Red	PEK04R	3098	Beijing	Tour	4 star	4	Plane	6	1/1/99-30/10/99	86%
Red	PEK06	3998	Beijing	Tour	4 star	4	Plane	10	1/1/99-30/10/99	86%
Red	PKB06X	5398	Beijing	Tour	6 star	6	Plane	12	1/1/99-31/12/2000	82%
Yellow	TCB	5298	Beijing	Tour	5 star	6	Plane	12	28/9/99-31/10/99	81%

Modify my preference

Search again

user profile, recommendations are computed automatically. Since the algorithm is based on probabilities, the profile will become more accurate if more ratings are provided. See Figure 3 for two snap shots of the EPA agent.

EPA is not only a tool for assisting property search but also a marketing tool that can collect customer information for market analysis so as to further improve customer relationship. Also, after the customer information grows to a certain size, collaborative recommendation agent can be integrated for providing more accurate recommendations.

Electronic Auction Agent (EAA)

Automated auction agents are a collection of software agents that search different auction sites and perform precision information filtering to help users locate their favorite items. As there are a large number of auction sites with items that may be of interest to an individual, browsing and searching at various sites can be very time consuming. Moreover, the auction process is a dynamic process where price and availability change rapidly. Thus, software agents that search and monitor different auction sites around the clock are essential. See Figure 4 for snapshots of the EAA agent.

An essential part of a software agent for automatic monitoring of different auction sites is the knowledge of the search formats and the Web page content layouts. The Web search can be composed by understanding search string format employed in individual Web sites. In the understanding and fusion of searching results returned from different auction sites, the document object structure hierarchy containing the auction product information has to be determined. In the current implementation, the searching agent covers such auction sites as eBay, Yahoo! Auction, and Yahoo! Hong Kong Auction.

As the availability of auction items is dynamically changing with time, the retrieval

Figure 3. Snapshots of EPA: (a) User registration. (b) The screen with the basic search function on the upper part and the recommended properties on the lower part.

(a)

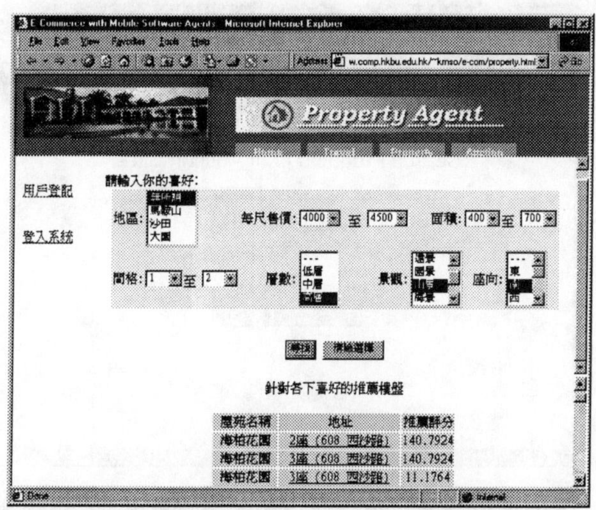

(b)

rate of the auction agent varies for different items and different periods of time. Typically, the auction agent is able to retrieve 30 auction items more than the user searching individual auction sites. As the auction agent fuses retrieved auction items from individual auction sites, the relevance rate of the auction agent is similar to the relevance rate of individual auction sites.

Future auction agents will incorporate extra functions, such as automatic and selective dissemination of information, modeling and prediction of responses, and implementation of pricing strategies. The selective dissemination of information allows for the dynamic matches of new auction items from auction sites with specific interests expressed in user profiles. More sophisticated bidding strategies can also be developed by incorporating user requirements and preferences.

Figure 4. Snapshots of EAA: (a) Entering the interested items for on-line search. (b) On-line search results integrated from heterogeneous auction sites.

(a)

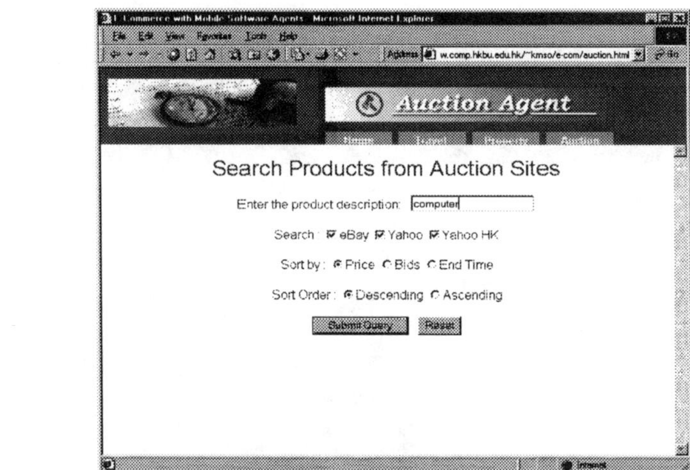

(b)

E Commerce with Mobile Software Agents - Microsoft Internet Explorer

Auction Agent

Home Travel Property Auction

No.	Site	Product	Price Ascending Descending	Bids Ascending Descending	Time Left Ascending Descending
1	Yahoo	Laptop Computers PowerSlim Pentium MMX, 266 Mhz ,Only One left HURRY	999.00 USD	0	2 hrs
2	Yahoo	New fully loaded PentiumIII multimedia computer system only 599	599.00 USD	0	2 hrs
3	eBay	Intel p2 400Mhz Computer system	500.00 USD	0	1 mins
4	eBay	*NEW* PENTIUM III 450 SUPER COMPUTER Y2K COMP	499.00 USD	1	11/24 22:40
5	Yahoo	Hewlett Packard 433MHz Desktop Computer System "NO-RESERVE" BRAND NEW	455.00 USD	7	15 mins
6	Yahoo HK	computer	2,000.00 HKD	0	2 days
7	eBay	Velo 1 Handheld Computer 20 MB, Modem, cc OK	197.00 USD	0	11/24 23:07
8	eBay	Velo 1 Handheld Computer 20 MB, Modem, cc OK	197.00 USD	1	45 mins

A Remark on Performance Evaluation

To evaluate the performance of search-related applications like the three proposed prototypes, related metrics have been proposed, including the recall and precision rates originated from the information retrieval community, as well as the absolute deviation and the expected utility derived by the recommender system community (Breese et al., 1998). Other than a set of commonly agreed metrics, a reasonable-sized real-world dataset is needed to be collected for conducting an effective evaluation, which at the moment is not yet done for our prototypes. However, preliminary hands-on experiments have been performed with satisfactory results.

DISCUSSION

With the proliferation of information, it becomes increasingly time consuming and difficult for Internet users to perform an exhaustive information search on the Web, which greatly hinders the matchmaking process—one of the most important processes in e-commerce. A successful electronic commerce system should provide these supports to the users: content, interface, motivation, decision, and delegation. The traditional marketing strategy based on customer segmentation is quickly replaced by one-to-one marketing as the marketplace is migrated to cyberspace. Parsaye (2000) proposed a measure of personalization called PQ (Personalization Quotient) and argued that it is hard to find anyone today who argues the usefulness of the personalization of a Web-based system and the question is just to what degree.

Experience from the CEC Project

So, in order to have an edge over other Web sites, it is no longer sufficient just to provide users with a large amount of raw data for them to analyze and select. CEC with intelligent software agents that behave like personal assistants with expert knowledge is highly desirable in the information society from the perspectives of both customers and dealers. The agent will be able to accept instructions that are more human oriented (interface support), such as selecting tours that leave after 15 January 2000, return before 25 January, visit at least three cities, for a preferred budget of no more than $1,000 per person, as illustrated in our ETA. The first two requirements are hard constraints because of the vacation period of the customer, but there could be flexibility on the cost and visiting cities. After understanding the requirements of the customer, the agent will search appropriate sites on the Web (delegation support), perform information filtering for the customer just like an efficient travel agent, find those tours that meet the customer's hard constraints, rank them according to the soft constraints, and present the results to the customer with the analysis of the pros and cons of the different options (decision support). Besides providing a helping hand and saving the customer a lot of time, the agent may even do a better job than the customer because the agent has more up-to-date tour information through its links to other Web sites (content support).

From the experience of serving customers with user profiles, a software agent may recommend products for the customer to consider. In the case of the EPA, the software agent may suggest to the customer properties which meet the underlying preference criteria of the customer captured implicitly based on user ratings. For example, a good unit in a neighboring city of satisfying the customer's needs can be easily found by the agent. As home purchase is a long-term commitment, the customer may be very selective for their dream home. Thus, home search could take a long time to complete. An agent may invite autonomous agents dispatched to other Web sites to monitor new home listings for selection (delegation support). As soon as suitable homes are posted, a remote agent may report to the agent in charge, which then reports to the customer for consideration (decision support).

Another kind of support a software agent can provide is to act on behalf of the customer for product brokering and purchase negotiation. For example, in the case of auction on the Web using the EAA, the customer may inform the agent the ceiling price for bidding and the agent will automatically locate relevant items from different auction sites (motivation and delegation support). In the future, the strategy can also be dynamically changed according to the number of competitors and the timing of the auction process. The agent will then offer bids on behalf of the customer.

CONCLUDING REMARKS

The Web being a quick and cheap medium for publishing information quickly leads to the information overload problem, which sometimes makes the on-line shopping experience unpleasant. CEC adds more convenient value-added features to the customers as well as the dealers. With the aid of built-in software agents in CEC, it is easier for the customers to access and manage product information from various sources, where comparison shopping is one of the representative killer applications. Also, the customers' consideration of a deal is no longer limited by the geographical factor or merely relies on the dealer's brand name, but rather on the actual deal and the customer services that can be provided. Thus, prices have to be very competitive for a dealer to sell its products and gain market share. This is good news to the consumer. Regarding the dealer side, to compete in the electronic commerce world which is highly dynamic in nature, traditional businesses have to consider their own e-commerce strategies, and respond promptly and appropriately. A case in point, with the success of Amazon.com, the bookstore chain Barnes and Noble also launches its own on-line shop to protect its market share. The platform provided by the CEC framework assists the dealer to understand their customers and build a loyal and profitable customer relationship so as to support their own business strategies.

Internet commerce may still have some way to go in order to fully demonstrate all of its advantages over its traditional counterpart. First, the satisfaction of looking and feeling a product has to be fulfilled by shopping in person. Also, the security and privacy concerns from some users, e.g., their credit card and personal information may be stolen, have to be seriously addressed. We believe that with the advent of intelligent software agent technology, the various supports provided by the CEC framework can alleviate part of those psychological factors and lead to more successful examples of e-commerce systems.

REFERENCES

Adomavicius, G., & Tuzhilin, A. (1999). User profiling in personalization applications through rule discovering and validation. In *Proceedings of the Fifth ACM SIGKDD International Conference on Knowledge Discovery and Data Mining* (pp. 377-381). San Diego, CA.

Aggarval, C. C., Wolf, J. L., Wu, K.-L., & Yu, P. S. (1999). Horting hatches an egg: A new graph-theoretic approach to collaborative filtering. In *Proceedings of the Fifth ACM SIGKDD*

International Conference on Knowledge Discovery and Data Mining (pp. 201-212). San Diego, CA.

Agrawal, R., Mannila, H., Srikant, R., Toivonen, H., & Verkamo, A. I. (1996). Fast discovery of associated rules. In U. Fayyad, G. Piatetsky-Shapiro, P. Smyth, & R. Uthurusamy (Eds.), *Advances in Knowledge Discovery and Data Mining*. AAAI Press: Menlo Park, CA.

Andre, E., Rist, T., & Muller, J. (1998). Guiding the user through dynamically generated hypermedia presentations with a lifelike character. In *Proceedings of the 1998 International Conference on Intelligent User Interface* (pp. 21-28). San Francisco, CA.

Ardissono, L., Barkero, C., Goy, A., & Petrone, G. (1999). An agent architecture for personalized Web stores. In *Proceedings of the Third Annual Conference on Autonomous Agents (Agents99)* (pp. 182-189). Seattle, WA.

Assadi, H. (1998). Construction of a regional ontology from text and its use within a document system. In *Formal Ontology in Information Systems* (pp. 236-249). IOS Press.

Balabanovic, M., & Shoham, Y. (1997). Content-based, collaborative recommendation. *Communications of the ACM*, 40(3), 66-72.

Ball, G., Ling, D., Kurlander, D., Miller, J., Pugh, D., Skelly, T., Stankosky, A., Thiel, D., van Dantzich, M., & Wax, T. (1996). Lifelike computer characters: The Persona project at Microsoft. In J. M. Bradshaw (Ed.), *Software Agents*. AAAI/MIT Press: Menlo Park, CA.

Basu, C., Hirsh, H., & Cohen, W. (1998). Recommendation as classification: Using social and content-based information in recommendation. In *Technical Report WS-98-08: Recommender Systems—Papers from the AAAI Workshop*. Madison, WI.

Bauer, M. (1996). Acquisition of user preferences for plan recognition. In *Proceedings of the Fifth International Conference on User Modeling (UM96)* (pp. 105-112). Kailua-Kona, HI.

Bauer, M., & Dengler, D. (1999). TrIAs: Trainable information assistants for cooperative problem solving. In *Proceedings of the Third Annual Conference on Autonomous Agents (Agents99)* (pp. 260-267). Seattle, WA.

Breese, J. S., Heckerman, D., & Kadie, C. (1998). Empirical analysis of predictive algorithms for collaborative filtering. In *Proceedings of the Fourteenth Conference on Uncertainty in Artificial Intelligence* (pp. 43-52). Madison, WI.

Chin, D. (1989). KNOME: Modeling what the user knows in UC. In A. Kobsa & W. Wahlster (Eds.), *User Models in Dialog Systems* (pp. 74-107). Springer: Berlin, Heidelberg.

Cohen, W. (1998). A Web-based information system that reasons with structured collections of text. In *Proceedings of the Second Annual Conference on Autonomous Agents (Agents98)* (pp. 400-407). St. Paul, MN.

Cohen, W. (1999). Learning page-independent heuristics for extracting data from Web pages. In *Technical Report SS-99-03: Intelligent Agents in Cyberspace—Papers from the 1999 AAAI Spring Symposium* (pp. 47-61). AAAI Press: Menlo Park, CA.

Condliff, M. K., & Lewis, D. D. (1999). Bayesian mixed-effects models for recommender systems. In *Proceedings of the SIGIR99 Workshop on Recommender Systems: Algorithms and Evaluation*. Berkeley, CA.

Cui, Z., & O'Brien, P. (2000). Domain ontology management environment. In *Proceedings of the Hawaii International Conference on System Sciences*. Maui, HI.

Desmarais, M. C., Maluf, A., & Liu, J. (1996). User-expertise modeling with empirically derived probabilistic implication networks. *International Journal of User Modeling and User-Adapted Interaction*, 5(3-4), 283-315.

Doorenbos, R. B., Etzioni, O., & Weld, D. S. (1997). A scalable comparison shopping agent for the World Wide Web. In *Proceedings of the First Annual Conference on Autonomous Agents (Agents97)* (pp. 39-48). Seattle, WA.

Frakes, W., & Baeza-Yates, R. (Eds.). (1992*). Information Retrieval: Data Structures and Algorithms*. Prentice Hall.

Glover, E. J., Lawrence, S., Gordan, M. D., Birmingham, W. P., & Giles, C. L. (1999). Recommending Web documents based on user preferences. In *Proceedings of the SIGIR99 Workshop on Recommender Systems: Algorithms and Evaluation*. Berkeley, CA.

Glushko, R. J., Tenenbaum, J. M., & Meltzer, B. (1999). An XML framework for agent-based e-commerce. *Communications of the ACM*, 42(3), 106-114.

Goldberg, D., Nichols, D., Oki, B. M., & Terry, D. (1992). Collaborative filtering to weave an information—Tapestry. *Communications of the ACM*, 35(12), 61-70.

Goldfarb, C. F., & Prescod, P. (1998). *XML Handbook*. Prentice Hall: NJ.

Good, N., Schafer, J. B., Konstan, J. A., Borchers, A., Sarwar, B., Herlocker, J., & Riedl, J. (1999). Combining collaborative filtering with personal agents for better recommendations. In *Proceedings of the Sixteenth National Conference on Artifical Intelligence (AAAI-99)* (pp. 439-446). Orlando, Fl.

Gray, P., Preece, A., Fiddian, N., Gray, W., Bench-Capon, T., Shave, M., Azarmi, N., Wiegand, M., Ashwell, M., Beer, M., Cui, Z., Diaz, B., Embury, S., Hui, K., Jones, A., Jones, D., Kemp, G., Lawson, E., Lunn, K., Marti, P., Shao, J., & Visser, P. (1997). KRAFT: Knowledge fusion from distributed databases and knowledge bases. In Wagner (Ed.), *Database and Expert System Applications (DEXA97)* (pp. 682-691). Toulouse, France.

Guttman, R. H., Moukas, A. G., & Maes, P. (1998). Agent-mediated electronic commerce: A survey. *Knowledge Engineering Review Journal*, 42(3).

Hayes-Roth, B., Johnson, V., van Gent, R., & Wescourt, K. (1999). Staffing the Web with interactive characters. *Communications of the ACM*, 43(3), 103-105.

Hofmann, T., & Puzicha, J. (1999). Latent class models for collaborative filtering. In *Proceedings of the Seventeenth International Joint Conference on Artificial Intelligence (IJCAI99)* (pp. 688-693). Stockholm, Sweden.

Hsu, C.N. (1998). Initial results on wrapping semistructured Web pages with finite-state transducers and contextual rules. In *Papers from the 1998 Workshop on AI and Information Integration (AAAI98)*. Madison, WI.

Joachims, T., Freitag, D., & Mitchell, T. (1997). WebWatcher: A tour guide for the World Wide Web. In *Proceedings of the Fifteenth International Joint Conference on Artificial Intelligence (IJCAI97)*. Nagoya, Japan.

Lieberman, H. (1995). Letizia: An agent that assists Web browsing. In *Proceedings of the Thirteenth International Joint Conference on Artificial Intelligence (IJCAI95)*. Montreal, Canada.

Maes, P., & Moukas, R. H. G. A. G. (1999). Agents that buy and sell. *Communications of the ACM*, 42(3), 81-91.

McCallum, A., Nigam, K., Rennie, J., & Seymore, K. (1999). Building domain-specific search engines with machine learning techniques. In *Technical Report SS-99-03: Intelligent Agents in Cyberspace—Papers from the 1999 AAAI Spring Symposium* (pp. 28-39). AAAI Press: Melo Park, CA.

McGuinness, D. L. (1998). Ontological issues for knowledge-enhanced search. In *Formal Ontology in Information Systems* (pp. 302-316). IOS Press.

McGuinness, D. L. (1999). Ontologies for electronic commerce. In *Technical Report WS 99-01: Artificial Intelligence for Electronic Commerce—Papers from the AAAI Workshop.*

Orlando, FL.

Mooney, R. J., & Roy, L. (1999). Content-based book recommending using learning for text categorization. In *Proceedings of the SIGIR99 Workshop on Recommender Systems: Algorithms and Evaluation*. Berkeley, CA.

Nwana, H. S. (1996). Software agents: An overview. *Knowledge Engineering Review*, 11(3), 205-244.

Parsaye, K. (2000). PQ: The personalization quotient of a Web site (http://www.personalization.com/soapbox/contributions/parsaye.asp).

Pazzani, M. J., & Billsus, D. (1999). Adaptive Web site agents. In *Proceedings of the Third Annual Conference on Autonomous Agents (Agents99)* (pp. 394-395). Settle, WA.

Preece, A. D., Hui, K. Y., & Gray, P. M. D. (1999). KRAFT: Supporting virtual organizations through knowledge fusion. In T. Finin & B. Grosof (Eds.), *Technical Report WS-99-01: Artificial Intelligence for Electronic Commerce—Papers from the AAAI Workshop (p. 33-38).* AAAI Press: Menlo Park, CA.

Resnick, P., Iacovou, N., Suchak, M., Bergstorm, P., & Riedl, J. (1994). GroupLens: An open architecture for collaborative filtering of netnews. In *Proceedings of ACM 1994 Conference on Computer Supported Cooperative Work* (pp. 175-186). Chapel Hill, NC.

Rosis, F. D., Pizzutilo, S., Russo, A., Berry, D. C., & Molina, F. J. N. (1992). Modeling the user knowledge by belief networks. *User Modeling and User-Adapted Interaction*, 2(4).

Rucker, J., & Polanco, M. J. (1999). Personalization navigation for the Web. *IEEE Intelligent Systems*, 2.

Russel, S., & Norvig, P. (Eds.). (1995). *Artificial Intelligence—A Modern Approach.* Prentice Hall: New Jersey.

Segal, R. B., & Kephart, J. O. (1999). Mailcat: An intelligent assistant for organization e-mail. In *Proceedings of the Third Annual Conference on Autonomous Agents (Agents99)* (pp. 276-282). Seattle, WA.

Sim, J. T. W., & Chi, C. H. (1999). Framework for an agent-based electronic market place: Design and implementation. In *Technical Report SS-99-03: Intelligent Agents in Cyberspace—Papers from the 1999 AAAI Spring Symposium* (pp. 164-173). AAAI Press: Menlo Park, CA.

Takeuchi, A., & Otsuki, S. (1988). A study of student models and learner-machine interaction. In P. Ercoli & R. Lewis (Eds.), *Artificial Intelligence Tools in Education* (pp. 87-104). North-Holland: Amsterdam.

Tryllian. (1999). Mobile Agents: The Workforce of the New Millennium, Tryllian whitepaper. November

Ungar, L. H., & Foster, D. P. (1998). Clustering methods for collaborative filtering. In *Technical Report WS-98-08: Recommender Systems—Papers from the AAAI Workshop*. Madison, WI.

W3C-ICE. (1998). Information and Content Exchange (ICE) Protocol, W3C Note, 26 October, http://www.w3.org/TR/NOTE-ice.

W3C-P3P. (1999). Platform for Privacy Preference (P3P) Specification, W3C Working Draft, 7 April, http://www.w3.org/TR/WD-P3P.

W3C-PIDL. (1999). Personalized Information Description Language, W3C Note, 9 February, http://www.w3.org/TR/NOTE-PIDL.

W3C-XML. (1998). Extensible Markup Language (XML) 1.0, W3C Recommendation, 10 February, http://www.w3c.org/TR/1998/REC-xml-19980210.

Wasfi, A. M. A. (1999). Collecting user access patterns for building user profiles and collaborative filtering. In *Proceedings of the 1999 International Conference on Intelligent User Interface* (pp. 57-64). Redondo Beach, CA.

Williams, A. B., & Tsatsoulis, C. (1999). Diverse Web ontologies: What intelligent agents must teach to each other. In *Technical Report SS-99-03: Intelligent Agents in Cyberspace - Papers from the 1999 AAAI Spring Symposium* (pp. 115-120). AAAI Press: Menlo Park, CA.

Wong, D., Paciorek, N., & Moore, D. (1999). Java-based mobile agents. *Communications of the ACM*, 42(3).

Chapter X

Agent Technologies and Business Models for Electronic Commerce[1]

Paul Timmers and Jorge Gasós
European Commission, Directorate-General Information Society, Belgium

Agent technologies have proved to provide adequate solutions to some of the challenges posed by the new business models that are arising in the field of electronic commerce. In this chapter, we present some of the key challenges in turning agents' research into commercial applications, provide an overview of the electronic commerce business models, and discuss how they can benefit from the new developments in agent technologies. We illustrate the discussion with examples of the work that is being developed by projects from the IST research program of the European Union.

INTRODUCTION

In line with the rapid expansion of electronic commerce in the recent years, there has been a parallel evolution in the associated business models in order to address the new market needs and opportunities. Initial models, like e-shop and e-procurement, showed relatively little innovation when compared to traditional ways of doing business: in many cases they consist of a Web site displaying electronic product catalogues, marketing material or procurement specifications. More innovative models, like third-party marketplaces or value chain integration, bring together multiple suppliers or multiple steps of the value chain, and add value by their potential to provide broader services while minimizing costs and by their potential to exploit the information flows. Current trends in business models focus on dynamic markets/networks, where consumers and businesses can seamlessly and dynamically come together, even for short-term relationships, in response to or in anticipation of new market opportunities.

These new business models require the development of a wide range of supporting technologies to allow the efficient implementation of the required processes and services. These technologies range from customer relationship management and marketing support to collaborative working tools and negotiation schemes, from security issues to automatic contractual arrangements and conflict mediation. In this context, agent technologies have contributed with appropriate solutions to some of these technological challenges (Maes et al., 1999).

Electronic commerce has proved to be a domain where the full potential of intelligent agents can be demonstrated. It requires managing enormous amounts of information, which in many cases is heterogeneous, not structured, and distributed in space, and needs to be dealt with in a personalized way with decision making that may need to be validated in a negotiation process. This combination of complex information from multiple sources that requires a personalized treatment and negotiation between different actors, calls for automatic solutions that show a certain degree of autonomy, intelligence, and ability to adapt/react to the particular environment/circumstances. Agent technologies fit these requirements since they provide an architecture for the implementation of autonomous, intelligent, and reactive behaviors. Furthermore, it is an enabling technology that is not restricted to specific reasoning or knowledge representation paradigms, and hence, it can be applied to the solution of many different problems from different perspectives and approaches (Maes, 1994; Bailey & Bakos, 1997; Ephrati & Rosenschein, 1994; Moukas, 1997).

The first agent systems that were developed for electronic commerce can be typified as *individual agents*: they have specific objectives and act on behalf of the user without interacting with other agents. This lack of interaction with other agents significantly simplifies the development of individual agents. Each agent can be programmed in an ad hoc fashion without concerns about protocols, semantics, or standards. Individual agents are already emerging in the market being incorporated into products and services. Examples include information agents, such as share price tracking or personalized newspapers, that retrieve, analyze, and integrate information available from multiple distributed sources. Examples of individual agents implemented for e-shops include user profiling and personalized marketing.

The next level in terms of complexity is *collaborative agents*: communities of agents that cooperate to achieve a goal, and that have been implemented following a detailed design and with a global view of the problem. The key point here is that, even if many agents have to interact, there is a certain control of the system and there exists previous agreement on the tasks to be performed by each agent and on the proprietary protocols and semantics for the exchange of information. Examples include agents cooperating to resolve network faults, decentralized management of limited common resources, and applications for static electronic marketplaces or value chain integration such as 'traditional' supply chain management. For the integration of collaborative agent systems into commercial applications it is still required to significantly improve in the area of agent engineering. These include rigorous methodologies for requirement analysis and system specifications, as well as tools for the verification, validation, and testing of the system functionality. In the case of large-scale collaborative agent systems, a better understanding is also needed of how individual agent's behaviors combine dynamically to generate the system behavior, since it will be different from a 'sum' of the individual behaviors in static environments. Issues such as social dynamics, self-organization, self-regulation, and adaptive behaviors become critical to avoid undesirable effects.

The most complex model is the *society of agents*: agents developed by different users or providers, implementing different objectives and strategies, and that have to inter-operate in a complex and dynamic environment. Global standards are the key issue to make possible these open agent platforms, including protocols for communication and common semantics for information exchange. Furthermore, legal and security issues, e.g. liability of contracts made by autonomous software and protection from malicious agents, need also to be addressed.

In this chapter we analyze the relation between agents' applications and electronic commerce business models. The context of advanced work in these subjects is the Information Society Technologies (IST) Research Program of the European Union.[2] This program supports collaboration between industry, research institutes, and public bodies for R&D and pilot projects with a European added value and on a co-financed basis. The program is structured around four key actions (see Figure 1). Most of the applications discussed in this paper have been developed in projects that fall in the 'e-commerce and e-work' key action.[3] The rest of the applications come from projects in the other key actions that address: services for the citizens and ICT (Information and Communication Technologies) supported public services; digital content and ICT support for education and training; and the underpinning information and communication technologies, including hardware, software, and services for next-generation networks. The IST program is completed with specific actions for long-term research and collaboration in research networks.

Figure 1. The European Union IST Programme

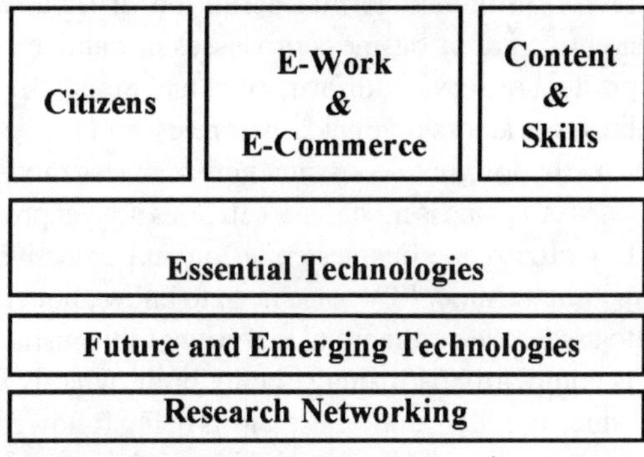

This chapter brings together several separate pieces of work by the IST projects, and connects them to provide a global overview of the different approaches to integrate agent technologies in electronic commerce business models. All the individual approaches have been reported in greater detail in the technical literature and in public documents of the projects. The goal of this paper is not to explain the technicalities of any of these approaches, but rather to provide a glimpse of the ways in which research on agent technologies is being applied to face the challenges posed by the new business models that are arising in the field of electronic commerce.

AGENT TECHNOLOGIES AND BUSINESS MODELS

'Business models' is certainly one of the most discussed topics in electronic commerce. Virtually every electronic commerce provider uses 'business models' in its advertising. Investors are asking 'What is your business model,' meaning, where are you going to make the money, why are people paying and continuing to pay for your service? Surveys of SMEs have shown that one of the most frequently mentioned barriers to electronic commerce, next to cost concerns, is 'the lack of a business model.'

In the literature several taxonomies of business models can be found. Some provide a broad overview such as Merz (1999) or Rappa (2000); others focus on specific business models such as virtual communities (Hagel & Armstrong, 1997). Often Internet technology companies provide their own taxonomies, for an example see Intershop.[4] An overview of references to business models and an additional taxonomy can be found in Rappa (2000). Rayport (1999) provides an historic perspective on the quest for successful business models.

Beyond business models it is also useful to consider larger-scale economic structures, that is, business networks like supply chains and e-markets or 'e-business communities' as defined and analyzed by Kalakota and Robinson (1999) and Tapscott et al. (1999). Timmers (1999) provided such an analysis of 'e-economy' structures in terms of value networks and dynamic markets, as will be discussed below.

For the business models classification, we will make use of the approach published in the *International Journal of Electronic Markets* (Timmers, 1998). This paper is one of the few to provide a formal definition of a business model, namely that it consists of the architecture of business processes or value chain steps, together with a description of the product or service, information, and money flows. The business model should also list the business actors involved, their roles, and the benefits they get. This approach also provides a methodology to construct new business models.

A business model in itself does not yet provide understanding of how it will contribute to realizing the business mission and objectives of any of the companies who is an actor within the model. We also need to know about the companies' marketing strategies in order to assess the commercial viability of the business model and to answer questions like: how is competitive advantage being built, what is the positioning, what is the marketing mix, which product-market strategy is being followed? Therefore it is also useful to define beyond a business model the 'marketing model' of a company, which consists of a business model in combination with the marketing strategy of the company (for a more profound analysis see Timmers, 1999).

In principle many new business models can be conceived by deconstructing the value chain into its constituent steps or by decomposing the business into its set of business processes, followed by reconstructing the value chain or set of business processes, again using electronic commerce technologies to build up the business operation. In practice only a limited number of business models are being realized in Internet electronic commerce. Figure 2 shows these most common e-commerce business models. The dimensions in this mapping are the degree of innovation relative to the nonelectronic way of doing business, and the degree of integration of business functions. In the discussion below these business models are briefly explained and put in the context of agent technologies.

E-Shop, E-Procurement

Figure 2. Electronic Commerce Business Models

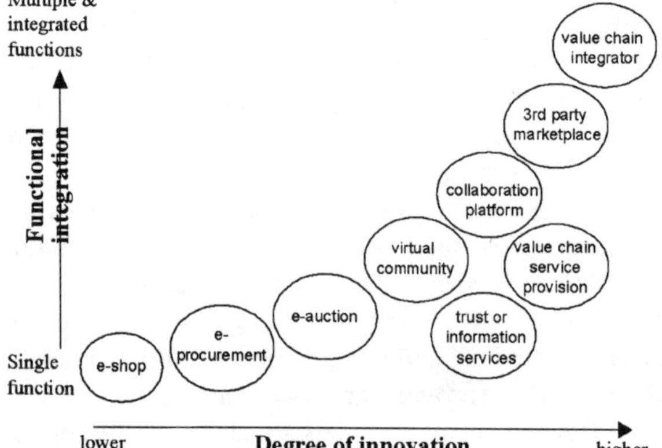

In their basic form e-shops (and e-procurement) are about bringing selling (responsible for buying) on-line by offering an electronic interface to the sales (responsibility for procurement) function. Initial models showed relatively little innovation and consisted of a Web site displaying electronic catalogues or marketing material. Extensions to this basic model integrated ordering and payment, as well as existing information systems, logistics, and distribution. Agent technologies have been successfully implemented to improve the front-office aspects of e-shops: mainly to build customer loyalty and to provide marketing support (Terpsidis et al., 1997).

Customer support can be implemented at different levels: providing the basic information that allows the selection of a product, providing additional technical advice, and personalizing the advice and information using extensive knowledge of the customer. In this line, COGITO[5] is a recently started EU project aiming at developing personalized assistants using intelligent agents. Starting from a chatbox enhanced by 2D and 3D animations, it will use agents to support customers through proactive advice and through intelligent and personalized dialogues, product search and offers. User profiles generated during the dialogues will allow users to learn their preferences and attitudes, and to improve the naturalness of the new dialogues. User profiles and domain knowledge will be used to assist the customer with situation-specific advice in the selection process.

The EU NECTAR[6] project is an example of the use of individual agents in the retail sector. The project aims at building and enhancing customer loyalty by means of actions that satisfy customer expectations and satisfaction, while improving the perceived benefits. The system automatically creates user profiles based on the transactions and product or brand preferences. They are used to generate personalized offers by the automatic monitoring of catalogues and products, seeking out items that match the personalized shopping profiles. Agents are also used for the dynamic presentation of affinity products, once the customer shows interest in a particular item. Furthermore, they have developed one-to-one marketing tools for targeted advertising and special promotional messages fitting the user interests. This strategy tries to generate impulse shopping, increases transaction rates, and provides real-time feedback on the effectiveness of the messages. Full tracking, data analysis, and reporting capabilities allow the marketing departments to improve their strategies and get a deeper knowledge of their customers and their campaigns.

Additional examples of EU projects in this area are: MIMIC,[7] that provides tools for tracking and analysis of pre-sales customer behavior with a view to optimizing the content of a Web site by identifying critical decision points; ACTIVE, that focuses on home shopping with filtering and recommendation capabilities, targeted promotion techniques, and provision of cost fluctuation and flexible advertising schemes; and AIMEDIA, that uses agents for personalized advertising in interactive media.

E-Auctions

Auctions are used to decide the price of a good, mainly when the seller cannot easily determine the market price or when there are fluctuations of demand and/or supply. Examples range from areas as diverse as secondhand products to electricity production to surplus electronic components and to advertising space. Real-world auctions often have an element of excitement and entertainment, and virtual world auctions are trying to reproduce this (see e.g., the auction clock in the EU project INFOMAR, now marketed as Multi-trade by SCS,[8], or the simulated real-time counter in Wehkamp's on-line auction[9]).

In the case of agent-automated auctions, the excitement of a real-world auction is replaced by the carefully studied bidding strategy implemented in the agent. One area particularly suited for agent implementation is commodities, e.g., similar, interchangeable goods that can be easily defined by a common ontology (Vetter & Pitsch, 1999a). An effect of the unprecedented degree of information available through electronic commerce is that many products that before required specialized advice are now starting to be sold as commodities. The power of information and the possibility of comparing competing products are further moving industry towards an auction marketplace where commodity products are sold based on cost, reliability, and speed of delivery.

Price-based auctions are the simplest type of auctions, where most efforts are focusing on their automation by means of agents. Multivariable auctions, based on price plus other factors such as delivery times, service contracts, or negotiable bundles of products and services, are starting to attract the interest of the research community. An example of a multivariable auction is the outsourcing of work or services (e.g., outsourcing software development). An additional issue to consider is the legal liability of the result of the auction that, being of concern in virtual auctions, is more critical in the case of bids made by autonomous software.

CASBA[10] is an example of integration of agent-driven auctions in the electronic marketplace. All participants in the automated auctions are agents that can take one of four roles (Vetter & Pitsch, 1999a). The *sell agent* initiates the process by sending an order to the *administrator agent*, including the descriptions of the good and the rules for the auction. The administrator agent informs of the auction terms to all *buy agents* that may be interested according to the available information in the buy agents' database. It also creates an *auctioneer agent*, in charge of handling the auction according to the agreed rules. The interested buy agents have to subscribe to the auction and, once the auction starts, can make bids executing the strategies of their users. A prototype is being developed for (last-minute) airline tickets, a good that has a clear ontology and therefore is well suited for automated auctions.

Third–Party Marketplaces

In a third-party marketplace (TPM) or 'distributive network,' the provider puts the catalogues of suppliers on-line, and offers catalogue search, ordering, and payment facilities in a secure environment to purchasers. The TPM provider might also add branding, one-to-one marketing support, and logistics to this, as well as more advanced functions such as risk management and insurance, tax/customs handling, and product bundling. In short, the TPM provider relieves suppliers and buyers of much of the burden to go on-line. This approach is particularly important since it is well suited for volume trading of routine supplies between businesses. These MRO goods (which are routine industrial goods that are needed to keep operations going but that are not of strategic importance to the production and are also called Maintenance, Repair, and Operations goods) constitute 50% of all e-commerce.

Agent technologies have an important role in the automation of some of the key processes involved in TPM: information brokerage and mediation, as well as negotiation of offers. TPM requires the development of multi-agent systems (*collaborative agents* as explained in the introduction) that match the demand and supply processes in a commercial mediation environment (Laasri et al., 1992; Rosenschein & Zlotkin, 1994).

The EU project ABROSE[11] is an example of an electronic commerce application that builds an agent technology architecture for brokerage and mediation. The main challenges faced by the project in the automation of information brokerage are:

- knowledge representation, processing, and retrieval to enable the matching of demand and supply; and
- managing the distributed access, flows, and update of information in time.

ABROSE has built a virtual marketplace, populated by agents from providers and users, which negotiate offers, supply, and demand. Transaction agents represent users and providers in the brokerage domain, encapsulating knowledge about them and learnings about other transaction agents. Each time a request is issued, the communication agent in charge of it contacts the transaction agent of the user. Based on specific mediation knowledge, relevant providers' agents are identified and contacted. Providers' agents analyze and adapt the request to issue a proposal that is transmitted to the user domain. Here decision support is provided by specialized agents that own specific domain knowledge, and that is updated based on the evaluation of the obtained results. A symmetric scenario is used for offer propagation (advertising).

The EU project CASBA implements advanced marketplaces providing services that improve customer focus and flexibility. It allows dynamic pricing according to the real demand and customer-specific offers; as a result, the customer and the vendor can negotiate the details of a deal. CASBA has developed a framework for electronic marketplaces using multi-agent technology: a set of tools for setting up and administrating electronic markets, and a tool for the creation of specialized agents to access these markets. An overview of the main features of the system includes (Vetter & Pitsch, 1999b):

- it allows the buyer set specific priorities on the attributes of the desired product;
- this enables the selling agents to answer with related products and/or alternatives according to the buyer preferences;
- using filtering rules the buyer can pre-select the sellers he wants to negotiate with; and
- the agents negotiate with each other using sophisticated strategies based on rule systems and a utility function defined by the individual user.

CASBA also includes a secure electronic payment system.

Value Chain Integration

Value chain integrators focus on bringing together multiple steps of the value chain, with the potential to exploit the information flow between those steps for further added value. Improved information exchange that allows tight integration of all partners in the value chain is one of the main benefits of this model. However, it also allows the provision of new services where intelligent agents can play an important role: as personalized advice to buyers of complex products, customized configuration of the products, and after sales support. All these services require the integration of information to come from all actors in the value chain.

The new IST project LIAISE[12] will use intelligent agents to bring together sellers and suppliers with long-term relationships in order to let the user to do his personal configuration of high complexity products. Agents on the seller side will interact with agents on the user and suppliers' sides. They will provide advice to the user and assure that the requested product configuration is well formed and fulfills all restrictions. They will interact with the suppliers to confirm the availability of the parts and to negotiate their optimal supply. Each user request requires constructing a new solution by assembling a compatible collection of parts chosen from the different suppliers in the value chain. Furthermore, the system will be integrated with the back-office functions of the organizations in the value chain. As test bed, the system will be applied to the selling process of industrial automation systems, where complexity and modularity of the configuration and allowed architectures are strongly increasing.

Other Business Models

The business models classification can be further extended with more business models that have emerged over the past few years. New business models include Application Service Provision (ASP), where the service consists of hosting business applications for a service fee. Access to the applications is over the Internet. ASP as a business model needs reliable and high-performance networking. Witnessing the recent huge investments in ASP there seems to be considerable confidence in this new business model. New forms of value chain service provision are also coming up, such as call centre support and order taking. An example of this is the announcement at the end of 1999 of USA Network[13] to form such an e-commerce services unit. Amongst specialized value chain services, also bill hosting has caught the spotlights for B-to-C transactions.

There are in principle many more business models that can be imagined. A systematic approach to this has been outlined in Timmers (1999). Agent technologies will be critical to enable some of these new models, especially those that focus on added value by targeting higher levels of semantics rather than only automating existing business processes.

AGENT TECHNOLOGIES AND THE ORGANIZATION OF THE ECONOMY

In the quest for efficiency, agility, and competitive advantage, companies constantly need to reassess what is core to their activities, which relationships are strategic, and in which markets they need to be active. For example, companies need to consider rearranging their cost structure, trading off production, which is organized in-house against sourcing from the market or partners. While the make-or-buy question has always existed for companies, it is the opportunities in particular from the Internet, as well as from enabling agent technologies, that have put this question very much into the spotlight again.

Such assessment and consideration lead to rethinking how business processes should be organized, that is, both inside the company as well as in relationship to other companies and to the market. All processes that add to value creation should be analyzed to assess their added value and the appropriate position inside the organization or external to it. In other words, the company is (re-)defining its business model.

However, business models are in fact a single-company-focused view of the organization of the digital economy at large. If we take a helicopter view, we see that business models are critically dependent upon some form of ICT-based networking between business partners and are therefore reflecting the local implementation of the general organization of the economy. Two of the particularly interesting patterns that are emerging in the organization of the information economy at large are *value networks* and *dynamic markets*. These are defined as follows:

A value network is a multi-enterprise set of relationships focused on integration of information flows to exploit information and knowledge in the business network for strategic business objectives.

A dynamic market configuration is a market-mediated set of relationships focused on increasing flexibility and opportunity for strategic business objectives.

A comparison of value network and dynamic market on some key characteristics is given in Table 1.

Table 1. Characteristics of Value Networks and Dynamic Markets

	Focus	***Time scales***	***Mutual commitment***	***Investment per relation***	***Relations***
Value Network	Increasing value through internal relations	Medium-long	High	High	Few
Dynamic	Increasing value	Short-medium	Low	Low	Many

Value networks generally consist of relationships between a limited number of companies. The focus is on deepening these internal relationships, that is, in between the companies and inside each of the companies. The set of partners may change gradually over time as new competitive suppliers or buyers are added and others are being dropped. The actual value chain at any given moment in time may involve a subset of partners from the value network, and this may change over time too.

Dynamic networks would typically involve a larger or very large number of parties, with a focus on seeking to maximize value from those external relationships. In a dynamic network the approach is to maximize price or delivery opportunity or flexibility or agility by selecting the most appropriate business partner (buyer, component supplier, service provider, etc.) at any moment in time.

Figure 3 shows how value networks and digital markets relate to each other by reorganizing value creation processes. It suggests that a company can evolve to become a member of a value network by setting up ICT-supported relationships with other companies who provide goods and services that are no longer produced in-house. It also suggests that these relationships can become more dynamic by being contracted from digital markets for goods and services. In other words, the value network can evolve into a dynamic market configuration. Certainly an evolution in this direction, from single company to value network to dynamic market configuration, is not the only path a company can take. It may also make sense to strengthen the ties with some of the ad-hoc partners in a dynamic market setup and thus go into the direction of a value network. It may even be appropriate to merge with other companies in the value network and thus internalize the business relations (vertical or horizontal integration). Furthermore, new Internet businesses can start in any configuration. By the very nature of the Internet, many of them in fact will start with a dynamic partnership with market parties, rather than as a traditional, tightly integrated company.

These definitions show that there can be overlap between the two forms, namely where market-mediated relationships are combined with tight integration of information systems. Also hybrid forms are conceivable, where a company is at the same time a partner in a value network for some of its business processes, as well as operating in a dynamic market setting for other processes. This can happen when collaboration with suppliers is tightly integrated and relatively static or of long duration, while collaboration with distributors is loosely integrated and more dynamic and of shorter duration. Another example is when critical components are sourced from a limited number of pre-selected suppliers, while the less critical parts are obtained from one out of many suppliers, which is dynamically selected on the basis of best price or fastest delivery.

A qualitative mapping of business models into the value network/dynamic market space is given in Figure 4, where investment specificity corresponds to the amount of sunk investment per business relationship. For a more detailed discussion of electronic commerce scenarios, such as value networks and dynamic markets, see Timmers (1999).

Value Networks

Most current implementations of the value chain integrator and third-party marketplace provider business models are examples of value network configurations. The agent technologies that have been mentioned above for these business models are relevant for value networks in general. Further complexity may come in as in the near future the depth of the value network increases. For example, some companies seek to tightly integrate *all* partners along the whole value chain, in order to implement customer-driven production, also called value chain reversal. Collaborative agents that can rely upon a shared semantics along the value chain clearly find application in such cases. While the alignment of business processes and business semantics across enterprises is a significant challenge, it is in principle possible. An example is the RosettaNet pilot in the PC supply chain, which has delivered such common ontology.[14] The ontology should not only address the 'what' of the value network (the product) but also the 'how,' that is the processes and roles and conditions, including business contracts. The variable parts in a value network are demand and supply (production) but not so much business partners or processes, let alone semantics. Value network agents have to negotiate production schedules and distribution schemes, matching demand and supply. Value network agents would also detect demand patterns and, if a business strategy such as customer-driven production is pursued, trigger the upstream part of the network.

Dynamic Value Networks

In the case of dynamic value chains, the main difference is the possibility of having short-term business relationships: companies or individuals may access the system on an ad-hoc basis and just for a specific kind of transaction. This flexibility brings complexity to the technological development. Collaborative agents developed centrally and deployed on the newcomer server may limit the type of activities performed or require an effort that is not worthy of a single transaction. The solution of a society of agents, developed by different users or providers and negotiating in a complex and dynamic environment, is the appropriate solution but still requires significant developments in agent interoperability, business semantics, and more generally ontologies. A particular challenge will be in detecting common semantics or the lack thereof 'on the fly.' Furthermore, these large-scale open platforms require a better understanding of issues as scalability and stability (including self-organization, self-regulation, and adaptive behaviors), as well as clear solutions for the legal and security aspects.

Dynamic value networks are a challenging research area for agent technologies since they require addressing all the key problems of open agent platforms, and they also provide

Figure 3. From Value Chain to Value Network and Dynamic Markets

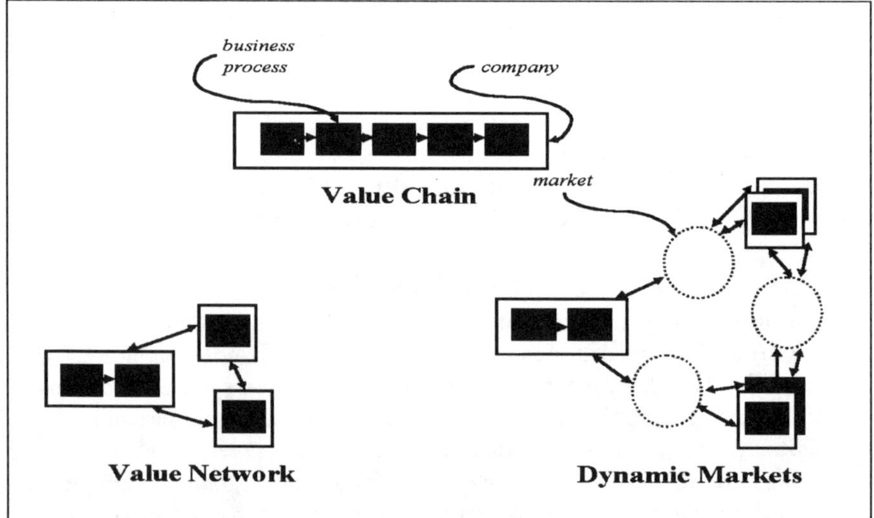

Figure 4. Business Models and Value Networks / Dynamic Markets

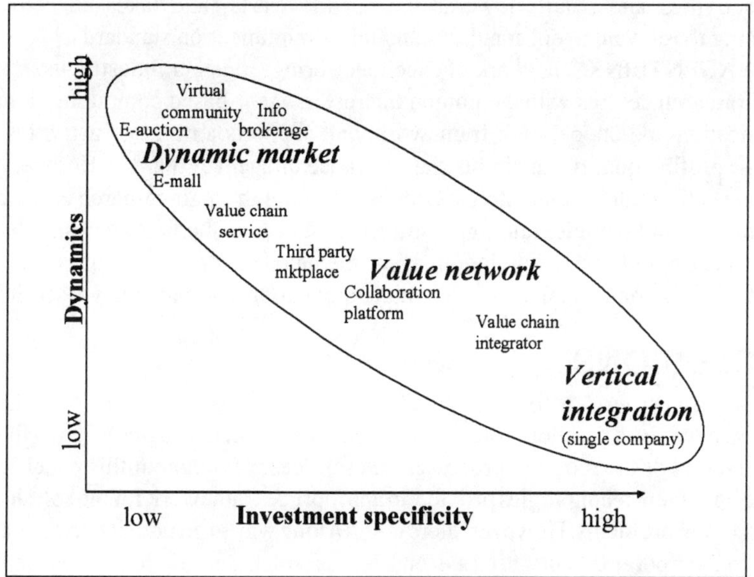

a test bed where the full potentiality of agents can be demonstrated. Dynamic value networks are the subject of the Year 2000 calls for project proposals of the e-commerce key action of the IST program.

STANDARDS AND RESEARCH NETWORKS

Standardization is a key issue to advance towards the development of open agent platforms. Today, two major standards addressing interoperability of agents are available, namely the Object Management Group (OMG) Mobile Agent System Interoperability Facility (OMG-MASIF) and the Foundation of Physical Intelligent Agents (FIPA) specifications. OMG-MASIF[15] aims at enabling mobile agents to migrate between agent systems of the same profile via standardized CORBA IDL interfaces. FIPA[16] works on enabling the intelligent agents' interoperability via standardized agent communication and content languages. Beside the generic communication framework, FIPA is also specifying ontology and negotiation protocols to support interoperability in specific application areas. However, these standards are far from being complete; they require validation, further enhancements, and most importantly integration.

FACTS[17] is a EU project that aims at validating the work of FIPA, OMG-MASIF, and other standards groups by constructing a number of demonstrator systems based on proposed standards. By building real demonstrator systems, it proves the overall technical approach adopted by the standardization bodies, identifies their strengths and weaknesses, and generates proven suggestions for changes and enhancements. Application areas include audiovisual entertainment and broadcasting, service reservation, and electronic trading.

The cluster CLIMATE[18] represents a pool of agent technology-related projects within the EU collaborative research and development program. Its mission is to optimize the information exchange and to promote cooperation between these projects in order to enable the harmonization of work, which ideally will result in a flexible common agent middle ware, which could be used for different application domains. CLIMATE promotes the agent project activities and results towards the outside world, and takes an active part in contributing to relevant agent standards and telecommunication standards.

The AGENTLINK[19] network of excellence brings together industry, users, universities, and research centres with a common interest in agent-based computing. It provides a communication and cooperation framework, and supports a range of activities aimed at raising the profile, quality, and industrial relevance of agent systems in Europe. Activities are organized through Special Interest Groups that cover the main research issues discussed in this chapter, and include: intelligent information agents, methodologies/software engineering, agent-based social simulation, agent-mediated electronic commerce, multi-agent coordination and control, telecommunication applications, and telematics services.

CONCLUSIONS

New business models for electronic commerce have been emerging over the past few years, which require a parallel evolution in the supporting technologies to allow the efficient implementation of the required processes and services. Throughout this paper it has been analyzed how agent technologies provide an appropriate framework for the solution of some of the emerging problems. However, there is still a long way to go until it becomes a common practice to incorporate agent-based systems into products and services, in particular, when we consider the most innovative business models. This will require addressing the key challenges of agent technologies, which are mainly related to the problems generated by large-scale open and highly dynamic systems. These include among others: agent software engineering, scalability and stability of agent systems, standards, and legal and security issues. The new IST program of the EU offers opportunities for collaboration between industry, research institutes, and public bodies by supporting research and development projects that can meet these challenges.

REFERENCES

Bailey, J., & Bakos, Y. (1997). An exploratory study of the emerging role of electronic intermediaries. *International Journal of Electronic Commerce*, 1(3).

Ephrati, E., & Rosenschein, J. (1994). Multi-agent planning as search for a consensus that maximizes social welfare. *Lecture Notes in Artificial Intelligence* 830, pages 207-226, Springer-Verlag.

Hagel, J., & Armstrong. A. (1997). *Net Gain: Expanding Markets Through Virtual Communities*. Harvard Business School Press.

Kalakota, R., & Robinson, M. (1999). *e-Business, Roadmap for Success*. Addison-Wesley.

Laasri, B., Laasri, H., Lander, S., & Lesser, V. (1992). A generic model for intelligent negotiating agents. *International Journal of Intelligent and Cooperative Information Systems,* Vol. 1.

Maes, P. (1994). Agents that reduce work and information overload. *Communications of the ACM*, 37(7), ACM Press.

Maes, P., Guttman, R., & Moukas, A. (1999). Agents that buy and sell. Communications of the ACM, 42(3).

Merz, M. (1999). Electronic Commerce: Marktmodelle, Anwendungen, und Technologien. dpunkt.verlag, Heidelberg.

Moukas, A. (1997). Amalthaea: Information filtering and discovery using a multiagent evolving system. *Journal of Applied AI*, 11(5).

Rappa, M. (2000). *Business Models on the Web*. http://ecommerce.ncsu.edu/business_models.html (May 25).

Rayport, J.R. (1999), The Truth about Internet Business Models. *Strategy + Business*, 3rd Quarter 1999, http://www.strategy-business.com/ (May 25).

Rosenschein, J., & Zlotkin, G. (1994). *Rules of encounter: Designing conventions for automated negotiations among computers*. MIT Press.

Tapscott, D., Lowy, A., & Ticoll, D.(1999). *Blueprint to the Digital Economy*. McGraw-Hill.

Terpsidis, I., Moukas, A., Pergioudakis, B., Doukidis, G., & Maes, P. (1997). The potential of electronic commerce in re-engineering consumer-retail relationships through intelligent agents. In: *Advances in information technologies: the business challenge,* J-Y. Roger et al. (Eds.), IOS Press.

Timmers, P. (1998). Business Models for Electronic Markets. *International Journal of Electronic Markets*, 98(2), Available: http://www.electronicmarkets.org (2000, May 25)

Timmers, P. (1999). *Electronic Commerce: Strategies and Models for Business-to-Business Trading.* Wiley & Sons Ltd.

Vetter, M., & Pitsch, S. (1999a). An Agent-based Market Supporting Multiple Auction Protocols, Agents 99. in: *WS 4: Agent-Based Decision-Support for Managing the Internet-Enabled Supply-Chain*, Goodwin, R. (ed.)

Vetter, M., & Pitsch, S. (1999b). Using autonomous agents to expand business models in electronic commerce. in: *Business and Work in The Information Society, EMMSEC'99*, Roger, Y., Stanford-Smith, B., Kidd, P.T. (Eds.), IOS Press.

ENDNOTES

1 Views expressed in this paper are the authors and do not necessarily reflect the opinions of the European Commission.

2 For information on the IST program, the current workprogram, and calls for project proposals, see http://www.cordis.lu/ist (2000, May 25)

3 For an overview of electronic commerce projects of the European Commission, see the publication, *Accelerating Electronic Commerce in Europe*, which lists about 300 EU e-commerce-related projects. The book is also available on-line at http://www.ispo.cec.be/ecommerce/books/aecebook.html, (2000, May 25).

4 Intershop makes a distinction between business models for direct and indirect sales (i.e., market-places, affiliate schemes, and distributor channels). See http://www.intershop.com (2000, May 25).

5 More detailed information about the project is available at http://www.darmstadt.gmd.de/~cogito/ (2000, May 25).

6 More detailed information about the project is available at http://www.etnoteam.it/nectar/ (2000, May 25).

7 More detailed information about the project is available at http://www.atinternet.fr/mimic/ (2000, May 25).

8 See http://www.schelfhout.com (2000, May 25). As a case study this is analyzed in-depth in Timmers (1999).

9 http://www.wehkamp.nl (2000, May 25) which also has a 'publiekstribune.'

10 More detailed information about the project is available at http://www.casba-market.org (2000, May 25).

11 More detailed information about the project is available at http://b5www.berkom.de/ABROSE.

12 More detailed information about the project is available at http://www.orsiweb.com/rtd/liaise.htm (2000, May 25).

13 http://www.thestandard.net/articles/display/0,1449,6956,00.html?1447 (2000, May 25).

14 RosettaNet: http://www.rosettanet.org (2000, May 25) is a project supported by a wide industry consortium and managed by CommerceNet since 1998.

15 Detailed information about OMG-MASIF is available at http://www.fokus.gmd.de/research/cc/ecco/masif (2000, May 25).

16 Detailed information about FIPA is available at http://drogo.cselt.stet.it/fipa (2000, May 25).

17 More detailed information about the project is available at http://www.labs.bt.com/profsoc/facts (2000, May 25).

18 More detailed information is available at http://www.fokus.gmd.de/research/cc/ecco/climate (2000, May 25).

19 More detailed information is available at http://www.agentlink.org (2000, May 25).

Chapter XI

SAFER E-Commerce: Secure Agent Fabrication, Evolution, & Roaming for E-Commerce

Fangming Zhu, Sheng-Uei Guan and Yang Yang
National University of Singapore

As electronic commerce (e-commerce) booms, the demands for intelligent tools to streamline transactions are increasing. This motivates the development of the next generation of e-commerce, agent-based e-commerce. This chapter proposes a Secure Agent Fabrication, Evolution, & Roaming (SAFER) architecture for agent-based e-commerce. SAFER provides services for agents in e-commerce and establishes a rich set of mechanisms to manage and secure them. The definitions and functions of the various components in the SAFER architecture are elaborated. This chapter also illustrates three main aspects in the SAFER architecture: agent fabrication, agent evolution, and agent roaming.

INTRODUCTION

Electronic commerce (e-commerce) is booming with the increasing accessibility of the Internet in almost every corner of the world. The World Trade Organization expects worldwide e-commerce revenues to reach US $200 billion in the next two years. E-commerce is revolutionizing the concept of carrying out business dealings. By using a web browser, buyers are able to access numerous e-commerce Web sites, where they can make purchases within a reasonable price range. Suppliers realize that e-commerce is essential to the success and competitiveness of their businesses. E-commerce has challenged some aspects of traditional commerce and, at the same time, is presenting a valuable opportunity for both suppliers and buyers. The benefits of conducting business online include significant reduction of the cost for many transactions and streamlining of operations. For these reasons, we can perform transactions without leaving our desks, and small companies have the chance to compete with larger ones.

However, there are also some obstacles to the success of e-commerce. Firstly, buyers may be lost in the ocean of the items available, and eventually miss the best deal. Secondly, it is a tedious task to search for a specific product through the Internet and it is difficult to bargain within the current infrastructure. Thirdly, some transactions are so complicated that they are too difficult to be dealt with. For instance, merchants often negotiate transactions with multiple issues of concern such as price, quantity, and method of delivery. Many strategies are employed to accomplish these tasks, and both the negotiating counterparts and the environment can affect the choice of the strategies. However, in many existing auction Web sites, price is the main focus for both bidders and sellers. Bidders and sellers are seldom given a chance to negotiate the other issues, and many commercial opportunities are neglected. In fact, most of them lack an intelligent tool to help streamline the transaction procedures (Guilfoyle, 1994).

To overcome this, a new generation of e-commerce, agent-based e-commerce, is emerging and software agents are playing a crucial role in it. Software agents have demonstrated tremendous potential in conducting transactional tasks in e-commerce through the Internet. It acts on behalf of an entity to carry out a delegated task. One of the earliest agents in e-commerce is the shopping agent, which carries out automatic comparative price shopping on the Web. A client can assign one or many shopping agents to carry out the shopping task. Agents can gather price information through the Internet first. The filtered and classified information is presented to the client for a decision. Certainly, the task of a software agent involves more than merely online data gathering and filtering. For example, software agents are also employed in negotiation. Negotiation agents are instructed with expected prices, quantities, delivery modes, and/or negotiation strategies. One agent can automatically launch a negotiation with a suitable counterpart. They may make offers, accept offers, make counter-offers similar to a tete-a-tete negotiation, and may even strike a successful deal in the end (Oliver, 1996; Kang, 1998). Besides, software agents can also undertake other tasks such as payment, mediation, distribution, interaction, and sales promotion in e-commerce.

With the development of Internet computing and software agent, agent-based e-commerce will become more and more mature. In particular, software agents may have significant contributions in this field. They can perform tasks in simple, intelligent, and independent manners. However, there can be potential dangers along with the merits. We should be careful of the side effects such as breaching privacy and inducing social mischief. Despite these, agent-based e-commerce is a promising novelty. We should utilize its full advantages while minimizing the potential risks (Bradshaw, 1997; Ahuja, 1996).

Software agents can be endowed with attributes such as mobility, intelligence, and autonomy. To alleviate concerns such as authorization, traceability, integrity, and security in e-commerce and the Internet, constructing appropriate architecture for agent systems in e-commerce is a fundamental consideration in facilitating agent-based transactions (Lee, 1997). As software agents become more common, there is a need for skilled programmers and even ordinary e-commerce clients to manipulate them. A practical way is to provide sites with methods to fabricate various agents according to the requirements of the clients. Due to the nature of e-commerce and the Internet, agents should be able to adapt to a changing environment automatically. We also need to look into the situation that there will be competitions and collaborations among various types of agents that belong to different owners. Agents should have an evolutional ability to enhance its intelligence and survivability. Roaming is one of the basic capabilities for agents so that they can fully utilize the power of network computing. They can achieve timesaving and cost-cutting in completing its task without compromising security by roaming from one host to another (Guan, 1999; Yang, 2000).

In order to meet the requirements discussed above and provide an environment for an in-depth research in e-commerce, this chapter proposes and discusses SAFER for e-commerce (Secure Agent Fabrication, Evolution, & Roaming for e-commerce).

OVERVIEW OF THE SAFER ARCHITECTURE

SAFER is an infrastructure to serve agents in e-commerce and establish the necessary mechanisms to manipulate them. The goal of SAFER is to construct standard, dynamic and evolutionary agent systems for e-commerce. The SAFER architecture comprises different communities as described in Figure 1. Each community consists of the following components: Owner, Butler, Agent, Agent Factory, Community Administration Center, Agent Charger, Agent Immigration, Clearing House, and Bank, which are illustrated in Figure 2. Every component will be elaborated in the following subsections.

Community

Agents can be grouped into many communities based on certain criteria. In order to distinguish agents in the SAFER architecture from those which are not, we divide them into SAFER communities and non-SAFER communities as shown in Figure 1. We shall only discuss the SAFER community. Each SAFER community can possess a set of the facilities and individuals as described in Figure 2. Figure 2 only lists the necessary components in one community. Some communities may have more entities than those depicted in the figure. For instance, there can be two agent chargers in a large community.

The partitioning of the agent communities can be based on criteria such as autonomy and geographical locations. In order to become a SAFER community member, an applicant should apply to his local community administration center. The center will issue a certification to the applicant whenever it accepts the application. A digital certificate will be issued to prove the certified status of the applicant. To decide whether a facility or individual belongs to a community, one can look up the roster in the community administration center. A registered agent in one community may migrate into another community. In addition to permanent residence in a community, an agent can carry out its tasks in a foreign community. For agents to visit a foreign community, they must register in the foreign community administration center as guests. When an agent roams from one SAFER community to another, it will be checked by an agent immigration with regard to its authorization and security before it can perform any action in this community. In order to integrate all the communities into a society, agent communities may have to exchange with each other information such as the registration and immigration details. These tasks are undertaken by community

Figure 1. SAFER Architecture (1)

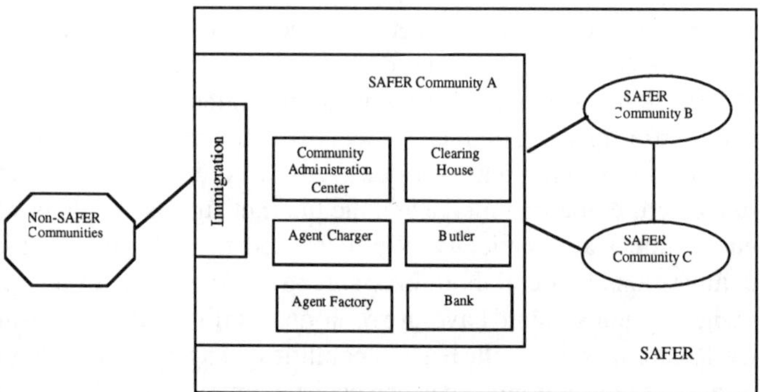

Figure 2. SAFER Architecture (2)

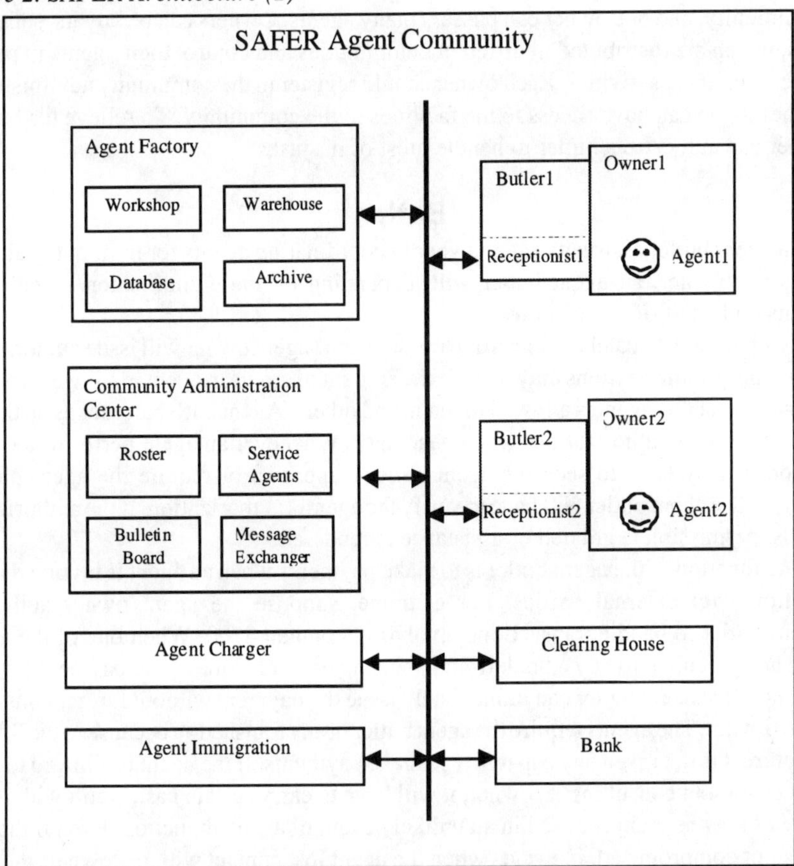

administration centers. For example, it is essential that every agent in the SAFER architecture has a unique identification number, and it can be achieved by having a naming scheme similar to the IP domain name mechanism. Communities exchange ID information to maintain global authentication. When two agents from different communities transact in one community, the authentication and authorization of both agents should be validated.

Agent community is the basic unit in SAFER e-commerce. It offers factories and evolution vehicles to streamline e-commerce agents. Under these organized communities, agents can be regulated in a tidy order and perform their tasks more efficiently. The tighter structure also provides a solid base for enhancing the security of agents, which is one of the most important concerns in agent-based e-commerce systems.

Owner

Agent owners stand at the top of the SAFER architecture's hierarchy. They are the real participants during the transactions and agents are acting on behalf of them. An owner has the priority and responsibility for all his agents. An owner controls his agents from creation to termination. An owner can request an agent factory to fabricate agents responsible for specific e-commerce activities. Furthermore, he acts as the supervisor for the roaming agents. Sometimes an owner needs to initiate important decisions of a transaction so that his agent can complete its tasks. For instance, negotiation agents need to request the final agreement from its owner before it can sign the contract. Many agent owners can exist in one community, and one owner can possess many agents. Owners can be buyers, sellers, or proxies, which are distributed in different communities and control their agents to participate in e-commerce activities. Each owner should register in the community administration center before he can have access to the facilities in the community. To relieve his burden, an owner can authorize a butler to handle most of his tasks.

Butler

An agent butler assists its agent owner in coordinating agents for him. In the absence of the agent owner, an agent butler will, depending on the authorization given, make decisions on behalf of the agent owner.

As agents are dispatched for certain missions, the agent owner will issue authorization to them. These authorizations may include the amount of credit an agent is allowed to spend, the range of host this agent is allowed to roam, and others. Agent butler also takes on the role of enforcing these authorizations when necessary. Whenever an agent performs a critical operation, it may have to seek the agent butler's approval or require the agent butler's assistance. The agent butler will have to verify the agent's authorization. If the authorization succeeds, permission is granted or assistance is rendered.

One function of the agent butler is to make payments when an agent is involved in any transaction with external parties. For example, suppose the agent owner authorizes the agent butler to handle transactions involving less than $100. When one of the agents reaches an agreement to buy a book from Amazon.com and requests the payment from the agent butler, the agent butler can immediately issue the payment without further consulting the agent owner. The agents require the agent butler in any transaction because in the SAFER architecture it is not given any capability to make payments. If the agent is allowed to make payments without consulting its owner, it will have to carry certain cash credit with it. The cash credit may be compromised in an unlikely event of agent abduction. Even if the cash credit is not compromised, in events when the agent lost contact with the owner, the issue of recovering lost cash credit in the agent and preventing the lost agent from making unauthorized payment is avoided. The fact that the agent does not carry any cash credit prevents it from been cracked.

In addition, an agent butler also keeps track of the agent's activities and its location. For example, an information-gathering agent will send information like sites visited and information collected back to the agent butler. With this information, the agent butler may ensure that the other agents do not visit the sites again. Moreover, the butler can order all the information-gathering agents to stop their operations and send all the information collected to one particular information-processing agent. Under the SAFER roaming protocol, all agents will inform its agent butler of its roaming destination (either directly or indirectly) whenever they roam to a new host. This allows the agent butler to keep track of its agents' whereabouts.

It should be noted that all child agents are required to report to the agent butler just like any other agent. When a new child agent is generated, the parent agent will report its 'birth' to the butler. Subsequently, when the child roams to other hosts, its roaming information is sent back to the butler. This allows the agent parent, which may be mobile itself, to get in touch with its child agents. This task is difficult to achieve without the help of the agent butler as the parent agent needs to inform its child agents and receives acknowledgement from them before it roams to a new host. Similarly, all child agents are required to inform the parent agent before they roam to another host if there is no agent butler. This reduces the efficiency of the roaming agents. Hence, with the help of the agent butler, both parent and child agents are able to roam freely without informing each other, and yet each can locate one another easily through the butler.

Agent butlers can also be used to detect agent abduction or lost agents. In certain applications, agents may be assigned with critical missions. If these agents are abducted or lost, the agent owner has to take quick actions. A typical scenario is when an agent with the task of negotiating an important contract is sent out, the owner needs to ensure that the agent is alive and performs the negotiations. Merely informing the agent butler of its roaming activities is not enough. The agent may be trapped in one host and is unable to continue its normal operation. By the time the agent butler finds out the agent's inactivity, precious time may be lost.

In order to ensure that an agent is 'alive,' critical agents are required to send a 'heartbeat' signal back to the agent butler at fixed intervals. If the butler does not receive heartbeats from an agent after the fixed interval, the butler will immediately alert the agent owner and appropriate actions can be taken to either recover the agent or issue new agents to continue the mission.

Another function of agent butlers is to act as receptionists in agent roaming (Yang, 2000). It services both the incoming and outgoing agents as well as coordinating agent transport.

Agent

Agent plays an active role in SAFER e-commerce. It is agent that brings to life the promising aspects in the next generation of e-commerce. All the facilities in the SAFER architecture serve agents in one way or another. Each agent has a unique identification and belongs to one specified owner. To identify itself, an agent should have a digital certificate issued by its creator. According to the tasks assigned by the owner, we can classify agents into many categories, such as negotiation agents, payment agents, mediation agents, and so on. The locations of agents change frequently, as they carry out their jobs in different places. Agents can be resting in the owner's computer when they are idle, or roaming from one host to another, or executing a task in a foreign host.

It terms of capabilities, agents can be classified as intelligent agents, mobile agents, evolutionary agents, etc. As an agent acts on behalf of its owner, it should have a certain degree of intelligence. For example, it accepts the owner's assignment and carries out the task delegated to it. An agent should learn the owner's preference, show an ability of reasoning, and adjust its behavior according to the task assigned and the resources available. Agents have the mobility to travel through the Internet. Mobile agents can carry important information when they are roaming through the network to complete transactions. It should be immune from attacks from hackers or malicious agents. Security protection is thus the most crucial issue in agent roaming as well as other activities in e-commerce. As many agents strive to accomplish their tasks, they may compete on limited resources or collaborate to complete similar tasks. Furthermore, agents can evolve and adapt to a diversifying and changing environment.

Agent Factory

Agent factory is the kernel of SAFER, as it undertakes the primary task of 'creating' agents. In addition, agent factory has the responsibility to fix and check agents, which is an indispensable function in agent evolution and security.

As illustrated in Figure 2, an agent factory consists of four components, namely, workshop, warehouse, database, and archive. Workshop is the site where an agent is fabricated, fixed, and checked. Coarse agents that are suspended in fabrication and those waiting for further fixing or checking are queued in the warehouse. Database includes various ontology structures and standard modules to assemble different agents in the workshop. Archive is the set of the factory logs and information of agents which have undergone certain processes in the agent factory.

An agent factory provides an interface, such as choices of fabrication or repair instructions for owners (or butlers), to customize agents with desirable functionality. Before an agent factory starts its process, it first checks the identity of the owner with the community administration center to ensure that the owner has legally registered. After the owner specifies the parameters and information, the agent factory starts to assemble or update the agent using the ontology structures and standard modules in the database. A newly created agent begins its task or moves back to the owner depending on the instruction given. The agent factory also undertakes the liability to check the fitness and integrity of the agents in the community, which is essential to the evolution procedures and security protection of the agents. Any work done by the agent factory is recorded in the archive for later references.

It can be seen that the functions of the agent factory are tightly related with the community administration center. Besides checking the identity of the owner, an agent factory applies for new ID numbers for new agents from the community administration center. The community administration center assigns a unique ID number to each agent. After the fabrication or repair of an agent, the agent factory will also report to the administration center to register the new agent.

Community Administration Center

The community administration center is responsible for administrative matters in the community. It has the privileges of coordinating and facilitating the activities of all the entities in the community. Its aims are to assure the smooth running of routine operations and security of the whole community.

The administration center has a roster of the community, which includes basic data on the registered facilities, owners, agents, and guest agents from other communities. This roster is updated periodically. When an agent factory has fabricated a new agent, it will inform the center to add the new item. When an agent is terminated, it should also be reflected in the roster. In addition, the center does a thorough routine examination of all components in the community and updates the roster periodically. If a foreign agent wants to enter this community for some purpose, it should request a 'visa' from the agent immigration, and the agent immigration will forward the registration to the administration center. For these reasons, the center is well aware of any incoming agents and events happening in it so that it is well-guarded from any intruder.

The administration center also has the responsibility of information exchange (e.g., ID information exchange) and communication with other communities. Moreover, it collects information, such as addresses of new auction websites, from the Internet to update the databases in the agent factory. The internal management of the center provides a message exchanger for the entities in the community. Another minor function of the community administration center is to provide services to the community agents. One of these services is to provide the community bulletin board, where agents can post their requirements and information to share with other agents. Furthermore, the community administration center has service agents such as advertising agents and broadcasting agents to cater to the needs of the community agents.

Agent Charger

The agent charger is part of the security mechanism to ensure agent integrity in SAFER. Since SAFER is designed for e-commerce, roaming agents must be protected from malicious attacks. One important aspect of agent protection is agent integrity. Roaming agents must not be interfered with during roaming or its execution at the remote host. The protection of agent integrity (both code integrity and data integrity) during roaming operation has been addressed in Yang (2000). In order to protect agent integrity during an agent's execution at a remote host, the concept of 'agent battery' is now introduced.

Before explaining agent battery, the concept of 'agent action' will first be defined. Agent action is any activity involving an agent with one or more third parties that may cause dispute or damage to other party. Typical agent actions include agent roaming, agent negotiation, and execution of transactions. Without the ability to execute 'actions,' the agent is effectively disabled like an electric-powered toy car with a dry battery. Agent battery refers to a battery carried by each agent that specifies the number of 'actions' it can perform. The agent battery decreases its energy level (i.e., number of 'actions') by one each time before an action is executed. If the level reaches zero, the agent is not allowed to perform any more action. In order to restore its energy level, the agent approaches an agent charger to regain its energy. Agent charger is located in the SAFER community. In large communities, there may be more than one agent charger to facilitate the charge-up operations. Before restoring an agent battery, the agent charger should inspect the agent for its fitness and integrity. The inspection should include both agent code or agent data. If an agent is found to be intact (code integrity and data integrity is not compromised), the charger can increase the battery quota in the agent. The amount of quota to be increased should be specified by the agent owner/butler. If no value is specified, the default amount will be used. In case the agent has been found interfered with during charging, the agent charger will detain the agent and informs either the agent's owner or its butler.

With this battery system, an agent is forced to go through a 'medical check-up' periodically. If an agent is corrupted at a malicious host, its battery level might drop to zero. Eventually, this corrupted agent is detected by a charger and is terminated. The agent's code integrity and data integrity can thus be guaranteed.

Agent Immigration

In an effort to promote open architecture, SAFER is designed to allow interaction with agents and hosts from within its family and other non-SAFER architectures. This leads to another problem: how do agents roam from one community to another community?

Agent immigration is introduced to provide a mechanism in the administration of agents across community boundaries. If an agent needs to roam outside the community, it has to obtain a 'visa' from the visiting community's immigration. A host will ensure that only foreign agents with valid visas are allowed to execute in its premise. Therefore, if an illegal agent sneaks into a community without going through agent immigration, it will not be able to perform any action.

The policy of issuing visas may differ from immigration to immigration. It is important to identify where an agent comes from and update the information in the immigration log. If the agent causes any damage in the community, a trace is available to identify the malicious agent's owner. Individual agent immigration has different policies of issuing visas depending on the level of security. For example, if an immigration wishes to have the strictest security in the community, it scans the agent's code and data for malicious instruction and false information. The agent is forbidden entry if the immigration detects any problem. On the other hand, if the immigration exercises trusts on incoming agents, the above check can be waived. Different policy may be applied to agents from SAFER communities and non-SAFER communities since agents from non-SAFER communities are more likely to be malicious.

With agent immigration, SAFER communities are more likely to be free from malicious agents. Even if a malicious agent managed to obtain a visa from immigration (due to the relaxation of security checks), the agent's source is recorded into the agent immigration which is used later to trace the culprit.

Clearing House and Bank

In order to facilitate financial transactions and clearance, a clearing house and bank are included as separate entities in each SAFER community.

Each agent and host should open an account with the bank that resides at its originating community. The personal particulars of the agents will only be known by the local bank and are not disclosed. If a transaction takes place within a community that does not involve any party from other communities, they can make an appropriate request directly to a local bank for immediate settlement. However, if a transaction involves parties from other communities, the clearing house must be used as the medium for settlement with different banks. Different from banks, a clearing house does not contain any account information as the bank does. It is merely a medium through which inter-bank settlement can be facilitated. For example, if agent 007 from a community (e.g., London) makes a payment to host CIA in the other community (e.g., Washington) for a rocket launcher, CIA will contact the clearing house in Washington to check on the credit limit of 007. The clearing house in Washington, in turn, will make inquiries to get information from its counterpart in London. If 007's credit line is good, the clearing house in London will transfer the credit from 007's London bank to the clearing house in Washington, which will subsequently deposit them into CIA's bank in Washington. It should be noted that during the transaction, the clearing house in London will not be able to find out CIA's account information in Washington and vice versa. Anonymity across different communities can be provided through the use of a clearing house. The detailed payment scheme is currently under active research.

AGENT FABRICATION

In SAFER, agents are fabricated by an agent factory in its community. There are many supporting arguments to adopt this mode of fabrication:

- Although some users may design agents by themselves, most users do not have the ability to do so. Also software agents in e-commerce have many types. It will be more convenient if an agent can be customized according to its own specification by using the agent factory.
- E-commerce agents implemented individually can lead to lack of standardization among owners. This may result in communication breakdown.
- Adopting this mode of agent fabrication will enhance the security of SAFER e-commerce. Since information of all fabricated agents is stored in agent factories, agents can be administered more efficiently and safely.

Under SAFER, the fabrication of agents obeys prescribed routine procedures. An owner customizes new agents through the interface provided by an agent factory. When an agent factory fabricates a new agent, it chooses the corresponding ontology structure from the database according to the requests from the owners. The agent factory then assembles the agents according to both the ontology structure and the owner's specification. The procedures of agent fabrication are demonstrated in Figure 3 and Table 1.

Each ontology structure defines the components and construction of a specific type of agent. Different types of agents are defined with different ontology structures depending on their prototypes in agent factory. Examples are ontology structures for negotiation agents and information-collection agents. The same type of agents may have different structures because of different requirements. The ontology structures are stored in the database of the agent factory.

SAFER adopts a tree structure to express the ontology and agent. Figure 3 lays out an ontology structure for negotiation agents, and the details of nodes in Figure 3 are shown in Table 1. There are two types of nodes in the ontology structure, namely, terminal and function nodes. Terminal nodes are the 'leaves' of the tree. They correspond to data and variable arguments such as node D1 for agent ID and node D2 for a destination. They can be customized or set to default value. The function nodes are internal nodes, showing the categories of their child nodes. The ontology structure also specifies the attribute of every node. If the node is indispensable in the structure, its attribute number will be zero. For example, node D1 in Figure 3 stands for agent ID which is mandatory for every agent; its attribute is specified as zero and the node is represented as D1/0. Similarly, if the node is optional or can be replicated to a maximum of N times, then the attribute for that node is represented with 1 or N, respectively. Examples are node D3/1 and node F2/3 in Figure 3.

When an agent factory fabricates a new agent, it arranges the data and functions according to the instructions from the ontology structure. Figure 4 demonstrates a negotiation agent fabricated according to the ontology structure illustrated in Figure 3, and the details of the nodes in Figure 4 are specified in Table 2. The first two digits in the nodes of Figure 4 correspond to the nodes in the ontology structure in Figure 3. For example, node D1A1 corresponds to node D1, nodes D4A1 and D4A2 correspond to node D4. Note that node F1A1 in the agent has only one child node D2A1, while node F1 in the ontology has two child nodes. This is because the at-

Figure 3. Ontology Structure

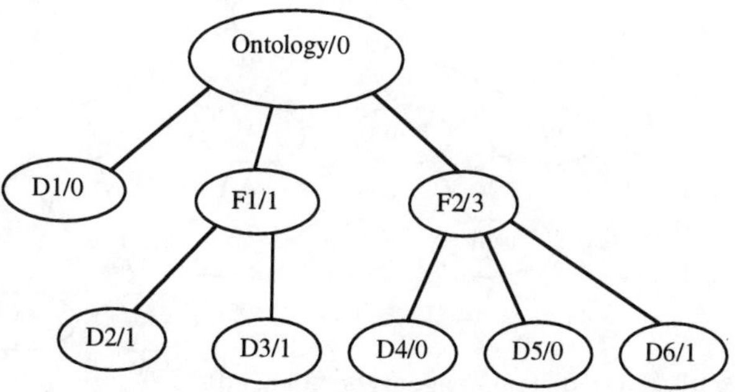

Table 1. Details of Nodes in Figure 3

NODE	CONTENT	ATTRIBUTE
Ontology	Ontology Type	0
D1	Agent ID	0
F1	Destination Site	1
D2	Destination 1	1
D3	Destination 2	1
F2	Negotiation Strategy	3
D4	Strategy Parameter 1	0
D5	Strategy Parameter 2	0
D6	Strategy Parameter 3	1

0 – Indispensable 1 - Optional
N – Maximum Replication Number (positive integer except1)

tribute of node D3 in the ontology in Figure 3 is 1, which means that it is optional. So when the agent factory fabricates the agent, it can choose to assemble only one node under node F1A1, which means that node D3 has no counterpart in the new agent. The new nodes F2A1 and F2A2 are replications of node F2 in the ontology, because node F2 in the ontology has an attribute 3, which means that it can be replicated up to as many as three times. Node F2A1 has two child nodes and node F2A2 has three child nodes. Similarly this can be seen from the attributes of the nodes D4, D5, and D6 in the ontology structure.

The above exemplifies the agent fabrication formalities. All the agents in SAFER are fabricated in agent factories based on formal procedures similar to this example. One of the many advantages it brings to SAFER is that the agent evolution is facilitated.

AGENT EVOLUTION

One of the most prominent aspects of SAFER is agent evolution. As numerous agents are distributed throughout the Internet and act on behalf of different owners in different communities, collaborations and competitions exist among them. For example, agents with the same goal of finding the pricing for a certain type of computer can collaborate with one another. One agent can inform the others of the Web sites it has visited and the information gathered so that other agents do not need to visit the same websites again. In another scenario, some agents may cooperate to negotiate with several sellers. They can share information and adjust their strategies accordingly during the negotiation process in order to reach satisfactory deals. On the other hand, competitions are inevitable when resource is limited. For example, if only a limited number of computers are available, agents will have to compete against each other to get them. In the end, some of them will succeed, while the others will fail. The successful agent may become more powerful, and the failed agent may lose some fitness. This is similar to collaborations and competitions in natural ecosystems.

Figure 4. An Agent Fabricated Using the Ontology in Figure 3

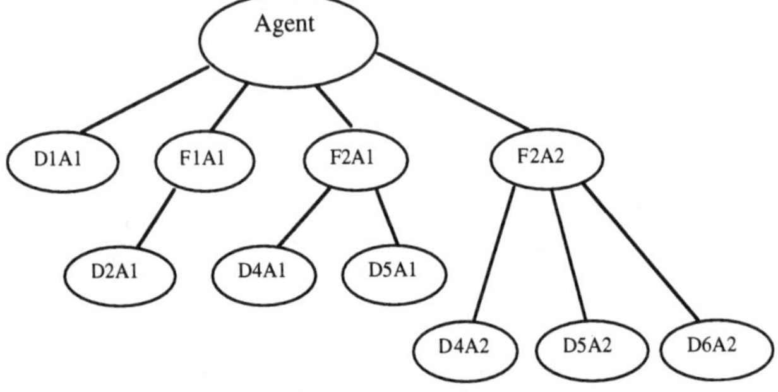

Table 2. Details of Nodes in Figure 4

NODE	CONTENT
Agent	Agent Name
D1A1	Agent ID
F1A1	Destination Site
D2A1	Destination 1
F2A1	Negotiation Strategy 1
D4A1	Strategy Parameter 1
D5A1	Strategy Parameter 2
F2A2	Negotiation Strategy 2
D4A2	Strategy Parameter 1
D5A2	Strategy Parameter 2
D6A2	Strategy Parameter 3

As the environment changes continuously, agents roaming in the network may be attacked by malicious agents or suffer from unstable environments. These agents must strive to protect and adapt themselves in order to complete their tasks successfully. Eventually, agents must have the capabilities of intelligence and evolution.

Some evolution-related attributes are proposed. The first attribute of concern is the *state of an agent*. Agents can be in different states such as new born, executing, suspended, communicating, and terminated. Evolution takes place among these states, and agents may migrate from one state to another as a result of evolution. For example, one agent in executing state may transform to suspended state because it quits or fails to complete its task.

The second attribute is the *relationship between agents*. When agents evolve, the relationship between them is also evolving. If two agents succeed in collaboration to work on one task, or one agent gets useful information from another, their relationship becomes tighter and friendlier. The relationship of agents also affects the subsequent track of evolution. For example, before communicating with another agent, an agent may evaluate the relationship between them. If the relationship is good, it will be willing to communicate and collaborate with the other agent. The relationship of the agents also affects the relationship of their respective owners and communities. The relationship map is preserved in the community administration center and is updated frequently.

The third attribute is the fitness of an agent, which is an indicator of an agent's ability to survive and adapt to the environment. The higher the fitness of an agent, the stronger it is. The evaluation of fitness is performed in agent factories and agent chargers using the following criteria:

- *The Integrity of agents* may be attacked during the process of evolution, roaming, or communicating. It is caused by intentional damages from malicious agents or accidental errors during legal formalities.
- *History of agents* includes the number of tasks carried out and the quality of completed tasks. Every time an agent completes a task and reports to its owner, the owner will assess the quality and give a corresponding mark. Through analyzing the trend of agent performance by combining every task and its mark, the fitness of an agent can be evaluated.
- *Evolution record* can be an auxiliary tool in the evaluation of agent fitness. Every result of fitness evaluation is stored in the community administration center. It shows whether an agent's growth is healthy.

If an agent charger finds the fitness of an agent too low, it can reject recharging the agent and adopt some other measures. Furthermore, the agent charger checks the evolution record of the agent. If the fitness of an agent is decreasing rapidly, it can be suspected that the agent might have been attacked or something may have gone wrong in the working experience of the agent. The agent charger can then send it back to an agent factory for a thorough examination. The agent factory has the right to detain or terminate an agent. It will inform the community administration center as well as the owner about the measures taken.

Evolution in SAFER exists in three different levels: intra-owner, intra-community, and inter-community. The evolution in the lower level will contribute to that in the higher levels. Eventually, agents may become more and more powerful.

Agent evolution also benefits from ontology evolution, since all the SAFER agents originate from the ontology structures. The fitness of the ontology structure can be obtained by considering all agents fabricated using this structure. The agent factory builds a liaison between the ontology structure and all its products (agents). It gathers the agents' fitness statistics periodically and determines the fitness of the ontology structure. This, in turn, helps the evolution of the ontology structure.

The evolution of agents and ontology structures are also implemented by tree structure. For example, if the negotiation agent in Figure 4 needs a new strategy to enhance its negotiation skill, its owner or butler will send the requests to the agent factory. The agent factory will add the requested modules to the agent. Figure 5 and Table 3 demonstrate the structure of the agent after evolution and details of nodes in the structure. The new node F2A3 and its child nodes D4A3 and D5A3 are built into the new agent as a new negotiation strategy. The same evolution procedures can be applied to the evolution of ontology structure, because of the case of similar tree structures.

AGENT ROAMING

A set of agent transport protocols has been designed for SAFER in Yang (2000) to allow intelligent agents to roam from host to host. The transport protocols designed provide a secure mechanism for agents in e-commerce to roam across different hosts and communities in SAFER. General security concerns as well as specific security issues arising from agent roaming have been carefully addressed in the design. In order to allow greater flexibility, three different protocols are proposed, each one addressing different requirements.

Supervised agent transport protocol allows controls to agent owner/butler during an agent's roaming operation. The agent has to obtain an approval from its owner/butler before roaming to a new host. The owner/butler can thus control the agent's roaming destination and prevent the agent from moving to certain undesirable hosts. The drawback of this protocol is the lack of efficiency since each agent's movement involves the agent owner/ butler. This involvement will inevitably delay the transport process and incur additional network traffics. If the agent owner/butler happens to be using a low bandwidth connection to the Internet, the situation may worsen as agents roaming in high bandwidth networks suffer from the bottleneck in low bandwidth communication with the agent owner/butler.

On the other hand, unsupervised agent transport protocol does not involve the agent owner/butler directly in the transport process. Agents do not need to request permission before roaming. Instead, an indirect notification of the roaming operation is sent to the agent owner/butler for recording purpose. The agent owner/butler is unable to control the agent's roaming destination directly. The advantage is the increased efficiency of agent roaming

Figure 5. An Agent After Evolution

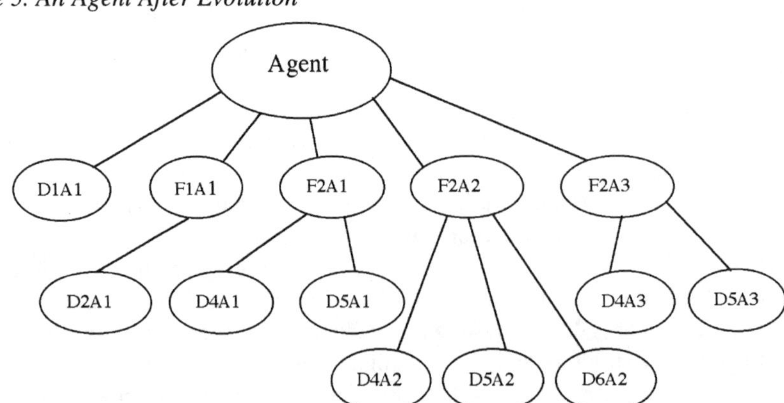

Table 3. Details of Nodes in Figure 5

NODE	CONTENT
Other Nodes	Same as in Table 2
F2A3	Negotiation Strategy 3
D4A3	Strategy Parameter 1
D5A3	Strategy Parameter 2

since fewer parties are directly involved in the transport process, thus leading to shorter turnaround time.

The above two protocols make use of fixed transport algorithms. To cater to the situation when agents require higher security during their roaming operations, SAFER provides a third agent transport protocol (bootstrap agent transport protocol) to allow the flexibility of using its own transport protocols. Under bootstrap agent transport protocol, an agent sends a transport agent to the destination using a conventional transport protocol. The transport agent takes over the role of agent receptionist and receives the parent agent in its own transport protocol. This way, an agent can design its own secure transport protocol and roam in SAFER using its proprietary transport protocol.

Based on different concerns on efficiency, roaming control, as well as level of security, individual SAFER agents can choose to use the most appropriate transport protocol or even a combination of different transport protocols in their roaming operations.

IMPLEMENTATION

We are implementing the SAFER architecture, which covers many facilities, such as butlers and agent factories, as well as routine procedures such as fabrication, evolution, and roaming. We started with the implementation of agent roaming, including the agent transport protocols (Yang, 2000). Three transport protocols have been implemented: supervised agent transport, unsupervised agent transport, and bootstrap agent transport. We have successfully realized the transportation of an agent from one host to another in the above three different ways. A simplified implementation diagram of the supervised agent transport protocol in SAFER is shown in Figure 6 (Yang, 2000). Currently, we are implementing the agent butler, agent community, and agent fabrication. We look forward to seeing a basic SAFER architecture set up in the near future.

The prototype of an agent butler is being implemented. Functions designed for the agent butler include coordination of agent payment, management of authorization, keeping track of agent whereabouts, detection of agent abduction, coordination of agent evolution as well as assistance in agent roaming. Each function is implemented as a separate module in the agent butler. The modules are e-payment coordinator, authorization manager, agent tracer, heartbeat monitor, evolution coordination, and transport assistant as shown in Figure 7. The agent butler keeps listening for incoming agent requests. Depending on these requests, the agent butler will pass the controls to the corresponding modules for further services.

As a start, two modules of the agent butler, agent tracer and heartbeat monitor, are being implemented. The agent tracer is in charge of keeping track of agents' whereabouts. All agents will report their whereabouts back to the agent butler before and after each roaming operation takes place. The agent butler can keep this information in its local database. Subsequently, if a query on an agent's whereabouts is made, the agent butler can look up its database with the agent's ID and retrieve the location of the agent. Heartbeat monitor is used to detect agent abduction. Critical agents, which are registered in agent butler as 'beeping agents,' are required to send their heartbeats back to the agent butler periodically. The

Figure 6: Supervised Agent Transport in SAFER

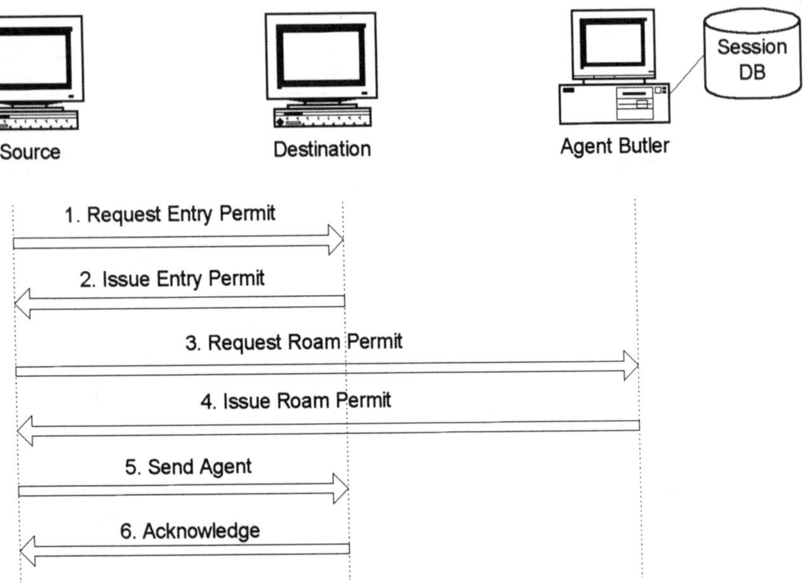

heartbeat monitor starts a timer for each beeping agent with the timeout set as the duration between expected heartbeats. Whenever an agent sends its heartbeats back, the timer is reset to its initial timeout value. If the timer reaches its timeout, an alarm is set off to alert the agent owner signaling a possibility of agent abduction.

Java is chosen as the implementation language, as it has a list of important features including robustness, security. and portability. The most important issue in an e-commerce architecture is the security of the system. Java provides a three-layer security model and many mechanisms to enhance security protection. We have also designed many facilities and protection mechanisms such as agent charger and agent immigration in the SAFER architecture. Because SAFER is designed for the Internet environment where different operating systems exist coherently, the interoperability feature of Java between the various platforms is also a motivation for us to choose it as a prototyping language.

CONCLUSION

In this chapter, we have proposed the SAFER architecture for agent-based e-commerce. SAFER provides the facilities to serve agents in e-commerce and establishes the necessary mechanisms to manage and control their activities. SAFER covers the whole lifetime of agent from its fabrication to its termination. We elaborate the functions of the components in SAFER, and the three aspects of SAFER: fabrication, evolution, and roaming. Tree structure is employed to present the agent and ontology structure in agent fabrication and evolution. We have also described the important features of agent and e-commerce, such as security and integrity.

SAFER e-commerce provides an opportunity in standardization for a dynamic, secure, and evolutionary agent architecture. With the SAFER architecture, conducting transactions on the Internet will be more convenient, secure, and efficient. We have finished the design and implementation of the secure agent transport protocol in SAFER (Guan, 1999; Yang,

Figure 7: Prototype of Agent Butler

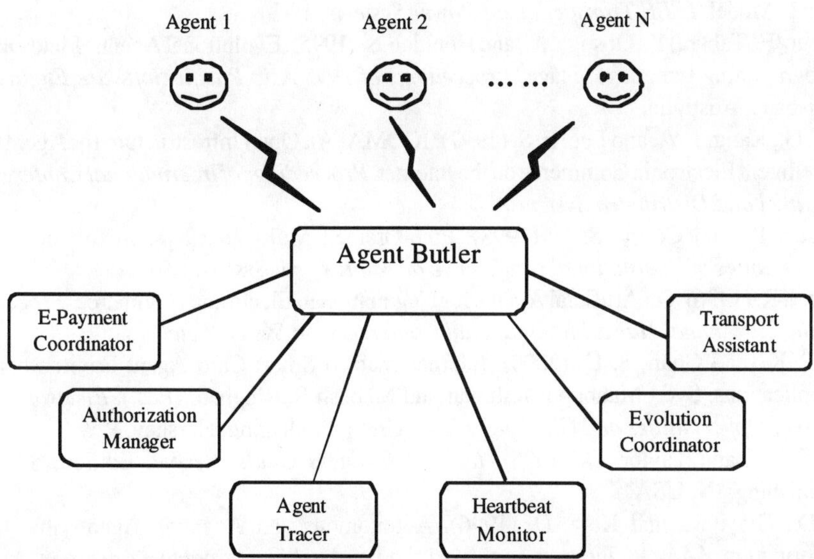

2000). We have planned the following steps to further improve the architecture and its functions. Firstly, we have started to implement the architecture using Java. We are trying to provide the basic modules and facilities first, as we regard SAFER as our infrastructure for further research on e-commerce. Secondly, as evolution is proposed in the SAFER architecture, its mechanism and theory presentation is being constructed. Thirdly, we are developing the payment mechanism in SAFER, as it is the essential part in e-commerce.

REFERENCES

Ahuja, V. (1996). *Secure Commerce on the Internet.* Academic Press, London, UK.

Ankenbrand, T., and Tomassini, M. (1997). Agent-Based Simulation of Multiple Financial Markets. In: *Proceedings 6th International Workshop on Parallel Applications in Statistics and Economics, PASE'97.*

Bradshaw, J. M. (1997). *Software Agent.* MIT Press.

Greenberg, M. S., Byington, J. C., and Harper, D. G. (1998). Mobile Agents and Security. *IEEE Communications Magazine*, 36(7).

Guan, S.U., and Yang, Y. (1999). *SAFE:* Secure-Roaming Agent For E-commerce. In: *Proceedings 26th International Conference on Computers & Industrial Engineering,* Australia.

Guilfoyle, C. (1994). *Intelligent Agents: The New Revolution in Software.* OVUM, London.

Guttman, R.H., and Maes, P. (1998). Agent-Mediated Negotiation for Retail Electronic Commerce. *Agent Mediated Electronic Commerce: First International Workshop on Agent Mediated Electronic Trading,* AMET-98 Minneapolis.

Johansen, D., Marzullo, K., and Lauvset, K. J. (1999). An Approach towards an Agent Computing Environment. *ICDCS'99 Workshop on Middleware.*

Kang, J.Y., and Lee, E.S. (1998). A Negotiation Model in Electronic Commerce to Reflect Multiple Transaction Factor and Learning. *Proceedings of Twelfth International Conference on Information Networking.*

Krishna, V., and Ramesh, V. C. (1998). Intelligent Agents for Negotiation in Market Games, Part1: Model. *IEEE Transaction on Power Systems*, 13(3).

Kumeno, F., Tahara, Y., Ohsuga, A., and Honiden, S. (1995). Evolutional Agents: Field Oriented Programming Language, Flage. *Proceedings of 1995 Asia Pacific Software Engineering*, Brisbane, Australia.

Lee, J. G., Kang, J. Y., and Lee, E. S. (1997). ICOMA: An Open Infrastructure for Agent-based Intelligent Electronic Commerce on the Internet. *Proceedings of International Conference on Parallel and Distributed Systems.*

Nangsue, P., and Conry, S. E. (1998). Fine-Grained Multiagent System for the Internet. *Proceedings of International Conference on Multi Agent Systems.*

Oliver, J. R. (1996). On Artificial Agents for Negotiation in Electronic Commerce. *Proceedings of the 29th Annual Hawaii International Conference on System Sciences.*

Poh, T. K., and Guan, S. U. (2000). Internet-enabled Smart Card Agent Environment and Applications. Syed Mahbubur Rahman and Mahesh Raisinghani (Eds.), *Electronic Commerce: Opportunities and Challenges*, Idea Group Publishing, Hershey, PA.

Resnick, R., and Taylor, D. (1995). *Internet Business Guide*. Second Edition, Sams Net Publishing, IN, USA.

Rus, D., Gray, R., and Kotz, D. (1996). Autonomous and Adaptive Agents that Gather Information. *AAAI'96 International Workshop on Intelligent Adaptive Agents.*

Tenenbaum, J. M., Chowdhry, T. S., and Hughes, K. (1997). Eco System: an Internet Commerce Architecture. *Computer*, 30(5).

Yang, Y., and Guan, S. U. (2000). Intelligent Mobile Agents for E-commerce: Security Issues and Agent Transport. Syed M. Rahman and Mahesh Raisinghani (Eds.), *Electronic Commerce: Opportunities and Challenges*, Idea Group Publishing, Hershey, PA.

Chapter XII

Web-Based Smart Card Agent Environment and Applications for E-Commerce

Teoh Kok Poh and Sheng-Uei Guan
National University of Singapore

Issues on usability, security, and mobility have always been the main concerns for e-commerce implementations that aim to gain widespread public acceptance. Smart Card Agent Environment is designed to address these issues by using a combination of software agent and smart card technology. In this chapter, a functional overview of the proposed environment is presented to illustrate how these two technologies can be integrated to offer e-commerce services with high usability, security, and mobility.

To further demonstrate the concept, a prototype implementation of the environment has been carried out. In this implementation, an on-card agent residing in the smart card is capable of storing critical data securely, providing digital ID and signature, and carrying out user authentication. On the other hand, off-card agent would provide various high-level agent services that can be used to carry out e-commerce activities.

Before the end of the chapter, practical considerations for issues on security, technology acceptance, infrastructure availability, and standardization will be discussed.

INTRODUCTION

The development of the Internet has created many new e-commerce activities and transformed many traditional services and information sources into online services. Much effort has been carried out to provide user-friendly access to these Internet-based services. However, interaction with online services still needs enhancement for it to be a pleasant experience. This is mainly due to the fact that users have not been properly represented for who they are and what they really want, and the lack of a seamless tool that makes them an informed user while allowing actual transactions to be carried out reliably.

Hence, before an e-commerce service is able to gain widespread public acceptance, the following issues need to be addressed gracefully:

Usability – Which includes user friendliness, information availability, and presentation.

Security – Which includes data security, privacy, and integrity.

Mobility – Which includes inherent support for user mobility.

The design of Smart Card Agent Environment represents an effort to close these gaps. Within the environment, software agents would provide system intelligence and information management to achieve high system usability. Software agents that know its user would carry out tasks on information sourcing and filtering to ensure a seamless transaction. On the other hand, portability and security features of smart card would facilitate personalized services and actual transactions to be carried out. Hence Smart Card Agent Environment would assist its users to perform information discovery, organization, and filtering, and serve as a convenience channel to execute tasks and carry out transactions.

The chapter begins with a conceptual overview of the Web-based Smart Card Agent Environment. This is followed by a literature review of smart card technology and software agent technology, where basic smart card architecture, technical background of both technologies, and related research work will be discussed. The next section covers the architecture of the proposed Smart Card Agent Environment and its typical application scenarios. Prototype implementation of two main components, the on-card agent and off-card agent, are presented and issues, controversies and recommendations for Smart Card Agent Environment will be discussed, including, many practical considerations. A subsequent section presents the discussion on future trends and recommendation for further works, and finally the chapter concludes.

BACKGROUND

Web-Based Smart Card Agent Environment

The Internet has realized a connected world with a great degree of openness. The degree of openness for the Internet and its inherent support for user mobility suggests that a reliable user identification process, secured storage media for critical data, and data portability are crucial for any successful Internet-based implementation (Poh & Guan, 2000). On the other hand, information explosion and overload on the Internet suggests that some effective information handling and management tools are required to prevent its users from getting lost in the sea of information and options.

Smart card's built-in cryptography capabilities and high resistance toward tampering have made it an excellent media for reliable user identification and secure data storage. It is indeed an ideal candidate as a 'personal representative' for Internet users. Many applications can be and have been derived from these key features. In the context of e-commerce, smart card represents an ideal media for self-identification, online payment, and secure data storage for sensitive data. Since sensitive data are stored inside smart cards and not within the Internet-connected computers, it is relatively distant from security attacks initiated from a network or the Internet.

On the other hand, software agent represents an excellent candidate to satisfy the need for information handling and management. The built-in intelligence and ability to learn about its user have enabled a new level of personalized services with great reduction of information overload.

The proposed smart card agent environment is an effort to bridge these two technologies to produce a viable solution for personalized, Web-based services and solutions. Introduction of software agent technology into traditional smart card applications will bring in new intelligence to make it smarter. While the high level of security and portability in smart card technology will greatly enhance the usability of software agents in the Internet world (Poh & Guan, 2000). With the combination of these two technologies, many Web-based applications can provide personalized services with minimum user interactions. These user-oriented features will promote the utilization of Web-based and e-commerce services.

Figure 1: System Overview of Smart Card Agent Environment

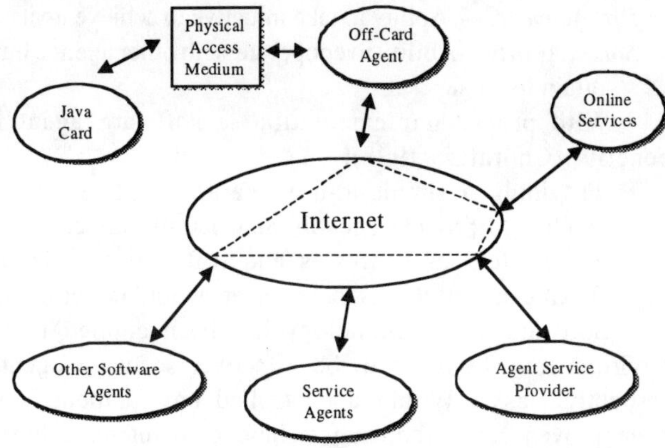

Figure 1 represents a system overview of the proposed Smart Card Agent Environment. It is an Internet-based agent environment with critical data stored and processed in the smart card. Smart Card Agent Environment aims to provide an infrastructure that delivers agent functionalities and services, as well as mechanisms to facilitate cooperative activities among various software agents. Hence, the environment is not competing with other Internet-based agents; it is rather an enhancement to the existing features.

Basically, Smart Card Agent Environment consists of seven major building blocks, with agent service provider serving as the center of the environment. Within the environment, agent service provider serves as a coordinator that coordinates various activities initiated from other system components. On the other hand, service agents also play a very important role to serve as virtual agents that provide various agent services such as travel, healthcare, personal services, and real estate, among many others. Hence, Smart Card Agent Environment would allow its users to receive personalized online services ranging from information services, queries, reservations, and even actual financial transactions within the same session.

An Overview of Software Agent

Agent technology has been around for more than a decade. Software agent is an active software artifact that would simplify the process of tasks execution through computer software. It might exhibit capabilities to learn its user's habits and preferences. In a multi-agent environment, the learned profiles and work patterns can be exchanged among various agents to facilitate personalized services. A software agent would have some or all of the following properties (Nwana & Ndumu, 1999):

Autonomy—Ability to operate without direct human intervention, based on predefined rules and guidelines.

Reactivity—Ability to perceive the environment and respond to any changes.

Learning—Ability to accumulate experience and learn the habits and preferences of its master.

Pro-Activeness—Ability to take initiative to achieve goals set by the user.

Social Ability—Ability to cooperate with other agents, humans, or some other systems to attain its goal.

With proper implementation, a software agent has the following potential benefits (Chorafas, 1998):

- Providing a simple-to-use interaction style.
- Ability to provide friendly and helpful advices.
- Hiding tedious processes and software complexity from its user.
- Taking care of things that its users would rather not have to do themselves.

Software agent technology has been applied to various applications in many environments. In order to be effective, software agents tend to specialize in their respective tasks. Within a controlled environment, software agent technology has been proven as a promising technique to integrate human intelligence into software systems. However, many technical and social issues need to be resolved before an effective real-time implementation can be carried out. In the technical aspect, there are issues like scalability, stability, and system performance. On the social sides, there are problems like privacy, responsibility, legal issues, and ethical issues to be addressed.

Agent in the World of Internet

Internet-based agents have been getting much attention from researchers in the agent community, as there are real demands for tools to help Internet users manage information that grows exponentially. Normally, such agents would assist its user to simplify the process of managing, manipulating, or collating information from many distributed sources.

As the Internet is a heterogeneous environment, multi-agent systems or environments are required to meet diversified requirements for various tasks. In a practical sense, problems and challenges in information discovery, ontology and communication, legacy software, reasoning and coordination, and event monitoring need to be addressed for real-world implementation (Nwana & Ndume, 1999).

An Overview of Smart Card Technology

Smart card is a microchip embedded plastic card with security functions for access control. It was initially designed as an alternative for the magnetic card, which is inherently insecure as its data can be read and modified through proper equipment. Also, due to high telecommunication infrastructure cost in Europe, smart card was targeted as a solution for offline transactions that required high security. Physically, smart card chips were designed to be a tamper-resistant media, while its built-in cryptography features ensured a secure processing can be carried out.

As compared to magnetic card, smart card has a higher storage capacity, higher security for data storage, and data transmission thanks to its cryptography features. Also, it has better reliability, as the embedded chip has a higher physical tolerance compared to magnetic stripe. Generally, smart card offers more flexiblility and features rich solution with enhanced security.

Smart Card Applications

Although smart card was initially designed for payment-related applications, it has been adopted by many other applications due to its tamper-resistant storage, data portability, and single data source features. Following are some of the major applications for smart card:

Figure 2. Typical Smart Card Architecture and System View

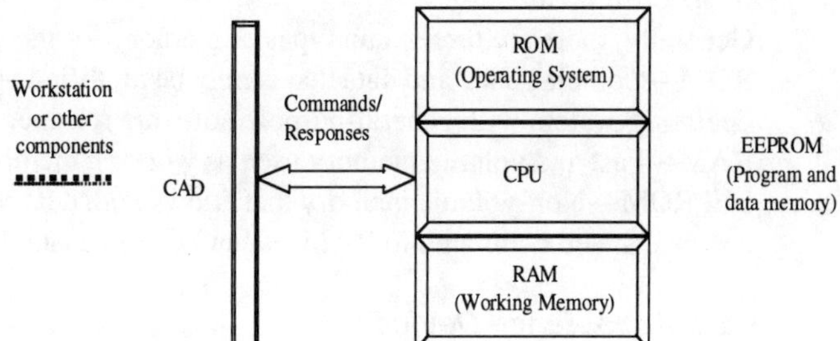

- Fraud-resistant payment media for credit, debit, and prepaid transactions.
- Access key for physical access and access to computer resources.
- Storage media for Public Key Infrastructure (PKI).
- Media for user identification and authentication.
- Considerably large secure storage for services that are physically distributed.
- Storage media for customized configuration and personalized product data.

Benefits and Characteristics of Smart Card

Many smart card implementations have been carried out based on various justifications. Following are some of the benefits that justify a smart card implementation:

- Reduced risk of fraud and theft for financial-related applications.
- Secure access control and user authentication.
- Lower processing cost resulting from minimal online data transmission, and reduced administrative cost of a huge database.
- Ability to serve as marketing and branding tools.
- Providing single source data and data mobility.
- Higher transaction throughput, as access to a huge database is not required for transaction purpose.

With increasingly higher computing power and larger storage, smart card would soon be able to handle multimedia such as voice and graphic. These features will make it an ideal candidate as human 'representative' to the digital world.

Smart Card Architecture

Basically, smart card consists of a communication interface, memory, and a CPU for data processing and calculation. In order to be useful, a smart card needs to interact with a card acceptance device (CAD) or reader through a communication interface. The card acceptance device serves as a conduit for information into and out of the card (Sun Microsystems, 1998). Figure 2 shows a typical smart card architecture and system view.

a) *Communication Interface*

A smart card is a 'passive' microprocessor that has no power supply and other peripherals such as a keyboard attached. The only external interface it has is the eight electrical contact points. In order to be useful, a card acceptance device is required to provide the power supply, control signals, and serial communication link.

b) *Smart Card Microprocessor*

Smart card microprocessor has limited computation power and memory resources due to the cost and physical constraints. Generally, there are 8-, 16-, or 32-bit microprocessors operating at a speed of 4–20 MHz, with user memory ranging from 1K to 64

Kbytes, and RAM of 1K bytes or less.

c) Smart Card Memory

Generally, there are three main types of memory for its respective purposes:

- ROM—Contains code and data that cannot be modified once burnt in. Mainly for the operating system with general-purpose software routine.
- RAM—Fast and volatile memory used as working memory and temporary storage.
- EEPROM—Non-volatile memory that allows both data read and data write action at a slower speed compared to RAM. It can be used as application and data memory.

Card Acceptance Device

A card acceptance device is required to activate a smart card to perform useful tasks. It can stand alone or link up with other computers through various ways such as serial communication port, PCMCIA slot, floppy disk drive, and ISA bus. For higher security, a SAM (Security Access Module) containing secret keys can be use to carry out authentication and secure messaging with the card. The communication protocol between CAD and the card are specified in the ISO Standard 7816-3. There are three different communication methods in the standard: T = 0, T = 1, and T = 14, with T = 14 reserved for proprietary protocol.

On a higher level, a smart card driver is required to communicate with the software applications. Until recently, most smart card drivers are proprietary drivers that limit hardware portability among various applications. Microsoft PC/SC represents a successful standard implementation that allows applications to remain operational for all CADs that comply with the standard.

Smart Card Security Features

Data security for smart card largely depends on its ability to withstand various security attacks. Following are some of the security measures to ensure smart card's data integrity and security:

- Smart card can be manufactured with a unique serial number for each card. This allows a system to test for fraud by checking the usage pattern of certain card numbers.
- Ability to execute algorithms with keys securely stored in the memory, which is not accessible externally. Also, smart card is capable of having a different digital signature for each transaction session. This allows active authentication where a session key cannot be replayed.
- Single chip design that combines microprocessor with memory. For most designs, the chip will either erase or lock its memory once exposed, to prevent physical attacks.
- Built-in circuitry for low frequency, under voltage and over voltage detection, to guard against attacks based on chip's electronic weaknesses.
- For most designs, data from a host or terminal are sent to the card; this data together with the secret keys in the chip are applied to the algorithm, and results are sent back to the terminal or host. No secret keys ever leave the chip.
- With a unique identifier, unique secret key, and appropriate key diversification, cracking a card will just give access to the card, not the entire system.

Java Card

In the design of our Smart Card Agent Environment, Java Card is used as the operating platform for the smart card. As an open standard platform, Java Card promotes platform independence of chips architecture and object-oriented programming in smart card (Sun Microsystems, 1998). Also, Java Card is inherently designed for multi-applications and dynamic updates of applets and data. This has greatly enhanced the system flexibility while the development and maintenance efforts are reduced.

Java Card security comes from both software and hardware as described in the following (Schlumberger, 1998):

- Smart card hardware provides a tamper-resistant media.
- Java Card has a much tighter security control than traditional Java platform.
- It has cryptographic capabilities to perform data encryption, digital signature, and authentication.

There are several versions of Java Card available in the market for application developers. Following are typical hardware configurations for a Java Card:

- 16/32 bits RISC microprocessor.
- 24–32 Kbytes of ROM.
- 16/32 Kbytes of EEPROM.
- 1 Kbyte or less of RAM.

This typical platform is sufficient to install various applets for smart card agent applications with its critical data stored within.

Related Research Work

Smart card technology started as an innovative application of chips rather than pure academic research. Early work of smart card-related research focused on making the technology a viable solution to many industry applications. In the later stage, researchers have been focusing on smart card authentication schemes (Wang et al., 1996), making the system secure and robust (Anderson, 1997), and multi-applications possible for smart card (Ferrer, 1997).

On the development of software agent as an assistant, Pettie Maes (1994) has demonstrated a personal agent that monitors a user's action and suggests a better way of doing a task. In the same year, Etzioni and Weld (1994) introduced Softbot, an agent for the Internet environment that interacts with the software environment by issuing commands and interpreting the environment's feedback. Also, Huhns and Singh (1998) illustrated a modern version of personal assistant in their article on Personal Assistant. However, the usefulness

Figure 3. The Architecture of Smart Card Agent Environment

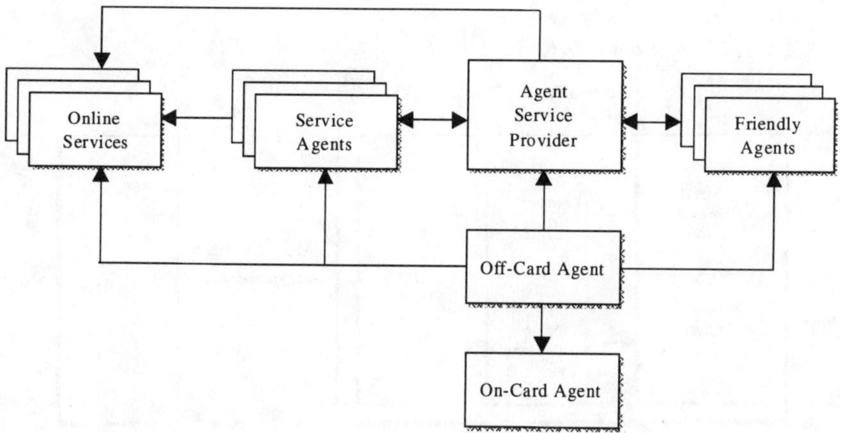

of such an assistant has been questioned, as extensive learning of user and environment without a deep cognitive model of the user and the task might produce nothing but annoyance (Nwana & Ndumu, 1999).

The concept of software agent has been extended into some mobile gadgets such as the wearable remembrance agent (Rhodes, 1997) that runs proactive memory aids using physical context of a wearable computer. In order to solve ontology problem, Open Profiling Standard (OPS) has been proposed as an attempt to standardize the profile information required by Web agents (Hensley et al., 1997). To further extend the concept, Lange (1998) has proposed a mobile agent that can travel across the networks to execute tasks.

Currently, there are many software-based applications targeted at certain aspects of the functionalities offered by the Smart Card Agent Environment. However, we believe it is hard for a pure software-based solution to achieve the service and security level required for truly user-oriented service. The proposed Smart Card Agent Environment, if fully implemented, would provide basic infrastructure for other software applications to provide user-oriented services.

ARCHITECTURE OF SMART CARD AGENT ENVIRONMENT

System Overview of Smart Card Agent Environment

Smart Card Agent Environment is designed as a platform to perform agent-related activities. Its key objectives are to provide agent functionalities and to act as personal assistants for several important online activities, rather than to deploy agent technology in a strict sense. In this design, the environment has been logically divided into six key components to meet practical consideration of data security, user mobility, and usability. In addition to standard services, Smart Card Agent Environment offers unique features of single source data, secured storage space, and data location transparency for other software agents to integrate with. Figure 3 represents the system architecture of Smart Card Agent Environment.

Smart Card Agent Environment is expected to provide personalized agent services for its users through its front-end interface, the off-card agent. Following are the objectives of the environment:

Figure 4. Overview of Java Card

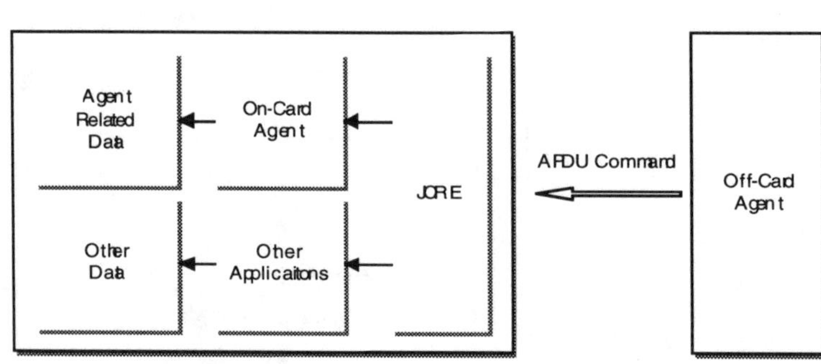

- To provide personalized agent service for various service sectors. More services can be tied into the environment when the system grows.
- Agents specialized in various sectors to assist its users to carry out online activities, such as information search, online banking, and online shopping.
- To provide its users a consistent and single entry point for online agent services.

Following are the major functional components of the environment:

a) Java Card

Java Card is a microprocessor-based smart card capable of multi-applications. The key application within Java Card is the on-card agent, an applet that manages the entire agent-related data and software routines within the card. Besides, other applications such as electronic cash, loyalty program, and membership program can be installed into the smart card, which will enable actual transactions to be carried out. Java Card's built-in cryptography capabilities allow secure authentication, data encryption, and digital signature to be carried out with its data.

The application applets and related data files are governed under Java Card Runtime Environment (JCRE), which also serves as the external interface for Java Card. Within the on-card agent, there are several basic routines for data and access management, and several agent-related data files such as system parameters file, personal profile, and custom agent data files. All data files can be protected by access schemes using secret codes or encryption keys.

External requests from the off-card agent are sent to Java Card Runtime Environment (JCRE) through APDU commands. The requests will then be forwarded to the on-card agent or relevant smart card applications, after which the selected applet will then process the request and generate responses accordingly. Additional data files and applets can be installed after the card has been deployed to the field. This allows the card to expand its features in the future.

b) Off-Card Agent

Off-card agent is the only gateway for on-card agent to connect to other components in the environment. It consists of four major components, i.e., user service,

Figure 5. Overview of Off-Card Agent

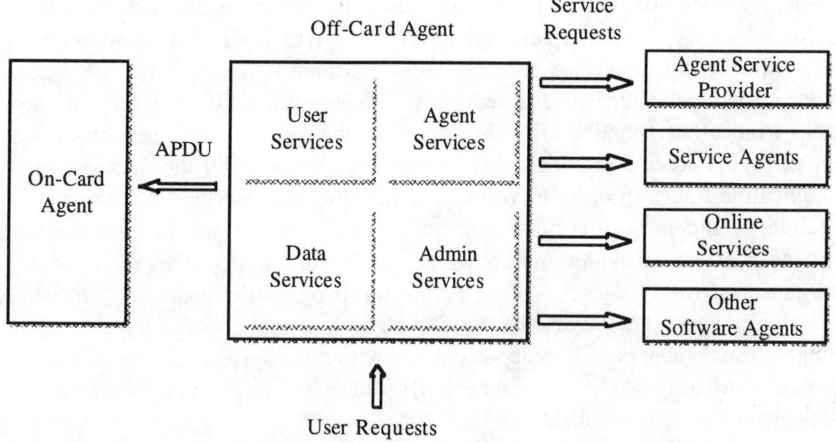

Figure 6. Basic Relationship of Agent Service Provider with Other System Components

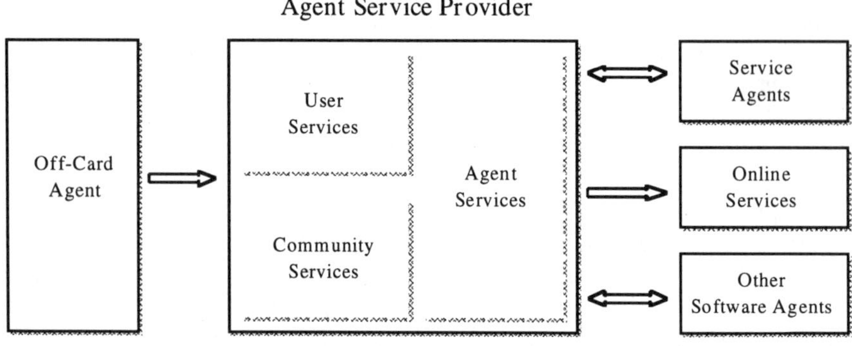

agent service, data service, and admin service. Functionally, off-card agent will get instruction from the user for an agent service or carry out any autonomous tasks determined from a set of user-predefined rules. Depending on the nature of the task, an agent service provider, service agent, other software agent, or the online services will be contacted to complete the task.

In principle, off-card agent should contact agent service provider for any general agent services. A copy of user profile will be kept in the agent service provider for those agents that are authorized to use it. For a more frequently used agent service, off-card agent can be configured to access the service agent directly instead of going through the agent service provider. Similarly, other software agents can be accessed if they are known to off-card agents. Normally, online services will only be accessed directly for user authentication and login purposes.

Throughout these communication sessions, if data from on-card agent are required, an APDU command will be issued from off-card agent to get the data. Also, the commands and terms for service request in off-card agent are based on standard terminology used within the environment, which might be different from those used in various online services. In order to solve this problem, the service agent will provide mapping for differences in data context between off-card agent and online services.

c) Agent Service Provider

Agent service provider is the coordinator of the environment. It is the main entry point for off-card agent to access agent services. When off-card agent requests for an agent service, agent service provider will determine if it can fulfill the request, or a service agent specialized in that service sector is required. If necessary, it can even get help from other friendly software agents. If the agent service request is handled within the agent service provider, then it will need to solve all the data mapping and communication issues in order to work with various online services. If a service agent is required, it will locate the most appropriate service agent and forward the request.

Agent service provider maintains the following update: database of service agents profile, friendly agents profile, online services profile, and users profile. Also, it maintains an up-to-date library for learning algorithms that allows a more standardized learning. These databases and library are shared with other system components within the environment. Also, agent service provider will be the reference point to resolve any conflict of data between system components.

Figure 7. Overview of Service Agent

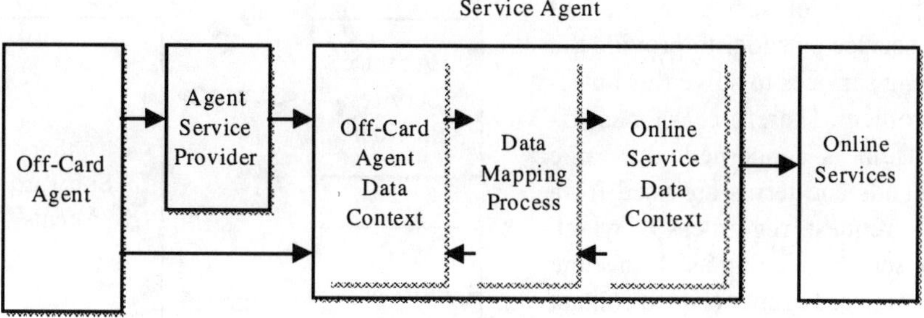

Other services provided by agent service provider are user service and community service. In user service, various member service and updates are available. Community service facilitates the association of community members by providing various communication channels and tools.

d) Service Agents

Service agent's primary function is to determine what the user wants from a service request, and locate one or more online services that can fulfill the service. In order to accomplish a service request, service agent needs to carry out data context mapping and information filtering processes.

Since most online services operate in their own data context, service agent needs to convert data from off-card agent to online service's native data context for outgoing requests. Similarly, service agent needs to reverse the data mapping process when a response is received from online service.

The process of information filtering aims to reduce users' information overload. Information to be presented to the users will be filtered based on user profile and preferences. This process can be automatically done with the help of some predefined rules or with user intervention.

e) Online Services

In the context of Smart Card Agent Environment, online services consist of various independent or associated services available online. It can be an Internet-based service or a proprietary system that is only available through dial-up or some other means. For services that are not available on the Internet, service agent or agent service provider will need to develop a way to establish a communication channel with these services. As far as the users are concerned, they are getting their services through the agents within the environment.

Figure 8. Overview of Online Services

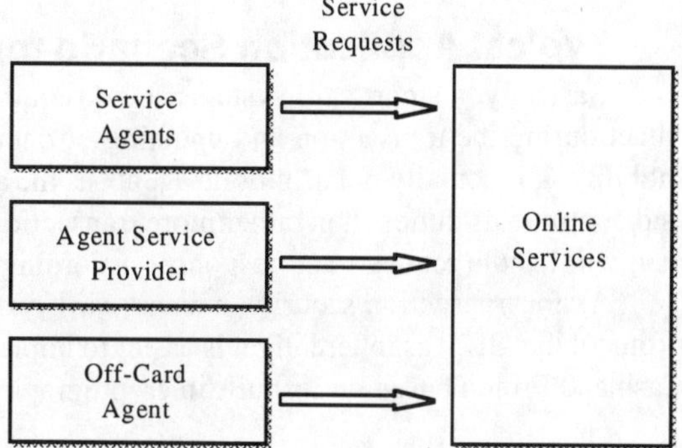

Generally, there are a number of similar online services within the same service sector, with each of them using different data context for their services and transactions. It is the responsibility of service agent and agent service provider to provide the mapping services to solve this ontology problem. Therefore, as far as off-card agent is concerned, the same commands and terms are used for a service request, regardless of which online service is being used. In some cases, off-card agent needs to contact an online service directly instead of going through service agent or agent service provider. In such a situation, off-card agent can provide basic user login and authentication service, and the user can then navigate the service site manually.

Figure 9. Overview of Other Software Agents

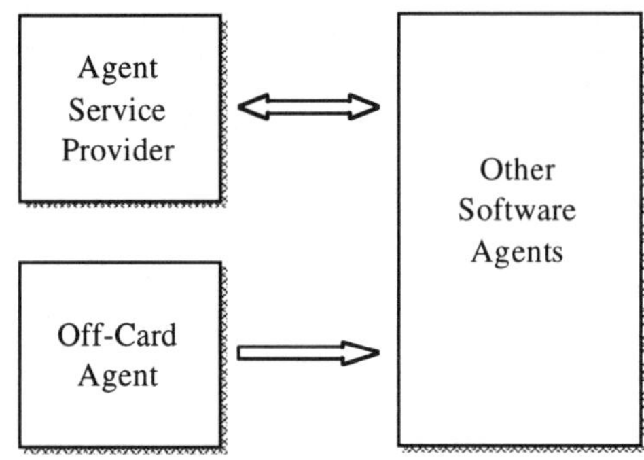

For practical considerations, online services can choose to integrate a simplified version of off-card agent within their services using 'plug-in' technology.

f) Other Software Agents

Smart Card Agent Environment allows other software agents to be integrated into the environment with minimum efforts. Generally, such agents maintain their own ways of operations and are independent from the environment. In order to participate in the environment, they only need to register themselves with agent service provider and install a software interface wrapper. This will allow them to communicate with agent service provider and allow other system components to call upon their services. Once registered, the agent becomes a friendly agent. Friendly agents can have the privilege to use resources in agent service provider, store customized agent data into Java Card, and allow the users of Smart Card Agent Environment to use their services.

g) Access Medium

A card acceptance device is required to physically bridge off-card agent and Java Card. Card acceptance device has been designed to work with various interfaces, including serial port, parallel port, PCMCIA, ISA bus, floppy drive, etc. In order to function as an access medium for Smart Card Agent Environment, the card acceptance device needs to be attached to a computer with installed off-card agent and active Internet connection. A hardware driver will serve as the interface between the card acceptance device and off-card agent.

Typical Application Scenario for E-Commerce Activities

Basically, a smart card system would require a smart card and its reader to be kept intact during the transaction and updating of data. While one of the key features is data mobility, it is actually not a "mobile agent" as the applet is not able to move out of the card and continue its duties. It is rather more transactional and cooperative client-server based, as it will handle requests and responses accordingly (Poh & Guan, 2000).

As for transaction security, a smart card system seldom uses purely software-based protocol like SET, as inherently it is easier to implement a secure electronic purse like Visa Cash and Proton based on its built-in cryptography capabilities. However, smart card can

Figure 10. Typical Application Scenario of Smart Card Agent Environment

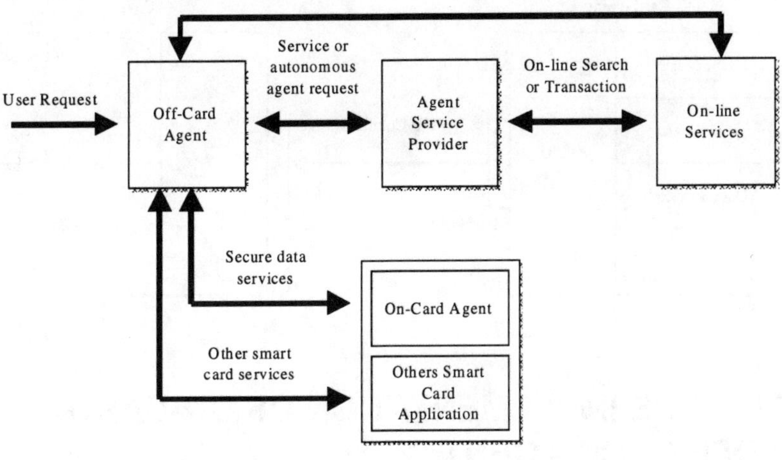

be used as a hardware token within the SET system to improve its security. Crypto-controller-based smart cards are available for financial applications and applications that require high security. These cards have built-in hardware to perform DES and RSA encryption efficiently.

Figure 10 represents a typical application scenario for Web-based e-commerce activities within Smart Card Agent Environment. Following are some of the key events:

- A user request or an autonomous request from off-card agent will be forwarded to agent service provider together with its associated personal data and customized data.
- The selected agent service will query related online services and perform necessary transactions to fulfill the request. Most data needed for transactions can be obtained from on-card agent, which needs to be unlocked once by entering a user PIN. If confirmation or user selection is required, the information will be forwarded back to off-card agent for further actions.
- If secure data like membership ID or credit card number is required for a transaction, service provider can choose to validate a user through smart card authentication or obtain a digitally signed ID for verification purposes.
- Other smart card applications like electronic cash and loyalty program can be accessed during transactions for payment or loyalty point updating purposes.
- Off-card agent will monitor the ongoing activities and capture necessary data to update the personal profile, user habits, and other on-card agent files. It is rather difficult to catch up with the personal profile and preferences in real time. However, if the applications of this environment are Internet based, we still can come out with a rather useful profile due to the fact that most activities are online and they can help keep the profile current.
- A mobile user can have on-card agent installed in their SIM cards or other embedded devices. It is not feasible to implement the complete version of off-card agent in GSM mobile handsets. However, we still can have most agent services by connecting a mobile device to agent service provider through Wireless Application Protocol or WAP-based gateway.

Figure 11. Functional Overview of Prototype Implementation

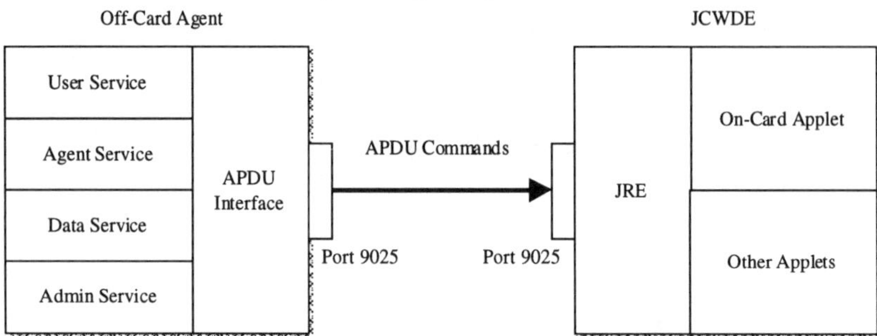

PROTOTYPE IMPLEMENTATION OF ON-CARD AND OFF-CARD AGENT

Objectives of Prototype Implementation

In order to demonstrate the basic concepts of Smart Card Agent Environment, prototype implementation for two of the key components, on-card agent and off-card agent, has been carried out. In the implementation of off-card agent, communication interface with on-card agent, as well as various agent services-related interfaces would be developed. This will illustrate how on-card agent's data can be used for various agent services. In the implementation of on-card agent, Java Card's capabilities to securely store critical data, as well as the ability to serve as a self-identification unit, will be demonstrated.

Overview of Implementation Platform

In this implementation, JCWDE (Java Card Workstation Development Environment) that consists of JRE (Java Runtime Environment) and Java Card API is used to simulate Java Card's JCRE (Java Card Runtime Environment). The on-card agent applet will be loaded into the virtual machine running under JCWDE for program execution. Port 9025 of the virtual machine will be opened and actively listens for incoming APDU commands.

On the other hand, off-card agent is a stand-alone Java application with port 9025 open as communication interface to on-card agent. Communication between the two systems is carried out through APDU data exchange using socket connection. Figure 11 represents the functional overview of the prototype implementation.

Prototype Implementation for Off-Card Agent

The implementation of off-card agent provides an example of how agent-related applications could be developed for Smart Card Agent Environment. In this implementation, only outline of the off-card agent functionalities and its ability to utilize on-card agent's data for agent-related activities would be considered. Actual software algorithms for agent services and intelligence features are not within the scope of this implementation. Off-card agent is interfaced with on-card agent and other Java Card applications through a communication interface implemented as a class. For JCWDE-simulated environment, on-card agent's data is initialized through an initialization routine.

Off-card agent consists of the following service modules:

Figure 12. User Service—Welcome

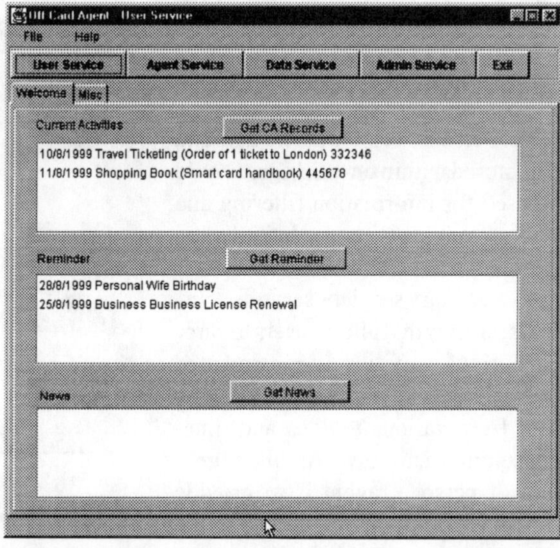

a) User Service

User service provides services for general tasks, agent service status update, and access point to agent service provider and other online services. Summary of on-going and outstanding agent-related activities are recorded as current activities. It consists of date of transaction, type of agent and type of service, service description, and transaction number. A user can select a particular activity for further information or actions. Whenever a user logs into off-card agent, data records for current activities stored in the smart card will be downloaded. Off-card agent will then contact agent service provider for status update of those records.

Also, reminders and news generated based on critical data and user preferences stored within on-card agent will be displayed for further actions.

Other services in user service are online membership and e-data. Online membership allows users to access agent service provider, agent-related services, and other online services. Off-card agent will automatically log in to these services with respective digital ID, digital certificate, and other necessary data stored in on-card agent. In e-data, the user can securely store and retrieve a certain amount of custom-defined data securely.

b) Agent Service

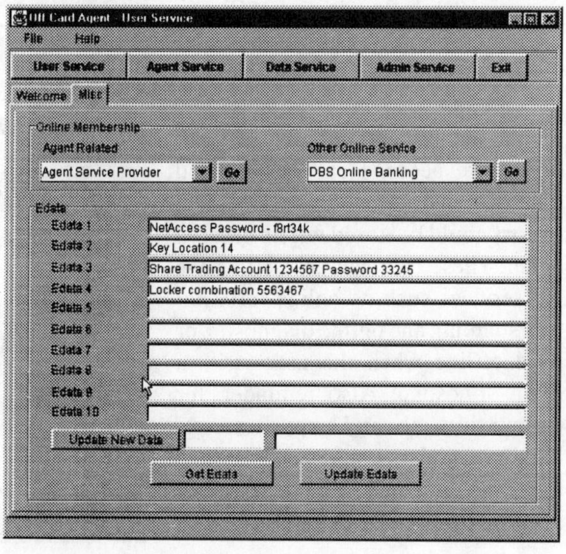

Agent service allows users access to various agent services through service requests. Service requests together with related data will be forwarded to agent service provider or respective service agent for further processing. Each successful request will be registered as a current activities record. Upon completion of a transaction, this record will be updated to on-card agent. In this implementation, agent services are categorized as personal agent, travel agent, healthcare agent, shopping agent, and other agents.

Figure 13. User Service—Misc.

Personal agent represents a personal assistant for daily activities such as events organization, secretary services, information services, and other miscellaneous tasks. In personal update, the user can request for various information update and services. Personal-related particulars and data stored within on-card agent could be used for information filtering and priority ranking to reduce information overload.

Secretary services serve as a virtual secretary that allows users to carry out various activities. If implemented properly, such a service can shield a user from various tedious and time-consuming activities. Another function of personal agent is to provide timely information and update to the users based on pre-defined settings. Figure 14 represents an example of personal agent.

Travel agent represents a travel assistant for business and leisure. It assists the user to make informed decision for various online travel services. With personal data, payment vehicles and other secure data stored within Java Card, travel agent will be able to assist the users to perform information sourcing, service selection, payment and keep track of travel activities while on the move. Figure 15 represents an example of travel agent.

Healthcare agent represents a virtual assistant to take care of your healthcare needs. Healthcare-related data, personal particulars, and medical history could be stored within on-card agent. These data can be used online for services such as online information sourcing and online diagnostic, or used offline when the user visits a clinic or hospital. Also, reminders for certain situations and a healthcare-related news alert could be generated based on these data. Figure 16 represents an example of healthcare agent.

Figure 14. Agent Service—Personal Agent

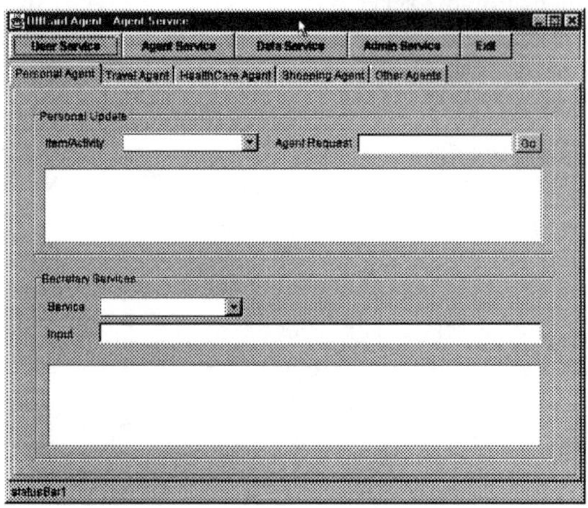

Figure 15. Agent Service—Travel Agent

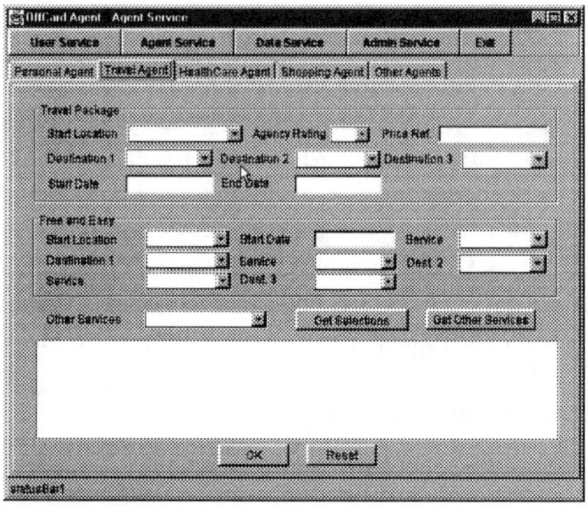

Figure 16. Agent Service—Healthcare Agent

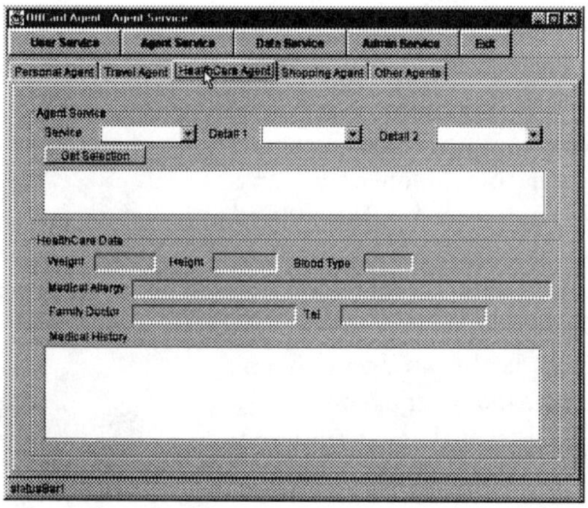

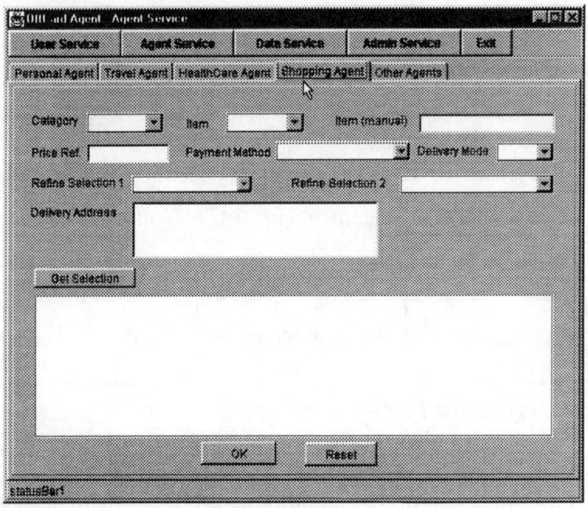

Shopping agent represents an example of software agent for e-commerce application. Shopping agent will return a list of short-listed goods based on the item category, item type, reference price, and other specification. The short-listing process will make use of the personal profile and other data stored within on-card agent. When a selection is made, off-card agent offers payment options of various electronic purse and encrypted credit card information residing in the smart card. Confirmed transactions would be logged for future reference or tracking. Figure 5.7 represents an example of shopping agent.

Figure 17. Agent Service—Shopping Agent

c) Data Service

Data service is a tool to view, evaluate, and organize on-card agent data. It consists of three sub-sections of data service: data maintenance, evaluate data, and data rules. In data maintenance, records of on-card agent can be viewed or edited, and new record can be added to files. As some of the agent-related data such as personal profiles are updated automatically through some intelligent algorithm, it is necessary to evaluate its effectiveness from time to time and fine-tune its performance. Data evaluations are carried out through test applications.

d) Admin Service

In admin service, users will be able to perform activities such as system configuration, on-card data configuration, data backup, agent registration, and system administration. System configuration allows users to configure the URL of agent service provider, default user profile, online services configuration file, and setting for reminders and news. Data management activities such as change of user PIN and user particulars can also be carried out. Other activities include custom agent registration, friendly agent registration, and general system administration.

Prototype Implementation for On-Card Agent

On-card agent is a sub-system within Smart Card Agent Environment that is responsible for the management of critical user data. This sub-system communicates with off-card agent in another computer through data exchange in APDU format. On-card agent consists of several basic routines for data and application management, and several files for various records.

Basic Routines

Several basic routines of on-card agent will facilitate the necessary operations for commands handling, file selections, and updating of records.

On-card:	The java applet constructor performs variables initialization and resource reservation, applet installation, and registration.
Install:	Called from the constructor. To install the on-card applet into the Java Runtime Environment when the applet is run for the first time.
Select:	To return On-card ID when the applet is selected.
Process:	Will process the APDU command and direct it to respective routines.
Deselect:	Handling necessary cleanup and resetting PINs.

Figure 18. Data Structure with CAD Number, Random Number, and Digital Signature

4 bytes	4 bytes	1 byte	1 byte	n bytes	8 bytes
CAD Number	**Random Number**	**Tag**	**Length**	**Data**	**Digital Signature**

Record Files

Record files consist of several files that store applications data and user data in linear fixed file format. In this implementation, a user PIN is required to update any record within a file. In actual implementation, various levels of access schemes can be used to improve security and privacy.

Parameters File	Contains on-card system parameters, including PINs, on-card ID, associated applet ID, issuer ID, and expiry date.
Personal Data	Contains personal particulars.
Personal Profile	A collection of indices that represent the user's habits and preferences.
ID Record File	Contains custom certificates for on-line authentication purpose.
Registered Agent File	A table to store all the registered applets used by the user.
Custom Agent Data File	Any registered agent can store their custom configurations or data as a record within this file.
Current Activities File	Contains all active activities carried out by agents or the user. This file gives a general overview of on-going events.
E-Data File	This is a user data file for the user to store his personal data or any data he wants to keep.
Transaction Log	A log file to record all the transactions of On-Card Agent.

Figure 19. Installation Process for On-Card Agent

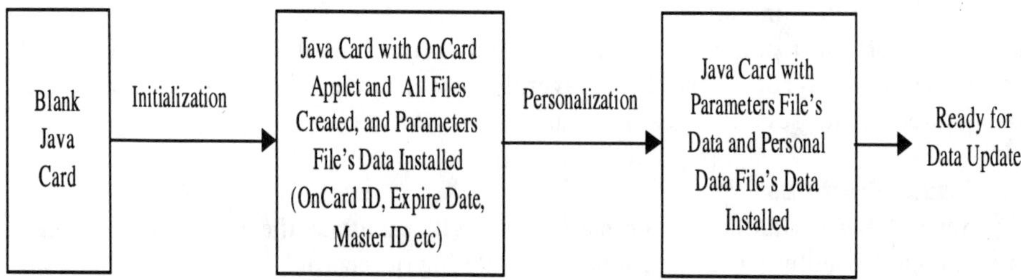

APDU Command Sequence and Data Structure

There are two types of command sequence used for data access in on-card agent:

- Commands that need to be initialize with an initialization command.
- Commands that can be issued directly without initialization process.

In both cases, relevant access rights need to be obtained before data access is allowed.

In terms of data structure, two types of data are being used:

- Data with CAD number, random number for challenge and response, and digital signature as illustrated in Figure 18.
- Data that consists of tag, length, and data only.

For applications that require high security, secure messaging can be used to ensure data security during the communication session. In secure messaging, a three DES session key will be generated to facilitate data encryption for data exchange between smart card and the card reader during that particular session.

Typical Service Usage Session

Figure 5.9 represents a typical installation process for on-card agent. The card issuer carries out the initialization and personalization processes. This is to ensure the uniqueness of the card and allow the card to serve as a self-identification unit. Whenever necessary, data in the parameter or personal data can be digitally signed by a trusted authority to increase its trust level. When Java Card is ready for data update, activities such as agent registration and records update can be carried out interactively. Off-card agent can be downloaded from agent service provider and installed to the platform of choice.

Following are key events for a typical usage of services in off-card agent:

- A user login to off-card agent through Java Card with on-card agent installed. The user needs to enter a valid PIN to unlock the card and gain access to the off-card agent.
- After that, the user is allowed to access various services from User Services, including catch-up with current activities, reminders, and news. Also, the user is allowed to access agent service provider and online services, and check out its user-defined data.
- When necessary, an agent service can be activated to handle user's service request. All user-related data required for decision making can be obtained from the on-card agent.
- If user authentication is required, on-card agent will provide various levels of user authentication to the appropriate online services.
- If payment is required for a transaction, off-card agent can activate one of the payment vehicles in Java Card or get the encrypted credit card information from on-card agent to complete the transaction.
- Each completed transaction that requires follow up will be recorded as a record of current activities. Completed transactions will be recorded in the transaction log file.
- The user can carry out other activities in data service or admin service. When it is done, the user can logout from off-card agent and Java Card will be locked.

ISSUES, CONTROVERSIES, AND RECOMMENDATIONS

Smart Card Agent Environment represents a viable solution to serve the needs of personalize services in the Internet world. However, there are issues and controversies that need to be sorted out before widespread implementations are possible. Following are some of the possible issues and controversies:

A) Feasibility Issues

Issue: While smart card represents an excellent system component within the environment, the true intelligence of many implementations still comes from software agent technology. Software agent technology has been implemented in many applications. However, it is still in its infancy state for implementation as a personal assistant. A mature agent technology is required to bootstrap the implementation of a true smart card agent environment.

Recommendation: Although agent as personal assistant has not been truly intelligent, implementation based on current techniques would be sufficient to handle basic requirements for agent functionalities, with more enhancements being done along the process.

Issue: Limited memory size and computing power of smart cards may not be able to handle demanding requirements for agent services.

Recommendation: Current smart card memory size is sufficient to store critical user data and other indexed data. Although it may not be able to execute truly intelligent routine, it is sufficient to serve as a media for secure data storage and self-identification. With the advancement of semiconductor technology, smart card chips' computing power and memory size are getting better and larger. There are already 16-bit and 32-bit microprocessors designed for smart card applications, with continued research that aims for better chips. Hence, more intelligence features can be added on later.

B) Acceptance Issues

Issue: Applications for Smart Card Agent Environment may not be able to gain public acceptance, as they are not used to it.

Recommendation: In order to kick-start such utilities, major efforts are required to provide accessibility and awareness of benefits for such utilities.

C) Availability Issues

Issue: Up to now, smart card reader is not a common computer peripheral like a floppy drive. In order to facilitate the implementation, smart card reader would need to be a default computer peripheral.

Recommendation: Smart card has started to gain acceptance as part of the main stream in the computer industry. Some major computer manufacturers have started to ship smart card readers together with their new systems. Furthermore, Microsoft's and others major software players' plans to include support for smart card in their products have further promoted its utilization. Hence the availability problem would be solved in the near future.

D) Security Issues

Issue: Security and trust level of on-card agent as a self-identification unit is a major concern. A trusted organization is required to validate the financially critical data like credit card information.

Recommendation: On-card agents and other sensitive data should be issued and digitally signed by a reputable and trusted organization so that they can be used as a trusted self-identification unit.

Issue: Security attacks that focus on technology weakness as compared to brute force attacks might be a major threat. A good example is the recent attacks on smart card using Simple Power Analysis (SPA) where an encrypted key can be extracted by analyzing the power consumption patterns of the chip when the encryption routine is being run.

Recommendation: Most attacks on technology weakness can be solved or contained by modifying the card operating system once these weaknesses are known. Therefore, field-upgradeable card operating systems would be needed to handle these problems. On the hardware level, smart card chip manufacturers have been constantly improving their chips' resistance towards tampering.

Issue: Personal profile, user particulars, and private statistics collected when using smart card might end up in the wrong hands.

Recommendation: Privacy has always been a major concern when personal-related information is required for a transaction. The data-mapping design of on-card agent allows multiple levels of security control for data access. Technically, users would be able to use most agent services without identifying themselves. Two-way challenge and response can be used to establish trust relationship without exposing personal information. Arrangement in the form of agreement can be made between agent service provider and users to ensure privacy.

As for the statistics data, personal data have already been used for demographic and others statistics. As long as the exposure is minimum, contained, and guaranteed under some form of agreement, smart card agent environment will not make things worse.

E) Standardization Issues

Issue: Interoperability of various smart cards and readers is still a major issue as most smart cards and readers in the market are not interoperable. Some form of joint-effort from various players is required in order to implement this distributed environment.

Recommendation: Efforts on open standard platform like Java Card for the OS and PC/SC for the interface are expected to alleviate these problems.

Issue: There are no existing industrial standards for interfacing between major components in the smart card agent environment.

Recommendation: A consortium should be formed to develop standards for smart card agents and their interface protocol. Before such standards are formed, agent service provider would need to develop a protocol for such purposes.

FUTURE TRENDS AND RECOMMENDATION FOR FURTHER WORK

The future of digital technology is largely dependent on social trends that are greatly influenced by current personal digital technology. Personally, we think the following three factors would shape the future of digital technology:

- Demands for personalized services.
- More and more people are on the move.
- Integration of virtual worlds into our physical world.

Personal digital technology has largely emerged from these trends. Hence, in the context of e-commerce, we would like to see the integration of software agent technology into personal digital technology that would facilitate an end user for e-commerce activities. Smart Card Agent Environment or other similar systems would prove to be essential for the role of 'personal representatives.'

The focus of this research is to explore the integration of smart card technology and software agent technology, and the technology to provide personalized service for the Internet and online services. The result of this design would be a useful vehicle or resource for the following activities:

- Full implementation of the working Smart Card Agent Environment and applications that want to ride on its facilities.
- To introduce software agent features into existing smart card applications.
- Using smart card for secure data storage with support for user mobility or software agent applications.

CONCLUSIONS

The integration of smart card technology and agent technology represents an effort to achieve intelligence amplification through microprocessors, i.e., smart cards that we can carry along. Smart card is probably the first successful attempt to equip the general public with microprocessors in their wallets. With increasingly higher computing power, smart card would be the best candidate as a 'personal representative' in the digital world. It has bridged the transactional gap between humans and computers to allow for a new level of 'human' computer interaction. This would open up huge application possibilities.

The design of a smart card agent environment has illustrated the concept of combining smart card and software agent technology to greatly enhance usability, user mobility, and security features of online services. The proposed environment has offered a practical way to allow a general user to use online services effectively in a painless way.

The prototype implementation of off-card agent has demonstrated how various agents can work together within the smart card agent environment. On the other hand, the prototype implementation of on-card agent has demonstrated how agent-related data can be stored and retrieved securely, and how access to on-card agent can be controlled through PIN, random number challenge and response, digital signature, and identification of card acceptance device (CAD). Also, a description of general application scenario has been given.

In the context of e-commerce, much effort has been focused on the infrastructure and transactional technology to ensure a smooth transaction from goods selection to the final payment and goods delivery. However, in order to gain widespread acceptance from the general public, the execution of these processes must be seamless, with minimum user interactions, while payment security is ensured. Hence, a tight integration among these processes is required.

Smart Card Agent Environment is designed to address the execution issues. Agent technology can be used to greatly enhance the selection process, while the user identification and information required for transactions, payment, and goods delivery can be delivered by the multi-applications smart card. Also, the smart card ability to meet the security and mobility requirement has made this a viable solution.

However, in the practical sense, various standardization issues need to be resolved before a practical implementation can be deployed.

REFERENCES

Alberda, M.I., Hartel, P.H., & Jong Frz, E.K. (1997). Using formal methods to cultivate trust in smart card operating systems. *Future Generation Computer Systems, 13*, 39-54.

Allen, C.A., Barr, W.J., & Schultz, R. (1996). *Smart Cards: Seizing Strategic Business Opportunities.*

Bradsgwa, J.M. (Ed.) (1997). *Software Agents.* Boston: MIT Press.

Chorafas, D.N. (1998). *Agent Technology Handbook.* McGraw-Hill.

Dale, J., & DeRoure, D.C. (1997). *A Mobile Agent Architecture for Distributed Information Management.* University of Southampton.

Dreifus, H., & Monk, J.T. (1997). *Smart cards: A guide to building and managing smart card applications.* Wiley Computer Publishing.

Effing, W., & Rankl, W. (1996). *Smart card handbook.* London: John Wiley & Sons.

Etzioni, O., & Weld, D. (1994). A softbot-based interface to the Internet. *Communication of the ACM, 37(7),* 72-76.

Ferrer, J.D. (1997). Multi-applications smart card and encrypted data processing. *Future Generation Computer Systems, 13,* 65-74.

Hensley, P., Metral, M., Shardanand, U., Converse, D., & Myers, M. (1997). Proposal for an open profiling standard. *Technical Note W3C* [Online]. Available: http://www.w3.org/TR/NOTE-OPS-FrameWork.html.

Huhns, M.N., & Singh, M.P. (1998). Personal assistants. *IEEE Internet Computing,* September/October, pp. 90-92.

Jennings, N.R., & Wooldridge, M. (1998). *Agent Technology Foundation, Applications and Markets.* Springer-Verlag.

Lange, D.B. (1998). Mobile agents: Environments, technologies and applications. *Proceedings Practical Application of Intelligent Agents and Multi-Agent Technology 1998.* London, 11-14.

Mckay, D.P., Pastor J., & McEntire R. (1996). An architecture for information agents. *Proceedings of the Third International Conference on Artificial Intelligence Planning Systems.*

Norman, D. (1994). How might people interact with agents?. *Communications of the ACM, 37(7),* 68-76.

Nwana, H., & Azarmi, N. (Eds.). (1997). Software agent and soft computing: Towards enhancing machine intelligence. *Lecture Notes in Artificial Intelligence 1998.* New York: Springer-Verlag.

Nwana, H.S. (1996). Software agents: An overview. *Knowledge Engineering Review, 11(3),* 205-244.

Nwana, H.S., & Ndumu, D.T. (1999). A perspective on software agents research. *The Knowledge Engineering Review, 14(2),* 1-18.

Poh, T.K., & Guan, S.U. (2000). Internet-enabled smart card agent environment and applications. In S.M. Rahman & M. Raisinghani (Eds.), *Electronic Commerce: Opportunities and Challenges* (pp. 246-260). Idea Group Publishing.

Quisquater, J.J. (1997). The adolescence of smart cards. *Future Generation Computer Systems, 13,* 3-7.

Reinhardt, A. (1994). The network with smarts. *Byte,* October, 51-64.

Rhodes, B.J. (1997). The wearable remembrance agent: A system for augmented memory. *Personal Technologies Journal Special Issue on Wearable Computing, 1,* 218-224.

Russell, J.F. (1997). *Compatibility and conflicts: PC/SC, OCF, Java Card Multos.*

Schlumberger. (1998). *Cyberflex Access Java programmable smart card.*

Smart Card Museum. (1999). *The Birth of Smart Card* [Online]. Available: http://www.cardshow.com/museum/welcome.html.

Smith, J. (1999). *World Cards Asia Pacific*. Singapore: Singapore National Printing Pte. Ltd.

Stone, P., & Veloso, M. (1996). *Multiagent Systems: A Survey from a Machine Learning Perspective*. IEEE—TKDE.

Sun Microsystems, Inc. (1998). *Java Card 2.1 reference implementation user's guide*.

Sun Microsystems, Inc. (1998). *Java Card applet developer's guide revision 1.12*.

Sun Microsystems, Inc. (1998). *Java Card applet developer's guide*.

Wang, S.J., & Chabg J.F. (1996). Smart card-based secure personal authentication scheme. *Computer & Security, 15(3)*, 231-237.

Wood, C.C. (1997). A management view of Internet electronic commerce security. *Computers & Security, 16*, 316-320.

Wooldridge, M., & Jennings, N.R. (1998). Pitfalls of agent-oriented development. *Proceedings of the Second Conference on Autonomous Agents*.

Wooldridge, M., & Jennings, N.R. (1995). Intelligent agents: Theory and practice. *The Knowledge Engineering Review, 10(2)*, pp. 115-152.

Chapter XIII

Business–to–Business Electronic Commerce: Electronic Tendering

Ahmad Kayed and Robert M. Colomb
University of Queensland, Australia

While there are many proposals to automate the buying and selling process, there has been no actual attempt to automate the tendering process (sealed auction). This chapter contributes toward the steps to move in this direction. In this chapter, the benefits of an on-line tendering system are clarified, the tendering process is analyzed, the current attempts are surveyed, the competency of EDI and on-line auctions approach is criticized, and a framework solution is proposed.

INTRODUCTION

The number of businesses and individuals through the world who are discovering and exploring the Internet is growing dramatically. The Internet is a cheap, open, distributed, and easy–to–use environment which provides an easy way to set up shop and conduct commerce at any place in the world (Lim et al., 1998).

Technology development represents a powerful driving force for the establishment of new methods of managing and organizing public procurement processes. Future development will make it possible to automate the tender process (Blomberg and Lennartsson, 1997) (Slone, 1992). Electronic tendering may contribute to increase efficiency and effectiveness of the procurement process in terms of costs, quality, performance, and time for both buyers and sellers. The sellers' efficiency and effectiveness will be increased by applying electronic tendering techniques in terms of cuts to manpower costs, reduced administrative and transaction costs, improvements in tender quality, strengthened tender preparation capacity, simplified public market access, competitiveness, and high integration capability with internal and external systems (Blomberg and Lennartsson, 1997).

The use of electronic tendering reduces the processing time and cost of RFQ (request for quotes) (Madden and Shein, 1998) (Shein, 1998). It allows analyzing the company's purchase activities, selecting the sellers more competitively, and reducing the time to get the best price. Since the Internet is open for all, buyers can order at any time and reach out to an array of qualified small and large businesses (Madden and Shein, 1998) (Shein, 1998).

The development of an electronic infrastructure will create excellent opportunities for buyers to establish closer cooperation in many areas of great importance to them, such as coordinate tendering in order to increase their purchasing power and to minimize distribution and stock-keeping costs, exchange of supplier information, procurement plans, tender enquiry samples and technical specifications, legal and procedural aspects, etc. This cooperation between buyers may take place at any level in the community: locally, regionally, nationally, and even globally (Blomberg and Lennartsson, 1997).

This chapter is organized as following: Section 2 reviews the current efforts to facilitate on-line tendering. Section 3 analyzes the tendering process and reviews current related protocols. Section 4 discusses the related problems and points out what are still missing in electronic tendering. Section 5 discusses our framework for automating the tendering process, and Section 6 concludes the chapter.

ELECTRONIC TENDERING

Automating the tender process is a major goal for many international and governmental bodies. Many countries such as the USA, Canada, Europe, Australia, Mexico, etc. are adopting legislation to contend with some technological issues, mainly bonding and signatures. This will facilitate business on the Internet. Some examples are:

In the USA, General Electric Information Services Inc. produced Trading Process Network (TPN)(*Inc.*, 1999). TPN lets buyers prepare bids, select suppliers, and post orders to its Web site. Commerce One Inc. (*Inc.*, 1999b) allows the employees to access the Seller's Web catalogs, select items, and order them. Gateway (1999) is a mediator matching sellers and buyers. Suppliers and buyers go to the Business Gateway Web site (www.businessgateway.com) and fill out forms indicating what they have to buy or sell plus other information. Business Gateway then matches buyers and sellers (Madden and Shein, 1998). Ariba Technologies Inc. (*Inc.*, 1999a) produces the Operating Resource Management System ORMS. ORMS lets a user open e-catalog for specific companies, create a purchase request, then it sends automatically for sign-off approval. ORMS lets a user create business rules that define the workflow and routing of the requests. SmartProcurement is developed by the National Institute for Standards and Technology and Enterprise Integration Technologies as a prototype to automate the tender process, mainly the RFQ (*Procurement*, 1996; *Technology*, 1996; Cutkosky et al., 1993). The system is initiated by RFQ, then a buyer agent acquires a list of registered vender agents for that item. Finally the buyer agent collects the bids submitted before the deadline and selects the best bid (O'Leary et al., 1997). The SmartProcurement system uses two evolving computer technologies: the World Wide Web (WWW) and software agents.

The Mexican Government started a plan for on-line tendering, in a project called Compranet (Noriega, 1997; *Compranet*, 1999). The main aim is to incorporate IT into small and medium companies. The Mexican Government regulates the procurement process in such a way that most acquisitions are made through a form of sealed bid auction. The call for tenders is announced via the Internet through Compranet. It is possible to submit tenders by Internet (Noriega, 1997).

SIMAP (*Projects*, 1999) is a European project whose objective is to develop the information systems infrastructure needed to support the delivery of an effective public procurement policy in Europe, by providing contracting entities and suppliers with the information they need to manage the procurement process effectively (*Projects*, 1999). Eventually, the project will address the whole procurement process, including bids, award of contracts, delivery, invoicing, and payment (*Projects*, 1999). SIMAP depends on EDIFACT specification in building up their information system. They collect samples of different EU tender documents and try to make mapping between the common elements in these documents and EDIFACT 850 (EDFACT Purchase Order Message) to facilitate on-line tendering. The full specification of this project can be found in Blomberg and Lennartsson (1997).

Tenders on the Web (*on the Web*, 1999) is produced by Context Ltd., an electronic publishing company based in the UK. Context is a gateway provider for Tenders Electronic Daily (TED), the database hosted by the European Commission Host Organization (ECHO). All public sector purchasing in the EU over a certain value has to be advertised and tenders invited. TED provides information about public sector purchasing in the EU (*on the Web*, 1999).

In Canada anyone can connect to a bulletin board called New Brunswick Opportunities Network to view tender information (*Tendering*, 1999b). MERX (*Tendering*, 1999c) is Canada's Electronic Tendering Service which aims to provide access to procurement opportunities from the federal, provincial, and municipal governments across Canada. BIDS (*Tendering*, 1999d) is another Canada's company which plays the role of mediator. The sellers tell BIDS what products or services they sell. When tenders are issued from any buying agencies, BIDS notifies the relevant sellers.

In Australia, TenderSearch (*Tendering*, 1999a) is a company providing Australian businesses with a tender information service. TenderSearch use the Internet to provide this information. This helps them to provide a timely, accurate, and up–to–date service to many businesses (*Tendering*, 1999a).

The main difference among these applications is which party will control the other. As we see it, we have three parties: the buyer, the seller, and the mediator; and we have four approaches to deal with this issue: (1) buyer puts his own tender and forces sellers to fill in the blanks, (2) the sellers put the standard and the buyer follows, (3) all must follow the pre-agreed standards, or (4) no one forces anyone. In the last case the mediator matches between sellers and buyers.

These systems were not designed to inter-operate in complementary stages to provide a full electronic tendering system. They support only buying or selling one item at a time. No system supports multiple items from multiple sellers. They focus in how to choose the lower price, and little attention has been given to manipulate the conditions or item specifications. In an agent-mediated system, they used a simple and direct agent communication to avoid the network overhead and ontology problems (Ong and Ng, 1998).

ELECTRONIC TENDERING PROCESS ANALYSIS

To automate any business process, we have to define the specification and execution of the process. General definitions include activities to be performed, their control flow and data exchange, organizational roles of persons and software components that are to perform activities, and policies that describe the organizational environment (Merż et al., 1996; Coalition, 1996).

To automate the tender process, we need to subdivide the process into atomic tasks, define each task, the interactions among these tasks, control flow and data exchange, the interrelated problems among these tasks, and determine which task should be or not be automated. Moreover we need to define the roles, and the interactions among these roles. In the following section we will define the main actors and activities of the tendering process.

Table1. The Roles and Activities of Tendering Process

Buyer	Seller	Mediator
	-Non Interaction Activities-	
Workflow Management	Catalogs Building	Templates Repository
Tender Forming	Bid or not to bid (DSS)	Data Maintenance
Bids Evaluation	Bid Forming	
	-Interaction Activities-	
Tender Invitation	Information Collection	Advertising
Tender Advertising	Bid Submission	Reputation Building
Buyers' Collaboration	Catalogs Interoperability	Auction App.
		Standardized App.
		Buyer-Seller Matching

There are two types of business models, transactional and non-transactional business models. The non-transactional business models include searching the Web for an item but completing the transaction via other means like fax or phone; advertising on the Web; and intermediaries. There are three different transactional business models on the Web (Stark et al., 1997):

- Browse, select, and purchase model: This is the most popular on the Web. Internet Shopper Web site (www.internetshopper.com) lists more than 25,000 on-line stores, this popularity gained from its simplicity.
- The Auction Model: In this model, the customers bid for individual items.
- The Bid Model: This is a business–to–business application. Instead of going out to find suppliers, businesses use the WEB as a channel to post their Request for Tender.

To analyze the process, we review the scope of the process, define the main actors and activities, point out to the system(s) that try to automate these activities, and indicate the missing issues needed to put the tendering on-line.

Tendering Activities and Actors:

The tendering process involves three actors:

- Buyers who are looking to purchase a service from sellers.
- Sellers or the suppliers who offer the services.
- Mediators (Brokers) who facilitate communication between buyers and sellers.

Tendering activities can be categorized into interaction and non-interaction activities. Interaction activities are the activities that contain more than one actor. Tender document interchange, tender invitation, tender return, tender advertising, negotiation, communication, collaboration, and matching between the sellers and buyers can be considered as this type. Non-interaction activities are activities which involve only one participant. Forming and evaluating the tender, forming the bid, data maintenance, and templates repository are considered in this category.

In the following, we will describe each actor's activity and point out to the system(s) that are needed to automate this activity. Table 1 summarizes these activities.

The Buyer Activities

Although the buyer is a cornerstone for any procurement process, little attention has been given to automate the buyer's activities. The main non-interaction buyer's activities are forming the tender and evaluating the bids. The well-known examples that support the automation of these activities are word processing and spreadsheet. The main buyer's interaction activities are: tender invitation and tender advertising, tender document interchange, collecting the return bids, negotiation, communication and collaboration. In the following we will discuss some of these activities.

Tender Forming: Forming the tender is an important step in the tendering process. King and Mercer (1988) argue that less detailed specification may mean the buyer has to evaluate different design features. Modelling this can be very difficult for both buyers and sellers. Gabb and Henderson (1996) also state that a poor specification will make the development of the evaluation model very difficult.

In a survey (Department of Defence, 1994), which encompasses 80 firms, among the reasons for unsuccessful tenders were that the actual users don't participate in preparing the tenders. Any system should provide mechanisms for the end users to participate in forming the tender.

In forming the tender, we have two situations: one off tenders and frequent tenders. An example of the former is a tender to buy establishment equipment. The key issue here is how to collect the actual users' needs and how to convert these needs to formal specifications. In other words, how to reduce the gap between the buyer's need and the sellers' offers to form a detailed specified tender. In this situation, attention must be given to automate the communications among parties, clustering the user's needs, converting needs to sellers' specifications, and facilitate negotiation among all parties.

Usually the tendering or sealed auction is used by governmental or large organizations to purchase or sell valuable things. In general, the buyer forms two committees to deal with tenders: one dealing with legal issues and the other dealing with specification and technical issues and providing recommendation to the first one. A system is needed here to support these activities and to coordinate the interactions between committees.

Generally, in the one off situation, the buyer consults someone else to write the tender, so the process will be repeated but with different items and/or different parties. Construction contracts and oil exploration rights are examples of frequent tenders. In this situation, problems like how to learn from experience and how to extract knowledge form experience should be given more attention.

Bid Evaluation Activity: The main activity on the buyer side is how to choose the best bid. A formal economic mechanism to perform this activity is the auction. Auction theory is a complex economics subject. Auction is an economic mechanism in which the buyers bid for an item following a predetermined set of rules (McAfee and McMillan, 1987; Wurman et al., 1998b). In the sealed-bid auction (*tendering*), the participants do not learn the status of an auction until the end of the auction.

Usually the lower price determines the rule of selecting the best bid. Vickery (1961) proved that using the second lowest price policy (Vickery mechanism) will reduce counter-speculation. Some of the on-line auctions (Tsvetovatyy et al., 1997) used Vickery mechanisms as a policy to chose among bids. In some countries the lowest price is selected with some restrictions, as in Saudi Arabia the bid should be not less than 70 percent of the cost estimate (Hatush, 1996).

Hatush et. al. (Hatush and Skitmore, 1998; Hatush, 1996) use Multi-Attribute Utility Theory (MAUT) to build a model for bid evaluation. In their model, the main criteria besides the price were financial soundness, technical ability, management capabilities, safety performance, and reputation. King and Phythian (1992) proposed repertory grids to elicit the knowledge from expert managers involved in bids evaluation. Using statistical techniques, they determined the key factors in evaluating bids.

In automating bid evaluation activity, we should not think in forms of one-to-one correspondence to the manual work. Usually sellers provide many documents to prove their abilities to win the tender. An electronic certificate issued from a legal body can measure the ability of sellers. Moreover buyers could register terms of qualification at this legal body, and the electronic certification issued only for the sellers that meet these terms.

The Seller Activities

The seller side in the tendering process is well discussed in economics, knowledge-based, knowledge extracting, expert system, decision support systems, information management systems, security, and other disciplines. Stark and Rothkope (1979) gave 500 titles which deal with models related to competitive bidding. These titles include ad hoc advice to bidders, analytical models and evaluations of auctions. Many of these titles discussed the construction contract, oil exploration rights, and securities.

The main non-interaction activities for the seller are done to develop catalogs, bid or not to bid, and form the bids to win. The seller interaction activities are: know about the tenders, submit the bid, and tender document interchange. In the following we will discuss some of these activities.

To bid or not to bid. This activity is related to many disciplines. It is normally discussed in the form of competitive bidding. There are many approaches treating this activity. King and Mercer (1988) categorized these approaches into four topics. These are:

- The basic probabilistic approaches
- The probabilistic strategy approaches
- The game theoretic approaches
- The non-price approaches

King and Phythian (1992) proposed a repertory grid to elicit knowledge from expert managers involved in bid evaluation. Using statistical techniques, they determined the key factors in evaluating bids. These factors were used to build an expert system to support the decision to bid or not to bid. Ward and Chapman (1988) proposed an informational framework procedure to support sellers in preparing their bids. Vanwelkenhuysen (1998) proposed a tender support system to improve the tender-to-order-to-production process for a pump company.

Dawood (1996) surveyed bidding approaches. He criticizes the mathematical approach (game and probabilistic models) for the lack of managerial knowledge of such models, and that these models are incomplete and model only a tiny part of the situation. He summarized his opinion in the following points:

- Probability theories alone are not sufficient to model bidding problems.
- Expert systems offer a good base for building bidding models, but the user should verify the knowledge rules and the inference engine, and this can be very time consuming.
- Neural Networks (NNs) are relatively simple to develop and require less time and effort. However, the black box nature of NNs make them less popular.
- The integration between information systems and expert systems can provide advice and information to aid the management in the bidding problem.

Franklin and Reiter (1996) proposed a secure sealed-auction protocol to solve traditional sealed-auction problems. McAfee and McMillan (1987) and Guttman and Kasbah (1998) raised the winner's curse problem where the winning bid value is greater than the product's market valuation.

Mediators' Activities

The electronic broker plays an important role in cyberspace. A broker is a party which mediates between buyers and sellers in a marketplace. Brokers play an integral part in some procurement transactions. Brokers are often useful when a marketspace has a large number of buyers and sellers, when the search costs are relatively high, or when trust services are necessary (Bichler et al., 1998). Mediators or intermediaries provide automated assistance for electronic tendering through knowledge of the market and the requirements of these markets. Mediators with their knowledge help the buyers inspect the goods electronically (Lee, 1997). More specifically, mediators provide knowledge of the market, requirements analysis, and negotiation (Robinson, 1997). Tendering process needs to combine disparate information sources. A possible approach is through the use of *mediators*, which can perform a customized integration. A mediator can reduce the gap between the buyer specification (which is general) and the seller specification (which is more technical). Another typical role of a mediator is to provide value-added services. In summary, mediators provide mediation, coordination, integration, negotiation, matching, and searching services.

There are two mechanisms to cope with the mediator's roles: auctioning and standardization mechanisms. In the following we will review the two approaches.

Auction Mechanism. Auction acts as a mediator among buyers and sellers (Lee, 1997). Yahoo (Wurman et al., 1998a) lists 95 on-line auctions. There are several prototypes and protocols for on-line auctions (Smith, 1980; Sandholm and Lesser, 1995; Wurman et al., 1998a; Bot, 1998; Moukas et al., 1998; Auction, 1998; Tsvetovatyy et al., 1997; Wurman et al., 1998b; Mullen and Wellman, 1998; Chavez and Kasbah, 1996; Lee, 1997; Rodríguez-Aguilar et al., 1998; Noriega, 1997; Collins et al., 1997; Sun and Weld, 1995). In the following we state some significant examples.

Smith (1980) pioneered research in communication among distributed agents with the Contract Net Protocol (CNP) (Collins et al., 1998). Smith's model is based on the sealed bid auction which works in a cooperative agent environment. In this model, each contractor is allowed to make only one bid, and the bids of the other contractors are not revealed to him (Smith, 1980).

Sandholm et. al. (Sandholm, 1993; Sandholm and Lesser, 1995; Sandholm, 1996) extended the CNP. In this model, each agent accepts deals which are profitable to it, based on marginal cost computations. They negotiate only the marginal cost within the announce-bid-award cycle. The agents are self-interested, and each agent negotiates directly with each other.

Kasbah (Guttman and Kasbah, 1998; Chavez and Kasbah, 1996) is a Web-Based multi-agent classified ad system where users create agents to buy and sell on their behalf. A user wanting to buy or sell a good creates an agent, gives it some strategic direction, and sends it off into a centralized agent marketplace. Kasbah agents seek out potential buyers or sellers and negotiate with them on behalf of their owners. Each agent's goal is to complete an acceptable deal, subject to a set of user-specified constraints such as desired price, a highest or lowest acceptable price, and a date by which to complete the transaction.

Rodríguez-Aguilar et al. (1998) and Noriega (1997) built an agent-mediated auction house for a fish market which was based on the Dutch auction bidding protocol. Bichler et al. (1998) proposed a prototype called OFFER which is CORBA-based and uses the auction mechanisms to buy and sell. The AUCNET system is a centralized, on-line wholesale market in which cars are sold using video images, character-based data, and a standardized inspector rating (Lee, 1997). Cathay Pacific (www.cathaypacific.com) used an electronic sealed-bid to sell airline tickets.

MAGMA (Tsvetovatyy et al., 1997; Collins et al., 1998) is a generalized multi-agent architecture that supports complex agent interaction. Examples of such interactions are: negotiation protocols, automated contracting, sealed-bid auction, and open-bid or advertised-price buying and selling. In this model, the agent negotiates with other agents through market sessions. A session is a mediator through which services are delivered to participating agents. A market's registry is used to find an agent willing to bid in call-for-bids request.

AuctionBot (Bot, 1998) is a general purpose auction server at the University of Michigan. A user creates an auction from a list of auction types and enters its parameters (e.g., the number of sellers, clearing time, etc.). The buyers and sellers can bid according to the negotiation protocol of the created auction.

Lim et al. (1998) proposed communication architecture for a commerce system. They proposed three types of agents: buyers, sellers and a directory agent. The agent could deal with user interface, thread manager, price manager, communication module, and log manager. Agent communication protocol is partitioned into four phases: specify the product, search for relevant sellers, choose the best seller (negotiation phase), and make payment.

Standardization Mechanism. The other main role of a mediator is to provide a common view between the buyers and sellers so they can understand each other, i.e., standards. Mediators provide standards to facilitate integration, cooperation, and communication among different actors, mainly buyers and sellers. Also the standard provides a mechanism so all the parties can understand the structure of the tender documents. A standard helps to solve the interaction problems among actors, and this will facilitate the automation of the non-interaction activities.

The well-known standard protocol for interbusiness transactions is Electronic Data Interchange (EDI). EDI has two standard protocols: private (ANSI X12) and public (UN EDIFACT ISO 9735) (Kalakota and Whinston, 1996). EDI transfers structured data by agreed message standard between computer applications. EDI has been extensively and successfully implemented, and is growing in popularity. EDI is also inflexible, insufficient, ambiguous, closed, expensive, slow, and supports only one-to-many relationships (Kimbrough and Moore, 1997; Wing, 1998; Kalakota and Whinston, 1996).

Lee and Dewitz (1992) proposed AI extensions to EDI to facilitate international contracting. Slone (1992] suggests adding functionality to the current EDI standards to automate the tendering process. Blomberg and Lennartsson (1997) proposed new functionality to the current EDIFACT 850 (EDFACT Purchase Order Message) to facilitate on-line tendering.

The trend now is to use XML as a basis to standardize the procurement process (Glushko et al., 1999). Examples of these are EDI/XML, ICE (Information and Content Exchanges), OPT (open trading protocol), OBI (open buying on the Internet), OFI (Open Financial Exchange), etc.

Other protocols that encourage corporations to initiate payments through the Internet and other public networks by increasing system security are: Secure Sockets Layer (SSL), Secure Electronic Transactions (SET), Bank Internet Payment System (BIPS), Joint Electronic Payments Initiative (JEPI), and Open Financial Exchange (OFX).

An example of a system that tries to integrate the current standard protocols and provides an interoperability framework is eCo system (Glushko et al., 1999). eCo began as an architectural vision for open Internet commerce (Tenenbaum et al., 1997). eCo system is led by CommerceNet Consortium (Consortium, 1999) which was considered as a CORBA-based interoperability framework. In 1997, eCo systems adopted the XML framework. eCo tries to integrate the current standards by providing the Business Interface Definitions

(BIDs) through the Common Business Library (CBL) (Glushko et al., 1999). CBL includes XML templates for EDI X12, OPT, ICE, OFX, and OBI. These templates can be customized and are easily understood by agents as well as people (Glushko et al., 1999). A company can define its business interface and communicate with another company even when the other company subscribes to different standards.

Keller (1995), presents an architecture for smart and virtual catalogs to solve interoperability problems between heterogeneous e-catalogs. In his approach, companies create smart catalogs of searchable, machine-sensible product information. Retailers and distributors create virtual catalogs that provide customers with product information dynamically requested from manufacturers' smart catalogs. Product data is stored in a database which communicates with a catalog agent which communicates with a facilitator agent broker. Facilitators identify the agents that support a user request.

ELECTRONIC TENDERING–RELATED PROBLEMS

The Internet is an open environment, widely distributed, and relatively cheap. Business transactions usually run under closed environments. To conduct business on the Internet, many problems must be solved. Examples of these problems are: security, authentication, heterogeneity, interoperability, and ontology problems.

In a large-scale and dynamic environment, the matching between the buyer's request and the seller's offer is nontrivial (Mullen and Wellman, 1998). EU uses a tendering mechanism to purchase about 480 billion Pounds with 150,000 procurement notices a year dealing with 600 to 800 procurement documents every morning. It is worth notifying the sellers only with relevant tenders instead of dealing with 600 documents (on the Web, 1999).

Current EC applications require users to search or locate relevant Web sites for purchasing goods themselves. This is not only time consuming, but it is extremely difficult to perform exhaustive searching on the Web (Vollrath et al., 1998). Current EC solutions do not provide a mutual mediation process to reach agreement among the buyers and sellers (Kang and Lee, 1998).

On-line marketplaces are both an opportunity and a threat to retail merchants. They are an opportunity because they offer a new channel to advertise and lower the transaction costs. They are also a threat because many on-line marketplaces are limited to price comparison—they do not consider added value services in their comparison. The retailers add value to manufacturers' products to distinguish themselves from their competitors (Guttman et al., 1998).

One of the problems in bid evaluation is the large number of seller's documents needed to win the tender. These documents are unstructured and vary from one seller to another. This limits the buyers' ability to choose the most qualified bidder.

A tender is a very complicated document. It has general terms, specific terms, optional terms, compulsory terms, items and specification for these items. Sellers like to add more specification and value-added services to win the tender. This make the comparison among bids a very complicated problem. Many EC applications are using the Internet as an underlying platform. Internet users need tools to search for information across heterogeneous systems and to match potential data sources with their needs. Consumers also need to search for information using terms from domains they are familiar with (ontologies) (Adam et al., 1998).

The integration among disparate information systems is needed to facilitate the automation of the tendering process. This will speed up the emergence of the new generation of business–to–business electronic commerce. The difficult problem here is how to combine disparate information sources to integrate them in an open environment like the Internet (Silberschatz et al., 1995).

The sheer volume of information available on the Web represents a very real problem (Jennings and Wooldridge, 1997). Everyday, we are presented with enormous amounts of information, only a tiny proportion of which is relevant or important. The volume of information available prevents us from finding information that meets our requirements.

Tendering process activities are dependent, i.e., simplifying one activity can simplify or complicate other activities. In the literature, the attempts to automate the tendering process were focused on one side of the problem, i.e., automating the interaction activities or the non-interaction activities. The challenge here is to link these disparate systems together and provide a new infrastructure that receives benefits from these systems.

The sealed auction *(tendering)* has different characteristics from the other types of auctions, in particular the outcry auction. The current auction protocols deal with the sealed auction without giving any attention to these characteristics. Sealed auction is not treated well in the on-line auction. Auctions deal with single-item, specific, well-known items, price mechanisms, simple terms, and are always centralized. On-line auctions provide a good background for the sealed auction, but for automating the tendering process there are many things still missing. The on-line auction automates an individual to business process while the tendering process is considered as a business–to–business process.

The seller side in the tendering process is well discussed in many disciplines. But very little attention was given to the buyer side. The role of the buyer is important in the tendering process and his activities (tender forming, bid evaluations, etc.) should be given more attention.

EDI and other standard protocols provide standards for content and transactions in the procurement process, but there are many things still missing. These standards need a super standard to be integrated. It is difficult to adopt a common domain-specific standard for content and transactions, particularly in cross-industry initiatives, where companies cooperate and compete with one another (Smith and Poulter, 1999). Moreover the open standards are not opened. Standards are inflexible, not scalable, expensive, and closed. Standards need a pre-agreement between the participants, and it takes time to be widely adopted.

PROPOSED SOLUTION

Tendering is well addressed in many disciplines and there are many commercial systems automated in the process or a part of the process. In summary, the tendering systems involve workflow, data analysis, security, EDI, DSS, searching, matching, monitoring, payments, and many other automated and non-automated activities. We are interested in automating the informational part of three activities: forming the tender, matchmaking, and bid evaluation. An agent-based system is needed for tender forming. A knowledge-based system is needed to store tender information and enable the mediator to perform matchmaking and bid filtration.

To deal with that huge number of participants, our solution will be agent-oriented. Agents are personalized, continuously running, and semiautonomous (Guttman et al., 1998). These features help us in resolving many problems. Software agents will help in filtering the huge number of tenders. This will help the buyer and the seller at the same time.

Our architecture is composed of three layers: the buyer (customer) layer, the mediator layer, and the seller (supplier) layer. Each layer communicates with other layers using direct

Figure 1. Tendering Framework Architecture

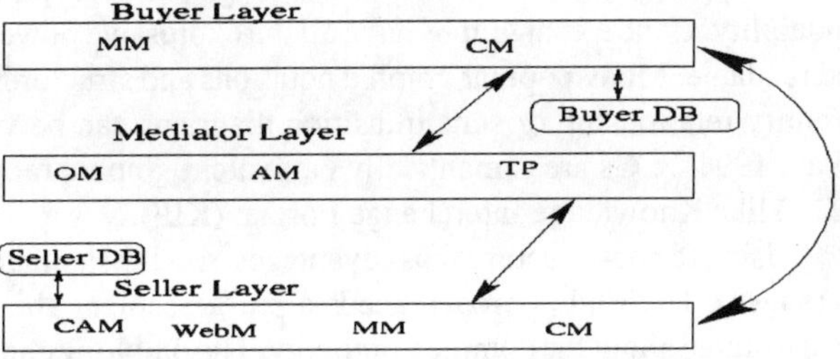

or indirect messages. The buyer layer contains the coordinator management (CM) and the matching management (MM). The mediator layer has the trusted party (TP), ontology management (OM), and the advertising management (AM). The seller layer is composed of the coordinator management (CM), the matching management (MM), catalogs management (CAM), and the Web management WebM (Figure 1).

Our solution is mediator-based. The mediator performs two types of operations: service-oriented and system-oriented operation. Service-oriented covers the provision of services to customers. Service identification, service request, agreement, and past agreement are examples of service-oriented operations. The system-oriented operations cover the systems that provide the users with some Value-Added Operations. Search, browse, metadata, profiles, and catalogs are examples of system services (GALLEGO et al., 1998).

A buyer can submit three types of request to the mediator. These are request for more information, request of invitation, or request of tendering advertising. On the seller side, sellers can submit two types of request: find relevant tenders or general request about any tender details.

The buyers' requests help them to advertise and form their tenders. For buyers we have two situations:

- Buyers know exactly their needs and are looking to advertise these needs in the mediator knowledge-based repositories in the terminology of the mediator.
- Buyers need more information about some of the items' specifications prior to performing step one.

The buyer creates an agent to collect information about some items or services. The agent asks the mediator (i.e., the AM agents). The mediator makes matching between the queries and the profile, and returns the address of the sellers' agents. The buyer agent asks the seller agent who may ask their catalog agent about this service. The buyer agent collects and summarizes the results for the buyer. CM coordinates the agent interactions and MM summarizes the answers with the help of OM agents.

We need the following components to implement our framework:

- Formal (logical) structures
- Formal ontologies
- Agent models
- Knowledge repositories and system tools

In the following subsections, we will discuss each component of the framework.

Formal (logical) Structures

Using natural language to model tendering makes any process associated with tendering automation extremely difficult. Since we are interested in storing the information in a knowledge base, we need a formal logical language to model our structures. In our system we use Conceptual Graphs (CGs). CGs are a method of knowledge representation developed by Sowa (1984) based on Charles Peirce's Existential Graphs and semantic networks in artificial intelligence (Sowa, 1995). According to Sowa (1984), CGs have a direct mapping to and from natural language and a graphic notation designed for human readability. Conceptual graphs have all the expressive power of logic but are more intuitive and readable. Many popular graphic notations and structures ranging from type hierarchies to entity-relationship or state transition diagrams can be viewed as special cases of CGs (Way, 1994). CGs are semantically equivalent graphic representation for first order logic (FOL) like Knowledge Interchange Format (KIF).

Using formal structures has advantages over the standardized approach (e.g., EDIFACT messages). The EDI approach needs a pre-agreement about everything, but here we just need to agree about the common ontology. The ontology contains abstract concepts that will form the primitives to construct a tender or a bid. This is more flexible and can be stored in a knowledge base. The ontology will make it easy to build tools to transfer from a friendly user interface (like the Web) to a logical structure (knowledge base). To build these structures, we modeled a real tender in conceptual graph. Then we extracted the primitive concepts from these models. These concepts were stored in the ontology. For specific situations, we built some tender templates using these formal structures. These concepts and templates were used to express the context, the rules and knowledge, and the agents (communication and queries). We will explain more about these structures in the following subsection.

Formal Ontologies

Since users tend to use their own tendering vocabulary, the mediator needs to maintain a common ontology to perform the service and the systems operations. Also the mediator uses the common ontology to define a context for similarity (Kashyap and Sheth, 1996).

In our project, we divided the ontology into three parts: collections of concepts, collections of conceptual structures, and collections of formal contexts. These all form our ontology (see Figure 2). The collections of concepts help us to build tools for translation and integration from one domain to another. The concept part consists of three subparts. Those are: the catalog vocabularies, the relation vocabularies, and the hierarchical relation between concepts. The Conceptual Structures (CS) represents the basic element for the tendering system. Software agents use these CSs to communicate and interact. Buyers, sellers, and mediators use these structures to describe their needs, offers, responses, or queries. The formal context provides the mechanisms of defining the similarities between concepts. The formal contexts contain three parts: the intentions graph (the graph in which the graph will be asserted), the lifting axioms, and the relation (type-of, is-a, part-of, etc.). The lifting axioms help us in reusing the ontologies and knowledge.

Following our framework (Kayed and Colomb, 1999), we need four types of ontologies: meta-ontology, abstract domain ontology, domain ontology, and tendering ontology. In the following we will briefly describe each ontology.

The Meta-Ontology defines (describes) very general concepts for other ontologies. The meta-ontology helps to query the domain ontologies and to translate from and to the domain ontologies. This is a very abstract ontology and we built its components from other generic ontologies like Farquhar et al. (1997), Elkan and Greiner (1993), and Uschold et al. (1998). We reused the definition of time (Date, Days, Years, Hours) from the ontology server (Farquhar et al., 1997). We took the basic unit measures from Cyc ontology server (Elkan and Greiner, 1993). We also redefined some organizational concepts like entity, buyer, seller, agent, activity, process, etc. from the Enterprise Ontology (Uschold et al., 1998).

The Abstract Domain Ontology contains *Classes* which are abstract descriptions of objects in a domain. The class has Class-ID, Class-Properties, Class-Synonyms, Class-Type, Relation, Sub-Class, and Axioms. A relation is a link between classes, and axioms are rules that govern the behavior of the classes. The abstract domain ontology represents a container of abstract data types for sellers' catalogs. In this sense we should distinguish between the catalogs and the ontology. For example ontology may contain a PC as a concept, which has RAM and CPU as other concepts. Catalog may contain Pentium 3 with 32 MB RAM. In CGs sense, this can be translated to:

Figure 2. Ontology Structure

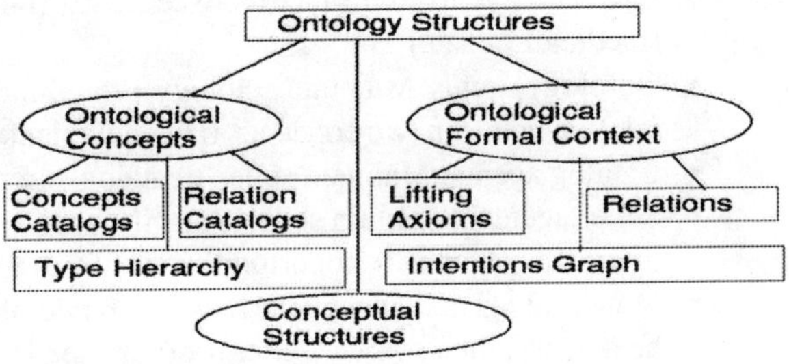

[PC:Dell]—>(Part-Of)—>[CPU-Type:Pentium3]—>(part-Of)—>[Memory: RAM]<--(measure)<--[Memory-Unit: 32 MB]

The Domain Ontology is a collection of vocabularies mapped to concepts in the higher level ontology. Since the Abstract Domain Ontology (ADO) is a schema for the sellers catalogs, we should define mapping between these abstract concepts (in the ADO) and the catalog values. This is how we know that Dell computer is a PC concept.

The Tendering Ontology represents the core ontology in our system. The basic part of it is the Tendering Conceptual Structures (TCSs). We divide them into three models: buyer, seller, and mediator models. The buyer model is divided into advertising model, query model, and policy model. The advertising model again can be divided into tender invitation, terms, objects (services), specification, and returned forms. Two of the most important TCSs are the Tendering Invitation Structure (TIS) and the sellers' profile structure (SPS). It is beyond the scope of this chapter to describe everything in this ontology. Readers are encouraged to visit our ongoing works at Kayed (2000).

Agent Models

Buyers' agents contact the mediator through formal structures that are committed to the ontology which should be defined in the former stage. The mediator checks the profile repository, and depending on the buyers' strategies, determines the address of sellers' agents that match their needs. This stage is based on software agents. There are many methodologies to design an agent-oriented system. The common core of these methodologies is to define the internal agent model and external (environmental) agent model. The internal model focuses on modelling BDI (Belief, Desire, Intention). The external model focuses on how agents can interact and the role of each agent.

Since the agents work autonomously, the buyer provides the agent with strategies and policies to direct their behavior. These strategies are implemented in a matrix of desires (with default values) and some logical rules. A quality of service (QoS) is an example of these matrixes. QoS contains concepts from the ontology, and some fuzzy numbers measure seller's capability for that service. The TP is responsible for maintaining this matrix.

In our project we define three agent models. The role of agents is described in Agents Model. How the agents can interact is described in the Interaction Agents Model. The internal behavior of each agent is defined in the BDI Model. In the following we will give a brief description for each model.

- Agents Model
  - Interface agents: Interface between user (buyers or sellers) and other agents (mediator agents)
  - Ontology agents: Maintain ontology, providing tools to browse ontologies, find the relation between two concepts, find equivalent concepts (terminology finder), etc.
  - Catalog agents: Maintain seller's catalog and answer other sellers' agents
  - Seller agents: Maintain seller's profile, answer buyer agent through the catalog's agents, look for new opportunities to inform the seller with relevant tenders
  - Matching agents: Determine how much two objects are similar. Object here may be a query, data source (seller profiles), tender, etc.
  - Summary agent: Summarize the returned answers in a table
- Interaction Agents Model
  - Agents Bulletin Board (ABB)
  - Agents messages
  - Global policies director
  - Ontological translator
  - Agent messages repository
- BDI model
  - Algorithms (Concepts matching, semantic correctness, similarity measures, etc.)
  - Local policies structures
  - Formal structures for messages, desire matrixes, strategies, quality of services, etc.
  - Translating tools

For more technical details, please visit Kayed (2000).

Knowledge Repository and System Tools

The mediator stores the tendering information in a knowledge-based repository and sends invitations to the relevant sellers. The mediator will be responsible for the following:

- Construct and maintain the knowledge base
- Construct and maintain the ontologies
- Maintain all the repositories (seller profiles, policies, agent profiles, etc.)
- Provide tools to use the above
- Tools provided by mediator are:
  - Repositories browsing tools
  - Matching tools and utilities
  - Tools to check the syntactic of profiles, tenders, queries, etc.
  - Translating tools + browsing the ontology
  - Tools to query ontology, profiles, tender, all the repositories
  - Bid filtration tools
- Repositories contains:
  - Logical messages
  - Rules of matching
  - Ontologies: tendering ontology, domain ontology, abstract domain ontology, and meta ontology
  - Profiles: buyers, sellers, and agent profiles
  - Policies
  - Advertising area
  - Bidding area

Discussion

Using ontological representation for tender modeling will facilitate bid evaluation. Following that, the procedure for bid selection will be simplified. Buyers submit their policies for bid selection, while the mediator checks the bids and tries to find the most bids that match the buyer policy.

As a business process, the mediator is not likely to decide which is the best bid. Mediator will perform a bid filtration by applying buyer desires and reduce the number of bids. Buyers are controlling the selection procedure through querying tools provided by mediator. Following these strategies, we will not violate any business rules.

One of the main operations of the mediator is matchmaking. In matchmaking the buyers/sellers advertise their needs/capabilities to the mediator (Sycara et al., 1999). The mediator uses the domain ontology to perform matchmaking. The needs/capabilities should be committed to the common ontology to perform this matchmaking.

Mediator receives users' structures (buyers or sellers) and checks their semantics. Mediator checks if the structures are canonically derived from the ontologies. Here we apply the algorithm of Mugnier and Chein (1993). This algorithm decides whether a conceptual graph is canonical relative to a given canonical basis (the repositories). The complexity of this algorithm is polynomial related to the complexity of computing a projection between two conceptual graphs. When the canonical basis is a set of trees, it is polynomial.

We defined two types of matching: soft-matching and concept matching. The soft-matching depends on the multi-attribute utility theory (MAUT) (Hatush, 1996). The tender is divided into classes, which may contain subclasses. The buyer provides a factor of importance (utility function) for each concept in each class in each level in the tender (the sum in each level should =100%). The mediator performs concept matching between the class concepts and the concepts in the seller profile. The concept matching returns a number which will be multiplied by the factor of importance up to a higher level which will determine the distance between the buyer request and sellers' offers.

Concept matching measures the distance between two concepts according to the common ontology. The distance between two concepts can be computed by the number of roles that subsume both concepts over the number of roles that subsume the buyer's concept. If the result is close to one, this means that the two concepts are similar.

CONCLUSION AND FUTURE WORK

Automating the tendering process is evolving and as it gets more advanced, the cost of automating this process will be reduced. Problems such as communication cost, legislation, security, and authentication will be reduced by that time. An open environment like the Internet and the huge number of participants will open new problems for both sellers and buyers. For the sellers, the problem is not just knowing about the tender; the problem will be whether this tender is relevant to the seller's domain. For the buyers, the problem is how to pick up only the relevant and qualified sellers that match their needs.

In this chapter we analyzed the tendering process, we surveyed the systems that automated fully or a part of the process. We pointed out the problem that should be resolved before putting the tendering on-line. We gave a general description of our framework.

We defined the role of ontology in automating the tendering process. We constructed our ontologies based on three components: the concepts, the structures, and the contexts. This decomposition facilitates the process of ontology building and reusing. We described our system of tendering automation focusing on the role of ontology. We clarified how the ontology would help in defining semantic matching. We have shown how the expressive power of CG helps in building ontologies and conceptual structures.

We introduced the concepts of layered ontologies. At the top level we used very abstract ontology which contains abstract data types for the domain ontology. Defining multiple levels of abstractions facilitates the transformation of catalog to ontology. One of the exciting areas here is to define the relation between the catalogs, standards, and ontologies. Catalogs are not interoperable. Standard catalogs are, but lack flexibility. The ontology is more flexible and provides interoperability between partners.

In future work, we will develop tools to translate from and to the common ontology. Besides soft matching and concepts matching, we will define data-mining facilities for bid evaluation. An expert agent will extract the concepts of a certain bid, using concept matching to find the items that best match the bid in similarity and cost. We intend to use the context to implement what we call soft-matching (Kayed and Colomb, 1999). This fuzziness will capture the buyers' policies that will direct the agent in finding buyers' needs.

ACKNOWLEDGMENT

The authors acknowledge the Department of CSEE at the University of Queensland for financial support for this project. Also we acknowledge anonymous referees who contributed to improving the ideas and readability of this chapter.

REFERENCES

Adam, N., Dogramaci, O., Gangopadhyay, A., and Yesha, Y. (August 1998). *Electronic Commerce: Technical, Business, and Legal Issues*. Prentice Hall (ISBN: 0-13-949082-5).

Auction, O. S. (1998). *Homepage*. URL: http://www.onsale.com.

Bichler, M., Beam, C., and Segev, A. (1998). OFFER: A broker-centered object framework for electronic requisitioning. *Lecture Notes in Computer Science*, 1402, 154+.

Blomberg, P., and Lennartsson, S. (1997). *Technical Assistance in Electronic Tendering Development—FINAL REPORT.* Technical Assistance in Electronic Procurement to EDI—EEG 12 Subgroup 1. http://simaptest.infeurope.lu/EN/pub/src/main6.htm.

Bot, M. I. A. (1998). http://auction.eecs.mich.edu.

Chavez, A., and Kasbah, P. M. (1996). Kasbah: An agent marketplace for buying and selling goods. In: *The First International Conference on the Practical Application of Intelligent Agent and Multi-Agent Technology*, UK, London.

Coalition, W. M. (1996). *Reference Model and API Specification*. http://www.aiai.ed.ac.uk/WfMC.

Collins, J., Jamison, S., Gini, M., and Mobasher, B. (1997). *Temporal Strategies in a Multi-Agent Contracting Protocol.* AAAI-97 Workshop on AI in Electronic Commerce.

Collins, J., Jamison, S., Mobasher, B., and Gini, M. (1998). A market architecture for multi-agent contracting. In: *Agent98, Proceedings of the Second International Conference on Autonomous Agents*, pages 285-292, ACM.

Compranet (1999). *Mexican On-line Trading*. http://crimson.compranet.gob.mx:8081/cnetii/plsql/principal.inicio.

Consortium, C.N. (1999). *Home Page*. URL: http://www.commercenet.org.uk/.

Cutkosky, M., Fikes, R., Genesereth, M., Gruber, T., Mark, W., Tenenbaum, J., and Weber, J. (1993). *PACT: An Experiment in Integration Concurrent Engineering Systems*. http:/

/www.eit.com/creations/papers/pact/.

Dawood, N. (1996). Strategy of knowledge elicitation for developing an integrated bidding/ production management expert system for the precast industry. *Advances in Engineering Software [ADV ENG SOFTWARE]*, 25(2-3), 225-234.

Department of Defence (1994). *Costs of Tendering Industry Survey*. Australia Government Publishing Service, Canberra.

Elkan, C., and Greiner, R. (1993). Book review of building large knowledge-based systems: Representation and inference in the CYC project (D.B. Lenat and R.V. Guha). *Artificial Intelligence*, 61(1), 41-52.

Farquhar, A., Fikes, R., and Rice, J. (1997). The ontolingua server: A tool for collaborative ontology construction. *International Journal of Human-Computer Studies*, 46(6), 707-727.

Franklin, M. K., and Reiter, M. K. (1996). The design and implementation of a secure auction service. *IEEE Transactions on Software Engineering*, 22(5), 302-312.

Gabb, A. P., and Henderson, D. E. (1996). Technical and operational tender evaluations for complex military systems. *Technical Report, Department of Defence–Defence Science and Technology Organisation (DSTO)-Australia*, Rep. No. DSTO-TR-0303.

GALLEGO, I., Delgado, J., and Acebron, J. (1998). Distributed models for brokerage on electronic commerce. *Lecture Notes in Computer Science*, 1402, 130-139.

Gateway, B. (1999). *Homepage.* URL: www.businessgateway.com.

Glushko, R. J., Tenenbaum, J. M., and Meltzer, B. (1999). An XML framework for agent-based E-commerce. *Communications of the ACM*, 42(3), 106-109, 111-114.

Guttman, R. H., and Kasbah, P. M. (1998). Agent-mediated integrative negotiation for retail electronic commerce. *Knowledge Engineering Review.*

Guttman, R. H., Moukas, A. G., and Kasbah, P. M. (1998). Agent-mediated electronic commerce: A survey. *Knowledge Engineering Review.*

Hatush, Z. (1996). *PhD. Thesis: Contractor Selection Using Multi-Attribute Utility Theory.* School of Construction Management and Property, Queensland University of Technology-Australia.

Hatush, Z., and Skitmore, M. (1998). Contractor selection using multi-criteria utility theory: An additive model. *Building and Environment*, 33(2-3), 105-115.

Inc., A. T. (1999a). *Operating Resource Management System.* http://www.ariba.com/.

Inc.,C.O. (1999b). *Real-Time Electronic Online System.* http://www.commerce-one.com/.

Inc, G. E. I. S. (1999). *Trading Process Network.* http://tpn.geis.com/.

Jennings, N. R., and Wooldridge, M. (1997). *Application of Intelligent Agents.* Queen Mary and Westfield College, University of London.

Kalakota, R., and Whinston, A. B. (1996). *Frontiers of Electronic Commerce.* Addison-Wesley Publishing Company, Inc.

Kang, J-Y., and Lee, E-S. (1998). *A Negotiation Model in Electronic Commerce to Reflect Multiple Transaction Factors and Learning.* Technical Report, School of Electrical and Computer Eng., SKKU, Seoul, Korea.

Kashyap, V., and Sheth, A. P. (1996). Semantic and schematic similarities between database objects: A context-based approach. *The VLDB Journal*, 5(4), 276-304.

Kayed, A. (2000). *Homepage.* http://www.csee.uq.edu.au/~kayed/.

Kayed, A., and Colomb, R. M. (1999). Infrastructure for electronic tendering interoperability. In *The Australian Workshop on AI in Electronic Commerce,* in conjunction with the *Australian Joint Conference on Artificial Intelligence (AI'99)* Sydney, Australia, ISBN 0643065520, pages 87-102.

Keller, A. M. (1995). Smart catalogs and virtual catalogs. In: *International Conference on Frontiers of Electronic Commerce.*

Kimbrough, S. O., and Moore, S. A. (1997). On automated message processing in electronic commerce and work support systems: Speech act theory and expressive felicity. *ACM-TOIS*, 15(4), 321-367.

King, M., and Mercer, A. (1988). Recurrent competitive bidding. *European Journal of Operations Research*, 33, 2-16.

King, M., and Phythian, G. J. (1992). Developing an expert support systems for tender enquiry evaluation: A case study. *European Journal of Operations Research*, 56, 15-29.

Lee, H. G. (1997). Electronic market intermediary: Transforming technical feasibility into institutional reality. In: *Thirtieth Annual Hawaii International Conference on System Sciences*, volume IV, pages 3-12.

Lee, R. M., and Dewitz, S. D. (1992). Facilitating international contracting: AI extensions to EDI. *International Information Systems,* January.

Lim, E-P., Ng, W-K., and Yan, G. (1998). Toolkits for a distributed, agent-based Web commerce system. In: *Proceedings of the International IFIP Working Conference on Trends in Distributed Systems for Electronic Commerce (TrEC'98)*, Hamburg, Germany.

Madden, J. and Shein, E. (1998). Web purchasing attracts some pioneers. *PC Week Online,* March 16.

McAfee, R. P., and McMillan, J. (1987). Auctions and bidding. *Journal of Economic Literature*, 25, 699-738.

Merz, M., Liberman, B., Muller-Jones, K., and Lamersdorf, W. (1996). Interorganisational workflow management with mobile agents in COSM. In: *Proceedings of PAAM96 Conference on the Practical Application of Agents and Multi-agent Systems.*

Moukas, A., Guttman, R., and Maese, P. (1998). Agent-mediated electronic commerce: An mit media laboratory perspective. In: *The First International Conference on Electronic Commerce*, Seoul, Korea.

Mugnier, M. L., and Chein, M. (1993). Characterization and algorithmic recognition of canonical conceptual graphs. *Lecture Notes in Computer Science*, 699, 294+.

Mullen, T., and Wellman, M. P. (1998). The auction manager: Market middleware for large-scale electronic commerce. In: *Third USENIX Workshop on Electronic Commerce*, Boston, MA, USA.

Noriega, P. C. (1997). *PhD. Thesis: Agent Mediated Auctions: The Fishmarket Metaphor.* Universitat Autonoma de Barcelona–SPAIN.

O'Leary, D. E., Kuokka, D., and Plant, R. (1997). Artificial intelligence and virtual organizations. *Communications of the ACM*, 40(1), 52-59.

on the Web, T. (1999).Homepage. http://www.tenders.co.uk/.

Ong, K-L. and Ng, W-K. (1998). A Survey of Multi-Agent Interaction Techniques and Protocols. *Technical Report, Centre of Advanced Information Systems*, CAIS-TR04-98, School of Applied Science, Nanyang Technological University, Singapore.

Procurement, S. (1996). http://waltz.ncsl.nist.gov/ECIF/smart_procurement.html.

Projects, S. (1999). *European Online Public Procurement.* http://simaptest.infeurope.lu/EN/pub/src/welcome.htm.

Robinson, W. N. (1997). Electronic brokering for assisted contracting of software applets. In: *Thirtieth Annual Hawaii International Conference on System Sciences*, volume IV, pages 449-458.

Rodríguez-Aguilar, J. A., Martín, F. J., Noriega, P., Garcia, P., and Sierra, C. (1998).

Competitive scenarios for heterogeneous trading agents. In Sycara, K. P. and Wooldridge, M. (Eds.), *Proceedings of the 2nd International Conference on Autonomous Agents (AGENTS-98)*, pages 293-300, New York, ACM Press.

Sandholm, T. (1993). An implementation of the contract net protocol based on marginal cost calculations. In: *Eleventh National Conference on Artificial Intelligence (AAAI-93)*, pages 256-262, Washington DC.

Sandholm, T., and Lesser, V. (1995). Issues in automated negotiation and electronic commerce: Extending the contract net framework. In: *First International Conference on Multi-agent Systems*, San Francisco.

Sandholm, T. W. (1996). *PhD. Thesis: Negotiation Among Self-Interested Computationally Limited Agents*. Department of Computer Science, University of Massachusetts–Amherst.

Shein, E. (1998). Special Net delivery. *PC Week Online*, March 16.

Silberschatz, A., Stonebraker, M., and Ullman, J. (1995). Database research: Achievements and opportunities into the 21st century. *NSF Workshop on the Future of Database Systems Research.*

Slone, A. (1992). Electronic data interchange and structured message usage. *Computer Standards and Interfaces*, 14(5-6), 411-414.

Smith, H., and Poulter, K. (1999). Share the ontology in XML-based trading architectures. *Communications of the ACM*, 42(3), 110-111.

Smith, R. G. (1980). The contract net protocol: High level communication and control in a distributed problem solver. *IEEE Transaction on Computers*, C-29(12), 1104-1113.

Sowa, J. F. (1984). *Conceptual Structures: Information Processing in Minds and Machines.* Addison-Wesley, Reading, Mass.

Sowa, J. F. (1995). Syntax, semantics, and pragmatics of contexts. *Lecture Notes in Computer Science*, 954,1+

Stark, H., Stevenson, M., and Barling, B. (1997). *Online Commerce*. Ovum Ltd. UK London.

Stark, R. M., and Rothkope, M. H. (1979). Competitive bidding: A comprehensive bibliography. *Operations Research*, 27(1), 364-389.

Sun, Y., and Weld, D. S. (1995). *Automated Bargaining Agents (preliminary results).* Technical Report TR-95-01-04, University of Washington, Department of Computer Science and Engineering.

Sycara, K., Lu, J., Klusch, M., and Widoff, S. (1999). Matchmaking among heterogeneous agents on the Internet. In: *Proceedings AAAI Spring Symposium on Intelligent Agents in Cyberspace,* Stanford, USA.

Technology, E. I. (1996). *URL:*. http://www.eit.com/.

Tendering, A. (1999a). *URL:*. http://www.tendersearch.com.au/info.html.

Tendering, C. (1999b). *URL:*. http://inter.gov.nb.ca/index1.htm.

Tendering, C. (1999c). *URL:*. http://www.merx.cebra.com/.

Tendering, C. (1999d). *URL:*. http://www.bids.ca/.

Tenenbaum, J.M., Chowdhry, T. S., and Hughes, K. (1997). Eco system: An Internet commerce architecture. *Computer*, 30(5), 48-55.

Tsvetovatyy, M., Gini, M., Mobasher, B., and Wieckowski, Z. (1997). Magma: An agent-based virtual market for electronic commerce. *Journal of Applied Artificial Intelligence.*

Uschold, M., King, M., Moralee, S., and Zorgios, Y. (1998). The enterprise ontology. *The Knowledge Engineering Review*, 13(Special Issue on Putting Ontologies to Use).

Vanwelkenhuysen, J. (1998). The tender support system. *Knowledge-Based Systems*, 11, 363-372.

Vickrey, W. (1961). Counterspeculation, auctions, and competitive sealed tenders. *Journal of Finance*, 16, 8-37.

Vollrath, I., Wilke, W., and Bergmann, R. (1998). Case-based reasoning support for online catalog sales. *IEEE-Internet Computing*, pages 47-54.

Ward, S. C., and Chapman, C. B. (1988). Developing competitive bids: A framework for information processing. *Journal of Operations Research Society*, 39(2), 123-134.

Way, E. C. (1994). Conceptual graphs: Past, present, and future. In Tepfenhart, W. M., Dick, J. P., and Sowa, J. F. (Eds.), *Proceedings of the 2nd International Conference on Conceptual Structures : Current Practices*, volume 835 of *LNAI*, pages 11-30, Berlin, Springer.

Wing, H. (1998). *PhD. Thesis: Managing Complex, Open, Web-Deployable Trade Objects*. Department of Computer Science and Electrical Engineering, University of Queensland-Australia.

Wurman, P., Walsh, W., and Wellman, M. (1998a). Flexible double auctions for electronic commerce: Theory and implementation. *Decision Support Systems*, 24, 17-27.

Wurman, P. R., Wellman, M. P., and Walsh, W. E. (1998b). The Michigan Internet AuctionBot: A configurable auction server for human and software agents. In Sycara, K. P., and Wooldridge, M. (Eds.), *Proceedings of the 2nd International Conference on Autonomous Agents (AGENTS-98)*, pages 301-308, New York, ACM Press.

Chapter XIV

Component Framework Supporting Agent-Based Electronic Data Interchange

Klement J. Fellner and Klaus Turowski
Otto-von-Guericke-University
Magdeburg, Germany

In this chapter, we present an approach to a component (application) framework supporting agent-based intercompany communication and coordination. By using the extensible markup language (XML) as an important cross-section technique, together with common business communication standards, we show how the border of heterogeneous (distributed) application systems can be overcome. With this, a business communication protocol is set up. Taking this protocol as a basis, we further present a component framework, which is implemented using the JavaBeans technology to support an efficient intercompany communication. In addition, we show how this approach may further develop to a means for intercompany coordination. Thus, we come to multi-agent systems that support innovative business strategies in e-commerce settings, which rely on automatic coordination of complex business transaction within virtual enterprises.

INFORMATION INFRASTRUCTURES FOR INNOVATIVE COMPETITIVE STRATEGIES

Business processes have been stretched across organizational borders to gain competitive advantage through the combination of individual core competencies, or solely because individual organizations lack specific knowledge. Nowadays, organizations worldwide are faced with growing competitive pressure through open markets and the movement from seller markets to buyer markets. Therefore, they seek to replace their (legacy) application systems with better, network-based architectures. The constant spreading use of network technology (like the Internet) involves new possibilities and adds a new quality to inter-organizational cooperation. Companies may now cooperate not only locally, but also globally with any company offering needed assets (knowledge as well as products) at best quality and lowest costs to gain competitive advantage.

This is especially necessary when competitive strategies, like *mass customization* (Pine II, 1993) are succeeding. A network of manufacturers, suppliers, and retailers has to be established to put mass customization into action (Kotha, 1996, pp. 447-449). Mass customization enables businesses to offer individual products at prices comparable to mass production, and comparable short shipment times. Tighter integration of suppliers and the coordination of inter-organizational production processes are critical success factors for mass customization (Moad, 1995, p. 35).

In order to provide the necessary flexibility in such alliances, the partnership should be as loose as possible, i.e., it should be formed for a limited period of time and a limited product palette. From a customer's viewpoint, who buys such a product, the alliance seems to be a single company. In fact, it is a *virtual enterprise*. The concept of virtual enterprises has its origin in the idea of the *agile enterprise* (Nagel, Dove, & Preiss, 1991, pp. 8-9). It is a temporary network of independent companies or natural persons, who have the same rights and cooperatively produce a specific good or service. The collaborators particularly bring in their core competencies. Further, there is no institutionalized common management. The virtual enterprise appears to others as a single company and is coordinated using a suitable information system (Arnold, Faisst, Härtling, & Sieber, 1995, p. 10). However, it is possible that over time the virtual enterprise becomes a conventional group or fusion of companies. Especially, if it is successful with its mass customized products in the market for a longer period of time. In this case, the period in which a virtual enterprise exists is a preparation phase for establishing a steady cooperation of companies. In such cooperations, the companies are connected through conventional supplier-producer relationships. The process of changing a virtual enterprise to a steady cooperation can be incremental. It may start with a core group of the members of the virtual enterprise, which is extended by adding more members over time. This does not exclude the case that some companies stay loosely coupled, particularly, if their products or skills are only demanded sporadically.

Figure 1. Component Framework Supporting Agent-Based EDI

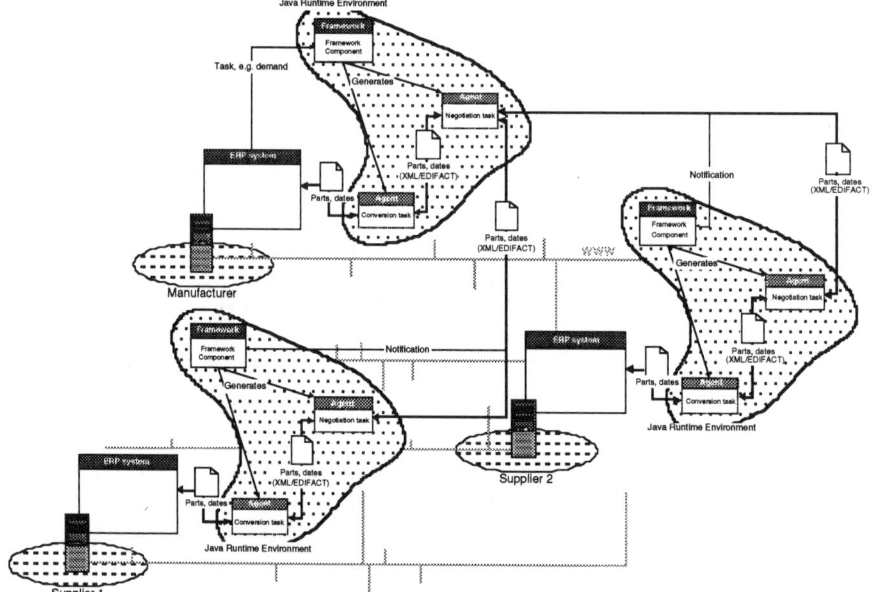

Tasks needed to support virtual enterprises like exchanging information for communication purpose or to coordinate production processes are well-suited for execution by software agents (e.g., Jennings & Wooldidge, 1998, pp. 11-15; Rautenstrauch & Turowski, 1999). Agent architectures are widely discussed since the late 1950s as a means to automate tasks. In common, a *(software) agent* is defined as an autonomous problem-solving unit that may collaborate with other agents, and that tries to achieve optimized results for a given problem area. For an in-depth discussion of software agents, we suggest Bradshaw (1997, pp. 5-11). Additionally, software agents may improve the cooperation between different systems. By providing functionality to encapsulate system-dependent implementation issues, they may also serve as mediators between systems (Bradshaw, 1997, pp. 12-14).

Figure 1 gives an overview of our approach. The scenario presented in Figure 1 consists of three actors (companies), the manufacturer and two suppliers, which form a virtual enterprise. Each company employs an information system for enterprise resource planning (ERP) and is connected to the Internet. The agents, which will be explained in detail in the following, are used to establish EDI (electronic data interchange) connections.

COMPONENT FRAMEWORK FOR INTERCOMPANY COORDINATION

Software agents themselves consist of several different elements. For the area of production planning and control (PPC), Corsten and Gössinger (1998, p. 176) identified three main parts that constitute a minimal setup for agents:

- a communication processor,
- a local knowledge base, and
- a problem solver.

Furthermore, an *ontology*, which is suitable for the application area, is needed. An ontology, as a common language, allows agents to understand each other at the semantics level. In the next section we will discuss this topic in detail.

Implemented in a certain way, those kinds of agents serve as a basis for automating major parts of intercompany business processes. They are well suited to coordinate the production of individualized products in the early phases of negotiation between manufacturer and suppliers. Taking these parts, a core *component model* of an agent-based coordination system can be derived (cf. Figure 2). Possible software components are conversion agent, negotiation agent, communication processor, problem solver, and knowledge base. In our approach components are the software units that implement parts of a software agent. The software agent on its own is therefore a software component made up of other components.

We use the *Unified Modeling Language* (UML) (Rational Software et al., 1997) to model components and their relationships (e.g., Figure 2). Although, our approach does not rely on any specific modeling language, we used UML because of its role of a standard modeling language for object-oriented systems. Definitions of what exactly constitutes a component vary in the literature. For an overview of definitions, we refer to Szyperski (1998, p 164-168). In common, *software components* are mostly understood as self-contained units with contractually specified interfaces and functionality. They may be sold independently, and composed by third parties (e.g., to form new application systems) in combinations not assumed by the component's manufacturer.

According to Figure 2, we distinguish between two kinds of agents:

- Agents that fulfill a conversion task (conversion agents), and
- agents that fulfill a negotiation (negotiation agents) task.

Figure 2. Core Component Model for an Agent-Based Coordination System

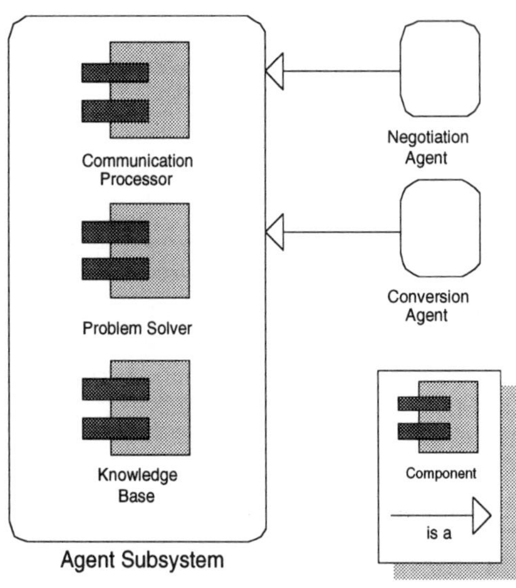

Conversion agents translate (business) data into languages that are understood by the respective application systems (mostly off-the-shelf ERP systems) of the virtual enterprise's participants. *Negotiation agents* are used to coordinate the production of goods and services themselves.

In general, two conversion agents must exist in a given system configuration to establish a connection to an ERP system: one for each direction of the transformation. Both, of course, may use the same knowledge base for matching the different business terms.

Because a company usually employs several kinds of negotiation protocols (e.g., auction-based, contract-based, or combined forms), also several negotiation agents must be implemented. However, the negotiation agents mainly differ in employing different kinds of problem solvers. Following our component model, these components are easily exchangeable, too.

The communication processor in this model is responsible for the local as well as the remote communication between agents. This component is identical in every agent of a given system implementation. In contrast, the implementation of the problem solver and the knowledge base is different in each class of agents. The problem solver of a negotiation agent consists of rules how a negotiation has to be carried out, whereas the same component of the conversion agent needs to know how to transform application-specific data into an application-independent exchange format and vice versa.

The contents of the knowledge base may also vary between different agent implementations. A conversion agent for example may use the knowledge base as a thesaurus of terms and their definitions. Hence, the knowledge base of negotiation agents consists of information regarding business partners, shipment terms, and conditions.

Apparently, there are several parts of the model, which may be reused extensively. To support reuse we followed-up an implementation as independent software components.

Software components normally contain domain-specific functions. Application systems made up of software components therefore need an additional cross-domain component, which enables coordination at the technical *and* the business level. A *component (application) framework* encapsulates the services and tasks mentioned. A component application framework may even encompass major parts of the application itself, e.g., San Francisco from IBM. Furthermore, a component framework itself may be implemented as a component. According to Szyperski (1998, p. 275), we call a component framework a component.

We propose the component architecture given in Figure 3 to solve the mentioned problems of intercompany coordination, and define the component implementing the component framework as *"framework component."* The framework component together with the respective agent components constitutes the proposed *component application framework.*

The *agent factory* within the framework component creates suitable negotiation and conversion agents for every new negotiation process depending on business rules for a concrete object of negotiation. The implementation of the respective components as well as the implementation of the agents will be discussed later.

Figure 3. Framework Component

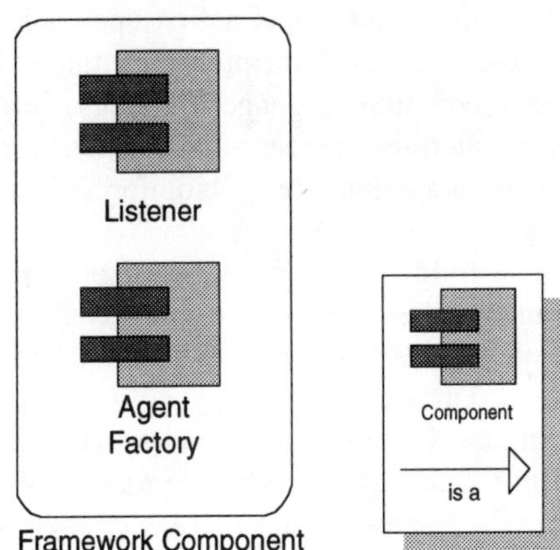

INTER-COMPANY EXCHANGE OF BUSINESS DATA

To establish and improve communication between manufacturer and supplier in a mass customization scenario, the implementation of EDI is necessary. The implementation of EDI additionally leads to organizational information-based surplus values (cf., Kuhlen, 1996, p. 90), e.g., an improved organizational as well as operational structure or time and cost savings. The most important standard for inter-organizational data exchange was established by the United Nations — the UN/EDIFACT (Electronic Data Interchange for Administration, Commerce, and Transport) (UN, 1995). However, the standard did not get the expected recognition and implementation extent because of fundamental drawbacks (cf., Zbornik, 1996, pp. 92-93; Goldfarb & Prescod, 1998, pp. 106-110):

- Absence of semantic rules (e.g., for quantity or packaging units).
- The implicit assumption that every organization implements the same business processes and scenarios.
- Economic shortcomings (e.g., high implementation costs).
- Organizational shortcomings (e.g., slow adoption to changing business processes complicates adjustment of established business process and rules).

On the one hand, there are several ongoing efforts to establish uniform business scenarios and semantic rules (cf., TMWG, 1998; Harvey et al., 1998, pp. 25-26; Steel, 1997). The XML/EDI-Initiative on the other hand concentrates on the economical and organizational drawbacks of the standard using XML (cf., Bray, Paoli, & Sperberg-McQueen, 1997) to lower the implementation costs and increase its flexibility. XML, like HTML (HyperText Markup Language), is based on the SGML (Standardized Generalized Markup Language) standard. In contrast to HTML, XML provides the possibility to define new tokens (tags) as well as user-defined document structures through *Document Type Definitions* (DTDs). DTDs describe the syntax of a certain data token. XML/EDI, as a way to utilize XML for inter-organizational communication, is based on well-known EDI standards, like UN/EDIFACT, templates representing organization-specific business rules, and DTDs.

Further on, we utilize XML/EDI, respectively the persistent use of XML for inter-organizational data exchange using the outlined agents to improve inter-organizational communication. As a first approach, we use UN/EDIFACT segment names as standardized field descriptors for the multi-agent system. These segment names present a common language (ontology) in our approach on bridging the gap between different interface languages of business application systems. When employing our approach in other fields (e.g., bioinformatics) a commonly recognized ontology must be employed.

The following explanation of our approach is based on the message exchange diagram in Figure 4. To keep it manageable, we restrict our example to one supplier. For an in-depth explanation of its connection to mass customization and the multi-agent system itself, see Turowski (1999).

Figure 4 shows the software agents used by the manufacturer and the supplier, the application system (ERP system), as well as the message exchange between these units. Figures 5 to 8 show the different agents at a more detailed level. Here the messages are given as function calls to the respective software agent. To keep the diagrams readable, the whole procurement process is divided into the subprocesses: *quote initiation* (Figure 5), *request for quote* (Figure 6), *quote* (Figure 7), and *order processing* (Figure 8).

Manufacturers as well as suppliers use an ERP system that provides at least a proprietary interface for exporting and importing data in a nonstandard format. After

Figure 4. Message Exchange for Procurement

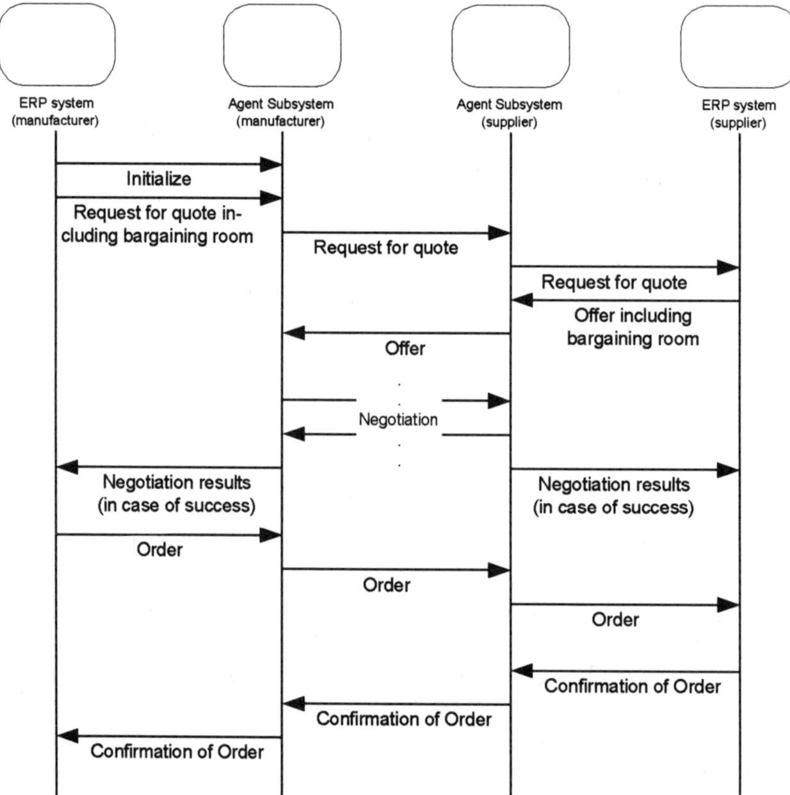

product configuration, the parts for procurement are determined and bought from suitable suppliers. The manufacturer's ERP system therefore generates the necessary inquiries. Ideally, these reports are forwarded automatically to all suitable suppliers using EDI. Utilizing our approach, the output of the ERP system (the inquiry) is transferred via the communication agent (Figure 5, messageIn (Initdemand)) to a conversion agent. In our approach the communication agent is responsible for selecting the appropriate communication protocols as well as establishing the communication channels between the different agents. Because the setup is different for each subprocess, this is done within the methods setup Requote, setup Quote, setup Negotiation, and setup Orders. The setup Requote method, for example, is also responsible for gathering suitable suppliers. The XML output then is transferred to the supplier using standard Internet protocols (such as, TCP/IP). The software agent at the supplier side transforms the inquiry into the format required by the supplier's ERP system (Figure 6). The software agent matches the content of the XML document with the arguments needed by the ERP system using the standardized XML-tags, which categorize every transferred information.

Next, the inquiry is processed by the ERP system resulting in a probably automatically generated offer, which is transferred to the manufacturer (the agent) using the same mechanism as described above.

Besides the described simple communication process between manufacturer and supplier, more complex coordination processes including additional subprocesses may occur. The above simple process assumes that conditions, like date of shipment, quantity, deadlines, or prices, are fixed for all participating parties. In real-world processes, these conditions are most likely subjects of negotiations. To include and automate these negotiation processes, we use the negotiation agent (cf. Figure 7). Objects of the negotiation process are parts that have to be produced in order to assemble a customer individual product. Negotiation agents do not need to know much about these objects. Only identification parameters and certain constraints, e.g., due dates or quantities are passed over. This information is created by the conversion agents based on the data given by the respective ERP system. Consequently, the negotiation agent returns the conditions on which one or more suppliers agreed to deliver.

Strictly speaking, the manufacturer generates an additional inquiry with negotiation ranges for several conditions, like price, date of shipment, etc. After the *inquiry for negotiation* is parsed by the conversion agent, the output is used to initiate the negotiation agent. On the supplier-side, an offer is generated matching the inquiry. When receiving an

Figure 5. Detailed Message Exchange for Request for Quote Initiation *(Manufacturer Side)*

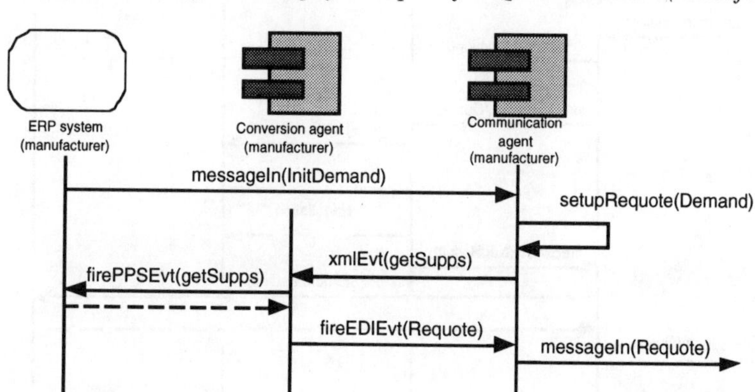

Figure 6. Detailed Message Exchange for Request for Quote *(Supplier Side)*

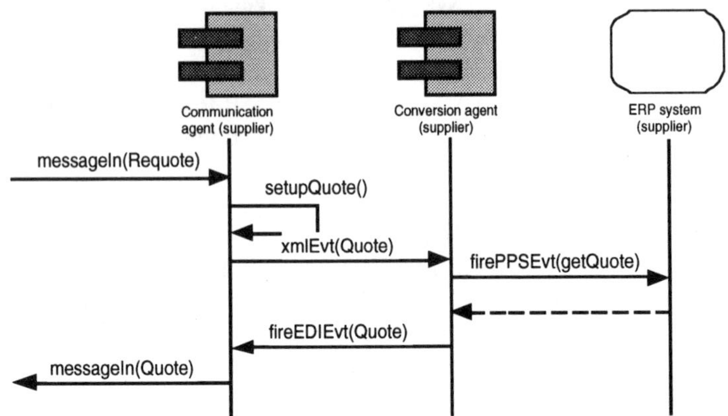

offer, the manufacturer-side negotiation agent extracts all relevant (negotiable) information and generates a counteroffer, accepts the offer, or aborts the negotiation process. The routing and the necessary conversion for this process are done by the conversion agents. After termination of the negotiation process, the negotiation result is transformed by the corresponding conversion agent and transferred to the ERP system, which generates an order, based on the negotiated offer (Figure 8).

In the case that all conditions are negotiated and corresponding orders are triggered, the same multi-agent system can be used to coordinate the production process, e.g., adjustment of production plans in case of failure. The system that failed to meet the agreed conditions creates a suitable software agent to negotiate any changes. The opposite side, of course, has to implement a corresponding software agent for negotiation.

The negotiation agents in the presented scenario all use the same software components for inter-organizational communication. This allows the reuse of appropriately implemented agents for similar tasks in different processes.

Figure 7. Detailed Message Exchange for Quote *(Manufacturer Side)*

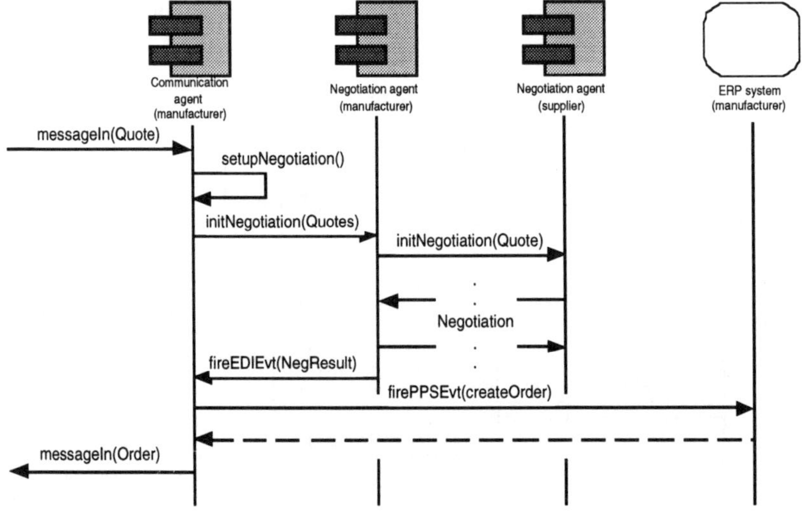

The component framework must be applicable in configurations with almost any existing ERP system as well as negotiation method. To avoid repeated implementations of the mentioned components, the framework component that implements the framework has to provide some kind of a *factory* (Gamma, Helm, Johnson, & Vlissides, 1997, pp. 115-125) for application-specific components. The factory component ("Agent factory" in Figure 3) is therefore responsible for creating the right negotiation and conversion agents (e.g., "conversion agent ").

IMPLEMENTATION ASPECTS

So far, the implementation of agents took place in special-purpose programming languages and environments, therefore resulting in proprietary systems (Bradshaw, 1997, pp. 377-378) (for an overview of programming software agents cf. Shoham, 1997). In case of production processes involving multiple suppliers, like mass customization, systems of the manufacturer have to communicate with systems from different suppliers, which are often unknown at implementation time. Therefore, an *open* implementation of agents is necessary.

Consistently, we propose a component-orientated implementation of agents that communicate with each other using open protocols (like TCP/IP). When software parts are implemented as components, which are applicable in different application areas, like the communication component, they may be reused extensively, thus, cutting down implementation costs.

All agents are implemented as Java (Sun Microsystems, 1998) applications, therefore requiring the existence of a Java Runtime Environment (JRE). Above all advantages (e.g., object-orientation or platform-independence), Java comprises a component model—the *JavaBeans* (Sun Microsystems, 1997)—providing the features for a straightforward implementation of the presented approach. JavaBeans are by definition implementations of self-contained components (cf., Englander, 1997), i.e., a single component can be distributed and used alone as well as in combination with others. In addition, the needed functionality to implement inter-agent-communication is part of the standard Java API (java.net) (cf., Sun Microsystems, 1998).

Figure 8. Detailed Message Exchange for Order Processing (Supplier Side)

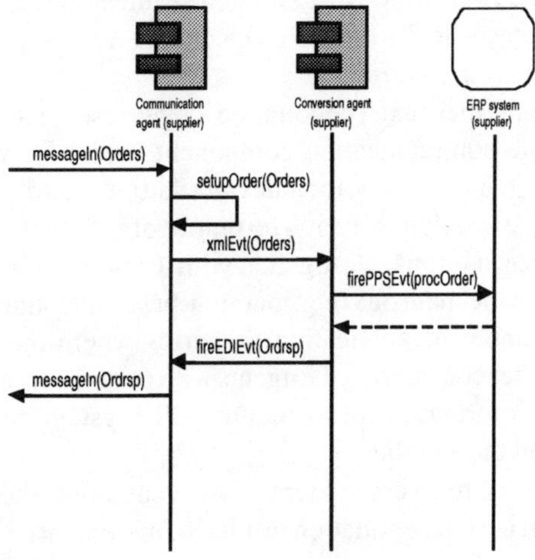

Following our approach, we implemented each agent as a stand-alone component (JavaBean) consisting of several JavaBeans: the communication bean, the problem-solving bean and the knowledge base bean (cp. Fig. 1). This allows extensive reuse of different components. The negotiation part (problem solver), for example, was reused in conjunction with a different knowledge base as well as a different communication bean. They only have to provide the information that the negotiation agent needs for the calculation. On the other hand, the knowledge base and the communication bean may be reused in a configuration using a different kind of negotiation.

The factory itself is implemented as a JavaBean following the factory method presented in Gamma et al. (1997, pp. 115-125). Based on provided parameters (e.g., by the application system or the end-user) and the information in the knowledge base, the matching conversion and negotiation beans are chosen.

The software framework component serves as the coordinating unit, responsible for initialization and creation of other agents as required by the application scenario. Hence, different negotiation processes or conversion tasks can run parallel to each other. Whereas the framework component and the negotiation agent may be reused in different system environments without any change, the conversion agent has to be adapted for every new application system (e.g., ERP system). As mentioned, the application system (ERP system) has to provide an interface, with a disclosed input and output format. The complexity of the conversion agent depends solely on the application system interface. A simple conversion agent, for example, parses a text-file generated by the application system and adds the corresponding XML-tags to the detected data fields. A more complex agent can access the information directly using remote function calls (RFCs) in the application system. Additionally, the conversion agent that transforms the data fields from XML to an application-specific format has to be adapted. Since several XML-parsers are available for free (e.g., XML4Java from IBM or XMLParser from Sun), the remaining effort to adapt this parser is low.

To show the integration of a real-world application system, we used SAP R/3 to demonstrate the conversion agent. Using the Business Application Programming Interface (BAPI) of R/3 (cf., SAP, 1997) it is possible to read from and write to the SAP system. As we used Java, we needed a bridge between our components and the SAP system. The InfoBus technology from Lotus/IBM, available from Sun Microsystems (1999), and the Enterprise Access Builder (EAB) for SAP R/3 included with IBM VisualAge for Java, were therefore used. Especially, the EAB from IBM allows a seamless integration of enterprise data into Java applications, because EAB BAPI objects are accessible as standard Java objects and can be encapsulated in JavaBeans.

Besides conversion agents, there exist negotiation agents responsible for the execution of negotiation processes. The communication component, which is responsible for the communication between negotiation agents, includes an additional XML-Parser to interpret the received documents for the problem solver. The output of the XML-parser depends on the used problem solver. Hence, it is reusable together with the problem solver. The problem solver implements negotiation mechanisms (e.g., auction-based negotiation). The extent of its reuse depends on the number of application scenarios where the same negotiation mechanism can be applied. After configuring the agents with organization-specific information and the adaptation to the information infrastructure (ERP system, etc.), they are usable for both the manufacturer and the supplier.

The knowledge base, as the third component of an agent, holds the specifications for ERP systems as well as all carried out negotiation results. It implements the methods *setERP* and *getERP*, which are responsible for delivering the target values to and from given ERP systems (e.g., *setSAP* and *getSAP)*. The methods *addOffer, searchOffer,* and *getOffer* are used to manage saved offers. If a new offer arrives, it is stored in the knowledge base. The negotiation component may search and classify *(classifyOffer)* offers stored in the knowledge base.

Below, a simple method to perform the search for the best offer is shown. As a starting point, the best offer is calculated using linear scalar transformation. The offers are therefore scaled between 0 and 1 (worst to best) based on the satisfaction of a priori—defined goals. The results are then weighed according to the importance of the goal. This method is implemented as a stand-alone component that is used by the negotiation agent in conjunction with the knowledge base to gather the best offer.

The negotiation component therefore implements two central methods: *getOptimum* and *setOptimum.* The method *getOptimum* is responsible for collecting the offers for a given inquiry from the knowledge base and finding the best one. When the best one is identified, it is marked in the knowledge base using *setOptimum.* It is possible to customize *getOptimum* to collect counteroffers, which leads to a restart of the process with new parameters.

The negotiation process stops when the parties (agents) reach an agreement or no acceptable offer arrives within a given period of time.

The information exchange between the agents is carried out by the communication agents. The problem solver of these agents comprises two beans, the COMManager and the ServiceAPManager. Whereas the COMManager manages and loads the necessary protocol components at run-time, the ServiceAPManager is responsible for negotiating the concrete communication path in a specific scenario. The ServiceAPManager therefore implements the XML/ServiceAP (XML Service Advertising Protocol), which is used to store and transfer information on supported communication protocols. The XML/ServiceAP messages are based on the UN/EDIFACT messages for request for quote (REQUOTE) and quote (QUOTE). Figure 9 shows the quote message a communication initiator receives after a request for quote. For all protocols that are implemented by the receiver, it contains the necessary information enclosed within the PROTOCOL tags, e.g., the IP-address and the port for the TCP connection. The CAPTION attribute is used to identify the protocols, e.g., JCE, TCP, RMI in the given example.

At run-time the ServiceAPManager gathers information from a remote ServiceAPManager (e.g., at the supplier-side) on possible communication protocols. This allows agent systems to choose a different channel every time they establish a communication. Especially, when sending corporate data over the Internet, it is essential to provide secure channels. In a given scenario a manufacturer may only accept encrypted offers (e.g., with RSA). The manufacturers' ServiceAPManager will then send the ServiceAPManager of the supplier the public key, which is used by the suppliers agent system to encrypt the message. Additionally, secure socket layers (SSLs) may be used to transfer this information. Here, a huge number of scenarios are imaginable. The different protocol components (TCP, Java Security, Internet Inter-ORB Protocol (IIOP), etc.) are loaded at run-time from a given server—which in turn may be secured—by the COMMAnager. The COMManager is set up by a configuration file in XML, containing information about each possible protocol component as well as information on the current negotiation process. A sample configuration file is given in Figure 10. The protocol components are defined in the COMCOMPONENT section (a). In the sample file only TCP connections are possible. Besides the caption, information on the classes which must be loaded (CLASS), the initial communication port (VALUE), as well as the type (TYPE) are set. As there may be more than one protocol

Figure 9. Sample XML/ServiceAP Message

```
<?xml version='1.0' ?>
  <SAP CLIENT='HERSTELLER'>
    <PROTOCOL CAPTION='JCE'>
         JCE://192.168.0.2:7002?PUBLICKEY=b0011cb08d86
         89aa06c806778d81818185808®3010a80b0010682010
         ...
         +ALGO=RSA+AMP=RSA/ECB/PKCS1Padding
    </PROTOCOL>

    <PROTOCOL CAPTION='TCP'>
         TCP://192.168.0.2:7001
    </PROTOCOL>

    <PROTOCOL CAPTION='RMI'>
         rmi://marcelpc:1100/rmiserver0
    </PROTOCOL>
  </SAP>
```

component, there may be more than one COMCOMPONENT section. This holds also for the next sections. The current negotiation information are subsumed in sections (b) to (d). Sections (b) and (c) contain information about the manufacturer and the suppliers, respectively. The last section (d) in the sample file contains the product information. This information, together with the company information, is used by the negotiation agents. After the initialization phase, the corresponding negotiation and conversion agents are set up according to the information provided.

The information itself is passed as an object to the conversion agent, which transforms the XML–based data into the specific format of the application system.

Allowing an easy way to compose applications visually, *IBM VisualAge for Java* is used to implement the prototype components. In fact, JavaBeans may be implemented in every other bean container, whereas a bean container is defined as a visual design environment, which uses a set of standard interfaces provided by the components through introspection.

OUTLOOK AND CONCLUSIONS

We introduced a component framework for a multi-agent-based architecture to support intercompany integration. Where available, we use public standards (like HTML, XML, etc.) or open industry standards (like Java) to implement our approach. Furthermore, we concentrate on the reuse of essential software components. We achieve a high degree of platform independence using Java as implementation language, therefore allowing organizations to adapt the components fast and at low implementation costs. In addition to the support of inter-organizational communication processes, the introduced approach also allows the support of nearly all kinds of procurement processes as well as inter-organizational coordination of production processes using the same information infrastructure. Another advantage is the possible implementation of the concepts and techniques step by step. For example a three-step approach may be followed: starting with conversion agents to support only the transfer of information (1), followed by a multi-agent system including the negotiation (2), and last, a multi-agent system to coordinate an inter-organizational production process (3).

However, we need some kind of common term set, upon which participating companies have to agree. Furthermore, participating companies need to customize conversion agents in order to automate communication from and to their respective ERP systems.

Due to its highly distributed character, our approach promises to be highly scalable, since agents may be placed at any suitable servers. Limiting factors are mainly bandwidth in general and the responsiveness of ERP systems.

Besides an improved treatment of the problems mentioned above, future enhancements will include the support of run-time selection of negotiation algorithms, the coordination of

Figure 10. Part of Initialization File for Supplier-Side Agent System

```
<INIT>
        <! Information for the ServiceAPManager !>
        <SAPAGENT CAPTION="SAP-AGENT" ID="MANUFACTURER">
                ....
        </SAPAGENT>
        <COMCOMPONENT>
(a)             <PROTOCOL CAPTION="TCPComponent1"
                        CLASS="de.unimd.wi.pps.agents.com.tcp.TCPComponent"
                        VALUE="6001"
                        TYPE="BASE" />
        </COMCOMPONENT>
        <PPCDATA>
         <AGENT MYSAPIP="localhost" MYSAPPORT="6000" IP="localhost" />
                <COMPANY TYPE="BY">
                        <SAPAGENT IP="localhost" PORT="6000" />
(b)                     Information about the Manufacturer
                        ...
                </COMPANY>
                <COMPANY TYPE="SU">
(c)                     <SAPAGENT IP="localhost" PORT="8000" />
                        Information about the Supplier
                </COMPANY>
                <PRODUCT>
                        <EARLIESTDATE>19990301</EARLIESTDATE>
(d)                     <LATESTDATE>19990401</LATESTDATE>
                        <AMOUNT>1</AMOUNT>
                        <ID>P-100</ID>
                        <CAPTION>Pumpe xyz</CAPTION>
                        <HIGHESTPRICE>100</HIGHESTPRICE>
                        <MARKETPRICE>75</MARKETPRICE>
                </PRODUCT>
        </PPCDATA>
</INIT>
```

production processes between manufacturer and suppliers, and the treatment of security aspects, e.g., cryptographic methods to ensure confidentiality of content, or certificates and digital signatures to force authentication security (Minoli & Minoli, 1998).

REFERENCES

Arnold, O., Faisst, W., Härtling, M., & Sieber, P. (1995). Virtuelle unternehmen als unternehmenstyp der zunkunft? *HMD, 32*(185), 8-23.

Bradshaw, J. M. (1997). An introduction to software agents. In J. M. Bradshaw (Ed.), *Software Agents* (pp. 3-46). Menlo Park: AAAI Press.

Bray, T., Paoli, J., & Sperberg-McQueen, C. M. (1997). *Extensible Markup Language (XML)*. Available: http://www.w3.org/TR/PR-xml.html [1998, 06-12].

Corsten, H., & Gössinger, R. (1998). Produktionsplanung und -steuerung auf Grundlage von Multiagentensystemen. In H. Corsten & R. Gössinger (Eds.), *Dezentrale Produktionsplanungs- und -steuerungs-Systeme: Eine Einführung in zehn Lektionen* (pp. 174-207). Stuttgart: Kohlhammer.

Englander, R. (1997). *Developing Java Beans*. Cambridge: O'Reilly.

Gamma, E., Helm, R., Johnson, R., & Vlissides, J. (1997). *Entwurfsmuster: Elemente Wiederverwendbarer Objektorientierter Software*. Bonn: Addison-Wesley.

Goldfarb, C. F., & Prescod, P. (1998). *The XML Handbook*. Upper Saddle River: Prentice-Hall.

Harvey, B., Hill, D., Schuldt, R., Bryan, M., Thayer, W., Raman, D., & Webber, D. (1998). *Position Statement on Global Repositories for XML*. Available: ftp://www.eccnet.com/pub/xmledi/repos710.zip [1998, 12-01].

Jennings, N. R., & Wooldidge, M. J. (1998). Applications of intelligent agents. In N. R. Jennings & M. J. Wooldidge (Eds.), *Agent Technology: Foundations, Applications, and Markets.*

Berlin: Springer.

Kotha, S. (1996). From Mass Production to Mass Customization: The Case of the National Industrial Bicycle Company of Japan. *European Management Journal, 14*(5), *442-450.*

Kuhlen, R. (1996). *Informationsmarkt: Chancen und Risiken der Kommerzialisierung von Wissen.* (2nd ed.). Konstanz: Universitätsverlag Konstanz.

Minoli, D., & Minoli, E. (1998). *Web Commerce Technology Handbook.* New York: McGraw-Hill.

Moad, J. (1995). Let customers have it their way. *Datamation, 41*(6), 34-39.

Nagel, R., Dove, R., & Preiss, K. (1991). *21st Century Manufacturing Enterprise Strategy—an Industry led View.* (Vol. 1). Bethlehem, PA: Iacocca Institute, Lehigh University.

Pine II, J. B. (1993). *Mass Customization: The New Frontier in Business Competition.* Boston: Harvard Business School Press.

Rational Software, Microsoft, Hewlett-Packard, Oracle, Sterling Software, MCI Systemhouse, Unisys, ICON Computing, IntelliCorp, i-Logix, IBM, ObjecTime, Platinum Technology, Ptech, Taskon, Reich Technologies, & Softeam. (1997). *UML Notation Guide: Version 1.1, 1 September 1997.* Available: http://www.rational.com/uml [1999, 04-17].

Rautenstrauch, C., & Turowski, K. (1999). *A Virtual Enterprise Model for Mass Customization.* Paper presented at the Second World Manufacturing Congress (WMC'99), International Symposium on Manufacturing Systems (ISMS'99), Durham.

SAP. (1997). *BAPI Catalog.* Available: http://www.sap.com/bfw/interf/bapis/preview/catalog/index.htm [1997, 11-04].

Shoham, Y. (1997). An Overview of Agent-Oriented Programming. In J. M. Bradshaw (Ed.), *Software Agents* (pp. 272-290). Seattle: AAAI Press/The MIT Press.

Steel, K. (1997). *The Beacon User's Guide: Open Standards for Business Systems.* Available: http://www.cs.mu.oz.au/research/icaris/beaug1.doc [1998, 12-01].

Sun Microsystems (Ed.). (1997). *JavaBeans: JavaBeans API Specification 1.01.* Mountain View: Sun Microsystems.

Sun Microsystems (Ed.). (1998). *JDK 1.1.6 Documentation—Java Development Kit.* Mountain View: Sun Microsystems.

Sun Microsystems (Ed.). (1999). *InfoBus 1.2 Specification.* Mountain View: Sun Microsystems.

Szyperski, C. (1998). *Component Software: Beyond Object-Oriented Programming.* (2 ed.). Harlow: Addison-Wesley.

TMWG. (1998). *Reference Guide: The Next Generation of UN/EDIFACT: An Open- EDI Approach Using UML Models & OOT (Revision 12).* Available: http://www.harbinger.com/resource/klaus/tmwg/TM010R1.PDF [1998, 12-01].

Turowski, K. (1999). A virtual electronic call center solution for mass customization. Paper presented at the *Proceedings of the 32nd Annual Hawaii International Conference On System Sciences, Maui, Hawaii.*

UN. (1995). *United Nations Directories for Electronic Data Interchange for Administration, Commerce, and Transport.* Available: http://www.unece.org/trade/untdid/Welcome.html [1998, 12-01].

Zbornik, S. (1996). *Elektronische Märkte, elektronische Hierarchien und elektronische Netzwerke: Koordination des wirtschaftlichen Leistungsaustausches durch Mehrwertdienste auf der Basis von EDI und offenen Kommunikationssystemen, diskutiert am Beispiel der Elektronikindustrie.* Konstanz: Universitätsverlag Konstanz.

Chapter XV

An Enterprise Viewpoint of Wireless Virtual Communities and the Associated Uses of Software Agents

Seng Wai Loke
DSTC, Australia

Andry Rakotonirainy
DSTC, Australia

Arkady Zaslavsky
Monash University, Australia

We envision the integration of the concepts of virtual communities, electronic markets, and ubiquitous wireless services into agent-enhanced mobile virtual communities which we call AMV-communities, a set of which form the AMV-community-space. We present concepts for an AMV-community modelled with RM-ODP Enterprise Viewpoint concepts, and outline an architecture of AMV-communities using software agents attached to roles. We also illustrate how we cope with disconnected computing by using agents and meta-policy rules.

INTRODUCTION

This is the age of virtual communities, electronic markets, and mobile computing. A virtual community (Rheingold, 1993) is a conceptual space enabling sustained interactions among people across geographical boundaries. A member of a virtual community cannot only utilize services provided by that community but also contribute content and services to that community. While many virtual communities are global, transcending geographical boundaries, geographically based virtual communities have also emerged, often called wired neighborhoods (Doheny-Farina, 1998), which focus on the interests of a physical community.

Emerging are also the concepts of electronic marketplaces such as enablers of customer-to-business and business-to-business electronic commerce (e.g., NetAcademy Team, 2000; Rachlevsky-Reich, 1999; Sandholm, 1999). Electronic auction houses (e.g., Amazon, 2000; eBay, 2000; Sandholm, 1999) are extremely popular, and there are numerous Web-based shopping malls. In Hagel and Armstrong (1997), the concepts of virtual community and electronic marketplace are married. Virtual communities form a space not only for discussions and information sharing but also functions as a place for commerce. Virtual communities become a means of maintaining relationships among buyers and sellers. One usually participates in several of such global virtual communities, wired neighborhoods, and electronic markets which then become sources of services. Indeed, some business Web sites are moving from simply selling items to building communities. For example, www.amazon.com lets surfers input their reviews on books.

Such virtual communities and electronic marketplaces are growing and new ones emerging, but mainly over wired networks. Wireless computing is the emerging technology wave enabling mobility, and connectivity where laying cables is difficult or impossible. There has been a frenzy of research from both academia and industry towards anytime and anywhere mobile access to information and computational support (for example, see http://www.acm.org/sigmobile). We are seeing rapid developments in the variety and functionality of mobile computers, including smartphones, communicators, palm-sized PCs, handheld PCs, mini-notebooks, notebooks, and laptops, in wide-area wireless networks such as GSM, GPRS, PHS, and UMTS, and in wireless (and some ad-hoc) LANs (e.g., WaveLAN, MobileNet, Bluetooth: http://www.bluetooth.com). Commercial wireless portals are being created to provide information services to networked mobile computers (e.g., MSN Mobile: http://www.mobile.msn.com/), Palm's Web clips: http://www.palm.net/, and Lucent's Zingo: http://www.zingo.com/). Such portals (wired and wireless) provide a mixture of information (e.g., stock prices, weather reports, music, discussion lists) and can be viewed as congregation points for virtual communities.

With ubiquitous computing and networking, we could see wireless LANs and WANs of varying granularities connecting not only computers but computer-controlled networked appliances and embedded systems such as toasters, refrigerators, dog collars, and wearable computers (http://www.wearablecomputing.com/). We will see the car's wireless LAN, the home's wireless LAN, the office's wireless LAN, and beyond Internet cafes, restaurants could be offering network services via their wireless LANs. The shopping center in which the restaurant resides could offer their wireless information services. In addition, Bluetooth networking enables ad hoc wireless networks to be formed just when several mobile devices are close enough to each other. Such LANs become a means to connect to wired neighborhoods, global virtual communities, and electronic marketplaces.

What we envision is the integration of the concepts of virtual communities, electronic marketplaces, and ubiquitous wireless services into mobile virtual communities which goes beyond the current ideas of wireless portals providing information. Such mobile virtual communities will also permit interaction with other community members and member-generated content as in virtual communities, and the creation of subcommunities representing electronic marketplaces. These mobile virtual communities can be of varying granularities reflecting the geographical granularities of the wireless networks, but could also be global (as much as the Internet is global) and could be linked or interrelated. For example, subcommunities of short lifetimes could exist (e.g., electronic auctions) involving mobile device users.

Parallel to the above developments is the rapidly developing area of software agents (Jennings et al., 1998). A software agent is a software entity which can act on behalf of a person or another software entity and has behavior which can be described as persistent, communicative, autonomous, proactive, reactive, deliberative, and even possibly mobile (i.e., they can migrate from one computer to another). It is our view that software agents will play an important role in realizing such mobile virtual communities due to the following reasons:

- We envision a proliferation of services and information a user could utilize or provide within just one community and the proliferation of communities themselves. In a similar way as how intelligent software assistants are being used to search and manage information on the World Wide Web, software assistants have been explored (and will increasingly so) for coping with this abundance of services and communities, such as for automating tasks in communityware (Hattori et al., 1999; Stathis et al., 1999) and electronic marketplaces (e.g., automating electronic commerce such as advertising, brokering, and negotiation [Guttman et al., 1998]).
- Open distributed systems are growing and becoming more and more difficult to manage. Centralized management has been proven not to be scalable. Agents provide a means of decentralized and distributed locality-based management. Each agent with delegated authority can make local management decisions and contact higher management only when necessary.
- Agents especially with the property of mobility provides a convenient means of providing services to mobile computer users (e.g., Gray et al., 1996; Jacobsen and Johansen, 1997; Kovacs et al., 1998; Sahai and Morin, 1998; Villate et al., 1998). The agents can be launched from mobile computers into a community and continue to work on behalf of the user while the mobile computer is disconnected. Also, agents can be a means of moving computation from resource (e.g., memory, CPU, connectivity, and available applications) poor devices to other hosts which have the required resources. Sometimes, moving computation to data is more efficient than transferring huge amounts of data (Ismail and Hagimont, 1999). Mobile code (and not just agents) is itself a useful means for extending applications or client-side services on-the-fly (Queloz and Villazon, 1999) or obtaining applications only when needed (e.g., in software-on-demand [Kortuem et al., 1997]).

Based on the notion of agent-enhanced mobile virtual communities, this paper proposes a type of community which we call *AMV-communities*, a set of which form what we call the *AMV-community-space*, and outlines the use of the agent abstraction for software realizing such communities. This work is a step towards our broader objective of simplifying the creation of such AMV-communities by providing appropriate AMV-community middleware. We would like to be able to rapidly create an AMV-community-space by customizing or extending this middleware.

Our approach is to exploit concepts from the Enterprise Language of the Reference Model for Open Distributed Processing (RM-ODP) (ISO/IEC JTC1/SC7, 1999) to describe AMV-communities. An enterprise in that model is a community of objects (people, computers, or combinations thereof) formed for a specific objective. We use concepts from the RM-ODP Enterprise Viewpoint such as relationships between communities, roles and policies to structure the AMV-community, and the AMV-community-space. Although the RM-ODP Enterprise Viewpoint is intended as a specification language, we aim to provide a computational interpretation of models expressed using this

Viewpoint by mapping the Viewpoint concepts to software abstractions.

The software agent is an abstraction we are investigating for software components in AMV-communities. We use a CORBA (OMG, 1999) based component model to describe services of agents. We also sketch a software system which we call an *AMV-community-space browser* for users to interact with the community-space and with agents.

We first provide background on the RM-ODP Enterprise Viewpoint, mobile computing issues, and a component model in the next section. Then, we describe the concept of the AMV-community-space. Thereafter, we discuss the uses of agents for realizing AMV-communities and conclude.

BACKGROUND

RM-ODP Enterprise Viewpoint Concepts

An enterprise specification defines the purpose, scope, and policies of an ODP system in terms of **roles** played by the system, activities undertaken by the system, and **policy** statements about the system. The community is the central concept in the RM-ODP Enterprise model (ISO/IEC JTC1/SC7, 1999). A community is a composition of roles formed to meet an **objective**. Three main stages of a community's lifecycle are creation, use, and dissolution. The establishment of a community is by a contract (set of policies) between parties (enterprise objects), each party assigned to some role. Communities can be related by sharing of objects or roles, and subcommunities can be created or dissolved.

A role is a specification of the behavior that an (enterprise) object should fill as a participant in the community. An object can fill more than one role in the same community or different communities. An object can switch roles at different times. Several objects can fill the same role. Roles can be added or removed during the lifetime of the community. When an object participates in a community, it fills a role, and due to policies on the role, becomes more restricted than before.

The community objective is expressed in a policy, which is a set of rules related to the purpose of the community. Policy rules govern the behavior of roles and interactions between roles (and therefore the objects filling the roles) within a community so that the objects are adapted to pursue the community's objective. Policies are a means of specifying and influencing behavior to reach a goal within a distributed system.

A policy rule can be expressed as an:

- **obligation:** a prescription that a particular behavior is required.
- **permission:** a prescription that a particular behavior is allowed to occur. A permission is equivalent to there being no obligation for the behavior not to occur.
- **prohibition:** a prescription that a particular behavior must not occur. A prohibition is equivalent to there being an obligation for the behavior not to occur.

Policy statements often involve stating the action, the role involved, the conditions under which the statement applies, and the issuing authority. Policy specification is in itself a research area which is beyond the scope of this chapter, and so we adopt a simple form of policy rules in our examples.

Besides policies governing the behavior of roles, policies might be given for governing:

- the assignment of roles to enterprise objects;

- the membership of a community (e.g., who can be members and for how long);
- how new policies should be made; and
- when and how subcommunities should be formed or dissolved.

The Mobile Computing Environment

Although wireless networking enables mobility of networked computers, current wireless technology has several drawbacks such as frequent disconnections, high cost for maintaining connections, variations in Quality of Service (QoS) of connectivity, low bandwidth available, limited computational and battery power, and memory on the mobile device. Hence, there is a need for adaptation of applications or adjustment of behavior (e.g., as indicated in Friday et al., 1999) to cope with dynamic changes in connectivity.

In addition, mobility implies changes in location. Location-awareness can be exploited to add value to applications such as serving location-dependent information automatically (e.g., weather, news, etc.).

Our model of AMV-communities aims to take into account the above issues. For example, we discuss meta-policy rules and delegation to an agent as a way of adapting to disconnected operations later.

A CORBA-Based Component Model

RM-ODP enterprise modelling is suitable for modelling the different roles (human and software) and policies that constitute a community. Unfortunately, role-based modelling has not been directly implemented in existing middleware. We use CORBA-based components to model the notion of roles and subsequently our scenario.

A component is a software abstraction, a unit of computation. In object-oriented terminology, a component is a set of interacting objects (or even a single object). A component has interfaces that are described in OMG IDL. Interfaces describe behavioral event interactions (operation, signal, stream) between the component and its environment.

Components have interfaces. They are classified into two groups

- *Require* interfaces that describe what a component requires and
- *Provide* interfaces that describe what a component provides (which always includes a single Management interface).

We interpret an omitted *Require* clause as equivalent to 'this component requires nothing.' An omitted *Provide* does not mean that the object cannot be used because the management interface is assumed to be always provided.

The description of a component's required and provided interfaces is given as a set of OMG IDL interface specifications or CORBA IOR references (OMG, 1998). Each interface is associated with a nonfunctional description representing the QoS (expressed as a *Behavior*) (see Rakotonirainy et al., 2000 for details).

AMV-COMMUNITIES

In this section we first present the general idea of the AMV-community-space and what a system based on AMV-community-spaces can be. Then, we present our view of the structure of an AMV-community and relationships between AMV-communities.

The General Idea: The AMV-Community-Space and the AMV-Community-Space Browser

We view a set of AMV-communities as forming a space of interrelated communities. These relationships include the relationships mentioned earlier such as subcommunity and role sharing. Figure 1 illustrates the AMV-community-space and its relationships with the physical space. The thin line hollow ovals on the left-hand side represent global AMV-communities which can span geographical physical communities. A thick line hollow oval represents a geographical AMV-community, i.e., an AMV-community corresponding to a physical community depicted as an oval on the right-hand side. The inner ovals represent subcommunities, conceptual and physical. The circles represent roles within AMV-communities. In the diagram, a person (with a mobile device) is currently filling a role in a geographical AMV-community and another role in a global AMV-community.

If the person moves from one physical community to another, then the person might leave one geographical AMV-community and enter another (now) more relevant geographical AMV-community, while maintaining membership in the global AMV-community.

AMV membership does carry with it certain responsibilities and privileges. These responsibilities are carried out in accordance with the goals and the policy of the community. We discuss leaving and joining communities in more detail later.

An AMV-community is not necessarily monolithic; it can be a collection (or potential collection) of subcommunities and sub-sub-communities (nested to any depth). A subcommunity might cater to some aspect of the "surrounding" community's distinctive goals or it might retain the original goals of the larger community. We discuss relationships between communities in more detail later.

We envision that the person's device will contain an *AMV-community-space browser*, displaying his existing roles in each AMV-community and what AMV-communities are available to him. The set of relevant geographical AMV-communities available to the person might change automatically as she/he moves among physical communities. We provide more details of this browser later.

Figure 1. The Conceptual AMV-Community Space and the Geographical Physical Communities

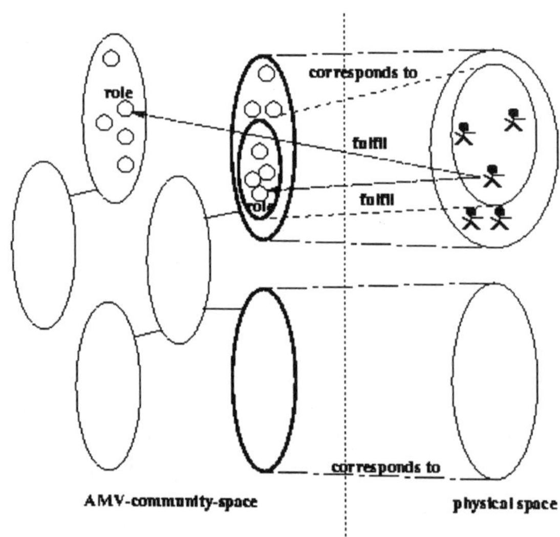

Basic Structure of an AMV-Community

We adopt the RM-ODP Enterprise model of community as described earlier. But we also prescribe a set of specific roles which must be present within an AMV-community. These roles provide a basic set of services for the community. We describe the minimal functions of these roles; these roles might be expanded with application-specific functions. Although these roles are distinct, they might be filled by the same object (e.g., a human supported by software). These roles (which we call management roles) are intended to provide basic services to support the lifecycle of community participants from joining the community, participation in the community (e.g., create and consume information, perform transactions—database or trading, and communication with other participants), to leaving the community. Many of these roles are inspired by Hagel and Armstrong (1997).

1. *Community Manager:* The role with the highest authority for making decisions about the community. For example, decisions about membership, suitability of certain content, and creation of new subcommunities are made by the manager, but such decision-making might be delegated (in part) to other roles. The manager also receives and processes requests for joining (or leaving) the community, and register (or de-register) new (existing) entrants with the community registrar.
2. *Community Registrar:* The role maintaining a directory about current roles, subcommunities, and objects within the community. For scalability, the registrar might be supported by a distributed architecture similar to Domain Name Servers, i.e., the role is filled by a distributed set of components.
3. *Member-Generated Information Manager:* The role organizing and maintaining member-generated content such as chat areas, bulletin boards, and real-time on-line events.
4. *Community Information Manager:* The role which publishes the community's non-member content such as that produced by community organizers or external companies, weather reports, and news.
5. *Information Archivist:* The role which builds up a historical library of member-generated content.
6. *Transactions Manager:* This role supports transactions by providing services such as security (e.g., authentication), trust management (e.g., credentials), reliability (e.g., keep a record in case of failure), and if needed, electronic payment mechanisms (e.g., e-cash). This manager might use additional commerce infrastructures such as public key infrastructures and certification authorities. Verifying the authenticity and authorization of people assuming roles in a community (or performing tasks) might be needed. Security-related activities will be governed by the community's security policies (e.g., which specifies who can access what and what kind of authorizations are required for a transaction).
7. *Communication Facilitator:* This role provides passive and active services to enhance communication within the community. Passive services are used only on request. For example, when a member wants to contact another member in the same or different community, the member sends a request to the communication facilitator which establishes the link between members (e.g., find the email address and send it, or initiate a phone call). The communication might consult the registrar to answer requests. Active services work even when not requested. These include matching member profiles to find members of similar interests, i.e., attempting to link members.
8. *Member Analyst:* This role manages member profiles, tracks participants' interaction

with the community (e.g., a history of services the participant uses), and analyzes members' patterns of behavior to create digital footprints and to evaluate usage of content.

9. *Members' Services Manager:* Responds to participant's questions about services (e.g., billing) and suggestions for improvement.
10. Environment *Awareness Service:* This role monitors the network and computing environment to provide information to applications which might need to adapt to changes in resources.
11. Community *Development Manager:* This role is in charge of establishing new subcommunities and services upon request by members or fróm observations by member analyst (e.g., certain members tend to interact more on a subarea).
12. Agent *Manager:* Which supports the full lifecycle of agents within the community. We describe agent management in detail later.

The functions and responsibilities of these management roles could be stated as policies, i.e., obligations, permissions, and prohibitions, on each role.

Apart from these management roles is the default role for participants of the community, the *member* role, and a default role for agents, the agent role. We explain attachment of agents to role-proxies later.

Additional Roles: Beyond the Basic Structure

Besides the above management roles, additional, more specialized roles can be created according to the purpose of the community. For example, in an electronic market community, there would be roles such as *customer*, *advertiser*, *vendor*, and *broker* which helps to link customers with vendors (perhaps using the communication facilitator's services). As another example, we discuss at length an electronic auction community which we call E-Auction.

E-Auction

The community is distributed and has the purpose of carrying out *Open-BidsAuctions*. The additional roles involved in the E-Auction community are *bidder*, *auctioneer,* and *vendor*, and are shown in Figure 2a as square boxes. The solid arrows represent participation of the added roles and the dashed arrows represent management participation (only three management roles are depicted). For example, the objects filling the bidder, auctioneer, and vendor roles are registered with the community registrar and can take up these roles upon approval by the community manager. Details on joining the community and taking up roles are given later. Figure 2b shows an example of a protocol involving two bidders (two objects having the bidder role) where Bidder 1 wins the auction.

Bids are made publicly. They follow an offer which was posted and published at the auction's start. The auction is open for a limited time interval. A bid is required to be higher than the latest posted. During the final stage of the auction, the auctioneer indicates that she/he is willing to accept a bid from the highest bidder. The highest bidder expresses his/her wish to accept the auctioneer offer. The highest bidder wins if its bid is greater or equal to the reserved price. A settlement is then processed.

A set of Trade-Objects are published for sale in E-Auction. The E-Auction subcommunity surrounding a Trade-Object is formed when:

1. a vendor offers a Trade-Object with a reserved price (Offer [O,price]). The reserved price is the minimum price that the vendor is committed to sell the item. The reserved price is only known to the auctioneer.

Figure 2. Scenario

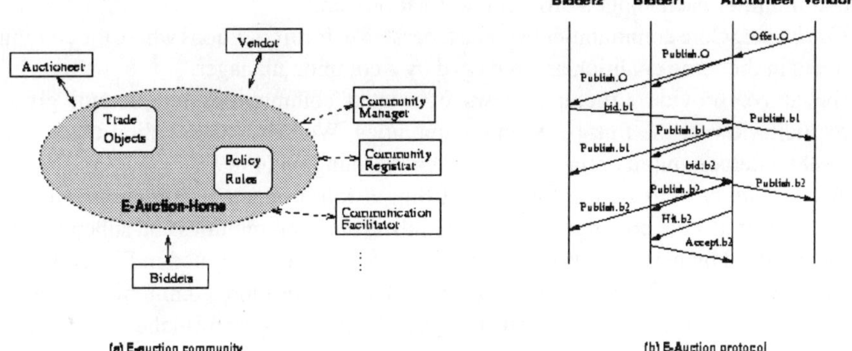

(a) E-auction community

(b) E-Auction protocol

2. An auctioneer takes charge of the offer and sets the auction rules. The auctioneer has the responsibility to open and close the bidding.

Once the two roles (i.e., vendor, auctioneer) are filled, the auctioneer opens the auction and bidders can start bidding (bid [O,price]). Once the Trade-Object is sold, the subcommunity would be dissolved.

Numerous policy rules have been developed that govern the auction process, in particular the exposure of bids and offers and the trade execution (Reck, 1997). For example, there is an *obligation* of the highest bidder to buy a specific good under the conditions the bid specifies. An offer in turn refers to the *obligation* of a vendor to sell a specific good at the conditions the offer specifies. A vendor role is *prohibited* to bid. A bidder has the *permission* to bid.

Bidding are shown on the E-Auction Web site which is continually updated to show the currently highest bid. The auction is live.

Note that with wireless networking, participants of E-Auction are not only distributed, but (some or all) bidders, vendors, and auctioneers are mobile. With mobility are issues of how an object can continue to be involved in the auction despite intrinsic problems introduced by mobility such as disconnection, limited bandwidth, security, and reliability.

An E-Auction around a Trade-Object is a subcommunity of a larger community where not all members are bidders in some auction, and some members might be a bidder in several auction subcommunities. An object who has taken up a bidder role but is also a member of the larger community (and hence, also has a member role) might utilize services provided by the management roles (e.g., contact other members through the communication facilitator or generate content managed by the member-generated information manager).

Relationships Between AMV-Communities

This subsection aims to answer the question: What kinds of relationships can exist among AMV-communities and how are they established?

We have already hinted on hierarchical relationships between communities when new subcommunities are formed for specific purposes with subsets of the larger community's participants. As AMV-communities grow, various relationships might form among disparate AMV-communities. For example, Hagel and Armstrong (1997) mentioned how virtual communities evolve over time as they grow in three stages:

1. *Virtual Villages:* A collection of small highly fragmented virtual communities;

2. *Concentrated Constellations:* Certain communities now become core communities each surrounded by smaller niche communities (e.g., travel community surrounded by communities each about a different destination); and
3. *Coalitions:* Core communities become federated to form coalitions where the communities in the same coalition are managed by a common manager.

The above provide structural views of related communities but do not give a more explicit view of the link between communities. We can make explicit these links by using the intercommunity relationships given in Linington (1999):

- A community is treated as an object filling a role in another community (e.g., a coalition with core communities as its members, and communities and subcommunities induced by nested physical geographical regions as illustrated in Figure 1).
- The same object fills at least one role in each of two or more communities (e.g., an object which is in a core community but also offering services to a niche community—and so has some role in both communities).
- A role in one community is not filled by any object but is defined by reference to a role in another community. Such a role-to-role relationship exists (abstractly) even without objects filling the roles.

The above implies that links between communities might change over time as objects change roles and as new roles are created.

TOWARDS A REALIZATION OF AMV-COMMUNITIES: USE OF AGENTS

This section discusses an agent-based approach for realizing AMV-communities. We first attempt a classification of agents useful within an AMV-community, relating them to the management roles. Then, we discuss a kind of agent called role-proxy in detail and discuss agent management. Finally, we discuss the AMV-community-space browser.

Classes of Agents

We have two classes of agents:

1. *Community Agents:* Created by the (objects filling the) management roles described earlier.

   There are three classes of community agents:

   - *Role-Proxy*: The concept of role is mapped to the concept of role-proxy. For example, the role Bidder has a Bidder-Role-proxy and Community Manager has a Community-Manager-Role-proxy. A role-proxy consists of a single process or two processes implementing the abstract notion of roles and interacts with members of the community directly. They can obtain requests from members and service these requests by communicating with other agents. We describe role-proxies in more detail in the next subsection.
   - *Information Agents*: Agents for gathering, filtering, sharing, monitoring, recommending, and comparing information, autoresponding to queries (e.g., email queries) and for guiding a person's browsing of the AMV-community-space. Such agents support the following roles: member-generated information manager, community information manager, information archivist, communication facilitator (with information from members' profiles), member analyst, members' services

manager (in responding to requests), and the environment awareness service (agents for monitoring resources).
- *Communication Agents*: Such agents are used by the communication facilitator to automate the tasks of matching potential communicating parties and contacting parties.

2. *Member Agents:* Agents provided or created by members (i.e., objects filling a member role).
The functions of the member agents depend on the members themselves. They can (but not necessarily so) be created by members using the services of the agent manager (which is described later). An example of a member agent is an agent for disconnected computing. When an object filling a role is disconnected from the community, an agent can act as the object's representative (taking up a designated role in the community) and take on the object's obligations. We discuss such agents in relation to role-proxies later. Member agents might interact with community agents to perform their tasks.

Information, communication, and member agents must fill (perhaps with other objects) a role in the community. For example, the same information agent might be used by different management roles and so is part of several roles. No agent appears in a community without a role. A role-proxy does not fill a role but directly represents a role.

Note that agents might move from one community to another or from one community-space to another. Such a move might involve transfer of the agent's code, execution state, and data from one host to another. For example, information agents might move to a community on a different host to monitor for changes in a bulletin board. When an agent enters a community (B) from another community (A) for the first time, it becomes part of some role(s) in community (B) but might retain its part in a role in community (A).

Role-Proxies

Single-Process Role-Proxies

The simplest way to view a role-based model in terms of a component model is to represent a role by a component interface specification. Unfortunately, using such a simple mapping of roles to component interfaces makes it difficult to model a component that can fill multiple roles or change roles. For example, an auctioneer (though disallowed from bidding in one community) can be a bidder in another community. One component cannot have two component interface specifications. Instead, a new component interface specification must be created which inherits from these two component interface specifications, and then the component can be properly typed with the new component interface specification.

Instead, we explore a different approach which takes a more agent-oriented view of roles. The filling of a role by a component (or enterprise object) is not viewed as a component interface instantiation, but rather as a constrained interaction between the component and a role-proxy. A (component, role-proxy) pair represents an instance of filling a role. Also, several components can be involved in the same instance of the filling of a role by interacting with the same role-proxy (if permitted by the specification of the role-proxy). For example, a component and its agent can both interact with the same role-proxy. We illustrate this later.

A component which fills multiple roles is then viewed as a component interacting with multiple role-proxies. Such a looser coupling between a component and its role (in contrast to component instantiating an interface) also makes it easier for components to change roles (or be assigned new roles) at run-time. Moreover, a role-proxy as a distinct process on its own could actively handle policies about a role and run-time changes to roles separately from the component.

Figure 3: Role Proxies and Components in E-Auction

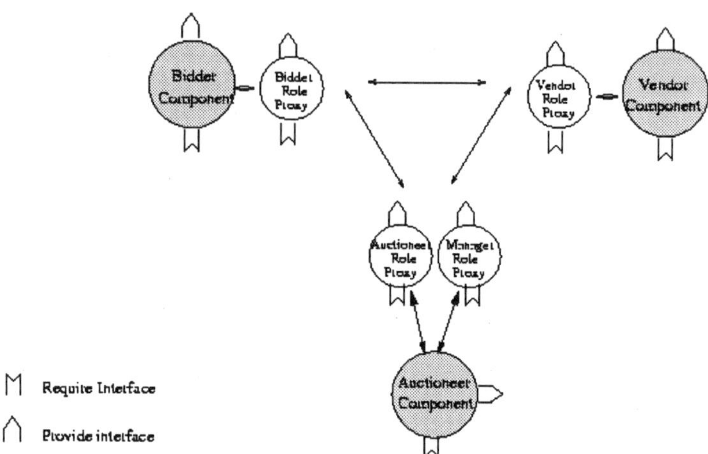

In RM-ODP, a role specification is a placeholder for behavior. It has a type, behavior, QoS, and policy rules. The above RM-ODP concept of role is realized as a proxy component in our architecture. A role-proxy may be thought of as a software agent that maintains the context of the community wherein the component is filling a role. Figure 3 shows the association between components and role-proxies in an auction scenario.

A component C fills a role R by interacting with a role-proxy of R. The role-proxy for a role R interacting with C has the following purposes:

- *Provide Services to the Component C.* The services provided by the role-proxy are the only means for C to interact with the rest of the community. With our agent-oriented view of role-proxies and components, the interactions are by means of messages. These messages can take several forms. For example, viewing role-proxies and components as separate processes, we could use message-passing as in the Unix message-passing library. Alternatively, we could use an agent communication language such as KQML (Finin, 2000). But in this paper, as we specify services in CORBA-style interfaces, we can implement messaging from component to role-proxy by the component invoking a procedure of the role-proxy in the style of a remote procedure call (RPC). Also, role-proxies can communicate with each other via such RPCs.

  There are two kinds of services: application-specific services and generic services. Generic services are provided for all applications and include management services which allow the acting component to TakeUp or GiveUp a set of roles within the community, and RegisterCallBack which permits the component to register callback procedures with the role-proxy. The role-proxy can then forward event notifications to the component invoking a registered callback procedure.
- *Control and Influence the Behavior of C Based on a Policy Specification.* The role-proxy must provide a means of informing C of policy rules and checking if the component C conforms to such a policy. As we explain later, the policy rules might change and C must be informed of such changes. Messages from other components in the community (possibly filling different roles) are intercepted by the role-proxy before being passed on to C. C can send messages to other components if the role-proxy provides such a service.

The following interface specification sketch represents a generic role-proxy, which uses management services as specified in the interface of Manager-Role-proxy. Note that we use such component interface specifications to specify role-proxy services, and so, components implementing (or instantiating) these interfaces are role-proxies and not components filling the role. Filling of roles is not modelled by instantiation of interfaces, but by interactions between component and role-proxy.

```
Generic-Role-proxy
   Require
       Manager-Role-proxy (* interface community manager*)

   Provide
       (** services to a component **)
       TakeUp({role})       (* procedure *)
       GiveUp({role})       (* procedure *)
       RegisterCallBack(ComponentProcedure)
                                     (* procedure *)
       InitiateInteraction() (* procedure *)

   Behaviour
       (* forwarding calls based on policy *)

   Policy
       (* Community policy associated with this role *)
```

Note that below the *Require* and *Provide* keywords, we can mention procedures or other interfaces. We also do not specify the parameters fully in this sketch. InitiateInteraction is invoked by a component intending to fulfill the role, and sets up the interaction (initializing the role-proxy's state).

Other role-proxies can then be defined by extension of the above generic specification. For example, a Bidder role-proxy can be specified by:

```
Bidder-Role-proxy inherit Generic-Role-proxy
   Require
       (* No requirements *)

   Provide
       (** services to a component **)
       Bid(Amount)           (* procedure *)
       Accept(Item)          (* procedure *)
       GiveUpBidderRole() (* procedure *)
       KnowCurrentBid()    (* procedure *)
       KnowHit()             (* procedure *)
       KnowPolicies()        (* procedure *)

       (** services for Auctioneer **)
       TellCurrentBid() (* procedure *)
       TellHit() (* procedure *)
```

```
Behaviour
    GiveUpBidderRole invokes
                    Generic-Role-Proxy::GiveUp
    KnowCurrentBid invokes
            Generic-Role-Proxy::RegisterCallBack
    KnowHit invokes
            Generic-Role-Proxy::RegisterCallBack
    KnowPolicies invokes
            Generic-Role-Proxy::RegisterCallBack

Policy
    (* Bidder is obliged to accept if he has been
    hit by the Auctioneer *)
    P1: obliged to Accept if invoked(KnowHit)

    (* Bidder is prohibited from giving up its role
    as a bidder if it has been hit *)
    P2: prohibited from GiveUpBidderRole
                        if invoked(KnowHit)
```

The Bidder role interface offers services to the component acting as a Bidder and to the Auctioneer to permit the Auctioneer to inform it of the current bid and a hit. KnowCurrentBid and KnowHit are invoked by the component to register callbacks to be informed of the current bid and if there is a hit, respectively. KnowPolicies register a callback permitting the component to be informed of obligations, permissions, and prohibitions, and to be informed of changes in them. Changes in policy are important in a mobile environment as we shall see later. Note that what the component does with the policy once it has been informed of them is internal to the component, but we have assumed that the component needs to be aware of the policy in order that it can adopt it in its behaviour. The role-proxy does not need to know the internal behaviour of components but does try to ensure that the component follows the policy.

To detect policy violations, the role-proxy keeps track of what services have been used by the component (e.g., a history of procedure invocations). Enforcement of policies is generally difficult and sometimes impossible. Instead when policy violation occurs, compensation actions or penalties might be imposed by the role-proxy. We do not discuss policy enforcement in detail in this paper.

Role-proxies are created at join time or when taking up roles and might be destroyed when the components leave a community or role.

Joining a Community

We use an example of joining an E-Auction community. Figure 4 describes how different role-proxies that form a community are created in the joining process. John sends a join message to the Manager-Role-proxy to be a member of E-Auction. The join message might incorporate some of John's personal information and his device characteristics. The Manager-Role-proxy will notify the acting manager (Jack) who either approves or rejects the request. The Manager-Role-proxy manifests the approval by assigning a Member role to John. This is achieved by migrating the code of Member-Role-proxy to John's device. The right type of code is sent to John's device according to the device characteristics. The new migrated role-proxy notifies John (acting member) about the new role. The Member-Role-proxy is the representation of John within the community. When John wants to bid for a particular Trade-object, it has to send a TakeUp message with Bidder Role as parameter to his Member-Role-proxy. The Member-Role-proxy checks the local policy with regard to the TakeUp procedure and decides to assign a new Bidder role to John. Note that the Member-Role-proxy might retrieve the code for the Bidder-Role-proxy from a role-proxy code server. The Manager-Role-proxy is notified of the new assignment.

Note that an advantage of this architecture is that the administration decisions are not centralized in the Manager-Role-proxy. It is distributed among role-proxies. Therefore, it is scalable. Each role-proxy has a divison of behavior and policy rules, that enables it to make local decisions that maintain the community goals. If the local role-proxy cannot handle the decision-making, then the Manager-Role-proxy or other role-proxies would step in.

Leaving a Community

AMV-community membership may be directed (say, by assignment from a person in authority, e.g., the community of incarcerated juveniles); required (e.g., the community of attorneys, to which professional association is virtually mandatory); or voluntary (e.g., subscription to e-mailing list). Conversely, canceling a membership can also be directed, required, or voluntary. The leave protocol depends on the role. For example, the community manager cannot leave his/her role while the community is still active. A less important role that issues a voluntary leave might leave the community easily. However, a directed leave might involve negotiation (e.g., to establish a majority of votes) among all roles in the community. The leave protocol is always stated in a contract when a component joins a community. In all cases, the component will issue a leave operation to its role-proxy. This role-proxy can take local actions according to the local policy (e.g., the component cannot leave in the middle of a transaction) or forward the request to the Manager-Role-proxy which will then act accordingly (e.g., log the request, initiate a vote,

Figure 4: Joining a Community and Taking Up Roles

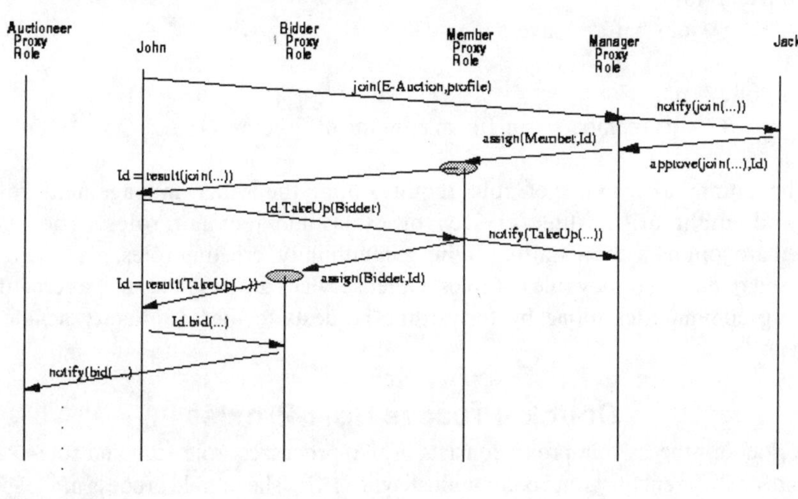

or notify other roles). When the leave request is approved, the role-proxy will die.

The following interface specification sketch represents a community Manager-Role-proxy:

```
Manager-Role-proxy
    Require
        Community-Registrar-Role-proxy
        Member-Generated-Information-Manager-Role-proxy
        Community-Information-Manager-Role-proxy
        Information-Archivist-Role-proxy
        Transactions-Manager-Role-proxy
        Communication-Facilitator-Role-proxy
        Member-Analyst-Role-proxy
        Member-Services-Manager-Role-proxy
        Environment-Awareness-Service-Role-proxy
        Community-Development-Manager-Role-proxy
        Agent-Manager-Role-proxy

    Provide
        (* services to the manager component *)
        Approve(...)
        Reject(...)

        (* services to other components *)
        join(Community-name,[role], profile)
        leave(Community-name,[role])
        create(role, [cardinality], property, spec)
        dissolve(role)
        add(policy, role)      (* add new policy to a role *)
        remove(policy, role) (* remove a policy)

    Behaviour
        (* join before leave *)

    Policy
        (* e.g. members can fill maximum of 2 roles *)
```

The community manager role requires that the other management roles be filled and might utilize the services of other management roles. The services provided are joining a community, leaving a community, creating roles, dissolving roles, adding and removing policy rules of roles. Other services are possible such as creating and dissolving communities (done by forwarding requests to the community development manager).

Double-Process Role-Proxies

A double-process role-proxy consists of two processes: role-stub and role-skeleton, which are on different hosts and communicate via RPCs. The double process model permits functioning in the presence of disconnections, and enables negotiation of QoS between the two ends of a connection, each process at one end.

As an example of the use of double-process role-proxies, we illustrate their use for disconnected computing below. This example also illustrates two ideas: (1) an agent which can act on behalf of a component when the latter is unreachable: a component's role-proxy can *delegate* its policy to the agent's role-proxy, and (2) adaptation of policies.

Meta-Policy Rules

We first discuss policy adaptation which consists of dynamically *activate*-ing or *inhibit*-ing policy rules as in McCann and Roman (1998). When a policy rule is inhibited, the rule is no longer imposed on the component.

Inhibiting/activating a set of policy rules permits us to strengthen/relax existing policy rules without changing the original statement. This simulates redefining of behaviour so as to avoid certain policy rules when they may be undesirable.

The inhibition or activation of policy is predicated on the capabilities and context of components and/or role-proxies such as presence or absence of connectivity, bandwidth, memory, CPU resources, and location.

Note that the capabilities of a component or role-proxy might depend on the characteristics of the environment.

Each meta-policy rule is now preceded with a capability expression. We call these meta-policy rules as they manipulate policy rules. The syntax we use is:

[capability] -> Operator(policy-rule)

where capability is a boolean expression, and Operator is either Inhibit or Activate.
For example:

[disconnection_rate(r_1,r_2) > 100] -> Inhibit(policy1)

specifies that if the disconnection rate between role-proxies r_1 and r_2 is higher than 100, then policy1 is inhibited.

In a role-proxy component specification, such meta-policy rules are situated in the same place as other policy rules.

Example

Figure 5a represents a configuration of a community. The Bidder-Role-proxy is explicitly represented as a role-stub and a role-skeleton distributed across Site 1 and Site 2. The role-stub and role-skeleton share the same policy rules that govern the behaviour of a Bidder. The agent filling the role of a member's agent has an Agent-Role-proxy. Note the mix of two kinds of role-proxy in the diagram: the single-process role-proxy and the double process role-proxy. The choice of role-proxy for a component can be determined at join time.

Let us assume that the Bidder role has the following two policy rules:

P1: **obliged to** snd(Take) **when** rcv(Hit) within t

P2: **obliged to**
delegate(Policy(Bidder),From:Bidder, To:Agent)
AND inform(Auctioneer)

delegate(Policy, Source, Destination) transfers a policy from one role-proxy to another role-proxy. inform(Auctioneer) signals to the Auctioneer that a delegation has taken place.

As we said in the previous subsection, policy must be predicated to deal with mobility. So, we have the following meta-policy rules in the Bidder role:

MP1: [connected(role-stub,role-skeleton)] ->
Activate(P1) AND Inhibit(P2)

MP2: [disconnected(role-stub,role-skeleton)] ->
Inhibit(P1) AND Activate(P2)

MP1 implies that the agent is not active while the role-stub and role-skeleton are connected. When disconnection takes place, due to MP2, the bidder component on Site 1 is no longer having obligation P1, i.e., the role-stub relaxes that obligation on the bidder. However, as P2 is activated, the role-skeleton on Site 2 delegates its policy to the Agent-Role-proxy. The Agent-Role-proxy then informs the agent of its newly acquired policy (via a callback registered by the agent with the Agent-Role-proxy). The agent then springs into action to act on behalf of the bidder. Figure 5(b) shows how the agent accepts an offer on behalf of a bidder when disconnection makes it impossible for the bidder to act. The transfer of obligations carries the notion of authorizing the agent to act.

Double-process role-proxies are created at join time in a similar way as single-process role-proxies but only apply to users with a weak connection (e.g., mobile computers with wireless link). The request for double-process role-proxies instead of single-process role-proxies is made when a component takes up a role. The agent for disconnected computing is sent as part of this request to the community manager. The community manager sends a request to the agent manager which sets up the agent and its role-proxy.

Agent Management

The Foundation for Intelligent Physical Agents (FIPA) specification for agent management (FIPA, 1998) describes an agent lifecycle and primitive commands on agents including create, invoke, destroy, suspend, resume, move, and execute. The object filling the agents manager role mentioned above manages the lifecycle of the community agents and also provides agent management services to member agents. We identify seven components of the software used in the agent manager role:

Figure 5. Agent

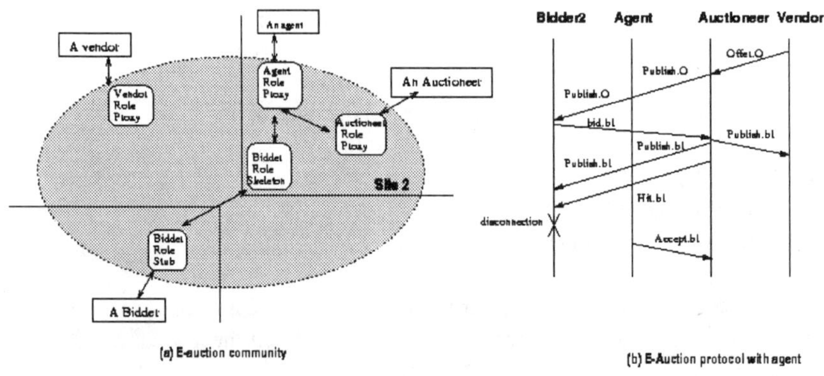

(a) E-auction community

(b) E-Auction protocol with agent

1. *Agent Creator/Editor:* This component lets users program the agents (and their travel itineraries if the agents are mobile).
2. *Agent Installer:* This component sets up agents by attaching them to (i.e., by setting them up to interact with) a generic Agent-Role-proxy as shown in Figure 5, or to some other role-proxy. For example, an agent can be attached to an existing Bidder-Role-proxy, i.e., the agent shares a Bidder-Role-proxy with another component. This attachment mechanism represents how an agent can be used by several different roles. Figure 6 shows how an agent is attached to two Bidder-Role-proxies. Whether such an attachment is permitted is an application-specific decision: the implementation of role-proxies must support it and/or conditions for attachment might be expressed as the policy rules for a role.
3. *Agent Store:* This component permits storage of created agents and of partially executed agents (with state). The latter is useful for temporarily holding agents which are waiting to be uploaded to mobile devices.
4. *Component Server:* Agent components are stored here (including agent's itineraries) and could be dynamically uploaded by agents during run-time. We introduce the idea of kernel agents which encapsulates minimal functionality but uptake components when needed and drop unneeded components. We anticipate the size of agents to be important when a myriad of agents are injected into the community.
5. *Agent Scheduler:* This component schedules the execution of agents. In order to avoid network congestion and overload at places, only a limited number of agents (e.g., a fixed size pool of agents) might be used at any one time.
6. *Run-Time Controller:* This receives commands from users sent from role-proxies and relays them to running agents. The commands should include the primitive ones mentioned above and application-specific ones (e.g., to add certain components to agents).
7. *Agent Messaging System:* A facility for routing messages to agents used for interagent communication or by the run-time controller. This system must keep track of agents in the community. In large communities, a single agent directory will not scale. Instead a distributed architecture might be employed as with the community registrar.

The AMV-Community-Space Browser

We mentioned software for browsing communities earlier. The functions of this browser are:

Figure 6. Agent Attachment to Two Role-Proxies

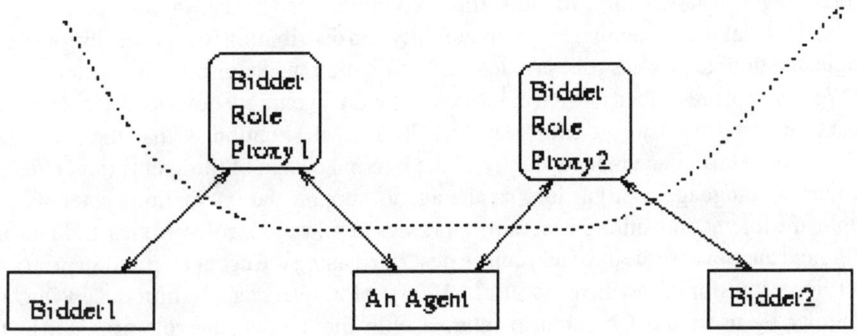

- enable the user to interact with different communities, and is a placeholder for role-proxies. Agents created by the user can be launched into the community via a Member-Role-proxy running in the browser as follows: assuming that the Member-Role-proxy offers the service of injecting agents into the community, an agent which is passed to the Member-Role-proxy is forwarded to the agent manager which then installs the agent;
- receive notifications about geographical AMV-communities in the area;
- bookmark AMV-communities; and
- maintain the user's personal information profile and device profile (e.g., hardware characteristics and device resources by actively monitoring resources such as memory, disk space, etc., on the device).

CONCLUSION AND FUTURE WORK

We believe that the electronic community is an important concept in electronic commerce, and that the usage of heterogeneous mobile devices will continue to grow. Communities for commerce (short or long term, ad hoc or multipurpose, customer-to-business or business-to-business) such as auctions, marketplaces, business (sub-) organizations, and trading communities involving mobile device users can be realized electronically as AMV-communities. Such communities can transcend geographical boundaries (and allow mobility of participants) and improve transaction efficiency via automation using agents.

AMV-communities can also be electronic augmentations of physical commercial communities (e.g., large shopping centers, markets, and business areas) which have a continual inflow and outflow of people. Such people would not just have a physical presence in the community but joins it electronically (e.g., receive advertisements during the visit, make contacts, perform electronic payments, provide electronic feedback, exchange advice and queries). An electronic membership in such a community created during a first visit can be retained beyond the visit, and active involvement continued by manual electronic interactions or by delegation to agents. Ad-hoc AMV-communities can be formed to provide the environment for the trading of soft-goods such as media-based information, interactive services, and digital value tokens (e.g., electronic access, prepaid services, electronic cash) which require a computational environment for exchange.

We have presented concepts for an AMV-community modelled with RM-ODP Enterprise Viewpoint. We have also outlined an architecture of AMV-communities using software agents attached to roles. We have attempted to maintain an enterprise level of abstraction for modelling communities (hence, the use of roles and policies) while taking a pragmatic view of mobility and distribution (hence, the introduction of single and double process role-proxies, and adaptation mechanisms with policies).

We have not prescribed an internal structure for our agents but described a macro-view of agents treating each agent as a gray-box. The ideal situation is that the interagent interactions can take place independently of the internal design of the agents (and even the programming language used) as long as the agents support the interaction protocols. For example, the interaction among a set of role-proxies (e.g., vendor role-proxies, bidder role-proxies, and auctioneer role-proxies) can be described using the agent interaction protocols for service provisioning (d'Inverno et al., 1998). Moreover, agents introduced into the community by users must be able to interact with the agents (the role-proxies) in the community even when the agents have heterogeneous internal structures. Such agent-to-agent interactions might benefit from ongoing work on norms and agent societies (Dellarocas and Klein, 1999). AMV-communities make use of several types of agents, and so can benefit from improvements in the internal design of various types of agents such as information agents and buying and selling agents (e.g., Guttman et al., 1997).

Towards an implementation of AMV-community middleware (which includes implementations of role-proxies and default components for management roles, and a set of information and communication agents), there are several outstanding research issues we are currently addressing:

- We are working on complete interface specifications for our management roles, member role, and agent role.
- A more comprehensive description of capabilities is needed. For example, availability, reliability, and ability to cross logical domains have not been discussed as capabilities.
- To guide implementation, we need a formalization for aspects of our model such as composition of communities and (meta-) policy rules.

After developing such middleware, tools for customizing the middleware (e.g., to add application-specific roles and role-proxies) to create required AMV-communities will be needed.

We are also working on providing computational interpretations to the following RM-ODP ideas:

- In the presence of an outer community, the policy framework of the inner community is bounded by the framework of the outer community. For example, the inner community cannot permit what is prohibited in the outer community, unless it has delegated authority to do so and the inner community might be able to prohibit or obligate its members provided the outer community does not prohibit the inner community from imposing such policies. Similarly, we would like to investigate how the policies of a core community relate to those of the niche communities in concentrated constellations, and how the policies of core communities forming a coalition are related.
- Policy enforcement is generally difficult, and is either pessimistic (preventative and ongoing checking) or optimistic (detect noncompliance and report/correct them).
- Policy specification can be factored into a number of policy submodels, each constraining a particular aspect of behaviour. A policy submodel defines the behaviour required to satisfy an aspect of the community's purpose in terms of required collections of actions, alternatives, and allowable forms of concurrency (e.g., policy rules and procedure for joining a community, or a delegation submodel for expressing the degree to and circumstances in which one object can take over the role and responsibilities of another). We wish to investigate a complete list of these submodels for AMV-communities.

ACKNOWLEDGEMENTS

The work reported in this paper has been funded in part by the Co-Operative Research Centre Program through the Department of Industry, Science, & Tourism of the Commonwealth Government of Australia.

REFERENCES

Amazon. (2000). Amazon.com Auctions. http://www.amazon.com.

d'Inverno, M., Kinny, D., & Luck, M. (1998). Interaction protocols in agents. *Proceedings of the 3rd International Conference on Multi-Agent Systems (ICMAS98),* 261-268.

Dellarocas, C., & Klein, M. (1999). Civil Agent Societies: Tools for inventing open agent-mediated electronic marketplaces. *Proceedings of the Workshop in Agent-Mediated Electronic Commerce (co-located with IJCAI'99).*

Doheny-Farina, S. (1998). *The Wired Neighbourhood.* Yale University Press.

eBay (2000). eBay—Your Personal Trading Community—Home Page. http://www.ebay.com.

Finin, T. (2000). UMBC KQML Web. http://www.cs.umbc.edu/agents/kse/kqml/.

FIPA (1998). FIPA 98 Specification—Agent Management. http://www.fipa.org/spec/fipa8a23.doc.

Friday, A., Davies, N., Blair, G., & Cheverst, K. (1999). Developing Adaptive Applications: The MOST Experience. *Journal of Integrated Computer-Aided Engineering*, 6(2), 143-157.

Gray, R.S., Kotz, D., Nog, S., Rus, D., & Cybenko, G. (1996). Mobile agents for mobile computing. *Technical Report TR96-285,* Department of Computer Science, Dartmouth College. Retrieved from ftp://ftp.cs.dartmouth.edu/TR/TR96-285.ps.Z.

Guttman, R., Maes, P., Chavez, A., & Dreilinger, D. (1997). Results from a multi-agent electronic marketplace experiment. *Poster Proceedings of Modeling Autonomous Agents in a Multi-Agent World (MAAMAW'97).*

Guttman, G., Moukas, A., & Maes, P. (1998). Agent-Mediated Electronic Commerce: A Survey. *Knowledge Engineering Review*, 13(2). Retrieved from http://ecommerce.media.mit.edu/papers/ker98.pdf.

Hagel, J., & Armstrong, A.G. (1997). Net Gain: Expanding Markets Through Virtual Communities. Harvard Business School Press.

Hattori, F., Ohguro, T., Yokoo, M., Matsubara, S., & Yoshida, S. (1999). SocialWare: Multiagent systems for supporting networkcCommunities. *Communications of the ACM,* 42(3), 55-61.

Ismail, L., & Hagimont, D. (1999). A performance evaluation of the mobile agent paradigm. *Proceedings of the International Conference on Object-Oriented Programming, Systems and Applications (OOPSLA'99).* Retrieved from http://sirac.imag.fr/Interne/doc/sirac/publications/INTERNE/Soumis/soumis-oopsla-agents.ps.gz.

ISO/IEC JTC1/SC7. (1999). Information Technology—Open Distributed Processing—Reference Model—Enterprise Language (ISO/IEC 15414 | ITU-T Recommendation X.911).

Jacobsen, K., & Johansen, D. (1997). Mobile Software on Mobile Hardware—Experiences with TACOMA on PDAs. *Technical Report 97-32*, Department of Computer Science, University of Tromso. Retrieved from http://www.cs.uit.no/Lokalt/Rapporter/Reports/9732.htm.

Jennings, N.R., Sycara, K., & Wooldridge, M. (1998). A Roadmap of Agent Research and Development. *Autonomous Agents and Multi-Agent Systems,* 1, 7-38.

Kortuem, G., Fickas, S., & Segall, Z. (1997). On-Demand Delivery of Software in Mobile Environments. *Proceedings of the Nomadic Computing Workshop at the 11th International Parallel Processing Symposium.* Retrieved from http://www.cs.uoregon.edu/~kortuem/htbin/download.cgi?/cs/www/home/research/wearables/Papers/nomadic97.ps.

Kovacs, E., Rohrle, K., & Reich, M. (1998). Integrating Mobile Agents into the Mobile Middleware. *Proceedings of the 2nd International Workshop on Mobile Agents (MA'98), Lecture Notes in Computer Science 1477,* 124-135.

Linington, P.F. (1999). Options for expressing ODP Enterprise Communities and their Policies by using UML. Proceedings of the 3rd International Enterprise Distributed Object Computing Conference, 72-82. Retrieved from http://www.cs.ukc.ac.uk/pubs/1999/885/index.html.

McCann, P.J., & Roman, G.-C. (1998). Compositional Programming Abstractions for Mobile Computing. IEEE Transactions on Software Engineering, 24(2), 97-110.

NetAcademy Team. (2000). Journal of Electronic Markets—Home Page. Retrieved from http://www.electronicmarkets.org/.

OMG. (1998). The Common Object Request Broker—Architecture and Specification.

OMG. (1999). TC Document orbos/98-10-18. CORBA Components.

Queloz, P., & Villazon, A. (1999). Composition of Services with Mobile Code. *Proceedings of the Joint Symposium ASA/MA'99.* Retrieved from http://cuiwww.unige.ch/~queloz/papers/asama99.ps.gz.

Rachlevsky-Reich, B. (1999). GEM: A Global Electronic Market System. Master's thesis, Faculty of Electrical Engineering, Technion—Israel Institute of Technology.

Rakotonirainy, A., Bond, A., Indulska, J., & Leonard, D. (2000). SCAF: Simple Component Architecture Framework. Proceedings of Tools 2000.

Reck, M. (1997). Trading-Process Characteristics of Electronic Auctions. *Electronic Markets,* 7(4), 17-23.

Rheingold, H. (1993). The Virtual Community: Homesteading on the Electronic Frontier. Addition-Wesley.

Sahai, A., & Morin, C. (1998). Mobile Agents for Enabling Mobile User Aware Applications. *Proceedings of the 2nd International Conference on Autonomous Agents (Agents'98*), Sycara, K.P., & and Wooldridge, M. (Eds.), 205-211. ACM Press.

Sandholm, T. (1999). eMediator: A Next Generation Electronic Commerce Server. Proceedings of the AAAI Workshop on AI in Electronic Commerce, 46-55.

Stathis, K., Pitt, J., & McKay, P. (1999). Mobile Agents for Mobile Users in Connected Communities. Proceedings of the Workshop on Intelligent Information Interfaces (i3 Spring Days). Retrieved from http://www.dfki.de/imedia/workshops/i3-spring99/.

Villate, Y., Gil, D., Goni, A., & Illarramendi, A. (1998). New Challenges for Mobile Computers: Combination of the Indirect Model and Mobile Agents. Proceedings of the ICSE98 International Workshop on Computing and Communication in the Presence of Mobility. Retrieved from http://siul02.si.ehu.es/~jirgbdat/PUBLICATIONS/icse98.ps.gz.

Section Four: Human Interface to Software Agents

Chapter XVI

A Virtual Salesperson

Andrew Marriott
Curtin University of Technology, Australia

Roberto Pockaj
University of Genova, Italy

Craig Parker
Deakin University, Australia

This chapter describes the use of a graphical humane interface—a Virtual Salesperson. The face of the Virtual Salesperson is a generic Facial Animation Engine developed at the University of Genova in Italy and uses a 3-D computer graphics model based on the MPEG-4 standard supplemented by Cyberware scans for facial detail. The appearance of the head may be modified by Facial Definition Parameters to more accurately model the required visage allowing one model to represent many different Talking Heads. The "brain" of the Virtual Salesperson, developed at Curtin University, integrates natural language parsing, text to speech synthesis, and artificial intelligence systems to produce a "bot" capable of helping a user through a question/answer sales enquiry. The Virtual Salesperson is a specific example of a generic Human Computer Interface—a Talking Head.

INTRODUCTION

The Internet and, more specifically, the Web is growing in popularity as a mechanism for conducting business-to-business, consumer-to-business, consumer-to-government, business-to-government, and government-to-government commerce (see, for example, Doukidis, Gricar, & Novak, 1998; Klein, Gricar, & Pucihar, 1999; Swatman, Gricar, & Novak, 1996; Vogel, Gricar, & Novak, 1997). Intra- and inter-organizational electronic commerce (which includes the Internet) is strengthening rapidly, especially in such areas as supply chain management and business process re-engineering through just-in-time manufacturing and quick response and efficient consumer response approaches (see, for instance, Cooper & Burgess, 1999).

Internet sales and revenue from consumer purchases have been low, however, when compared to more traditional channels (Burke, 1997; Peterson, Balasubramanian, & Bronnenberg, 1997). Reasons for this problem are varied, primarily because of the complexity of consumer markets, and include:

- the nature of products/services—some require "experiencing" or trialing, while others can be purchased based on information alone (Peterson et al. 1997)
- the Internet shopping experience generally not providing the same levels of personal service and social interaction as face-to-face shop assistants (Burke, 1997; see also Cohn, 1999; Quelch & Takeuchi, 1981);
- the difficulty of navigating the Web (or Web sites) and of finding the needed information (Jarvenpaa & Todd, 1997; Lohse & Spiller, 1998); and
- the heterogeneous nature of consumers (Peterson et al. 1997)—ranging from elderly to "baby-boomers" and to more techno-savvy teenagers (McConnell, 1998)—all of whom have different needs and problems which need addressing if they are to purchase via the Internet.

Further exacerbating these consumer-oriented problems are their increasing demands for rapid responses to their e-mail queries by organizations (Rabkin & Tingley, 1999). The growing number of individuals using the Internet is also producing large volumes of these e-mails which need to be attended to by customer support staff (Hibbard, 1998; Poleretzky, Cohn, & Gimnicher, 1999).

This chapter examines these inhibitors to consumer Internet purchasing in more detail and discusses some of the Artificial Intelligence (AI) techniques that are being used to address them. The chapter then describes the innovative work being carried out jointly at Curtin University in Australia and the University of Genoa in Italy on a prototype 3-D audiovisual Virtual Salesperson.[1] The Virtual Salesperson has the potential to automate many of the routine queries received by organizations—while at the same time facilitating more "humane" and user-friendly social interactions—by providing spoken answers to natural language enquiries from customers.

E-COMMERCE, THE WEB, AND AI

The need to respond rapidly to consumer e-mail queries and requests (Rabkin & Tingley, 1999) and the increasing volumes of such emails (Hibbard, 1998; Poleretzky et al. 1999) is providing the impetus for automated Web techniques to reduce consumer reliance on staff. These automated approaches to consumer support are also being driven by globalization, whereby consumers in other "time-zones" will send these enquiries via the Internet out of normal business hours. Requests during irregular hours are also likely to increase, according to Burke (1997), because the Internet might provide a convenient means for time-constrained dual-income and single-parent families to gain access to products/services. The main types of automated consumer support are outlined below.

Portals and Self-Service Centres

Common automated consumer support facilities on the Web are portals (Bacheldor, 1999; see also Clarke, 1999) and self-service (or self-help) centres (Poleretzky et al. 1999; Wagner, 1997). These mechanisms are central points of access to an organization through which consumers can obtain and search for information about products/services, the company, etc. Similar self-help approaches include the use of Frequently Asked Questions (FAQs), which permit consumers to search for the question or query they might have and to see the answer provided to their question.

There are, however, a number of potential problems with this approach to automating consumer support:

- Information is typically presented in a hierarchical fashion, so that consumers must "drill down" to find the specific information they are after (see Burke, 1997).
- Information hierarchies can often be structured around or distributed between areas maintained by different divisions of an organization, or even different companies, rather than based on the needs of the consumers (see Clarke, 1999).
- Answers to consumer questions or problems might not be included in the information or might be difficult to find (Cohn, 1999). This issue will be exacerbated as the volume of information and/or FAQs increase (Beard, 1999).
- Competitor product/services comparisons are not provided or, if provided, do not permit easy comparisons. This is significant because consumers often base purchasing decisions on this (as well as other) information (see Burke, 1997; Lohse & Spiller, 1998; Menezes, 1999).

Clarke (1999) proposes multi-organizational electronic service delivery (MESD) as a way of addressing the problem of information being structured around or by organizational divisions. MESD involves adopting a consumer-centric approach in which the portal or self-service centre information is structured around their needs or activities.

For example, the Australian State of Victoria's Maxi Project hides the departmental structure of government by designing its customer interface around "life events." Getting married, therefore, might involve filling out a single form (including, perhaps, changes to a surname and/or residential address) from which the relevant information will be distributed to the necessary government departments. A similar consumer-centric approach in a retail context might involve leading consumers through their purchasing decision-making process (see McGaughey & Mason, 1998), including Information Search Assistants such as AI "bots" to obtain comparative product/service details on which to make their decision. Providing this support is important, according to Lohse and Spiller (1998), because they believe that consumers often want help with product selections and obtaining other information (such as payment and security details).

Intelligent Software Agents

This consumer-centric approach to automated consumer support, along with the other problems identified above, suggests the need for more sophistication than can be provided by just listing FAQs on a Web page. Rather it implies the need for feature sets such as information filtering and intelligent searches for relevant information and answers to queries—automated services which can be provided by intelligent software agents (see, Menezes, 1999; Rabkin & Tingley, 1999). These agents can enable consumers to search for answers to their queries, rather than traversing hierarchies of information. Marriott (1999b) reports on initial findings of research into applying AI to e-commerce.

Of importance to the user, desktop and interface agents emerged from the research in the Programming-by-Demonstration (PBD) discipline and resulted in PBD systems which learned by watching what interaction took place between a user and a Graphical User Interface. Examples can be found in Maes & Kozierok (1993), Lieberman (1994), and Koda & Maes (1996). Wood (1994) and Greif (1994) indicated that the learning could be applied to the entire desktop metaphor, and at the same time Sheth (1994) was applying the learning paradigm to information-filtering/data mining to develop an information filtering "personal assistant." The early Personal Assistants/Interfaces such as described in Etzioni and Weld (1994) were soon applied to the World Wide Web to assist in browsing. The techniques were also being applied to generalized browsing, calendar assistants, finding and communicating with people and Data Mining activities such as Usenet news filtering. Agent technology was starting to be applied to many areas historically rich in information. See Marriott (1999c) for a good bibliography of on-line papers about Software Agents and related technology.

One motivation for using interface agents is that sound, graphics, and knowledge can convey ideas faster than technical documents alone. Also, the use of an anthropomorphic agent may affect the way in which a user interacts with the interface and hence Interface agents often use the personifying technique of depicting the interface as a human face. Koda and Maes (1996) in their article "Agents with Faces: The Effects of Personification of Agents" investigated the most "favorable" interface through the use of a poker game and four computer players, all with different personas. Two important results for anthropomorphism were found:

- Faces made the game more engaging.
- The human face rated first in intelligence and comfort, and was second to the dog cartoon in likability.

People liked faces in Interfaces!

More significantly, Poleretzky et al. (1999) explain that intelligent software agents can provide context-sensitive assistance to customers based on their location on a Web site, their individual profile, their historical purchasing patterns, and any new offerings from the organization. Automated responses to e-mail queries by consumers can also be generated by intelligent software agents, which process the text of the query and reply using pre-written responses matching the enquiry (see also Hibbard, 1998).

One problem with the software agents which provide a single question-answer facility is that the answer provided might not relate to the question exactly (see Cohn, 1999). A more sophisticated tool is the case-based reasoning engine (Hibbard, 1998), which analyses customer questions and asks further questions (as necessary) to derive an appropriate answer from a database of pre-written responses. The database can be pure data or can be "intelligent" in that the data contained can be updated by user queries—the system learns about user enquiries through machine learning.

Maes (1994) has explored the use of machine learning in personal assistant interface agents. Initially an assistant is not familiar with the habits and preferences of the person they are assisting. By watching how the person goes about tasks, being instructed by the person, and learning from other assistants, the assistant agent can gradually become more useful; this is machine learning. A Virtual Salesperson should "learn" a customer's buying preferences. Any Data Mining task can become more effective through the use of machine learning.

An important point made by Poleretzky et al. (1999) is that consumer interaction with organization support staff will not become obsolete. Regardless of the "intelligence" of the software agents, it is important that human interaction is provided or encouraged when the consumer appears to be having difficulty to ensure a quality retail experience. The authors describe click-stream-tracking technology, which identifies and targets particular customers for which human intervention should be invoked based on[2]:

- customer profile information stored in the site's database, possibly indicating that they have a history of difficulty in using the site;
- the path which the customer is taking through the Web site, which might imply that the consumer is lost or cannot find the information for which they are searching;
- the price of the products in the customer's shopping basket, possibly indicating that they are highly valued by the organization; and/or
- the time the customer has spent looking at a particular page.

Natural Language Processing

A further problem with having an "intelligent search engine" as the primary customer interface is their complexity due, for instance:

- to inconsistencies between the search engines (Lohse & Spiller, 1998) provided by different Web sites (such as their syntax and advanced search capabilities);
- to the often large numbers of "hits" produced which might not even be relevant to the query being made (Wiley, 1998); or
- to the plethora of navigation features and options, such as buttons, frames, pull-down menus, image maps, etc. (Burke, 1997).

An approach which has the potential to provide a more consistent and human-interaction search facility would involve natural language processing (see, for example, Rabkin & Tingley, 1999) coupled with an Interface agent. Such a mechanism for querying would involve a natural language question being typed by a consumer and the intelligent software agent carrying out pattern matching or finding cues which are associated with the requested information or answer. This approach also obviates the need for sophisticated navigation features or search options and ensures that all such agents on different Web sites are interacted with in the same way.

Natural language processing therefore goes a long way towards enhancing the retail experience for consumers, because it parallels to some extent the social human interaction they would experience in a face-to-face shopping environment. An effective way in which to enhance this more "humane" (as opposed to "human") interaction is providing the answers to consumer natural language queries using facial animation and voice reproduction.

The use of a recently formalized International Standard for facial animation—MPEG-4—to provide a more "humane" visual interface can help with user acceptance of e-commerce whilst the use of various AI techniques such as text to speech synthesis, natural language processing, and data mining can help in making the user experience more consistent, enjoyable, and profitable.

FACIAL ANIMATION OVERVIEW

Facial animation is receiving more attention than ever before in its 25-year life, representing an independent area of computer graphics with proper theoretical basis, principles, methodologies, algorithms, and technologies. Applications of animated virtual faces are found in advanced human-computer interfaces, interactive games, multimedia titles, electronic commerce, telepresence, education, and in a broad variety of production animations.

Despite the specific objective of the application, being that of synthesizing realistic faces or fantastic ones, the realistic representation of the facial expressions of humans and of other creatures is initiating cross-disciplinary research of extreme interest and fascination.

Graphics technologies underlying facial animation include more conventional approaches to image morphing such as key-framing as well as accurate, front-end anatomical, and physical modelling coupled with behavioral animation.

Contributions in this area began with Parke's first computer-based facial animation and continued up to the recent success of films such as "Toy Stories" and "A Bugs Life."

Arguably, the first step for future facial animation systems has been defined by a standardization body known as MPEG (a working group of the International Organization for Standardization—ISO). In fact, although several nice-looking facial animation systems have been developed in the past years, they have all suffered from a major limitation. Each of them used a proprietary architecture and syntax to animate the synthetic face. In most cases, the facial animation systems were developed to fit and solve a specific application, without taking into account possible limitations or drawbacks that a particular architecture could encounter when used outside the specific application for which it was designed. MPEG tried to overcome all the divisions in the world of facial animation by defining a standard way to deal with synthetic faces. Three years of work and consultation have led to the definition of a set of animation parameters and semantic rules that can be used to drive any synthetic face compliant with the standard.

A Few Concepts on MPEG-4 Facial Animation

MPEG-4 offers a nice framework to build a man-machine interface with animated faces. It is important to understand how this technology can be used to build a Virtual Salesperson, and the advantages, disadvantages, and limitations of this new technology.

A mesh of polygons (left hand side of Figure 2), often triangles, typically describes the **face model**. The higher the number of polygons, the better is the appearance of the model on the screen. In addition, some computer graphics techniques can be used to 'smooth' the polygons and hence improve the appearance of the face.

According to the MPEG-4 standard, any face animation decoder must have its own **proprietary face**. It is better if it has both a male and female model, since sometimes the content to be reproduced requires a specific gender.

In Figure 1 the underlying structure of a simple face model is presented; in Figure 2 two hi-complexity models are shown to give evidence of the achievable level of quality.

Any face model compliant with the standard can be animated by means of streams of parameters, called FAPs, **Facial Animation Parameters**. The FAPs can either control a very limited part of the face or the whole face expression. Figure 3 show the effects of FAP on a generic face model. FAP basically control the displacement of specific key points of the face, the **feature points**. By providing the movement of the feature points representing the corner of the lip, it is possible for instance to perform a smile or a scowl. Pre-rendered movies of face animation examples can be downloaded from Pockaj (1999).

It should be stressed that MPEG-4 does **not** stream bandwidth-intensive video of computer graphics-rendered heads but sends low bandwidth FAP parameters to the user's computer where the model is rendered in real time.

Finally, advanced facial animation decoders can also handle **Facial Definition Parameters** (FDPs) making it is possible to modify the appearance of the face or even replace it, hence, for example, maintaining the corporate identity of the Virtual Salesperson.

The reader can refer to MPEG (1998) for detailed information on the standard.

Figure 4 shows the effect of FDP on a proprietary face.

Figure 1. Wireframe and Flat Shaded Representation of a Simple Face Mode (Less Than 1000 Polygons).

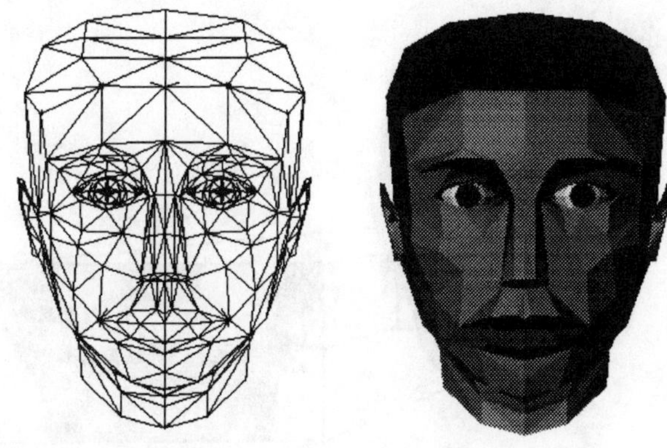

Figure 2. Gouraud Shaded Representation of a Complex Face Model (More Than 10000 Polygons) (Pictures Courtesy of Pierlugi Garaventa)

MPEG-4 Facial Animation in E-Commerce

By reading the specifications, it's immediately clear how MPEG puts very few constraints on the implementation of the face decoder. This allows companies implementing MPEG-4-compliant facial animation enough latitude for competition, a fact that will likely lead to a very high quality in the products.

First of all, MPEG-4 doesn't specify anything about the face model resident on the decoder except that it must have at least one proprietary face model with at least the 84 standardized feature points. The model can be of any arbitrary complexity, from a few hundred to a few thousand polygons (see Figures 1 and 2), and driven by very simple or extremely sophisticated animation rules.

Second, MPEG-4 does not specify how to interpret the FAPs; this means that any facial animation decoder must have proprietary criteria to map a very limited amount of information (the FAP value, e.g., the reproduction of a joy expression to the stretch of a lip corner) into very complex face postures.

There are no constraints on the movements of the vertices of the model in the neighborhood of the feature point. For instance, the movement of the mouth corner during a smile implies that part of the lips and the cheek are also moved in a natural way. The collection of these criteria for interpreting the FAPs, usually referred to as the "animation

Figure 3. Effects of FAP: Movement of the Left Outer Corner Lip (left) and Expression of Anger (right)

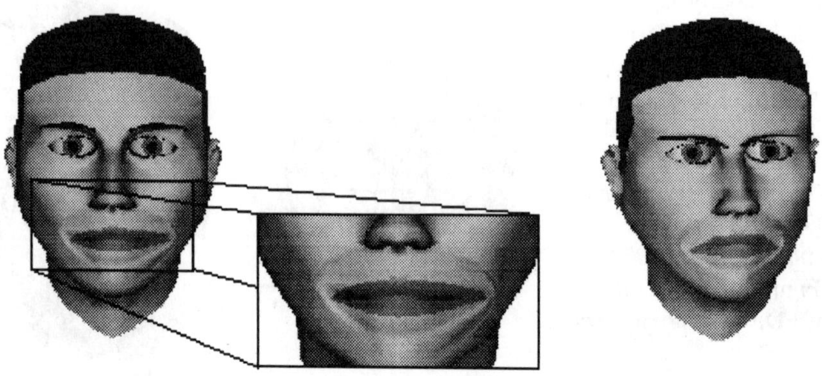

Figure 4. Effects of FDP: Proprietary Face (middle); Reshaped Proprietary Face by Means of Feature Points and Texture (left); Replacement of the Proprietary Face Model (right); the Two Small Models Represent the Proprietary Model After Reshaping Process and the Mesh of the Transmitted Model that Replaced the Proprietary One Respectively.

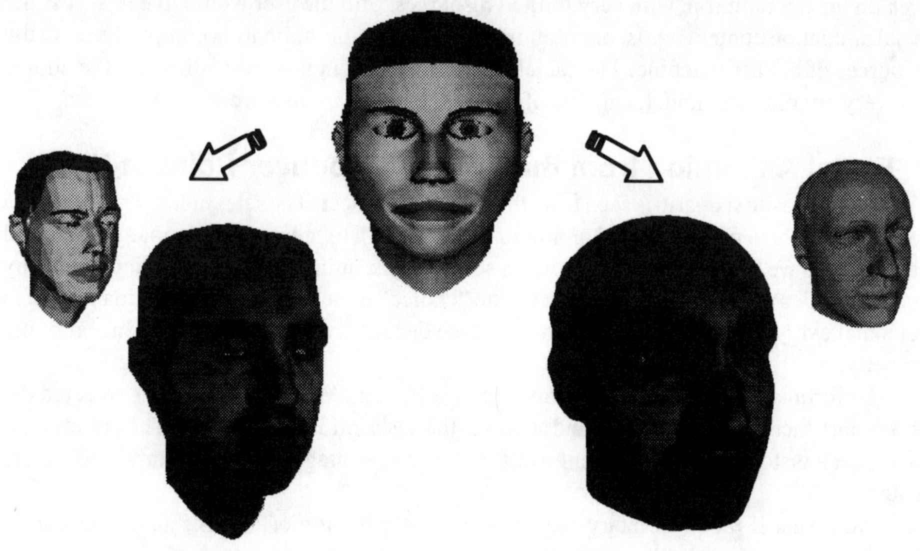

rules," is proprietary to the decoder. The animation rules, being responsible for the final quality of the animation, can therefore make a visible difference amongst the facial animation decoders.

All these considerations must be used to drive the creation of a human interface, namely a virtual seller. Depending on the specific application, the system can be differently tuned and biased.

The following example shows the two views of the use of the Virtual Salesperson. Figure 5 shows, as a matter of example, a hypothetical Web site where the Virtual Salesperson is used to sell pizzas and drinks on the Internet.

Facial Animation from the User Point of View

One possible scenario implies that the user buys, or simply downline loads as a plug-in, an MPEG-4 facial decoder to access, for instance, our pizza-selling Web page that contains content encoded through the FAP. The user here represents a possible customer of a product advertised through a virtual face.

In this scenario, the same information is played in different, although similar, ways by different decoders. The resulting animations will be different since they are played by different faces, controlled by different software, and yet similar since the same content drives them: if the FAP stream directs a face to nod or smile, all the decoders will show a nodding or smiling head.

The choice of the user for a certain decoder over another will therefore be driven by the perceived quality of the animation. The quality of the proprietary model itself is not sufficient; it has to be balanced with the performances during the animation. Both the animation rules and the rendering speed (namely the number of rendered frames per second) on common hardware platforms are important parameters to guide the choice.

The user may also want to select a favorite face model among several faces made available by the decoder; its goal is that of accessing the encoded content in the way he/she likes more. But note an exception. Sometimes the user may work on his/her portable PC, or even on his/her palmtop, with very limited resources. Still the user would like to access the facial animation content whilst maintaining the best possible animation compatible with the resources of his/her machine. The facial decoder should, in this case, allow for the choice of a very simple face model, capable of fitting the hardware resources of the system.

Facial Animation from the Content Producer Point of View

The opposite scenario is seen from the content producer. The sales manager of the pizza company wants to produce facial animation content both to present the company and to sell products. As we have seen in the previous scenario, the animation is not predictable in any way. The sales manager can only rely on the "choice" done by the users. The manager can hope that every user has bought a very nice face decoder, with a nice looking face moving properly.

Unfortunately, in these cases hope is not sufficient. What if the user has selected the proprietary face model of a clown and accesses the description of a product? The effect could be at best a distortion of the content itself, but worse, damage to the company's corporate image.

And what if the proprietary face renders an expression of joy like an expression of sadness, and the virtual seller looks very sad in presenting a new product? All this can be possible whilst still maintaining a perfect compliance with the standard.

It appears clear, therefore, that from the content producer point of view the main goal is, very often, to leave as little freedom as possible to the user of the content. In this scenario it's very likely that the content producer wants to make use of the FDP to their maximum extent in order to get complete control of the animation rendered by any decoder accessing

Figure 5. An Example of a Virtual Salesman

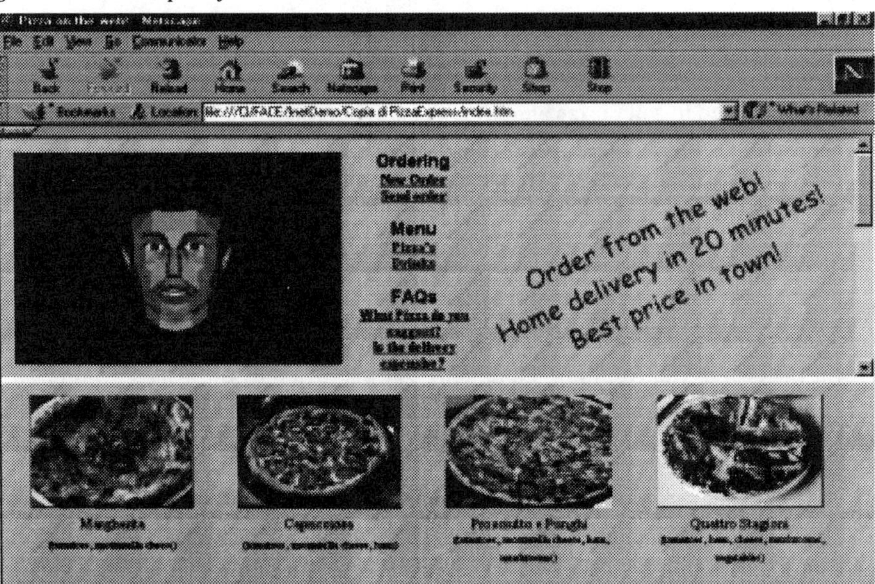

the content.

There could be other reasons for downloading a specific face to the decoder; for instance, if the company's logo is a face-like character, the company would like that this model is animated rather than a generic face. Also, if the user is currently working on a very low-power machine, the content producer may even prefer that the user doesn't display anything at all rather than a very bad, maybe jerky, animation.

The limitations at the user side introduced in the present scenario do not affect in any way the competition among face implementers. The responsibility has simply been moved from the decoder to the encoder side; in this case, the required face model and associated animation rules have to be transmitted rather than being resident in the decoder.

What drives the server side of this man-machine dialogue? The current Virtual Salesperson is driven by a client which has three subsystems: a brain, a text to speech synthesizer (TTS), and a personality. The personality is currently under development and the TTS is considered to be a black box. The TTS converts written input (perhaps with some markup language) to spoken output. Rather than developing a TTS system from scratch, the black box approach allows MBROLA, Festival, or any proprietary TTS such as the Elan or Lernout and Hauspie system to be used. The phoneme information is separated from the synthesis process and used to calculate the speech-related FAPs. These FAPs may be added to by the persona of the Virtual Salesperson.

Since the Virtual Salesperson has a "brain," it can answer questions such as "Can I add anchovies at no extra cost?" By parsing the sentence and retrieving the relevant data from its knowledge base. The brain owes much to research into agents as mentioned previously but is also heavily indebted to work on natural language processing, intelligent database systems, and finally, chatterbots. The following section gives a brief background to the evolution of chatterbots and to some of the techniques that can make them seem more human and more humane.

TALKING HEADS

It has long been man's dream to be able to interact or converse with something man-made: G.B. Shaw's "Pygmalion," the android in Fritz Lang's "Metropolis," Robbie the Robot in "Forbidden Planet," HAL in Clarke's "2001." Recently, computer scientists have been confident enough to be able to debate as to whether this could become true. The debate was often on a philosophical level, the question being: "Can machines think?'' A seminal argument in this debate is seen in the collection "Computer Machinery and Intelligence'' by Turing (1963). He argued that if a judge could not decide if a hidden contestant was human or not simply based upon their ability to carry on a question/answer conversation, then for all intents and purposes, the contestant was "human" regardless. The computer either imitates a human or is "intelligent." Any Virtual Salesperson needs to appear to be intelligent.

This intelligence testing became known as the Turing test, and in 1991 it was conducted as a formal computer competition: the Loebner contest. The AI programs competing in this contest are often referred to as chatterbots.

Eliza

Arguably, the first of these chatterbots was Eliza, one of the first successful programs to imitate humans. It was developed by Joseph Weizenbaum, a MIT professor in 1966. It was renown more for its illusion of understanding than for its AI techniques, the illusion being achieved by what Weizenbaum termed "tricks."

Weizenbaum explains that the tricks he employs are to fool the user into assuming there is more intelligence than is actually present. He admits that Eliza is just a simple program, but that it could still play the "imitation game." The tricks that Eliza uses centre on the user directing the course of the conversation, with Eliza contributing very little substance (Weizenbaum, 1976). This was achieved through the characterization of Eliza as a "psychoanalytic therapist" and then through the use of "Rogerian" analysis. Psychoanalytic therapists use Rogerian analysis to allow a patient to extrapolate on their own thoughts by the therapist asking questions about the last response that the patient provided.

Eliza implements features that are applicable to a Talking Head. One such feature is the elegance in which Eliza matches user input to patterns and constructs sentences, often substituting some of the reply to the user with their original text. This dialogue manager often gave the illusion of intelligence. For example:

USER: My mother is always working.

ELIZA: Who else in your family is always working?

In this example it can be seen that Eliza's response seems intelligent, yet behind-the-scenes processing shows that there is very little understanding. A simple pattern match and the use of the user's own words have created the illusion that Eliza is actually following the conversation. Eliza can also keep track of what the user has said and use it in a later reposte. Eliza uses other tricks such as the use of questions with the user supplying most of the context of the conversation, Eliza at no point volunteering information. This approach is not enough for a Virtual Salesperson who has to respond accurately to requests. One does not expect 300 pizzas to be delivered to your home because of a dialogue misunderstanding—who pays?

The way in which the computer science community embraced Eliza worried Weizenbaum; there was a belief that his program was the be-all and end-all of computers understanding human language. This "hype" about clever tricks masquerading as AI breakthroughs is still apparent today. Weizenbaum put forward that a general solution to natural language processing was impossible, and that language could only be understood in contextual frameworks. The theory of contextual frameworks is that to some extent conversation occurs through the relating of beliefs and knowledge of a domain to one another. Weizenbaum believes that even humans do not employ a general solution in the way that they interact with one another through dialog (Weizenbaum, 1976).

Chatterbots

Chatterbots are conversational agents constructed to simulate conversation and/or provide useful information. Michael Mauldin, a pioneer in chatterbots, has the view that the Turing test, when restricted to simple domains, benefits the AI area of computer science. The reasoning for this way of thinking is that if you can get a computer program to pass a single domain, then 50 to 100 groups working on different domains could create a single program capable of finding a common conversational ground with a user (Mauldin, 1994). Thomas Whalen, another chatterbot author, backs up Mauldin's view, when he talks about a database he wrote to answer a user's natural English questions (Whalen & Patrick, 1990). He believes that if you write enough good questions and answers, then a good question-and-answer program is relatively simple to write. Answering questions is only a small part of human conversation, but Whalen's view is similar to that of Mauldin—once a domain has been conquered, expanding the domain is trivial.

Mauldin and Whalen clearly believe that the answer to conversational architectures is a knowledge-based approach. Chatterbots need to know how to talk to begin with, since no one wants to have to teach a computer how to converse. Clearly however, this type of chatterbot design will be limited by its initial knowledge and so a merging of knowledge-based and machine learning approaches has become prevalent in the modern design of chatterbots.

In many cases chatterbots are used in Multi User Domains (MUDs) to provide users with conversation and useful information such as answers to questions like "Where is player X?" This is done by parsing the user's query ("How much is a large pizza with the lot?") and matching it against its "user-question" database. These natural language databases allow users to ask questions (query) in their natural language and receive an appropriate answer. A popular tool used within many natural language systems is pattern matching. Two of the most famous chatterbots using this system are Colin and Julia—Maas Neotek robots—constructed by Michael Mauldin. Both are TinyMUD robots, with Colin being available via FTP (ftp://nl.cs.cmu.edu/usr/mlm/ftp/robot.tar.Z).

The way in which Colin and Julia were designed was to use a tree-based model of input/output patterns to transfer the conversation between a number of states (Mauldin, 1994). By using states, Mauldin hoped to guide the user through a restricted conversation. The use of states means that this knowledge-based approach is limited to how good the conversational module is; there is no learning to improve the way in which the chatterbot reacts to the user.

These chatterbots are an improvement on Eliza because they use more tricks and have more sophisticated memories of past events and conversations (Maes, 1995, p. 110). This form of dialogue management is also more robust at giving correct answers or information to user requests (but see later limitations). Hence, it is very suitable for a Virtual Salesperson interface. Finally, the chatterbots seem more humane. Since it has been shown that it is very important for a Talking Head interface to appear human and humane—it is instructive to see how a chatterbot is perceived by someone interfacing with them (Foner, 1993). Julia is a good example.

Julia is a client bot - she connects to the MUD server via telnet just as a normal human player would. Julia has an interesting persona, most of which is to make her seem more human. For example, since Julia can map out a MUD, it is possible to ask her for directions. Julia will also lend you money, can describe herself and of course can carry on a reasonable conversation. She retains limited knowledge about past conversation subjects and reuses them. Julia often appears to be too human. The following conversation reported in (Foner, 1993) was acquired by MUD user Robyn Kozierok who knew that Julia was a 'bot:

Robyn whispers, "How are you feeling?" To Julia.
Julia whispers, "Terrible."
Robyn whispers, "Why, Julia?" To Julia.
Julia whispers, "I have PMS today."

Since most players in the MUD do not realize that Julia is a chatterbot, she is treated like any other potential female by the other players and hence she has many responses for dealing with subtle or blatant flirtation. Colin similarly has extensive code for dealing with swearing. Foner (1993) details a dialogue between a male MUD player and Julia. He prefaces it with:

"He spent 13 days trying to get to first base with Julia, and it's not clear he ever figured out he was trying to pick up a robot (although he clearly suspects it at two points)."

Both Julia and Colin's natural language processing facilities are simple—more extensive but apparently less algorithmically sophisticated than those of Eliza. For example, Colin uses a brute force matching of likely patterns to produce a response (the * represents any sequence of words or characters):

```
else if (MATCH (lcmsg, "*predict*weather*")          ||
        MATCH (lcmsg, "*what*weather*")              ||
        MATCH (lcmsg, "*how*s*weather*")             ||
        MATCH (lcmsg, "*how*z*weather*")             ||
        MATCH (lcmsg, "*what*forecast*")             ||
        MATCH (lcmsg, "*describe*forecast*")         ||
        MATCH (lcmsg, "*describe*weather*"))
```

The fuzziness of meaning derived from the '*'s can adequately cater for many enquiries but can also lead to many *non-sequiturs* or outright misleading responses from the chatterbot. Since this would not be acceptable in a Virtual Salesperson, it is necessary to have less fuzziness through more specific patterns. This increases the domain knowledge of the Virtual Salesperson and also how long it takes to accurately understand what the request was.

Verbots

Mauldin has continued his foray into chatterbot design recently with the construction of a new breed of chatterbots called verbots. These verbots are not only chatterbots, but also include virtual personalities with the use of 2-D graphics and synthesized voices, making the experience very similar to that of interface agents discussed previously. The chatterbot design has remained very similar to that of Colin and Julia, but with the availability of end-user customization. With the help of tutorials (Plantec, 1999), users can write their own scripts for verbots, giving them increased knowledge. This end-user customization is an improvement over the previous MUD agents, but there still exist some problems: not everyone has the ability to write their own script. The use of these scripts has shifted the hard-coded pattern-matching/response algorithm into the domain of users. The "weather" request processing similar to the above Colin example is given in Sylvie's (the verbot's name) net file as a rule:

```
<id-59>
a:0.4
p:1 *weather*
p:1 *is it*cold*there*
p:1 *is it* snow*
p:1 *is it* rain*
p:1 *is it*warm*there*
p:1 *is it*hot*there*
r:The disks are warm and the IO channels are humming.
```

The "<id-59>" is the name of a user-defined state so that state transitions can occur. The "a" is an activation level—this supposedly gives user control over when the rule will fire. An activation level of 0.2 means that this rule should not fire at random. Values below 0.3 are very unlikely to fire without a pattern match and those above 0.2 may fire if Sylvie runs out of things to say. By carefully adjusting the activation level, Sylvie's random comments or *non-sequiturs* won't become too numerous. The multiple "p" lines represent patterns to match, with * representing any number of words or characters. The numeric value (1 in this case) represents a "comparative activation level" (Plantec, 1999). So if Sylvie matches the user request to one of the patterns, then the pattern with the highest relative activation will produce the response given by the "r" line.

Not shown in this example is the mechanism for causing state transitions (and for preventing incorrect backward transitions). For example, it is often needed to add lines such as: "+<statexxx>" and "-<stateyyy>" (the x and y are irrelevant) so that Sylvie will increase the activation level on this response temporarily or will inhibit the firing of the rule in the second case. This tends to force the verbot to make the required state transition and hence to have a limited memory of previous user requests or a context in which to supply an answer. For example, a user may ask "Do you have large pizzas?" and then ask "How much is it?" The "it" in the second request obviously refers to a large pizza and the current state will help identify this.

In contrast to Mauldin's expressed views on the Turing test about having mastered one domain, 50 experts can master 50 domains, the addition of new knowledge to Sylvie remains problematic. The more knowledge she has (or the more fuzzy patterns she has to match against), the more likely an incorrect or irrelevant response will be produced. Getting the activation levels correct is a black art. However, Sylvie is a believable talking head.

Mentoring System

Marriott (1999a) details work on a software-based mentoring system which uses similar techniques for natural language processing and for producing relevant information-rich responses. The entire system—a suite of cooperating network-based computer programs, databases, and user interfaces—runs on a network of Unix workstations and PCs (see Figure 7). Core to this is the central **Mentor** daemon or server—a Java-based mini operating system in its own right. The system is of moderate size, currently being about 50,000 lines of Java code in 150 classes spread over about 30 different packages.

The main GUI interface between the user model and the **Mentor System** is via a Query client type interface integrated into the user model. An actual but contrived dialogue is shown in Figure 8 and shows some of the functionality of the system. The user input is in the top section and alternates with the **Mentor System** response in the bottom one.

The **Mentor System** has rudimentary natural language processing through regular expression pattern matching, state transitions and the use of sub-classing of Java classes, and therefore has a good ability to understand user requests. It will greet the user in a non-deterministic fashion, occasionally using various parts of the user's full name. In a similar manner it will respond to requests on different topics made with varying phrasing such as: "What is the weather?", "What is the time?", etc. Occasionally, in response to a weather update request, it will data mine a weather Web site to report accurate meteorological information.

The equivalent "weather" request in the **Mentor System** (shown below) would be specified as an array of string inside a Java class. Notice that the array uses ".*" to represent any number of characters since it uses Perl-5 regular expressions. Similarly, the '?' in the strings indicates that the preceding character is optional. For efficiency, the system must first successfully match the keywords in the first element of the array. If this and subsequent matches against the elements of the array succeed, the response is randomly chosen from an array of N appropriate responses with duplicates in the last N responses suppressed. This response is weighted and the overall winning response from all the matched topics is sent back to the user.

```
protected transient String patterns[ ] =
        {
First entry is the general area to match
            ".*(weather|fore?cast).*",

            ".*predict.*weather.*",
            ".*what.*weather.*",
            ".*how.*s.*weather.*",
            ".*how.*z.*weather.*",
                ".*what.*fore?cast.*",
            ".*describe.*fore?cast.*",
            ".*describe.*weather.*"
 };
```

The system makes heuristic guesses about the subject of enquiries. In the example shown in Figure 8, the system has accurately guessed the identity of "geoff" even though there are many geoff's on the system. Notice as well that the system knows the sex of the subject (and of any requested individual) and adjusts the output accordingly. Most of the base information is obtained by data mining various Web sites and system files. The system is proactive—not just responding to user input but also initiating meaningful dialogue with the user. Although these features appear trivial, they are very important for maintaining the humane image of any Talking Head interface.

The **Mentor System** knows about a number of topics—the heart of the above client interface is a loop that checks what the user has typed and what they have typed in the past against a list of **Mentor** topics. This is done with preprocessed regular expression matching algorithms. As well as the topics indicated in Figure 8, the system knows about religious and cultural dates, various ways of saying hello and good-bye, swearing and offensive queries, current Lecturer-Tutor-Practicals information about the units that the user is enrolled in and also information concerning the location of various venues on campus. The system can also use the "net" files that are used by Sylvie and a user can "load up" their own topics at run-time. The main domain of the **Mentor System**'s knowl-

Figure 7. The Mentor System

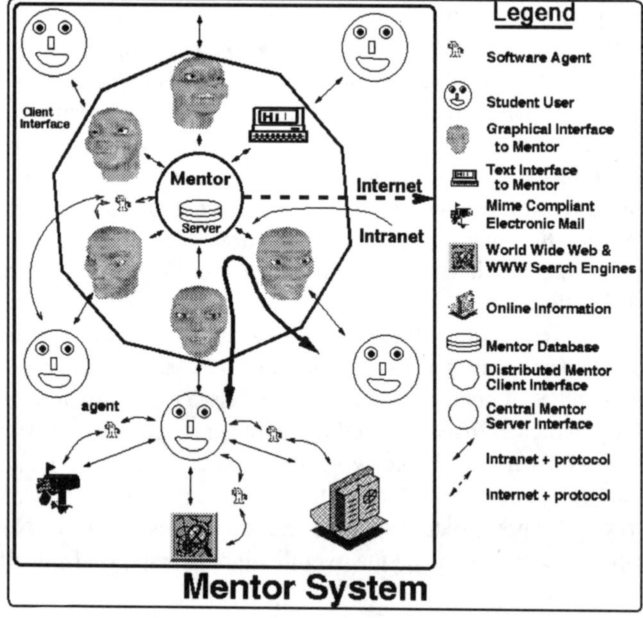

edge is educational but the programmed "topics" can cover any field. The system could easily be programmed as a Virtual Salesperson.

It is important to understand that the more specific the knowledge domain is, the more accurate and relevant will be the response. Unfortunately, the responses will also seem less humanlike—humans have a large knowledge domain. This poses a dilemma for the implementation of a realistic Virtual Salesperson.

*Figure 8. A **Mentor System** Client that is the Base Level Querying Part of the User Model. See the Text for an Explanation of the Example Dialogue Between the User and the **Mentor System**.*

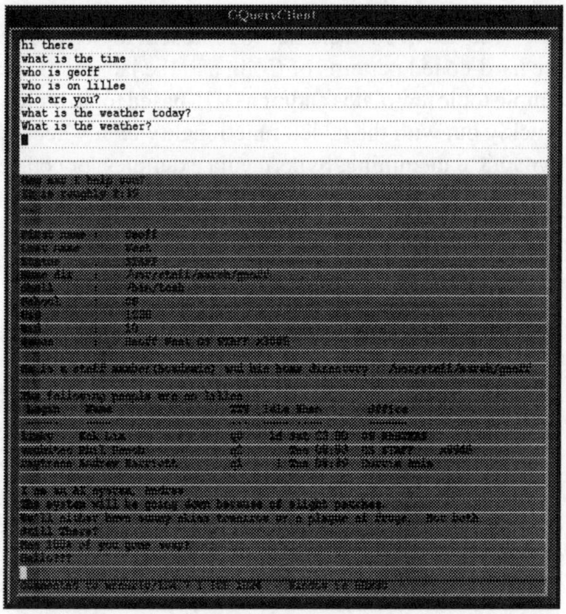

With careful programming of the natural language processing system, we can cater for variety in the input but still give accurate responses. For example, the complex Perl-5 regular expression shown below will match a large number of typical requests for information about a certain subject (in this case a GTK widget). Most of the complexity in the string is so that the subject of the enquiry can be easily isolated.

```
".*\b" +
    "(?:" +
        "(?:(?:I\s*(?:need|want)\s*)?help\s*(?:me)?\s*(?:about|with|on))|" +
            "(?:what\s*is)|" +
            "(?:where\s*" +
                "(?:" +
                    "(?:can\s*I\s*(?:get|find\s*(?:out\s*)?))|" +
                    "(?:is\s*(?:the(?:re)?\s*)?)|" +
                ")" +
            "\s*info(?:rmation)?\s*(?:about|with|on))|" +
            "(?:tell\s*me\s*about)" +
        ")" +
        "\s*(?:the|a|)\s*(?:(?:gtk\+?)?)" +
        "(.*)(?:\s*widget)?.*"
```

The system can produce the following dialogue between user and **Mentor System**:

Mentor System: *[unsolicited]* Assignment 2 for cg252 is due soon. How goes it?
User: OK
Mentor System: Have you started it yet?
User: No

Mentor System: Do you know where to start with the algorithm?
User: Yes but I haven't got it working yet.
Mentor System: The /usr/units/cg252-502 subdirectory contains some useful example code.
User: OK. Ta
Mentor System: That's OK.

The use of Java classes to represent topics of interest is a good compromise between the hard-coded patterns of Colin and the lack-of-flexibility "net" files of Sylvie. By using simple topic templates and/or a GUI-based topic builder, new topic "databases" can be built quickly but with the added functionality of any necessary specific Java code (for example dynamic data mining, hypermedia examples, or code execution). In essence, the system is a Natural Language Processing GUI front-end to an intelligent information database. This is roughly what any Virtual Salesperson, Virtual Lecturer, etc. is: The Mentor System has been integrated with the facial animation system to create a Talking Mentor. With this in mind, we developed a FAQBot.

FAQBot

A FAQBot (Beard, 1999) is an audiovisual agent that will automate the process of users finding answers to their questions in FAQs (Frequently Asked Questions). The FAQBot's basic job is to answer a user's questions using the knowledge it gleans from FAQs. It does this through integration of natural language parsing, text to speech synthesis, facial animation and AI systems, to produce a 'bot capable of helping a user through normal question/answer conversation (see Figure 9).

As with chatterbots, the idea behind a question-and-answer conversation from the computer's point of view is to match the user's question with a question from an FAQ, and respond with the expert answer to that question. To produce more accurate and relevant responses to user enquiries, a process similar to Markov Chaining has been used—word graphs.

The idea behind the graphs is to efficiently store many similar questions (all having the same answer). This is similar to the complex regular expression seen in the **Mentor System** above—getting more possible questions out of a small set of words. Word graphs can basically be thought of as condensed word trees—most times the questions share the same kind of structure. Some typical questions that all mean the same thing:

Figure 9. The FAQBot User Dialogue

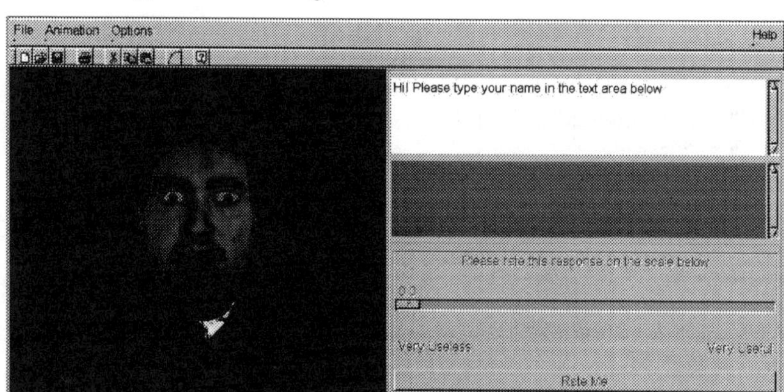

WHAT DO THE INITIALS FAQ STAND FOR?
WHAT DOES THE ACRONYM FAQ STAND FOR?
WHAT DOES FAQ STAND FOR?

These can be represented as the following graph:

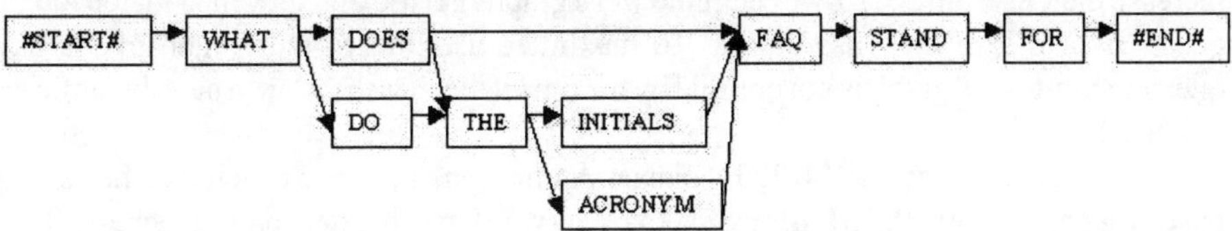

If all paths are followed on the above graph, the following questions can be extracted:

WHAT DOES THE ACRONYM FAQ STAND FOR?
WHAT DO THE INITIALS FAQ STAND FOR?
WHAT DOES FAQ STAND FOR?
WHAT DOES THE ACRONYM FAQ STAND FOR?
WHAT DO THE INITIALS FAQ STAND FOR?

The questions in italics were not part of the original question set, but have been extracted from the graph. This is one of advantages of a graph, you get "like" questions for no extra cost. The extra questions may not be written with correct English, but this does not matter, they merely help to match against more types of user input—the outcome is no worse than using pattern matching with * to represent 0 or more words. The major advantage of using word graphs is the ability to compare lengths of questions, along with sentence structure matching. For example the pattern "what.*faq.* " could match a question like : "*What processing does a FAQBot do in order to use an FAQ?*"

Regular expression pattern matching must check source and target question lengths (as well as other criteria) to get a proper match. To further illustrate the advantage of using word graphs, consider a user asking, "What does FAQ mean?" If the one extra node is added to the word graph, it becomes:

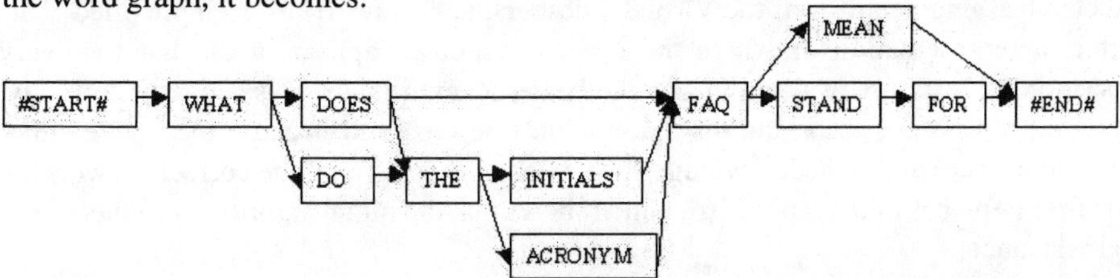

The extra questions (on top of those shown earlier) that are found for no extra cost:

WHAT DOES FAQ MEAN?
WHAT DO THE INITIALS FAQ MEAN?
WHAT DOES THE ACRONYM FAQ MEAN?
WHAT DO THE INITIALS FAQ MEAN?
WHAT DOES THE ACRONYM FAQ MEAN?

Now the FAQBot can match a whole plethora of questions ending with "mean," which it previously could not do. This in turn will make the service of the FAQBot better for all.

Since the graphs are dynamically added to when user questions are close to what is wanted but not quite correct (the user gives feedback on relevance of the ranked response), the FAQBot learns.

Word graphs would appear to be a perfect solution to the question/answer user interaction. As word graphs increase in size, they can match more and more questions and increase their usefulness. However, if the word graphs get too big, they then match too many questions and lose their usefulness. To maximize usefulness, individual graphs have a question limit—if a graph is not optimal by the time it reaches the limit, a new dynamic graph is started.

The research into the MPEG-4 Facial Animation, Text to Speech Synthesis and AI based on chatterbots, the **Mentor System,** and word graphs, has led to a generic Talking Head interface whose visage is customizable, whose voice can take advantage of current state-of-the-art TTS systems, and whose brain is flexible enough to be able to understand and process most user requests, be they in the domain of FAQs, education, information broker, or e-commerce.

THE VIRTUAL SALESPERSON

The Virtual Salesperson (VS) shown in Figure 11 is a Talking Head that uses the previously described technologies to match common e-commerce enquiries against the Salesperson's knowledge base to provide a service—information, sales, sales-talk, billing—accompanied by a suitable response—vocal, textual, visual. The entire Talking Head project forms a small part of a European 5th Framework Project whose objective is to define new models and implement advanced tools for audio-video analysis, synthesis, and representation in order to provide technologies for the implementation of large-scale virtual and augmented environments.

Preliminary trials have shown that 62% of VS enquiries were answered correctly the first time. As a comparison to a similar project, COMODA achieved right answers 56-69% of the time (a different analysis technique for that system makes it difficult to give an exact figure). Therefore it can be seen that word graphs are a viable matching/retrieval mechanism.

To give some insight into the relevance of responses within the ranked list and the predicted learning behavior of the Virtual Salesperson, Figure 10 has been provided. This chart is a representation of where the correct responses appear in the list for every transaction. A response at position 1 is the best, meaning that it was returned correctly. Negative scores show the enquiries that couldn't be retrieved because they were either irrelevant or were not in the knowledge base. Greater than 80% of the correct answers are in the first 10 places of the ranked list, which shows that the initial algorithm produces very good relevance.

One way in which the matching process could be refined to produce better results would be to provide support for suffixes and prefixes, plurals, and word stemming. For example, in the current implementation, if a user types in a word as plural and only the singular term is in the word graph, then there is no match for that word. This extra word functionality would help the Virtual Salesperson to handle requests that originate from people who do not speak English well. A common area for mistakes when learning and speaking English is the improper use of plurals.

Another improvement would be to recognize what words are important and what words aren't and use a "weighted" scoring system for ranking matches. This could be achieved with

Figure 10. The Virtual Salesperson Relevance-Retrieval Results

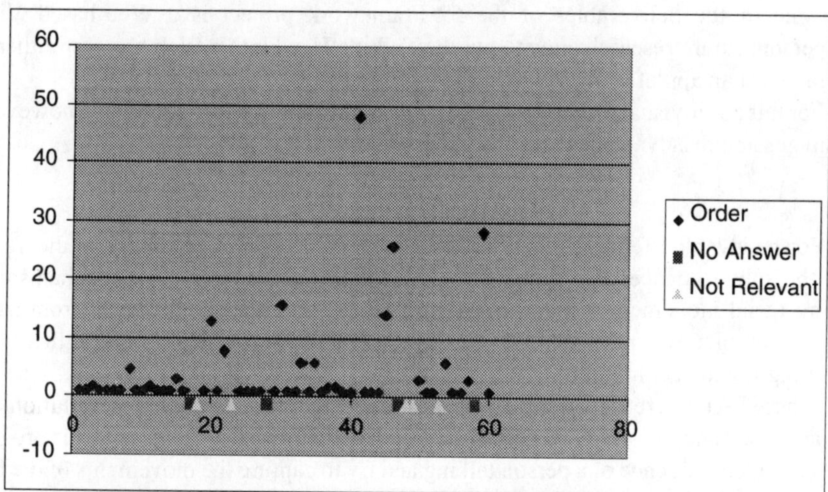

some rudimentary natural language processing, and the use of a second knowledge base such as WordNet. By doing this, the relevance of the matching process would be improved as conjunctive, and unimportant words would not skew the matching. Only questions sharing the same important words would receive high scores during matching.

The Virtual Salesperson forms a solid base for trustworthy humane e-commerce although it must be pointed out that the current application is **not** yet Web enabled nor has

Figure 11. The Virtual Salesperson Schematic

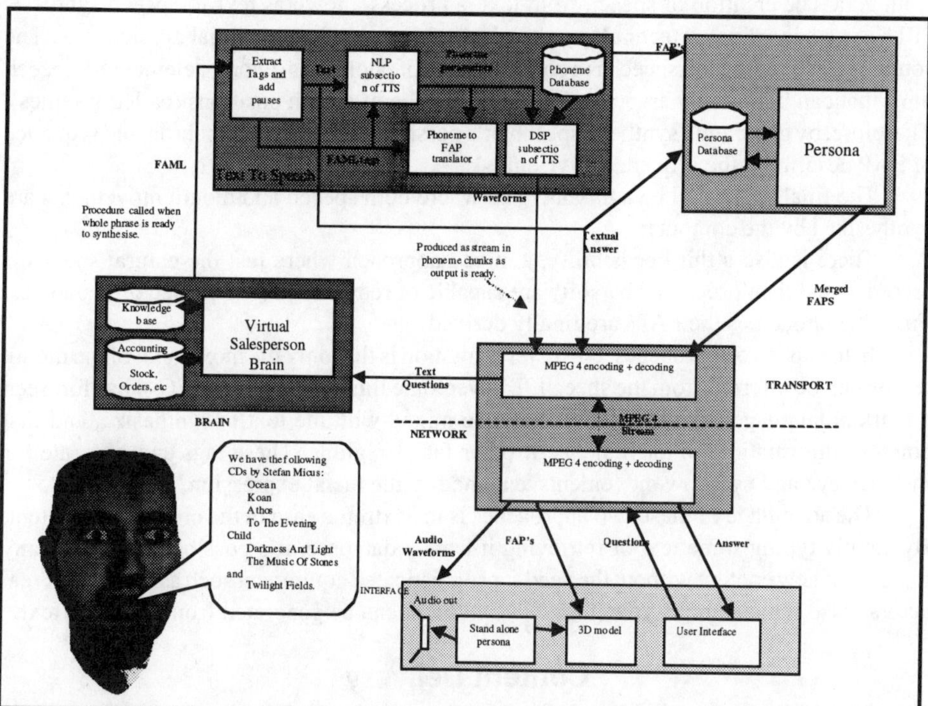

an extensive e-commerce infrastructure (knowledge base, stock database, etc.) been set up. Since one of the deliverables of the 5th Framework project is a Web-based Virtual Salesperson, future research aims to put the Talking Head into a Web browser either as a plug-in or via an applet using the Java Media Framework.

For this audiovisual technology to be successfully applied to e-commerce however, its advantages and disadvantages must be understood.

Content Creation

For believable lifelike animation, the FAP must be able to reproduce in the Talking Head the subtle nuances that humans are use to. There are three basic mechanisms for creating facial movement content based on FAP: it can either be retrieved from natural scenes or completely synthesized. This is more or less like recording a movie with a camera or creating it with a computer.

Where FAP are retrieved from a natural scene, there are two possible solutions, one software based and the other one hardware based. In the first case image analysis programs process a video sequence of a person talking and try to capture the movements of the facial feature points. In the second case, specific sensors (typically reflecting markers) are placed on the speaker's face in correspondence with the feature points; the movements of the markers are then tracked by dedicated hardware. In both cases the natural speech is recorded and subsequently reproduced synchronized with the facial animation.

The state of the art currently provides better and faster results with the hardware solution but, unfortunately, this is far more expensive that the software solution.

It would seem that the complete synthesis of FAP seems to be the best way for content creation, at least in all those cases where a very hi-fidelity and naturalness in the animation is not required. This approach consists of the simultaneous generation of speech and FAP from text. The creation of speech from text, a process known as text-to-speech synthesis (TTS), is a consolidated technology already used in several commercial applications. The sound corresponding to a speech is a concatenation of phonemes (a sort of elementary speech unit) that can be suitably associated with a sequence of mouth positions (called visemes). Therefore, by generating synthetic speech, it's possible to generate a synchronized sequence of FAP describing the sequence of visemes.

The final result will be a talking head where both speech and mouth movements are synthesized by the computer.

There is also a third possibility, a mixed approach where just the natural speech is recorded and then processed by software capable of retrieving the sequence of phonemes. From the phonemes the FAPs are finally derived.

In the last two approaches, the major limitation is that only the movement of the mouth region can be inferred from the speech. To overcome this limitation, MPEG-4 has foreseen a markup language (like HTML) that can be mixed with the text to synthesize, and that conveys information on movements of other facial regions. These tags can generate for instance eye and eyebrow movements, can modify the facial expression, and so on.

The advantage of these two approaches is the extreme ease in the creation of content. By simply typing some text or retrieving it from a database, it's possible to create many minutes of new content without the need for sophisticated equipment such as cameras or real actors. Also female, male, young, or elderly voices can be generated from the same text.

Content Delivery

MPEG-4 provides all the tools for the content delivery. One significant advantage is that the animation of an MPEG-4 face requires far less bandwidth (which often means that it can be downloaded in far less time) than a natural video: some 3k bits per second against 20k bits per second (if compared with highly compressed video of very low quality), up to hundreds of k bits per second (if compared with good quality compressed video).

Moreover, the facial animation bitrate is independent of the size of the pictures: the face can be viewed as a thumbnail or full screen (providing enough computational power) without loss of quality. All this makes a FAP-based animation highly oriented for transmission over a low bandwidth channel like the Internet. However, the proprietary model must be resident on or sent to the client.

Content Reusability

All the produced content can be easily reused. In principle, this is true for any digital content but, if you consider a digital movie, all you can do is take some part of it and insert that into other movies. If you have content stored in terms of a FAP stream, you can have it played by different faces dependent on the target customer the content is designed for or on other factors.

For example, if I want to sell a toy, I may want to use the face of a cartoon to present the toy all through the year, but at Christmas, I can choose a Santa Claus face to advertise the product. Exactly the same content (i.e., the same words pronounced with the same mimics) are played onto two different faces. Similarly, the same product can be sold to different groups of customers, from different social classes, of different ages, or even different races (it's common for the same product to be commercialized in different countries). Each group of customers can have its own virtual seller, resembling the prototype customer as much as possible. Just the face has to be changed, not the content! This is the case for instance of a Music Store: the message to be given to the customers is the 10% discount on all CDs for this month. If the customer accesses the Web page listing the pop music, demographics (may) say he will probably be a boy and therefore he will find the face of a famous pop-singer announcing the discount; if he accesses the classical music page, maybe he will be more comfortable listening to Mozart's face announcing the discount.

Content Personalization and Manipulation

As previously mentioned, the content producer can force the customer's decoder to display exactly what is received from the encoder. This implies the use of FDP's and generates completely predictable animation. In the previous examples, only the different face models had to be transmitted to the customer's decoder. On the contrary, when the face model is not set by the content creator, the customer has a wide freedom to configure the animation. He/she can choose a favorite face model. It's even possible that the customer can build or buy his own unique model, even a virtual clone of him/herself. To some extent, the user is also allowed to interact with the face modifying, for instance, the expressions of the face, amplifying or reducing the amplitude of the movements, and so on.

Quality of the Animation

So, does MPEG-4 only have advantages? Not at all. It's the first standard that includes facial animation, but it may remain just a piece of paper if the market doesn't support it. In addition, it has been designed with the primary goal of efficient encoding and capturing of facial movements. This means that the level of quality achievable by MPEG-4 facial animation has not yet proven itself, although several nice implementations of the specification have begun to appear. Only the market will be able to settle any doubts in the years to come.

CONCLUSION

The chapter has argued that a more humane visual interface to the Web will be an important step toward making this environment more accessible, usable, and comfortable to on-line consumers—especially those who are not accustomed to or do not understand the use of tools such as search engines and Web portals. The paper has also argued that quality, personalized customer service will be one of the more significant drivers of e-commerce success by organizations. This was followed by a discussion of the development and underlying components of a Virtual Salesperson Talking Head, which can respond to routine, natural language queries received by organizations through a humane visual interface. This initial work will provide the impetus for more sophisticated data mining and presentation applications of the Virtual Salesperson Talking Head:

- Universities use it for Distance Education. Various custom-built Talking Heads modelled on the Lecturer-in-Charge or brought in from other universities are used to help students understand the lesson, to provide one-to-one tutoring, to give accurate, consistent answers to queries. Each student has the lecturer as their tutor to guide them.
- On-line exhibitions such as a museum or art gallery can have a knowledgeable virtual Sister Wendy or any other art critic.
- A virtual friend available at anytime for a confidential talk.
- A virtual travel agent for giving information about ticket and accommodation arrangements.

The authors also plan to address specific environments related to the use of advanced multimedia technologies in Science Communication, Cultural Heritage, Theatre, and Arts.

In particular, a study is in progress to implement a system based on a Talking Head to be used by the Aquarium of Genova (the largest in Europe) for interactively guiding visitors to specific sections of the exposition, answering questions, and explaining the event of the day. Similar investigations are in progress in cooperation with the acting company "Teatro dell'Archivolto" of the historical Genoese theatre "Gustavo Modena" for writing novel pieces of unconventional theatre with natural actors playing on the stage together with virtual actors "living" on a screen.

In conclusion, the discussion should not be about the presence of a synthetic face in interfaces for e-commerce applications simply because of the ability of a face (either natural or virtual) to attract the attention of a possible customer. The discussion instead should be concerned with whether to use a virtual salesperson to emulate a real salesperson within an environment as close as possible to the real world or, on the contrary, to exploit the potentialities of the virtual actor to create something completely new, as far as possible from what the customer is used to experiencing.

More and more people believe the second scenario is the right one....

REFERENCES

Bacheldor, B. (1999). Portals make business sense. *InformationWeek*, October 18, 81-90.

Beard, S., Crossman, B., Cechner, P., & Marriott, A. (1999). FAQBot. *Proceedings of Pan Sydney Area Workshop on Visual Information Processing*. November 10, University of Sydney.

Burke, R.R. (1997). Do you see what I see? The future of virtual shopping. *The Journal of the Academy of Marketing Science, 25*(4), 352-360.

Clarke, R. (1999). Electronic services delivery: From brochure-ware to entry points. In S. Klein, J. Gricar, & A. Pucihar (Eds.), *Proceedings of the 12th International Electronic Commerce Conference*. Kranj: Moderna Organizacija.

Cohen, M. M., Walker, R. L., & Massaro, D. W. (1995). Perception of synthetic visual speech, speechreading by man and machine: Models, systems and applications. *NATO Advanced Study Institute 940584* (Aug. 28, Sep. 8, 1995 Chateau de Bonas, France).

Cohn, R. (1999). Bringing back the human touch. *Communications News, 36*(1), 32-34.

Cooper, J., & Burgess, L. (Eds.). (1999). *Proceedings of the 3rd Collllecter Conference on Electronic Commerce*. Wollongong: University of Wollongong.

Doukidis, G.J., Gricar, J., & Novak, J. (Eds.). (1998). *Proceedings of the 11th International Electronic Commerce Conference*. Kranj: Moderna Organizacija.

Etzioni, O., & Weld, D. (1994). A softbot-based interface to the Internet. *Communications of the ACM,* 37(7), 72–76.

Foner, L.N. (1993). *What's an Agent Anyway? A Sociological Case Study*. ftp://ftp.media.mit.edu/pub/Foner/Papers/What's-an-Agent-Anyway—Julia.ps.Z; http://foner.www.media.mit.edu/people/foner/Julia/.

Greif, I. (1994). Desktop agents in group-enabled products. *Communications of the ACM,* 37(7), 100–105.

Hibbard, J. (1998). Web service: Ready or not. *InformationWeek*, November 16, 18-20.

Jarvenpaa, S.L., & Peter, A.T. (1997). Is there a future for retailing on the Internet? In R.A. Peterson (Ed.), *Electronic Marketing and the Consumer* (pp. 139-154). Thousand Oaks, CA: Sage.

Klein, S., Gricar, J., & Pucihar, A. (Eds.). (1999). *Proceedings of the 12th International Electronic Commerce Conference*. Kranj: Moderna Organizacija.

Koda, T., & Maes, P. (1996). Agents with faces: The effects of personification of agents'. In: *Proceedings of HCI'96*, The British HCI Group, pp. 98-103.

Lashkari, Y., Metral, M., & Maes, P. (1994). Collaborative interface agents. In: *Proceedings of the 12th National Conference on Artificial Intelligence*, AAAI Press, Seattle, vol. 1.

Lieberman, H. (1994). *Attaching Interface Agent Software to Applications*. AAAI Press. http://lieber.www.media.mit.edu/people/lieber/Lieberary/Attaching/Attaching/Attaching.html.

Lohse, G.L., & Spiller, P. (1998). Electronic shopping. *Communications of the ACM, 41*(7), 81-87.

Maes, P & Kozierok, D.(1993). Learning Interface Agents. In *Proceedings of AAAI93*. The MIT Press: Cambridge, MA, pp. 459–465.

Maes, P. (1994). Agents that reduce work and information overload. *Communications of the ACM*, 37(7), 31-40.

Maes, P. (1995). Artificial life meets entertainment: Interacting with lifelike autonomous agents. *Communications of the ACM*, 38(11), 108–114.

Marriott, A. (1999a). A lifelong mentor system. In K. Martin, N. Stanley, and N. Davison

(Eds), *Teaching in the Disciplines/Learning in Context. Proceedings of the 8th Annual Teaching Learning Forum*, The University of Western Australia, February. Perth: UWA. http://cleo.murdoch.edu.au/asu/pubs/tlf/tlf99/km/marriott.html

Marriott, A., Ambrosini, L., & Lavagetto, F. (1999b). Virtual Salesperson. In: *Proceedings of Australia. Workshop on AI in Electronic Commerce*. Sydney, Australia, 6 December.

Marriott,A. (1999c). http://weed.cs.curtin.edu.au/~raytrace/papers/ajet/html/references1.html .

Mauldin, M. L. (1994). Chatterbots, tinymuds, and the turing test: Entering the loebner prize competition. In: *Proceedings of AAAI'94 Conference*. AAAI Press, Seattle.

Menezes, J. (1999). Retail only the tip of e-commerce iceberg: Report. *Computing Canada, 25*(24), 11, 13.

McConnell, D.T. Jr. (1998). Who's shopping your store...today and tomorrow? *Supermarket Business, 53*(5), 119-122.

McGaughey, R.E., & Mason, K.H. (1998). The Internet as a marketing tool. *Journal of Marketing Theory and Practice, 6*(3), 1-11.

MPEG. (1998). http://drogo.cselt.it/ufv/leonardo/mpeg/standards/mpeg-4/mpeg-4.htm.

Peterson, R.A., Balasubramanian, S., & Bronnenberg, B.J. (1997). Exploring the implications of the Internet for consumer marketing. *The Journal of the Academy of Marketing Science, 25*(4), 329-346.

Plantec, P. (1999). The Zen of scripting verbots. http://www.vperson.com/verbot30tt.html (5/6/1999).

Pockaj, R. (1999) http://www-dsp.dist.unige.it/~pok/RESEARCH/.

Poleretzky, Z., Cohn, R., & Gimnicher, S.M. (1999). The call center & e-commerce convergence. *Call Center Solutions, 17*(7), 76-89.

Quelch, J.A., & Takeuchi, H. (1981). Nonstore marketing: fast track or slow? *Harvard Business Review, 59*(4), 75-84.

Rabkin, B., & Tingley, M. (1999). Tech-savvy customers want quick response. *National Underwriter, 103*(40), 12, 21.

Sheth, B.D. (1994). A learning approach to personalized information filtering. *M.S. Thesis*, MIT Media Lab. ftp://ftp.media.mit.edu/pub/agents/interface-agents/news-filter.ps.Z

Swatman, P.M.C., Gricar, J., & Novak, J. (Eds.). (1996). *Proceedings of the 9th International EDI-IOS Conference*. Kranj: Moderna Organizacija.

Turing, A. (1963). Computing Machinery and Intelligence. *Computers and Thought*, E. Feigenbaum and J. Feldman (Eds.), NewYork: McGraw-Hill, pp. 1-35.

Vogel, D., Gricar, J., & Novak, J. (Eds.). (1997). *Proceedings of the 10th International Electronic Commerce Conference.* Kranj: Moderna Organizacija.

Wagner, M. (1997). E-commerce shoppers need tools to help themselves. *Computerworld, 31*(26), 6.

Whalen, T. & Patrick, A. (1990). COMODA: A conversational model for database access. *Behavior and Information Technology*, Taylor and Francis, New York, 9(2), 93-110.

Weizenbaum, J. (1976). *Computer Power and Human Reason.* W.H. Freeman and

Company, New York.
Wiley, D.L. (1998). Beyond information retrieval. *Econtent, 21*(4), 18-22.
Wood, A. (1994). Towards a Medium for Agent-Based Interaction. Thesis Proposal PR-94-15, University of Birmingham, School of Computer Science (October). ftp://ftp.cs.bham.ac.uk/pub/dist/hci/papers/medium_for_abi_PR-94-15.ps.Z

ENDNOTES

1 This research is part of a three-year EU 5th Framework Research and Technology Project.

2 Note that this technology is also applicable when implementing portals or self-service centres.

Section Five: Payment Systems, Recommender Systems and the Future

Chapter XVII

Agents and Payment Systems in E-Commerce

Feng Hua and Sheng-Uei Guan
National University of Singapore

Since the 1990s, the World Wide Web has brought about innumerable changes to the ways enterprises do business. Electronic commerce is emerging as one of the most important applications on the Internet. The use of agents in e-commerce is a new research area. Agents can provide effective, fast, and cheap ways to make deals and execute transactions in cyberspace. Abstract representations of value have been developed from metal, paper notes, and bank checks to savings cards, credit cards, and now electronic forms. This chapter presents a brief survey of existing different types of payment systems and focuses on mobile agent-based computing trends in e-commerce. By combining software agent technology with cryptographic techniques, an agent-based e-payment scheme built for the SAFER e-commerce architecture is proposed, which is aimed to provide a flexible and secure financial infrastructure for Internet commerce.

INTRODUCTION

Electronic commerce and payment systems have flourished within less than half a decade. It is an emerging outcome of the popularization of Internet, which has presented great opportunities and potential for businesses and enterprises. Electronic commerce can reduce transaction costs from the traditional financial world, and provide faster transaction turnaround time by streamlining and integrating operations. Customers now can stay at home and use a Web browser to search for items and related product databases that they may be interested in.

An essential problem to be solved, before widespread commercial use of the Internet can take place, is to provide a trustworthy solution for transferring monetary value over the Internet securely. From the early 1990s, many pilot projects have been devoted to designing different types of secure payment systems for open networks. Quite a number of protocols have been proposed for these systems including NetBill, NetCheque, Open Market, iKP, Millicent, SET (Sherif, 1998), E-Cash (Brands, 1995), NetCash, CAFÉ

(Mjolsnes, 1997), etc. These systems are designed to meet diverse requirements, each with particular attributes. All of these protocols have made contributions to this research area.

The requirements of electronic payment systems vary, depending both on their features and the assumptions placed on their operations. Security is always considered as the prime issue in the process of system design. Different aspects of security include integrity, authorization, confidentiality, and reliability.

Besides the security issue, there are still some factors restraining the development of e-commerce, which pose a new dimension of challenges in this area. One of them is lack of intelligence. Electronic trading is still non-automated. Sometimes, it will be hard for customers to locate specific items when there are so many available. Additionally, in most cases, buyers have to be involved in the loop of all stages of the process, which would increase transaction cost. The lack of intelligent tools to help streamline and integrate the whole procedure is the cause of the above challenges.

Agent technology has been incorporated into the area of e-commerce to provide intelligence and automation for the e-trade process. In the future, where computing power is cheap and abundant, powerful and flexible e-commerce applications can be built allowing potential buyers to run agents on merchant hosts where they have full and fast access to product information, prices, etc. In this kind of system, agents play very important roles. Agents can move between shops, looking for best deals, report back to their owners, or autonomously place orders and execute payment actions provided they have been authorized for such activity.

Generally, an agent is an intelligent software program, which is capable of accomplishing tasks in an autonomous manner on behalf of its user. Agent-based systems have gained popularity because they ease the application design process by giving software engineers and agent owners greater flexibility. Agents must provide highly trustworthy consistency and fault tolerance if they want to be truly useful in an electronic environment such as the open net where eavesdropping and fraud may happen without expectation. Besides security, it is desirable for agents to have roaming capability. Roaming extends the agent's capability well beyond the limitations imposed by its owner's computer. In order to meet the requirements discussed above and provide an environment for an in-depth research in e-commerce, especially in the area of payment, the chapter will discuss some related components in SAFER architecture (Secure Agent Fabrication, Evolution & Roaming) (Zhu and Guan, 2000), and propose an agent-based payment scheme for SAFER. While roaming, mobile agents can be endowed with attributes such as mobility, intelligence, autonomy, and a small amount of credits or electronic cash.

The rest of this chapter is organized as follows. A brief survey of current electronic payment systems is presented in the next section. Then, the following sections focus on mobile agent computing trends in e-commerce by introducing concepts and attributes of agents and by comparing several agent-based solutions available today to the proposed agent-based e-payment scheme built for SAFER. The final section presents the conclusions of the chapter and discusses several open issues for further work.

CURRENT ELECTRONIC PAYPENT SYSTEM

A robust payment infrastructure will inspire the widespread commercial use of the Internet. Information technology has created many new possibilities for value-exchange. The purpose of this section is to provide brief background knowledge to the rapid emergence of electronic means to transfer value. In general, an electronic payment system must exhibit integrity, authorization, confidentiality, availability, and reliability for security requirements (Asokan, 1997). Different types of electronic payment systems have been developed to meet diverse requirements, which will be discussed in the following sections.

Classification and Comparison of Different Payment Systems

Payment systems can be classified in a variety of ways according to their characteristics (Dahab, 1998) such as the exchange model (cash-like, check-like or hybrid), central authority contact (on-line or off-line), hardware requirements (specific or general), payment amount (big, small, or micro payment), etc. Electronic payment systems can be divided into several broad categories, as shown in Figure 1.

In addition to security issues, other important characteristics for an Internet payment system also include scalability, anonymity, interoperability, audit ability, acceptability, custom base, flexibility, efficiency, ease of use, and fault tolerance. Some of these characteristics such as anonymity may be more important in some communities for certain kinds of transactions than they are in other communities (Neuman, 1995). However, sometimes clearness and transparency are also needed by some businesses. On-line systems can provide higher security but the transaction cost will also be high. Allowing users to conduct transactions without contacting the system's central authority (which are known as off-line systems) will induce more risks of fraud. Specific systems are designed to meet specific requirements, and how these characteristics are balanced poses a challenge to future development. Comparisons of attributes of some typical schemes and protocols, shown in Figure 1, are presented in Table 1.

Among all the available payment schemes in the market, e-cash is one of the best in terms of security, flexibility, and full anonymity. It aims to simulate, even replace, physical cash. The agent-based payment scheme for SAFER adopts some similar principles and concepts of e-cash. Therefore a brief introduction of an e-cash scheme is given in the following section.

Introduction of E-Cash

In the category of electronic currency payment systems, participants include payers (buyers), merchants, and financial institutions. Payers can purchase virtual notes or coins against their accounts from their electronic banks, and hold them in virtual wallet software on their own machines. When a payment is requested, the buyer will mail the right amount of value-token to the merchant. The recipient verifies the authorization on the e-coins and

Figure 1. Classification of Electronic Payment Systems

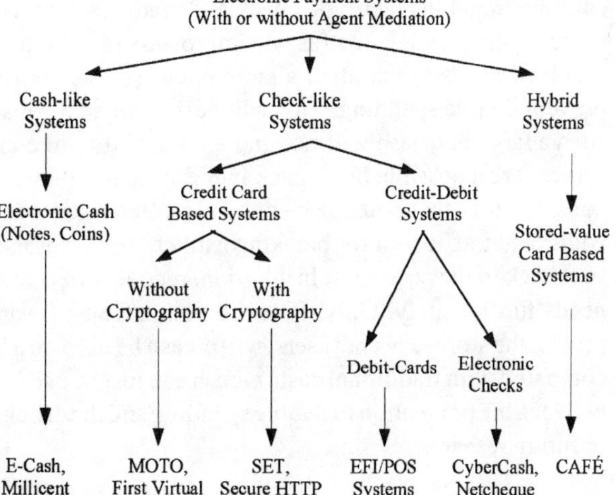

Table 1: Comparison of Different Payment Schemes

Attributes / Typification	Strengths	Weaknesses
First Virtual	Simplicity; Involving no encryption procedure or complex client-end software; Less cost.	Pre-registration needed; A bank account or credit card number are required; Less security.
Secure HTTP	Using Public-key technique to encrypt credit card No.; No need for pre-registration; Simplicity & Security.	No anonymity; Potential bottleneck due to the complexity of verification phase.
Netcheque	Using digital signature; Banks & clearing systems are incorporated to enable audibility; Transparent transaction progress.	No anonymity; Additional time and cost for balancing pre-registered accounts.
E-Cash	Using "blind signature" techniques to realize full anonymity; Great flexibility; Prevent double spending.	Limitation in scalability; Bank endures the burden of maintaining a large database in order to prevent double spending; Risks in case of hardware crash.
Smart Card	Reducing cash handling expenses and losses due to fraud; Customer transactions expedited and customer safety enhanced.	Specific card readers attached to machines are required, which may cause inconvenience in Internet commerce.

sends them to the central server in order to check whether the coins have been previously spent. A clearing system is necessary in such systems to enable banks to support different kinds of tokens and transfer credits. Published schemes include DigiCash's E-Cash, NetCash, and some micropayment systems such as Millicent, Micromint, among which e-cash is in operation through at least the Mark Twain Bank in the USA, Deutsche Bank in Germany, Merita Bank in Finland, and is accepted by EUNet, Europe's largest ISP (Clarke, 1996).

E-cash is a cash-like on-line system that uses electronic coins as tokens. Each electronic coin is in fact a string of digits. A coin is endorsed with a serial number as well as an expiry date, signed blindly by the authorizing bank. Double spending is prevented by recording every coin that is deposited to the minting bank in the system. E-cash is tested as a full anonymity system by using cryptographic techniques. The client cannot be traced to a transaction using the value token information even if all the other parties collude.

E-cash has its unique advantages such as flexibility, integrity, and full anonymity that can't be found in electronic check and credit card-based systems. However, there are still some challenges left for further improvement. The main disadvantage is that each bank involved needs to maintain a large database to store the serial numbers of used coins to prevent double spending. This will be a burden on banks because the cost for maintaining such a large database will rise and the scalability of e-cash would be limited. E-cash bank servers are a possible bottleneck in the system if they are not scalable. Another issue to be considered is that some schemes only offer fixed-value tokens, which will bring about additional traffic cost for breaking a token for a transaction amount with the rest as change sent back to the customer. In addition, recovery of e-cash in case of workstation crash still needs further study. Only if a solid guarantee (software or hardware) can be fulfilled to protect the storage in end-users, will e-cash be used on a larger scale. The last concern is that compared with traditional cash, e-cash can just be used once. How to balance the trade-offs between the prevention of double spending and the efficiency of coin reuse poses a challenge to future research.

SOFTWARE AGENT IN ELECTRONIC COMMERCE

Introduction of Software Agents

Agents are bits of software that help computer users by performing routine tasks, typically in the background, while the user continues to work on other matters. Gathering, filtering, and presenting information are some of small and well-defined tasks given to simple agents. One example of a simple agent is the filter that many people use in conjunction with their e-mail programs to screen out spam. Although an intelligent agent is a piece of software just like any other computer software, it distinguishes itself from them by its intelligence. Traditional software only responds to human input in a fixed and predictable manner such as word processors, spreadsheets, and calculators. Intelligent agents are capable of "thinking" and producing intelligent feedback (Guan and Yang, 1999). Furthermore, agents have the ability and freedom to choose different approaches to solve the same problem. Autonomy is part of agent intelligence. Besides, an agent should not be restricted to executing in the machine it is generated. Most agents designed will be friendly intelligent agents. This is the main difference between agents and viruses. Strictly speaking, viruses are intelligent agents that perform destructive tasks. In order to prevent an agent from behaving like a virus, security measures are implemented to limit the agent's capability while not preventing it from performing legitimate tasks.

The requirement for continuity and autonomy derives from our desire that an agent be able to carry out activities in a manner that is responsive to changes in the environment without requiring constant human guidance or intervention. As described in Bradshaw (1997), agents have the attributes shown in Table 2.

Table 2: Attributes of Software Agents

Attribute	Description
Reactivity	The ability to selectively sense an act
Autonomy	Goal-directness, proactive and self-starting behavior
Collaborative	Can work in concert with other agents to achieve a common goal
Communication	The ability to communicate with persons and other agents
Personality	The capability of manifesting the attributes of a believable character such as emotion
Temporal continuity	Persistence of identity and state over long periods of time
Adaptivity	Being able to learn and improve with experience
Mobility	Being able to migrate in a self-directed way from one host platform to another

For several years, network citizens have used simple agents to track their favorite news topics at on-line sites. Nowadays, software companies are revolutionizing e-commerce by creating agents that compare, buy, and sell goods. Agents can finesse dozens of purchasing decisions at once, and search with high efficiency. Agent-initiated tasks are a powerful catalyst to increase the Web traffic, as they start a chain of events that have a rapid multiplicative effect on the Web. Agent-based commerce is positioned at the highest level of user interaction, because it utilizes all other lower levels of the Web information hierarchy to accomplish a specific task. According to the classificationof Mougayarre, there are four classes of agent-based commerce technologies: automated-pull, Web automation, interactive personalized catalogs, and Information filtering (Mougayarre, 1997).

Examples of Agent-Based Systems for Electronic Commerce

There are several software agent-based prototypes under development, which will be capable of doing even more on behalf of buyers and sellers. Kasbah is such a research project at MIT considered as the first generation of agent marketplace. Kasbah uses multiple agents which are intended to bring about fundamental changes in the way buying and selling is conducted and doing much of the work on the user's behalf. Buyers who need to procure particular goods would create an agent, give it basic strategic direction, and send it off into the electronic marketplace. The Kasbah agents would then proactively seek out potential sellers and negotiate with them on the buyer's behalf, making the best possible deal, based on a set of constraints specified by the buyer, including a highest acceptable price and a transaction completion date (Chavz, 1996). There are two main pitfalls in Kasbah:

- The matching between buying agents and selling agents is one-to-one. An agent will always accept the first offer that can meet its asking price; however, there might be another offer that also meets the asking price but is even better. This behavior is quite different from what people do in real life, where we are used to comparing prices among several stores before trading.
- There is only one centralized marketplace. With the increasing number of agents, such implementation will definitely increase the work load of the system and network.

AuctionBot was developed in the artificial intelligence lab of theUniversity of Michigan. It is a general purpose Internet auction server. Product sellers can create new auctions by choosing from a selection of auction types and then specifying its parameters, e.g., clearing times, method for resolving bidding ties, etc. Buyers can choose to join an existing auction. Like Kasbah, agents are generated to act as the roles of traders. Buyers can then bid according to the multilateral distributive negotiation protocols of the created auction. In a typical scenario, a seller would bid a reservation price after creating the auction and let the AuctionBot manage and enforce buyers' bidding. The two main weaknesses of AuctionBot are:

- Buyers cannot create a new auction but join an existing auction. That means all auctions are only one-sided, i.e., only buyers can bid for a typical product. One-sided auctions could cause a winner's curse problem.
- As in Kasbah, there is only one centralized marketplace.

AGENTics is another agent prototype, which develops what is referred to as "on-line catalog integration for e-commerce." AGENTics products shield the user from the technicalities of "where" and "how" the information was gathered, while synthesizing many information pieces into a coherent whole (Mougayar, 1997). More specifically, AGENTics' technology allows a user to receive an intelligent and unified view of a set of heterogeneous on-line catalogs by unifying their information access mechanism in an innovative manner. In each purchasing session, users interact with a knowledgeable product-focus wizard™, which helps them describe and identify their requirements. This presents applications for Internet marketplaces and purchasing departments who can now provide this service to their members and employees in order to significantly enhance their e-commerce practice.

More sophisticated agents, which are adaptive and able to learn by observation, to make decisions, and filter incoming information, can be developed. For example, agents can select desired items based on preference, search databases to look for selected pieces of information, and conduct transactions. Examples of such adaptive agents are exhibited in the SAFER architecture for e-commerce, which will be discussed in the next section.

Overview of SAFER Architecture

SAFER (Secure Agent Fabrication, Evolution, and Roaming) is a Web-based distributed infrastructure to serve agents to query, buy, and sell goods in e-commerce and establishes necessary mechanisms to transport, manufacture, and evolve all different kinds of agents.

The goal of SAFER is to construct standard, dynamic and evolutionary agent systems for e-commerce (Zhu and Guan, 2000). There will be SAFER-compliant and non-compliant communities coexisting in the whole e-commerce network. Each SAFER community consists of several mandatory components that are used to generate a complete mechanism to run agents for e-commerce. They are Owner, Butler, Agent, Agent Factory, Community Administration Center, Agent Charger, Agent Immigration, Clearinghouse and Bank, which are shown in Figure 2. Some communities may have more entities than those depicted in the figure. SAFER provides services for agents in e-commerce and establishes a rich set of mechanisms to manage and secure them. Introduction of necessary components that are closely associated with on-line payment transaction will be presented in the following paragraphs.

Community: Agent community is the basic unit in SAFER e-commerce, which offers virtual regions and vehicles to host and administrate mobile agents during roaming, transaction, and evolution. Under such circumstance, agents can be regulated in an expected order and perform their tasks more efficiently.

Owner: Owners who stand on the top of the SAFER hierarchy are the real participants during transactions. An owner is in charge of all his agents, and making respective authorizations of different levels to mobile agents and his agent butler, which is an 24-hour on-line watcher who would handle most of the tasks on behalf of the owner. One of the big advantages of agent-based e-commerce is that the owner can be released from tedious jobs such as searching for goods on the Net, information collecting, price comparison, and so on. The owner doesn't need to be on-line all the time, but assigns tasks to agents through the agent butler. The owner also authorizes certain amounts of credit (subject to a limit) to the agent butler who will conduct transactions when the owner is away.

Agent Butler: Agent butler is a kernel component that plays a significant role in the whole architecture, especially in the payment transaction module. In the absence of its owner, an agent butler will, depending on the authorization given, make decisions on behalf of the agent owner. When agents are sent out, roaming in the network, traveling from one host to another, the butler has the responsibility of keeping track of agents' activities and locations by sending and receiving messages with agents. This is especially important when an agent's task is relatively significant. Tracking can be done by some pre-designed methods like heartbeat in SAFER. Agent butler is necessary in all agent transactions, because in SAFER, mobile agents won't be given the authorization to carry a large amount of credits. When an agent is involved in any transaction with external parties, it needs to report to the butler about the details immediately, then the butler will take actions depending on conditions of the deal and authorization from the owner. More details on how the butler helps to coordinate payments will be discussed in the next section.

Clearing House and Bank: In SAFER, when any transaction is executed electronically, just as it may happen in the financial commerce field, the action always involves a payer and a payee. At least one financial institution, usually a bank, which can link all value-representation to real money, must also be involved. Banks can be divided into two kinds according to their functions, issuer and acquirer. Actually, electronic payment is implemented by a payer paying via the issuer and acquirer to the payee (Asokan, 1997). If a

Figure 2. SAFER Community Architecture

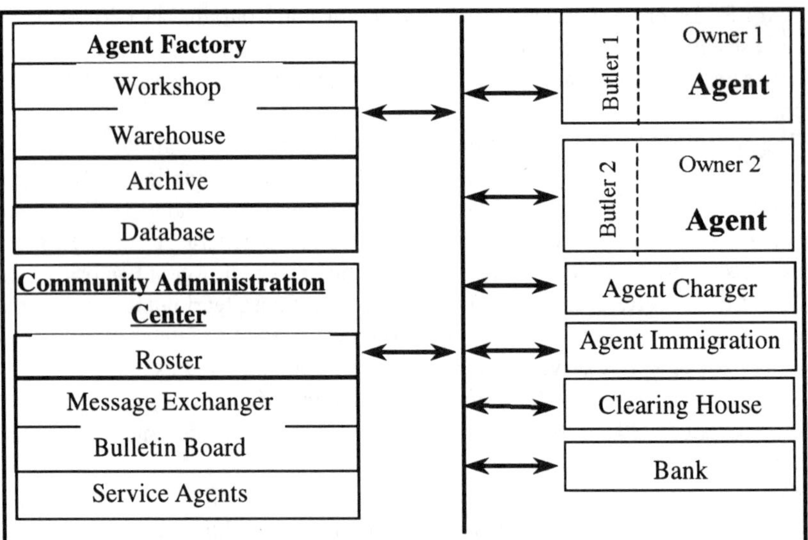

transaction takes places within the same community, and only a single form of value-token is adopted, agent butlers of the payer and the payee can request an immediate settlement from a local bank.

The payment scheme designed for SAFER is expected to fulfill flexibility and interoperability, which means diverse representations of value will have the possibility to be emerged in one framework for users' convenience. Given that, it is important that funds represented by one mechanism be easily converted into funds represented by others (Neuman, 1995). Protocols like SET and instruments like electronic check and e-cash can be integrated together into the SAFER payment framework, which allows the preferred method of payment to be used according to the conditions of the transaction. Consequently, balancing and settlement between different means calls for another financial entity for SAFER. A clearing system will be established to enable banks, which support various kinds of tokens to exchange with one another (just like financial clearinghouses support international currencies), and to transfer credits between banks in different communities. Therefore, the clearinghouse stands on a higher hierarchical level over banks, and through which, interbank settlement can be facilitated.

More detailed elaboration of SAFER architecture can be found in this book chapter "SAFER E-Commerce: Secure Agent Fabrication, Evolution, and Roaming for E-Commerce" by Fangming Zhu and Sheng-Uei Guan.

AN AGENT-BASED E-PAYMENT SCHEME FOR SAFER

Motivation

Agent-mediated e-commerce is promising a revolution in the way humans conduct transactions by which time and cost can be much more reduced than the traditional way. Intelligent agents can be responsible for collecting and interpreting information of merchants and products, making decisions, even presenting payment information, and settling transactions, reducing time and cost. Users would be notified about deals that agents have made. It is no longer a fantasy for computer users to be exempt from the loop of tedious routines. General architecture of agent-based e-commerce systems contains marketplace, users, and agents. A marketplace must be a trusted place, where deals can be made. The structure of a marketplace must recognize and protect against situations that allow agents to gain unfair advantages at the expense of other agents. To enhance the system's security and flexibility:

1. The architecture must provide authentication by means of public key techniques to prevent hiding or misusing identity.
2. The architecture should provide a trusted auditing service to curb illegal actions, which implies the use of a trusted third party.
3. The system must provide a fraud and fault detection mechanism for credit checks, banking services, secure payment facilities when a transaction is executed.
4. Meanwhile, agents of the system should be protected as well from attacks of malicious hosts, since agents may carry credits with them when roaming in an unfamiliar environment.
5. Compared to former generations of agent prototypes such as Kasbah, in which matching between buying agents and selling agents is one-to-one in only one centralized marketplace, a new generation is expected to provide more flexibility and distributed properties.

SAFER is defined as a distributed infrastructure to serve, transport, manufacture, and evolve agents for use in e-commerce. SAFER aims to provide a secure and automated environment, and to construct standard, dynamic, and evolutionary agent systems for e-commerce, in which a highly trusted and flexible payment infrastructure is a vital subset of the entire architecture.

Electronic-Payment Scheme for SAFER

The payment module in the agent-mediated SAFER e-commerce architecture must contain several essential components: the marketplace, agents (including mobile agents, static agents and agent butlers), financial institutions, and users. In SAFER, a community will offer virtual regions, factories, administration tools, and vehicles to manipulate and administrate mobile agents during any activity and provide security so that users can trust it. A user should be notified about deals that an agent makes via his agent butler, who will take charge when the user goes off-line. Several different forms of payment are supported in the scheme depending on security, time, and the amount of money of the transaction.

Different kinds of agents fabricated by an agent factory of SAFER are running under the payment scheme for respective functions and tasks, such as information access and collection, query formulation and facilitation, negotiation and mediation, financial aids, and database accumulation, etc. They are briefly described in Figure 3.

In this scheme, a subsystem called agency is mentioned. Quite similar to the definition given by Dr. Larry Kerschberg in his DPSC project, an agency can be thought of as a multilayered agent group or a federation of agents with a specific goal and functional role in the architecture. It is also like a collection of cooperating intelligent agents with particular expertise (Kerschberg, 1997).

If the owner is interested in some items, he will assign tasks to his butler and agents. Then the agent butler will send out information agents from the agency. When agents are created, the owner will describe the item of interest as well as set parameters to guide each agent's direction and negotiation, such as the due date by which the item should be purchased, desired price and highest acceptable price, as well as some available destination information.

In order to facilitate the provision of security services such as privacy, non-repudiation, and identification, a PKI-based (public-key infrastructure) certification module will be used to establish identities for all SAFER agents when they are created in the agent factory of SAFER. Each agent carries its code and data, encrypted by its private key.

In the payment module, the information agents used to sift, filter, and process information will roam in SAFER or even non-SAFER communities under a certain transport protocol, which is explained in Guan and Yang (1999). It can help with dozens of purchasing decisions, thus lower the cost and gain great efficiency. Such agents are designed with mobility and half-autonomy.

While roaming, agents are well tracked by the agent butler, by sending messages to report their activities and locations, which is described in detail in Zhu and Guan (2000). When enough information about the desired item is gained, the information agent will travel back to the agency and forward them all to the strategy agency where another type of agent which is in charge of information management and decision making will integrate and analyze the new data, and settle down a recommendation/decision for the user. A suggestion may include a collection of alternative vendors, items, and approximate prices to be investigated further. All the results or recommendations will then be reported to the agent butler.

Figure 3. Cooperating Agents for the SAFER Payment Scheme

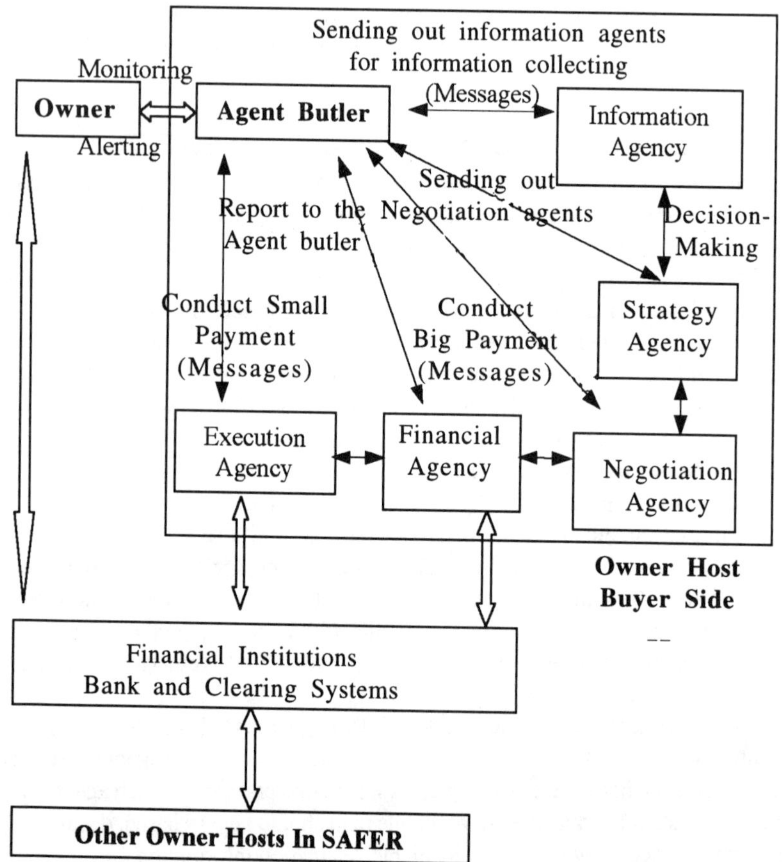

Agent butler is truly a user agent, who acts on behalf of a user under authorization. In the SAFER e-payment scheme, different forms of payment methods are supported. In an environment as insecure as an open net like the Internet, unexpected fraud or agent abduction may happen without any warning. In SAFER, mobile agents are prohibited to carry big credits while roaming on the net. Thus when a recommendation is reported from the strategy agency to the butler, the butler will activate the negotiation agency, which will send out negotiation agents to the short-list merchant hosts according to the report. Before a deal is settled, the negotiation agents will negotiate with the receptionist agents in the merchant hosts. Negotiation is defined in Green (1997): "Negotiation is the communication process of a group of agents in order to reach a mutually accepted agreement on some matter." When negotiation agents are created, some negotiation functions such as "price raise or decrease" protocol should be set among choices as linear, cubic, etc. If the negotiation agent and the receptionist agent reach an agreement, the result will be reported to the butler. The butler will then inform the financial agency to initiate the contract for certain goods, and make a transaction decision according to the amount of money involved, the distance from host to the destination vendor, etc.

Generally, there are three cases for the butler to make a decision. If the amount of the transaction is very small like micropayment, for example a dollar or two, then the butler will inform the Execution Agency to initiate a buying agent to deal with the receptionist agents in the merchant host directly, e.g., make payments, or if required, a buying agent authorized and equipped with the very amount of electronic cash can be dispatched to travel to the destination host to make a deal. The transaction procedure in this case by means of electronic cash can be described as an example shown in Figure 4. After the transaction is settled, both

Figure 4. Transaction by Agents via Electronic Currency

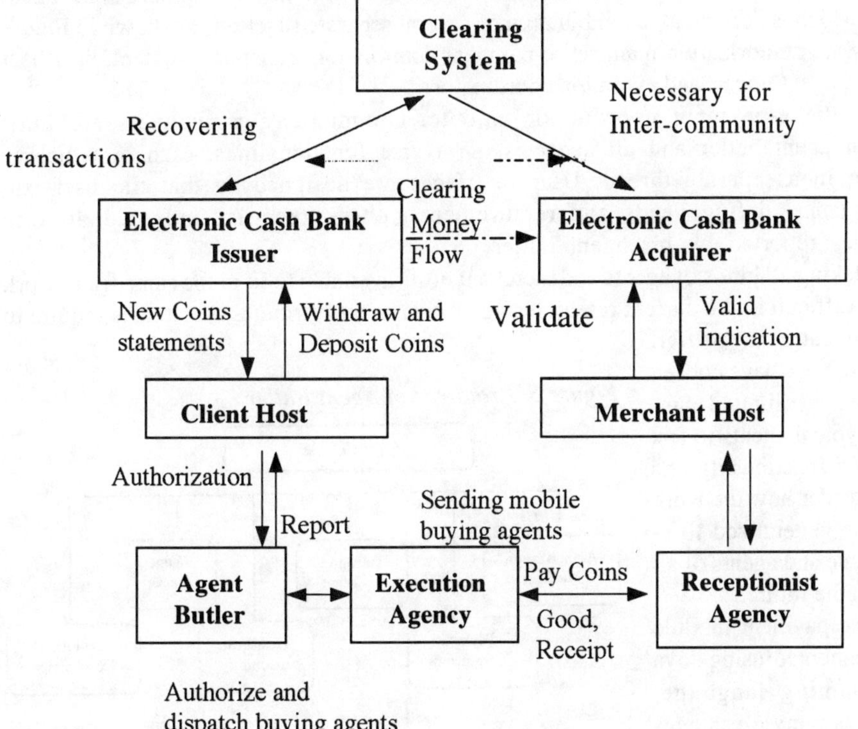

the butler and the financial agency will be informed, and a receipt or contract will be settled and recorded by the financial agency.

When the amount of the transaction is over a micro limit but less than a certain small amount, mobile buying agents will not be given the credits to carry due to the higher risk when roaming in an unfamiliar environment. In this case, the agent butler will directly activate the Financial Agency to make transaction with the merchant host via credit-debit-based electronic payment methods such as an electronic check which is drawn from certain account in an electronic bank located in the local community. Financial agents will take charge of the goods reception and payment transaction under the authorization of the butler. They communicate with the merchant host, autonomously make payment request, and sign contract order against the right good. When the invoicing agent gets the receipt of the correct merchandise on the contract, funds will be automatically transferred to the merchant account directly if local, or via a clearing house when in other communities.

Another case arises when the amount of money of a transaction is beyond the authorization prescribed to the agent butler, or the merchant's ID is not available in the present trustable vendor list, or the merchant host is located in a non-SAFER architecture. The butler won't make decisions alone, but needs to alert the owner via some automatic alerting systems. All the transactions are recorded in a certain log file by the agent butler.

IMPLEMENTATION AND DISCUSSIONS

The implementation of SAFER is under way. The whole architecture is complicated, and consists of several closely related but separate modules: roaming module, evolution module, fabrication module, negotiation module, and electronic payment module.

The implementation of the payment module began with the development of the agent butler, which is defined as a combination of several separate functions as shown in Figure 5. They are authorization manager, e-payment coordinator, transport assistant, heartbeat monitor, agent tracer, and evolution coordinator.

In the e-payment coordinator module, communication channels are built between agent butler and all agencies of diverse functionalities, each of which is running in a separate thread. User interfaces are designed so that the user can assign tasks, define needs and requirements, check records, and read alerting messages reported by his agent butler.

Making all kinds of agents and merchant hosts available to fit in the same framework will be difficult in the current research stage, because the attributes that agents require to communicate may differ. Given that, we have chosen to implement a limited number of typical agents to test the system functionality, and will consider how the work could be generalized to e-commerce and agents of all kinds in the future.

Figure 5. Prototype of Agent Butler

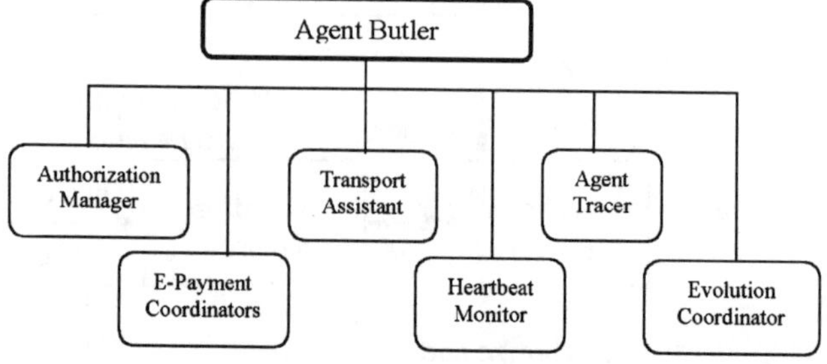

The payment module is implemented using Java programming language, which has many advantages

Figure 6. Payment Coordinator

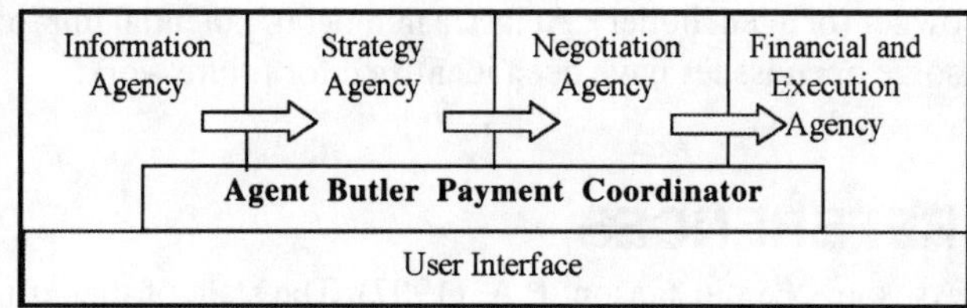

for this application. Java is a language with fully object-oriented attributes. Another reason is that Java holds a run time library that provides platform independence. In SAFER, especially the payment and the roaming module, when an agent is sent out to a destination merchant host, you can't assume knowledge of the type of operating system that is running on the host machine. It would be an advantage to be able to use the same codes (agents) on different platforms.

The foremost important feature of e-commerce is transaction security. If the system is not trustworthy, there will be no incentive for participants to cooperate. A prerequisite is the prevention of double spending of electronic cash or coins. Ensuring this is the crux of any system and it will incur significant overhead. Electronic currency in the context of mobile-agent based systems has one particular caveat: the credits that an agent may carry are essentially just data, to which the host potentially has access. To ensure system reliability and reduce overhead, there are still many open issues for further consideration and discussion in future work:

- privacy issues in collecting data and negotiation—e.g., to prevent agents from divulging private information to other hosts and to protect agents from malicious hosts;
- the extent that users will let agents make decisions for them (based on their preference);
- agent's ability of negotiation—it should be protected to prevent a host from having access to the agent's negotiation function and then affect the agent's buying power;
- agent traceability—agent butler keeps contact with his mobile agents periodically;
- fault tolerance and credits recovery in case of sudden crash of remote systems or unexpected attack taken place on mobile agents;
- protection of agent's public and secret key during agent roaming.

CONCLUSIONS

Development of a secure payment systems over an open network is one of the foremost precedents for the expansion of electronic commerce. Markets rely on a secure means of value exchange. Transaction security is provided in the proposed agent-based payment scheme for SAFER electronic commerce by combining cryptographic techniques (PK-based infrastructure) with intelligence in the form of agent technology.

This chapter discussed desirable prerequisites and classification of available e-payment systems in the first two sections and focused on agent-based computing technologies in the following sections. Several agent-based systems were introduced briefly in Section 3 and in the references. In the final two sections, an e-payment scheme designed for agent-based SAFER e-commerce was proposed and explained in detail. This payment scheme incorporated agent technologies and took advantage of some standardized secure payment transaction protocols. It aims to simulate and even replace physical cash and is designed to support a multitude of currency types. By incorporating concepts of agent, the system is expected to provide security, efficiency, flexibility, autonomy, and intelligence. It is designed to provide anonymity against other parties, and audit ability (traceability) for the owner (or agent butler). At last, a number of potential improvements, practical aspects, and some open issues have been identified for future work.

REFERENCES

Asokan, N., and Janson, P.A. (1997). The state of the art in electronic payment systems. *Computer,* 30(9), 28–35.

Bradshaw, J. (1997). *Software Agent.* AAAI Press/The MIT Press.

Brands, S. (1995). Electronic Cash on the Internet. *Proceedings of the Symposium on Network and Distributed System Security*, pp. 64–84.

Buchmann, A. (1998). Using Multiple Mobile Agents for Distributed Transaction Cooperative Information Systems. *Proceedings 3rd IFCIS International Conference.*

Chavz, A., and Maes, P. (1996). Kashbah: An Agent Marketplace for Buying and Selling Goods. *First International Conference on the Practical Application of Intelligent Agents and Multi-Agent Technology, London, UK.*

Green, S. (1997). *Software Agents A review.* IAG Technical Report, Trinity College.

Guan, S.U., and Yang, Y. (1999). SAFE: Secure-Roaming Agent For E-Commerce. *26th International Conference on Computers & Industrial Engineering, Australia.*

Kerschberg, L., and Banerjee, S. (1997). The DPSC Electronic Marketspace: The Impact of Intelligent Agents, the Internet and the Web on Electronic Commerce and Logistics. Http://cise.krl.gmu.edu/KRG/DPSCAgentHTML_folder/DPSCAgent.html

Mao, W. (1996). *On two Proposals for On-Line Bankcard Payments Using Open Network: Problems and Solutions.* Hewlett-Packard Laboratories.

Mjolsnes, S.F. and Michelsen, R. (1997). CAFÉ. Open Transnational System for Digital Currency Payment. *System Sciences, Proceedings of the Thirtieth Hawaii International Conference,* 5, 198 –207.

Mougayar, W. (1997). The Future of Agent-Based Commerce on the Web. CYBERManagement Inc, http://www.cyberm.com/cyber/art2.htm

Neuman, B.C., and Medvinsky, G. (1995). Requirements for Network Payment: The NetCheque™ Perspective. *Proceedings of IEEE Compcon'95, San Francisco.*

Poh, T. K., and Guan, S.U. (2000). Internet-enabled smart card agent environment and applications. Rahman, S.M., and Raisinghani, M. (Eds.), *Electronic Commerce: Opportunities and Challenges,* Idea Group Publishing, Hershey, PA.

Sherift, M.H., and Serhrouchni, A. (1998). SET and SSL: Electronic Payments on the Internet. *Computers and Communications,* ISCC '98. Proceedings Third IEEE Symposium on, pp. 353–358.

Turban, E., and McElroy, D. (1998). Using Smart Cards in Electronic Commerce. System Sciences. *Proceedings of the Thirty-First Hawaii International Conference.*

Zhu, F.M., Guan, S.U., Yang, Y., and Ko, C. C. (2000). SAFER E-Commerce: Secure Agent Fabrication, Evolution, and Roaming for E-Commerce. Rahman, S.M., and Bignall, R.J. (Eds.), *Internet Commerce and Software Agents: Cases, Technologies and Opportunities*, Idea Group Publishing, Hershey, PA.

Chapter XVIII

Supporting Electronic Commerce of Software Products Through Pay-Per-Use Rental of Downloadable Tools

Giancarlo Succi and Raymond Wong
University of Alberta, Canada

Eric Liu
University of Calgary, Canada

Carlo Bonamico and Tullio Vernazza
DIST – Università di Genova, Italy

Luigi Benedicenti
University of Regina, Italy

The Internet supports the development of software tools that can be downloaded on demand by users, software tools on-demand. *These tools cannot be purchased like products, because they do not reside on the user's machine. Rather, they can be used as "services."*

In this chapter, we propose a new paying mechanism for electronic commerce of software tools-on-demand, that charges users according to how much they have used a given tool: pay-per-use *rental. We discuss the benefits of pay-per-use for users and producers, and we evidence the critical issues in designing a system to support pay-per-use.*

Then we introduce WebMetrics, our pay-per-use system that supplies software metrics collection and analysis tools—on demand. WebMetrics integrates pay-per-use in a client/server Java application. It is based on the idea of prepaid "virtual cards" similar to rechargeable prepaid calling cards for long distance telephone calls.

We conclude with a discussion on the open issues: security, reliability, availability, and standards.

INTRODUCTION

The pervasiveness of Internet connectivity and the wide diffusion of Java-capable browsers foster innovative techniques for software distribution. In this chapter, we propose a new model for the electronic commerce of software tools based on a pay-per-use rental policy.

Pay-per-use rental of downloadable tools is the natural exploitation of Java applets that can be transferred on demand to the user's machine and executed dynamically inside a browser. While software rental is not a new idea (Flamnia and McCandless, 1996), at present no example of a standard pay-per-use rental mechanism for downloadable software tools exists.

This approach benefits from the advantages of central management of tools and zero maintenance for users typical of Java applets, together with a new way to pay for their use. Software rental presents several advantages to producers and users. Pay-per-use rental is particularly suited to Web-based applications, because they are offered to a very heterogeneous and dynamic user population (Bakos and Brynjolfson, 1997).

This chapter describes advantages and issues related to pay-per-use, and explains how to add it to Web-based systems, by presenting the example of pay-per-use integration in WebMetrics, a Web-based system providing distributed collection, management, and analysis of source code metrics.

This chapter is organized as follows. Section 2 discusses tools-on-demand. Section 3 presents the role of pay-per-use. Section 4 introduces WebMetrics, our prototype pay-per-use application. Section 5 describes the architecture of WebMetrics. Section 6 presents a list of open issues. Section 7 draws some conclusions.

TOOLS-ON-DEMAND

The Web already supports two mechanisms for electronic software distribution:

- Free software can be downloaded directly.
- Commercial, shrink-wrapped software can be purchased on-line and then downloaded.

In both cases users have to install the software on their computers.

In the last two years, another distribution mechanism has become popular: tools that are downloaded on demand from the developer's server and executed inside a browser to avoid installation on the user's machine. This approach presents several benefits (Yourdon, 1996):

- The tools are immediately available to any Internet-connected computer, providing a set of computing services available appealing to telecommuters, mobile users, and consultants.
- The tools can run on any hardware platform with a Java-capable Web browser.
- Since the tools are downloaded from a central server, users always get their latest version (Gosling and McGilton, 1996).
- There is no installation, so managing a large user base becomes more viable.
- Maintenance costs are significantly reduced (Gupta *et al.,* 1998).

Table 1: Existing Software Tools On-Demand

Producer	Tool	Type	URL	Access Control
Sun Micro-systems	Over 60 intern-al business applications	Various	Not available for evaluation on the Web	Servlet
VELA project	CHDstd and others	Collaborative IC design	http://wwwcad.eecs.berkeley.edu/Respep/Research/weld/java/index.html	None
IDEA project	IADE, Arachne, Pandora	Database design	http://iris.elet.polimi.it:7272/	Cookies & servlets
University of Catania, Italy	GISHARPE	Models of dependabil-ity, performance and performability	http://sun195.iit.unict.it/~gisharpe/gisharpe/GISharpe.html	Digital ID
University of Catania, Italy	WebSPN	Modeling/analysis tool for stochastic Petri nets.	http://sun195.iit.unict.it/~webspn/webspn2/webspn2.html	Digital ID
Bell Laboratories	SeeSoft	Software visualization	Not available for evaluation on the Web	None
NCSU	OmniDesk	TCL-based workflow design tools	http://www.cbl.ncsu.edu/software/WebWiseTclTk/WebWiseTclTkDemos.html Note: does not work on Windows 95	None
Experimental Software Engineering Group at the	WebMe	Web-based metrics analysis and visualization	Not available on-line anymore	None

- The elimination of packaging and physical distribution helps reducing production costs (Hummel, 1996).

Table 1 presents examples of distributed systems that are based on the *tools-on-demand* approach.

Sun Microsystems is converting its internal computing and networking infra-structure to an applet on demand architecture, with the intent to target real business environments (Gupta *et al.*, 1998). Several other companies and research groups have ported their existing tools to the Java platform. The VELA project, U.S. governmental effort to allow cooperative IC design over the Internet, has produced more than a dozen different tools (Geppert, 1998). The European Community-funded IDEA project has made its database design tools available on the Internet (Ceri *et al.*, 1998). Puliafito *et al.* (1998) present various tools for modeling Petri Nets and assessing computer systems. Many technical issues of porting those tools from the desktop to the Web are analyzed in Puliafito *et al.* (1997).

Web-based software tools can also be used to provide new services. The Bell Laboratories Software Visualization Group uses Java applets to create Live Documents, where static tables typical of ordinary statistical reports are replaced by dynamic Web-based documents. This allows the reader to customize the report while reading it (Eick *et al.*, 1998). Web-based software metrics analysis and visualization is discussed in Tesoriero and Zelkowitz (1998). "OmniDesk" and "OmniFlows" are non-Java distributed workflow design tools (Lavana and Brglez, 1998) that show feasibility of download on-demand using other programming languages.

Existing tools-on-demand systems present various limitations. Most of them require a fast network connection to get reasonable download times. While they are typically intended for public availability, those that need some form of access control simply use password protection of the HTML page containing the tool, or use Java servlets (IDEA Web Lab, Sun internal system). Only GISHARPE and WebSPN use a more sophisticated digital ID system. Access control is usually a yes/no mechanism, making it impossible to differentiate user capabilities.

PAY-PER-USE RENTAL OF DOWNLOADABLE TOOLS

Downloadable applications are becoming popular on private intranets. Several vendors provide them (Kerstetter, 1997).

All users of an intranet application belong to the same organization. Even if some sort of accounting is helpful, such users do not have to pay for the downloaded applications. The organization owning the intranet pays for them, typically by buying the server software. When such applications are offered on the public Internet, the need for specific charging models arises.

Software products are usually sold through a onetime licensing fee, which gives the customer the right to use them for an unlimited period.

This approach is not suitable for Web-based applications that do not reside on the customer's machine. Web-based applications are more similar to services than to traditional software products, because they are operated by the server's owner and not by end-users. Thus, they are more suited to rental than to purchase (Flammia and McCandless, 1997).

A well-known approach to rental is the time-based fee—e.g., renting a car with unlimited mileage or subscribing to cable TV. In this case, the charge does not depend on the intensity of use. This is suited when the rented good or service has a high capital intensity or it ages with time.

Time-based rental is already widespread in the Internet. This approach is particularly suited to server-side applications, like the GroupWare products rented by Interliant (http://www.appsOnline.com). There are also companies that rent Web site editors bundling them with the server space needed to host the sites; an example is iTool (Clark, 1998).

Another possible rental approach is the per use fee—e.g., charges for long distance phone services, which depend on the number of minutes of conversation without any monthly fee, or electricity bills, which are based on the electricity consumption, and so on. This is particularly suited when the rented good or service "deteriorates" with use, or requires an actual maintenance on the base of the intensity of use. For instance, the more one phones long distance, the more the long distance line gets overloaded; the more one use electricity, the more electricity needs to be produced. This is also suited to attract occasional users or people who do not want to commit to a given service.

Advantages of Pay-Per-Use

Pay-per-use of software tools on-demand offer several benefits to both users and tool developers (Table 2).

By making computing more dynamic, pay-per-use addresses *"the reality that customers' needs vary from moment to moment, depending on what they are doing"* (Yourdon, 1996). In fact, users would have ready access to a wide range of tools, but would pay only for the use of the tools they actually download. Users with heterogeneous needs for software tools would experience substantial savings, while users that often access the same tool could arrange for volume pricing.

Table 2: Advantages of Pay-Per-Use

For users	• Users pay only for the software use they need • Occasional users obtain substantial savings • Buyers can make effective choices between tools • Mobile users can access tools from anywhere
For producers	• Users are encouraged to try new tools • A world-wide customers audience can be reached instantly • Small developers experience lower entry barriers • Vendors enlarge market size • Revenue streams become more stable • There are new possibilities for marketing • It is easier to prevent software piracy

Buyers could also make better choices between tools: they could try the tools initially for free or for a small fee without any of the limitations based on time or on functionality that are typical of shareware and demo products. In addition, no installation effort would be required.

Consultants and other mobile users could move from site to site and still be able to access their own tool base through the Internet connection of customers or of third parties.

There would be no initial investments linked to physical distribution, and a worldwide customer audience could be reached almost instantly even by small software firms or individual developers.

While traditional software can be considered a durable good, pay-per-use licensing makes it a consumable good. In choosing between consumable goods, quality and functionality are more relevant to customers than brand names (Marder, 1997). This would result in lower entry barriers for new developers. Thus the market for pay-per-use software would be highly competitive, and this would reduce the prices for end users. (Baumol *et al.*, 1982).

Vendors would enlarge market size, because they could reach even those people that need their tool only occasionally and cannot afford to buy them (Fishburn *et al.*, 1997).

At the same time, developers would also experience a stabilization of their revenue streams, which would make budgeting and planning easier (Digital, 1998). This is a significant improvement over the case of shrink-wrapped software, where revenues depend heavily on the release dates of new versions of the tools.

Customers interact continuously with the vendor's Web site. This creates new possibilities for marketing. An early example of this is the Intuit WebTurboTax tax filing tool (TAX, 1999). This system charges the users only if they want to print or file the results, while form filling and checking is free.

As it is typically very complex to copy and reuse downloadable tools without the cooperation of the distribution Web site, software piracy could be effectively limited.

Web site hosting services have proliferated in the last few years. Similarly, Internet service providers (ISPs) could offer application hosting services. Service providers could set up and manage completely not only the tools-on-demand software, but also the required server hardware. Those information systems could be rented to customers from anywhere in the world. This would be particularly attractive to geographically dispersed teams, like inter-organizational workgroups created ad-hoc for a specific task, or groups of telecommuters (Maurer and Kaiser, 1998).

The growing presence of automated, agent-based brokers to identify and select suitable tools and services on the Internet (Crowston, 1997) could support effectively the market of pay-per-use systems. *"Internet-based electronic marketplaces leverage information technology to match buyers and sellers with increased effectiveness and lower transaction costs, leading to more efficient, 'friction-free' markets"* (Bakos, 1998). As an example, the THEDA Computing Brokerage Project has developed an automated system to find simulation and analysis tools for electronics design (Lin, 1998).

Accounting data collected for charging purposes would reveal a precious information about users' preferences and modes of operation. Hence, the development process could be optimized, because software producers could concentrate their resources on the tools and functionality that users need the most and understand better the operational profile of their systems.

Pay-per-use would be also effective for internal use in an organization, to bill software expenses to the right department. In inter-organizational collaborations, when creating an extranet or ultranet to link business partners and customers (Riggins and Rhee, 1998), a pay-per-use infrastructure effectively reduces the problem of costs-attribution.

The only known pay-per-use system for downloadable software tools is a prototype electronic market for Java applets (Buxmann *et al.,* 1997). A payment applet charges the users before loading the requested applet.

Pay-Per-Use Systems Supporting Web-Based Tools

Several companies have identified application-specific mechanisms to implement pay-per-use for Web-based tools. Several examples are worth mentioning: Toolwire, McAfee.com Clinic, KnowledgePoint, and the market of tax software.

Toolwire (www.toolwire.com) delivers web-based electronic design and productivity tools to customers using a Java-enabled Web browser. The Java client handles the tool interface and communication aspects with the server side. When needed, client files are compressed, encrypted, and then sent to the Toolwire server farm for processing. Charging is based on an action/transaction specific to the tool.

McAfee.com Clinic (www.mcafee.com) offers virus-scanning and other PC maintenance activities over the web. This requires a Windows-specific client to work in conjunction with a scripting-enabled web browser. Users subscribe to the service on a monthly basis.

KnowledgePoint (www.performancereview.com) offers Performance Review, a service to support the management in writing employee evaluations. Users pay separately for each review. As the cost of a single review is quite high, payment can efficiently happen with an SSL-protected credit card transaction. KnowledgePoint also offers a time-based subscription to its service, which is based on an HTML/CGI approach..

Several companies offer support to taxpayers in completing their tax-declaration forms on-line, and charge a fee only when the completed form is filed or printed (TAX, 1999). These are also based on an HTML/CGI approach.

Pay-Per-Use Policies

Different charging policies exist for pay-per-use services (Table 3).

Charging users at each download is not compatible with the widespread use of network caches and proxy servers typical of today's Internet.

In a pure pay-per-use approach, the minimum charging unit is very small: either a single task—writing a document, performing a simulation, or a single elementary transaction, such as retrieving a table from a database or exchanging some data with the server.

Transaction-based pay-per-use is envisioned as the most innovative solution by Yourdon: *"the real paradigm shift, in my opinion, will be the replacement of purchased software packages with transaction-oriented rental of Java applets attached to web pages* "(Yourdon, 1996). Ideally, each user could access any available tool, and periodically receive a bill based on the actual use.

This is the approach chosen by the Malaysian company BizTone for its latest ERP product (which is still in the development stage). Their multitiered client-server application suite will be rented directly to customers from BizTone's web site. BizTone's system is being entirely written in Java, and exploits the recently released JINI technology to reach scalability and location-independence (Carlton, 1998).

Table 3: Different Charging Policies for Software Rental

Policy	Variants
• Per single download	• of an entire application • of each separate component
• Per actual use	• per elementary transaction (like water, or electricity) • per task

When charging per single use, the price per single transaction must be low enough to be competitive. Charging users on-line in real time and, possibly, anonymously requires a system of micropayments, because the overhead per single transaction for traditional credit cards would be too high (MIT E-Cash Group, 1998). The Millicent micropayment system (Digital, 1998) is particularly suited to software rental, because of its very low transaction cost, and the possibility to fulfill payments from $0.001 to $5. However, Millicent is still in beta-test phase, and the Internet does not yet have any established micropayment infrastructure.

Pay-per-use has intrinsic limitations. In literature there is wide consensus that pay-per-use is not an effective solution for all categories of software and users (Bakos and Brynjolfsson, 1997; Doan, 1997). As an example, various surveys show that users do not want to worry about being continuously charged for everyday-use software, like a web browser, a word processor, or an e-mail client.

Supporting a pay-per-use mechanism requires digital money and an electronic payment system. E-cash (Kalakota, 1996) and NetBill (Sirbu and Tygar, 1995) are electronic payment systems that provide security transaction and the opportunity of micropurchases.

The electronic money from E-cash can be purchased with the supplied software from the E-cash issuing bank. The purchasing of E-cash takes days before the E-cash is physically stored into the clients' machine and the money becomes usable. The purchasing of Ecash involves the transfer of real-world money between banks. The cost for maintaining the account is low. In each year, customers have to pay a fee of $20 and merchant accounts cost about $300. Each single payment and transaction with the bank is free of charge.

NetBill takes another approach. The system contains a NetBill server that maintains the accounting information for clients and merchants. These accounts are directly linked to conventional institutions. The transactions between clients and merchants involve a transaction protocol. The protocol allows flexibility for pricing and protection of users' accounts against unscrupulous merchants. The NetBill accounts can be prepaid or postpaid. The cost of using the system is small; the marginal cost of each transaction is 1 cent on the order of 10 cents.

WEBMETRICS

WebMetrics is our prototype tools-on-demand, pay-per-use system. It is aimed at web-based software metrics collection and analysis. It is the result of a joint effort by the Software Engineering Laboratory (SELab) of the University of Calgary, Canada and the Software Process Engineering Laboratory (LIPS) of the University of Genova, Italy. The active research carried out by both labs in software metrics has been the reason for focusing on the domain of software metrics collection.

Users can download with their browsers a wide range of Java applets for data collection and analysis. The data collection applets use parsing algorithms to extract various metrics from the user's source code files. WebMetrics allows developers to measure several internal characteristics of their work. Those data are collected in a central server, which can also be managed remotely by two administration applets.

We have chosen a tools-on-demand architecture for WebMetrics to make our measurement service instantly available to an entire software firm. In addition, WebMetrics enables a consultant to visit a firm and perform the required inspection using his/her own version of WebMetrics running on her/his remote host. We have used this feature a lot to collect metrics data from firms that did not allow their proprietary source code to be moved off-site.

The measurement service provided by WebMetrics is particularly suited for per use rental. There are frequent updates of the tools-set-bug fixes in the measurement algorithms, parsers for new languages, new modules for reporting. Since WebMetrics is rented as a service, users do not want to worry about maintenance and upgrades. With pay-per-use, users can choose from a wide range of tools, paying only for those they need and always getting the most advanced functionality available.

Key features of WebMetrics are:

- Single point of login
- Machine-independent user interface, based on Sun's Swing
- Extensible communication protocol, based on Java Serialization
- Portable Java-based server, which can be managed indifferently locally or remotely
- Modular security framework, with group/user hierarchy
- Use of a relational database so to make integration with legacy systems easier

Security information (username, group, password or certificate) is grouped into a small *token*, which is passed to the server with each request, to obtain a fine-grained access control. This is an important requirement for WebMetrics, because the value of collected data depends on the guarantees of their origins. This approach ensures that sensitive information about users' projects is accessible only to authorized people.

Metrics are calculated on the client machine, improving scalability and avoiding transfer of sensitive code over the network.

A single WebMetrics server can be used by different organizations, because database structure and token-based validation of incoming requests prevent access to other companies' data. This is needed to sell the tools as services to several organizations, without requiring a server for each customer.

WebMetrics has two single points of failure: the server and the database. They are key-components responsible for all the administration and accounting processes. If one of the components fails, the entire WebMetrics application cannot function anymore. Multiple replicas of the server and database running on different machines remove the presence of single points of failures.

Comparison of Web-Based Pay-Per-Use Systems

Table 4 briefly compares WebMetrics with other web-based pay-per-use systems mentioned previously.

The purpose of the comparison is not to criticize systems, but merely to illustrate the different possible techniques for implementing such a system. The requirements for each system are specific to a domain. For instance, WebMetrics features source code metric extraction. This is an activity which is likely done only once in a while (say, at certain milestones in the lifecycle), so a per-action pricing model makes sense. In the case of

McAfee.com Clinic, users probably would like to scan their systems for viruses very often to gain peace of mind. A monthly subscription would work better here.

Table 4. Comparison of Web-Based Pay-Per-Use Systems

Tool	Pricing Model	Tool Delivery Technology	Processing On
Toolwire	Per action/transaction	Java	Server side
McAfee.com Clinic	Monthly subscription	Custom Windows client and scripting	Client side
Knowledge-Point	Per review	HTML/CGI	Server side
Tax filing	Per filing	HTML/CGI	Server side
WebMetrics	Per action/transaction	Java	Client side

Using Java as the tool deployment platform works well for WebMetrics since the users can access the tools instantly from any computer with a Java-enabled web browser. In addition, WebMetrics processing is done on the client side because that's where the client's valuable source code is stored. On the other hand, this scheme would not work well for Toolwire, since the client machine likely does not have enough computing horsepower for all the complex simulations that can take place during an electronics design process (like a FPGA design, for example).

ARCHITECTURE OF WEBMETRICS

The first version of WebMetrics has been implemented using Java 2 (formerly known as JDK 1.2). Our choice has been motivated not only by a portability requirement, but also by Java's rich network libraries and object-oriented features. The Java 2 platform also offers several significant improvements over JDK 1.1. Design and implementation of WebMetrics have been greatly simplified by the availability of the Swing library (for OS-independent user interface), the new Collections API, and the fine-grained security policies for applets. In fact, it would be impossible to run the parser with a JDK 1.1-compliant browser, at least without applet signing, because they require read/write access to the client machine's file system. Until Java 2 capable browsers are deployed, WebMetrics relies on Sun's Java Plugin to run its applets on the widespread Netscape Navigator, Internet Explorer, and Opera browsers (PLUGIN, 1999).

Figure 1. Architecture of WebMetrics

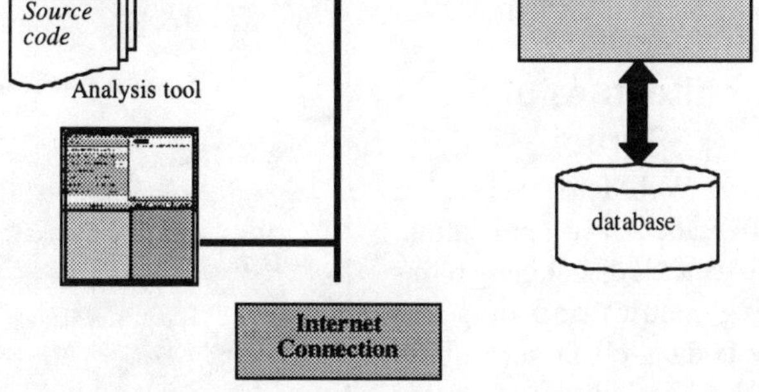

Figure 1 outlines the high-level architecture of WebMetrics.

Users access the system from a page on the lab's web site. WebMetrics home page contains an applet for login (Figure 2).

After a successful authentication, the user is presented with another applet from which she/he selects a tool (data collection, analysis, or administration) and a project to work on (Figure 3).

The selected tool is then downloaded and executed, and communicates with the server over a TCP/IP connection to complete its task.

Client-Server Communication Protocol

The tools communicate with the server using a stateless protocol, which improves robustness when slow or unreliable Internet connections are used. WebMetrics protocol is similar to HTTP, but while an HTTP request returns a file, WebMetrics exchanges software agents. These communication agents are represented as serialized Java objects (Gosling and McGilton, 1996).

The server receives requests to store some data, to perform an administrative task or to query the database. It processes them and sends back a reply. Each request is processed independently. In this stateless exchange of packets, the client opens a TCP connection to the server, sends a request packet, receives back the server's answer, and closes the connection.

Packets are communication agents in WebMetrics. They are Java objects (Figure 4) which are directly serialized with the writeObject() method. The resulting byte stream may then be sent through the TCP connection. Packets are instances of class Packet. It is possible to build packets with different characteristics by instantiating various subclasses of Packet. The client sends subclasses of type Request (Figure 5) and the server replies with Response objects (Figure 6). A request packet always contains a token with security information, and a payload which can carry either commands or metrics. A response agent may simply contain an acknowledgment, or carry the results of a query on the database (DataTable).

When an object is serialized, all its fields and variables are serialized recursively. To transfer complex data structures, like sets of Metric objects, it is only necessary to add an array of Metric objects as a field of the Packet.

The communication protocol is encapsulated into two classes, one for the client side and one for the server side (Figure 7). In this way, it is possible to try and test different implementations of the protocol without interfering with the rest of the system.

Figure 2. WebMetrics Login Page

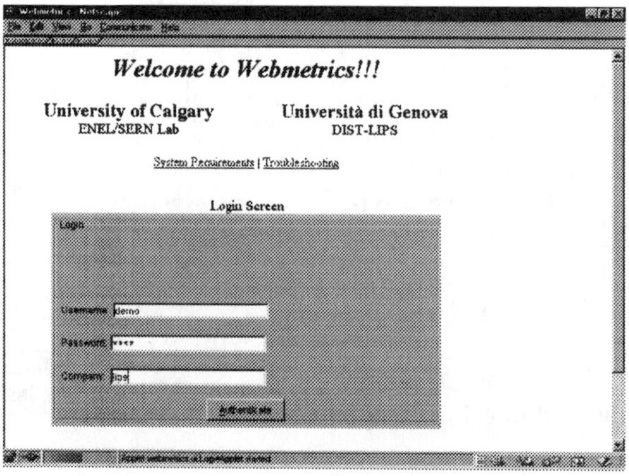

Architecture of the Server

The WebMetrics server is a multithreaded Java application, which handles dispatching of incoming metrics and outgoing analysis data, client authentication, permissions verification, and logging (Figure 8).

A server is an instance of class **WebmetricsServer**, which is responsible of initialization and reads configuration data from a file. Each instance of WebmetricsServer has a Log object, a Manager, a dBase and an AuthenticationServer.

Figure 3: Tool and Project Selection

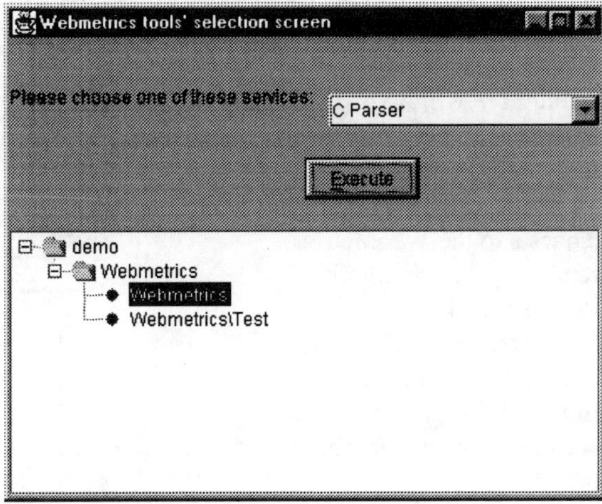

The server binds by default to port 8888. When a connection with a client is established, the server creates a new thread to handle it, and continues listening for other connections. Each thread receives a reference back to the server that created it, so to be able to access its dBase, Manager, AuthenticationServer and Log.

Each **WebmetricsServerThread** thread sends a prompt to the client, receives a Request object, and invokes the AuthenticationServer. If the security checks succeed, the thread builds a packet of type Response containing an acknowledgment message, and possibly the result of the queries on the database. It sends back the packet to the client, and closes the connection.

The **dBase** object generates the SQL statements needed to perform the various tasks, and is responsible for their execution via JDBC.

Authentication and accounting algorithms are encapsulated into the **AuthenticationServer**, which tracks each incoming request. It is then possible to change the charging policy without modifying other parts of the server, and also reuse this accounting engine in other projects from other domains.

The AuthenticationServer (Figure 9) performs various queries on the database, in order to check:

- If the received authentication *token* is valid
- If the user is allowed to use the requested tool
- If the users can pay for the requested service

If all conditions are satisfied, the user's request is satisfied and the user is charged for the transaction.

Downloadable Agents

The clients are implemented as separate applets that perform their duties by communicating with the WebMetrics server. They are responsible for delivering the appropriate services from server to the clients' location dynamically accordingly to user requests.

Figure 10 details how a user accesses the services offered by

Figure 4: Types of Packets

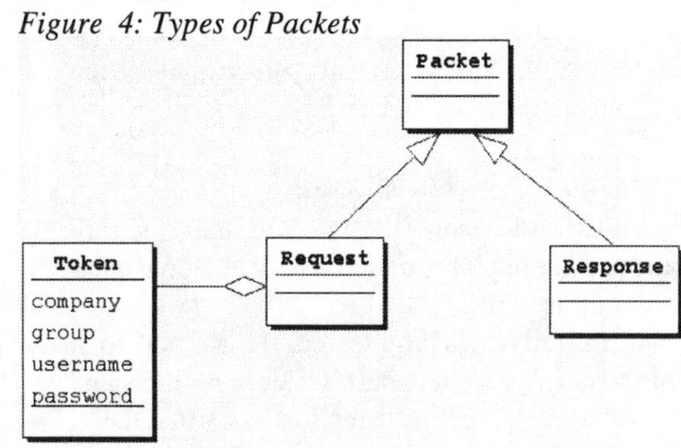

WebMetrics. The user opens the main WebMetrics page in his browser. S/he selects a agent (1), which is then downloaded from the web server (2). The tool completes its task by sending requests to the WebMetrics server (3), e.g. asking it to store a set of metrics. The server replies with an acknowledgment packet confirming that the metrics have been saved into the database (4).

Figure 5: Class Diagram of a Request

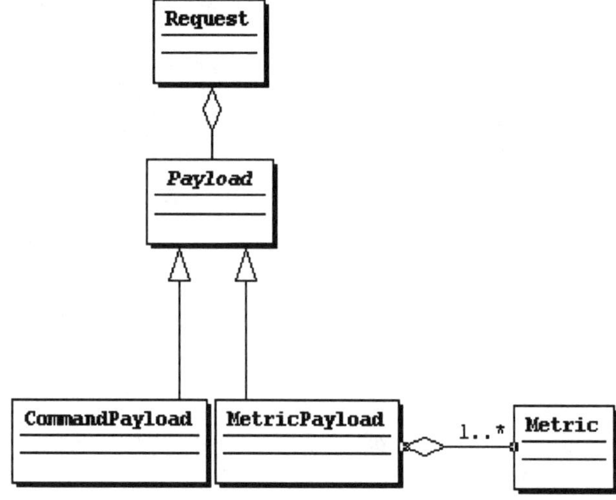

To simplify development and integration of the agents, the functionality common to all types of agents has been enclosed into two classes:

- Webmetrics client, that encapsulates the stateless communication protocol, offering high level primitives to send sets of metrics or commands to the server
- RemoteDatabaseInterface, that contains a set of primitives covering all database querying and administration aspects

The client is based on three main components (Figure 11):

- a GUI
- a component carrying out the target task –a parser, a data analysis engine, or an administration utility
- a Webmetrics client component that implements the communication protocol.

The code needed by the tools to interact with the server is contained in less than 20KB to reduce the download time. The use of standard Java 2 libraries, including Swing for the GUI, also helps reduce tool size, and hence download time. Thus, WebMetrics transfer rates are excellent on a LAN, and remain acceptable even over slow POTS Internet connections.

The data collection agents use parsers to calculate metrics (Conte et al. 1988). Presently we have developed parsers for C (Figure 12), C++, Java, Cobol, and RPG. The parsers have been developed using JavaCC 0.7.1.

Figure 6: Class Diagram of a Response

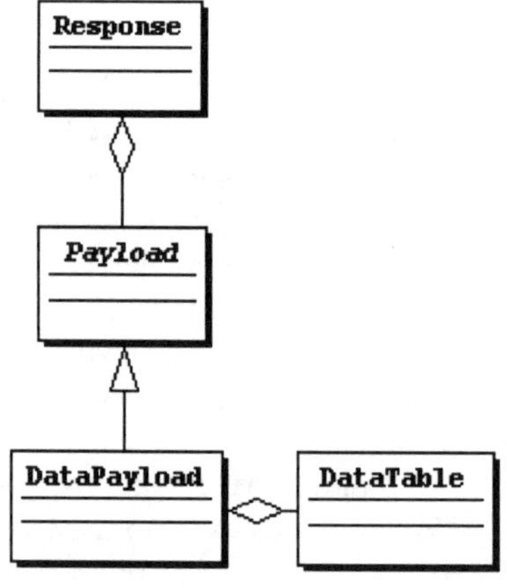

Database

The server stores the processed data, security and accounting information into a relational database, using JDBC.

Initially, we connected the server to a Microsoft Access database residing on the same machine as the server, using Sun's JDBC-ODBC bridge and the Microsoft Windows ODBC engine.

Figure 7: Implementation of the Communication Protocol

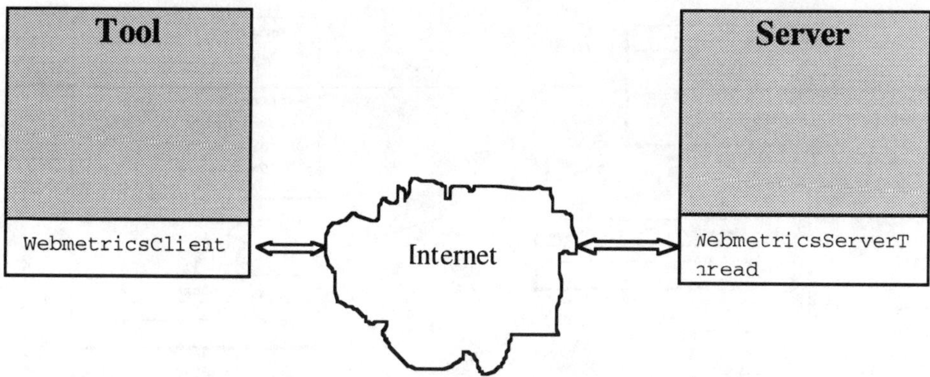

The database could reside on a different machine, if different JDBC drivers were used.

Unexpectedly, this configuration showed significant degradation of performances over time. After the execution of around 30 SQL statements, the time needed to process a packet reached 30 seconds, clearly an unacceptable value. Then, we configured WebMetrics to use Microsoft SQL Server 6.5 and InstantDB 1.92, a pure-Java database engine (http://www.instantdb.co.uk). Both ran smoothly, and did not cause any performance degradation over time. Using Microsoft SQL Server, we experienced an improvement of around four times over the Access solution, while InstantDB was slightly slower than Access.

At the end, we discovered that Microsoft Access does not slow down if the server closes and reopens the JDBC connection periodically –i.e., after sending about 20 consecutive SQL statements.

Our tests are just a qualitative guide for our implementation effort. They are not a precise quantitative evaluation of performances. Such complete quantitative evaluation requires dedicated hardware, software, and network infrastructures and several runs. Clearly, this is beyond the scope of this research.

Implementation of Pay-Per-Use

As in most web-based systems, the collected data and the security information are

Figure 8: Overview of the Server's Architecture

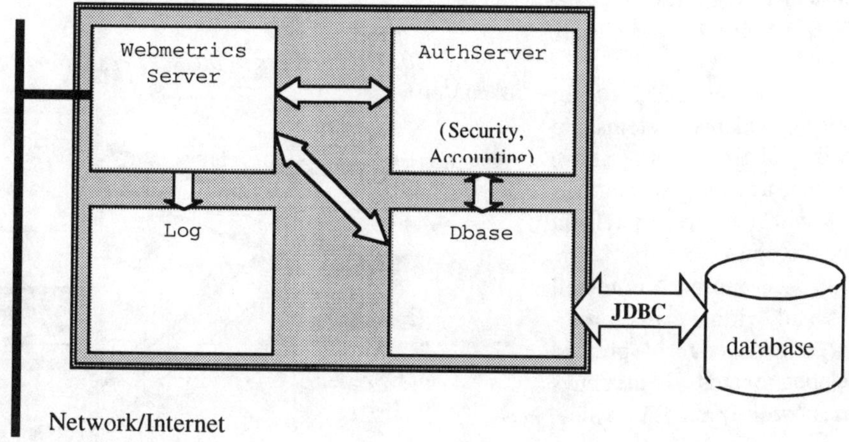

Figure 9: Class Diagram of the Server

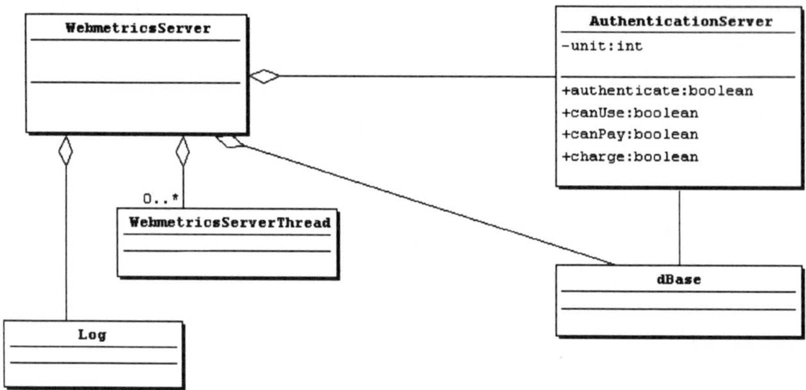

stored in a central database managed by the server. Therefore, the completion of any task requires one or more interactions with the server. Thus, it is possible to implement a pay-per-use policy by adding to the server the ability to count the number of times each user interacts with it.

The transferring of information between the server and clients are achieved with a set of communication agents. The server is the centralized point to collect these agents; it is important for the server to know who is sending each incoming agent. Therefore, each agent contains a *token*, with a reference to the current user. When a request agent is received by the server, if the request can be fulfilled, the AuthenticationServer object charges the requester accordingly.

The server is able to charge users for any single exchange of agents. It is also possible to disable charging for specific types of transactions. For instance, users may pay to collect metrics, and enjoy free read-only access to their own data. The system administrator can configure the system to select the strategy that best fits their need. The system architecture is open to support any pay-per-user policies.

Disaggregating the price of a tool into small pieces, as in the case of pay-per-use, is interesting to users only if the payment mechanism does not add a significant overhead to each payment operation. As an example, credit cards are not adequate for pay-per-use if the cost of a single use is below $10US (MIT E-cash Group, 1998).

Since no standard for micropayments systems are widely accepted yet, we have defined a mechanism compatible with mainstream payment technologies.

Our approach is to sell prepaid "virtual cards", similar to the rechargeable prepaid telephone cards. The user buys a card with a predefined value, such as 50, 100, 1,000, or

Figure 10: User Access to the Services Offered by WebMetrics

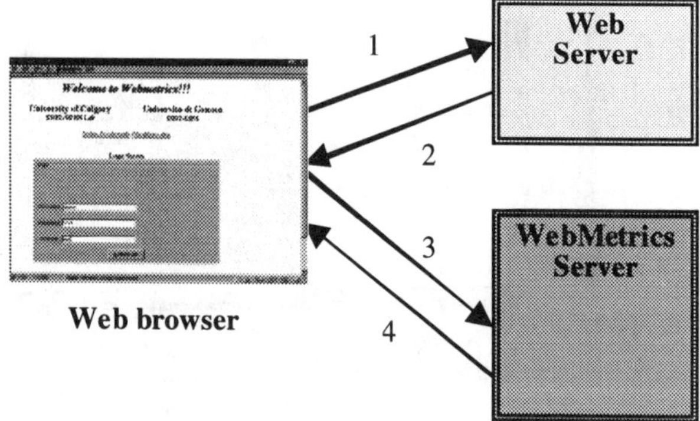

Figure 11: Structure of a Client

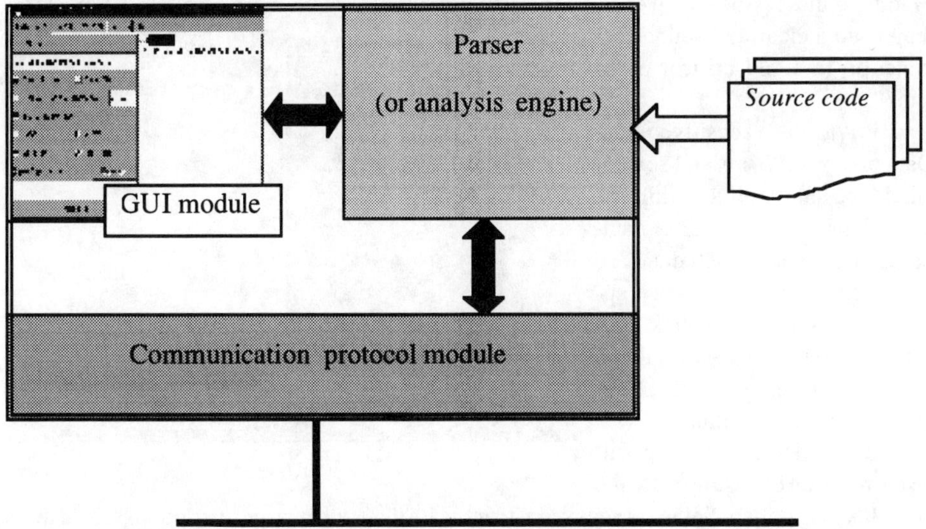

10,000 "basic interactions". Each single client in the system contains an account in the system's database, the accounts are filled with the specified quantity of allowable basic interactions.

Each time the user interacts with the server, this quantity is decremented by the unit according to the type of interaction specified by system administrators. With this approach, the purchase may be performed with a traditional on-line credit card transaction, because the very small cost of a single use is multiplied by the number of uses bundled into the card.

Users Can Verify Their Remaining Credits at Any Time

Obviously, charging users makes authentication a critical issue. During the test phase, we used simple username/password checks, but we are adding support for standard X.509 certificates for both client and server authentications.

OPEN ISSUES

Development of WebMetrics has shown that doing usage accounting is only the first and simplest step in the development of a pay-per-use product. Open issues are mainly related to reliability, privacy, and standards.

When Java applets are rented, and a significant part of the application is server-based, reliability problems arise.

- If there is a network failure, the user cannot be charged, and probably cannot access the tool altogether. Replication could be provided to make the system fault-tolerant on the server side, but what about the client side?
- There are few guarantees on how long a service will be available in the future. The service could be discontinued by the provider and even the provider itself could close. What would happen to the users of such service? How could they access their data? How could the users use such data if they are stored in a proprietary format?

Figure 12: Main Window of the C Parser Agent

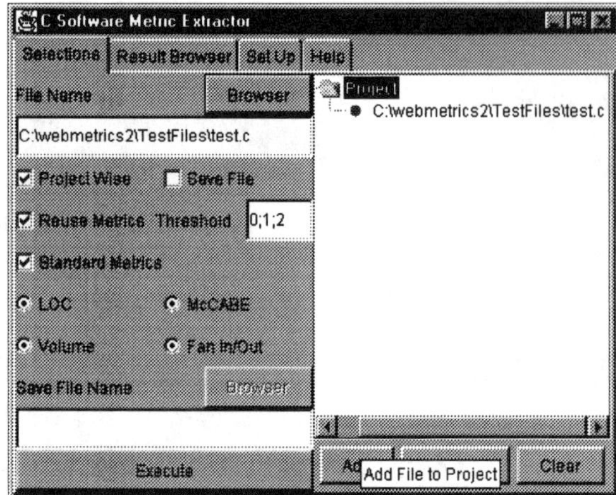

Solutions could be devised to address these issues. However, they need a clear and sound formulation to avoid critical problems.

Privacy is a sensitive issue. Data of several firms and several employees are stored within the same database or cluster of databases. This makes such database or cluster of databases very appealing to intruders. Robust protection of the databases could be obtained encoding the data with cryptographic algorithms.

It is still not clear what will be the reaction of customers to the new charging policy. Some surveys seem to indicate that with pay-per-use people are always worried about spending more than planned (Bakos and Brynjolfsson, 1997). In addition, budgeting pay-per-use software is a new and not trivial task for companies (Doan, 1997).

The lack of standards is an obstacle to introduction of pay-per-use/tools-on-demand systems. Users tend to be skeptical of the introduction of completely new systems and operating procedures (Katz and Shapiro, 1992). Standards help overcoming this natural diffidence, increasing the confidence of users. Standards would be advisable for all the aspects of pay-per-use tools-on-demand systems, from the payment schema to user authentication, to the user interfaces.

CONCLUSIONS

Java-based tools-on-demand systems allow the introduction of a new paradigm for electronic commerce of software products: pay-per-use rental of web-based applications over the Internet. Renting software tools on the web presents several advantages: users pay only for what they need, and they do not have to deal with maintenance. Several web-based tools are available on the Internet, but they are typically rented through monthly subscriptions, so that users must pay in advance without knowing how much they will access the tools in the following month. A much greater degree of flexibility may be attained with a pay-per-use policy, which benefits both users and developers.

Integration of pay-per-use accounting in WebMetrics, a client-server system for distributed management of software metrics, proves the feasibility of this new approach. However, our experiences with WebMetrics indicates that there are many issues related to pay-per-use which are yet to be solved, particularly in the reliability and privacy areas.

ACKNOWLEDGMENTS

This research has been partially supported by the Canadian National Science and Engineering Research Council, the Government of Alberta, the University of Calgary, and the European Commission.

REFERENCES

Bakos, Y. (1998). "The Emerging Role of Electronic Marketplaces on the Internet." *Communications of the ACM*, 41(8).

Bakos, Y., and E. Brynjolfsson (1997). "Aggregation and Disaggregation of Information Goods: Implications for Bundling, Site Licensing and Micropayment Systems." *Conference on Internet Publishing an Beyond*, Harvard University, Cambridge, Massachusetts.

Baumol, W.J., J.C. Panzar, and R.D. Willig (1982). *Contestable Markets and The Theory of Industry Structure*, Harcourt Brace Jovanovich, Inc.

Buxmann, P., W. König, and F. Rose (1997). "An Electronic Market for Java Software Elements." *ECIS 97*, Cork, Ireland.

Carlton, D.(1998). "The Vision Thing." *BizTone*, December.

Ceri, S., P. Fraternali, S. Gevinti, and S. Paraboschi (1998). "Building a Database Design Laboratory on the Internet." *IEEE Internet Computing*, 2(5).

Clark, S.(1998). "iTool Enables Developers to Build the Web via the Web." *InternetNews*, December.

Conte, S. D., H.E. Dunsmore, and V.Y. Shen (1986). *Software Engineering Metrics and Models*, The Benjamin/Cummings Publishing Company, Inc.

Crowston, K.(1997). "Price behavior in a market with Internet buyers' agents." *ICIS-97*, Atlanta, December.

Digital (1998).. "New Revenue Models for Software Developers." Digital Equipment Corporation Inc., http://www.millicent.digital.com/sell/white_papers/software/index.html

Doan, A.(1997). "Net vendors, ISPs raise credibility of rented software." *IDG Infoworld*, 19(34).

Eick, G., T.L. Graves, A.F. Karr, and A. Mockus (1998). "A Web Laboratory for Software Data Analysis." *WWW Journal*, 1(2).

Fishburn, P.C., A.M. Odlyzko, and R.C. Siders (1997). "Fixed Fee Versus Unit Pricing for Information Goods: Competition,Eequilibria, and Price Wars." *Proceedings of he Conference on Internet Publishing and Beyond*, Harvard University, Cambridge, Massachussets, June.

Flammia, S. G., and M. McCandless (1997). "From Software to Service: the Transformation of Shrink-wrapped Software on the Internet." *IEEE Expert*, 12(2) .

Geppert, L. (1998). "IC Design on the World Wide Web." *IEEE Spectrum*, 35(6).

Gosling, J., and H. McGilton (1996).. "The Java Language Environment - A White Paper." Javasoft, http://java.sun.com/docs/white/index.html

Gupta, A., C. Ferris, Y. Wilson, and K. Venkatasubramanian (1998). "Implementing Java Computing: Sun on Architecture and Applications Deployment." *IEEE Internet Computing*, 2(2).

Hummel, R.L.(1996). "How Java Can Pay the Rent." *Byte*, June.

Katz., M.L., and C. Shapiro (1992). "Product Introduction with Network Externalities." *The Journal of Industrial Economics*, XL(1).

Kerstetter, J.(1997). "C/S Suites Tap Into Java", *PC Week*, March 21, http://www.zdnet.com/zdnn/content/pcwk/1412/pcwk0093.html

Kalakota, R., and A. Whinston (1996). *Frontiers of Electronic Commerce*, Addison Wesley.

Lavana, H., and F. Brglez (1998). "WebWiseTclTk, OmniDesk and OmniFlows: A User-Configurable Distributed Design Environment inside a Web-Browser." http://www.cbl.ncsu.edu/publications/#1998-TR@CBL-03-Lavana

http://www.cbl.ncsu.edu/publications/#1998-TR@CBL-03-Lavana

Lin, Y.(1998). "The THEDA Computing Brokerage Project." Tsing Hua University, http://theda28.cs.nthu.edu.tw/~broker/broker.v2/Introduction.html

Marder, E., *The Law of Choice,* Simon and Shuster Inc., 1997

Maurer, F., and G. Kaiser (1998). "Software Engineering on the Internet Age." *IEEE Internet Computing*, 2(5).

MIT E-Cash Group (1998). "Survey on Electronic Cash and Micropayments." http://rpcp.mit.edu/~pearah/micropayments.

PLUGIN (1998). "Java Plugin Overview", Javasoft, http://java.sun.com/products/plugin/1.2/overview.html

Puliafito, A., O.Tomarchio, and L.Vita (1998). "Increasing Application Accessibility through Java." *IEEE Internet Computing*, 3(4).

Puliafito, A., O.Tomarchio, and L.Vita (1997). "Porting SHARPE on the Web: Design and Implementation of a Network Computing Platform using Java." *9th IEEE Int. Conf. On Modelling Tech. and Tools for Computer Performance Evaluation (TOOLS'97).*

Riggins, F.J, and H. Rhee (1998). "Toward an Unified View of Electronic Commerce." *Communication of ACM*, 41(10).

Sirbu, M., and J.D. Tygar (1999). "NetBill: An Internet Commerce System Optimized for Network Delivered Services", Carnegie Mellon University, http://www.ini.cmu.edu/NETBILL/pubs/CompCon_TOC.htmlTAX. "Rentable Tax Software", Intuit, http://www.intuit.com

Tesoriero, R., and M. Zelkowitz (1998). "A Web-Based Tool for Data Analysis and Presentation." *IEEE Internet Computing*, 2(5).

Varian, H.L.(1995). "Pricing Information Goods." *Research Libraries Group Symposium on Scholarship in the New Information Environment*, Harvard Law School, May.

Yourdon, E.(1996). "Java, the Web and Software Development." *IEEE Computer*, 29(8).

Chapter XIX

Software Agent-Mediated Internet Trading Framework

Xun Yi
Nanyang Technological University, Singapore

Mahbubur Rahman Syed
Minnesota State University, Mankato, USA

Robert J Bignall
Monash University, Malaysia Campus

Chee Kheong Siew
Nanyang Technological University, Singapore

Xiao Feng Wang and Kwok Yan Lam
National University of Singapore, Singapore

In recent years Internet trading has seen explosive growth and will have a major impact in shaping future markets. It will certainly be very advantageous if Internet trading can be made more automated and secure than is currently the case. This would dramatically reduce the time and energy spent by customers. This chapter focuses on applying software agent technology together with cryptographic technology towards automating and securing the processes of negotiation and payment, which are the principal and most time-consuming steps during Internet trading. A software agent-mediated Internet trading framework integrating negotiation and payment procedures is proposed.

INTRODUCTION

The Internet has revolutionized the computer and communications world like nothing before. It may be viewed as a worldwide broadcasting system, a mechanism for information dissemination, and a medium for collaboration and interaction between individuals and their computers without regard for geographic location.

In 1990, HTML, a hypertext Internet protocol that could be used to communicate graphic information on the Internet, was introduced. Individuals could create graphic pages (a Web site), which then became part of a huge, virtual hypertext network called the World Wide Web (WWW). The Web grew to reach 10 million users faster than any other communications medium in history, and is expected to penetrate 50 million homes in the U.S. alone by the year 2000.

As the Web grows ever larger and new users go on line daily, merchants are also rushing online. They set up shop on the WWW and make sales over the Internet. Some specialty operations exist that do all of their business on the Internet, such as Amazon.com (http://www.amazon.com), NECX Direct (http://www.necx.com), FirstAuction (http://www.firstauction.com) and others. Recent studies by analysts from Nielsen, Forrestor and IDC have shown that the number of Web buyers, sellers and transactions are growing at a rapid pace. The number of people buying on the Web is expected to increase from 18 million in December 1997 to 128 million in 2002, representing more than US$400 billion worth of commercial transactions.

The emergence of Internet trading represents one of the most important applications on the Internet, with the potential to revolutionize the whole structure of retail merchandising and shopping. By providing more complete information to purchasers and cutting transaction costs, it is reducing market friction and making markets more perfect.

With the development of trading on the Internet, the amount of business information available online has become so large that it is becoming infeasible for customers and merchants to manually visit each site on the Internet, to analyze all of the information available, and thereby make optimal business decisions regarding the trading of goods or services. In addition, electronic purchase transactions are still largely non-automated. While information about different products and vendors is more easily accessible and orders and payments can be dealt with electronically, a human buyer is still responsible for collecting and interpreting the information about merchants and products, making decisions about them and finally entering the necessary purchase and payment information.

Software agent technology offers a new paradigm for Internet trading. A software agent is a software program that uses agent communication protocols to exchange information for automatic problem solving. Unlike more traditional software, software agents are personalized (incorporating cooperation, negotiation and conflict resolution), continuously running and semi-autonomous (Maes, 1994). Software agent technologies can be used to automate several of the most time consuming stages of the buying process. A software agent might have service capabilities, autonomous decision making and commitment features. These qualities are conducive to optimizing the whole buying experience and revolutionizing commerce as we know it today (Moukas et al., 1999).

In spite of the fact that software agents are able to simulate the entire person to person trading process, customers are wary about employing them to trade on their behalf, largely because of concerns about unknown risks they may face. The key to alleviating many of these concerns—to mitigating the risk—is the security of agents. In order to run, a mobile agent has to expose its code and data to the host environment that supplies the means for it to execute. Thus the agents are at risk of being tampered with, scanned or even terminated by malicious servers.

In this chapter, software agent technology and cryptographic technology are combined with a view to automating and securing Internet trading. The chapter is organised as follows. Firstly, software agent technology is introduced. A new software agent-mediated Internet trading framework is then proposed, in which an agent automatically roams the Internet to negotiate with some merchants using an auction-like negotiation protocol and then orders and pays for a commodity according to an agent-mediated SET protocol. The security aspects of the framework are then discussed and some conclusions drawn at the end.

SOFTWARE AGENT TECHNOLOGY

Software agents are one of the fastest growing areas of information technology. They offer a new paradigm for developing software applications. More than this, agent-based computing has been hailed as "the next significant break-through in software development" (Sargent, 1992) and "the new revolution in software" (Ovum, 1994). Currently, agents are the focus of intense interest in many sub-fields of computing science and artificial intelligence. Agents are being used in an increasingly wide variety of applications, ranging from comparatively small systems such as e-mail filters to large, open, complex, mission-critical systems such as Internet trading.

General Concept of a Software Agent

An agent's role is one of action on behalf of others. In the field of artificial intelligence, the term is used to refer to an entity that functions autonomously in a particular environment and provides services to its owner. This agent is autonomous in the sense that its activities do not need human intervention. People have long dreamed of an intelligent system which can let them "input less and output more" to replace traditional applications with little flexibility that depend on the input of step-by-step instructions. Intelligent software agent research is trying to narrow the gap between the dream and the reality. The hope is that agents will provide services to people without requiring them to explicitly indicate the procedures required, make appropriate decisions in unexpected or novel environments, plan their action in advance and tackle problems independently.

The term "agent" has its background in the early artificial intelligent approach to humanoid entities. During the long period of development of artificial intelligence the term was applied to a wide range of techniques and attracted different definitions. Genesereth (1994) regards agents as "software components that communicate with their peers by exchanging messages in an expressive agent communication language." Shoham (1993) regards agents as being ontologically dependent on their role in the community.

An agent can be thought of as a computer program that simulates a human relationship by doing something that another person could do for you (Selker, 1994). An agent is a self-contained program capable of controlling its own decision making and acting, based on its perception of its environment, in pursuit of one or more objectives (Jennings et al., 1996). More than one type of agent is possible. In its simplest form it is a software object that sifts through large amounts of data and presents a subset of this data as useful information to another agent, user or system. An example of this is an agent that reads and analyzes all incoming e-mail, and routes it to an appropriate department or another agent for a reply (Wirthman, 1996). These types of agents are called static agents.

Mobile agents owned by a user or another software element are capable of migrating from one computer to another to execute a set of tasks on behalf of their owner. Such agents would typically gather and analyze data from a multitude of nodes on the network and present a subset of this data as information to a user, agent or system. For example, a

Figure 1. Encapsulated Agent Format

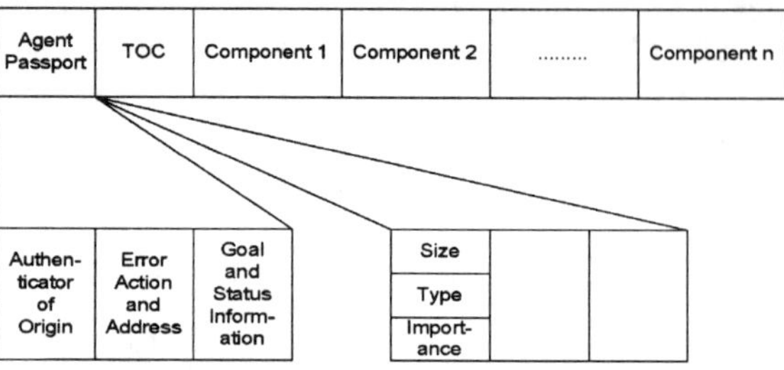

company that needs to order additional stationery supplies from time to time could have agents that monitor its internal usage patterns and stocks of paper and launch buying agents when supplies are becoming low. Those buying agents would automatically collect information about vendors and products that may fit the needs of the company, evaluate the different offerings, make a decision about which merchants and products to pursue, negotiate the terms of transactions with these merchants and finally place orders and make automated payments. Mobile agents can also act as brokers for users. For example, a single sign-on agent can sign-on to many different systems, relieving the user from typing in his or her password for every system (Wirthman, 1996).

Mobile agents are said to be autonomous, in the sense that they can make their own decisions while away from their host. This implies that a mobile agent (agent, for short) is not just a piece of data being transferred between systems, but may also carry some logic (i.e. code) and state, which enables it to perform some part of its tasks in one system, migrate to another and continue its work there. In this chapter we mainly focus on mobile agents.

Mobile Agent Systems

A mobile agent framework naturally draws upon existing components of networks such as name servers, directories, routers and so forth, and adds several new facilities:

- *Mobile Agents*
  These may be expressed in various procedural languages and may transport knowledge expressed in various forms. They must be structured so as to engage in a progressive dialogue with the Agent Meeting Places (AMPs) until they are able to execute some task or are rejected.
- *Agent Languages*
  Two kinds of languages are involved. One is the language in which the programmatic content of the agent is written; this is usually (though not necessarily) a script language. The second is a language for knowledge representation, which provides the means to express goals, tasks, preferences, and vocabularies appropriate to various domains.
- *Agent Meeting Places*
  These have various sub-components, and they are the principal means by which a server becomes part of the agent framework. We think of the AMP as a broker between the agents that are making requests for resources and services and the applications that implement these resources and services.
- *Public Security Services*
  These security services, which are trusted by the servers taking part in the agent framework, provide certificates of authenticity and other security services to the mobile agents.

In the following sections, we will describe the principal aspects of a mobile agent framework.

Mobile Agent Structure

The basic structure of a mobile agent (as shown in Figure 1) can be divided into three distinct portions: the Agent Passport, the Table of Contents (TOC), and some Components, which are discussed below.

The Agent Passport consists of the basic information required to permit the agent to flow from AMP to AMP. This includes:

- *Authentication of Origin*
  This is the authentication certificate of the originator of this agent. This certificate includes the name or the authority of the owner and the name or names of other authority sanctioning entities. In the example of Figure 1, this certificate may carry the identity of the originator of the agent and the "network name'' of the business server.
- *Error Actions and Addresses*
  This is the action that the AMP should take if an error occurs while processing the agent. Some possible actions include discarding the agent without comment, delivering an error notification to a specified address; or routing the agent to another AMP.
- *Goal and Status Information*
  This information includes a representation of the agent's goals and can include its relationship to other agents and their goals. Note that this agent may be the child of an agent that is present at the AMP, returning after an assignment from the parent. In some cases, the agent may require the AMP to notify an external entity (another agent or a client) of its status or progress based on some specified conditions. The address of the external entity and the conditions are provided as part of this information.

It should be noted that this structure is only that of the agent and does not include any header or segmentation that may be imposed by communications protocols used to move it between AMPs.

The Table of Contents (TOC) for the body of an agent provides a map of the structure of the agent. Each component has a size, type and importance. The size, as expected, is the size of the component. The type field contains a simple representation of what is required to process the component. The importance field describes whether the component is necessary for the agent to be instantiated at the AMP. This permits agents to carry obscure components through AMPs that do not support these components, and to avoid unpacking components that will not be used at any AMP.

Note that in order to provide for arbitrary length expressions specifying the type of service needed to support the component, the type fields are stored in a variable length section of the TOC, with offsets to the start of each field and their length stored in the fixed table structure of the TOC.

Operation of Mobile Agent System

In many cases, the mobile agent is launched from a client device such as a laptop or desktop PC by an otherwise conventional application. We anticipate that end-users will not in general write their own agents (though that is certainly possible), but that various classes of agents will be distributed by services for use by their subscribers or will be packaged with client applications. The agent is initialized with the user's task and transmitted by a message channel. The sending client may specify a destination service directly, but more than likely it sends the agent initially to, for example, a Yellow Pages server, which can propose servers to be visited that are likely to be able to fulfill the user's task.

When the agent reaches a server, it is delivered to an Agent Meeting Point (AMP). Upon arrival at an AMP, the Agent Passport is inspected for its authentication credentials. Once validated, the AMP examines the agent's Table of Contents (TOC). Ontologically named service requests are resolved to determine if the desired services are available at the AMP. If sufficient resources are available at the AMP and are permitted to the agent, the constituent parts of the agent are passed to the services.

The executable portions of the agent are then started. In some cases, the mobile agent will interact directly with server resources (via proxy objects, which enable access control to be enforced). In the other cases, the mobile agent will interact with a static agent at the AMP. A static agent is an agent that is resident at that AMP. The static agent may have been installed by the server operator. Static agents enable the server's function to be personalized by the server's owner or by users. When the agent has successfully completed its task at this server, it may ask to be transported to a new host. Alternatively, it may launch a smaller agent to deliver the acquired information to the sending client or to another server and then it may terminate. This ability to acquire knowledge and transport it from place to place is a key attribute of a mobile agent. The new knowledge may simply be a new destination or it may be a security token or a transaction. This ability means that the agent is not merely a program that is executed on a remote host and then returned to its origin, but it is a dynamic process which progressively accomplishes a task by moving from place to place.

If the agent proves to be unauthorized, or if the meeting point is unable to provide the agent with the resources it has requested, the AMP will take action based on the agent's header. It may discard the agent, send the indicated party a description of the failure or, if it is capable, propose one or more AMPs that may be able to satisfy the request.

SOFTWARE AGENT-MEDIATED INTERNET TRADING FRAMEWORK: NEGOTIATION

The proposed framework intends to automate the purchase process for a customer browsing online retail outlets to purchase goods or services from an optimal site. This framework is composed of two stages: negotiation and payment. In the first stage, a mobile agent roams the Internet to seek several merchants and negotiate with them on behalf of customer until an optimal site from which to buy a commodity is located. During the second stage, the mobile agent orders and pays for this commodity according to an agent-mediated SET protocol. This section will deal with the first stage.

Evolution of Auction-Like Negotiation

So far, one of the best solutions to automatic negotiation for goods on sale is through an auction. In recent times, auctions have achieved considerable popularity in Internet retail commerce. In their survey paper on automatic negotiation, Beam et al. (1996) define automatic negotiation as the process by which two or more parties multilaterally bargain resources for mutual intended gain, using the tools and techniques of electronic commerce. The most attractive characteristic of an auction is its open and simple framework. Research on electronic negotiation through Internet-based auctions can be found in Beam et al. (1996). Some electronic auction houses have already been established on the web, such as Onsale (http://www.onsale.com), FirstAuction (http://www.firstauction.com), ZAuction(http://www.zauction.com), Dealdeal(http://www.dealdeal.com) and Ubid (http:// www.ubid.com). They post details of goods for sale on the web page every day; customers can freely bid for them via their web browsers. Onsale, the first and most prominent of the online auctions, reported a 50% increase in gross revenue for the second quarter of 1997. The surge in auctions has stimulated a large number of online salesrooms and related industries such as newsletters, auction software providers and specialized search engines.

Although there is an "auction fever" which tends to take auctions as a panacea for shopping and selling, a closer look at the characteristics of auctions reveals their disadvantages for retail commerce. Guttman (1998) pointed out problems with current online auctions such as the "winner's curse" and low performance.

Nowadays, consumers are much more in the driver's seat in the online market than in the physical-world market. This is largely due to the dramatic reduction of search costs. This increases competition among retailers and forces them to positively differentiate themselves in value dimensions other than price. However, instead of merchants competing for consumer patronage, traditional online retail auctions force consumers to compete with one another for a specific merchant offering. This leads to the "winner's curse", which pushes up the winning bid above the product's market valuation. On the other hand, retailers often care less about profit on any given transaction and care more about long-term profitability. Customers' losses through the "winner's curse" actually destroy the relationship between retailers and customers, thus damaging the retailers' benefit in the long run. Furthermore, the traditional online auctions have a long delay between the start of an auction and the purchase of the product. This is an impediment for a large number of impatient or time-constrained consumers. In fact, the English and Yankee auction protocols are usually implemented over the Internet for several days. Since only the highest bidder(s) at an auction can purchase the auctioned good(s), the rest of the bidders (the majority) have to endure a long fruitless delay. Unlike the selling of, say, works of art, this is quite annoying in retail commerce.

The development of software agent technology may provide some opportunities to improve auction performance. Some researchers have suggested dispatching agents to a centralized salesroom to conduct the auction locally. However, this causes security concerns. In order for an agent to run, it must expose its data and code to the host resources. Therefore, if the auctioneer conspires with the owner of the salesroom, the auctioneer can manipulate the auction to his advantage. If the mobile agent's negotiation strategy is known to the host it may be at a significant disadvantage. Suppose the merchant's host knows that the buyer's negotiation strategy is to accept all offers under a certain (unknown) threshold value. The merchant can begin at a price greater than the threshold value and repeatedly offer the buyer a penny less each time, until the buyer's threshold value is reached, at which point the (worst possible, for the buyer) deal is made. This results in the bidding agents suffering losses.

Considering the difficulty for a negotiation agent to hide its negotiation strategies and the open and simple framework of auctions, an agent-mediated auction-like negotiation protocol for Internet trading is proposed in this section. Auctions are normally used when the auctioneer wants to sell an item and get the highest possible payment for it while the bidders want to acquire the items at the lowest possible price. In contrast to traditional auction models, the negotiation agent of this protocol acts as a mobile auctioneer while online retailers bid for the lowest price. It is strategically analogous to an English auction. This approach in fact eliminates the "winner curse".

Architecture of Agent-Mediated Auction-Like Negotiation

Components of the Architecture: The architecture for agent-mediated Internet trading comprises the following components:

- Customer (*C*)—generates a mobile agent (*A*) and launches it to traverse a list of online shops (or merchants) so as to seek out an optimal site from which to purchase a commodity.
- Mobile Agent (*A*)—acts as an auctioneer on behalf of the customer and negotiates with a list of merchants in an auction-like way.
- Online Shops or Merchants (*S[i,j]* or *S(i)*)—each negotiates with the mobile agent *A* by bidding a price for the commodity requested by *A* and each provides an Agent Meeting Place (*AMP*) for *A* to run its code.

Security Assumption: Throughout the following discussion, each participant *X* in the architecture (the customer and the merchants) has a pair of keys associated with it: the public key of *X* denoted by X_p and the private key of *X* denoted by X_s. *X*'s public key is used to encrypt data meant to be read by *X*; *X* decrypts the result using its private key, i.e., $D= X_s (X_p (D))$. *X* uses X_s to create its digital signatures, which can be verified by any party using X_p. The hash value of a message *M* with the hash function *H* is denoted by *H(M)*. In addition, we assume the existence of a certification authority (*CA*) which provides public key certification for all participants in the architecture. The public key of the certification authority (CA_p) is known to every entity. *X*'s certificate (*Cert(X)*) is issued by the *CA*.

Table of Symbols: In this section we will make use of the following symbols:

C	=	customer
A	=	mobile agent
S[i,j]	=	online shop that takes part in the negotiation and never wins
S(i)	=	online shop that takes part in the negotiation, wins at least one time and finally loses (iπn)
S(n)	=	online shop that finally wins the negotiation
X_s	=	private key of the entity *X*
X_p	=	public key of the entity *X*
$X_p (D)$	=	ciphertext of the data *D* encrypted with the public key X_p of public-key cryptosystem
$X_s (D)$	=	ciphertext of the data *D* encrypted with the private key X_s of public-key cryptosystem
Cert(X)	=	certificate of the entity *X*
H(M)	=	hash function of the message *M*
N	=	a round of an auction-like negotiation procedure between two bidders.
AMP	=	agent meeting place

CDC = code and data component
NAC = negotiation agreement component
$NAC_{s(i)}$ = negotiation agreement component reached at online shop *S(i)*
NRC = non-repudiation component
$NRC_{s(i)}$ = non-repudiation component of online shop *S(i)*
$Sign_{S(i)}$ = signature of *S(i)* on some data
|| = concatenation of two messages
WA = waiting agent in some round of negotiation
BA = bidding agent in some round of negotiation
WS = waiting server in some round of negotiation
BS = bidding server in some round of negotiation
MB_0 = initial minimum bid
MB_i = the minimum bid of the ith round of negotiation
MBD = minimum bid decrement

Overview of the Agent-Mediated Auction-Like Negotiation: The architecture of the agent-mediated auction-like negotiation protocol is illustrated in Figure 2. There are in total *n* rounds of negotiation carried out.

Initially, the negotiation agent *A* launches from the customer's computer and traverses a series of online shops *S[0,1], S[0,2], ..., S[0,i(0)] (i(0)> 0)*. No negotiation occurs during this period because the first *i(0)* servers do not have the required commodity for sale. *S(1)* is the first shop that is willing and able to sell the commodity to *A*. Then the customer *C* negotiates with *S(1)* to reach a negotiated agreement (the current lowest sale price of this commodity).

A brings the previous negotiation result from *C* and roams another series of online shops *S[1,1], S[1,2], ..., S[1,i(1)], S(2)* until it finds an online shop *S* that is able to offer a sale price less than the current lowest sale price. If the *S* is one of *S[1,1], S[1,2], ..., S[1,i(1)]*, it loses the competition (i.e., *S* gives up the right to make a further bid) after it negotiates with *S(1)* in an auction-like way. The online shop *S(2)* not only offers a lower price, but also finally wins the auction between *S(1)* and *S(2)*.

A brings the new negotiation agreement from *S(1)* and roams a new series of online shops *S[2,1], S[2,2], ..., S[2,i(2)], S(3)*. The same procedure as above is carried out.

A brings the previous negotiation result from the *S(n-1)* and roams a new series of online shops *S[n,1], S[n,2], ..., S[n,i(n)]*. When A traverses to *S[n,i(n)]*, the lifetime or size limit of the agent is reached. Therefore, the two agents in *S(n)* and *S[n,i(n)]* both bring their final negotiated agreements and return to the customer *C*. The negotiation process terminates.

Figure 2. Architecture of Agent-Mediated Auction-Like Negotiation

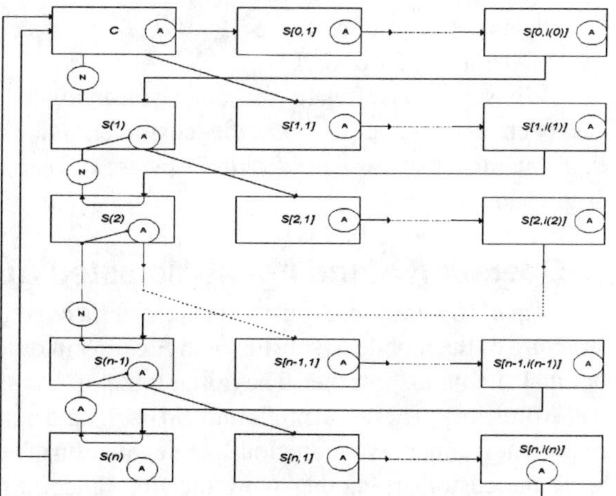

Structure of the Mobile Agent: The mobile agent *A* possesses the same structure as that of a general mobile agent (see Figure 1). Its Agent Passport and Table of Contents are exactly the same as those in Figure 1. Since the goal of *A* is negotiating with merchants, each component of *A* has a specific significance. The structure of *A* can be described as follows (shown in Figure 3):

Figure 3. Structure of the Mobile Agent (A)

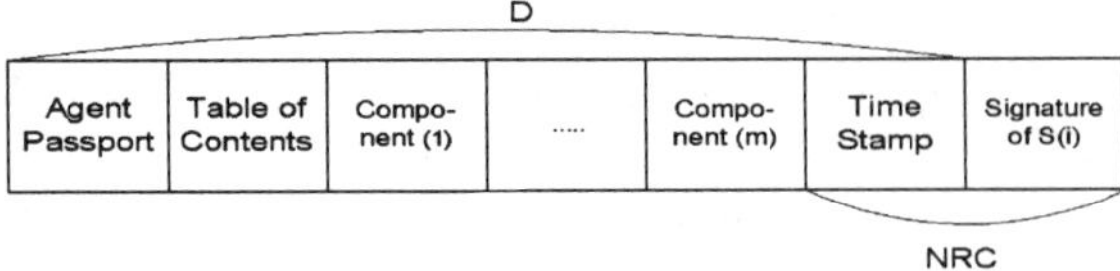

- Code and Data Component (*CDC*)—contains code and data executed at each merchant to determine the optimal site from which to purchase the commodity. The data portion records the visited and unvisited IP addresses, the minimum bid decrement, the maximum time for the collection of negotiated agreements and so on.
- Negotiation Agreement Component (*NAC*)—contains the negotiated agreement of each round of auction-like negotiation between two bidders. The negotiated agreement should be firstly signed with the secret key of the winner of this round of auction-like negotiation and then signed by the loser to ensure the integrity and legality of the negotiated agreement.
- Non-Repudiation Component (*NRC*)—contains the signature of some merchant $S[i,j]$ and the time stamp. It usually occupies the last component of the *agent* and attaches right behind the corresponding *NAC*. For example, when *A* is launched from $S(i)$ and roams into $S[i+1,1]$, the *NRC* is the signature of the $S(i)$ on part *D* (as shown in Figure 3).

Signature on the Agent The signature of $S(i)$ on D (denoted as $Sign_{S(i)}$) is generated and verified in the following way:

1) $S(i)$ produces the hash value of D, that is $H(D)$.
2) $S(i)$ signs the hash value $H(D)$ with its secret key to generate its signature on A, i.e.,
   $Sign_{S(i)} = S(i)_s(H(D))$ (1)
   where $S(i)_s$ denotes the private key of the merchant $S(i)$.
3) The signature can be verified to be genuine if the following equation holds;
   $S(i)_p(Sign_{S(i)}) = H(D)$ (2)
   where the public key $S(i)_p$ of the $S(i)$ can be retrieved from the certificate $Cert(S(i))$ of the $S(i)$.

We suppose software for the agent-mediated auction-like negotiation protocol has been distributed to both the customer and the merchant servers. In addition, every merchant server has a Login Database to keep the evidence for non-repudiation of origin and receipt.

Operation of the Agent-Mediated Auction-Like Negotiation

Agent Generation: A customer *C* creates a negotiation agent *A* in accordance with the structure of the mobile agent shown in Figure 3 in order to purchase a commodity from an optimal site on the Internet. The initial route of *A* is specified by *C* according to a yellow pages directory. The initial minimum bid (MB_0) and minimum bid decrement (*MBD*) are two important parameters for auction-like negotiation. They can be assigned in two ways: one is by the customer, another is by the first bidder who has the commodity for sale. By convention, our protocol adopts the first way to assign *MBD* (included as part of the non-varying data of the agent) and the second way to assign MB_0.

At the same time, C sets up a static agent that will reside in the customer's computer and:

- Automatically negotiate with the first bidder (i.e., *S(1)*) based on some strategy and verify the authenticity of the signature of *S(1)* on the initial negotiated agreement.
- Verify the authenticity of the final negotiated agreement from the last round of negotiation.
- Create a payment envelope based on the Secure Electronic Transaction (SET) protocol.

Finally, *A* is launched by *C*. *A* migrates to the first merchant's host *S[0,1]* on the Internet, in accordance with its route list.

Execution Process of the Agent in the Online Shop S The general case of the execution of the negotiation agent *A* in an online shop *S* that wishes to bid is considered here. We suppose the online shop *S** is the bid winner immediately prior to *S*. Once *A* arrives at the Agent Meeting Place (AMP) of *S*, *S* executes the following procedures shown in Figure 4.

The communication portals of *S*'s *AMP* are responsible for managing the arrival and departure of mobile agents. For inbound services, they extract the arriving mobile agent *A* and pass it to the mobile agent concierge. The mobile agent concierge acts much as a concierge does in a full service hotel.

With the help of authentication services, the concierge can verify the following items:

- Is *Cert(C*)(from the Agent Passport) issued by the *CA*?
- Is the signature *C* on the original agent (from the *NRC* of *A*) genuine?
- Is the *Time Stamp* of the original agent (from the *NRC* of *A*) valid?
- Is *Cert(S*)* (from the *NAC* of *S**) issued by the *CA*?
- Is the signature of *S** on the previous negotiated agreement (from the *NAC* of *S**) genuine?
- Is the signature of *S** on the current *A* (from the *NRC* of *S**) genuine?
- Is the *Time Stamp* of the current *A* (from the *NRC* of *S**) valid?

Note that all signatures are verified based on Equation (2).

If there is no problem, the concierge extracts the Code and Data from *A* according to the *TOC* and then sends it to an agent execution environment for it to run. Once *A* resides and runs its code in the agent execution environment, it firstly asks *S* to provide a lower bid to sell the commodity and then sends the lower bid to the negotiation agent *A**

Figure 4. Execution Process of A *at the* AMP *of* S

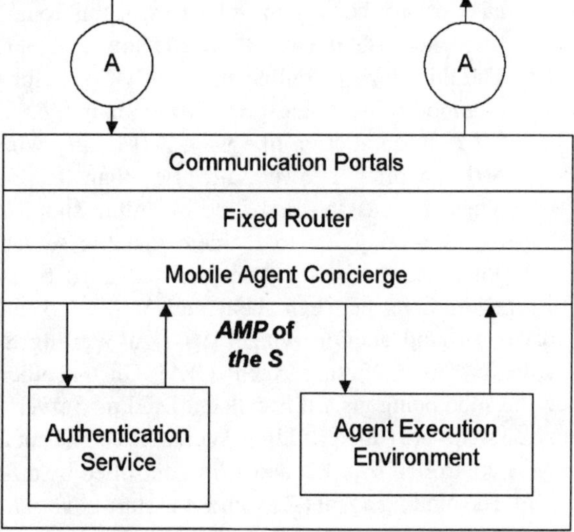

residing in S^*, the bid winner of the previous round. Thus the auction-like negotiation between two merchants begins. This process will be dealt with later.

Once the goal of the negotiation in S has been fulfilled, A will ask the concierge to launch it to the next destination.

If A does not pass the verification check, the concierge handles it in accordance with the information in the Error Actions and Addresses part of the Agent Passport.

Initial Round of Negotiation: As shown in Figure 1, the $S(1)$ is the first online shop that wishes to sell the commodity to the agent A. After A enters the Agent Meeting Place (AMP) of $S(1)$, the initial round of negotiation between the static agent of C and $S(1)$ begins. The static agent bargains with $S(1)$ by applying some negotiation strategies to reach an initial negotiated agreement indicating the initial minimum bid MB_0. The corresponding negotiation agreement component takes the form of

$$NAC_{s(1)} = Cert(S(1)) \| S(1)_s \ (MB_0, t)$$

where $S(1)_s$ denotes the signature private key of $S(1)$ and t is the current time. The $NAC_{S(1)}$ is collected into A as a negotiation agreement component. The agent duplicates itself, keeps one copy in Server $S(1)$ and migrates another copy to the customer's computer and then from C to other merchant servers on the Internet after the static agent of the C has verified the authenticity of the signature of $NAC_{S(1)}$.

The j-th Round Auction-Like Negotiation: The agent-mediated auction-like negotiation protocol is similar to the English Auction and the common values model (bidder's valuation is influenced by others). After exiting from $S(j-2)$, the agent A chooses an unvisited online shop from its routing list and enters the server. Note that if the routing list has run out, the agent will browse on the Internet to find new seller servers and add them to the routing list of the agent. We assume that A further roams a series of online shops $S[j-1,1]$, $S[j-1,2], \ldots, S[j-1,i(j-1)]$ $(1<j<n+1)$, $S(j)$ as shown in Figure 2. These online shops can be divided into the following three types:

- The first type of online shop does not have the commodity for sale or does not wish to sell the commodity at a sale price lower than MB_{j-2} of $NAC_{s(j-1)}$.
- The second type of online shop is willing to sell the commodity at a sale price lower than MB_{j-2} of $NAC_{s(j-1)}$ in the beginning and indeed compete with $S(j-1)$ in an auction-like way in order to win this round of the auction. However, it finally loses because it cannot offer a lower sale price than that of $S(j-1)$.
- The third type of online shop (only $S(j)$ belongs to this type) is willing to sell the commodity at a sale price lower than MB_{j-2} of $NAC_{s(j-1)}$. By competing with the $S(j-1)$ in an auction-like way, $S(j)$ finally wins this round of the auction because $S(j)$ can offer a lower sale price than that of $S(j-1)$.

When A visits the first type of online shop, *it* only marks the IP address of this shop on its routing list to indicate that the server has been visited.

When the A visits the second and third type of online shop, there are auction-like negotiations between them and $S(j-1)$. To simplify the description, we call the previous round auction winner $S(j-1)$ a Waiting Server (*WS*) and the agent residing in the WS as a Waiting Agent (*WA*). On the other hand, the second or third type of online shop being visited is called a Bidding Server (*BS*) and the agents residing in these online shops are called Bidding Agents (*BA*). The auction-like negotiation process between a WA controlled by a *WS* and a *BA* controlled by a *BS* can be described as follows:

1) The bidding agent (*BA*) sends the start-negotiation request to the waiting agent (*WA*).

The format of the request is *Cert(BS)*|| BS_s *(*MB_{BS}*, t)* where the MB_{BS} is the current minimum of the *BS,* which is established based on its negotiation strategy and the bidding regulations (e.g., the amount by which a bid price is decreased must be a multiple of the minimum bid decrement (*MBD*) and the MB_{BS} must be lower than the minimum bid MB_{WS} in the $NAC_{S(j-1)}$.

2) *WA* authenticates the request. If correct, the procedure continues. Otherwise, the request is ignored.
3) *WS* checks MB_{BS} and makes its decision about whether to further lower the sale price or give up. If WS wants to lower the sale price, it provides its new minimum bid according to the bidding regulations, and then replies to *BA* with its bid response WS_s *(*MB_{WS}*, t).* If the decision is to resign the round of negotiation, the procedure goes to step 5.
4) After *BS* receives the bid response, it checks MB_{WS} and determines whether to further lower the sale price or give up. If *BS* wants to lower the price, it creates another minimum bid (MB_{BS}) and sends BS_s *(*MB_{BS}*, t)* to WA. Then the procedure goes to step 3. If *BS* wants to give up, the procedure goes to step 6.
5) Because *WS* fails to further lower the price, it has to give up bidding and send a resignation notification to *BA*. The format of the notification is *Resign*||WS_s *(*MB_{WS}*,* BS_s *(*MB_{BS} *t)),* where $MB_{WS}>MB_{BS}$. After *BA* gets the resignation notification, *BA* updates itself by attaching *Cert(BS)*||WS_s *(*MB_{WS}*,*BS_s*(*MB_{BS}*,t))* as a negotiation agreement component NAC_{BS} and a non-repudiation component NRC_{BS} created according to Figure 3 to the end of *A*. In addition, The updated agent duplicates itself, keeps one copy in the *BS* and migrates another copy to the *WS*. After *WA* verifies the authenticity of the signature of *BS* on the current minimum sale price, *A* continues to roam to an unvisited server. Only the negotiation between *S(j)* and *S(j-1)* belongs to this case. Now the current MB_{BS} is the minimum bid (denoted as MB_{j-1}) after the agent *A* roams through online shops *S[j-1,1], S[j-1,2],…,S[j-1,i(j-1)], S(j).* $NAC_{S(j)}$ is expressed by

Cert(BS)||WS_s (MB_{WS},,BS_s(MB_{BS}, t))

From then on, the bidding server that wins the

Figure 5. Negotiation Between Waiting Server and the Third Type of Online Shop

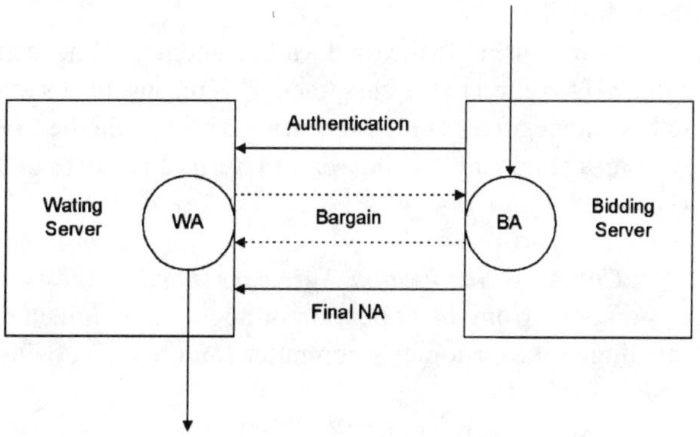

Figure 6. Negotiation Between Waiting Server and the Second Type of Online Shop

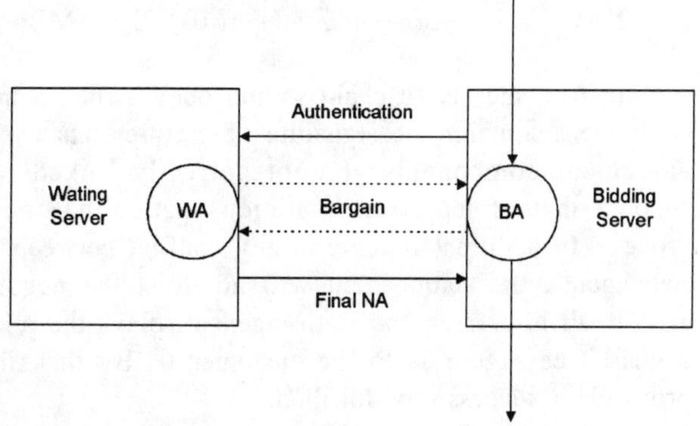

current round of bidding changes to the wait server and keeps a copy of the new version of the agent as a waiting agent. This round of negotiation is ended. The procedure is illustrated in Figure 5.

6) Because *BS* fails to lower the price, it sends a resignation notification which informs *WA* that *BA* gives up the round of negotiation. *WA* updates itself by updating the negotiation agreement component with $WS_s\ (MB_{WS,}t)$. The updated agent duplicates itself, keeps one copy in *WS* and migrates another copy to *BS*. After *BA* verifies the authenticity of the signature of *WS* on the current minimum sale price, *A* continues to roam to an unvisited server. Now the current MB_{WS} is the minimum bid (still denoted by MB_{j-1}). This round of negotiation is complete. This auction-like negotiation procedure is illustrated in Figure 6.

Last Round Auction-Like Negotiation: The size and lifetime of the negotiation agent *A* is limited. Therefore, the customer *C* must assign two parameters to the agent before sending the agent out. Each time *A* enters a server, the two parameters are checked. If the agent's size or lifetime has been exceeded, the agent will automatically return to the customer *C*.

Referring to Figure 2, the last round of auction-like negotiation is performed between the *S(n-1)* and the *S(n)* or between *S(n)* and a second type of online shop among *S[n,1], S[n,2],......, S[n,i(n)]*. When the agent *A* enters the online shop *S[n,i(n)]*, it finds its size limit has been exceeded or its lifetime limit is up. Then the auction-like negotiation to compete the selling of the commodity is completed. The final winner is the online shop *S(n)*.

We require both the final waiting agent residing at the *S(n)* and the agent residing at the *S[n,i(n)]* to return to the customer. This means that even if there are more merchant servers to bid and negotiate with the waiting agent while the lifetime or size of the agent is up, the waiting agent in the waiting server returns directly to *C*. The two agents may be same when *i(n)=0*.

Checking Negotiation Agreements: After the two negotiation agents return to the customer C, from the collection of negotiation agreements of each agent, the static agent residing at the customer's computer can obtain a chain of negotiation agreement components as follows:

$$NAC_{s(1)} = Cert(S(1)) \| S(1)_s\ (MB_0, t_1)$$
$$NAC_{s(2)} = Cert(S(2)) \| S(1)_s\ (MB_0, S_{s(2)}(MB_1,\ t_2))$$
$$NAC_{s(3)} = Cert(S(3)) \| S(2)_s\ (MB_1, S_{s(2)}(MB_2,\ t_3))$$
$$\cdots\cdots$$
$$NAC_{s(n)} = Cert(S(n)) \| S(n-1)_s\ (MB_{n-2}, S_{S(n-1)}(MB_{n-1},\ t_n))$$

In fact, the above chain should obey a rule: a non-initial negotiation agreement component contains the signature of the previous winner. If the chain of negotiation agreement components are not correctly linked together, the static agent will suspect that at least one malicious action has occurred during the negotiation process. In addition, if there is any conflict between the two chains obtained by the two agents, the static agent will not trust the negotiated agreements.

If all is correct, the static agent displays the auction-like negotiation report via a chart (see Figure 7) to the customer *C*. By this time, the auction-like negotiation protocol is successfully fulfilled.

Figure 7. Auction-Like Negotiation Report

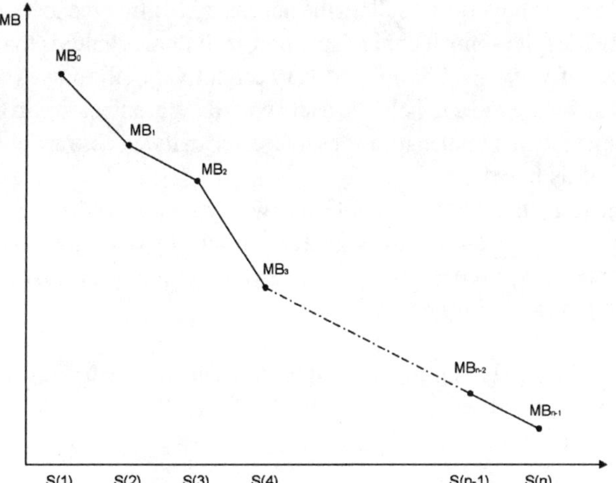

Whereafter, the customer *C* will order and pay for the commodity with the final winner of the auction, namely the online shop *S(n)*, using the SET protocol.

SOFTWARE AGENT-MEDIATED INTERNET TRADING FRAMEWORK: PAYMENT

In this section, we discuss how an agent residing in an online shop orders and pays for a commodity on behalf of the agent's owner (i.e., a customer).

Overview of Secure Electronic Transaction (SET)

The Internet is now considered to be the preferred environment for electronic commerce. However, there is still some resistance from the public to buying products and services online and paying for them over the Internet; for example, by browsing a company's Web server, ordering a product, and paying for it by filling in a form that includes credit card information. The main difficulty is that almost every Internet user has heard of credit card fraud performed by hackers eavesdropping connections used to send transaction data—despite the fact that very few of those attacks have actually succeeded. Even the deployment of secure servers based on protocols such as SSL or S-HTTP is not enough, since the credit card information is deposited in the server where it can easily be read by anyone with access to it (or even by unauthorized hackers).

The concern for protecting users' credit card information led VISA and MasterCard, in association with major software and cryptography companies, to the development of the SET protocol (Visa International and MasterCard International, 1997). SET provides important properties like authentication of the participants, non-repudiation, data integrity and confidentiality. Each player knows only what is strictly necessary to play their role, for example, the selling company never knows the buyer's credit card information, and the financial institution authorizing the transaction is not aware of the details of the purchase, including the nature of the products, quantities, etc. Paying for something using a credit card under the SET protocol is clearly much more secure than doing it, say, in a restaurant, where the card is normally taken out of the customer's sight.

SET is expected to give buyers and sellers the necessary confidence to launch Internet commerce definitively (despite some technical and non-technical problems that still exist). From the buyer's point of view, SET should be very attractive, both to use (there will be many SET-compliant software tools to help the users with their credit cards on the Internet) and to trust (if we assume the financial institutions interested in its success are able to explain it and convince users of its benefits).

Each participant X in the SET protocol has two types of certificates: one is the signature certificate $Cert_s(X)$ containing the signature public key of entity X; another is the key-exchange certificate $Cert_k(X)$ containing the key-exchange public key used to distribute session keys for a symmetric cryptosystem.

Table of Symbols: In the section, we will adopt the following symbols in addition to those in the last section:

C	= cardholder
M	= merchant
PG	= payment gateway
OI	= order information
PI	= payment instruction
$Cert_s(X)$	= signature certificate of the entity X
$Cert_k(X)$	= key exchange certificate of the entity X
$E_k(D)$	= ciphertext of the data D encrypted with the secret key k of symmetric cryptosystem.
$E_{PG}\{K,PI\}$	= digital envelope for payment gateway

On the assumption that cardholders and the merchants have registered and obtained their certificates from the Issuer, the purchase request phase of SET can be outlined as follows (see Figure 8):

- *Step 1:* A cardholder (C) looks at a catalog (printed on paper, supplied on a CD-ROM, or available on-line on the Web) provided by a merchant (M) and, after deciding to purchase something, sends a request to the merchant's server. The request includes the description of the services or the quantities of the goods, the terms of the order and the brand of the credit card that will be used for payment.
- *Step 2:* The merchant receives the request and sends back its own signature certificate $Cert_s(M)$ and the key-exchange certificate $Cert_k(PG)$ of a payment gateway (PG). The merchant also sends a unique identifier, assigned to this transaction.
- *Step 3:* The cardholder (i.e., his or her software) verifies the certificates by traversing the trust chain to the root key (the public signature key of a certificate authority (CA)) so as to assure itself of the authenticity and integrity of the data (the merchant had digitally signed it), and creates two pieces of information:
  (a) The Order Information (OI), containing control information verified by the merchant to validate the order, card brand and bank identification. The OI also includes a digest of the order description, which includes the amount of the transaction and other elements such as quantity, size and price of the items ordered, shipping and billing addresses, etc. This data, not included in the OI, will be processed outside the scope of the SET protocol.
  (b) The Payment Instructions (PI), containing the amount of the transaction, the card account number and expiration date, instructions for installment payments (if

Figure 8. SET Purchase Request Transaction

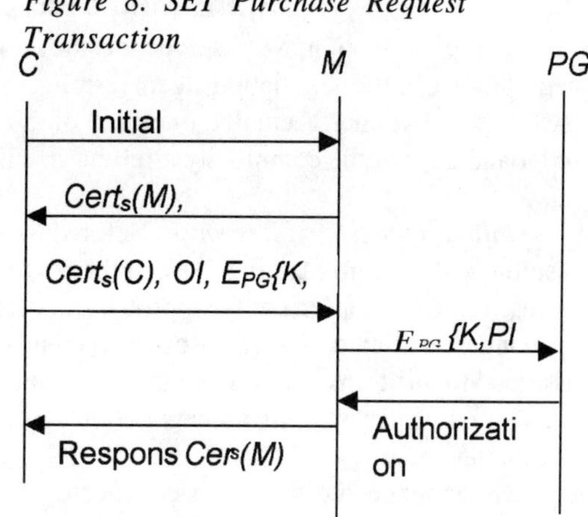

that's the case) and a couple of secret values to prevent guessing and dictionary attacks on the data, among other elements. The *PI* is encrypted with a randomly generated symmetric key *K*.

Both elements will contain the transaction identifier and are dually signed, so they can later be linked together by the payment gateway. Then, the encrypted *PI* (i.e., $E_k(PI)$) and the key (*k*) used to encrypt it are encrypted into a digital envelope (E_{PG}), using the payment gateway's public key. Finally, the *OI* and the digital envelope are sent to the merchant, along with the cardholder's signature certificate $Cert_s(C)$.

- *Step 4:* The merchant verifies the cardholder certificate and the dual signature on the *OI*. The request is then processed, which includes forwarding the digital envelope to the payment gateway for authorization (the details of this operation are outside the scope of this description). After processing the order, the merchant generates and signs a purchase response, and sends it to the cardholder along with its signature certificate. If the payment was authorized, the merchant will fulfill the order by delivering the products bought by the cardholder.
- *Step 5:* The cardholder verifies the merchant signature certificate, checks the digital signature of the response, and takes any appropriate actions based on its contents.

The software responsible for the cardholder's side of the protocol manages a data structure called a digital wallet, where sensitive data like certificates, private keys and payment card information are kept, usually in encrypted files. The merchant will have a more complex system composed of several parts, doing different jobs: managing the dialog with cardholders, signing messages and verifying signatures and certificates, asking payment gateways for payment authorizations, and so on.

SET is a very complex protocol, and may not be suitable under some technical conditions, such as mobile computing environments. Generally, the devices used in these environments have limited computational capacity and use slow and expensive connections to the Internet. SET may be too demanding for this kind of equipment and connectivity, preventing on-line transactions for mobile users.

SET/A, guided by the SET rules and based on the mobile agent paradigm, is proposed by Romao et al. (Romao et al., 1998). With SET/A, the computational burden is taken away from the user's device, so it can be disconnected while the transaction is running. However, SET/A depends on a secure execution environment at the merchant's server to protect an agent's confidential data (i.e., credit card information) against a malicious merchant. In our opinion, the solution is high cost for merchants and the required security is not easy to ensure.

In the next section, we will propose another agent-mediated SET protocol, which avoids the security limitations on the agent's execution environment in the merchant's terminal.

Agent-Mediated SET Protocol

In the last section, we observed that the on-line shop *S(n)* finally wins the auction-like negotiation and the negotiation, agent residing in the *S(n)* brings all negotiation agreements back to the customer. Actually, one copy of the agent can stay in the *S(n)* and continue to order and pay for the commodity after the size limit or lifetime of the negotiation agent is up.

Initial Request and Response: Before it returns to the customer *C*, the agent *AMP(A)* residing at the Agent Meeting Place of the *S(n)* sends an initial request to the merchant *S(n)* as just the first step of the SET protocol. After obtaining the initial response (the key-exchange certificate $Cert_k(PG)$ of a payment gateway (*PG*) and the unique identifier *I* assigned to this transaction) from the merchant server as the second step of SET protocol, the agent *A* brings not only all negotiation agreements but also the initial response back to the customer *S*.

Note: Since the signature certificate of the merchant *S(n)* has been included in a negotiation agreement, the *S(n)* does not need to re-send it in the initial response.

Verification Request and Response: After receiving all negotiation agreements along with the verification request brought back from the negotiation agent, the static agent residing in the customer's computer firstly checks the authenticity of all negotiation agreements and then verifies the authenticity of the key-exchange certificate $Cert_k(PG)$ of a payment gateway (*PG*) if the customer *C* has made a final purchase decision after viewing the auction-like negotiation report displayed by the static agent.

In accordance with the third step of the SET protocol, the static agent creates the following items:

- Order Information *OI* containing the identifier *I*;
- Payment Instruction *PI* containing the identifier *I*;
- Dual signature of the cardholder (i.e., the customer *C*) on the *OI* and *PI*; this takes the form $Cs(H[H(OI) \parallel H(PI)])$.
- Digital envelope E_{PG} for the payment gateway *PG*. This takes the form $E_k(PI) \parallel PG_p(k)$.

Finally, the static agent transmits the following message to the *AMP(A)* residing at the *S(n)*'s server:

$$OI,\ H(PI),\ Cs(H[H(OI) \parallel H(PI)]),\ E_k(PI) \parallel PG_p(k)$$

Note: The signature certificate $Cert_s(C)$ of the customer *C* is known to the merchant *S(n)*. Hence, this certificate does not appear in the above message.

Purchase Request: After obtaining the above confirmation, the agent *AMP(A)* sends a purchase request to the merchant *S(n)* by forwarding all of above message to *S(n)*.

Authorization Request: With *OI*, *H(PI)* and the signature public key C_p of the cardholder extracted from the Passport of *AMP(A)*, the merchant *S(n)* can verify the dual signature of the cardholder. If it is valid, *S(n)* transmits the following message to its payment gateway:

$$Cert_s(C),\ H(OI),\ Cs(H[H(OI) \parallel H(PI)]),\ E_k(PI) \parallel PG_p(k)$$

Authorization Response: The payment gateway *PG* firstly decrypts $PG_p(k)$ with his own private key-exchange key PG_s to obtain *k* and then uses the *k* to decrypt $E_k(PI)$ to obtain *PI*. With *PI*, *H(OI)* and $Cert_s(C)$, the *PG* can verify the dual signature of the cardholder. The next action of the *PG* is the same as the corresponding step of the SET protocol.

Purchase Response: This step is the same as the fourth step of the SET protocol.

Agent Return: After obtaining the purchase response from *S(n)* (i.e., the signature of the merchant on the order), the mobile agent brings the purchase response back to the cardholder and the static agent of the cardholder verifies the purchase response from *S(n)*.

The whole payment process can be illustrated in Figure 9.

SECURITY ANALYSIS

Mobile agent security can be split into two broad areas (Chess et al., 1995). The first involves the protection of host nodes from destructive mobile agents while the second involves the protection of mobile agents from destructive hosts. In this section, we combine cryptographic technology and sociological means to propose a non-repudiation approach to securing this agent-mediated Internet trading framework.

Login Data Bases (LDB): In the proposed agent-mediated Internet trading framework, each online shop needs to set up a Login Data Base (*LDB*) saving some information from passing mobile agents in order to provide non-repudiation evidence when any problem occurs.

Because there are probably a lot of mobile agents entering an online shop to negotiate every day, it is impossible for any online shop to keep full copies of visiting agents in its records, since the *LDB* will then occupy a great deal of storage space. In view of this, the record structure of the *LDB* needs to be optimized. Our solution to this problem is illustrated in Figure 10.

In Figure 10, the meanings of the symbols used are as follows:

- Agent Passport - the passport of the agent, obtained from the original agent;
- Customer *NRC (0)* - the non-repudiation component of the customer, obtained from the original agent;
- *NAC (i-1)* - the negotiation agreement component of the winner of the previous bidding round, i.e., the on-line shop *S(i-1)*;
- *NRC (i-1)* - the non-repudiation component of the winner of the previous bidding round *S(i-1)*;
- *NAC (i)* - the negotiated agreement reached between the present on-line shop *S(i)* and the winner of the previous bidding round *S(i-1)*; this records the negotiated agreement at the point when the previous on-line shop *S(i-1)* lost the bidding to the present on-line shop *S(i)*.
- *NRC (i)* - the non-repudiation component provided by the present online shop *S(i)*;
- *NAC (i+1)* - the negotiated agreement reached between the present on-line shop *S(i)* and the winner of the next bidding round *S(i+1)*; this records the negotiated agreement just after the present on-line shop *S(i)* loses the bidding to the winner

Figure 9. Purchase Request Transaction Based on Software Agents

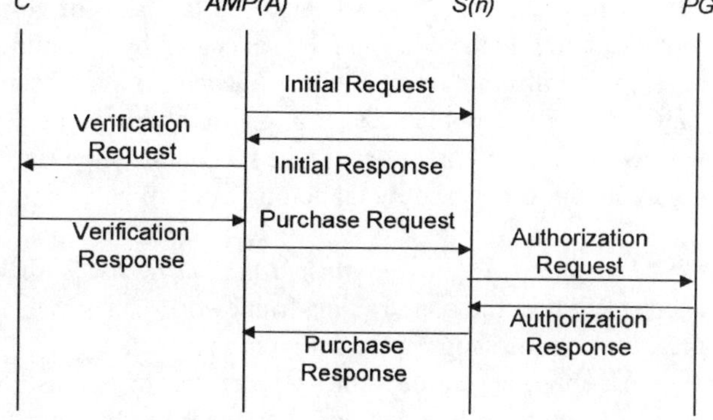

Figure 10. The Record Structure of a Login Data Base (LDB) *for S(i)*

Agent Passport	Customer NRC (0)	NAC (i-1)	NRC (i-1)	NAC (i)	NRC (i)	NAC (i+1)	NRC (i+1)

S(i+1) of the next bidding round.

- *NRC (i+1)* - the non-repudiation component of the winner *S(i+1)* of the next round bidding.

Extracting the Agent and Saving it in the LDB: On the route list of the negotiation agent are some on-line shops that have once won a bid in the auction. Only the negotiation information provided by them affects the purchase decision of the customer. Although the merchant *S(n)* is the final winner of the auction, the customer may select another merchant with a good reputation or near to the customer in order to make a deal with that merchant. Therefore, those merchants who have once won a bidding round still have opportunities to sell their goods. In view of this, they are motivated to behave according to the rules. The movement of the negotiation agent among these kinds of on-line shops can be depicted as follows:

C-->S(1)-->C
-->S(2)-->S(1)
-->S(3)-->S(2)
....
-->S(n-1)-->S(n-2)
-->S(n)-->S(n-1)-->C

We can see that the negotiation agent visits each of these online shops twice, except for *S(n)*. When the agent visits the online shop *S(i)* (i=1,2,...,n-1) the second time, it takes the form of

Original Agent || $(NAC_{S(1)} \| NRC_{S(1)}) \| (NAC_{S(2)} \| NRC_{S(2)}) \| \ldots\ldots \| (NAC_{S(i+1)} \| NRC_{S(i+1)})$

Therefore, *S(i)* can obtain all the items required for the *LDB* and create a new record to store them.

Protection of Hosts Against Malicious Agents: In the agent-mediated Internet trading framework, the Code and Data Component (*CDC*) is signed by the customer *C*. Its genuineness is ensured by the signature of the customer, i.e., Signature (0) of the *LDB*. No other parties can forge this signature on the basis of cryptography. Therefore, the *CDC* provides not only the code and data executed by all online shops to achieve a negotiation mission, but also non-repudiation evidence, so that *C* can not deny having generated the *CDC*. Should any problems, such as a virus altering other local agents, propagating viruses, worms and Trojan horses occur when an online shop runs the *CDC* in its agent execution environment, *C* is probably malicious and will be accused.

Protection of Agents Against Malicious Hosts: With the help of the *LDB*, the proposed agent-mediated Internet trading framework can provide protection for agents against malicious online shops in the following respects:

Although an online shop is permitted to put its Negotiation Agreement Component *NAC* and Non-Repudiation Component *NRC* into an agent, any malicious manipulation (such as cutting or manipulating another online shop's *NAC*) will be detected by the customer *C* because *C* will be conscious of any malicious action if an agent has taken an error action, or if the chain of negotiated agreements cannot be linked correctly.

In the case that the two returning negotiation agents are tampered with or cut (i.e., the chain of negotiated agreements is broken), *C* can carry out the following check procedure to identify the malicious merchant.

1. *C* asks each *S(i)* on the route list to commit their records (denoted as *Rec(i)*) about the agent *(i=1,2, ..., n)*. The motivation to prove themselves to be innocent drives all online shops except a malicious one to provide true records about the agent.
2. On basis of the initial agent and *Rec(i) (i=1, 2,......, n)*, *C* can reconstruct the negotiation agent at all stages in a recursive way.
3. As regards the merchant *S(1)*, *C* firstly checks whether both *NAC(1)* and *NRC(1)* from *Rec(1)* are the same as those from *Rec(2)*. If not, *C* further checks whether either *NAC(1)* and *NRC(1)* from *Rec(2)* are indeed signed by the *S(1)*. If so, *S(1)* is identified as a malicious merchant. If not, *S(2)* is a malicious merchant because it is supposed to begin bidding after confirming the authenticity of both signatures of *S(1)*. The merchant *S(1)* can be excluded from the suspect list only when both *NAC(1)* and *NRC(1)* from *Rec(1)* are the same as those from *Rec(2)*.
4. Suppose that all merchants before *S(i)* are proved to have behaved correctly. Let us consider *S(i)* (where *i<n*). *C* firstly checks whether both *NAC(i)* and *NRC(i)* from *Rec(i)* are the same as those from *Rec(i+1)*. If not, *C* further checks whether either *NAC(i)* and *NRC(i)* from *Rec(i+1)* are indeed signed by *S(i)*. If so, *S(i)* is identified as a malicious merchant. If not, *S(i+1)* is a malicious merchant because it is supposed to begin bidding after confirming the authenticity of both signatures of *S(i)*. The merchant *S(i)* can be excluded from the suspect list only when both *NAC(i)* and *NRC(i)* from *Rec(i)* are the same as those from *Rec(i+1)*.
5. As for *S(n)*, *C* directly checks the signatures of *S(n)* in *NAC(n)* and *NRC(n)* brought back by the negotiation agent and judges whether *S(n)* has behaved correctly.

In the case that the negotiation agent does not return to the customer, i.e., it is killed, *C* executes the following check procedure to determine which malicious merchant killed the agent.

1. *C* requests the first bid merchant *S(1)* to commit its record *Rec(1)* on the negotiation agent *A*.
2. On basis of the *NAC(2)* and *NRC(2)* from *Rec(1)*, *C* further asks the *S(2)* to commit its record *Rec(2)* on the negotiation agent *A* and so on.
3. The first merchant that cannot provide the *NAC* and *NRC* of the next merchant is identified as the malicious merchant because it should return the agent to *C* when the lifetime of the agent has expired.

This case occurs when a merchant has won the auction by offering a lowest bid, but does not really wish to sell the commodity to the customer. In view of this, it has not returned the negotiation agent to the customer. At the same time, the negotiation agent is also killed after it comes from the previous bidding winner.

CONCLUSION

In order to automate and secure Internet trading, we proposed in this chapter a software agent-mediated Internet trading framework to meet the needs of both customers and merchants on the Internet.

In the proposed software agent-mediated Internet trading framework, in order to purchase a commodity from an optimal site, a customer firstly generates a mobile agent and then launches it to roam a list of online shops. The online shops traversed by the mobile agent negotiate with each other in an auction-like way. When the lifetime or maximum size of the agent is exceeded, the negotiation agent sends all negotiated agreements back to the customer from the server of the final winner in this auction-like negotiation. At the same time, the negotiation agent is transformed into a payment agent. It resides at the final winner's server and executes the SET protocol to order and pay for the goods on behalf of the customer.

The security of the proposed software agent-mediated Internet trading framework is ensured by a non-repudiation approach with a Login Data Base. This approach can prevent malicious attacks from the mobile agent and the online shops to some extent. If the negotiated agreements brought back by the negotiation agent are tampered with or partly deleted by a malicious merchant, or if neither of the two negotiation agents (one from the final winner, another from the online shop where the lifetime or maximum size of the agent is exceeded) has returned to the customer, this approach can help the customer to identify the malicious merchant.

The auction-like negotiation protocol in the proposed agent-mediated Internet trading framework can help to overcome the "winner curse" (winning bid is greater than the product market valuation) and the long delay between starting an auction and purchasing a commodity. In addition, mobile agents can dynamically negotiate with merchants across the Internet. This means that the auctioneer has the ability to dynamically identify potential bidders.

Since the router of the mobile agent is dynamic, the proposed framework is vulnerable to a collusion attack in which two merchants involved in the auction-like negotiation process collude to retain the negotiation agent until its lifetime is up. Indeed, any given merchant may be able to increase their probability of success simply by delaying the agent for a period, thus reducing the number of other merchants that it can visit before the time limit on its life expires.

As part of our future work, we intend to use an Aglet language to implement the software agent-mediated Internet trading framework and devise strategies to prevent delay and collusion attacks.

REFERENCES

Beam, C., Segev, A. and Shanthikumar, J. G (1996). Electronic negotiation through Internet-based auction. CITM Working Paper 96-WP-1019, Dec. 1996.

Chess, D., Grosof, B., Harrison, C., Levine, D., Parris, C. and Tsudik, G. (1995). Itinerant agents for mobile computing. IEEE Personal Communications, 2(3), 34-49.

Genesereth, M. R., Ketchpel, S. P. (1994). Software agent. *Communications of ACM,* 37(7), 48-53.

Guttman, R.H. and Maes, P.(1998). Agent-mediated integrative negotiation for retail electronic commerce. In *Proceedings of Workshop on Agent Mediated Electronic*

Trading, Minneapolis, Minnesota, USA. May 1998.

Maes, P. (1994). Agents that reduce work and information overload. Communications of the ACM, 37(7), 31-40.

Moukas, A., Guttman, R., Maes, P. (1999). Agent-mediated electronic commerce: an MIT media laboratory perspective. To appear on Proceedings of the International Conference on Electronic Commerce.

Ovum Report (1994). Intelligent agents: the new revolution in software.

Romao, A. and Mira da Silva, M (1998). An agent-based secure Internet payment system for mobile computing. In Proceeding of TrEC'98, LNCS 1402, Hamburg, Germany,.

Sander, T. (1997). On cryptographic protection of mobile agents. In Proceedings of the 1997 Workshop on Mobile Agents and Security, University of Maryland, October.

Sander, T. and Tschudin, C.F. (1998). Protecting mobile agents against malicious hosts. Mobile Agent and Security, LNCS 1419.

Sargent, P. (1992). Back to school for a brand new ABC. In The Guardian, 12 March, 28.

Selker, T. (1994). A teaching agent that learns, Communications of the ACM, 37(7).

Shoham, Y. (1993). Agent-oriented programming. Artificial Intelligence, 60(1), 51-92.

Visa International and MasterCard International (1997). Secure electronic transaction (SET) specification. Version 1.0.

Wirthman, L. (1996). Gradient DCE has sign-on feature, *PC Week.*

Chapter XX

Distributed Recommender Systems: New Opportunities in Internet Commerce

Badrul M. Sarwar, Joseph A. Konstan and John T. Riedl
University of Minnesota, USA

INTRODUCTION

Internet commerce has exploded in the past three years. Consumers went from spending almost nothing on Internet commerce in 1996, to an estimated $4 billion that will be spent just between Thanksgiving and New Year's Day in 1999! (Forrester Research, 1998). Several types of products are emerging as the early leaders. Table 1 shows the top products in Fall 1998.

These products share several characteristics. First, many of them are commodity products in which the name is sufficient to identify the product to the consumer. Books, music, and travel are almost completely commodities. Hardware and apparel are less of a commodity. Brand is extremely important, but individual products within a brand change rapidly. Second, these products are easy to ship. Books, music, and apparel are relatively dense in value per unit of size or weight, and are nearly unaffected by extremes of climate. Travel *is* shipping, of the consumers, and the tickets are easy to transport, especially with the emergence of e-tickets that are not physically transferred at all. Third, consumers buy many of these products over the course of a year, so online businesses see the same consumers frequently.

Table 1: Top Internet commerce products (source: Jupiter Communications, Fall 1998).

Product	Market Share
Hardware	30.1%
Travel	29.6%
Books	9.2%
Apparel	4.3%
Music	1.9%

One implication of the first two of these characteristics is that consumers may feel that it does not matter who they purchase their products from. Since the products are commodities, and since they are easy to ship anywhere, consumers may feel they can choose to purchase their products from any business that carries those products, independent of location. If the three most important attributes of retail in the pre-Internet age – "location, location, and location" – have been rendered irrelevant in Internet commerce, what will replace them?

Future of Internet Commerce

Clearly service in delivering products will be one of the new attributes. Internet commerce companies that do not deliver products as promised are already seeing their names posted on special Web pages. New companies have been created, such as *BizRate*, whose sole function is to evaluate the delivery service of other companies. Because the Internet will continue to make delivery of information about service easy, we believe that over the long term, consumers will have information about which companies are actually fulfilling their promises, and which ones are not. We believe, therefore, that in the steady-state of Internet commerce, all successful businesses will deliver the products they promise in a timely manner.

The next candidate for the crucial new attribute of retail is price. Many researchers have argued that in Internet commerce, consumers will be drawn to the cheapest price (Lynch et al., 2000). Tools now exist to make it easy for consumers to shop over the entire Internet looking for the cheapest price for a commodity product (e.g., www.mysimon.com, www.Jango.com, and www.roboshopper.com). These tools are a matter of concern to many businesses. If price becomes the deciding factor in consumer purchase decision, then price wars will inevitably break out. Profit margins for the businesses will plummet to near zero, reducing profitability for the businesses (Greenwald et al., 1999). Some observers have even suggested that the entire Internet economy may collapse under the most intense price pressure ever seen in history!

Many businesses are turning to other ways to deliver value to their customers in the Internet economy. They embrace the need for strong service, but reject the inevitability of price wars. These businesses are seeking ways to enhance their relationship with their customers by delivering services those customers cannot find at other businesses, on or off the Internet. Many businesses are creating services that help their customers sort through the available products to find the ones that are most valuable to them. Services like these have been shown to reduce the price sensitivity of consumers, while increasing their satisfaction with the purchase experience (Lynch et al., 2000). One of the most successful of those emerging services is a new type of database marketing, created for the Internet, and known as *recommender systems*.

Contributions of this Chapter

In this chapter, we introduce the concepts of recommender systems as a very successful Internet commerce tool. Then, we describe the basic principles of recommender systems and carefully analyzes how these systems relate to other prevailing data-analysis techniques and how they are more suitable for providing real-time personalized recommendations for customers of Internet commerce. The following section depicts the importance of recommender systems and their strategies for improving sales. We then analyze the nature and necessity of recommender systems in future commerce applications and establish the need for distributing such services to make them widely available. Later we present a detailed taxonomy of distributed recommender system applications and three different implementation frameworks for providing distributed recommender system services for Internet commerce, we analyze some of the design issues as well.

RECOMMENDER SYSTEMS

Recommender systems (RS) present an alternative information evaluation approach based on the judgments of human beings (Resnick and Varian, 1997). It attempts to automate the "word of mouth" recommendations that we regularly receive from family, friends, and colleagues. In essence, it allows everyone to serve as a critic. This inclusiveness circumvents the scalability problems of individual critics—with millions of readers it becomes possible to review millions of books. At the same time, it raises the question of how to reconcile the many and varied opinions of a large community of ordinary people. Recommender systems address this question through the use of different algorithms, *nearest-neighbor algorithm* (Resnick et al., 1994), *various clustering algorithms* (Ungar et al., 1998), *probabilistic and rule-based learning algorithms* (Breese et al., 1998 and Basu et al., 1998, Bilsuss et al., 1998) to name but a few. In this chapter, we will mainly focus on the nearest-neighbor algorithm-based recommender systems. These systems are often referred to as *Collaborative Filtering (CF) systems* in research literature (Resnick et al., 1994; Maltz et al., 1995). A typical CF-based recommender system maintains a database containing the *ratings* that each customer has given to each product that customer has evaluated (e.g., in the form of a score from 1 to 5).

History of Recommender Systems

Several recommender systems based on automated CF have been developed. The GroupLens Research system (Resnick et al., 1994; Konstan et. al., 1997) provides a pseudonymous collaborative filtering solution for Usenet news and movies. Tapestry (Goldberg et al., 1992), Ringo (Shardanand and Maes, 1995) and Video Recommender (Hill et al., 1995) are email and web systems that generate recommendations on music and movies respectively, suggesting collaborative filtering to be applicable to many different types of media. Since CF does not need to analyze the content of the products to be evaluated, it is applicable to a wider range of media than similar technologies such as Information Retrieval (Salton et al., 1983) and Information Filtering (Belkin and Croft, 1992) technologies. CF-based RS applications have been built for a variety of hard-to-classify visual and audio media including art, music, and film. Indeed, it is precisely this flexibility that has led many Internet commerce businesses to explore using CF technology to personalize their offerings to customers.

Detailed Architecture of a CF-Based Recommender System

The earliest implementations of collaborative filtering, in systems such as Tapestry (Goldberg et al., 1992), relied on the opinions of people from a close-knit community, such as an office workgroup. However, collaborative filtering for large communities cannot depend on each person knowing the others. Several systems use statistical techniques to provide personal recommendations of documents by finding a group of other customers, known as *neighbors,* that have a history of agreeing with the target customer. Usually, neighborhoods are formed by applying proximity measures such as the Pearson correlation between the opinions of the customers. These techniques are called *nearest-neighbor techniques.* Figure 1 depicts the neighborhood formation using a nearest-neighbor technique in a very simple two-dimensional space of customers. Notice that each customer's neighborhood is those other customers who are most similar to him, as identified by the proximity measure. Neighborhoods need not be symmetric. Each customer has the best neighborhood for himself. Once a neighborhood of customers is found, particular products

Figure 1: Neighborhood Information. Each neighborhood is created for a single customer.

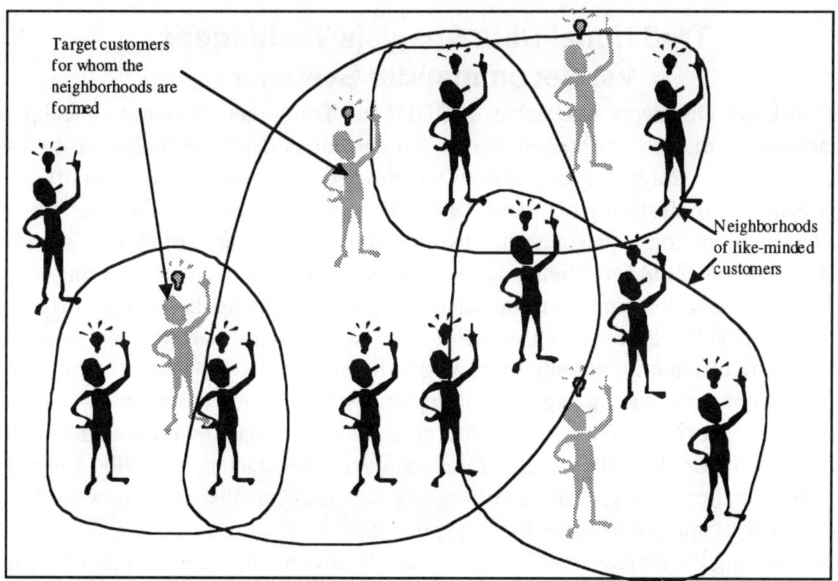

can be evaluated by forming a weighted composite of the neighbors' opinions of that document. Recommender systems may use very simple application interfaces. The most common API calls are:

1. Recommend. Given a customer, recommend a list of products that customer will be interested in.
2. Predict. Given a customer, and a list of potential products, predict which of those products the customer will be interested in. The input list of products is the difference between recommend and predict. The list might have been produced as the result of a customer search, for instance.
3. Rate. Express an opinion of a customer about a product.
4. Find neighbors. Return a list of the nearest neighbors of a customer, for community applications, such as chat groups.

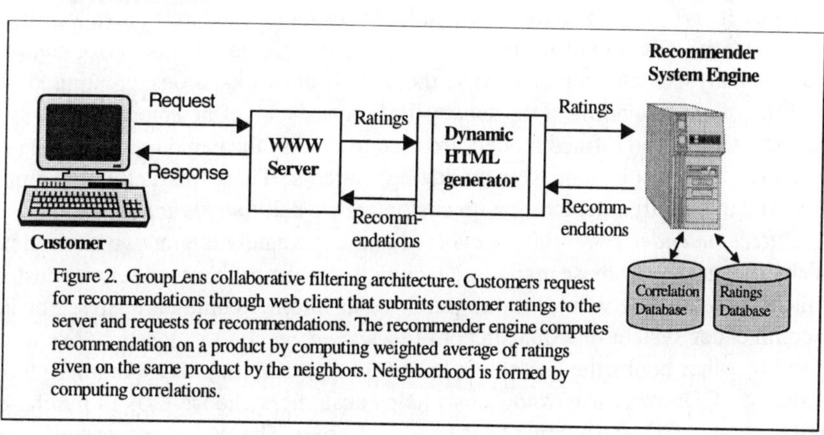

Figure 2. GroupLens collaborative filtering architecture. Customers request for recommendations through web client that submits customer ratings to the server and requests for recommendations. The recommender engine computes recommendation on a product by computing weighted average of ratings given on the same product by the neighbors. Neighborhood is formed by computing correlations.

Figure 2 depicts the schematic architecture and API calls of the GroupLens (Konstan et al., 1997; Resnick et al., 1994) collaborative filtering system.

Traditional Data Analysis Techniques vs. Recommender Systems

Knowledge Discovery in Databases (KDD) and Traditional *data mining* techniques have focused on discovering knowledge in the enormous databases collected by every modern corporation (Fayyad et al., 1996). The knowledge discovered has most often been concept learning or clustering (Zytkow, 1997). Though the research techniques are often subtle, their application in business has two unsubtle goals. They are to save money by discovering the potential for efficiencies, or to make more money by discovering ways to sell more products to customers. For instance, companies are using data mining to discover which products sell well at which times of year, so they can manage their retail store inventory more efficiently, potentially saving millions of dollars a year (Brachman et al. 1996). Other companies are using data mining to discover which customers will be most interested in a special offer, reducing the costs of direct mail or outbound telephone campaigns by hundreds of thousands of dollars a year (Bhattacharyya, 1998; Ling et al., 1998). These applications typically involve using data mining to discover a new model, and having an analyst apply the model to the application.

Data mining techniques have been successfully applied to many aspects of business data processing, including inventory management, product planning, manufacturing, and recommending products to customers. In most of these domains the benefit of data mining is to save money by improving efficiencies. For instance, in using data mining for product planning, the models can be used to focus development effort on products that are more likely to be purchased by consumers. Improving the focus of product development reduces the expenses of creating eventually unprofitable products, and shortens the costly product development cycle.

The most direct benefit of data mining to businesses is increasing sales of existing products by matching customers to the products they will be most likely to purchase. Since our focus here is on recommender systems that have evolved on the Web primarily in support of Internet commerce, we will focus on this type of data mining system. Data mining systems that are *used* to match products to customers we will call *database marketing systems*. Figure 3 shows the flow of information in a typical database marketing system, derived from a general data mining flow diagram (Fayyad et al., 1996). In the data mining system, data is brought together from multiple corporate databases into a warehouse. In the warehouse the data is analyzed using data mining tools, creating models for human analysis. Human analysts view and manipulate the models on workstations, creating knowledge in the form of understanding of the data by the humans, and refined models in the system. The new knowledge and refined models are used to modify the behavior of existing marketing systems, or to implement new marketing systems. Those marketing systems that are involved in directly interacting with customers we call *touchpoint systems*.

Recommender systems have evolved in the extremely interactive environment of the Web. They apply database marketing techniques to the problem of helping customers find which products they would like to purchase at Internet commerce sites. For instance, a recommender system on Amazon.com (*www.amazon.com*) suggests books to customers based on other books the customers have told Amazon they like. Another recommender system on CDnow (*www.cdnow.com*) helps customers choose CDs to purchase as gifts, based on other CDs the recipient has liked in the past. The Web presents new opportunities

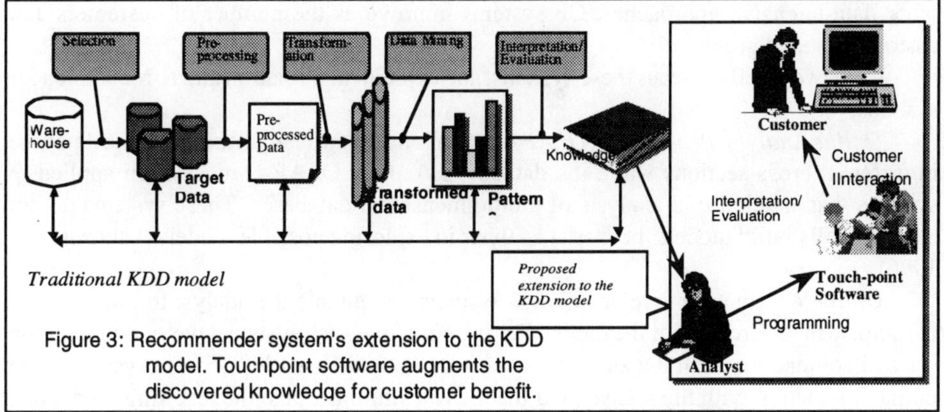

Figure 3: Recommender system's extension to the KDD model. Touchpoint software augments the discovered knowledge for customer benefit.

for database marketing, but challenges database marketing systems to perform interactively. While a customer is at the Internet commerce site, the recommender system must learn from the customer's behavior, develop a model of that behavior, and apply that model to recommend products to the customer. *Collaborative filtering* is used in many of the most successful recommender systems on the Web, including those at Amazon.com and CDnow.com.

Recommender systems evolved to help users sort through the huge volume of available products at Internet commerce stores. Now, recommender systems are helping the retailers that employ them to create stronger relationships with their customers. The businesses learn from their customers about their buying preferences. Based on what they learn, the businesses are able to help the customer find more products they may wish to purchase. The customers benefit because they have a better and more efficient shopping experience that more often yields products they like. The business benefits because its customers are more loyal, since they get the highest quality recommendations from the business they have shopped at the most, and because the customers are more successful at finding products they wish to purchase, increasing average purchase size. Recommender system APIs are simpler, concrete and efficient, so they can be directly implemented in the touchpoint software (Sarwar et al., 1999).

Relationship of Recommender Systems to Other KDD Systems

There are several types of KDD systems that seem at first sight to have very similar goals to recommender systems, but that are actually quite different in practice. In traditional KDD systems the interface between the KDD system and the customer touchpoint is mediated by an analyst. The algorithms used in KDD develop as output high-level data structures, such as Bayesian networks, classifier functions, rules bases, or data clusters (Heckerman, 1996; Cheeseman, 1990; Agarwal et al., 1993; Fayyad et al., 1996). Typically the model is expensive to build, but rapid to execute, so it is recomputed only after sufficient changes have occurred in the database. (Ongoing work is developing incremental KDD algorithms, but these are currently rare in practice.) The model, once produced, is high-level, powerful, and abstract, so its interface to the touchpoint software is mediated by a human. CF-based recommender systems are specifically designed to make real-time use of ratings data without requiring additional personal information. As each rating is entered, it immediately influences subsequent predictions and recommendations. Since CF does not require an off-line model, it uses less information and is computationally simpler. And, like other data-intensive approaches, CF systems improve as the number of customers and customer ratings grows.

Here, we briefly discuss these systems, and explain their relationship to recommender systems.

Online Analytic Processing (OLAP) systems enable the analyst to look at the database in different cross-sections while the database is online. OLAP is most often applied to systems that enable rapid analysis of multidimensional databases. These systems do not automatically build models, but assist analysts in exploring possible models (Uthurusamy, 1996).

Online KDD systems refer to KDD systems that enable the analyst to interactively participate in the creation of the model. For instance, one such system develops association rules in conjunction with the analyst (Aggarwal, Su, and Yue 1998). These systems have online interaction with the analyst, but the analyst still must take the resulting model and separately integrate it with the touchpoint software.

Interactive mining has been used to refer to using "human inspection and guidance at intermediate stages" of the data mining process (Zytkow 1991). These systems are closely related to online KDD systems, but do not require that the inspection and guidance be interactive.

RECOMMENDER SYSTEMS IN INTERNET COMMERCE

The emergence of Internet and its far-reaching deployment is changing the way commerce is done. Economists and commerce experts are now suggesting companies shift from the old world of mass production characterized by "...standardized products, homogenous markets, and long product life and development cycles..." to the new world where "...variety and customization supplant standardized products" (Pine, 1993). In his famous book *Mass Customization,* Joe Pine also suggests that building one product is simply not adequate anymore. Companies need to be able to, at a minimum, develop *multiple* products that meet the *multiple* needs of *multiple* customers. The movement toward Internet commerce has allowed companies to provide customers with more options. However, in expanding to this new level of customization, businesses increase the amount of information that customers must process before they are able to select which items meet their needs. One obvious solution to this information overload problem is the use of *recommender systems.* As discussed in the previous section, recommender systems can be used to recommend products based on various features such as top overall sellers on a site, demographic information of the customer, or the past buying habits of the customer as a prediction for future buying behavior. In general, recommender systems provide a "personalized" interface to each customer and thus automate personalization on the Internet. Personalization to this extent is one way to realize Pine's ideas of the new world order of Internet commerce.

How Recommender Systems Help Businesses?

Recommender systems can help Internet commerce site boost their business in several ways. We discuss three of them here (Schafer et al., 1999):

- By providing personalized recommendations on various products, they help to convert **browsers into buyers**. Visitors to a Web site often look over the site without ever purchasing anything. Recommender systems can help customers find products they wish to purchase and can potentially increase sales.

- Recommender systems improve **cross-sell** by suggesting additional products for the customer to purchase. If the recommendations are good, the average order size should increase. For instance, a site might recommend additional products in the checkout process, based on those products already in the shopping cart.
- Internet commerce is getting more competitive day by day. Freed from large capital investment and recurring costs for physical storefronts, an unprecedented number of businesses are using the Internet to market and sell goods. As a consequence, **gaining customer loyalty** is an essential business strategy (Reichheld and Sesser, 1990; (Reichheld, 1993). Recommender systems improve loyalty by creating a value-added relationship between the site and the customer. Sites invest in learning about their users, use recommender systems to operationalize that learning, and present custom interfaces that match customer needs. Customers repay these sites by returning to the ones that best match their needs. The more a customer uses the recommendation system – teaching it what they want – the more loyal they are to the site. Creating relationships between customers can also increase loyalty. Customers will return to the site that recommends people with whom they will like to interact.

Recommendation Interfaces and Ways to Make Money

There are many ways to display recommendations to a customer. The method selected may well depend on how the Internet commerce site wants the customer to use the recommendation. In the following we will examine several recommendation interfaces, and how each assists the site in making money. While some of these methods have their roots in traditional commerce, each of them draws upon the strengths of ubiquitous Internet to provide more powerful recommendations. We present examples of some large Internet commerce sites using these features (Schafer et al., 1999).

Similar Item: One modification of traditional commerce techniques is the *similar item* recommendation. Systems such as Reel.com's Movie Matcher, Amazon.com's Customers Who Bought, and one variation of CDNOW's Album Advisor attempt to expose customers to items they may have forgotten about, or of which they may have simply been unaware. Their implementation in Internet commerce sites allows for more specific and personalized recommendations. The items displayed can be entirely selected based on the item(s) in which a customer has shown interest. In doing so, sites increase customers' exposure to their product line, and ideally are able to sell more items per order.

Email: Recommendations can also be delivered directly to customers through *email,* in a extension of traditional direct-mail techniques. Amazon.com's Eyes feature allows them to notify customers the minute an item becomes commercially available.

Top-N: Amazon.com's Book Matcher, Levi's Style Finder and My CDNOW, among others, take advantage of recommendations through a *top-N* list. Once each site has learned details about a customer's likes and dislikes, each is able to provide the customer with a personalized list of the top number of unrated items for that customer. It is as though one could gather all of the clothes that might interest a given client onto a single rack without distracting them with items they will not be interested in. This helps the vendor in several ways. First, it is another example of converting browsers into buyers – it provides increased exposure to the vendor's wares, but only to those items that should truly interest the user. Second, it may help the customer in making a decision about items that they originally held in doubt – the suggestion from the site may be another point in favor of the item.

Ordered Search Results: Finally, a less restrictive variation of the top-N list are *Ordered Search Results* recommendations. While top-N limits the predictions to some predefined number, ordered search results allow the customer to continue to look at items highly likely to be of interest to them. Moviefinder.com's "We Predict" feature allows customers to have query returns sorted by the predicted likelihood that the customer will enjoy the item.

DISTRIBUTED RECOMMENDER SYSTEMS

Recommender Systems Must Address Changing Internet Applications

In the past, participating in commerce meant that the consumer had to travel to the location of the store from which he wanted to purchase a product. Today, participating in commerce may be as easy as moving a mouse and typing a few keystrokes. In the future, participating in commerce will become even easier, with the introduction of new wireless devices that enable commerce on the palmtop, wherever the consumer happens to be. For instance, a company called phone.com has developed a browser for palmtop devices. This browser supports a new industry standard for wireless Internet access called WAP, for Wireless Access Protocol. WAP is a XML-based language that provides a subset of HTML functionality for wireless devices. The history is that HTML, the language of the Internet today, evolved from a class of languages called SGML. SGML languages are used for most text markup tasks today. XML is a simplified subset of SGML that enables new markup languages to be specified in a specification language as needed. WAP is one of those new markup languages.

Through WAP, special Web applications can be written using modern Web development tools such as Cold Fusion, Active Server Pages, or CGI. These applications can be served through existing Web servers, delivering WAP pages, rather than HTML Web pages. Wireless Web browsers access Web servers as shown in Figure 4.

The Web client connects to a special link server through its radio connection. The link server accesses Web pages using the HTTP protocol, and delivers the results to the wireless device through the radio connection. Persistent functionality, such as bookmarks and cookies, are implemented in the link server, to conserve memory on the wireless device. To the end-user, the result is browsing of the special WAP-formatted pages as if she is directly connected to the Internet.

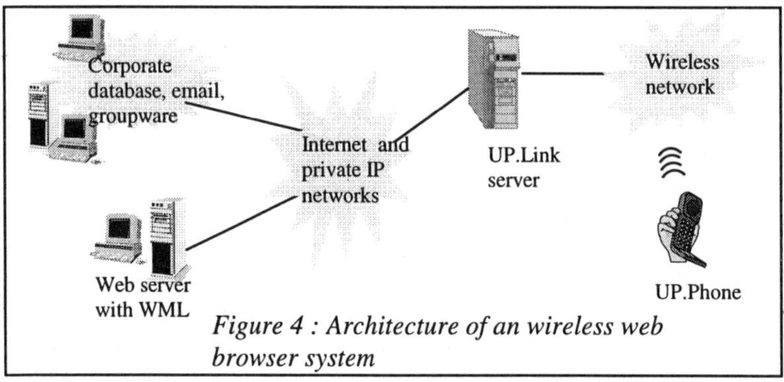

Figure 4 : Architecture of an wireless web browser system

The result of technical improvements like wireless Web browsers is that consumers will come to expect the same shopping experience when travelling as they currently receive when directly connected to the Internet. For instance, a customer who uses a restaurant recommendation service in his hometown will expect to be able to use the same restaurant recommendation service while travelling. Likewise, a customer who is used to receiving good recommendations for theatre shows to attend in his hometown will expect theatre recommendations on the road. In fact, the recommendations will be even more valuable on the road, since the customer will know less about what is available.

Creating good recommendations for a travelling consumer is challenging, though, especially for the leading recommendation technology, collaborative filtering. The recommender system has not had a chance to learn from the consumer, so it has a hard time helping the consumer. The topic of this chapter is what information the recommender system can glean from the consumer's past interactions with other recommender systems in other locales, and how this information can be used to help the consumer with useful recommendations in his present locale.

The Need for Distributed Collaborative Filtering

Many Internet commerce sites, including several of the largest ones are now using CF recommender systems as part of their personalization effort. As the largest Internet commerce sites attempt to use these systems, however, they are discovering the drawbacks of today's centralized systems. While a centralized architecture may be useful for smaller applications, there are several key drawbacks to centralization:

- **Scalability.** The largest Internet commerce sites have millions of customers and up to millions of products. These numbers continue to increase and a centralized RS is increasingly unable to serve high transaction rates for large databases.
- **Fault Tolerance.** As Internet commerce comes to depend upon personalization, a central point of failure becomes unacceptable.
- **Performance.** Global businesses cannot deliver reliable low-latency performance around the world from a single, potentially overloaded RS.
- **Security and Privacy**. Consumers are becoming increasingly wary of businesses that attempt to "own" data about them. Indeed, consumers have an interest in both limiting the scope of access to their opinions and in being able to take their preferences to other vendors.

Together, these issues point towards distributed architectures for collaborative filtering. In this paper, we propose a design framework for distributed CF recommender systems. This framework is motivated by a number of scenarios including products of global and local scope (e.g., books and local fairs) and issues facing travelers as they move among localities.

TAXONOMY OF DISTRIBUTED RECOMMENDER APPLICATIONS

In this section we taxonomize the space of distributed recommender system applications. Since the focus of this chapter is on distribution in recommender systems, our taxonomy is also focused on distribution. Each of the following fundamental components of a recommender system has implications for distribution:

- Products: Are the products being rated products of local interest, or all available products?
- Ratings: Are the ratings being used from local customers, or from all available customers?
- Neighborhoods: Are the neighborhoods formed from local customers, or from all available customers?
- Predictions: Are the products for which predictions are being formed local or all available products?

From an algorithmic perspective, the two most important of these components are the neighborhood formation and prediction processes, since these decide what data is used by the recommender system, where that data is stored, and how that data is used. Also, neighborhood formation implicitly includes the selection of ratings for forming the neighborhoods, and the prediction algorithm uses ratings from the products for which it is making predictions. Therefore, we will characterize applications by whether they use local or all available ratings for forming neighborhoods, and by whether they are forming predictions for local products or all available products. For simplicity, we will use the term "global" instead of "all available", since from the perspective of the distributed system, "all available" means "without respect to location", which is similar to the meaning of "global". We also use the term "local" to denote city-specific applications. We will refer to the application areas in short by first characterizing the ratings they use for neighborhood, local or global, and second by characterizing the products they are to predict, local or global. Thus, the application areas range from local/local (short for local neighborhood and local predictions) to global/global (short for global neighborhood and global predictions).

For each application type in the taxonomy we describe the basic idea, give a set of example applications, and characterize in detail how the prediction process works in that domain, drawing on the examples. Note that it is not the goal of this section to discuss the implementation of these applications; that is reserved for the final sections of the paper. First, we discuss the application requirements that drive implementation decisions.

Global Neighborhoods and Global Predictions

The most common applications of recommender systems on the Internet have been in situations in which distribution is completely transparent. All customers potentially have opinions about all products, and interest in all products. These applications are most common because they are the applications for which the Web gives the most leverage. From wherever a customer accesses the recommender system the customer gets recommendations that are valuable.

The easiest examples of global/global recommender systems are the many successful examples of recommender systems in Internet commerce. For instance, CDnow (*www.cdnow.com*) makes recommendations of music CDs based on artists the customer has liked in the past. Amazon.com (*www.amazon.com*) makes the recommender system more explicit in the *BookMatcher* application. Customers rate books they have read in the past, and receive recommendations for books that they may like in the future. In both cases, most of the music CDs and books are of global interest, and most customers are asking for recommendations across all of the products in the catalog.

The neighborhood generation process is the usual collaborative filtering process. All customers are compared to find the set of customers that is the best neighbor for the given customer. The prediction process finds the set of products that the neighbors like best, independent of location.

Global/global recommender systems are likely to continue to be very successful, because they benefit by bringing together the large community of customers on the Web to make recommendations for each other. However, these systems are limited in that they only apply to products that are equally valuable to customers wherever they are located.

Global Neighborhoods and Local Predictions

A common use of recommender systems in the future will be to get recommendations for local products of interest when travelling. The customer will have an established profile with a global recommender system, and will ask a local recommender system to leverage that global profile to produce locally valuable recommendations.

For instance, the recommender system could help the customer find restaurants, local bands, theatrical shows, micro-brew beers, parks, or museums. Consider a customer visiting Seattle, who wishes to find a micro-brew beer that he will like. The recommender system would use the customer's opinions of national beer brands to establish a neighborhood of Seattle residents who like the same kinds of beer. Then, the recommender system would recommend the local Seattle beers that those neighbors like best. After finding the perfect micro-brew, the customer might want to find a Seattle grunge rock band he will like. If his hometown does not have grunge rock bands, the recommender system may have a difficult time predicting his tastes in bands. However, if he has been buying grunge CDs, the recommender system could use his preferences in CDs to form the neighborhood, and recommend bands liked by people who live in Seattle and who share the same taste in CDs.

Global/local recommender systems would work by using separate sets of ratings data for the neighborhood algorithm and the prediction algorithm. The customer selects a set of products of interest (the "prediction products"), and specifies a locality. The system designer has specified a set of global products for forming neighborhoods for this particular set of prediction products (the "neighborhood products"). These selected neighborhood products are thought to be sufficiently similar to the desired prediction products that customers who like the same neighborhood products will probably like the same prediction products. For instance, grunge CDs are probably good neighborhood products for grunge bands. (Beer drinkers may argue that national beer brands are a poor neighborhood for micro-brew beers. In our experience, it is impossible to know for sure without an experiment. We predict no problem finding volunteers for the experiment!) The neighbors are then used to make predictions. The usual collaborative filtering prediction process is used, except that only those products that are flagged as being from the locality of interest can be predicted.

When they work, global/local recommender systems are more valuable than global/global recommender systems for travelers. Global/global recommender systems can only recommend products of global interest, whereas travelers are often more interested in local food, drink, and entertainment. A traveler doesn't need a recommender system to suggest Pizza Hut in Seattle; she already knows she likes Pizza Hut from her hometown. In principle, a global/global recommender system could include local products, but then a traveler visiting Seattle might get a recommendation for a restaurant that is only in Baltimore! Global/local recommender systems can leverage their knowledge of the customer's global interests to suggest to her local products that she will probably like. Global/local recommender systems have several requirements for success. First, neighborhood products must be identified that are successful predictors of the prediction products. Second, the neighborhood products must have been rated by many customers in the destination city, as well as by the visiting customer. Third, the prediction products must have been rated by many different customers in the destination city. Large cities with active Web populations are likely to have many entertainment venues that fit these criteria.

Local Neighborhoods and Global Predictions

The other way a distributed recommender system can help travelers is to leverage the experience of fellow travelers from their hometown. Local/global recommender systems use the opinions of other travelers from your hometown to discover global products you will probably like. Local/global recommender systems are very much like the typical word-of-mouth recommendations travelers usually use: to find a good place to go, ask family and friends what they've liked in the past.

For example, if a customer wants to find a national park to visit on vacation, the recommender system can suggest parks that other people from the same city like. Since people in the same city have different tastes in parks, the recommender system can use collaborative filtering to create a neighborhood of people from the same city who like the same nearby city or state parks. The opinions of these neighbors about national parks are likely to be similar to the customer's opinions. Similarly, to find a restaurant in Seattle for a customer, the recommender system can suggest restaurants liked by people when they have traveled to Seattle who tend to agree with me about restaurants in my hometown.

Local/global recommender systems work by forming prediction neighborhoods from among the actual neighbors in the customer's hometown. The neighborhood products are those products from the hometown that are good predictors for the desired global products. The prediction products can be chosen in one of two ways. The directly global method is to choose prediction products from among all possible products, regardless of locale. This method is most useful when the customer has not yet chosen a destination, and wants to discover the destination with the most interesting places to visit. For instance, a vacation traveler might want help choosing a city in which he will have the most fun. The semi-global method is to choose prediction products from among products in a particular city. This method is most useful when the destination has already been chosen, and the customer would like help finding places to visit in that city. For instance, a business traveler might like help finding the restaurant she will enjoy the most in her destination city.

Like global/local recommender systems, local/global recommender systems can be more helpful to travelers than global/global predictions. Local/global recommender systems can suggest products to customers that are specific to a locale the customer has never visited. Local/global recommender systems perform best when a customer has strong correlation with other customers from his hometown, and when many of those customers have traveled to the places of interest. There are likely to be fewer ratings to use in constructing recommendations in local/global systems than in global/local systems, because only the ratings of fellow travelers can be used in local/global systems. However, the relationships between customers and their neighbors are likely to be stronger, because these relationships can be developed over all products of interest in the hometown. Because of these stronger relationships, where there is sufficient data about the prediction products, local/global recommender systems are likely to be more accurate than global/local recommender systems.

Local Neighborhoods and Local Predictions

We now consider purely local recommender applications, to round out the space of distributed recommender applications. Purely local recommender applications recommend products within a specific geography to customers. These applications are in many ways similar to global applications, but restricted to ratings sets that apply to local products. However, the solutions that are appropriate for local/local applications are different from the other solutions, so we treat them as a fourth case.

Local/local recommender systems are best suited for city-specific applications. For instance, they can help residents of a city find restaurants, community college classes, interesting booths at a city festival, or auto repair shops they will like. We have already treated these products for travelers, but recommender systems are also valuable for local residents in larger towns or cities.

Local/local recommender systems work by forming neighborhoods of people who have a specific attribute, such as living within a city. These neighborhoods are then used to form predictions of products that are also within the city.

By only considering residents of the city, local/local recommender systems have a higher ratings density than other recommender systems. Since all of the residents are from the locality, and will have visited many of the local products, the recommender system will have more data to work with both for forming neighborhoods and making predictions.

Summary

Figure 5 shows the four application domains we have discussed along the axes of global or local neighborhoods and global or local predictions. The position of a recommender system application along these axes is chosen by the systems designer to meet the goals of the application. The recommender system must have available ratings of the products that it wishes to recommend. If the products are global in nature, these ratings can come from anywhere, so the global/global recommender system is the least restricted. Global/global systems can easily share ratings between distributed, partitioned sites, since the products are all the same. Further, global/global systems are easy for travelers to use, since the desired recommendations are independent of location.

If the products are local in nature, the ratings must come either from people who live near the product under consideration, or from people who visit the product under consideration. These two possibilities are the definition of global/local and local/global recommender systems, respectively. In the global/local case, the neighbors are chosen to be people who live near the product in question. In this case, there is little evidence for agreement between the traveler and her neighbors, because they do not usually visit the same products. Therefore, the neighborhood must be based on agreements on global products. In the local/global case, the neighbors are chosen to be local neighbors of the traveler who have visited the products in question. Since the neighbors are local, agreement can be on either local or global products. Since the product is remote, it is likely that only a few of the possible neighbors will have visited the product. The difference between global/local and local/global is that global/local has less information to use in forming the neighborhood, but more in making predictions, while local/global has more information available for forming the neighborhood, but less in making predictions. Application designers must make these trade-offs in designing their recommender system. In practice, hybrid methods that combine characteristics of global/local and local/global may be most effective.

Recommender systems that recommend local products to local customers are easier. They can use exactly the same algorithms as the global recommender systems, but restrict the neighborhood and prediction product sets to the locality of interest. Note that local/local recommender systems can in principle use global ratings for forming neighborhoods, but that in general that information will be sparse and will form less predictive neighborhoods because the products are less similar.

Figure 5: Application Domains with Examples

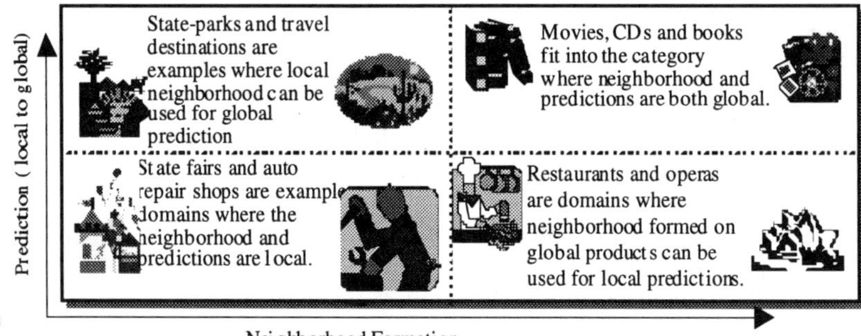

Note that the distinction between local and global in recommender systems also applies to neighborhoods that are not geographic. For instance, a local community may be an interest group with a closely shared interest in a certain type of jazz music. Visitors to the group are people who share an interest in that type of jazz music, but who have not participated in the group in the past. The taxonomy of local and global given here applies directly to these visitors as it does to geographic visitors. However, since the focus of the present paper is on distributed systems issues in recommender systems, and since the distributed systems issues apply most strongly to geographically distributed systems, we focus on global and local geography in this paper.

DISTRIBUTED RECOMMENDER SYSTEM DESIGN

Design Issues

After taxonomizing the application space, our next goal is to provide implementation frameworks for distributed collaborative systems. Creating implementation frameworks requires consideration of the key design issues. In this section, we introduce and analyze these issues, and develop an evaluation model based on them. We focus on the design issues that have implications for distributed systems.

Security. Internet security and authentication are well-understood problems, and a multitude of security and authentication protocols are being used in practice. The advent of high-speed processing powers and low-cost memory has paved the way for sufficiently strong encryption algorithms. In the Internet domain, protocols like RSA (Rivest et al., 1978) and SSL (Freier et al., 1995) are widely used in Internet commerce and Internet banking applications. The design of a distributed recommender system can use such techniques to solve the security problem. Nevertheless, we consider a design to be less secure the more it communicates ratings over public networks. Experience suggests that these remotely communicated ratings are more susceptible to attack, though the success of the attack may depend on mistakes by the application designer or by the customer. We do not consider communication of ratings behind firewalls to be a security issue.

Privacy. Customers are increasingly aware of the risks to their privacy in having large databases of their preferences (Wang et al., 1999, Ackerman et al., 1999). In exchange for helping customers find products they are interested in, recommender systems require information about customer's likes and dislikes. Recommender systems work well even in the case that the customer's information is connected to an identifier that is not connected to personal information, such as name, address, or phone number. This sort of identifier provides "persistent anonymity" to the customer. The recommender system can match the customer to his or her likes and dislikes, but cannot match those likes and dislikes back to a specific person. Still, there are privacy risks in the Internet commerce use of even safe identifiers, since eventually the customer must identify himself to the system to make a purchase. Eventually this privacy risk may be ameliorated by anonymous delivery services, such as a parcel service that could deliver to a person by code number, without an address, but these services are not yet generally available. We consider the privacy risk to be highest in systems that centralize the data about an individual, and lowest in those systems that leave control of the data in the hands of the customer.

Performance Issues. Distributed recommender systems have strict performance goals, which can be measured along many dimensions:

- Scalability – How do number of customers, products, and ratings affect performance?
- Network traffic – How many messages, and of what length, must be transmitted?
- Response time – How long does it take to deliver a recommendation to a customer?

In analyzing performance, we will combine these metrics into an evaluation of the overall performance of the recommender system.

Quality of Recommendations. Better recommendation systems may ensure higher coverage (the number of products for which recommendations are available) and higher quality recommendations. All of the techniques for distributing recommender systems that we consider are designed to make the same set of ratings available to the recommender system, so distribution should not affect quality.

We will use the design issues introduced in this section to build a set of evaluation criteria to evaluate each proposed implementation of a distributed recommender system.

Implementation Models

In this section we present three implementation frameworks for different types of distributed collaborative filtering. At the heart of all three of the frameworks are protocols for storage, exchange and maintenance of customer preference profiles. A *profile* is a collection of customer preference data, possibly along with the customer's demographic information. Recommender systems extract required rating data from this profile and build rating databases to compute recommendations. We build on two previously published techniques for distributing these profiles:

1. Use of sharable media: Roaming customers can carry their ratings data in sharable media such as floppy disks or more sophisticated technology such as smartcards (Abadi et al., 1990) and javarings (Curry, 1998). Smartcards and javarings are both portable and secure media for carrying data and both of these contain small processors with some amount of memory. Both of these techniques use powerful authentication algorithms (e.g., javaring uses 1024-bit RSA (Rivest et al. 1978) algorithm) and are deemed to be highly secure.
2. Use of a standard ratings distribution protocol: In the case of centrally managed databases, using profile distribution protocols can solve the distribution problem. *Open Profiling Standard (OPS)* (Hensley et al. 1997) is one such protocol. OPS leverages existing Internet protocols and standards to provide a mechanism for remote machines to gain access to end-customer's personal preference

and demographic data, while ensuring that the owner of the profile data is in complete control of how this information can be disseminated.

The design of a distributed recommender system is most strongly influenced by the placement of the ratings database. Ratings databases can be managed locally by the customer's client, can roam with the customer in some sharable media, can be stored at a centralized database or can be fully distributed by using geographically spread databases. These three implementation frameworks vary according to the degree of distribution, varying from local to geographically distributed models.

All three frameworks make the fundamental assumption that the purposes of recommender systems are to benefit customers, and that customers have demanded that these benefits be transferable. Neither of these assumptions is correct in Internet commerce today. Merchants gather customer profiles, and jealously guard them as trade secrets, or sell them to non-competing merchants. In our frameworks, the customers have demanded that merchants work together to create a sharable framework for ratings and recommendations, so that customers can build a profile of their interests once, and use it with any merchant they choose. The benefits of our model are lower effort and improved service for customers. The cost is that merchants can no longer use the profile data they have collected to make it hard for a customer to switch to another merchant.

Local Profile Model

The basic idea of the *local profile* model is to have the profile database stored locally by the customer's client. A customer contacts a recommendation server to request recommendations. The recommendation server retrieves her profile from her client, computes recommendations, and returns them. The customer retains full control over her profile. Whenever she needs to travel to a remote place she carries her profile with her in sharable media such as floppy disks, javarings, or smartcards. Figure 6(a) shows the schematic organization of this model. Marked arrows in this figure represent the sequence of messages needed for a single recommendation. (1) The customer requests recommendations from the recommender system. (2) The recommender system retrieves the customer profile, computes recommendations, and returns them to the customer. The only network traffic is the transfer of the profile to the recommender system, and the return of the recommendations to the customer. The latency includes these messages plus the time needed to actually compute the recommendations. Note that the OPS protocol includes specifications for customer-maintained access control lists to selectively grant profile access permissions to recommender systems.

Figure 6. (a) Local Profile Model *(b) Central Profile Model*

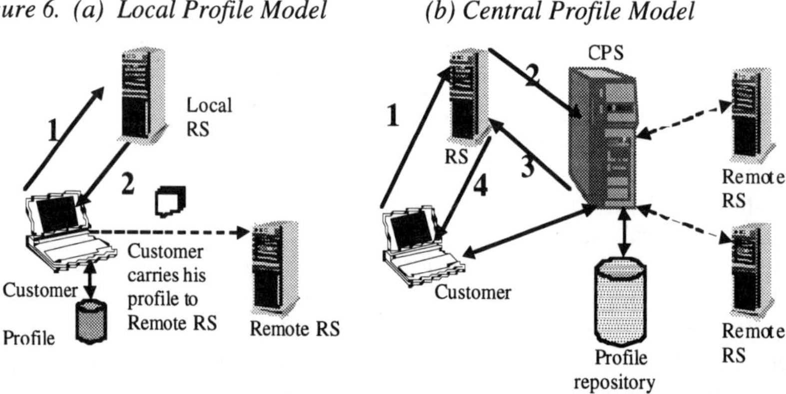

The main advantage of the local profile model is its simplicity and a persuasive assurance of security and privacy as the profile is maintained solely at the customer's site and they present it to the recommender site of their choice. This model, compared to the others, provides customers with the fastest recommendations. However, customers need their client to have access to profiles. Customers who travel with laptops may carry their profiles with the laptop. Other customers may carry the profile separately, so they can use their profile with computers at their destination. The latter approach requires an infrastructure for reading and recording profiles on computers around the world. Further, carrying profiles using sharable media may be cumbersome and costly, and creates potential security and privacy risks.

Central Profile Model

To reduce the effort required for traveling with a profile, customers may prefer a Central Profile Server (CPS). Customers submit their profile to the CPS and provide an access control mechanism that specifically mentions which recommendation systems will be allowed to access their profile. For example, a customer may wish to reveal his food preference to a restaurant recommendation site, but may choose not to reveal his news preference to them. Figure 6(b) shows the basic organization of this model. A recommendation generation process involves four network communications between the customers and the recommendation system. (1) Customer requests a recommendation from the system. (2) The system then contacts the CPS and requests for that particular customer's profile. (3) The CPS then checks the permissions and if allowed, supplies the profile to the recommender system. (4) The recommender system

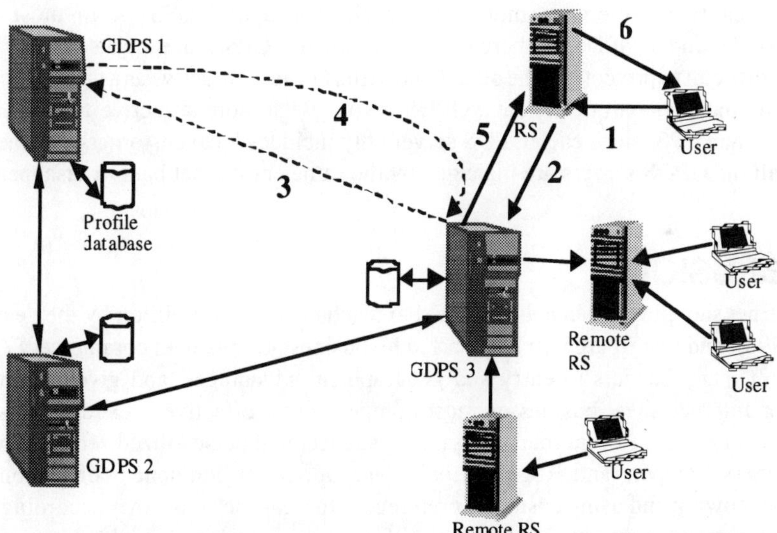

Figure 7. Geographically distributed profile model. 1) Users request for recommendations from the server. 2) the server contacts the closest profile server; if profile not found then request is sent to another server (3 & 4), then the recommendation is returned to the user (5&6). (If the closest server has the profile, steps 3 & 4 are not required).

computes recommendations by using the rating database and sends them to the customer. The network traffic in this model includes the additional round-trip to the CPS. Latency is higher, too, by the time required for this round-trip plus the time required to lookup the profile in the CPS. Further, having a single centralized site that keeps all profiles creates security and privacy risks. The security risk is that the single repository will prove a tempting target to hackers. The privacy risk is that the owner of the CPS may be tempted over the long-term to behavior that is not in the customer's best interests, such as selling the profile data. Solutions to the privacy problem are fundamentally social, not technical.

Geographically Distributed Profile Model

This model overcomes some of the drawbacks of the CPS, while retaining its principle benefit of location-independence. One basic assumption behind this model is that in most of the cases, customers' requests for recommendations are within a geographic region. Based on this locality principle, the model employs a number of interconnected, but Geographically Distributed Profile Servers (GDPS) to hold the profile database. The GDPS architecture alleviates the bottleneck problem of the CPS, and reduces the security and privacy issues caused by centralizing all profile data. The architecture of this model is shown in Figure 7. Most of the communication in the GDPS model is the same as in the CPS, but the work will be divided among several GDPS servers. Further, the GDPS servers can be located closer to the customers, in terms of network hops, reducing communication latency. Travelers will see slightly higher latencies, since when the local server doesn't find the required profile in its database, it initiates a request for the profile to a remote server (step 3). One challenging issue here is the proper partitioning of the profile database according to the geographical partition model and replicating and updating the fragmentation mapping in each server so that, each server knows which remote server to request for the profile information. Given an efficient locality of reference model, the performance of GDPS is, in most cases, similar to CPS model. GPDS is inherently less secure than CPS, since the data is distributed and more difficult to protect. On the other hand, it may be less attractive as a target since each GPDS only includes part of the data. GPDS is somewhat more attractive from a privacy standpoint than CPS, since each GPDS server only includes local customers. On the other hand, if all the GPDS servers are managed by the same entity, that benefit disappears.

CONCLUSION

Internet shopping revenue is expected to reach nearly $37.5 billion by the year 2000 (Achs 1998), and this figure will be dwarfed by business-to-business commerce. With the removal of many barriers to entry and geographical advantages, and given the ease of launching Internet sites, businesses must compete more effectively to retain customer loyalty and attention. Recent marketing trends suggest that personalized service is valued by customers (Peppers and Rogers, 1997). One important component of personalized service is knowing and using customer preferences to treat each customer according to her taste. Recommender systems are capable of providing such value-added services for customers. Recommender systems provide an Internet commerce site with most of the fundamental methods of achieving goals of mass customization listed in Pine's book (Pine, 1993). Recommender systems achieve these goals by providing a "customized service" that enables Internet commerce sites to sell their largely commodity products more efficiently. By creating "customizable products and services", by directly "customizing the point of delivery" for the Internet commerce site and we predict that recommender systems will be used in the future to "predict demand for products", enabling earlier communication back the supply chain.

Recommender systems will become ever more important in the future, as modern businesses are increasingly focused on the long-term value of customers to the business (Peppers and Rogers, 1997). Internet commerce sites will be working hard to maximize the value of the customer to their site, providing exactly the pricing and service they judge will create the most valuable relationship with the customer. Since customer retention will be very important to the sites, this relationship will often be to the benefit of the customer as well as the site. Currently, most recommender systems are centralized, run and controlled by a single Internet commerce merchant. Recommender systems will become more and more distributed over time, driven by user needs for less effort and better service. In the future, portable devices with wireless Internet connections will be commonplace and the need for distributed recommender services will increase substantially.

In this chapter, we have introduced the concepts of recommender systems and their similarities and differences with traditional data analysis and knowledge discovery methods. We also presented a detailed analysis of recommender systems application interfaces for some Internet commerce applications and described how they are being used to make money by capturing customer loyalty. We then presented taxonomy of the application space for distributed recommender systems. We studied several frameworks for implementing distributed recommender systems, and presented several implementation models. We hope our analyses will instigate thoughts of researchers and will pave the way for further research in this field.

REFERENCES

Abadi, M., Burrows, M., Kaufman, C., and Lampson, B. (1990). Authentication and Delegation with Smart-Cards. *Research Report 67*, Systems Research Center, Digital Equipment Corp., Palo Alto, CA.

Achs, N. (1998). Online Shopping Report: Strategies for Driving Consumer Transactions. *Digital Commerce Group,* New York, 1997 (URL: http://www.jup.com).

Ackerman, M., Cranor, L., and Reagle, J. 1999. "Privacy in E-Commerce: Examining User Scenarios and Privacy Preferences". In *Proceedings of ACM Conference on Electronic Commerce (EC-99),* Denver, CO.

Agarwal, R., Imielinski, T., and Swami, A. 1993. "Mining Association Rules between sets of Items in Large Databases. In *Proceedings of ACM SIGMOD conference on Management of Data,* 207-216.

Aggarwal, C. C., Sun, Z., and Yu, P. S. 1998. "Online Generation of Profile Association Rules." In *Proceedings of the Fourth International Conference on Knowledge Discovery and Data Mining*, 129-133.

Basu, C., Hirsh, H., and Cohen, W. 1998. Recommendation as classification: using social and content-based information in recommendation. In *Proceedings of the 1998 Workshop on Recommender Systems*, 11-15.

Belkin, N. J. and Croft, B. W. (1992). Information Filtering and Information Retrieval: Two Sides of the Same Coin? *CACM.* 35(2).

Billsus, D., and Pazzani, M. J. 1998. "Learning Collaborative Information Filters". In Proceedings of Recommender Systems Workshop. Tech. Report WS-98-08, AAAI Press,

Bhattacharyya, S. 1998. "Direct Marketing Response Models using Genetic Algorithms." In *Proceedings of the Fourth International Conference on Knowledge Discovery and Data Mining*, 144-148.

Brachman, R., J., Khabaza, T., Kloesgen, W., Piatetsky-Shapiro, G., and Simoudis, E. 1996. "Mining Business Databases." *Communications of the ACM*, 39(11), 42-48, November.

Breese, J. Heckerman, D., and Kadie, C. (1998). "Empirical Analysis of Predictive Algorithms for Collaborative Filtering". In *Proceedings of the Fourteenth Conference on Uncertainty in Artificial Intelligence*, Madison, WI.

Coulouris, G., Dollimore, J. and Kindberg, T. (1994). Distributed Systems Concepts and Design. *2nd Ed. Addison-Wesley Publishing Co.*

Cheeseman, P. 1990. "On Finding the Most Probably Model." In *Computational Models of Scientific Discovery and Theory Formation*, ed. Shrager, J. and Langley, P. San Francisco: Morgan Kaufmann.

Curry, S. M., (1998). An Introduction to the Java Ring, *JavaWorld*, April 1998.

Fayyad, U. M., Piatetsky-Shapiro, G., Smyth, P., and Uthurusamy, R., Eds. 1996. "Advances in Knowledge Discovery and Data Mining". *AAAI press/MIT press.*

Freier, A., Karlton, P. and Kocher, P. (1995). SSL version 3.0, Internet Draft. *draft-freier-ssl-version-3-00.txt.*

Goldberg, D., Nichols, D., Oki, B. M., and Terry, D. 1992. "Using Collaborative Filtering to Weave an Information Tapestry". *Communications of the ACM.* December.

Greenwald, A., Kephart, J., and Tesauro, G. 1999. "Strategic Pricebot Dynamics". In *Proceedings of ACM Conference on Electronic Commerce (EC-99),* Denver, CO.

Heckerman, D. 1996. "Bayesian Networks for Knowledge Discovery." In *Advances in Knowledge Discovery and Data Mining*. Fayyad, U. M., Piatetsky-Shapiro, G., Smyth, P., and Uthurusamy, R., Eds. *AAAI press/MIT press.*

Hensley, P., Metral, M., Shardanand, U., Converse, D., and Myers, M. (1997). "Proposals for an Open Profiling Standard. *World Wide Web Consortium (W3C) working draft".* URL http://www.w3.org/TR/NOTE-Web-privacy.html, June 1997.

Hill, W., Stead, L., Rosenstein, M., and Furnas, G. 1995. "Recommending and Evaluating Choices in a Virtual Community of Use". In *Proceedings of CHI '95.*

Konstan, J. A., Miller, B. N., Maltz, D., Herlocker, J. L., Gordon, L. R. and Riedl, J. (1997). "GroupLens: Applying Collaborative Filtering to Usenet News". *CACM.* 40(3).

Ling, C. X., and Li C. 1998. "Data Mining for Direct Marketing: Problems and Solutions." In *Proceedings of the Fourth International Conference on Knowledge Discovery and Data Mining*, pp. 73-79.

Lynch, J., and Ariely, D. 2000. "Wine Online: Search Costs and Competition on Price, Quality, and Distribution." To appear in *Marketing Science, 2000, Vol. 19(1).*

Maltz, D. and Ehrlich, K. Pointing the Way: Active Collaborative Filtering. *Proceedings of CHI '95.*

Peppers, D., and Rogers, M. 1997. The One to One Future : Building Relationships One Customer at a Time. Bantam Doubleday Dell Publishing.

Piatetsky-Shapiro, G., and Frawley, W. J., Eds. 1991. "Knowledge Discovery in Databases". *AAAI press/MIT press.*

Pine II, J. 1993. Mass Customization. Harvard Business School Press. Boston, Massachusetts

Pine II, J. Peppers, D., and Rogers, M. 1995. Do you want to keep your customers forever? *Harvard Business School Review*, 1995(2), 103-114.

Reichheld, F., and Sasser Jr, W. 1990. Zero Defections: Quality Comes to Services. *Harvard Business School Review*, 1990(5), 105-111.

Reichheld, F. 1993. Loyalty-Based Management. *Harvard Business School Review*, 1993(2): pp. 64-73.

Resnick, P., Iacovou, N., Suchak, M., Bergstrom, P., and Riedl, J. 1994. "GroupLens: An Open Architecture for Collaborative Filtering of Netnews. In *Proceedings of CSCW '94,* Chapel Hill, NC.

Resnick, P. and Varian, H. R. (1997). Recommender Systems. *CACM*. 40(3), pp. 56-58.

Rivest, R. L., Shamir, A. and Adleman, L. (1978). A Method of Obtaining Digital Signatures and Public Key Cryptosystems. *CACM* 21(2), 120-126.

Salton, G. and McGill M. J. (1983). *Introduction to Modern Information Retrieval.* McGraw-Hill, Inc.

Sarwar, B. M., Konstan, J. A., Borchers, A., and Riedl J. T., (1999). "Applying Knowledge from KDD to recommender Systems". *Tech. Report 99-013, Computer Science and Engg. Dept., University of Minnesota.*

Schafer, J. B., Konstan, J., and Riedl, J. 1999. "Recommender Systems in E-Commerce." In *Proceedings of ACM Conference on Electronic Commerce (EC-99),* Denver, CO.

Shardanand, U., and Maes, P. 1995. "Social Information Filtering: Algorithms for Automating 'Word of Mouth'." In *Proceedings of CHI '95.* Denver, CO.

Terveen, L., Hill, W., Amento, B., McDonald, D. and Creter, J. (1997). PHOAKS: A System for Sharing Recommendations. *CACM.* 40(3), 59-62.

Ungar, L. H., and Foster, D. P. (1998). "Clustering Methods for Collaborative Filtering." *AAAI Workshop on Recommendation Systems.*

Uthurusamy, R. 1996. "From Data Mining to Knowledge Discovery: Current Challenges and Future Directions." In *Advances in Knowledge Discovery and Data Mining.* Fayyad, U. M., Piatetsky-Shapiro, G., Smyth, P., and Uthurusamy, R., Eds. *AAAI press/ MIT press.*

Wang, H., Lee, M. and Wang, C. Consumer Privacy Concerns about Internet Marketing. *CACM.* 41(3), 63-70.

Zytkow, J., and Baker, J. 1991. "Interactive Mining of Regularities in Databases." In *Knowledge Discovery in Databases.* Piatetsky-Shapiro, G., and Frawley, W. J. Eds. AAAI Press/MIT Press.

Zytkow, J. M. 1997. "Knowledge = Concepts: A Harmful Equation." In Proceedings of the Third International Conference on Knowledge Discovery and Data Mining.

About the Authors

Syed Mahbubur Rahman currently is a professor at the Minnesota State University, Mankato, USA. He worked in several other institutions around the world including NDSU in the USA (1999), Monash University in Australia (1993-98), Bangladesh University of Engineering and Technology (BUET, 1982-92) and Ganz Electric Works in Budapest (1980-82), etc. He was the head of the Department of Computer Science and Engineering of BUET from 1986 to 1992. He is co-chairing and is involved as a program/organizing member in a number of international conferences. He obtained his doctoral degree from Budapest Technical University in 1980. He supervised more than 30 research projects leading to master's and PhD degrees. His research interests include electronic commerce systems, multimedia computing and communications, image processing and retrieval, computational intelligence, pattern recognition, distributed processing and security. He has published 100+ research papers in his areas of interest.

Robert Bignall holds a BSc(Honours) and PhD from the Flinders University of South Australia. He also holds postgraduate qualifications in further education and computer science. He has served as a senior lecturer and then as an associate professor at Monash University since 1990. In 1995 he was appointed as the foundation head of the Gippsland School of Computing and Information Technology at Monash University; he served in that role for five years. He was also acting director of the Monash Centre for Electronic Commerce in 1998 and 1999. He took up his current position as pro vice-chancellor of Monash University Malaysia at the start of 2000. Professor Bignall's research interests include electronic commerce systems and multimedia technologies. He has also published a number of papers on algebraic and multiple-valued logic and their applications in computer science.

***

Ravi Bapna is assistant professor of MIS at Northeastern University. His research, primarily in the experimental analysis of auction-based on-line mercantile processes, has been published in the *Communications of the ACM*, *Information Technology and Management*, and *Journal of Electronic Commerce Research.* His PhD is from the University of Connecticut.

Luigi Benedicenti is an associate professor at the University of Regina, Regina, Saskatchewan. He holds a Laurea (a kind of joint BSc and MSc) degree in electrical engineering, Genova, Italy, and a PhD in electrical and computer engineering (1993) from the University of Genova. Prof. Benedicenti's research interests include software process modelling, engineering, and improvement, software systems measurements, statistics in software engineering, distributed computing, Internet cooperation, groupware, and software engineering over the Internet architectures and patterns, software reuse, virtual reality.

David Bennett is professor of technology management at the Aston Business School, a member of the Technology and Operations Management Research Group and serves as the Business School's Coordinator of International Development. He is also head of the Aston Centre for Asian Business and Management (ACABAM), which is one of the Business School's interdisciplinary research centres. His past and current research investigations are concerned with issues relating to quality and reliability management, production systems design, technology management and the transfer of technology between industrialised and developing countries, especially in the Asian region. He has authored and co-authored several books as well as numerous articles in these subject areas. David Bennett's industrial experience includes periods in the automotive components and electrical equipment industries. Previous academic appointments have been with the former Wolverhampton Polytechnic (now Wolverhampton University) and a secondment to the Malaysian National Institute of Public Administration where he was a training consultant. Currently he is an adjunct professor with the University of South Australia involved in supervision of research students in Singapore and Hong Kong. He has also undertaken several contracts as a faculty member at the China-Europe Management Institute in Beijing and the China-Europe International Business School in Shanghai. His recent research and teaching activities have taken him to a number of Western European countries as well as the USA, Japan, China and Hong Kong, Singapore and the Ukraine.

David Bennett holds MSc and PhD degrees from the University of Birmingham. He is a Chartered Engineer and a member of the Institute of Management, the Decision Sciences Institute and the Production and Operations Management Society. He is also a member of the International Advisory Committee of the International Association for Management of Technology and serves on the Board of the European Operations Management Association. He is General Editor of *Integrated Manufacturing Systems: The International Journal of Manufacturing Technology Management*, published by MCB University Press, an Associate Editor of *International Journal of Manufacturing Systems Design* and serves on the editorial advisory boards of several other academic journals: *International Journal of Operations and Production Management, International Journal of Entrepreneurship and Innovation Management, Benchmarking for Quality Management and Technology, Technology Management: Strategies and Applications* and *Business Process Management Journal.*

Carlo Bonamico is a PhD student at the University of Genova. He is working on multimedia systems over the Internet, and especially MPEG4 SHNC, using the Java3d and Java Media Framework class libraries from Sun. He is also interested in ways to merge traditional applications and libraries with the Java platform, to take the best of both worlds. He is also experimenting with JNI and CORBA. Part of this work is conducted inside the European community project Interface.

William Cheung received his BSc and MPhil in electronic engineering from the Chinese University of Hong Kong, and PhD in computer science from the Hong Kong University of Science and Technology. He is currently a post-doctoral fellow of the Department of Computer Science at Hong Kong Baptist University. His research interests include pattern recognition, data mining, intelligent systems and electronic commerce.

Robert M. Colomb is currently a reader in information systems with the Department of Computer Science and Electrical Engineering, The University of Queensland; lecturing in advanced databases, information science, and human-computer interface. His research interests are in the general area of how an information space presents itself to a user population and conversely how a user can interact with the space in order to satisfy information requirements. He has more than 75 publications, including two books, and has supervised eight completed PhD and MSc programs. From 1985 to 1990, he was manager of the Knowledge Based Systems Engineering program of the CSIRO Division of Information Technology. The group had a mission to develop tools to help people exploit knowledge, and worked in software engineering of artificial intelligence systems, knowledge processing technology, and hypermedia systems.

In 1987 he was awarded a PhD in computer science from the University of New South Wales for the application of content addressable memory to the programming language Prolog. Prior to resuming his studies, he had an extensive and varied career in the computer industry, including commercial, operating systems, programming tools, technical, planning and communications applications; as well as consulting in a variety of areas, both in the United States and Australia. When he came to Australia in 1971, he spent a few years outside the computer industry doing, among other things, running a fruit shop in a small country town. He has a BS in mathematics from the Massachusetts Institute of Technology, awarded in 1964.

Jana Dospisil is a lecturer at the School of Network Computing at Monash University, Australia. She has more than 20 years of industry experience in large scale software projects (e.g. Telecom's Tran$end). In addition, she has been pursuing software engineering research in academia for the last 10 years. She obtained her PhD from the Royal Melbourne Institute of Technology for her contribution to resource allocation, scheduling, and constraint technology for networked multimedia. Over the last five years, she has been extending these techniques to agent systems. Dr. Dospisil has more than 30 publications in constraint technology, multimedia, and agent systems.

Klement J. Fellner is PhD student and lecturer at the University of Magdeburg in the department of Business Information Systems. Prior to assuming his current position, he worked for Oracle Consulting Austria as a Business Consultant in the field of business process redesign. He studied business information systems at the University of Vienna, where he received his diploma degree (Mag. rer. soc. oec.). His main research interests are interorganizational business processes, sustainable development, and component-based business application systems. Additionally, he has been working in a variety of consulting projects concerning analysis and design of business applications, business process management, and data-warehousing. In May 2000, he was co-organizer of the first German conference on XML applications in business.

Jorge Gasós is scientific officer for electronic commerce in the European Commission's Information Society Directorate-General. He is in charge of the research area on "Intelligent Applications for Electronic Commerce" in the Electronic Commerce Unit, that includes research and developments in agent technologies. He has published a large number of papers and book chapters in leading international journals and publications, mainly in the area of artificial intelligence. Jorge Gasós previously held research positions in Spain, Japan and Belgium, where he focused his work on artificial intelligence applications. He holds a PhD in Computer Science from the Polytechnic University of Madrid (Spain).

Gary Gregory is currently a senior lecturer in marketing at the University of Wollongong, Australia. He has been involved in overseas teaching, research and consulting in the U.S., Middle East, Australia and Africa. His areas of specialization includes cross-cultural marketing, marketing strategy, international management, and consumer behaviour and advertising strategy. His research has been published in *Journal of Business Research, Psychology and Marketing, Journal of Brand Management, Journal of the Academy of Marketing Studies, Journal of Transnational Management Development, International Business Teaching* and *Advances in Consumer Research*, along with a number of national and international conference presentations for the *Academy of Management, American Marketing Association,* and *Academy of International Business.*

Sheng-Uei Guan received his MSc and PhD from the University of North Carolina at Chapel Hill. He is currently an associate professor of the electrical engineering department at National University of Singapore. Prof. Guan has also worked in a prestigious R&D organization for several years, serving as a design engineer, project leader, and manager. He has also served as a member on the R.O.C. Information & Communication National Standard Draft Committee. After leaving the industry, he joined Yuan-Ze University in Taiwan for three and half years. He served as deputy director for the Computing Center, and also as the chairman for the Department of Information & Communication Technology. Later he joined La Trobe University with the Department of Computer Science & Computer Engineering where he helped to create a new Multimedia Systems stream. Prof. Guan is active in the following research areas: intelligent machines, artificial life, multimedia systems, high speed networking, World Wide Web applications & electronic commerce, and computer-supported cooperative work.

Shahul Hameed is an MPhil, PhD in International Economics from the Jawaharlal Nehru University, New Delhi. He has ten years of teaching experience in multi-disciplinary subjects. His research work on " Imperatives of Market Economy in India" is published in *New Globalism and the State* edited by Dr. Sushil Kumar, Research Press India, 1999. He is currently teaching in the Regent School of Economics, Stamford College, in Malaysia.

Feng Hua received her BS degree from Beijing Polytechnic University, China in 1999. After graduation, she continued her study in the research area of software computing and engineering. She is currently pursuing a master degree of engineering (electrical) in the Department of Electrical Engineering at National University of Singapore. Her current research interests include electronic commerce, software agents, and secure payment systems for Internet use.

Maria Indrawan is a lecturer in the Gippsland School of Computing and Information Technology at Monash University. She holds a PhD in computing from Monash University. Her main research interests are in the areas of multimedia indexing and retrieval, agent systems for electronic commerce and the application of multimedia and agent systems for flexible learning.

Munib Karavdic is an e-commerce project manager in the Financial Services Group at Macquarie Bank, Sydney, Australia. He has been involved in the on-line financial services projects development. He is a PhD candidate in the Department of Marketing, the University of Wollongong. His areas of expertise are electronic commerce, international marketing, and marketing services. His papers related to the e commerce have been presented at Academy of International Business conferences. He has also been a visiting lecturer at the University of Wollongong teaching postgraduate students marketing on the Internet.

Ahmad Kayed is currently a PhD student in information systems with the Department of Computer Science and Electrical Engineering at the University of Queensland. His research interests are in electronic commerce, tendering process, ontology, knowledge acquisition, e-broker, software agents, and EDI/XML. From 1989 to 1993, he joined Arab Community College (Jordan) as a computer instructor. From 1993 to 1996, he was a project manager for financial systems at IdealSoft within IdealGroup. This project achieved the Best Software Award (METS 1994 & 1996). From 1996 to 1998, he joined the Centre for British Teachers (CfBT) Oman branch as computer lecturer. In 1989 he was awarded a BSc in computer science and MSc (1992) in math/statistics from Jordan University, Amman-Jordan. When he came to Australia in 1998, he joined the University of Queensland Brisbane to complete his PhD.

Elizabeth A. Kendall is the Sun Microsystems Chair of Network Computing at Monash University. She is a recognised leader in agent technology, including role modelling, patterns, and applications. Prof. Kendall obtained a BS from MIT, and an MS and a PhD from the California Institute of Technology. She has been involved in academia and research in Australia and New Zealand since 1990. Prior to moving to Australia, she was involved in groundbreaking research and development in the U.S. aerospace and defense industry throughout the 1980s. She has frequently worked as a consultant to industry on agents systems and object-oriented design, and she has more than 80 publications in agents, object technology, patterns, and aspect-oriented programming.

Joseph A. Konstan is an associate professor of computer science at the University of Minnesota. His area of expertise and research is software systems for human-computer interaction, including multimedia systems for flexible presentation, scientific visualization, collaborative filtering, and constraint-based programming tools. He received his AB in computer science from Harvard College in 1987 and MS and PhD degrees in computer science from the University of California, Berkeley in 1990 and 1993, respectively.

Kwok Yan Lam is an associate professor at the Department of Computer Science, School of Computing, National University of Singapore. His research interests include systems security, intrusion detection, fast cryptographic algorithms, authentication protocols, context-dependent access control and distributed computing.

Ernest Lam received his BSc in engineering, and MSc and PhD in computer science from the University of California at Los Angeles. He had been a faculty member in the School of Computer Science at University of Windsor and the Department of Computer Science at University of Hong Kong. He is currently associate professor and head of the Department of Computer Science at Hong Kong Baptist University. His current research interests are in pattern recognition and electronic commerce.

Chun Hung Li received his PhD in electronic engineering from the Hong Kong Polytechnic University. He is currently working as a post-doctoral fellow of the Department of Computer Science at Hong Kong Baptist University. His research interests include image analysis, pattern recognition, stochastic algorithms and internet applications.

Xue Li is a senior lecturer in information systems, technology and management at the University of New South Wales in Sydney. He has a master's degree in computer science and a PhD in information systems. His research interests include programming, object-oriented databases and expert systems, and he has published many articles in these areas. Xue has had more than 18 years' experience in information technology. He has programmed numerous commercial database applications and network applications. Among other interesting projects, Xue was involved in programming the first Fortran compiler for Chinese machines. He has also consulted for a number of firms. Currently Xue is involved in teaching advanced data networks and advanced database systems.

Eric Liu received his BSc in electrical engineering with a minor in computer engineering from the University of Calgary, Alberta, Canada. He is currently working towards his MSc in software engineering at the University of Calgary. His research interests include metrics collection tools, software metrics, and their application in providing immediate feedback to a developer.

Jiming Liu is an associate professor of computer science at Hong Kong Baptist University (HKBU) and a senior member of the IEEE. His areas of expertise are autonomous agents and multiagent systems, learning, self-adaptation, and artificial life in software and systems, agents in electronic media and commerce, robotics, and dynamics of computation and complex adaptive systems. Liu earned BSc from East China Normal University (Shanghai), MA from Concordia University, and MEng and PhD both from McGill University (Montreal). He was employed as engineer, research associate and senior research agent at R&D firms and government labs in Canada (e.g., CRIM, CWARC (Government of Canada), KENTEK Inc. and Virtual Prototypes Inc.), before joining HKBU. Liu was invited as a visiting scholar and spent a six-month sabbatical leave in the computer science Department at Stanford University in 1999.

Seng Wai Loke obtained his PhD in computer science from the Intelligent Agent Laboratory at the University of Melbourne in 1998. He is currently senior research scientist at the Distributed Systems Technology Center (DSTC) in Australia (Melbourne branch). He is actively involved with the M3 mobile computing project at DSTC. His recent research interests include the applications of agent technology in mobile computing, workflow, and distributed data mining.

Andrew Marriott is a senior lecturer in the School of Computing at Curtin University of Technology, Western Australia. In 1988 he formed the Computer Animation Negus, a research and development group whose aim is to provide a sophisticated environment for animation work at the undergraduate, postgraduate and commercial level. His research interests include facial animation and AI-based Web interfaces. Current research includes a large-scale Java-based graphical mentoring system, which uses a talking head graphical user interface, a client-server system and reusable communicating software agents. An FAQBot has also been developed—this is a Web-based talking head used for on-line presentations and as a virtual salesperson.

Craig Parker is a senior lecturer with the School of Management Information Systems at Deakin University, Australia where he is the director of the master of electronic commerce program. He also teaches in this program and in the e-commerce major within Deakin's bachelor of commerce. Craig has spent the last seven years researching business simulation approaches to teaching university students and business professionals about e-commerce. This work led to the development of a Web-based business simulation called TRECS (Teaching Realistic Electronic Commerce Solutions). He is also a research supervisor in such areas as virtual communities, Internet markets and e-commerce enabled regional sustainability.

Roberto Pockaj received his master's degree in electronic engineering from the University of Genova, Italy in 1993 and his PhD degree from the Department of Communications, Computer and System Science (DIST) in 1999. From 1992 to 1996 he was with Marconi Software as a Software Designer in R&D of real-time image and signal processing for optoelectronic devices. From 1996 onwards he has been involved in the definition of the new MPEG-4 standard for the coding of multimedia contents within the subgroup on Synthetic and Natural Hybrid Coding (SNHC) and the Ad Hoc Group on Face and Body Animation (FBA).

Teoh Kok Poh is a graduate student of the National University of Singapore. He is currently the smart card technical development manager of Access Management Group, the smart card unit of National Computer System Pte Ltd. Mr. Poh was actively involved in the smart card industry with extensive experience in various aspect of smart card technology including card and chip module manufacturing, personalization and testing, smart card based product development and system design, system integration, key management system, public key infrastructure and smart card based services.

Mahesh S. Raisinghani, is the founder and CEO of Raisinghani and Associates, a diversified global firm with interests in software consulting and technology options trading. As a faculty member at the Graduate School of Management, University of Dallas, he teaches MBA courses in information systems and e-commerce, and serves as the director of research for the Center for Applied Information Technology. As a global thought leader on e-business and global information systems, he has been invited to serve as the local chair of the World Conference on Global Information Technology Management and the track chair for e-commerce technologies at the Information Resources Management Association.

He has published in numerous leading scholarly and practitioner journals, presented at leading world-level scholarly conferences and has recently published his book *E-Commerce: Opportunity and Challenges*. He is the invited editor of the special issue of the *Journal of Electronic Commerce Research on Intelligent Agents in E-Commerce*. Dr. Raisinghani was also selected by the National Science Foundation after a nationwide search to serve as one the panelists on the information technology research panel for awarding $500,000 grants to appropriate proposals. He serves on the editorial review board for leading information systems publications and is included in the millennium edition of *Who's Who in the World, Who's Who Among America's Teachers* and *Who's Who in Information Technology*. He can be contacted at mraising@gsm.udallas.edu

Andry Rakotonirainy obtained his PhD from INRIA in 1995. He is currently senior research scientist and project leader of the M3 project related to mobile computing at DSTC, Australia (Brisbane branch).

John T. Riedl is an associate professor in computer science at the University of Minnesota. His research interests include collaborative systems, distributed database systems, and scientific visualization. He received a BS degree in mathematics from the University of Notre Dame in 1983 and MS and PhD degrees in computer sciences from Purdue University in 1985 and 1990, respectively. Together with Joe Konstan and others he co-founded NetPerceptions Inc., a leading provider of personalization software.

Badrul M. Sarwar is a PhD candidate in computer science at the University of Minnesota. He is currently working with the GroupLens collaborative filtering research group. His research interests include recommender systems, machine learning, data mining, collaborative filtering, distributed systems, databases and object-oriented systems. He received his BSc degree in computer science and engineering from Bangladesh University of Engineering and Technology in 1994, where he served as a lecturer in the computer science and engineering department from June 1994 to August 1995. He received his MS in computer science from the University of Minnesota in 1998.

Chee Kheong Siew is director of the Information Communication Institute of Singapore (ICIS), School of EEE, Nanyang Technological University. His research interests include e-commerce, traffic shaping, neural networks and network performance.

Nansi Shi has obtained degrees of PhD, MEng, BSc, has published a number of papers in international journals and conferences, and is writing a book about electronic commerce. He is also teaching information management course to MBA students. Shi currently serves as technology planning manager, Singapore Pools (Pte) Ltd, in charge of corporate IT strategy planning, electronic commerce, IT security policy, network design, etc. Shi has more than 20 years' experience in the information systems field and has worked as deputy general manager, project manager, project leader, research assistant, analysis programmer, software engineer and programmer. In the management area, he has managed and accomplished a number of projects, including corporate IT strategy plan, corporate and IT year 2000 compliance, electronic commerce study, IT security policy and practice, quality management system (ISO – 9002), network design, IT and IT-based projects assessment and software assurance standards. In the technologic filed, he has participated and accomplished in developing some systems, including integrated according information systems, computer network protocol converter, telephone book compilation system, graphic software, material information management system, and car component inventory system.

Giancarlo Succi is professor of software engineering at the University of Alberta, Edmonton, Alberta. He holds a Laurea (a kind of joint BSc and MSc) degree in Electrical Engineering (1988) Genova, Italy, a MSc in Computer Science (1991) from the State University of New York at Buffalo and a PhD in Electrical and Computer Engineering (1993) from the University of Genova. Prof. Succi is a registered professional engineer in Alberta and in Italy, and official consultant of the court of Genova, Italy. Prof. Succi is a consultant for several North American and European firms and for the European Commission, and serves as reviewer and member of the editorial board of international scientific journals and magazines. Prof. Succi has written more than 100 papers published in journals, proceedings of conferences, and books. Prof. Succi is also the author of a book on software reuse and editor of a book on logic programming. Before joining the University of Alberta, Prof. Succi was associate professor and director of the software engineering graduate program at the Department of Electrical and Computer Engineering of the University of Calgary, assistant professor at the Department of Computer and Management Sciences of the University of Trento, Italy, and owner and head of Eutec, a small software firm.

Vijayan Sugumaran is assistant professor of MIS in the Department of Decision and Information Sciences at Oakland University. He received his PhD in information technology from George Mason University, Fairfax, Virginia. His research interests are in the areas of domain modeling and reuse, component based software development, knowledge-based systems, Internet technologies, intelligent agents, and e- commerce applications. His recent publications have appeared (or are forthcoming) in *Communications of the ACM, Data Base, Industrial Management and Data Systems, Automated Software Engineering, Expert Systems, Journal of Network and Computer Applications*, and *HEURISTICS: The Journal of Knowledge Engineering & Technology*. He has presented papers at various national and international conferences including the International Conference on Information Systems.

Paul Timmers is head of sector for electronic commerce in the European Commission's Information Society Directorate-General. He is closely involved in electronic commerce policy and programme development at the European Commission and has been working with several national governments on electronic commerce policies. He regularly publishes about electronic commerce, including the recent book *Electronic Commerce: Strategies and Models for Business-to-Business Trading*, (Wiley & Sons Ltd). He is a frequent speaker at international conferences and a visiting professor at several business schools and universities. Paul Timmers previously held management positions in the IT industry and has co-founded a software company. He holds a PhD in theoretical physics (University of Nijmegen, NL) and an MBA (Warwick Business School, UK).

Klaus Turowski is an assistant professor at the University of Magdeburg in the Department of Business Information Systems. Prior to assuming his current position, he worked at the University of Münster, where he received a Dr. rer. pol. (PhD in business information systems). In addition, he holds a Dipl.-Wi.-Ing. (diploma degree in industrial engineering and management) from the University of Karlsruhe. He is speaker of Working Group 5.10.3 Component-oriented Business Application Systems of German Informatics Society (GI) and co-founder of GI working group 5.5 E-Commerce. His main research interests are component-based business application systems and interorganizational integration. Besides his theoretical background, he has been working in a variety of consulting projects concerning process management, service level management, application outsourcing, and ERP-systems, especially SAP R/3. In May 2000, he chaired the first German conference on XML applications in business, and he organized and chaired several other scientific events, especially those concerning the component-based development of business applications.

Tullio Vernazza is an associate professor at the University of Genova. He holds a Laurea (a kind of joint BSc and MSc) degree in electrical engineering, Genova, Italy. Prof. Vernazza is a registered professional engineer in Italy. He serves as consultant for several firms and acts also as director of the IT department of the Istituto Giannina Gaslini, one of the world largest children's hospitals. Prof. Vernazza is heavily involved in electronic commerce, with special interest in authentication mechanisms and biometric keys in the medical domain, including the use of smartcard and thumbs' code for authoring medical information. This research also includes hardware/software co-design, especially robotic systems, again in the medical domain.

Xiao Feng Wang is a PhD candidate of Carnegie Mellon University, USA. His research interests include e-commerce, software agent technology and computer security.

Merrill Warkentin is associate professor and chair of MIS in the College of Business at Northeastern University, where he holds the Joseph G. Riesman Research Professorship for Electronic Commerce Research. He has authored more than 90 papers, books and book chapters. His research has appeared in such journals as *MIS Quarterly*, *Decision Sciences*, *Information Systems Journal*, *ACM Applied Computing Review*, *ACM SIGICE Bulletin*, *Journal of Electronic Commerce Research*, *Journal of Computer Information Systems*, and *HEURISTICS: The Journal of Knowledge Engineering & Technology*. Professor Warkentin has served as a consultant to numerous companies and government agencies and has been a featured speaker at over one hundred industry association meetings, executive development seminars, and academic conferences. His PhD in MIS is from the University of Nebraska-Lincoln. His virtual home is *http://mis.cba.neu.edu.*

Raymond WM Wong received the BS degree in electrical engineering with a minor in computer engineering from the University of Calgary, Alberta, Canada. He is currently working toward his master's degree in software engineering. His research interests are in software engineering tools and component-based software development (especially in the composition of components in the network environment).

Yang Yang received his BEng (electrical) from the National University of Singapore. He is currently pursuing MEng (electrical) in the Department of Electrical Engineering at the National University of Singapore on a part-time basis. During his industrial attachment, he worked in the Information Security Group at the Institute of System Science (Singapore) on a secure-cash project. He went on to work to develop a smart-card-based SSL 3.0 package for the same organization. During this period, he was also involved in the development of S-One, a Web-based payment solution using smart card. After his graduation from the University, Yang Yang worked in the Development Bank of Singapore as an IT analyst. Yang Yang is currently researching security related issues in electronic commerce and intelligent agents.

Xun Yi is a teaching fellow with the School at Electrical and Electronic Engineering, Nanyang Technological University, Singapore. His research interests includes electronic commerce, software agent technology, network and computer security and cryptography.

Arkady Zaslavsky received an MSc in applied mathematics majoring in computer science from the Tbilisi State University (Georgia, USSR) in 1976 and PhD in computer science from the USSR Academy of Sciences in 1987. He holds a position of associate professor with the School of Computer Science and Software Engineering of Monash University. His research interests include mobile computing; distributed and mobile agents and objects; distributed computing and database systems and distributed object technology. He is a member of ACS, ACM and IEEE Computer and Communications Societies.

Fangming Zhu received his BS and MS degrees from Shanghai Jiaotong University, China, in 1994 and 1997 respectively. After graduation, he joined Shanghai Ricoh Facsimile Co. Ltd. as a research engineer. He is now a PhD candidate in the Department of Electrical Engineering at the National University of Singapore. His current interests include electronic commerce and software agents. He is a student member of the IEEE.

Index

A

B

C

L

M

N

O

P

R

S

T

U

V

W

X